THE
AFRICAN AMERICAN
ENCYCLOPEDIA

THE
AFRICAN AMERICAN
ENCYCLOPEDIA

Volume 6

The Sport of the Gods – Zydeco

Index

Editor

MICHAEL W. WILLIAMS

Marshall Cavendish
New York • London • Toronto

Published By
Marshall Cavendish Corporation
2415 Jerusalem Avenue
P.O. Box 587
North Bellmore, New York 11710
United States of America

∞ The paper in these volumes conforms to the American National Standard for Permanence of
Paper for Printed Library Materials, Z39.48-1984.

Library of Congress Cataloging-in-Publication Data

The African American encyclopedia / Michael W. Williams, editor.
    p.   cm.
  Includes bibliographical references and index.
  1. Afro-Americans—Encyclopedias. I. Williams, Michael W. (Michael Warren)
E185.A253   1993
973′ .0496073′003—dc20   93-141
ISBN 1-85435-545-7 (set)   CIP
ISBN 1-85435-551-1 (volume 6)

PRINTED IN THE UNITED STATES OF AMERICA

Contents

Sport of the Gods, The (pb. 1901, serial; 1902, book): Novel by Paul Laurence DUNBAR. Set about 1900, this racial protest work portrays a middle-class family of southern blacks who are the victims of racial prejudice. Having served a wealthy white businessman for twenty years, the family is torn apart following the father's sentencing by the white employer to ten years of hard labor for a theft he did not commit. When the truth comes out one year later, he is released from jail and the family is reinstated on the employer's estate.

Sports: Most of humankind's athletic ability developed out of survival needs. Gradually, tribal groups began to use athletic feats to measure boys' passage into manhood. Men needed certain skills in order to survive, and performance of these feats indicated possession of those skills. Men began to compete, both intra- and intergroup, in their performance of these feats. Contests were sometimes used to minimize conflict between tribes, taking the place of warfare or reducing the rivalries that could lead to war.

Historical Summary. Among ancient African tribes, athletic feats were used during manhood rituals and were part of special celebrations held during the year, particularly at harvest time. Team competition in wrestling was commonplace, and wrestlers generally were accorded great honors within their villages.

Athletics also were an important aspect of the American slave's life. Slaves were not permitted much recreational time, although some slaves were allowed Saturday afternoon to do their personal chores, and Sunday was considered a day of rest by even the most harsh masters. In addition, most slaves were given brief holidays from toil after harvest time and during the Christmas holidays; slaves owned by devout masters also enjoyed other religious holidays.

Slaves often engaged in physical contests with other slaves. During the festival seasons such as harvest and Christmas, athletic competitions, including races and wrestling matches, were organized. On occasion, white masters would amuse themselves by arranging to have their slaves fight one another. These matches, which seldom were fought with rules or referees, often ended in death.

Slaves continued to fight at their masters' bidding until the Civil War ended the institution of SLAVERY. Since that time, African American men and women have attempted to prove their worth in all areas of American life, including the battlefield and the sports arena, sometimes under the most dire circumstances.

Boxing. The first sport in which African Americans were able to achieve success was BOXING. It was the custom in the old South for wealthy plantation owners to send their sons to England to be educated; at the time, boxing was considered a gentleman's sport in England. As a result, many of these young southerners learned boxing skills, mainly for use in self-defense. When those young men returned to their homes in the South, however, it was often almost impossible for them to find sparring partners.

Many young masters thus began to train their personal male slaves in the art of boxing. Slave boxers soon became so proficient at the sport that competitions were held between the champions of various plantations. Victorious African American boxers earned considerable money for their masters, who often wagered large sums of money on these matches, and earned special privileges for themselves. A number of slaves were even able to gain their freedom in this way, and some earned a living by boxing as freedmen in the North and in England.

Boxing champion Henry Armstrong in 1937. (AP/Wide World Photos)

The first known African American boxing champion was Joe Lashley, who had recorded fights in 1792 and 1796. Of his match against Tom Treadway on June 13, 1796, it was written that "During the contest, the African showed great agility, excellent bottom and a thorough knowledge of the art not to be exceeded by the most skillful among boxers." Bill Richmond became the first celebrated African American boxer. Brought to the attention of a British military commander in 1777, Richmond was taken back to England, where he became a hero to the English working classes. Richmond fought—and won—his last fight in 1818, at the age of fifty-six.

Richmond's achievements inspired another African American, Tom MOLYNEUX. Said to have been the son or grandson of famous boxing slaves from Virginia, Molyneux was born in 1784 in South Carolina. He earned his freedom and eventually made his way to England, where he gained considerable fame. So great was his fame that many black boxers used his name to give themselves credibility. One such fighter was Jim Wharton, who made a great amount of money fighting as Molyneux.

George Godfrey was the first heavyweight champion among African Americans. Godfrey was scheduled to fight John L. Sullivan, the white heavyweight champion of the 1880's, but Sullivan refused to box against Godfrey, or Charles Hadley, or any other good boxer of African heritage. Significantly, the first black boxing champion in any division recognized by the United States was a Canadian, George Dixon.

In 1908, Jack JOHNSON became the first African American to win the world heavyweight boxing championship when he knocked out Tommy Burns in the fourteenth round of a bout held in Sydney, Australia. The boxing world tried to find a "great white hope" to topple Johnson, but Johnson proceeded to defeat a succession of white challengers. Johnson flouted the racial mores of his times, and he was hated by many whites, particularly for his involvement with white women. In 1912, Johnson was convicted on largely trumped-up charges of violating the Mann Act, and he fled to Europe, where he spent the next few years putting on exhibitions and fighting a few matches. On Apr. 5, 1915, in Cuba, Johnson lost to white fighter Jess Willard; some observers believed that Johnson threw the fight.

After the breaking of boxing's color line, African American men achieved success in all weight divisions. Scores of black boxers have won championships, and many, such as Henry ARMSTRONG, Joe LOUIS, Sugar Ray ROBINSON, Muhammad ALI, Joe FRAZIER, Larry Holmes, and Mike TYSON, rank among the sport's all-time greats.

Baseball. BASEBALL, a peculiarly American adaptation of primitive stick-and-ball games, evolved into its modern form during the nineteenth century. During the Civil War, baseball spread throughout the North and the South and was encouraged by the military leaders of both the Union and Confederate armies as an excellent recreational outlet for soldiers and prisoners alike. It was also during the North-South conflict that baseball became widely played by African American slaves and freedmen.

After the Civil War, African American men continued to play baseball, and many became expert at the sport. In the northern states, there was a higher level of organization, because African American athletes were not hindered by the hostility generated by RECONSTRUCTION or the intrusion of the BLACK CODES. In the North, as a result, African American baseball players formed their own leagues and played "colored" championship series that determined the best teams. As far back as 1867, some of these teams were playing all-white teams in exhibition games. In the South, however, African American players were forced to mask their serious interest and skill in the game by performing minstrel shows on the baseball diamond.

The racial chaos following the Civil War took its toll in a number of ways. In baseball, race was injected into the charter of the National Association of Baseball Players. When that group became the National Association of Professional Baseball Players in 1871, the ban against African American ballplayers was omitted, but the exclusionary policy continued as an unwritten "gentlemen's agreement."

Despite this, African Americans did play in the white leagues. John W. "Bud" Fowler was the first know African American to earn a salary in organized baseball. Fowler was born in Cooperstown, N.Y., now well known as the permanent home of the Baseball Hall of Fame. Fowler—who could play any position, including pitcher—spent the years from 1872 to 1897 playing all over the country, primarily with white teams. He began his career with the Newcastle, Pa., team, but by 1885, he was playing with the Keokuk, Iowa, team in the Western League.

There were at least thirty other African American men playing in the white leagues before 1900. Among them were Moses Fleetwood WALKER, an OBERLIN COLLEGE graduate, who became the first African American major league player in 1884, when he was signed to catch for the Toledo Blue Stockings of the American Association. Five weeks later, his brother, Welday Walker, signed to play the outfield with the same team. Robert Higgins pitched for the Syracuse, N.Y., team in 1887 in the International League.

These early African American players were met with all forms of racism. Further, there was a concerted effort, led by Adrian "Cap" Anson, the manager and star first baseman for the Chicago White Stockings, to purge black ballplayers from the major leagues. Within nine years, African Americans were out of organized baseball, as racism—bolstered by the "SEPARATE BUT EQUAL" doctrine set down in the Supreme Court decision in *PLESSY V. FERGUSON*—took its toll.

There were, however, a few whites who attempted to circumvent the ban on African Americans in baseball. While managing the Baltimore Orioles, John McGraw tried unsuccessfully to pass off second baseman Charlie Grant as a Cherokee Indian with the name of Charlie Tokohama. When McGraw joined the New York Giants in 1902, he brought with him an African American trainer, Ed Mackall, and before World War I, he hired Andrew "Rube" Foster as a pitching coach.

Buck Leonard starred in baseball's Negro Leagues. (National Baseball Library, Cooperstown, NY)

For most of the first half of the twentieth century, though, blacks in professional baseball were limited to playing in the Negro Leagues, the name given to a loose collection of leagues and teams that flourished before 1949. Playing before largely black crowds in the East, Midwest, and South, Negro League teams featured such stars as Josh GIBSON and Buck LEONARD, who were widely regarded as comparable to the best white players.

Major-league baseball, though, remained lily white until after 1945, when Jackie ROBINSON was signed by Branch Rickey to play for the Brooklyn Dodgers' Triple A farm team, the Montreal Royals. On Apr. 15, 1947, Robinson made his debut in a Dodger uniform. By the end of the season, he had compiled an impressive record, and in the process had proven that African American men could be as good as their white counterparts in baseball.

Despite Robinson's quick success, some major-league teams were slow to integrate their rosters. It was more than another decade before all major-league teams had African American ballplayers. Many black stars, including Roy CAMPANELLA, Don NEWCOMBE, Monte IRVIN, Willie MAYS, Hank AARON, Ernie BANKS, Larry DOBY, and Satchel PAIGE, were recruited out of the Negro Leagues. Faced with the loss of their best players and, after the breaking of baseball's color line, deprived of their reason for existing, the Negro Leagues quickly disappeared.

By 1980, more than one-fourth of all major-league players were African Americans. As black players attained equality on the field, a push began to integrate the front offices and managerial staffs of major-league teams, but the effort met with minimal success. By the 1990's, only a handful of African Americans held major-league managerial and front-office positions.

Horse Racing. Like boxing, horse racing was first introduced to African Americans during slavery. When the sport of horse racing spread throughout the South, plantation owners began to import and breed thoroughbreds, turning over the chores of grooming, feeding, breaking, exercising, and training the horses to their slaves. It was also the slaves who rode the horses to victory or defeat. Unfortunately, although official records were kept of the winning horses and their owners, the names of the JOCKEYS and trainers were not included, so the feats of those early African American sportsmen are lost to history.

Following the Civil War, African American men continued to excel at horse racing. At the first Jerome Handicap at Belmont Park in 1866, a rider known simply as Abe won, riding a horse called Watson. Abe also rode a horse named Merrill to victory at the third Travers Stakes, at Saratoga Springs in 1866. Fourteen of the fifteen jockeys in the first Kentucky Derby—held at Churchill Downs in Louisville in May, 1875—were African Americans, including the winning rider, Oliver LEWIS, who rode a horse called Aristides.

The most celebrated African American jockey was Isaac Burns MURPHY, who was born in 1861. Murphy won his first race at the age of fourteen, and by his early twenties, he was on a $10,000 retainer so that a particular horse owner could have first call on his services. Murphy rode three winners in the Kentucky Derby—Buchanan in 1884, Riley in 1890, and Kingman in 1891—a record that stood unmatched for forty years.

In 1896, the year Murphy died, Willie Simms won the Kentucky Derby on a horse named Ben Branch, and two years later, he won again on Plaudit. Simms went to England and became the first American jockey to win on an English course with an American horse, owner, trainer, and equipment. Jimmy Winkfield was the jockey with the best winning record in the Kentucky Derby, with two victories, one second, and one third in four starts. His victory on Alan-a-Dale in 1902 was the last by an African American jockey for more than ninety years.

During the early twentieth century, there were many noted African American jockeys, including Alonzo "Lonnie" Clayton, James "Soup" Perkins, John H. Jackson, Robert "Tiny" Williams, Anthony Hamilton, Henry J. Harris, and William Porter. Several jockeys, including George B. "Spider" Anderson and Bud Haggins, went on to become excellent steeplechase riders. Jockey Jimmy Lee rode six winners in one day at Latonia in 1909, and he twice rode five winners in one week. In 1911, Jesse Conley was the last African American of his era to ride in the Kentucky Derby, finishing third on a mount named Colston. After that, African Americans were systematically excluded from horse racing. JIM CROW LAWS and practices had brought an end to the illustrious history of the African American jockey.

Football. The first intercollegiate FOOTBALL game was played four years after the end of the Civil War, between Princeton and Rutgers. Shortly thereafter, Harvard, Yale, Cornell, and the University of Michigan also established football teams. Although black colleges did not organize football teams until the 1890's, African American athletes were probably playing intramural football before then. In 1892, Biddle University and Livingston College became the first black colleges to play each other; they were soon followed by Howard, Lincoln, Tuskegee, Atlanta, and Shaw.

Football began as a college sport, and even today the vast majority of professional football players are drafted from college teams. Consequently, football, more than any other sport, created the first real opportunities for African American men as coaches and assistant coaches, at more than one hundred private and land-grant institutions. Black college football also gave southern African American athletes the chance to exhibit their skills on the gridiron.

Great rivalries quickly developed between schools, such as that between Howard and Lincoln (Pennsylvania) or between Tuskegee and Wilberforce. Kentucky State, Morris Brown, Florida A&M, Southern, Langston, and Xavier were other football powerhouses that drew large followings. Football scholarships to black colleges and universities also provided the entry for many young African American men into the fields of medicine, law, dentistry, business, teaching, and social work.

Before the exploits of the gridiron heroes from black institutions were chronicled, African Americans were starring on football teams at predominantly white schools in the North and Northeast. Among the first to be recognized was William Henry Lewis, a center on the Amherst team who was chosen for Walter Camp's All-American team in both 1892 and 1893. Because athletic eligibility rules were not rigid in those days, Lewis was also the captain of the football team at Harvard while he was in law school. Lewis went on to become the first African American to be admitted to the American Bar Association.

Numerous African American football players came out of college to play in the early years of professional football. Among them was Frederick Douglass "Fritz" POLLARD of Brown University, who played for the undefeated Akron Pros in the American Professional Football Association (APFA) in 1920. Pollard became the first African American professional football coach in 1923, after the APFA evolved into the National Football League (NFL). The renowned singer and actor Paul ROBESON was an All-American player at Rutgers; Robeson went on to play professionally with the Hammond Pros, the Akron Pros, and the Milwaukee Badgers, a team that had three African American players.

Other outstanding early black professional players included John Shelbourne from Dartmouth, who played with the Hammond Pros; Edward "Sol" Butler from Dubuque, Iowa, who first joined the Rock Island Independents before playing with the Hammond Pros in 1924 and again in 1926; James Turner, who followed Robeson to the Milwaukee Badgers in 1923; Jay Mayo "Inky" Williams, a teammate of Pollard at Brown who joined the Hammond team from 1923 to 1924; Fred "Duke" Slater, from the University of Iowa, who played with the Rock Island team, the Milwaukee Badgers, and the Chicago Cardinals; the University of Oregon's Joe Lillard, who played with the Cardinals in 1932 and 1933; and Ray Kemp, who played with the 1933 Pittsburgh Pirates.

The professional African American football player disappeared after 1933, when George Preston Marshall, the owner of the Washington Redskins, George Halas, the owner of the Chicago Bears, and Art Rooney, the owner of the Pittsburgh Pirates, entered into an agreement to exclude them from professional teams. The nation was four years into the Great Depression, and the team owners rationalized that black men should not be able to earn more money than white men. Twelve years later, in 1946, the National Football League had to compete with the fledgling All-America Football Conference, which had signed a number of African American athletes; in response, the NFL once again included African American players on its rosters.

Racism in football—both collegiate and professional—persisted, although blacks came to account for more than half of the NFL's players. African Americans make up a large majority of the league's linebackers, defensive backs, and running backs, but the so-called thinking positions—quarterback, center, kicker, and punter—have remained basically white, despite the fact that dozens of African American players have starred at those positions for college teams.

dominantly white institutions were African American. Black employment in the front offices of NFL teams has been equally sparse.

Track and Field. It was more difficult for racist practices to keep African Americans out of TRACK-AND-FIELD events, which are largely based on individual, rather than team, effort. Although track-and-field contests—especially foot races—had gone on for centuries, the start of the modern Olympic Games in Athens, Greece, in 1896 was the primary impetus for modern organization of the sport.

No African Americans competed in the modern Games until the 1904 Olympics in St. Louis, Mo., where George POAGE of the University of Wisconsin won a bronze medal in the 400-meter hurdles. On the national scene, African

Jesse Owens' achievements in track-and-field events are legendary—on one day in 1935, he set or tied four world records, a feat that may never be duplicated. (AP/Wide World Photos)

As of 1991, there were only two African American head coaches in professional football, and only one in ten of the NFL's assistant coaches was black. On the college level, fewer than 2 percent of the head coaches at pre-

American athletes began to excel in track-and-field events. In 1912, Howard P. Drew won national titles in the 100-yard dash and the 220-yard dash. Sol Butler, from Dubuque, Iowa, won the Amateur Athletic Union (AAU)

title in the broad jump in 1920, beginning a domination of the event by African American men. In a thirty-six-year span, African Americans won twenty-six AAU championships in the broad jump, with DeHart HUBBARD of Cincinnati winning six consecutive AAU titles from 1922 to 1927.

An endless stream of superb African American track-and-field athletes followed Poage, and their accomplishments are legion. Jesse OWENS' performance at the May, 1935, Big Ten meet in Ann Arbor, Mich., may have been the greatest one-day accomplishment in track history. Although Owens fell down a flight of stairs and injured his back shortly before the meet, after heat applications and hot baths, he jumped 26 feet, 8¼ inches, a world record; ran the 100-yard dash in 9.4 seconds, typing his own world record; ran the 200-yard dash in 20.3 seconds, another world record; and ran the 220-yard low hurdles in 22.6 seconds, also a world record—and he performed these feats in less than one hour. Owens went on to star at the 1936 Olympics in Munich, Germany, where he became the first athlete to win four gold medals in a single Olympics, setting two world records and tying an Olympic record in the process.

At the 1960 Olympic Games in Rome, Italy, another African American, Wilma RUDOLPH, became the first American woman to win three gold medals. Rudolph won the 100-meter and 200-meter dashes and came from behind as the anchor leg of the 400-meter relay team to win her third gold.

At the 1984 Los Angeles Olympics, Carl LEWIS duplicated Jesse Owens' feat of winning four gold medals. Lewis won the 100-meter dash, won the 200-meter dash in an Olympic-record 19.8 seconds, took first place in the long jump, and won a fourth gold as part of the men's 400-meter relay team in a world record time of 37.83 seconds.

International competition in the sprint races, inclusive of the hurdles, came to be dominated by African American men and women, as did the long jump and the triple jump. For many years, it was held that black runners could win races only at short distances, but John Woodruff destroyed part of that myth when he won a gold medal in the 800-meter run at the 1936 Olympics. When John Borican, a student at Virginia State College, beat the legendary white runner Glenn Cunningham twice in the 1,000-yard run, and Frank Dixon of New York University won the prestigious Millrose Mile, the myth was shattered. By the late 1960's, many Africans had emerged as among the world's best runners at the longer distances.

Basketball. BASKETBALL was invented by James A. Naismith in 1891, and the game grew rapidly in popular-

ity in the United States. As in other sports, however, there was an early unwritten rule that blacks and whites should not play on the same teams, or against one another. African Americans did sometimes play on predominantly white college teams, although they were often banned from competing when their teams played southern schools. Some excellent early black collegiate basketball players were Wilbur Woods of Nebraska, John Johnson of Columbia, Paul Robeson of Rutgers, Maynard Garner of Hamilton College, John and Samuel Barnes of Oberlin, and Ralph J. BUNCHE of the University of California at Los Angeles (UCLA).

At black colleges, basketball flourished, even though competition was limited primarily to games against other black schools. Despite their exclusion from mainstream college basketball, superb black players developed, particularly at Xavier University in New Orleans, where the starting five players during the mid-1930's were all from Wendell Phillips High School in Chicago. The team won sixty-seven games and lost only two in four years, a remarkable achievement.

In the early years, professional basketball for African Americans was limited to traveling teams. There were many African American teams, but only two became well known. Organized in 1922 by Bob Douglas, the Renaissance Big Five (also known as the Harlem Renaissance "Rens") won their first professional game on Nov. 11, 1923; until the team disbanded after the 1948 season, the Rens, in the words of Douglas, "treated the fans to the classiest basketball in the world."

The other well-known black professional team was the HARLEM GLOBETROTTERS, organized in 1926 in Chicago by a white man named Abe Saperstein as the Savoy Big Five. Saperstein renamed the team the Harlem Globetrotters and took it on the road. The team proved to be so good that it had difficulty finding teams to play against. Saperstein devised a strategy whereby the team would play seriously for the first part of each game, then slow the game down and switch to clowning around—tactics similar to the skilled yet minstrel-like antics African American baseball players were sometimes forced to employ when playing white teams.

At the end of World War II, the Renaissance Big Five and the Harlem Globetrotters were still in business. The Globetrotters were primarily entertainers, while the HARLEM RENS were still playing competitive basketball against all comers. The Rens became a memory, however, when they joined the white National Basketball League as the Dayton (Ohio) Rens in mid-December, 1948, and finished the season with a 14-26 record. Dayton fans refused to accept an all-black team, and the league's refusal to allow the team to move to another city led to the team's demise.

After World War II, thousands of African American veterans took advantage of the G.I. Bill to attend white colleges and universities outside the South, and many played collegiate basketball. Soon, blacks were playing on previously all-white professional teams, beginning with the drafting of Charles "Chuck" COOPER, an All-American forward from Marquette University, on Apr. 25, 1950, by the Boston Celtics, a National Basketball Association (NBA) team.

While Cooper was the first African American drafted to play pro basketball, Earl Lloyd, a center-forward from all-black West Virginia State College, was the first to actually play in the NBA when he suited up for the Washington Capitols, one day before Cooper took the floor with the Celtics. That same year, the New York Knickerbockers purchased Nat "Sweetwater" Clifton from the Globetrotters.

During the 1950's, many NBA teams began to sign African American players. The Globetrotters' Saperstein responded by refusing to allow his team to play in some NBA cities, because he thought his control over his ballplayers was being challenged. The NBA owners persevered and signed more Globetrotter players, including the legendary Wilt CHAMBERLAIN.

African American men have been extremely successful in basketball, financially and otherwise. Blacks make up about half of the players in college ball and more than three-fourths of the players in the NBA. Blacks have found far greater opportunities in coaching and management in basketball than in baseball or football, and African American businessmen and former basketball stars have made serious bids to purchase NBA teams.

Basketball is also a popular sport for female athletes. Although women's college basketball programs are not as well financed as men's, most major schools field women's teams. Black women stars such as Cheryl MILLER and Lynette WOODARD have excelled in both collegiate and Olympic competition.

Tennis. In tennis, the road was very rocky for African Americans. African American colleges began organized tennis competition in the late 1800's, and by 1916, they had formed the American Tennis Association (ATA). The ATA held its first national tournament at Druid Hill Park in Baltimore, Md., in 1917. Individual African American tennis players performed very well in the years prior to World War II at schools including the City College of New York, the University of Chicago, and the University of Illinois.

Yet it took the outstanding play of Althea GIBSON to begin to erase the color barrier in tennis. Gibson, the ATA women's champion, in 1950 became the first African American invited to play at the U.S. National Championship at Forest Hills, N.Y. Gibson went on to win both the U.S. championship and the Wimbledon championship in 1957 and again in 1958, and she won the French Open in 1956. In 1975, Arthur ASHE became the first African American man to win at Wimbledon. The most successful African American tennis player in the 1980's and 1990's was Zina GARRISON, who defeated Steffi Graf to advance to the 1990 Wimbledon final match and was herself defeated by Martina Navratilova.

Tennis great Arthur Ashe displays his Wimbledon trophy. (AP/Wide World Photos)

Golf. Golf, like tennis, was considered a sport for the elite, although John Shippen, the first professional African American golf professional, entered the third United States Open in 1896 at the age of eighteen. Many African American men were hired as caddies for white players, and some became very proficient at the game. There were enough black golfers to form the black UNITED GOLFERS

ASSOCIATION (UGA) in the 1920's, and an African American tournament was established in 1926.

For much of the twentieth century, African American golfers either played on inferior black private courses or waited for "Caddy Day" at white courses and clubs in order to play on good eighteen-hole courses. In 1948, John F. Law sued for the right to use the municipal golf courses in Baltimore. He won his case, and within the next decade, most of the public courses in the United States were integrated.

Professional golf has remained a largely white sport, although black professionals such as Charlie SIFFORD, Lee Elder, and Calvin PEETE have achieved notable successes. One of the reasons for the relatively low representation of blacks in professional golf is the fact that many Professional Golf Association (PGA) tournaments are played at private clubs, and many of those clubs, particularly in the South, have had race-restricted memberships. By 1990, pressure had been put on many PGA clubs to integrate their memberships; some clubs withdrew their facilities from the PGA tour rather than integrate.

Competitors in Other Sports. African Americans have performed with merit in other sports as well. Stock-car racer Wendell SCOTT is well known in the field of auto racing, and Cheryl GLASS was the first African American female professional race-car driver in the nation. In 1986, George Branham III became the first African American to win a Professional Bowling Association (PBA) tournament. In the 1984 Olympics, Nelson Vails parlayed the skills he honed as a bicycle messenger to win a silver medal in the cycling sprints.

In the field of gymnastics, Ron GALIMORE became the first African American gymnast to win a National Collegiate Athletic Association (NCAA) championship. Debi THOMAS became the number-one figure skater in the United States in the mid-1980's and won a bronze medal in the 1988 Olympics. John DAVIS was among the greatest weightlifting champions of all time; from the late 1930's until 1953, Davis won numerous national and world championship competitions, including gold medals in the 1948 and 1952 Olympics. African American Odis Wilson, Jr., and his younger sister Alicia have won numerous professional water-skiing tournaments.—*Philip G. Smith*

SUGGESTED READINGS:

• Ashe, Arthur, Jr. *A Hard Road to Glory: A History of the African American Athlete Since 1946.* New York: Warner Books, 1988. Tennis star Ashe offers brief biographies of African American champions in every sport. A substantial reference section gives their statistics. This handsome and thorough book features photos of some of the athletes, an index, and a bibliography. Two companion volumes carry the history of African American athletes back to 1619.

• Chalk, Ocania. *Black College Sport.* New York: Dodd, Mead, 1976. Chalk delves into the history of African Americans in collegiate sports as far back as 1881, when Moses F. Walker joined the Oberlin College baseball team. This study covers the last half of the nineteenth and the first part of the twentieth century. Includes many fascinating old photographs and an index.

• Chalk, Ocania. *Pioneers of Black Sport: The Early Days of the Black Professional Athlete in Baseball, Basketball, Boxing, and Football.* New York: Dodd, Mead, 1975. This book could be considered a sequel to Chalk's other work, although it was published a year earlier. Follows the progress of African American athletes from college to professional sports. Most of the coverage is of the twentieth century, up until the late 1960's. Includes statistical data and an index.

• Green, Tina Sloan, Alpha Alexander, and Nikki Franke. *Black Women in Sport.* Reston, Va.: AAHPERD Publications, 1981. This slim volume contains several essays and some biographies. Its chief interest lies in the résumés and personal statements provided by the athletes themselves.

• Young, Andrew Sturgeon Nash. *Negro Firsts in Sports.* Chicago: Johnson, 1963. Contains valuable information about the Negro Leagues, early black boxers, and a few female athletes. The text has the naïve, hopeful tone of the very beginning of the Civil Rights movement.

Spottswood, Stephen Gil (July 18, 1897, Boston, Mass.—Dec. 1, 1974, Washington, D.C.): Clergyman. Spottswood was pastor of churches in several states before he was elected as a bishop of the AFRICAN METHODIST EPISCOPAL ZION CHURCH in 1952. He served as chairman of the board of the NATIONAL ASSOCIATION FOR THE ADVANCEMENT OF COLORED PEOPLE from 1961 until his death.

Stadler, Joseph F.: TRACK AND FIELD athlete. Stadler was, with George POAGE, one of two black athletes to compete in the 1904 Olympics. He won a silver medal for the standing high jump and a bronze medal for the standing triple jump. Both events have since been discontinued.

Stallings, George Augustus, Jr. (b. Mar. 17, 1948, New Bern, N.C.): Religious leader. Stallings founded the Imani Temple African American Catholic Congregation in 1989 in response to alleged insensitivity of the Roman Catholic church to the spiritual and cultural needs of African Americans. By 1992, the organization had churches in Philadelphia, Pa., Washington, D.C., and Norfolk, Va., and had approximately fifteen hundred members.

Stanford, John Henry (b. Sept. 14, 1938, Darby, Pa.): Military officer. Stanford did his undergraduate work in political science at Pennsylvania State University, receiving a B.A. in 1961. He was a member of the Army Reserve Officers' Training Corps, and after graduation was commissioned as a second lieutenant. Later, Stanford earned an M.S. in personnel management/administration from Central Michigan University (1975).

As an Army officer, Stanford was a platoon leader, fixed wing aviator, chief of the electrical section of the Army Transportation School, and executive assistant to the secretary of defense. His citations include the Defense Distinguished Service Medal, the Legion of Merit, and the Distinguished Flying Cross. He reached the rank of major general before retiring in 1991.

Staples, The: Soul group of the early 1970's. Consisting of master guitarist Roebuck "Pops" Staples; his daughters

Mavis (lead singer), Cleo, and Yvonne; and Pervis Staples, the group began its career as a family gospel act in the mid-1950's, achieving moderate success. In the early 1970's, the Staples switched from gospel to soul and achieved phenomenal success with million-selling hits such as "Respect Yourself" (1971), "I'll Take You There" (1972), "If You're Ready (Come Go with Me)" (1973), and "Let's Do It Again" (1974), the biggest hit of the group's career. The Staples continued to record, but did not again attain the success of the early 1970's.

Star of the Morning (pr. 1963): Biographical drama by Loften MITCHELL. Subtitled *Scenes in the Life of Bert Williams*, the historical play concerns the struggles and life experiences of the famous black entertainer and comedian Bert WILLIAMS, who starred in numerous black musicals with George WALKER.

Star Trek: The Next Generation (Synd., 1987-   ): Television science fiction/adventure series. This sequel to the original *Star Trek*, set in the twenty-fourth century, features a new spaceship with an expanded multiethnic

Master guitarist "Pops" Staples and his three daughters performed as a popular soul group in the early 1970's. (AP/Wide World Photos)

crew. African American actors portray three leading characters of different races. Human Lieutenant Geordi La Forge (LeVar BURTON) is a blind helmsman whose vision is enhanced by high-tech electronic glasses. Guinan (Whoopi GOLDBERG), an alien whose planet was destroyed by the Borg, is now the proprietor of the ship's lounge as well as a close friend of the captain. Lieutenant Worf (Michael DORN), the first Klingon to serve aboard a Federation starship, was rescued as an infant from a Klingon-Federation battle site, was reared on Earth by human parents, and is frequently instrumental in negotiations between Starfleet and his violent home planet.

Stargell, Wilver Dornel "Willie" (b. Mar. 6, 1941, Earlsboro, Okla.): BASEBALL player. Playing his entire twenty-one-year major league career with the Pittsburgh Pirates, Stargell led his team to victories in the 1971 and 1979 World Series. He won the Most Valuable Player award in 1979. A member of baseball's Hall of Fame, Stargell tied Stan Musial for sixteenth place on baseball's home run list, with 475.

Baseball Hall of Famer Willie Stargell hit 475 career home runs. (National Baseball Library, Cooperstown, NY)

Starr, Edwin (Charles Hatcher; b. Jan. 21, 1942, Nashville, Tenn.): Singer. A recording artist for Motown, Starr never became one of the company's big stars, but he made several hit records in the late 1960's and 1970's. His Wilson PICKETT-style voice went over well with fans. His early hits include "Stop Her on Sight" and "Headline News" in 1966 for Ric-Tic, then "Twenty-five Miles" in 1969, when Motown bought Ric-Tic. Perhaps best known for his strident antiwar song "War," released in 1970, Starr made his passionate feelings about peace into a hit disco dance tune. Starr left Motown in 1972, eventually signing with Twentieth Century. His 1979 song "H.A.P.P.Y. Radio," from the album of the same name, was a hit with listeners. Starr consistently was sought as a live performer, especially in Great Britain.

Step Brothers, The: Tap dance team. A top act from the 1920's through the mid-1960's, the Step Brothers won distinction with acrobatics and flashy tap. Unlike other brother acts of their day, the Step Brothers were not actually brothers. They were talented dancers in a group whose membership often changed. Maceo Anderson and Al Williams cofounded the group; over the years, Red Gordon, Sherman Robinson, Sylvester Johnson, Freddie James, Prince Spencer, Flash McDonald, and other dancers passed through the ranks of the Step Brothers.

Initially a teenage trio, the Step Brothers first appeared with bandleader Duke ELLINGTON at the COTTON CLUB in the late 1920's. By the 1930's, the group had became a quartet, renamed the Four Step Brothers and billed as "Eight Feet of Rhythm." Known for its diversity and sheer durability, the group incorporated singing, comedy, and the latest dance trends—from flips, splits, and dance acrobatics to BOOGIE WOOGIE and jitterbug-style tap—into the routine. Their trademark was the challenge dance, a tradition from Harlem street corners in which each dancer tries to outdo others in a solo, while onlookers clap their hands and stomp their feet to keep time.

Each new member of the Step Brothers introduced changes into the act. When Freddie James joined the act in 1939, he became its star for four years. In 1941, Prince Spencer added slides to the routine, and Flash McDonald brought elements of Afro-Cuban dancing when he became a member in 1943.

The Step Brothers appeared in numerous motion pictures, including the Abbott and Costello film *It Ain't Hay* (1943), *Rhythm of the Islands* (1943), *Greenwich Village* (1944), *That's My Gal* (1947), and *Here Come the Girls* (1953).

In their long and versatile career, the Step Brothers toured the world four times. They danced for the queen of England and the king of Thailand, and they played every major nightclub and theater in the United States, including Radio City Music Hall, the APOLLO THEATER, and the Paramount Theater. They also were the first African American performers to appear on many American stages that previously had been the exclusive terrain of white entertainers.

Stewart, Bennett McVey (Aug. 6, 1914, Huntsville, Ala.—Apr. 26, 1988, Chicago, Ill.): U.S. representative from Illinois. Stewart was raised in Alabama and was graduated from high school in Birmingham. He remained in Birmingham for college, graduating with a B.A. degree in 1936 from Miles College. After graduation, Stewart took a position as assistant principal at Irondale High School in Birmingham. In 1938, he returned to Miles College to serve on the faculty as an associate professor of sociology. He left teaching in 1940 to join Atlanta Life Insurance Company. He became an executive with the company and moved to Chicago in 1950, when he was promoted to be the company's director for the state of Illinois. Stewart retired from the company in 1968.

Upon retirement, Stewart became a building inspector for the city of Chicago from 1968 to 1970 and served in the city's department of urban renewal as a rehabilitation specialist. He was elected to the Chicago city council in 1971 as an alderman from the city's Twenty-first Ward. Stewart later was elected to serve as Democratic committeeman from that ward in 1976 and served until 1978.

After U.S. congressman Ralph METCALFE died in October of 1978, the Democratic committeemen from Illinois' First Congressional District were authorized to select the party's candidate to fill the remainder of Metcalfe's term. Stewart was selected to run, and he defeated former alderman A. A. Rayner in the November election. Stewart took his seat in Congress on Jan. 3, 1979, and was appointed to serve as a member of the House Committee on Appropriations. During his term in Congress, Stewart advocated emergency appropriations to provide low-income housing residents with financial assistance in paying their home heating bills and supported loan guarantees to stave off bankruptcy for Chrysler Corporation, a major employer providing fifteen hundred jobs in Stewart's district. He reintroduced Ralph Metcalfe's resolution to designate February as Black History Month, a measure which eventually was approved.

Stewart ran for reelection in 1980 but was defeated in the March Democratic primary by Harold WASHINGTON, who went on to win the election in November. Stewart completed his term in Congress and returned to Chicago, where he served as interim director of the city's Department of Intergovernmental Affairs from 1981 to 1983. He then retired from public office and remained a resident of Chicago until his death.

Stewart, Chuck (b. 1927): Photographer. Stewart studied photography at Ohio University, then moved to New York City. He is best known as a photographer of jazz musicians, both in his studio and on stage. He photographed virtually every major jazz musician active between 1950 and 1980.

Stewart, David Keith (b. Feb. 19, 1957, Oakland, Calif.): BASEBALL player. This right-handed pitcher won at least twenty games in every season from 1987 to 1990. On June 29, 1990, he pitched a 5-0 no-hit victory for the Oakland Athletics. Stewart won two games in the 1989 World Series. A recipient of the Roberto CLEMENTE Award, Stewart has contributed to many charities, including relief after an earthquake on Oct. 17, 1989, interrupted the World Series in Oakland.

Outstanding pitcher for the Oakland Athletics, Dave Stewart. (National Baseball Library, Cooperstown, NY)

Stewart, Frank (b. 1949, Nashville, Tenn.): Photographer. Stewart holds a B.F.A. in photography from Cooper Union and specializes in fine arts photography and photojournalism. He has taught at the State University of New York at Purchase and at the Studio Museum in Harlem. Stewart was one of the ten photographers commissioned by the Los Angeles Olympic Committee and has worked on various film projects.

Stewart, Maria Miller (1803, Hartford, Conn.—Dec. 17, 1879, Washington, D.C.): Abolitionist. Orphaned when she was five years old, she was bound out as a servant and began her struggle to educate herself. After moving to Boston, Mass., in the early 1820's, she met James Stewart, whom she married in 1826. Widowed three years later, she overcame her grief only after an intense religious conversion which transformed the balance of her life. Stewart became an outspoken proponent for William Lloyd Garrison in 1831 and for the moral and intellectual uplift of African Americans. She was among the first women in the United States to challenge conventional thinking on women's role in society, speaking before audiences and arguing for the right of women to be religious teachers and active combatants in the struggle for racial and political justice. In 1834, she moved to New York City, where she continued teaching, writing, and working for abolition. In 1863, she moved to Washington, D.C., and began working for the Freedmen's Hospital, becoming its matron by the early 1870's. Despite declining health, she remained an active teacher and Episcopalian apostle and published her antislavery, religious, and autobiographical writings.

Still, William (1821, Shainong, N.J.—1902): Abolitionist. Still was the youngest son of escaped slaves. Largely self-educated, he moved to Philadelphia, Pa., while in his early twenties, was married, and eventually gained employment in the Pennsylvania Society for the Abolition of Slavery, rising from janitor to journalist and finally to chairman of the society. Still's carefully kept records describing the fugitive slaves arriving in Philadelphia were published in his book *The Underground Railroad* (1872). By his own count, he helped 649 slaves to obtain freedom.

Still, William Grant (May 11, 1895, Woodville, Miss.—Dec. 3, 1978, Los Angeles, Calif.): Composer. Still is considered to be the preeminent African American composer. He was the first African American to conduct an orchestra, the New Orleans Philharmonic Symphony, in the Deep South, and became the first African American to conduct a major U.S. orchestra, the Los Angeles Philharmonic, in 1936. His *Afro-American Symphony*, written in 1931, was the first symphony of full length written by an African American to be recorded by a major record company.

Stir Crazy (Columbia, 1980): Film directed by Sidney POITIER. Richard PRYOR and Gene Wilder reteamed after their success in *Silver Streak* (1976) to make this comedy,

set in prison. Falsely accused of bank robbery, the pair receive life sentences and must use their wits to adapt to prison life. Georg Stanford BROWN has a supporting role as a gay inmate. The film's chief appeal lies in the comedic talents of its two stars.

Stitt, Edward "Sonny" (Feb. 2, 1924, Boston, Mass.—July 22, 1982, Washington, D.C.): Saxophonist. A consistently important jazz musician, Stitt often has been linked with Charlie PARKER and BEBOP music. He began

Sonny Stitt performs at the Newport Jazz Festival in 1963. (AP/Wide World Photos)

his career in the 1940's, playing with legendary trumpeter Dizzy GILLESPIE and his group. He also performed in the 1950's with Norman Granz's Jazz at the Philharmonic. He led his own combos in the 1950's and 1960's, traveling throughout the United States as well as in Europe. For the last thirty years of his performance career, however, he most often was a solo act.

Stitt's association with the early bebop music and its progenitors brought him a steady and devoted following. His performances reminded listeners of his claim to fame within the crowded pantheon of jazz. As the jazz that originated in the 1940's and was developed in the 1950's and 1960's grew subservient to the rock and roll of the 1960's and beyond, important jazz figures such as Stitt tended to fade from the public consciousness. Stitt was conscious of his musical identity. He switched from the alto saxophone to the tenor, in fact, to avoid comparisons between his music and that of Charlie Parker. Stitt proved to be equally talented on the tenor, alto, and baritone saxophones.

Stoakes, Louise (b. Malden, Mass.): Track sprinter. Stoakes, known as "The Malden Meteor," and teammate Tyde Pickett were removed from the 1932 Olympic 400-meter relay team and replaced with two white runners whom they had beaten in time trials. U.S. coaches replaced Stoakes with a white athlete again for the 1936 Olympics. She is the first African American woman to make an Olympic team, even though she never was allowed to compete.

Stokes, Carl Burton (b. June 21, 1927, Cleveland, Ohio): Politician. Carl Stokes became the first African American elected mayor of a major American city when he won Cleveland's 1965 mayoral race. In office, Stokes was charismatic, articulate, and knew the issues concerning Cleveland residents. He believed that democracy could work, that he could attain positive reform in Cleveland politics, and that he could create a better city for all Cleveland residents. Stokes also became the first African American to hold high offices in all three branches of government—legislative, executive, and judicial.

Youth and Early Adulthood. Stokes's father died when Carl was two years old, leaving Carl's mother and grandmother to rear both Carl and his brother, Louis. Stokes's mother worked as a domestic, and the family eked out a living on welfare.

The Stokes brothers were greatly influenced by their mother's encouragement to get an education and to make something out of their lives (Louis later became a member of the U.S. House of Representatives). Carl's education, however, was interrupted when he dropped out of Cleveland East Technical High School at the age of seventeen. Street life was so enticing that he became a pool hustler.

Street life, however, paled for Stokes, and by July, 1945, dissatisfied with his circumstances and realizing that he was going nowhere, he joined the Army. At the completion of his military service, which included a tour of duty in Germany, he quickly realized that, as his mother had said, an education was indispensable if he was to achieve success. He therefore returned to high school, earned his diploma, and enrolled in college. While attending college, he worked as a state liquor enforcement agent

and was responsible for closing down illegal establishments in African American neighborhoods. He soon transferred to the University of Minnesota and was graduated with a B.S. degree in 1954. Stokes later attended law school at night while serving as a probation officer during the day. He was graduated in 1956 and set up a law practice, but he soon turned toward politics.

Political Life. Stokes commenced his political career in 1962, when he became the first African American Democrat elected to the Ohio legislature. Elected to two terms in the state legislature, he began to set his sights on the mayoral seat in Cleveland. The decades preceding Stokes's quest for the mayoral job saw the city's population change; more and more whites left the city, while the black population increased. By 1965, Cleveland was one-third black, and the growing black community meant a greater pool of potential voters that Stokes could mobilize behind him. He entered the 1965 mayoral election as an independent candidate, since the local Democratic Party organization backed incumbent Ralph Locher. He nearly pulled off an upset in the predominantly white electorate, losing by slightly more than twenty-two hundred votes, less than 1 percent of the total. The election was of great value in providing more experience for Stokes and his supporters and enabling him to assess his chances in a second attempt at the mayor's seat in 1967.

Stokes entered the 1967 mayoral election knowing that he needed a solid turnout from the African American community and that he had to make greater inroads among white voters. Many voters were attracted to Stokes by his personal charm, his charisma, and his knowledge, command, and articulation of the issues. In addition to these qualities, his strategy for attracting whites was to neutralize their fear of an African American taking control of the city. Stokes chose to downplay the race issue and ventured to Cleveland's west side, which was virtually all white, in order to curry support. He claimed that voters should base their support of him on his ability and should not let race interfere in their choice. In the black community, efforts were made to increase registration of voters and to see that residents actually cast their votes.

As Stokes was the first African American to campaign seriously for mayor in Cleveland, many residents were concerned about his ability to prevent racial disorders. Racial tension in Cleveland and throughout the country had risen during the previous years, and racial disturbances had erupted across the nation between 1964 and 1966. Cleveland's Hough community had been the scene of one of these racial disorders in 1966, and voters wondered if Stokes would be able to defuse Cleveland's racial tension.

After being elected the mayor of Cleveland in 1968, Carl Stokes was faced with a confrontation between po-lice and black nationalists in the city's Glenville community. (Library of Congress)

In the 1967 primary election, Stokes, running with the reluctant support of the local Democratic Party, finally defeated incumbent Locher. He then faced Republican Seth Taft in the general election. Taft was a descendant of a former president, while Stokes was a descendant of slaves. The most controversial moment of the campaign came during a debate between the two candidates. The issue of race was present throughout the campaign; everyone in the city knew that a black candidate and a white candidate were running against each other for mayor, but both candidates were reluctant to talk about racial issues. At the debate, though, Stokes decided to bring the issue before the people. He remarked that political experts claimed that Taft would win the election because he was white. The audience loudly booed Stokes, and staff members of both candidates believed that the campaign had shifted in favor of Taft. Despite this political gaffe, Stokes recovered and defeated Taft, becoming the first African American elected mayor of a major American city.

Campaign's Aftermath. The new mayor saw his election as a victory for egalitarianism; he viewed himself as a poor boy who had risen from poverty to occupy the highest office in the city. Cleveland's African American community was ecstatic that one of their own had become mayor; Stokes's election seemed to demonstrate that, like other ethnic groups in the past, African Americans were gaining their place in the political world.

Stokes's early months in office went well and were highlighted by the introduction of his Cleveland: NOW! program, which involved citizens in housing projects, youth programs, city planning, and urban renewal. Also noteworthy, in relation to later events, was Stokes's assistance in preventing the city from exploding into riots during the aftermath of the Martin Luther KING, JR., assassination, as many other large American cities did.

The honeymoon period for the mayor ended in July, 1968, with an outbreak of violence in Cleveland's Glenville community. Although BLACK NATIONALISM was not a strong force in Cleveland, a black nationalist group led by Fred Ahmed Evans fired on policemen in the Glenville neighborhood, and for several days, the area was plagued by looting. The Ohio National Guard was called out, and when peace was restored, seven people were dead, fifteen had been wounded, and two million dollars in damage had been done. Stokes, in a controversial decision during the riot, had kept all white officers and the National Guard out of the Glenville area while he led several African American leaders into the riot district in order to reduce tension and to prevent additional deaths. He was bitterly criticized for this decision by many on the police force and by some members of the white community. His

popularity in the white community suffered, and Stokes himself admitted that the incident haunted the rest of his administration. Not only did funds for his projects dry up, but the city's resolve to make strides in race relations was stymied. Many African Americans recognized the violence as an unfortunate incident but also realized that resentment had existed in the black community for some time over perceived harassment by members of the police force.

Achievements. The Glenville incident notwithstanding, Stokes won reelection in 1969. His achievements during his two terms as mayor were impressive. While he served as mayor, there were more public-housing units constructed than during any other period in recent Cleveland history. Funds were made available for small entrepreneurs and for minority businesses, and Cleveland adopted an equal employment opportunity ordinance in 1969 to guarantee fair employment practices by firms contracting business with the city. Stokes was the first Cleveland mayor to appoint blacks to high-level public offices, and he increased the number of blacks working for the city. The mayor was instrumental in getting the DEPARTMENT OF HOUSING AND URBAN DEVELOPMENT to release more than $11 million in federal funds earmarked for Cleveland but held up during Locher's administration. The most extensive program in Stokes's administration, however, was Cleveland: NOW!, a multimillion-dollar project in which citizens were asked to participate in varied programs, from raising funds to establishing day care centers, with the objective of building up and rejuvenating the city. Stokes also was responsible for the formation of the Twenty-first Congressional District Caucus, an organization of political leaders that could be used to continue an African American presence in Cleveland politics.

Life After Politics. Stokes left Cleveland's political scene after refusing to seek a third term in office, and he turned his sights on a journalism career. In 1972, he became the first African American newscaster to appear on a daily basis in New York City, and in 1978, he won an Emmy Award from the New York chapter of the National Academy of Television Arts and Sciences.

In 1983, Stokes, who had returned to Cleveland in 1980 to practice law, successfully ran for election as a municipal court judge. With his election to the bench, Stokes had served in all three branches of government—legislative, executive, and judicial.—*Lester S. Brooks*

SUGGESTED READINGS: • Elliot, Jeffrey M., ed. *Black Voices.* San Diego, Calif.: Harcourt Brace Jovanovich, 1986. • Masotti, Louis, et al. *Shoot-Out in Cleveland.* New York: Bantam Books, 1969. • Nelson, William E., and Philip J. Meranto. *Electing Black Mayors*. Columbus: Ohio State University Press, 1977. • Stokes, Carl B. *Promises of Power, Then and Now*. Cleveland: Friends of Carl B. Stokes, 1989. • Weinberg, Kenneth G. *Black Victory: Carl Stokes and the Winning of Cleveland*. Chicago: Quadrangle Books, 1968.

Stokes, Louis (b. Feb. 23, 1925, Cleveland, Ohio): Politician. After service in the Army in World War II, Stokes attended Case Western Reserve University and Marshall College of Law in Cleveland. He subsequently became one of Cleveland's most successful black lawyers.

In 1967, Stokes's brother, Carl, gained national attention when he was elected mayor of Cleveland, the first African American to be elected mayor of a major American city. In the same year, Louis Stokes's legal career led him into politics. He represented Charles P. Lucas, a black Republican, in a suit against the Ohio legislature that charged that it had gerrymandered the state's congressional district boundaries to divide black voting strength and prevent the election of minority candidates. The case eventually reached the Supreme Court, where Stokes won a court order requiring the redrawing of the state's congressional districts. In 1968, Stokes bested a crowded field to win the Democratic nomination for Ohio's new Twenty-first District on Cleveland's east side. He then went on to win the general election, against Lucas. Stokes was the first African American to be elected to Congress from Ohio. He won subsequent reelections by large margins.

In Congress, Stokes enjoyed a long career that saw him become one of the House's most influential members. He rose to be one of the senior majority members on the powerful House Appropriations Committee. A liberal Democrat, Stokes was chairman of the Congressional Black Caucus and a consistent and effective spokesman on minority affairs. He stressed the need to broaden educational and employment opportunities. Stokes was also a member of the House Permanent Select Committee on Intelligence, in which capacity he played a prominent role in the House investigation of the Iran-Contra scandal in 1987. The House's trust in Stokes is evidenced by the fact that he twice served as chairman of the House Ethics Committee. In 1992, this position thrust him into the spotlight when it was revealed that many members of the House, including Stokes himself, had written checks against insufficient funds in their accounts in the House bank.

Stone, Toni (b. 1921?): Female BASEBALL player. Stone, in 1953, appeared in about fifty games for the India-napolis Clowns, a Negro American League franchise noted for its publicity stunts. According to league records, Stone, who played second base, batted .243. She may have been the only female player in the Negro Leagues.

Toni Stone is believed to be the only woman to play baseball in the Negro Leagues. (National Baseball Library, Cooperstown, NY)

Stono Rebellion, The: The largest slave uprising in colonial North America occurred southwest of Charleston, S.C., in September, 1739. The Stono Rebellion (named for the river where it began) was eventually quelled after the loss of some sixty lives and the destruction of several plantations. Although unsuccessful, the episode illustrated the tenuousness of white control and led to permanent adjustments in the attitudes and behavior of white South Carolinians. It marked a turning point in the history of the colony's black population.

Background. Colonial South Carolina was a slaveholding society with a substantial black majority. As a result of the development of rice cultivation—a labor-intensive enterprise—in the 1690's, white planters had become increasingly dependent upon black workers. By 1739, blacks outnumbered whites nearly two to one among the colony's 56,000 inhabitants. Most were slaves, and a sizable proportion had recently been imported from Africa. Moreover, most slaves worked on large plantations owned by absentee masters, who spent much of their time away in Charleston. There was increasing tension between the races and a spreading anxiety on the part of whites, who had a very real fear of slave revolt.

The possibility of slave escape was equally real. Only coastal Georgia, some two hundred miles of largely unsettled terrain, lay between South Carolina and Spanish Florida. Throughout the early months of 1739, a rising number of slaves had managed to flee the colony and find their way to the Spanish fort at St. Augustine. Such defections were encouraged by the Spanish, who one year earlier had offered asylum to runaway blacks from the British colonies rather than return them as officials demanded. White South Carolinians feared that their slaves were conspiring to rise up and leave the colony by force.

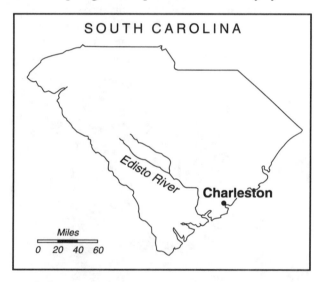

SOUTH CAROLINA

Edisto River

Charleston

Miles
0 20 40 60

Rebellion. The Stono Rebellion began in the early morning hours of Sunday, Sept. 9, 1739, when some twenty slaves gathered near the western branch of the Stono River in St. Paul's parish, twenty miles from Charleston. The conspirators, many of whom were Angolans, also hoped to make their way to St. Augustine. Led by a slave named Jemmy, they proceeded to the Stono Bridge and sacked a general store. After seizing gunpowder and several guns, they executed the two storekeepers and left their victims' heads upon the front steps. Once armed, the rebels moved on to a nearby house, plundering and burning it and killing the owner and his two children.

The band of slaves then turned southward along the main road to Georgia and St. Augustine. Proceeding along this route, they came to a tavern before dawn; because of the tavernkeeper's reputation for kind treatment of his slaves, his life was spared. Moving on several miles, the rebels burned at least five plantation houses, killing every

white they captured. A man named Bullock eluded their grasp. One white planter, Thomas Rose, was hidden by his slaves. Not all bondsmen flocked to the rebel band; some were forced to join to keep the alarm from being spread. Many, though, were voluntarily recruited. As the numbers increased, confidence rose. Before long, two drums were found, a banner was raised, and shouts of "Liberty!" were heard. The company may have numbered fifty or more by this time.

About 11 A.M., Lieutenant Governor William Bull and four companions came within view of the rebels while returning to Charleston on horseback for the opening of the legislative session. Bull and company immediately wheeled about and, although several blacks pursued them, managed to escape unharmed. By then, the alarm had been sounded. Had the slaves been able to capture Bull or to evade pursuit for a few days while their numbers increased, the rebellion might have seriously threatened or even overthrown slavery in South Carolina, changing the course of American history. The rebels' failure to do either soon brought defeat.

Turning Point of the Rebellion. Late on Sunday afternoon, after pursuing but failing to apprehend Bull and his companions, the rebels halted in a field not far from the Edisto River. Their number now approached one hundred. They may have stopped for a variety of reasons—overconfidence, exhaustion, intoxication from stolen liquor, or a desire to allow other slaves time to join their band. This proved to be a fatal mistake. Alerted to the insurrection, a contingent of armed and mounted white planters located the rebels about 4 P.M. and opened fire. The slaves were caught off guard. Some hesitated, a few fired back, many fled. At least fourteen blacks were killed or wounded in the confusion. Others were quickly seized and shot while attempting to return to their plantations. Victorious whites severed the heads of some of the rebels and set them on mileposts along the main road as a warning to other recalcitrant slaves.

At least thirty of the rebellious slaves escaped. The entire colony was quickly armed, guards were posted at key ferry points, and militia companies conducted intensive manhunts. Most of the fugitives were captured and executed within a week. After several days of pursuit, one militia company caught up with the largest rebel band some thirty miles closer to the Georgia border. A few of the rebels remained at large for months or even years, but they had been effectively dispersed. The unsuccessful insurrection had resulted in localized property damage, the deaths of twenty-five whites and thirty-five blacks, and a surge of white terror.

Consequences. The Stono Rebellion confirmed the

worst fears of South Carolina's white minority. In the wake of the uprising, colonial officials moved quickly to reassert white control and to lessen the likelihood that slaves would flee to Florida or rise in revolt. This effort entailed three distinct changes in the system of slave supervision within the colony.

First, the colonial assembly approved and rigorously enforced a comprehensive new slave code, one of the most stringent in the hemisphere. The Negro Act of 1740, as it was known, became the basis of South Carolina's system of slave control for more than a century. The law curtailed many of the personal liberties that slaves had enjoyed in the colony for several generations, including the freedom to assemble, to move about, to grow their own food, to earn money in their leisure time, and to learn to read. It mandated careful surveillance of black activity and established stiff fines for masters who failed to keep their slaves in line. It also removed jurisdiction over slave manumissions from individual planters and placed it in the hands of the assembly.

Second, the assembly sought to alter the ratio of blacks to whites by imposing a prohibitive duty on new slaves carried into the colony from Africa and the West Indies. This action brought quick results. Although slavers had unloaded more than one thousand blacks a year in South Carolina during the 1730's, slave importations slowed to about a tenth of that number in the decade that followed. The duties collected were used to encourage white immigration from Europe. The SLAVE TRADE into the colony would resume its prerebellion dimensions by 1750, but as a result of the limited importation of the intervening decade, newly arrived slaves would never again constitute such an overwhelming proportion of the colony's total population.

Finally, South Carolina authorities attempted to eliminate the escape routes that slaves used to reach Spanish Florida. They waged war on the Spanish, hoping to punish them for their meddling and, if possible, to drive them from the region, where their proximity to the British colonies proved a perpetual incitement to slave escapes. They persuaded Georgia officials to rigorously police the most convenient passages through that colony. South Carolina strengthened its own slave patrol system, making service in the patrols a required part of militia duty and dividing the colony into well-organized beats. This permanently changed the nature of slave resistance in South Carolina. After the Stono Rebellion, seditious slaves could no longer simply flee across the frontier to Florida. They were left with but two options—feigned submission or armed struggle.—*Roy E. Finkenbine*

SUGGESTED READINGS: • Littlefield, Daniel C. *Rice and Slaves: Ethnicity and the Slave Trade in Colonial South Carolina*. Baton Rouge: Louisiana State University Press, 1981. • Sirmans, M. Eugene. "The Legal Status of the Slave in South Carolina, 1670-1740." *Journal of Southern History* 28 (November, 1962): 462-473. • TePaske, John T. "The Fugitive Slave: Intercolonial Rivalry and Spanish Slave Policy, 1689-1764." In *Eighteenth-Century Florida and Its Borderlands*. Edited by Samuel Proctor. Gainesville: University Presses of Florida, 1975. • Weir, Robert M. *Colonial South Carolina: A History*. Millwood, N.Y.: KTO, 1983. • Wood, Peter H. *Black Majority: Negroes in Colonial South Carolina from 1670 through the Stono Rebellion*. New York: W. W. Norton, 1975.

Stormy Weather (Twentieth Century-Fox, 1943): Film directed by Andrew Stone. A showcase for the talents of Lena HORNE and dancer Bill ROBINSON, the film also includes in its cast Cab CALLOWAY and his band, Dooley

Lena Horne and Bill "Bojangles" Robinson starred in the 1943 film Stormy Weather. *(Museum of Modern Art/Film Archive, NY)*

Wilson, Ada Brown, the NICHOLAS BROTHERS, Coleman HAWKINS, and Fats WALLER, performing "Ain't Misbehavin'." The story is told in flashbacks as the now-retired Corky (Robinson) reminisces about his career and his on-again/off-again romance with Selina (Horne). The story is based loosely on Robinson's life.

Straight Out of Brooklyn (Samuel Goldwyn Company, 1991): Film written and directed by Matty RICH. This bleak story of a young black man's attempt to free himself from a life of poverty by committing a crime marked Rich's feature film debut. Longing to free himself from a dismal future and a family life marked by his father's anger and domestic violence, the teenaged Dennis (Lawrence Gilliard, Jr.) plans a crime that he hopes will make him rich.

Strawberry, Darryl (b. Mar 12, 1962, Los Angeles, Calif.): BASEBALL player. Strawberry ranks as one of baseball's African American superstars. Breaking into the major leagues with the New York Mets in 1983, Strawberry proved to be a power hitter, setting a Mets home run record of 39 in 1987 and tying it in 1988. In 1991, he joined the Los Angeles Dodgers as one of the highest paid free agents of all time, earning more than $4 million a year.

Darryl Strawberry became a star baseball player with the New York Mets. (New York Mets)

Strayhorn, Billy (Nov. 29, 1915, Dayton, Ohio—May 31, 1967, New York, N.Y.): Pianist, arranger, and com-

poser. Strayhorn's career is tied to the band and music of Duke ELLINGTON. From the time that he joined the band in 1939 as a pianist, arranger, and lyricist until his departure in 1965 (because of serious illness), he wrote arrangements and collaborated with Ellington in practically every phase of the band's life.

Ellington was one of the most influential musicians in the development of big bands and their music, a process beginning in the 1930's and not exhausting itself until the 1960's. One cannot underestimate the influence of the Ellington group, from the ensembles to the individual artists. Throughout the most fruitful and exciting years of the group's development, Strayhorn was a guiding force. Strayhorn's progressive inclinations probably moved the band in directions Ellington would not have taken without Strayhorn's influence.

In addition to his collaboration with Ellington on arrangements and compositions, Strayhorn composed on his own the lyrics and melodies of superb works. "Lush Life" (1938), a ballad recorded by countless popular singers in the United States and abroad, is but one of his beautiful pieces. He wrote "Take the A Train" (1941), the theme song of the Ellington band, familiar to audiences worldwide as a signature piece of American swing music, Ellington style. Approximately two hundred compositions have been attributed to Strayhorn, either alone or in collaboration with Ellington. Listeners sometimes could not tell whether Ellington or Strayhorn had written a particular song.

Street, The (1946): Novel by Ann PETRY. *The Street* portrays an ambitious, self-reliant African American mother who, after her divorce, moves into a run-down Harlem apartment with her son. Her hopes of improving her situation are shattered when she is manipulated by those around her. She ends up killing a man and fleeing Harlem, leaving her son behind.

Student Nonviolent Coordinating Committee (SNCC): Organized in April, 1960, to coordinate the activities of students involved in protest activities, such as SIT-INS, and voter registration. Student leaders, who were hesitant to join with traditional CIVIL RIGHTS groups, formed SNCC after an organizing conference on Apr. 15-17, 1960, on the Shaw University campus in Raleigh, N.C. Initially, SNCC was dedicated to practicing nonviolent protests. The contrast between well-groomed, peaceful sit-in demonstrators and hate-filled attackers proved successful in drawing national support to the movement. The group urged a "Jail, No Bail" campaign beginning in February, 1961, in which arrested protesters would stay in jail rather than paying fines or getting out on bail. In the early years, SNCC was a democratically operated, multiracial organization. A wave of young white people flowed to the South to work with SNCC, in an atmosphere in which everyone's contribution to the decision-making process was considered.

Carmichael was named as head of SNCC on May 19, 1966, succeeding John LEWIS, who then resigned from the group in July. Under Carmichael's leadership, SNCC adopted the Black Power concept, which served to alienate SNCC from middle-class African Americans and erode its base of support among northern white liberals.

H. Rap Brown, the head of the SNCC, conducts a press conference. (Library of Congress)

By 1964, some members of SNCC were losing patience with the nonviolent strategy. These individuals, exemplified by Stokely CARMICHAEL (Kwame Toure), felt more aggressiveness in response to southern white reactionaries and southern institutions. Eventually, Carmichael's more militant position came to dominate SNCC. Tensions began to rise between African American and white members, and white members began to leave the organization. In addition, SNCC male leadership began to take on beliefs and positions that diminished the female leadership roles.

After 1963, SNCC's most important work was in the area of voter registration. Facing intense resistance, it succeeded in registering African American VOTERS throughout the South. SNCC also founded the MISSISSIPPI FREEDOM DEMOCRATIC PARTY and attempted to gain seats at the 1964 Democratic National Convention.

SNCC began to focus activities on northern cities following the breakdown of segregation throughout most of the South and the passing of the VOTING RIGHTS ACT OF 1965. Its effective leadership, including Carmichael, left to pursue other interests. H. Rap BROWN, who continued to call for confrontation with the American system, took over leadership on May 12, 1967, and in the summer of 1969 changed SNCC's name to the Student National Coordinating Committee. Brown indicated that the group would retaliate violently if required to do so. Shortly thereafter, SNCC became all but defunct, as Brown's legal problems left him little time to work with the group.

Studio Museum of Harlem (HARLEM, N.Y.): Regarded as the most important repository in the United States for contemporary black art and African and Caribbean folk art. After its opening in 1969 as a gathering place for artists who needed working space, the studio became known as a cultural center. It expanded to become a concert hall, lecture hall, and assembly hall. The studio moved in 1980 from its original location above a liquor store into what had been an office building.

Stylistics, The: Singing group. The Stylistics were famous during the early 1970's for their smooth, harmonious love songs. The group (Russell Thompkins, Jr., Airrion Love, James Smith, Herbie Murrell, and James Dunn) was formed in 1968 in Philadelphia, Pa., the members' hometown. After singing in local nightclubs, they achieved national fame in 1971 with their hit record "You Are Everything." Among their million-selling records are "People Make the World Go Round" (1972), "Betcha By Golly, Wow" (1972), and "You Make Me Feel Brand New" (1974).

Substance Abuse: Substance abuse is a major problem in American society; in 1989, public opinion polls reported that Americans believed that drugs constituted the most serious crisis facing the nation. While drug and alcohol abuse affects Americans from all walks of life, black residents of inner-city neighborhoods are particularly at risk. Many inner-city blacks have experimented with alcohol and drugs; some have become addicted to these substances as a form of personal escape from depressing and overwhelmingly bleak environments. In 1989, a Justice Department report on drug-related arrests in 21 cities showed that black arrests for drug possession exceeded those recorded for whites; in 1990, blacks constituted 40.7 percent of all arrests for drug violations, a figure that is nearly 3.5 times greater than their estimated 12.1 percent proportion of the American population. These arrests are evidence of an alarming trend within the African American community—a cycle of exposure and addiction that threatens to destroy the aspirations and achievements of an entire generation of African Americans.

Environmental Factors. It is difficult to separate the distribution and use of drugs from the host of other problems that grip the black underclass: POVERTY, crime, unemployment, ACQUIRED IMMUNE DEFICIENCY SYNDROME (AIDS), and the breakdown of the family structure. Because many black urban residents find themselves excluded from socially acceptable opportunities for success, self-validation, and self-fulfillment, they find themselves developing alternative routes to gain these objectives. The strain of growing up in impoverished and deprived circumstances pushes many black adolescents to join neighborhood gangs. Gang activity has increas-

ingly become linked with the drug trade and other forms of organized crime, providing access to drugs and alcohol and promoting drug experimentation among gang members.

Drug Use Among Adolescents. In the United States, exposure to drugs and alcohol has become common among young people in their early teens. The 1990 *National Household Survey on Drug Abuse* indicated that white adolescents were somewhat more likely than black adolescents to have tried or recently used drugs such as inhalants, hallucinogens, cocaine, marijuana, and alcohol. Black adolescents were more likely than whites to have experimented with or recently used PCP and crack. Among black teenagers between the ages of 12 and 17, 4.5 percent admitted to having used inhalants, generally considered a first step toward experimentation with hardcore drugs.

While problems exist among black and white teenagers, the high rate of social experimentation with drugs and alcohol among black adolescents is most often connected with difficulties they face in urban schools. Boredom, alienation, poor grades, and a general belief that academic achievement is an impossible and unrealistic goal—all of these factors tend to push black adolescents to drop out of school. Lacking a high school diploma, these dropouts find that their job opportunities are extremely limited. Unemployment in turn contributes to feelings of hopelessness for which black teenagers seek solace in illegal drugs. In many cases, this drug abuse leads to violent criminal behavior.

Link Between Drug Use and Crime. Drug and alcohol abuse may be linked to criminal activity in two ways. First, substance abuse may decrease inhibitions and make the user act in a more aggressive manner; both of these factors tend to increase a person's potential for committing crimes. A recent survey of police reports indicated that 27 percent of violent black offenders were perceived to be under the influence of drugs or alcohol while committing criminal acts. Second, while addiction itself is not a necessary cause of criminality, many offenders commit criminal acts in order to obtain the money to purchase alcohol or illegal drugs. Results from a Rand Institute survey showed that a majority of violent career criminal offenders in the United States had a history of heroin use, often in combination with alcohol or other drug use. In addition, a study of heroin users in Harlem conducted in the early 1980's indicated that serious addicts committed more crimes, including robberies and burglaries, than did occasional users.

Drug Abuse and Health Problems. Malnutrition and respiratory problems are among many of the health problems that may result from drug addiction. In addition to expected health problems resulting from long-term drug use, users may suffer from other ailments, including vision impairment, musculoskeletal disorders, skin disease, frequent colds, and tooth and gum disease. Health complications may occur as an indirect result of drug dependence. Users who turn to prostitution to support their habit have an increased susceptibility to sexually transmitted diseases. When drug users share intravenous (IV) hypodermic needles, syringes, and other drug paraphernalia, they may become ill and die as a result of an infection, such as hepatitis or AIDS, transferred into the bloodstream from tainted drug equipment. Illegal drug use is not solely confined to ghetto residents; professional athletes who may be abusing anabolic steroids in order to improve their sports performance also suffer from health complications as a result of their drug dependence.

War on Drugs. During the 1980's, a massive antidrug movement was launched to publicize the serious effects of both occasional and long-term substance abuse. The prevalence of cocaine, especially in the concentrated and easily ingestible form of crack, was blamed for increased homicides, street robberies, and family violence and neglect. Not only was there new concern over the long-term health effects of cocaine abuse on the user, but scientific studies began to document alarming physiological damage inflicted upon infants who had been exposed to crack and other drugs while in their mothers' wombs. In response, the Reagan Administration pledged itself to mounting a "war on drugs" by passing more stringent laws and increasing the federal funds and manpower used to combat drug smuggling and distribution. The government was also in the forefront of the media campaign against drugs with First Lady Nancy Reagan's "Just Say No" program, which focused its efforts on improving drug education efforts in elementary and secondary schools.

Drug Treatment Efforts. While the economic resources available to most black drug abusers are insufficient to cover the cost of most detoxification and personal therapy programs, some drug offenders are required to participate in prison detoxification programs and other users seek help from neighborhood treatment programs. Efforts are also being made to create family-centered solutions to drug addiction. In addition to providing medical and psychological treatment, these programs devote their resources to keeping children in parental custody and providing shelter and job counseling in order to alleviate the frustration of poverty while parents are in recovery. The Center for Family Health, run by the nonprofit D.C. Institute in Washington, D.C., is one such program. Sup-

ported by private funds as well as Medicaid, the program costs $20,000 annually per family, but if rehabilitation and prevention are successful, this expense is small compared to the estimated annual outlay of $100,000 to provide hospital care for an abandoned, drug-exposed infant.

Conclusion. As documented above, substance abuse is a major factor in the tragic life circumstances of many inner-city blacks. Since rehabilitation of drug users is a costly final step in the effort to combat substance abuse, many experts have proposed that funding be targeted for preventive efforts that could intervene before drug experimentation and addiction begin. These proposals include programs to rescue black students at risk of dropping out of school, programs to educate teenage mothers about the perils of neonatal drug addiction, and programs to provide job training and improve employment skills. Some critics have pointed out that such community-based prevention programs would eliminate the demand for drugs at its source, resulting in a more effective "victory" than has yet been made with the huge budgets devoted to capturing and prosecuting drug distributors during the Reagan and Bush administrations. Whatever solutions are proposed, it is clear that many young African Americans will continue to succumb to the destructive enticements of drugs and alcohol until decisive action is taken to improve their self-image and their socioeconomic status.—*Judith Ann Warner*

SUGGESTED READINGS: • Bell, Peter. *Chemical Dependency and the African American: Counseling Strategies and Community Issues.* Center City, Minn.: Hazelden, 1990. • Brunswick, A. F. "Young Black Males and Substance Abuse." In *Young, Black and Male in America: An Endangered Species*, edited by Jewelle Taylor Gibbs. Dover, Mass.: Auburn House, 1988. • Elliot, D. S., D. Huizinga, and S. S. Ageton. *Explaining Delinquency and Drug Use.* Boulder, Colo.: Behavioral Research Institute, 1982. • Jaynes, Gerald D., and Robin M. Williams, Jr., eds. *A Common Destiny: Blacks and American Society.* Washington, D.C.: National Academy Press, 1989. • U.S. Congress. House Select Committee on Narcotics Abuse and Control. *Intravenous Drug Use and AIDS: The Impact on the Black Community.* Washington, D.C.: U.S. Government Printing Office, 1988.

suburbanization: Movement to the outlying areas of cities. African Americans became more urbanized between 1920 and 1970 as they moved to cities to obtain employment. The proportion of black people living within central cities began to decline in the 1970's, following an earlier trend among white people. This suburbanization can be viewed as representing such ideals as open housing, freedom of movement, and ability to choose housing that balances family needs such as education and living space with cost and proximity to employment. Jobs also were moving to the suburbs and the purchase of a home was easier there than in central cities, encouraging suburbanization.

From 1970 to 1980, the total suburban population grew by 17.3 percent, but black suburbanites grew in number by 49.4 percent. By 1988, more than one-fourth of black people in the United States lived in the suburbs. In 1970, 4.8 percent of all suburbanites were black, but by 1980 that figure had reached 6.1 percent. The rising number of black people who had reached middle-class income status contributed to this movement, as did the rising number of open housing laws. In 1971, the NATIONAL ASSOCIATION FOR THE ADVANCEMENT OF COLORED PEOPLE (NAACP) filed suit against Oyster Bay, N.Y., charging that zoning laws effectively shut out black people by prohibiting building of apartments. President Richard Nixon promised to enforce antidiscrimination laws but would not force low-cost housing into suburban communities that did not want it.

Suburbanization can be viewed as a positive step in community integration, but it has not proved to be as effective for African Americans as it has for Asian and Hispanic Americans, according to a study by Douglas S. Massey and Nancy A. Denton published in the *American Journal of Sociology* in November, 1988. Those researchers found that black people did not experience as large an increase in interracial contact after moving to the suburbs as did Asian and Hispanic Americans.

Sudarkasa, Niara (Gloria Marshall Clark; b. Aug. 14, 1938, Fort Lauderdale, Fla.): University professor and administrator. In 1987, Sudarkasa became the first woman to be president of LINCOLN UNIVERSITY, the oldest HISTORICALLY BLACK COLLEGE in the United States. In her earlier academic life, she won a Ford Foundation Scholarship for Early Admission to College, attending FISK UNIVERSITY from 1953 to 1956 and transferring to OBERLIN COLLEGE, from which she earned her A.B. in 1957. Her M.A. (1959) and Ph.D. (1964) in anthropology are from Columbia University.

From 1960 to 1963, Sudarkasa held a Ford Foundation Foreign Area Training Fellowship, which she used to study the Yoruba language and the role of Yoruba women in the marketplace. She studied at the University of London, then lived in a Yoruba village in Nigeria. Her publications include works on African women, West African migration, African American families, and market activities of Yoruba women.

From 1963 to 1964, Sudarkasa was a fellow at the Committee for the Comparative Study of New Nations at the University of Chicago. She became an assistant professor at New York University in 1964, teaching there until 1967, when she became an assistant professor at the University of Michigan at Ann Arbor. She reached the rank of full professor in 1976, becoming the first black woman to achieve that rank in the school's division of arts and sciences. From 1981 to 1984, she was director of the university's Center for Afro-American and African studies. She then was named as associate vice president for academic affairs. In that position, she initiated, evaluated, and monitored the recruitment and retention of minority students.

Niara Sudarkasa was named president of Lincoln University in 1986, the first woman to fill that position at the oldest historically black college in the United States. (Harlee Little)

In 1977, Sudarkasa married John Clark, an inventor, sculptor, and contractor. It was then that she began using her new name. The name of Sudarkasa, she says, came from her marriage. "Nia" is a Swahili word meaning "purpose," and Niara is an adaptation meaning "woman of purpose."

Lincoln University announced its selection of Sudarkasa

as president on Sept. 29, 1986. She began serving in 1987. Among her stated goals as president were to maintain ties with the African continent. Toward that goal, she planned to add to the school's collection of African materials and to open an African museum. She also continued to stress the school's strong programs in science.

Sugar Hill Times (CBS, 1949): Television musical variety show. Harry BELAFONTE headlined this showcase for African American talent, which had as regulars Willie Bryant, Timmie Rogers, the Jubileers, and Don REDMAN and His Orchestra. Of the six broadcasts, four were of an hour's length and two were half-hour telecasts. The first two programs were respectively entitled *Uptown Jubilee* and *Harlem Jubilee*.

Suicide, The (pr. 1967): Play by Carol Freeman. This drama in one act is set in a ghetto apartment where a quiet vigil is being held to honor a death. A loud, disrespectful neighbor, however, refuses to turn down her radio, turning the wake into a noisy quarrel.

Sula (1973): Novel by Toni MORRISON. The work deals with the lives, families, and strong friendship ties of two black women who are separated for ten years. Sula goes to the city to get an education, while Nel gets married and remains in the small town. Their friendship turns to hatred after Sula seduces Nel's husband.

Sullivan, Leon Howard (b. Oct. 16, 1922, Charleston, W.Va.): Religious leader and community organizer. Sullivan was educated at West Virginia State College, from which he received the B.A. degree in 1943. He attended Union Theological Seminary in 1945 and received an M.A. degree from Columbia University in 1947. Virginia Union University also granted him an honorary doctorate of divinity. Ordained a Baptist minister in 1941. Sullivan gained prominence as pastor of Zion Baptist Church in Philadelphia, Pa. (1950-1988), as a community organizer, and as founder (1964) and director of the Opportunities Industrialization Centers of America, Incorporated (OIC), which became a national institution operating in one hundred cities in the United States.

Having been a part of A. Philip RANDOLPH's threatened march on Washington program to obtain jobs for African Americans, and having served as an aide to Adam Clayton POWELL, JR., in his campaign for Congress, Sullivan was well prepared for the role he would play in the Philadelphia community movement which he initiated. He was the major figure behind the Philadelphia Four Hundred, an alliance of African American ministers who led a

Leon Sullivan has played many roles in his life, from minister to community organizer to businessperson. (AP/Wide World Photos)

successful selective buying campaign in the early 1960's. The campaign spurned local businesses that discriminated in employment. The technique was so successful that it spread to other cities, such as Atlanta, Detroit, and New York. Sullivan then organized the OIC as a means of providing African Americans with the skills and training needed to fill the jobs that opened up.

Sullivan's prestige led to his selection as a member of the board of directors of General Motors in 1971. He was the first African American to participate in the direction of a United States automobile company at that high a level. In 1976, the Leon Howard Sullivan Chair was established in the school of social welfare at the University of Wisconsin. Sullivan received the Franklin D. Roosevelt Four Freedoms Medal in 1987. The Leon Howard Sullivan Scholarship Fund was established at Bentley College in Massachusetts in 1988.

Sullivan, Louis Wade (b. Nov. 3, 1933, Atlanta, Ga.): Educator and government official. Shortly after he won the 1988 election, President-elect George Bush named Sullivan as United States secretary of health and human services, thus making him the highest-ranking African American in the Bush Administration and the only African American in the cabinet.

Sullivan was the younger of two sons of political activist and undertaker Walter Wade Sullivan and schoolteacher Lubirda Elizabeth Sullivan, who cofounded the NATIONAL ASSOCIATION FOR THE ADVANCEMENT OF COLORED PEOPLE. Sullivan distinguished himself at Morehouse College and was graduated magna cum laude in 1954. He won a scholarship to Boston University Medical School and was graduated cum laude as the only African American in the class of 1958. On completing residency at New York Hospital-Cornell Medical Center, he won a fellowship in pathology to Massachusetts General Hospital in Boston in 1960. In 1961, he obtained a research fellowship to Thorndike Memorial Laboratory at Harvard Medical School, and two years later he began an academic career as an instructor of medicine at Harvard.

From 1964 to 1966, Sullivan was assistant professor of medicine at New Jersey College of Medicine. He returned to Boston University as assistant professor and codirector of hematology at the university's medical center. He became associate professor in 1968 and full professor of medicine and physiology in 1974. He cofounded the Morehouse-affiliated medical school, which trained physicians for the rural South and urban America, where doctors were in scarce supply. As dean, he steered the program to a fully accredited four-year institution under the name of the Morehouse School of Medicine, one of the only three black medical schools in the country. He led the school in researching health problems to which African Americans are especially at risk, such as SICKLE CELL ANEMIA, hypertension, and some forms of CANCER. He also founded the National Association of Minority Medical Educators. As secretary of health and human services, Sullivan supervised a $400 million budget and was known as a hands-on administrator. He showed great sagacity in handling controversial issues related to abortion and the right to life, antitobacco laws, funding for the arts, and other government-funded programs.

Sullivan, Maxine (Marietta Williams; May 13, 1911, Homestead, Pa.—Apr. 7, 1987, New York, N.Y.): Singer. Sullivan began her musical career as a vocalist with the big band of Claude Thornhill in 1937. Her recording of the Scottish folk song "Loch Lomond" (1937) appealed to popular taste for sweet, folk music. An immediate success, it unfortunately typecast her as a singer of folk or semiclassical music.

Sullivan appeared in two Hollywood film musicals, *Going Places* (1938), in which she introduced the song "Jeepers Creepers" with Louis ARMSTRONG, and *ST. LOUIS BLUES* (1939). She was also in the Broadway show *Swingin' the Dream* (1939), with Louis Armstrong and Benny Goodman. Sullivan performed in small jazz ensembles, most notably with saxophonist John Kirby and his combo, which specialized in low-key, quiet jazz, what has been called "chamber jazz." She married Kirby in 1938, and they starred in a radio program, *Flow Gently, Sweet Rhythm*, beginning in 1940. She eventually settled upon a solo career, singing at jazz clubs and occasionally performing on valve trombone and flugelhorn. She was divorced from Kirby, then married Cliff Jackson in 1950.

Singer Maxine Sullivan recorded big band, folk, and jazz music and appeared in several Hollywood and Broadway musicals. (AP/Wide World Photos)

During the 1950's, Sullivan embarked on another career, training as a nurse. She shifted her appearances to community-oriented activities, most notably services among the urban deprived. She concentrated on community service and performance in her later life but occasionally appeared at jazz clubs and jazz festivals, performing with the World's Greatest Jazz Band of Bob Haggart and Yank Lawson. She also toured the United Kingdom and was recorded by the British Broadcasting Corporation.

Summer, Donna (LaDonna Gaines; b. Dec. 31, 1948, Boston, Mass.): Singer and composer. After launching a singing career from Germany, Summer became the biggest star of the 1970's disco trend in the United States.

Known for long compositions with a beat-driven melody, she managed to appeal to disco, rock, and pop music fans.

Born into a family of five sisters and one brother, Summer sang in churches as a child and made her professional debut at Boston's Psychedelic Supermarket in 1967. At the age of eighteen, she landed a singing role in a production of the rock musical *Hair* in Munich, Germany. While in Europe, she also sang in the Vienna Folk Opera's version of *PORGY AND BESS*, worked as a backup singer at Munich's Musicland Studios, and recorded several hit records.

Summer earned acclaim in the United States with the 1975 release of a controversial tune, "Love to Love You Baby," a seventeen-minute erotic single full of moans and heavy breathing. It became a major disco hit, ranking high on both the pop music and rhythm-and-blues charts. Soon after, Summer abandoned her high-pitched, breathy vocal style and recorded a series of top-selling hits including "I Feel Love" (1977), "MacArthur Park" (1978), "Bad Girls" (1979), and "Hot Stuff" (1979).

In 1978, Summer appeared in the disco film *Thank God It's Friday* and won a Grammy Award for her recording of "Last Dance" from the film's sound track. In the late 1970's, her duet "No More Tears (Enough Is Enough)" with singer Barbra Streisand reached number one on the pop charts. By 1982 Summer had received eight gold and two platinum albums in addition to ten gold and two platinum singles.

In the 1980's, Summer entered a new phase of her musical career. She traded her sexy, fantasy-like disco image for a devoutly Christian one. Her first song with a born-again Christian message appeared on her 1980 album entitled *The Wanderer*. Similarly, her music moved away from the modern electronic sound of disco and began to resemble more traditional forms of African American soul music.

Summers, Edna White (b. Sept. 4, 1919, Evanston, Ill.): Supervisor of Evanston, Ill. White attended Roosevelt University and the University of Wisconsin-Milwaukee before returning to settle in her hometown of Evanston. She was elected as alderman on the Evanston city council in 1968 and served until 1981. In 1974, she was employed as a social services worker for the state of Illinois, and she continued in this position until 1985. She became supervisor for Evanston Township in 1985, a position equivalent to mayor, and was the first African American woman to attain this post in the state of Illinois.

Sunday, Elisabeth: Photographer. Sunday became active as a photographer in Oakland, Calif., in the early 1980's. She traveled for four years in Europe and Africa taking pictures. She has taught workshops in France and Switzerland as well as in California, and she has produced several limited edition portfolios of her work.

Super Fly (Warner Bros., 1972). Film directed by Gordon Parks, Jr. One of the first of what would be labeled "black exploitation" or "BLAXPLOITATION" pictures, the film stars Ron O'NEAL as Youngblood Priest, a drug pusher who plans to leave his chosen profession once he gets rich from one last deal. Carl Lee plays his partner, Charles McGregor is Fat Freddie, and Curtis MAYFIELD provided the film's popular musical score.

Supreme Court and Civil Rights, The: The Supreme Court was established by Article III of the Constitution as the head of the judicial branch of the federal government. The Court has jurisdiction over all cases in law arising under the Constitution and under federal law, over controversies between citizens of different states or between one state and another state, over disputes between a state and the federal government. The Court has no power to enforce its decisions, however, and its authority and power are subject to limitation by the executive and legislative branches of government. Yet the Court has been the most significant institution in the development of social policies regarding CIVIL RIGHTS and equality in American history, because it is the final arbiter of the constitutionality of all laws and presidential orders.

Pre-Civil War to Plessy v. Ferguson. The Supreme Court has been the pivotal branch of government in the pursuit of equality for all Americans. Depending on the Court's conservative-liberal composition and the sociopolitical milieu, the Court has been either a lifeline for or an oppressive anchor to the African American and minority communities' quests for equality. Historical analysis of the Supreme Court's decisions on civil rights for African Americans shows that early civil rights laws often enjoyed limited success before the Supreme Court reinterpreted these laws to invalidate their effectiveness.

In the first major case before the Court on the constitutionality of SLAVERY, *Dred Scott v. Sandford* (1857), the Supreme Court considered the question of whether a slave became free upon temporary residence in a free territory. The Court held that the Constitution did not include African Americans as citizens, and therefore, African Americans could not claim any of the rights guaranteed by the Constitution.

In 1863, President Abraham Lincoln signed the EMANCIPATION PROCLAMATION, which freed all slaves in the southern states. In 1866, the THIRTEENTH AMENDMENT, which formally abolished slavery, was passed and signed. The Civil Rights of Act of 1866 established citizenship for all former slaves. In 1868, the FOURTEENTH AMENDMENT, which guaranteed due process and equal protection of the Constitution for all citizens, was passed. In 1870, the FIFTEENTH AMENDMENT was ratified, prohibiting the denial of the right to vote on the basis of race or previous condition of servitude. The Civil Rights Act of 1875 guaranteed that all persons within the jurisdiction of the United States were protected from discrimination in the use of public accommodations because of race, color, or previous servitude. The thrust of these laws was to destroy slavery forever and to lay the foundation for full citizenship for African Americans.

did not violate the equal-protection clause of the Fourteenth Amendment. The decision created the legal basis for the subjugation of African Americans for much of the twentieth century.

The Warren Court and Equality. In 1953, Earl Warren became the chief justice of the Supreme Court. The Warren Court marked a new era in defining and extending constitutionally guaranteed civil rights. In the fifteen years after 1953, the Court set many new precedents that greatly expanded the civil rights of African Americans and other protected groups. In its decision in *BROWN V. BOARD OF EDUCATION* (1954), the Court reversed the "separate but equal" doctrine. The case was litigated by Thurgood MARSHALL, who was later to become the first African

The Supreme Court's decision in Brown v. Board of Education—*that the concept of "separate but equal" schools for white and black students was invalid—spawned a crisis in Little Rock, Ark.* (The Associated Publishers, Inc.)

In response to such legislative acts, the Supreme Court made several decisions over the next thirty years that effectively nullified these major gains. The civil rights cases of 1883 involved five cases raising the issue of whether the denial of accommodation in hotels and theaters to blacks violated the constitutional guarantees of the Thirteenth and Fourteenth Amendments. The Court decided that such denial did not violate these amendments. It also found that the Civil Rights Act of 1875, prohibiting discrimination in public accommodations, was unconstitutional. Concluding this significant retreat, the Court's decision in *PLESSY V. FERGUSON* (1896) relegated African Americans to second-class citizenship for the next half-century. In its decision, the Court ruled that "SEPARATE BUT EQUAL" facilities for white and black passengers on a train

American Supreme Court justice. The Court ruled that segregated educational facilities were inherently unequal and violated the equal-protection clause of the Fourteenth Amendment.

From the early 1950's to 1968, African Americans and their allies engaged in massive protests demanding equality. In response to the Civil Rights movement, three major civil rights initiatives became law: Congress passed two civil rights law, the Civil Rights Act of 1964 and the Voting Rights Act of 1965, and President Lyndon Johnson signed Executive Order 11246.

The Voting Rights Act. The VOTING RIGHTS ACT of 1965, which has been hailed as the most significant social legislation of the twentieth century, prohibited the use of any practice or procedure that would deny any citizen the right to vote. In the area of voting and the participation of African Americans in the political process, the Court made several landmark decisions that became the principles of the Voting Rights Act. *In Gomillion v. Lightfoot* (1960), the Court ruled that the drawing of new city

Civil Rights Act and Affirmative Action. The Civil Rights Act of 1964 contained Title VII, which prohibited unlawful discrimination in employment on the basis of race, color, religion, sex, or national origin. In 1972, the act was extended to cover most federal, state, and local

The civil rights protests of the 1960's, in which many African American demonstrators put their lives on the line, resulted in the Civil Rights Act of 1964. (AP/Wide World Photos)

boundaries to exclude African American voters violated the equal-protection clause of the Fourteenth Amendment. The Court decided in *Baker v. Carr* (1962) that the unequal apportionment of population among state legislative districts was a constitutional issue and therefore was within the jurisdiction of the federal courts. In *Gray v. Sanders* (1963), *Wesberry v. Sander* (1964), and *Reynold v. Sims* (1964), the Court enumerated the constitutional principle of "one man, one vote," which required all county and state legislators to be elected from districts roughly equal in population. The impressive increase in the numbers of African Americans occupying elected positions is testimony to the impact of these decisions.

government employers and educational institutions. President Johnson, recognizing that it would require many years of litigation before the Civil Rights Act could become effective, signed Executive Order 11246, which required government contractors to engage in AFFIRMATIVE ACTION to address discrimination in employment against African Americans and other minority groups. Affirmative action regulations required the hiring of minority group members in accordance with their availability within a geographical area, targeted goals, or quotas, demonstrating the results of affirmative action policies and programs, and targeted promotions and training opportunities based on proportional representation.

In the first major affirmative action case, the Supreme Court in *University of California Regents v. Bakke* (1978) approved the use of race as a factor in the selection process for admission to universities. In *Kaiser Aluminum v. Weber* (1979), the Court upheld the use of voluntary affirmative action programs by private employers to redress manifest racial discrimination. These two cases established the legality of applying affirmative action laws and policies to state and private employers.

In the major decision involving employment discrimination, *Griggs v. Duke Power Company* (1971), the Court established the legal precedent that any selection procedures, tests, or criteria that disproportionately excluded minorities from employment were unlawful unless such criteria could be shown to be job-related and dictated by business necessity. The most significant impact of the *Griggs* decision was the enumerated principle that the effects, and not the intent, of a selection procedure determined whether it was unlawful.

The Rehnquist Court. The civil rights successes of the 1950's, 1960's, and 1970's were followed by a full retreat by the executive and federal branches of government in ensuring full equality; overtly racial political appeals led to the election of presidents committed to overturning the legacy of the Warren Court. By the mid-1980's, through the selection of conservative justices, the Supreme Court had become an obstacle to the aspirations for equality of African Americans and other disadvantaged groups.

During the 1988-1989 term, the Court, headed by Chief Justice William Rehnquist, made several decisions on equal employment opportunity law that eviscerated earlier antidiscrimination laws. The *Griggs* precedent was overturned by the Court in *Wards Cove Packing Company, Inc. v. Atonio* (1989). Under the *Griggs* standard, once the racially disparate impact of a job-selection process had been shown, the employer in question was required to show a nondiscriminatory reason for the process. The *Wards Cove* decision shifted the burden of proof from the employer to the plaintiff; it also limited the use of statistical evidence as proof of discrimination. In another major case, *Patterson v. McLean Credit Union* (1989), the Court overruled earlier interpretations by limiting the Civil Rights Act of 1866 to apply only to discrimination in hiring; the Court ruled that the act did not apply to any discrimination that occurred during employment.

In 1991, Congress passed the Civil Rights Act of 1991, which overturned the Supreme Court's decisions in the 1989 cases. Adverse rulings by the Rehnquist Court, however, suggested that African Americans and other minority group members would need to rely on Congress for

support in the continuing struggle for equality.—*Richard Hudson*

SUGGESTED READINGS: • Altschiller, Donald, ed. *Affirmative Action*. New York: H. W. Wilson, 1991. • Baum, Lawrence. *The Supreme Court*. 2d ed. Washington, D.C.: Congressional Quarterly Press, 1985. • Bell, Derrick A., Jr. *Race, Racism, and American Law*. 2d ed. Boston: Little, Brown, 1980. • Ginger, Ann Fagan. *The Law, the Supreme Court and the People's Rights*. Rev. ed. Woodbury, N.Y.: Barron's, 1977. • Goode, Stephen. *The Controversial Court*. New York: J. Messner, 1982.

Supremes, The: Most successful of the "girl groups" in soul/rhythm-and-blues music in the 1960's and 1970's. The Detroit teenagers from the Brewster-Douglass housing project first sang as the Primettes, taking their name from the Primes, who evolved into the TEMPTATIONS. The girls signed with Motown Records in 1961. Florence Ballard, Diana ROSS, and Mary WILSON then changed the name of their group to the Supremes.

The Supremes' recording career started slowly, and none of the early records was a real hit. In 1963, Motown paired the group with the writing and producing team of HOLLAND-DOZIER-HOLLAND. The Supremes' career took off with the release of "When the Lovelight Starts Shining Through His Eyes" in 1963. In 1964 and 1965, the group established itself at the top of American popular music with five straight number-one hits: "Where Did Our Love Go," "Baby Love," "Come See About Me," "Stop! In the Name of Love," and "Back in My Arms Again." Three more number-one releases followed in 1966 and 1967: "You Can't Hurry Love," "You Keep me Hangin' On," and "Love Is Here and Now You're Gone." In 1967, Ballard left the group and was replaced by Cindy Birdsong. Number-one songs continued, including "The Happening" (1967), "Love Child" (1968), and "Someday We'll Be Together" (1969).

Lead singer Diana Ross attracted increased attention, and in 1967 the trio was renamed Diana Ross and the Supremes. In 1970, Ross left the group for good to pursue a successful singing and acting career. She was replaced by Jean Terrell. The Supremes continued to record with some success into the late 1970's.

At their peak, the Supremes were the most successful American singing group of the day. Their success could be attributed to Holland-Dozier-Holland's producing style, which provided lush instrumental backgrounds, and the compatibility of the group with Ross's high lead voice. Usually sheathed in long gowns, the Supremes were less choreographed than other Motown groups, depending on coordinated hand and arm motions for visual effect. Efforts by the group to cross over into other areas of music were not very successful. The 1981 Broadway show *DREAMGIRLS* is based on the Supremes' story. After numerous personnel changes, the group dissolved in 1976.

Sutton, Percy Ellis (b. Nov. 24, 1920, San Antonio, Tex.): Politician. Sutton became a major participant in New York City politics when he was elected president of the borough of Manhattan in 1966. As borough president (until 1977), Sutton had two votes on the city's Board of Estimate, which allocates funds for municipal departments and services. This position made Sutton one of the most influential black people in the United States. Sutton, an attorney, also served in the New York state assembly.

Sutton, as a practicing attorney following his release from the United States Air Force, was involved actively in CIVIL RIGHTS cases. Much of this was done in collaboration with the NATIONAL ASSOCIATION FOR THE ADVANCEMENT OF COLORED PEOPLE (NAACP). Sutton was director of the New York branch of the NAACP in 1961 and 1962. He received some of his experience with United States laws in the area of civil rights through his position as a trial advocate judge in the United States Air Force.

During his brief tenure as a state assemblyman (1964-1966), Sutton organized other African American representatives into a bloc that won them membership on major committees. His organizational abilities and political knowledge served Sutton well in his capacity as borough president. As borough president, Sutton drew attention to urban problems and directed efforts to solve them. He also increased citizen participation in government. Sutton was a believer in citizens using the system to advance their interests. For example, in 1963 he formed, along with Charles RANGEL, the Harlem Democratic Club (later the Martin Luther KING, JR., Club), which has hundreds of volunteer workers.

Following his tenure as borough president, Sutton devoted his energies to the media business. Sutton understood the power of media to advance the interests and well-being of African Americans. Sutton formed groups that purchased the *Amsterdam News*, an African American newspaper. In 1977, Sutton became owner and chairman of the board of the Inner-City Broadcasting Company, which owns radio stations throughout the country.

Sutton, Pierre Montea "PePe" (b. Feb. 1, 1947, New York, N.Y.): Broadcasting company executive. Sutton became chairman of Inner City Broadcasting Corporation (ICBC), a successful African American broadcasting company, in 1990. The company was founded in 1972 upon the purchase, by Sutton's father and a group of investors, of a single AM radio station in Harlem. Sutton's father, Percy, whose vision guided the company through the subsequent acquisition of nine radio stations, the purchase and renovation of the legendary APOLLO THEATER in Harlem, and a $70 million cable television deal, named Sutton as the first president of the corporation in 1977.

ICBC purchased WLIB-FM, the sister station to its first acquisition. Upon changing the call letters of the station to WBLS-FM, ICBC made it the corporation's flagship station. It would set the standard for African American radio in the United States, and it became the premier black radio station.

Sutton's father retired as chairman of ICBC in December, 1990, leaving the corporation in Sutton's hands. Sutton had been directing the corporate affairs of the organization's radio stations for many years. Sutton's charge as chairman was to nurture his father's vision to establish ICBC as a multimedia empire. The core business of the corporation remained the radio stations. The acquisition of the Apollo Theater provided an impetus for ICBC to branch out into record production, artist management, music publishing, concert promotions, theater

Taking over the company founded by his father and others in 1972, Pierre M. Sutton became the chairman of Inner City Broadcasting Corporation, in 1990. (Inner City Broadcasting Corporation)

productions, television syndication, and magazine publishing. ICBC's most successful effort with the Apollo purchase was the production and syndication of the program *It's Showtime at the Apollo!* This show is a syndicated broadcast of the weekly amateur night held at the Apollo Theater.

Sutton, who was graduated with a bachelor of arts degree from the University of Toledo in 1968, has held leadership roles in various civic organizations such as the Minority Investment Fund, National Association of Black Owned Broadcasters, Harlem Boy Scouts, Alvin Ailey Dance Foundation, and Better Business Bureau of Harlem.

Swanson, Howard (Aug. 18, 1907, Atlanta, Ga.—Nov. 12, 1978, New York, N.Y.): Composer. Swanson gained national recognition in 1949 with the performance of his song "The Negro Speaks of Rivers." In 1950, his *Short Symphony* was performed by the New York Philharmonic Orchestra. Other works include *Night Music* (1950), *Music for Strings* (1952), *Vista No. II* (1969), and several songs with poems by Carl Sandburg, Vachel Lindsay, and Langston Hughes as lyrics.

Sweet Honey in the Rock: Female vocal group founded in Washington, D.C., in 1973 by Bernice Johnson Reagon. The group performed gospel and other black music unaccompanied. Its songs protested social evils and addressed humanitarian issues. The group's concerts were signed for those with impaired hearing.

Sykes, Brenda (b. June 25, 1949, Shreveport, La.): Actress. Sykes was reared in Los Angeles, Calif., from the age of six. She attended the University of California at Los Angeles and was married to musician Gil Scott-Heron. Sykes made appearances on such television programs as *Room 222*, *The Streets of San Francisco*, and *Mayberry R.F.D.* before obtaining the role of college student Brenda MacKenzie in the syndicated series *Ozzie's Girls* (1973). She also had a recurring role in the dramatic series *Executive Suite* (1976-1977).

A popular supporting actress of the 1970's, she played in such films as *The Liberation of L. B. Jones* (1970), *Black Gunn* (1972), and *Cleopatra Jones* (1973). In 1971, she starred in the interracial romance *Honky*, but she achieved greater fame for another interracial liaison in *Mandingo* (1975). In this antebellum melodrama, Sykes portrays a slave involved in a sexual relationship with the son (Perry King) of a plantation owner. Although critically denounced, this popular film led to a sequel, *Drum* (1976), in which Sykes was featured in a small role.

Sylvers, The: Singing group. Part of the 1970's craze for family singing groups, the Sylvers were a nine-member

The Sylvers in 1984, a family singing group popular in the 1970's. (AP/Wide World Photos)

collection of brothers and sisters. They released several albums and had a few minor disco hits but never reached the level of stardom of the JACKSON 5 or the Osmonds. By the early 1980's, the group had slimmed down to five members and was signed to Solar Records. It developed a sophisticated style not unlike that of the group Chic, including rich melodies, smooth vocals, and crisp production. The Sylvers released a lively album, *Concept*, in 1981.

Sylvester (Sylvester James; c. 1946, Los Angeles, Calif.—December, 1988, Oakland, Calif.): Singer. Flamboyant disco star Sylvester's brand of high-camp style enabled him to cross over from gay disco fame to mainstream appeal at the peak of the disco craze. He began his singing career as a child gospel star before moving to San Francisco during the height of 1960's psychedelia. He joined a nightclub group known as the Cockettes, in which he honed the elaborate and campy style of dress for which he became known. In 1977, he was signed to Fantasy records, for which he recorded *Sylvester*. The album's combination of disco rhythms and soulful ballads sung in his trademark falsetto style set the stage for his enormously successful second album, *Step Two*, which was released in 1978 and included two hit singles, "(You Make Me Feel) Mighty Real" and "Dance (Disco Heat)."

Sylvester's entourage included two large-sized backup singers, Martha Wash and Izora Rhodes, who became known as Two Tons of Fun and who recorded on their own for Fantasy. Martha Wash went on to become a well-known voice on recordings of other groups, including C+C Music Factory and Black Box. When the disco craze died out, Sylvester went on to do session work with such notables as Herbie HANCOCK and Jeanie Tracy. He later was diagnosed with ACQUIRED IMMUNE DEFICIENCY SYNDROME and worked hard to educate the black community about the disease, finally succumbing at the age of forty-two.

Syphilis: A sexually transmitted disease caused by a spiral-shaped organism called *Treponema pallidum*. Most medical historians contend that syphilis was not introduced to Europe until the fifteenth century, when Columbus' men returned with it from the New World. Some diagnoses of leprosy prior to that time, however, may have been misdiagnoses of syphilis. Whatever its origins, this disease has been a source of morbidity and mortality for many Americans. According to some authorities, African Americans have been at greater risk for the disease than other ethnic groups.

From around 1865 to 1890, physicians often attributed poor health among blacks to syphilis. Most agreed that through education, African Americans could overcome the disease and lead healthy lives. By the turn of the century, however, as race relations deteriorated throughout the United States, members of the medical community were more likely to believe that black people were more susceptible to syphilis than others as a result of their supposed rampant immorality and ignorance. Syphilis became perceived as an African American disease that the race had brought upon itself.

As in the case of other serious diseases, scientific

Because syphilis is often spread by prostitutes, many white doctors in the early twentieth century believed that "immoral" black men were more susceptible to the disease than other groups. (AP/Wide World Photos)

medicine gave physicians the means to control syphilis. In 1905, scientists identified the organism that causes the disease. Later, laboratory tests were developed to diagnose the disorder, and an array of drugs was used to combat it. All segments of the population benefited: Even African Americans, who appeared to be a syphilis-ridden race, found new hope for cure.

In 1932, the United States Public Health Service undertook an infamous study of the effects of untreated syphilis. Using approximately three hundred black male residents of Macon County, Ala., as human guinea pigs, researchers studied morbidity and mortality among untreated syphilis victims. During the course of the Tuskegee Study, as it came to be known, the subjects who were in the later stages of the disease received neither new drug therapies nor older therapies. As one historian of medicine stated, the study was nontherapeutic and simply examined the course of untreated syphilis among black males. The Tuskegee Study, however, must be seen as an aberration in the conquest of sexually transmitted diseases.

By the 1980's, the incidence of syphilis had declined among all segments of the population, an indication that the disease could be controlled successfully among all ethnic groups. A resurgence of syphilis appeared to be under way in the United States around 1987. This increased incidence, however, might well be attributed to better reporting and a raised consciousness level regarding all sexually transmitted diseases during the ACQUIRED IMMUNE DEFICIENCY SYNDROME epidemic.

Syreeta (Syreeta Wright; b. 1946, Pittsburgh, Pa.): Singer. Syreeta began her career at Motown Records as a secretary and backup singer. A single, "I Can't Give Back the Love I Feel for You," was released in 1968 but made little impact. In 1970, Stevie WONDER heard her singing in the office and walked in to offer her a song to sing. They began writing songs together, and by the time her first solo album came out in 1972, they were a couple. Although their marriage broke up by the time of her second album, *One to One* (1974), they remained friends. It was three years before Syreeta cut a third album for Motown. She remarried and cut a fourth album, titled *Rich Love, Poor Love* (1977), featuring G. C. Cameron. The venture yielded several hit singles. When Billy PRESTON signed on at Motown in 1978, he and Syreeta sang a duet together for the sound track to the film *Fast Break* (1979). They completed a duo album in 1981, *Billy Preston and Syreeta*. Their work together also resulted in several hit singles, including "It Will Come in Time" and "With You I'm Born Again."

System of Dante's Hell, The (1965): Novel by Amiri BARAKA (LeRoi Jones). The autobiographical fiction in this work projects experiences drawn from the author's life and deals with Western culture's impact on African Americans, their EDUCATION according to Western traditions, and the ensuing ambivalence and confusion that they experience. Such education, Baraka believes, alienates African Americans from their roots and causes feelings of racial inferiority.

T

T. and T. (Syndicated, 1987): Television detective drama. MR. T portrayed T. S. Turner, a detective and former boxer who worked for attorney Amanda Taler (Alex Amini). Although his character ostensibly preferred a suit and tie, Mr. T spent part of every episode in studded leather gear, as the criminals he pursued were more likely to be intimidated by leather than by pinstripes. Not surprisingly, the series was a failure.

Tadlock, Robert: Costume designer. Tadlock began working Off-Broadway as a costume designer in the 1950's. One of his more notable assignments was the design of costumes for the play *Mercy Drop* in 1973. In addition to costume design, Tadlock paints and owns an art gallery.

Singer Johnny Nash played a troubled black teenager in the film Take a Giant Step. *(The Museum of Modern Art/Film Stills Archive, NY)*

Take a Giant Step (United Artists, 1958): Film directed by Philip Leacock. Singer Johnny NASH plays a troubled black teenager from an affluent family who searches for a place for himself in both the black and the white communities. Beah RICHARDS and Frederick O'NEAL play the boy's parents, Estelle Hemsley his grandmother, and Ruby DEE the family maid, to whom he turns for comfort. The film lacks dramatic impact, but it is earnest and well intentioned in its treatment of the young man's problems.

Take 6: Gospel-oriented, a cappella jazz vocal group. Its mixture of jazz chord structures, gospel lyrics, and mas-

terful vocalization techniques make Take 6 an important component in the musical traditions of the African American community.

Take 6 was formed at Oakwood College, a small Christian school in Huntsville, Ala., in 1980. It was there that the members of the group met and formed a group named Alliance. The group performed in local churches and could be found rehearsing in dormitory bathrooms or any other place with adequate acoustics. When three of the original members graduated, Claude V. McKnight, Mark Kibble, and Mervyn Warren were joined by Cedric Dent, David Thomas, and Alvin "Vinnie" Chea in the renamed Take 6.

In 1987, the group played a concert for gospel record companies. Representatives from only two gospel labels came to the concert, but Jim Norman of Warner Bros. records attended. He was impressed immediately with the group's style. Take 6 signed with Warner Bros. in that year. It also signed with Reunion records, a gospel label, in order to saturate both the pop and the gospel markets.

The group's first album, *Reprise*, brought critical acclaim from the gospel and jazz communities. The group gained exposure through church and jazz festival performances. Acclaim also came from established members of the music community such as Lena HORNE, Quincy JONES, Anita BAKER, and Stevie WONDER.

Even as the group experimented with timing changes, jazz-based arrangements, and a cappella style, the focus of the group's performances did not change. Through its songs and its members' life-styles, Take 6 continued to express the joy and need for salvation that is central to its members' religious beliefs as Seventh-day Adventists. The group would not perform on the Sabbath between Friday and Saturday nights, as that religion dictates. The members' shared goal is to live clean and righteous lives. When questioned about success, they give credit to the Lord.

Taking of Miss Janie, The (pr. 1974): Play by Ed BULLINS. The drama, set on a Southern California college campus, centers on the rape of a California beach girl by her black friend. It won the New York Drama Critics Circle Award in 1975 as best American play of the year.

Talented Tenth: Concept of W. E. B. DU BOIS that the most capable one-tenth of African Americans should be given higher education and leadership training. The Talented Tenth would then be responsible for the economic and cultural elevation of all African Americans. Du Bois feared an overemphasis on industrial education and believed that African Americans should be trained as teachers and professionals rather than solely as industrial workers. The phrase "Talented Tenth" was used in print first in 1903.

Tambourines to Glory (pr. 1963): Morality play by Langston HUGHES. Set to gospel music, the drama deals with the efforts of two women, Essie Belle Johnson and Laura Wright Reed, to establish a storefront church in Harlem. They are assisted in their efforts by a disguised devil.

Tampa Red (Hudson Woodbridge; Dec. 25, 1900, Smithville, Ga.—Mar. 19, 1981, Chicago, Ill.): Blues guitarist. Still in his youth when orphaned, Woodbridge moved to Tampa, Fla., to live with his maternal grandmother. He also took his mother's family name, Whittaker, but would soon be dubbed "Tampa Red" for his red hair and for the city where he spent his younger years. A self-taught slide guitarist, Tampa Red began to play in juke joints and honky-tonks up and down the Florida gulf coast in the early 1920's.

About 1925, Tampa Red moved to Chicago, Ill., where he would spend the rest of his life. In his early days in Chicago, Tampa Red sang and played on the streets when he could not secure club work. By 1928, he had made his first recordings, on the Paramount label. He did some solo recording, but also played as part of The Hokum Boys (with Thomas A. "Georgia Tom" DORSEY) and with Ma RAINEY, Madlyn Davis, Victoria Spivey, and others. One recording with Dorsey for the Vocalion label, "Tight Like That," was a major hit. Over the next four years, Tampa Red and Georgia Tom worked together, playing all manner of small engagements in the Chicago area, including work at juke joints, dance halls, rent parties, and vaudeville theaters. By the early 1930's, Tampa Red was fronting his own band, The Chicago Five, and had moved to the Bluebird label after having made numerous recordings with Paramount and the Vocalion/ARC label group. Throughout the rest of the decade and into the early 1940's, Tampa Red worked at various Chicago nightclubs (especially the C & T Club) solo, and with Big Bill BROONZY, Big Maceo, and others. The popularity of Tampa Red's brand of music—acoustic slide guitar—had begun to decline, however, with the discovery of the electric guitar by Chicago bluesmen. Following a stint in Gary, Ind., working local clubs with Sunnyland Slim,

Tampa Red returned to his usual round of club dates in Chicago, working places such as The Zanzibar, Sylvio's, The 708 Club, and The Peacock Lounge, while continuing to record, now with the Victor label.

After the death of his wife, Francis, in 1953, Tampa Red's involvement with music withered as he struggled with alcoholism. He was hospitalized frequently for treatment of the disease in the latter half of the 1950's. Tampa Red did, however, record on the Prestige-Bluesville label in 1960 and worked sporadically through the 1960's. He finally retired to a Chicago nursing home in 1974, having won a secure place in the annals of blues music.

Tanner, Henry Ossawa (June 21, 1859, Pittsburgh, Pa.—May 25, 1937, Etaples, France): Painter. Tanner is one of the most important and renowned modern African American artists. His paintings include landscapes, seascapes, biblical figures, and studies of African Americans. His works have been acclaimed for their experimentations with light and color and for the fresh, nonstereotypical representations of African Americans. He was the first African American in the National Academy of Design.

Tanner's father, Benjamin Tucker Tanner, was made a bishop of the AFRICAN METHODIST EPISCOPAL CHURCH in 1888; his mother was a former slave who conducted a school in the family's home in Pittsburgh. One of the most important developments in Tanner's early life was his family's move to Philadelphia in 1866. It was there that Tanner became interested in becoming an artist, after watching a landscape painter at work in Fairmont Park. His interest was deepened after he read an article about America's need for painters of seascapes. He became less interested in this genre and by age thirteen turned his talents to painting animals. This wide-ranging interest in different genres later would be reflected by various phases of Tanner's adult career.

Although Tanner's parents discouraged him from pursuing a career as a painter—his father wanted him to be a minister—in 1880 he began one of the most important episodes of his life, studying at the Pennsylvania Academy of the Fine Arts, where he was the only African American student and where his teacher was the important American artist Thomas Eakins. After leaving the academy in 1882, Tanner struggled to make his career, exhibiting his works and infrequently selling them.

The next major event in Tanner's life came in 1891, when he went to France to study painting. Tanner would spend most of the rest of his life in France. The period of the early to mid-1890's was marked by some of Tanner's most renowned paintings, studies of African Americans which include *The Banjo Lesson*, *Old Couple Looking at a Portrait of Lincoln*, and *The Thankful Poor*. Some art critics have emphasized the greatness of Tanner's subtle yet complex renderings of African Americans in contrast to the patronizing or racist stereotypes produced by many white artists of the era.

In the mid-1890's, Tanner became interested in painting biblical subjects, an interest which lasted the rest of his life. Some of the acclaimed paintings of this genre include *Daniel in the Lion's Den* and *Christ and Nicodemus on a Rooftop*. Toward the turn of the century, Tanner's paintings began to express the influences of Impressionism and of Symbolism. *Salome* is one such painting.

was an attorney in private practice in Tacoma, Wash., from 1955 to 1978. He served on the board of visitors of the University of Puget Sound Law School and was a member of the school's national board of directors from 1962 to 1968. In 1978, President Jimmy Carter appointed Tanner to serve on the federal bench as U.S. district judge for the Western District of Washington State.

Tap (Tri-Star Pictures, 1989): Film directed and written by Nick Castle. Gregory HINES stars as Max Washington, a former convict who is torn between returning to a life of crime or pursuing a career as a tap dancer. A standout among the supporting players is Sammy DAVIS, Jr., mak-

As Max Washington, Gregory Hines shared the screen with legendary tap dancers in the 1989 film Tap. *From left: Arthur Duncan, Pat Rico, Harold Nicholas, Steve Condos, Sandman Sims, Henry LeTang, Hines, and Sammy Davis, Jr.* (AP/Wide World Photos)

Tanner, Jack Edward (b. November, 1919): Federal judge. Tanner attended the University of Puget Sound Law School, where he received his law degree. After passing the Washington State bar examination, Tanner

ing his final film appearance. The film also features appearances by such famed tap dancers as Harold NICHOLAS, Howard "Sandman" SIMS, Bunny BRIGGS, and Jimmy SLYDE.

Tap Dance Kid, The (pr. 1984): Musical by Charles Blackwell. The work, performed at Broadhurst Theatre, addresses the frustrations and aspirations of a black middle-class family living in a Manhattan duplex and searching for upward mobility. The protagonist, a ten-year-old boy named Willie, dreams of becoming a tap dancer when he grows up. His thirteen-year-old sister, Emma, wants to be a lawyer. Their father is opposed to Willie's ambitions because he believes that black people did not get anywhere until they stopped dancing and started working.

Tar Baby (1981): Novel by Toni MORRISON. The protagonist, an African American model orphaned at the age of twelve and educated at the Sorbonne, is torn between white society, of which she is part, and black society, from which she feels cut off. She struggles to find her identity and assert her individuality amid pressure from each side to subscribe to its culture.

Tarrant, Caesar (1755?-1796?): Sailor. Tarrant was a Virginia slave who was put to service by the American Navy in the Revolutionary War because of his experience as a pilot on the Chesapeake Bay. He probably was at the wheel of the *Patriot* when it and its crew were captured by the British. The Virginia legislature set him free in 1789 as a reward for his service.

Tarry, Ellen (b. Sept. 26, 1906, Birmington, Ala.): Author. As a journalist in New York City, she was executive secretary of the Negro Author's Guild and a member of a writers' group organized in 1937 by Claude McKAY, a poet associated with the HARLEM RENAISSANCE. During World War II, she was a staff member of the National Catholic Community Service. She has published *The Runaway Elephant* (1950), illustrated by Oliver Harrington, who created "Bootsie," a cartoon character renowned in the African American press. Her other books include her autobiography, *The Third Door* (1955), and *The Other Toussaint* (1981), a biography of Pierre Toussaint.

Tatum, Art, Jr. (Oct. 13, 1909, Toledo, Ohio—Nov. 5, 1956, Los Angeles, Calif.): Jazz pianist. Tatum suffered severely impaired vision from a very early age. He was completely blind in one eye and possessed only limited sight in the other. As a teenager, he attended the Toledo School of Music, but he was largely self-taught at the piano, relying on the "teachings" of piano rolls, recordings, and the radio. His commitment led to his memorization of many Fats WALLER compositions and perfor-

mances. By 1936, he was playing professionally in Toledo and Cleveland, Ohio. By 1932, he had made his way to New York City, and in 1933 he made his first recordings. Increasingly, over the remainder of the decade and into the 1940's, Tatum became known as jazz's virtuoso performer on the piano. His performances on radio, and in clubs in Chicago, New York, and Los Angeles, brought him to a wide audience.

Art Tatum, jazz pianist, was largely self-taught despite his severely impaired vision. (AP/Wide World Photos)

The critical appreciation Tatum received from writers and musicians, however, always seemed to be greater than the development of a true popular following. In 1943, Tatum formed a trio similar to Nat COLE's, signing on with bassist Slam Stewart and guitarist Tiny Grimes, hoping to attract the popular following that so far had eluded him. The experiment had mixed success, but Tatum's continued brilliance at the piano was clear. His solo recordings made for producer Norman Granz in the early 1950's were seminal in jazz history.

Tatum's work has influenced pianists as diverse as Herbie HANCOCK and Oscar PETERSON, and artists on other instruments, such as saxophonist Charlie PARKER, were also affected positively. Tatum's improvisations were usually alterations of popular standards, but he remained close to the tradition of the blues. He is also known for his playful parodies of many classical works.

Tatum, Reese "Goose" (b. May 3, 1921, Calion, Ark.—Jan. 18, 1967, El Paso, Tex): Basketball player. A versatile athlete, Tatum excelled in BASEBALL, FOOTBALL, and BASKETBALL. He began his athletic career in 1941 as a player on a black baseball team in Minneapolis-St. Paul, Minn. In 1942, team owner Abe Saperstein approached Tatum to play for another of his enterprises, the HARLEM GLOBETROTTERS basketball team. Tatum agreed. Except for three years of armed service, and until 1955, Tatum's showmanship was central to the entertaining athleticism of the team and its fan appeal. His style of holding the ball one-handed above his head before passing or shooting has been copied by National Basketball Association greats Connie HAWKINS, Wilt CHAMBERLAIN, and Kareem ABDUL-JABBAR.

After Tatum left the Globetrotters in 1955, he organized his own team, the Harlem Magicians, and played with it until his health declined in the mid-1960's. He was famous for his seven-foot arm span.

Taylor, Charles Robert "Charley" (b. Sept. 28, 1942, Grand Prairie, Tex.): Football player. A star athlete for Arizona State University, Taylor was the Washington Redskins' first draft choice in 1964, when he was named as National FOOTBALL League (NFL) Rookie of the Year. He caught fifty-three passes that season, an NFL record for a running back. Taylor was then switched to wide receiver. He played in eight Pro Bowls and one Super Bowl over his career, retired from the NFL in 1977, and was inducted into the Pro Football Hall of Fame in 1984.

Taylor, Gardner Calvin (b. June 18, 1918, Baton Rouge, La.): Baptist clergyman. Taylor earned his A.B. from Leland College and his Bachelor of Divinity from OBERLIN COLLEGE. He was ordained in 1939. Between 1938 and 1947, he served as pastor in Elyria, Ohio, New Orleans, La., and Baton Rouge, La. In 1948, he served as dean and professor at the Colgate-Rochester Divinity School.

Taylor was pastor of the Concord Baptist Church in Brooklyn for more than thirty years, beginning in 1948. He delivered the Lyman Beecher lectures at Yale Divinity School in the 1975-1976 academic year. Active in the New York State Democratic Committee, he was also the first Baptist and first African American to head the Protestant Council. Among his books are *How Shall They Preach* (1977), *The Scarlet Threat: Nineteen Sermons* (1981), and *Chariots Aflame* (1988).

Taylor, Hobart, Jr. (b. Dec. 17, 1920, Texarkana, Tex.): Taylor was on a number of important governmental

President Johnson appointed Hobart Taylor executive vice-chairman of the Committee on Equal Employment Opportunity. (AP/Wide World Photos)

commissions as well as serving as a member of the board of directors or as counsel to various businesses. He received his B.A. degree from Prairie View College, an M.A. from HOWARD UNIVERSITY, and an LL.M. from the University of Michigan. He was appointed as executive vice chairman of the Committee on Equal Employment Opportunity by President Lyndon Johnson, who also named him to the board of Export-Import Bank. Besides being a partner in a law firm in Detroit, Mich., he became a board member of Eastern Airlines, Aetna Life and Casualty Company, Standard Oil, and Westinghouse Electric Corporation.

Taylor, John Baxter, Jr. (Nov. 3, 1882, Washington, D.C.—Dec. 2, 1908): Runner. Taylor set a collegiate record for the 440-yard dash while attending the University of Pennsylvania, with a time of 48.8. He was Amateur Athletic Union champion in 1907. In 1908, he won an Olympic gold medal for the 4 × 400-meter relay with a time of 3:29.4. His career was cut short by typhoid pneumonia, of which he died only five months after winning the medal.

Taylor, Johnnie (b. May 5, 1938, Crawfordsville, Ark.): Singer. Brought up in the gospel traditions of his church,

Taylor was introduced to secular music through the recordings of his neighbor, Little Junior Parker. Taylor has also cited local country blues artists such as Rice "Sonny Boy WILLIAMSON" Miller and his radio programs as inspiration.

Taylor's first recordings were in the mid-1950's, with a Chicago-based group called the Five Echoes, which recorded DOO-WOP songs on the Chance label. He began to distinguish himself later in the decade with a gospel quartet called the Highway Q.C.'s, singing lead on a number of tracks including "Somewhere to Lay My Head" for the Vee Jay label.

In 1957, Taylor replaced legendary gospel and pop vocalist Sam COOKE in the SOUL STIRRERS, recording extensively with that group as it rose to the status of the nation's best-selling gospel group. Taylor became an ordained minister during this period. He left the Soul Stirrers and began recording pop and RHYTHM AND BLUES on Cooke's Sar label, releasing a minor hit, "Rome Wasn't Built in a Day," in 1964. The label ceased operations after Cooke was murdered in 1964.

Shortly after this unsettling period, there was a confusing turn of events. A West Coast singer named Johnny Young began billing himself as "Little" Johnny Taylor, releasing the hit "Part Time Love" while capitalizing on the other Taylor's marginal successes as a gospel singer. Johnnie Taylor then turned the tables by singing his namesake's hit, billing himself as Little Johnnie Taylor and catapulting himself into the national limelight as a pop and rhythm-and-blues star.

By 1966, Taylor had signed with the fledgling Stax label in Memphis, Tenn. He became a mainstay for the label that would soon set the standards in the world of progressive rhythm and blues. He was paired with ex-Motown session guitarist, producer, and songwriter Don Davis. The result was his 1968 smash single "Who's Making Love," which reached number one on the rhythm-and-blues charts and number five in pop. He would remain with Stax until its forced bankruptcy in 1975.

In 1976, Taylor had a number-one hit on CBS with "Disco Lady," one of the first certified platinum singles ever and the beginning of a successful tenure with the label. After a brief sojourn with the Beverly Glen label, which released "What About My Love," Taylor signed with Malaco, a Jackson, Miss., label. He recorded on that label into the 1990's.

Taylor, Koko (Cora Walton; b. Sept. 28, 1935, Memphis, Tenn.): Blues singer. In 1953, Taylor began to travel along the club circuit. Her gravelly voice and wry sensuality

Laurence Taylor was a number one draft pick for the New York Giants football team in 1981. (Courtesy New York Football Giants, Inc.)

have earned her nearly every award available to a blues singer, including a 1985 W. C. Handy Award as entertainer of the year. She has also accumulated a number of best-selling songs beginning with "Wang Dang Doodle," a 1965 gold record.

Taylor, Kristen Clark (b. 1959?, Detroit, Mich.): Political appointee. Taylor grew up in Detroit as the youngest of seven children and was graduated from Michigan State University. At the age of twenty-three, she served as the only African American woman on the start-up staff at *USA Today*. In 1986, she became senior writer for the vice presidential press office of George Bush. While in Washington, D.C., Taylor met and married Lonny Taylor, Sr., who worked as chief of staff for a Republican congressman.

Upon winning the presidency, Bush appointed Taylor to serve as White House director of media relations. Although press secretary Marlin Fitzwater had primary responsibility for the president's interviews with the Washington press corps, Taylor arranged for presidential interviews by other members of the print and broadcast media and was responsible for briefing Bush on issues that came up at press meetings and luncheons. She coordinated a White House luncheon with African American publishers to help foster better relations between Bush and the black-owned media.

Taylor, Lawrence "L. T." (b. Feb. 4, 1959, Williamsburg, Va.): Football player. After a stellar career with the University of North Carolina, Taylor was the number-one draft pick for the New York Giants of the National FOOTBALL League (NFL) in 1981. During his rookie season, he was named as Associated Press (AP) Defensive Player of the Year and NFL Rookie of the Year. In 1982, he won an unprecedented second consecutive award of AP Defensive Player of the Year. He was named as National Football Conference (NFC) Defensive Player of the Year in 1983 and again in 1986. His defensive play helped the Giants beat the Denver Broncos in Super Bowl XXI. He holds the record for the most quarterback sacks.

Taylor, Marshall W. "Major" (Nov. 26, 1878, Indianapolis, Ind.—June 21, 1932, Chicago, Ill.): Bicycle racer. The first widely known U.S. black athlete, Taylor overcame constant discrimination by cycling officials to win the world one-mile title in Montreal, Canada, in 1899. In 1900, he was recognized as the best sprinter in the nation, having won the consecutive U.S. professional sprint championships and the 1899 world professional sprint championship. He retired in 1910 and wrote poetry and an autobiography, *The Fastest Bicycle Rider in the World* (1928).

Taylor, Mildred D. (b. 1943, Jackson, Miss.): Author of children's novels. She received her bachelor's degree from the University of Toledo and attended graduate school at the University of Colorado. Inspired by her father's stories of African American slaves who retained their dignity despite their servitude, Taylor wrote a trilogy chronicling African Americans' attempts to establish themselves after SLAVERY. The first novel, *Song of the Trees* (1975), was named the Outstanding Book of the Year by *The New York Times*; the second, *Roll of Thunder, Hear My Cry* (1976), received the Newbery Medal. In 1981, Taylor published *Let the Circle Be Unbroken*, the final novel of the trilogy. Her work also includes *The Road to Memphis* (1990).

Taylor, Noel C. (b. July 15, 1924, Bedford City, Va.): Mayor of Roanoke, Va. Taylor was graduated with honors from Bluefield State College with a bachelor of science degree in 1949. He took positions as a teacher and an elementary school principal with the Bedford City Public Schools between 1949 and 1952. He received a bachelor of divinity degree in 1955 and a doctor of divinity degree in 1959 from Virginia Seminary and College. Taylor was ordained into the ministry of the Baptist church and was appointed pastor of the First Baptist Church in Clifton Forge, Va. He served from 1955 to 1958. He was pastor of First Baptist Church in Norfolk, Va., from 1958 to 1961 before being appointed as pastor of High Street Baptist Church in Roanoke in 1961. In 1963, he earned his master of arts degree in religious education from New York University.

Taylor was first elected to the Roanoke city council in 1970. He served as vice-mayor from 1974 to 1975 and was elected mayor of Roanoke in 1975.

Taylor, Susan L. (b. Jan. 23, 1946, New York, N.Y.): Journalist. Taylor began her working life as an actress

Susan Taylor, journalist, addresses the New Jersey Black Issues Convention in 1986. (AP/Wide World Photos)

and licensed cosmetologist. She then became involved in free-lance beauty and fashion writing. She was a free-lance beauty writer for *Essence* magazine in 1970 and became its beauty editor in 1971. That department was broadened to include fashion. Taylor became editor-in-chief of *Essence* in 1981 and vice president of Essence Communications in 1986, acting as host of its television program.

Taylor, Theodore (b. June 23, 1921, Statesville, N.C.): Author. Before he began his career as a children's writer, Taylor was a journalist and a screenwriter. He also worked as a merchant marine and a boxing manager. He is best known, perhaps, for his children's novel, *The Cay* (1969), about a boy on a life raft in the Caribbean. *The Cay* won numerous major awards, including the Jane Addams Children's Book Award, the Lewis Carroll Shelf Award, and the Commonwealth Club of California Silver Medal. In 1974, *The Cay* was produced for television, starring James Earl JONES as Timothy, the black man who befriends the boy. The book subsequently came under fire as having a racist depiction of black people.

Taylor, William "Billy" (b. July 24, 1921, Greenville, N.C.): Jazz pianist. Taylor was reared in Washington, D.C. Jazz pianist, composer, arranger, conductor, author, and educator, Taylor has supported jazz as a member of the National Council on the Arts and as a board member of the American Society of Composers, Authors, and Publishers (ASCAP).

Jazz musician Billy Taylor is known for his highly expressive and technically masterful piano renditions. (Roy Lewis Photography)

Taylor studied classical piano with Henry Grant and received a B.A. in music from Virginia State College in 1942. Migrating to New York City in the 1940's, he secured a Fifty-second Street engagement with the leg-

endary Ben WEBSTER. Taylor also worked with Dizzy GILLESPIE, Charlie PARKER, Machito, and Don REDMAN.

In 1951, Taylor began working at BIRDLAND as house pianist, establishing a record for the longest run at the club. He received the first International Critics Award as best pianist. During the 1950's, he performed with Billie HOLIDAY, Oscar Pettiford, Lee Konitz, and Roy ELDRIDGE. Taylor formed his own trio, which at times in its more than forty years included Ed Thigpen, Earl May, Victor Gaskin, and Freddie Waits.

In 1965, Taylor cofounded and served as executive director for Jazzmobile, Inc. Taylor hosted jazz programs for WLIB and WNEW radio in New York and served as general manager for WLIB, a black-owned station. In the 1980's, he hosted *Jazz Alive* for National Public Radio. Active in television, he conducted the orchestra for *The David Frost Show* between 1969 and 1972, and during the 1980's he began appearing on the CBS *Sunday Morning* program.

Taylor composed more than three hundred songs, including "I Wish I Knew How It Would Feel to Be Free" as well as the "Suite for Jazz Piano and Orchestra." Versatile in the performing arts, he appeared in *The Time of Your Life*, a Broadway hit. Taylor earned a doctoral degree in music education from the University of Massachusetts in 1975. Author of more than a dozen books and numerous articles, he published *Jazz Piano: History and Development* (1982).

As a pianist, Taylor is known for his highly expressive and technically masterful piano renditions, revealing the influences of Nat "King" COLE and Art TATUM. Among his more than thirty recordings as a leader are *Piano Panorama* (1951), *Sleeping Bee* (1969), and *Where've You Been?* (1980). During the early 1990's, Taylor devoted his time to composing and solo performances.

Teague, Robert "Bob" (b. Jan. 2, 1929, Milwaukee, Wisc.): Newscaster. Author of the autobiography *Live and Off-Color: News Biz* (1982), Teague has had a diverse career, including time as a Big Ten halfback during his college years for the University of Wisconsin and writing the stage work *Soul Yesterday and Today*, based upon Langston HUGHES's work. He was a newspaper reporter before he went to work for the National Broadcasting Company in 1963. He has appeared on several late-night news programs.

Teenage Pregnancy: The United States has the highest teenage fertility rate of any Western industrialized nation. U.S. teenagers also have the highest abortion rate among teenagers in developed nations. In fact, nearly one million

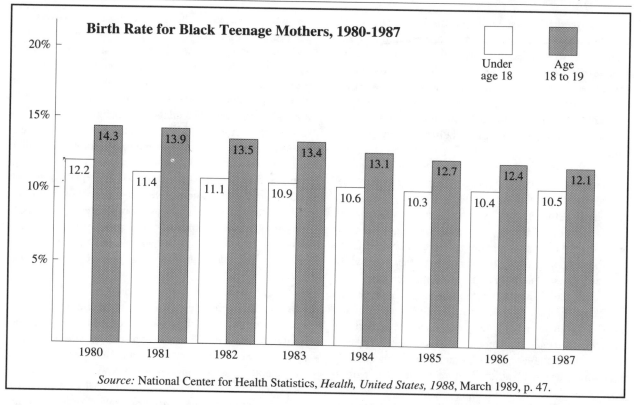

Birth Rate for Black Teenage Mothers, 1980-1987

Under age 18 — Age 18 to 19

Year	Under age 18	Age 18 to 19
1980	12.2	14.3
1981	11.4	13.9
1982	11.1	13.5
1983	10.9	13.4
1984	10.6	13.1
1985	10.3	12.7
1986	10.4	12.4
1987	10.5	12.1

Source: National Center for Health Statistics, *Health, United States, 1988*, March 1989, p. 47.

teenagers become pregnant each year in the United States. Roughly half choose abortion.

Although there has been a decline in the teenage birthrate, the fact that so many pregnant teenagers choose to bear and keep their children has compelled public and scholarly attention. Another trend causing alarm is that marriage rates among pregnant teenagers have fallen sharply. Researchers and policymakers also worry about teenagers' children, who, many believe, are at risk of health and social problems because they are the "babies of babies." In addition, because older women are having fewer children, policymakers worry about the resulting high proportion of all babies that will be born to teenage mothers.

Although U.S. teens have higher rates of pregnancy and childbearing than their counterparts in other developed nations, their sexual behavior is similar. So, while there are high rates of premarital sexual activity among U.S. teenagers, these rates are similar to those of other countries. African American teenagers have had higher rates of premarital sexual activity than have whites, yet the gap is narrowing; premarital sexual activity among African American girls is diminishing at the same time that it is increasing among white teenage girls. For example, although African Americans exhibit the highest rates of sexual activity and out-of-wedlock births, the rate

of increase in sexual activity for white girls doubled in the 1970's and has continued to increase. Overall, however, African Americans have teenage pregnancy rates that remain twice as high as those of whites.

Determinants of Teenage Pregnancy. Sexual activity alone does not explain national differences in rates of teenage pregnancy. Rather, sexual activity in respect to contraceptive practice must be analyzed to understand racial differences in U.S. pregnancy rates and differences between rates in the United States and other developed nations. Since the level of sexual activity among U.S. teenagers is similar to that of other Western teenagers, the difference in pregnancy rates is explained by researchers as resulting from greater contraceptive failure among U.S. teenagers.

Teenage girls in the United States are less likely to use contraception than their counterparts in other Western nations are. Among U.S. teenagers, moreover, African American girls are less likely to use contraception than whites are. Nevertheless, African American teenagers' fertility does not, by itself, account for the higher fertility rates among U.S. teenagers. For explanations of contraceptive behavior, researchers have examined family backgrounds, community values, and educational aspirations.

African American families often do not conform to the

white patriarchal nuclear family norms. Researchers find, however, that African American teenage daughters are more likely to confide in their mothers about concerns related to sexual activity and contraceptive failure than are whites. Furthermore, there is considerable variance in social norms regarding premarital sexual activity in African American communities. Such variances seem to be primarily related to religious beliefs and peer-group culture.

Many scholars theorize that cultural norms prohibiting premarital sexual activity are absent among groups that exhibit high rates of such behavior and high rates of unwed parenthood. Studies document the perception, common among African Americans, that black communities do not condemn unwed mothers. Such studies do not show, however, that black communities approve of premarital sexual activity and unwed motherhood.

Overall, data from studies examining the determinants of teenage motherhood suggest that there are dramatic racial differences in the levels of teenage sexual activity, contraceptive use, and teenage abortion rates. At every stage in this sequence, African Americans are more likely than whites to make choices that lead to teenage parenthood.

Conservative Values. Ironically, the African American community is noted for its opposition to premarital sexual behavior based on traditionally conservative attitudes toward sexuality. Many teenagers ignore or disregard conservative attitudes toward premarital sexuality; ironically, too, conservative attitudes may affect rates of pregnancy by inhibiting the use of contraception by teenagers. For example, parents with conservative views toward sexuality may be uncomfortable with or opposed to discussing contraception with their children. African Americans are less likely to be informed about contraception than are whites; given these findings by researchers, it is not surprising that sexually active African Americans are more likely to become pregnant than sexually active whites are.

The data on abortion are contradictory: African Americans are noted for voicing negative views toward abortions, yet are slightly more likely than whites to have abortions if they become pregnant. This may result from the fact that attitudes toward abortion do not always prevail when teenagers are faced with unintended pregnancies. U.S. teenagers overall exhibit the highest abortion rate among teenagers in any developed nation; their high fertility rates are not the result of antiabortion sentiments, since teenage women as a group have almost as many abortions as they do live births in a given year. Again, scholars point to ineffective or irresponsible con-

traceptive behavior as the major cause of full-term teenage pregnancies and assumption of teenage motherhood.

Educational Expectations. Scholars look at the general social conditions facing teenagers to try to establish why they would fail to use contraceptives and why they might choose to become mothers. One of the phenomena that appears significant is teenagers' expectations of educational achievement and its outcome. In various studies, researchers have found that one explanation for higher fertility rates among African Americans might be that, compared to whites, they have lower expectations for educational achievement. Even though increasing numbers of African Americans are completing high school, relatively few have expectations of going on to participate in HIGHER EDUCATION. Whites who do not expect to go on to college are also more likely to engage in premarital sexual activity.

African Americans, in comparison to both Hispanic and non-Hispanic whites, are the most likely teenagers to consider having a child out of wedlock. They are also likelier to voice preferences for having a child before the age of twenty, though they expect to marry at a later age. In general, those teenage women who would have the most to lose by having a child out of wedlock at a young age are least likely to engage in premarital sexual activity or to contemplate an out-of-wedlock birth.

Consequences of Teenage Pregnancy. Traditionally, scholars have argued that early pregnancy is likely to reduce educational attainment, which in turn may negatively affect labor-force participation. Many scholars believe that early parenthood leads to POVERTY and may perpetuate cycles of poverty.

Others counter this argument by saying that many dropouts leave school for reasons other than pregnancy such as racism, family problems, and estrangement from school. They point to changes in dropout rates among teenage mothers, following the passage of legislation in 1972 that prevented schools from forcing pregnant girls to withdraw. Passage of such legislation and a concurrent increase in school attendance during and after pregnancy has caused some scholars to question the assumption that young women who become mothers are destined to begin a cycle of poverty or to continue in the cycle.

Most scholars agree that teenage pregnancy has health implications for the children of teenage parents. Such pregnancies often lead to low-birth-weight babies who may suffer from a variety of health problems. Some propose to solve this by improving young mothers' understanding of, and access to, the health-care system.

Summary. Overall, there is a widely held assumption that early childbearing results in poverty as a consequence of interrupted education and economic burdens that inexperienced, unskilled single mothers are often ill-equipped to shoulder. Yet while many in the academic community still maintain the view that teenage childbearing begins or continues a cycle of poverty, teen mothers and their parents do not always agree. This opposing perspective on the effects of teenage motherhood is not surprising in communities in which unemployment and reliance on public assistance are common and in which the possibility of college attendance continues to be very limited.

The prevailing view is that teenage pregnancy is a problem. Yet some contend that teenage mothers simply experience the same problems confronting any single mother, including the frequent lack of financial support from their children's fathers. For African American teenage mothers, such financial problems are often accentuated by the high rates of unemployment among African American teenage males. Such troubles may be offset by reliance upon extended family network resources; these, however, are often already strained.—*Sharon Elise*

SUGGESTED READINGS: • Dash, Leon. *When Children Want Children: The Urban Crisis of Teenage Childbearing.* New York: William Morrow, 1989. • Hendricks, Leo E., and Teresa A. Montgomery. *Teenage Pregnancy from a Black Perspective: Some Reflections on Its Prevention.* Washington, D.C.: Institute for Urban Affairs and Research, Howard University, 1986. • Jones, Dionne J., and Stanley F. Battle, eds. *Teenage Pregnancy: Developing Strategies for Change in the Twenty-first Century.* New Brunswick, N.J.: Transaction Books, 1990. • Moore, Kristin A., Margaret C. Simms, and Charles L. Betsey. *Choice and Circumstances: Racial Differences in Adolescent Sexuality and Fertility.* New Brunswick, N.J.: Transaction Books, 1986. • Williams, Constance Willard. *Black Teenage Mothers: Pregnancy and Child Rearing from Their Perspective.* Lexington, Mass.: Lexington Books, 1991.

Television: Virtually every home in the United States has a television set. For most Americans, television is the primary source of daily entertainment, news, and information and a public forum for debating ideas. Combining the popular arts of film, radio, theater, and literature, television has emerged as the dominant medium in American popular culture.

Noting the medium's central place in American life, television programmers have attempted both to mirror and help shape the popular mood by providing a variety of programs: daily news, feature documentaries, dramas, sports events, talk shows, variety programs, and situation comedies. In the midst of this television fare lies the portrayal of African Americans, and network television's popular portrayals of African Americans have been met with broad-based criticism. It is only through an ongoing dialogue between African Americans, other concerned communities, and the television industry that the medium has moved toward constructive change in its portrayals of African Americans.

The Formative First Decade. By 1948, when the mechanics of television broadcasting had been ironed out and the medium was becoming available to a wide cross section of American viewers, public discussions in print and broadcast media had already involved questions of how African Americans would be portrayed on television. The popular mood of post-World War II America (an era in which the fight against fascism was fresh in the minds of the public) suggested portrayals free of the bias that characterized popular literature, radio, theater, and film. Civil rights organizations, literary magazines, and entertainment personalities called for television, as the ultimate public medium, to destroy negative stereotyping and effectively quell racial discrimination through the presentation of positive images and factual information.

Television, however, was conceived as a business, and it depended upon the financing of advertisers and sponsors. Postwar, reform sentiments were superseded by advertisers' concerns not to alienate the widest cross section of consumers. Despite protests by many inside and outside the television industry, television programmers found it most profitable to broadcast the stereotypical images of African Americans that had gained popularity in other profit-based media. Most of these stereotyped characters found a home in situation comedies such as BEULAH (produced from 1950 to 1953 on ABC) and AMOS 'N' ANDY (shown from 1951 to 1953 on CBS), in which African American characters exhibiting unflattering, antisocial qualities maintained enough popular support to keep such programs on the air for several seasons.

The notable exceptions to these portrayals were few and far between. These nonstereotyped portrayals were primarily found in variety shows, sports programs, a few failed features, occasional documentary shorts, and a limited number of local productions.

The Civil Rights Era. Perhaps the most significant and unwitting challenge to television's portrayals of stereotyped African Americans came as a result of the sheer impact of televised images of the CIVIL RIGHTS movement that gained national attention in the 1960's. Images of African Americans being physically and verbally attacked while they protested against racial discrimination proved fortuitous for those who wanted progressive change both inside and outside the television industry. In addition to nightly news coverage, there were a number of documentaries, usually produced for feature news programs, which provided comprehensive analysis of topical issues affecting African Americans as well as in-depth interviews with civil rights leaders.

These timely news features, coupled with the insistent protests that began in television's formative years, gave television programmers the go-ahead for using African Americans in increasing numbers of unstereotyped roles. Initially meeting with some localized resistance, networks cautiously included occasional roles for African Americans in feature programs and drama specials. Eventually, by the second half of the 1960's and the early 1970's, network television featured African Americans starring or costarring in some nineteen feature series; an equal number of series featured African Americans as significant supporting-cast members. Two of the most

outstanding of the series, featured on NBC, were *I Spy* (1965-1968)—the first network drama series to feature an African American as star—and the situation comedy *Julia* (1968-1971). These programs, which focused on conscientious professionals and socially agreeable characters, were typical of television's new commitment to African American portrayals that were devoid of the minstrel-type characterizations of the previous decade.

While the new portrayals were applauded for their lack of stereotypes, most were also criticized for their refusal to deal with specific African American social, economic, and cultural themes. At the height of the Civil Rights movement, viewers, civil rights advocates, and media organizations alike were troubled by portrayals that seemed to indicate that social and economic equality were not to be gained through changes in public policy and practice but through compliance and individual achievement.

It was public advocacy and individual achievement

Good Times *explored issues of black family life*. (AP/Wide World Photos)

The Cosby Show *depicted an affluent African American family.* (AP/Wide World Photos)

that would compel the television industry to make significant inroads in the employment of African American professionals in front of and behind the cameras in the civil rights era. More and more African Americans appeared as reporters, correspondents, news anchors, and camera operators, especially since white personnel often avoided racially explosive situations. Additionally, small but ground-breaking steps were being made as African Americans joined the ranks of television writers, directors, producers, and executives, increasing expectations for a new era of bias-free, issue-oriented, and culturally concerned programming.

Exploring Ethnicity. Television programmers in the 1970's and early 1980's did attempt to present more African Americans in programs that revolved around relevant social, economic, and racial themes. Most of these themes, however, were presented in the television comedy format—a format long criticized for its tendency to humorize rather than explore problems. While some supported these comedies because the humor was drawn from elements of African American culture, many also felt that these portrayals ridiculed rather than satirized the culture, revived jokes based solely on race, and often recalled the minstrel-type portrayals of 1950's television. Nevertheless, such comedies as SANFORD AND SON, THE JEFFERSONS, and GOOD TIMES were extremely popular, many placing among the nation's top-rated programs throughout most of their unprecedented runs.

In the less-common dramatic specials, African American portrayals depicted fact-based, historical, and often heroic stories and characterizations. Perhaps the most memorable of these dramas was ROOTS, an eight-part ABC miniseries that explored the story of an African American family from SLAVERY to emancipation and that became the most-watched drama in American television history. Meanwhile, the Public Broadcasting Service (PBS) gained national attention, and from its noncommercial focus came a number of news journals and feature-length documentaries that were often written, directed, and produced by African Americans. Commercial networks' nonfiction coverage was much more infrequent.

It was children's television that would introduce some of the most marked changes in television's portrayals of African Americans in this era. Series such as PBS's *Sesame Street* and CBS's *Fat Albert and the Cosby Kids* made substantial use of African American actors and characters while providing educational information, teaching personal and social responsibility, and portraying harmonious racial environments. Many of these programs set new standards for children's television while simultaneously acting as supplements to formal education.

Finally, the television industry continued to improve its record on the hiring of African Americans in nonperformance roles in front of and behind the cameras, a trend that caused many to expect more sophisticated characterizations in all television genres.

Characterization Versus Caricature. By the mid-1980's, television had begun a distinctive move toward complex characterizations of African Americans in all of its genres. Such programs as THE COSBY SHOW, a 1984-1992 NBC series, proved that even situation comedies could be based on complex characterization and yet provide sophisticated humor while maintaining a popular audience (*The Cosby Show* was number one for its first five seasons). Alongside comedic characterizations, more and more dramatic series and specials such as the 1989 miniseries THE WOMEN OF BREWSTER PLACE featured African American lead characters and dealt sensitively with a wide variety of social, economic, and culturally specific issues. In addition, an increasing number of documentaries, of which the 1986 six-part PBS series *Eyes on the Prize* was exemplary, provided comprehensive explorations of African American history and culture.

Mid-1980's and early 1990's television was also characterized by an influx of African Americans into genres where they had not previously played a significant role. This was illustrated by such talk and variety shows as THE OPRAH WINFREY SHOW and ARSENIO, both of which were hosted by African Americans and consistently ranked number one in their categories, and the 1989 debut of the first African American soap opera, *Generations*.

Criticism of mid-1980's and early 1990's television tended to be more targeted. Individual documentaries, dramas, and comedy episodes were criticized for overlooking the historical development of stated problems, for not presenting a wide enough range of African American perspectives, or, in the case of some comedy skits on feature programs, for insensitive, caricature-like portrayals. Nevertheless, such later television portrayals of African Americans met with great support from a wide cross section of American viewers, with programs featuring African Americans as leads, costars, hosts, anchors, writers, directors, and producers ranking as some of the most popular on television.

Conclusion. Television has grown along with other popular media in reforming its portrayal of African Americans, a consequence of the growing amount of information on African American people and perspectives, public criticism and debate, the influx of African Americans into influential media positions, and the evolution of the television industry itself. The development of numerous progressive African American portrayals and nonperformance positions in television serves as a model for the infusion of previously excluded minorities and perspectives into all American media.—*Monique S. Simon*

SUGGESTED READINGS: • Barnouw, Erik. *Tube of Plenty: The Evolution of American Television.* 2d rev. ed. New York: Oxford University Press, 1990. • Bogle, Donald. *Blacks in American Films and Television: An Illustrated Encyclopedia.* New York: Garland, 1988. • Brooks, Tim, and Earle Marsh. *The Complete Directory to Prime Time Network TV Shows: 1946-Present.* 4th ed. New York:

education. He worked as a blacksmith. He is famous for inventing the toggle harpoon, nicknamed the "Temple toggle iron," in 1848. The harpoon was immensely popular in the whaling industry. Temple, however, had not patented his invention, and he died poor.

Temptations, The: One of the most versatile and successful singing groups of the 1960's and 1970's. Formed from members of several other groups, the Temptations was organized in Detroit, Mich., in 1961. By 1963, the group had signed with Motown Records and taken the form that would produce most of its early hits: Paul

The Temptations enjoy themselves during a radio interview. (Oggie Ogburn)

Ballantine Books, 1988. • MacDonald, J. Fred. *Blacks and White TV: Afro-Americans in Television Since 1948.* Chicago: Nelson-Hall, 1983. • McNeil, Alex. *Total Television: A Comprehensive Guide to Programming from 1948 to the Present.* 3d ed. New York: Penguin Books, 1991. • Winship, Michael. *Television.* New York: Random House, 1988.

Temple, Lewis (1800, Richmond, Va.—1854, New Bedford, Mass.): Inventor. Lewis never received a formal

Williams, Melvin Franklin, Otis Williams, Eddie KENDRICKS, and David RUFFIN.

In 1964, the group scored its first hit, "The Way You Do the Things You Do," produced by Smokey ROBINSON, which went to number eleven on the charts. The following year, "My Girl" became the group's first number-one single. A series of other hits followed, with *Cloud Nine* (1968) winning a Grammy. In the 1970's, both "Just My Imagination" (1971) and "Papa Was a Rollin' Stone" (1972) were number-one hits. By this time, the group had undergone major personnel changes, losing its two lead singers. Ruffin left the group in a dispute with Motown management in 1967 (being replaced by Dennis Edwards), and Kendricks left to pursue his own career in 1971. New members kept the group going into the 1990's, however. In 1982, Ruffin and Kendricks rejoined the group for an album, *Reunion*, and a concert tour.

At their peak, the Temptations was among the most successful soul/rhythm-and-blues groups. Its mellow gospel background was nicely supplemented by Kendricks' falsetto and Ruffin's earthy baritone, giving the group considerable range. Most of the Temptations were former athletes, and the dance routines during live performances were among the most acrobatic in the business. Many considered the live shows to provide the best combination of music and visual entertainment of any soul group. In 1966, Norman Whitfield began producing the group's recordings and cultivated its versatility. In the later 1960's and 1970's, the group's style changed, with songs embodying greater use of brass in their instrumentation and subjects that were more topical. "Papa Was a Rollin' Stone" is considered by some critics to be one of rock music's most moving statements about the problems of inner-city families.

Tenafly (NBC, 1973-1974): Television detective drama. One of four rotating elements in the 1973-1974 edition of the NBC Wednesday/Tuesday Mystery Movie, this ninety-minute dramatic series focused on an idealized and idealistic private detective. From nine to five, Harry Tenafly (James McEachin) was dedicated to his work and his coworkers, but he left them at the office each night to return to his loving wife, Ruth (Lillian Lehman), and son, Herb (Paul Jackson).

Tenspeed and Brown Shoe (ABC, 1980): Television detective drama. Broadway veteran Ben VEREEN played E. L. Turner, better known as "Tenspeed," a con artist who chose to become a detective in order to meet his parole requirements. His partner, Lionel Whitney, or "Brown Shoe" (Jeff Goldblum), was as naïve as Tenspeed was slick, and he depended on Tenspeed to get through each case. Despite a glitzy promotional campaign and an initially large audience, the series did not last long.

Terrell, Mary Church (Sept. 23, 1863, Memphis, Tenn.—July 24, 1954, Annapolis, Md.): Civil and women's rights activist. Born into a wealthy family of former slaves, she was educated in Ohio. She was graduated from OBERLIN COLLEGE in 1884 and completed an M.A. in 1888. She also studied languages in Europe; this background proved

useful in her later political activities.

She taught at Wilberforce University and in Washington, D.C., schools before marrying school principal Robert Heberton Terrell in 1891. The Harvard-educated Terrell was a lawyer and somewhat independent protégé of Booker T. WASHINGTON. He served as a municipal court judge in Washington, D.C., from 1910 until his death.

Terrell strengthened her public activities after her marriage, spurred on by the lynching of her Memphis friend, Thomas Moss, in 1892. She gained appointment as one of the first black women on the District of Columbia school board (1895-1901 and 1906-1911), headed the prestigious Bethel Literary and Historical Society, and cofounded the Washington Colored Women's League. Later, Terrell worked with Margaret Murray Washington in national and international club movements. Terrell became the first president of the National Association of Colored Women in 1896, retaining the office until 1901.

Mary Church Terrell was a longtime participant in civil and women's rights movements. (The Associated Publishers, Inc.)

Terrell broke with Booker T. Washington over his acquiescence to Theodore Roosevelt's punishment of black soldiers after the BROWNSVILLE INCIDENT of 1906. She attended the founding conference of the NATIONAL ASSOCIATION FOR THE ADVANCEMENT OF COLORED PEOPLE, which both her husband and Washington avoided. She also participated in the woman's suffrage movement, entered into Republican Party politics, and attended international conferences on peace and women's rights.

Even into her eighties, Terrell maintained her life of protest against bigotry, waging a long, successful campaign to integrate the Washington Association of American University Women. She also chaired the Coordinating Committee for the Enforcement of the District of Columbia Anti-Discrimination Laws in 1949, seeking to revive antisegregation laws of the 1870's and picketing local establishments that discriminated against African Americans. Terrell's autobiography, *A Colored Woman in a White World*, appeared in 1940. She wrote several other books about African American history.

Terrell, Tammi (Thomasina Montgomery; 1946, Philadelphia, Pa.—Mar. 16, 1970, Philadelphia, Pa.): Singer. Terrell wanted to study medicine and major in psychology at the University of Pennsylvania, but her musical talent came to the attention of Luther Dixon, who signed her away from academia to Sceptre/Wand records, where she made her recording debut in 1961. She sang briefly with the James BROWN Revue before being signed to Motown in 1965 under her married name of Tammi Terrell. "I Can't Believe You Love Me" was a debut hit for her in 1966 and was followed by "Come on and See Me."

Motown paired Terrell with Marvin GAYE, and their three-year singing partnership put them at the top of the charts. "Ain't No Mountain High Enough" and "Your Precious Love," both released in 1967, set the pace of their work together. Gaye's rich, vital voice made a perfect complement to Terrell's sweet, soulful voice. Their vocal union produced further hits. "Ain't Nothing Like the Real Thing" and "You're All I Need to Get By" are now considered classics in pop music. At the peak of their popularity, Terrell began to suffer violent headaches. Operations showed a malignant tumor. Her treatment appeared successful, and she resumed performing only to collapse in Gaye's arms while onstage one night. Their last hit together, "The Onion Song," was released posthumously in 1970. Motown followed it with a collection of Terrell's greatest hits.

Terry, Lucy (1730, West Africa—1821, Sunderland, Vt.): Poet. Terry was brought from Africa as a slave. She is considered to be the first African American poet, although she is not the first African American to have published poetry. She lived, sequentially, in the state of Rhode Island, Deerfield, Mass., and Sunderland, Vt. She is the author of only one known poem, "Bars Flight," narrated by her to a second party in 1746 and published

in 1893. It narrates an account of a settlement being attacked by Native Americans.

Tharpe, Sister Rosetta (Rosetta Nubin; Mar. 20, 1915, Cotton Plant, Ark.—Oct. 9, 1973, Philadelphia, Pa.): Vocalist, guitarist, and pianist. Tharpe was the first African American gospel singer to extend her musical career beyond the confines of the black church community into the venues of nightclubs and lounges. Musically innovative, she popularized gospel by fusing it with jazz and blues rhythms. Classified as "pop gospel," her sound is credited with paving the way for the rhythm-and-blues era. She primarily sang gospel, but she successfully adapted her material to appeal to jazz, blues, and folk music audiences.

Tharpe was reared within the black Holiness church by her mother, Katie Bell Nubin, a traveling evangelist and a musician of considerable merit. Nurtured by an ecstatic religion that emphasized song and dance as a form of worship, Tharpe was, by the age of six, already a master of the guitar and the gospel repertoire. It was in this atmosphere of unbridled spiritual energy that Tharpe developed a unique style of showmanship that would provide the impetus for her lifelong career.

With the widespread acceptance in the 1930's of modern gospel, combined with the simultaneous rise of the recording industry and of radio, Tharpe's exuberant singing, enhanced by her blues-driven guitar accompaniment, was showcased on Decca records. Her first recording, "Rock Me/Lonesome Road," achieved pop status on Billboard's charts, instantly establishing her as a leading gospel singer. Astute in business, she capitalized on this success by touring with such jazz bands as Cab CALLOWAY's COTTON CLUB Revue, the Lucky Millinder Band, and Sammy Price's trio. She sang with a wide range of performers, from the DIXIE HUMMINGBIRDS and Madam Marie KNIGHT to Benny Goodman, MUDDY WATERS, and even country-and-western singer Red Foley. "Trouble in Mind," "Up Above My Head," and "God Don't Like It," among other recordings, earned her recognition as a jazz artist.

In the 1950's, Tharpe's bright career dimmed somewhat after she violated church ethics by singing the blues in nightclubs. Subsequently shunned by the black church community, she toured Europe for a year, where she sang her diverse repertoire to enthusiastic fans. Eventually, however, she returned to her church, though not with the same level of support as before. For the remainder of her career, she worked both by recording (one album earned her a Grammy nomination) and by touring, mostly in small rural churches in the South.

That's My Mama (ABC, 1974-1975): Television sit-com. When his father died, Clifton Curtis (Clifton DAVIS) inherited not only his father's Washington, D.C., barber-shop, but also his mother's meddlesome influence. "Mama" Eloise Curtis, portrayed by Theresa Merritt, pressured him to settle down and start a family, just like his sister, Tracy (played first by Lynne Moody and later by Joan Pringle), and her husband, Leonard (Lisle Wilson). Theodore Wilson, Jester Hairston, DeForest Covan, and Ted LANGE played Clifton's friends and customers.

Theater: The first known appearance of an African American character in American theater was in 1769, when Lewis Hallam appeared in BLACKFACE in *The Padlock*. Other plays of the late eighteenth century featured a variety of African American characters. A play in 1798 called *The Triumph of Love* introduced a shuffling, cackling black servant, and an unfortunate stereotype was created.

The AFRICAN GROVE THEATER was formed in 1820 by James Hewlett and began performing Shakespeare before mixed audiences in 1821. Hewlett was a fine tragic actor, but his company was forced to close because of attacks by white hooligans. With the destruction of that company and the departure of the great Ira ALDRIDGE for Europe came the end of an early opportunity to develop a significant African American theater.

The early nineteenth century also saw the beginning of the tradition of interspersing "black-dialect" songs into regular plays. By the 1820's, George Nichols had popularized "Zip Coon" and George Washington Dixon was impersonating African Americans in songs. In 1823, Edwin Forrest, a white actor, blackened his face in *The Tailor in Distress* and was praised as offering "the first realistic representation of the plantation Negro."

Minstrelsy. In 1828, Thomas "Daddy" Rice, a white performer, began to imitate the singing and shuffling of a black person and created a popular act called *Bone Squash*. He is credited with initiating the character of Jim Crow. Imitations of Rice followed. P. T. Barnum added Ethiopian "breakdowns" to his shows, and in 1843 Daniel Emmett brought his Virginia Minstrels to the New York stage. White men in its performances wore blackened faces and gala costumes, and they told jokes for white audiences. The era of minstrels was officially launched.

In minstrelsy, a large group of men sat or stood in a half circle, with a master of ceremonies in the middle acting as a straight man while on each side of him were the musicians. The language and music were parodies of the distinctive new styles that African Americans had developed after being deprived of their African heritage.

African Americans as Theater Characters. African Americans also appeared as characters in the theater. In spite of the good intentions of the abolitionist play *Uncle Tom's Cabin*, it too helped to establish stereotypes, such as the mischievous Topsy and the all-forgiving Uncle Tom. Another theatrical type was the "tragic mulatto," such as in Dion Boucicault's *The Octoron*. It further insulted blacks by establishing a "white" beauty standard. Other African American characters that appeared before and soon after the Civil War were mostly servants and minor personages.

By the 1880's and 1890's, a more balanced treatment slowly emerged, beginning with Steele Mackaye's play *A Fool's Errand* in 1881, and culminating with Edward Sheldon's *The Nigger* in 1910. Sheldon's was one of the few plays up to that time to appear on Broadway with a story line about an African American.

Ben Vereen, shown rehearsing for Pippin, *extended a long tradition of African American stage dancers and actors.* (AP/ Wide World Photos)

African American Actors. Theatrically, the most significant development following the Civil War was the appearance of African Americans as entertainers, at first in the minstrel tradition, where they were a caricature of a caricature, and later in their own unique form. In 1898, Bob Cole wrote, directed, and produced *A Trip to Coontown*, a musical with a plot that broke with the minstrel tradition by telling a story through music, song, and dance. Produced in New York City, it provided a model for others to follow.

After the turn of the century, Bert WILLIAMS became one of the most popular black performers of all time, starring in such well-known shows as *Abyssinia* (1906), written by Jesse Shipp, *Bandanna Land* (1908), *Mr. Lode of Kole* (1911), and various editions of *Ziegfeld's Follies*. The years 1909 to 1917 saw the rise of the Harlem Theater movement, with shows by African American artists written for their own audiences at such theaters as the Crescent, the Lafayette, and the Lincoln.

With the production of Eugene O'Neill's *THE EMPEROR JONES* in 1920, with Charles GILPIN cast as Brutus Jones, black characters played by black actors became accepted in the theater. Many other plays followed, including O'Neill's *ALL GOD'S CHILLUN GOT WINGS* (1924), starring Paul ROBESON, Paul Green's *In Abraham's Bosom* (1926), Dubose and Dorothy Heyward's *Porgy* (1927), and Lew Leslie's *BLACKBIRDS OF 1928*, which starred the great dancer Bill "Bojangles" ROBINSON and was followed by *Blackbirds of 1929* with Eubie BLAKE. Black theater flourished in the 1920's.

In 1930, although the Depression curtailed theatrical activity, some black plays were produced. One of the most successful was Marc Connelly's *THE GREEN PASTURES*. This was followed by worthy efforts such as Hall Johnson's *RUN, LITTLE CHILDREN* (1933), John Wexley's *They Shall Not Die* (1934), Langston HUGHES's *MULATTO* (1935), and the musical *PORGY AND BESS*.

The 1930's also saw a number of attempts to found a permanent African American theater. Such distinguished artists as Rose McClendon, Dick Campbell, Richard Huey, and Venezuela Jones contributed greatly to the effort. One of the most important organizations of the late 1930's was the "Negro Unit" of the FEDERAL THEATRE PROJECT, which was an arm of the Works Progress Administration, President Franklin D. Roosevelt's program to put people back to work.

The numerous productions of the 1930's included such works as George McEntee's *The Case of Philip Lawrence*, J. Augustus Smith's *Turpentine*, Rudolph Fisher's *The Conjure Man Dies*, and William Dubois' *Haiti*. The most highly acclaimed production was the Orson Welles–John Houseman offering of *Macbeth*, set on a West Indian Island and featuring an all-black cast, among whom were Canada LEE, Jack Carter, and Edna Thomas. The Rose McClendon Players gave a noteworthy production of William Ashley's *Booker T. Washington*, and *Mamba's Daughters* (1939) introduced the great Ethel WATERS.

In the 1940's, Richard WRIGHT's novel *NATIVE SON* (1940) was adapted by Paul Green to the stage, with Orson Welles directing and Canada Lee playing the lead. Paul Robeson played *Othello* to great acclaim, Ethel Waters continued in *CABIN IN THE SKY*, and in 1943 *CARMEN JONES* captivated New York audiences. Moreover, *Anna Lucasta* scored a big success on Broadway, *Deep Are the Roots* held a long run, and Robert Ardrey's *Jeb* received much attention. Experimentation took place Off-Broadway, giving a number of opportunities to black artists. The AMERICAN NEGRO THEATRE, founded in 1940, was part of this experimental movement.

Lorraine HANSBERRY's award-winning *A RAISIN IN THE SUN* (1959) with Sidney POITIER and directed by Lloyd RICHARDS brought black theater to international attention.

Black Theater Movements. In the 1960's, the African American theater movement arrived, accepting the integrity and dignity of the black experience and refusing to compromise with white sensibilities. In 1964, Amiri BARAKA and others founded the Black Arts Repertoire Theatre School in New York City and produced a number of black plays. Although it dissolved, it provided a model for black arts organizations across the country. In 1968, the Negro Ensemble Company was established, with Douglas Turner WARD as artistic director and thirteen permanent company members. It also instituted a training program for actors, directors, and playwrights. In 1967, the New Lafayette Company, headed by Robert Macbeth, was started in Harlem.

The 1960's and 1970's saw the advent of many new African American theater artists, including such playwrights as James BALDWIN (*BLUES FOR MISTER CHARLIE*, 1964), Amiri Baraka (*The Toilet*, 1964; *DUTCHMAN*, 1964), Lonne ELDER III (*CEREMONIES IN DARK OLD MEN*, 1969), Ed Bullins (*Clara's Old Man*, 1965), and Charles GORDONE (*NO PLACE TO BE SOMEBODY*, 1969).

As a result of increased opportunities, the 1980's saw the arrival of even more African American theater talent. One of the most important newcomers was August WILSON, whose award-winning plays included *MA RAINEY'S BLACK BOTTOM*, *FENCES*, *JOE TURNER'S COME AND GONE*, *THE PIANO LESSON*, and *TWO TRAINS RUNNING*.—*Tony J. Stafford*

SUGGESTED READINGS: • Brown-Guillory, Elizabeth. *Their Place on the Stage: Black Women Playwrights in America.* New York: Greenwood Press, 1988. • Craig, E. Quita. *Black Drama of the Federal Theater Era: Beyond the Formal Horizons.* Amherst: University of Massachusetts Press, 1980. • Hatch, James V., and Omanii Abdullah, eds. *Black Playwrights, 1823-1977: An Annotated Bibliography of Plays.* New York: R. R. Bowker, 1977. • Mitchell, Loften. *Black Drama: The Story of the American Negro in the Theatre.* New York: Hawthorn Books,

General Lucius Theus retired from the military in 1979 and then became director of civic affairs for the Bendix Corporation in Southfield, Mich. (U.S. Air Force)

1967. • Sanders, Leslie Catherine. *The Development of Black Theatre in America: From Shadows to Selves.* Baton Rouge: Louisiana State University Press, 1988.

Theatre Owners Booking Association: Vaudeville circuit. The association was an African American vaudeville circuit organized in Chattanooga, Tenn., in 1920. The original theaters of the circuit were located primarily in the Midwest and South, in black sections of major cities. The circuit provided steady work for many famous entertainers such as Pigmeat MARKHAM, Ethel WATERS, and Bill "Bojangles" ROBINSON. Economic difficulties forced the circuit to disband during the Depression era.

Their Eyes Were Watching God (1937): Novel by Zora Neale HURSTON. The protagonist, a strong and romantic black woman, tells her life story to a close and affectionate woman friend. She explains how she struggled through three marriages in order to find fulfillment and a sense of purpose in her life. She finally finds happiness by rejecting her society's attitudes toward security, materialism, and hierarchies, and by making her own decisions and controlling her own life. The novel is a vital account of the life of uneducated and rural African Americans in the South during the period and of black gender roles.

Theus, Lucius (b. Oct. 11, 1922, near Bells, Tenn.): Air Force officer. Theus joined the Air Force in 1942 and was commissioned as a second lieutenant in 1946. He advanced to the rank of major general in 1975. He was the squadron adjutant at Tuskegee Air Force Base in Alabama in 1946, then moved to posts in Germany, France, and Greece before returning to the United States in 1958. He was the comptroller and deputy base commander at Cam Ranh Bay, Vietnam, from 1966 to 1967. He served as a data automation staff officer at the Pentagon from 1967 to 1974, then was commander of the Air Force Accounting and Finance Center and director of accounting and finance at the headquarters of the U.S. Air Force in Denver, Colo. He retired from military service in 1979 to become assistant corporate controller and corporate director of civic affairs for the Bendix Corporation of Southfield, Mich. He has been an instructor in business administration. He holds an M.B.A. from George Washington University (1957) and was enrolled in the advanced management program at Harvard University in 1969.

Thigpen, Lynne (b. Joliet, Ill.): Actress. Thigpen landed her first major role in the stage version of *Godspell*, and also appeared in the 1973 film. She had roles in *Lean on Me* (1989) and *Tootsie* (1982), among other films. She appeared in several television series in the 1980's, and in the 1990's played a district attorney on *L.A. Law*, while also playing The Chief on the Public Broadcasting Service children's show *Where in the World is Carmen Sandiego?* Thigpen also directed that geography quiz show.

Third Life of Grange Copeland, The (1970): Novel by Alice WALKER. The work traces the protagonist of the title, a black sharecropper, through three generations as he searches for identity and dignity. It examines the realities of racism in the South and deals with the frustrations of black men, the deterioration of the family, domestic violence, and adultery.

Thirteenth Amendment: Amendment to the U.S. Constitution prohibiting SLAVERY. Ratified in 1865, it outlawed slavery or involuntary servitude except as punishment for a crime for which a person had been convicted by fair trial. The prohibition applied to the United States and areas within the country's jurisdiction. Congress was given the power to pass laws to enforce the prohibition.

Thomas, Bettye Collier (b. 1943, Macon, Ga.): Historian, museum director, and educator. She is best known for her scholarly endeavors in African American women's history. From 1977 to 1989, she developed and administered the Bethune Museum and its archives in Washington, D.C. In 1979, she coordinated the first national scholarly research conference on black women's history, held at the museum and funded by the National Endowment for the Humanities. In 1989, she became the first director of the Center for African American History and Culture at Temple University in Philadelphia.

Thomas, Carla (b. 1942, Memphis, Tenn.): Soul singer. Thomas was the most prominent female soul artist of the 1960's before the emergence of Aretha FRANKLIN. Thomas' first record, "Cause I Love You," a 1960 duet with her father, Rufus THOMAS, was the first Memphis soul hit and helped to establish Memphis' Stax Records as the dominant soul music record company. Her hits include "Gee Whiz" (1961), "B-A-B-Y" (1966), and "Tramp" (1967), a duet with Otis REDDING.

Thomas, Clarence (b. June 23, 1948, Pinpoint, Ga.): Supreme Court justice. Thomas' father abandoned the family when Thomas was two years old, and Thomas was sent to be reared by his maternal grandparents at the age of seven. Thomas was educated at an all-black Catholic grade school and later at a boarding-school seminary. He attended college at Immaculate Conception Abbey for one year before transferring to Holy Cross College. Thomas was graduated with honors from Holy Cross and received his B.A. degree in 1971. He was admitted to Yale Law School and received his J.D. degree in 1974. Upon graduation, Thomas moved to Missouri, where he was admitted to the state bar. He served as assistant attorney general for Missouri under Attorney General John C. Danforth from 1974 to 1977. In 1977, he became an attorney for the Monsanto Company, serving until 1979.

Thomas' career in Washington, D.C., began when Danforth, who had since been elected as a senator from Missouri, selected Thomas to serve as his legislative assistant from 1979 to 1981. Upon Danforth's recommendation, President Ronald Reagan appointed Thomas to serve as assistant secretary for civil rights in the U.S. Department of Education. In 1982, Thomas was appointed chairman of the U.S. EQUAL EMPLOYMENT OPPORTUNITY COMMISSION (EEOC). He served in this post until 1990. President George Bush appointed Thomas to the federal bench on Mar. 6, 1990. Thomas became U.S. circuit judge for the District of Columbia Circuit of the U.S. Court of Appeals.

Thomas' next judicial appointment came in July of 1991, when President George Bush announced that he had selected Thomas to replace retiring justice Thurgood MARSHALL on the U.S. Supreme Court. Senate hearings on Thomas' appointment began shortly thereafter, and Thomas' judicial record and positions on such issues as AFFIRMATIVE ACTION, school prayer, and abortion were scrutinized. The hearings became the focus of national attention when a Federal Bureau of Investigation report was leaked to the press. The report contained allegations of sexual misconduct and harassment by Thomas, made by Anita HILL, an African American professor of law at the University of Oklahoma who had been an assistant to Thomas when he was the head of EEOC. As a result of the ensuing controversy, the committee reconvened the hearings to investigate Hill's charges. The Senate panel was unable to determine Thomas' guilt or innocence and voted by a narrow margin to recommend to the full Senate confirmation of Thomas' nomination. Thomas was confirmed by a vote of 52 to 48 in the full Senate on Oct. 15, 1991.

Thomas, Debi (Mar. 25, 1967, Poughkeepsie, N.Y.): Figure skater. Approximately sixty million American

Debi Thomas during her freestyle routine at the 1988 Olympics. (AP/Wide World Photos)

television viewers—a number rivaling the audience for the Super Bowl—watched "The Battle of the Carmens" in the 1988 Olympics in Calgary, Alberta, Canada. The combatants were Thomas and 1984 Olympic champion Katarina Witt of East Germany. Each skated to music from Bizet's *Carmen*. At the end of the competition, Witt took the gold medal and Thomas finished behind Canada's Elizabeth Manley to earn a bronze.

Thomas' career prior to the 1988 Olympics was one of great achievement. That she is the first African American—in fact, the first person of African ancestry—to achieve such a level of success in figure skating is only part of her significance. She was one of the most accomplished figure skaters of her generation, something borne out by her many championships. Thomas won the United States national championships in 1986. That same year, she went on to win the gold medal at the World Championships, defeating Witt. The following year, plagued by problems with her Achilles tendons, Thomas won the silver medal at both the United States and World championships. In 1988, Thomas became the first dethroned national champion in fifty-four years to reclaim her title at the United States championships. It is clear, therefore, that although the 1988 Olympics may have introduced Thomas to a wider audience, her career prior to that was one marked by distinction.

Another distinguishing mark of Thomas' life and career is that while competing at these championships she was a pre-med student at Stanford University. Thomas' attitude toward combining the two provides an important message: "Things like the importance of an education and being whatever you can be give me an inner strength to pull things off on the ice." Her success in school and in sports made Thomas an ideal role model not only for African Americans but for all people, regardless of race. Thomas never believed, however, that she suffered for lack of a role model. Her communication of this attitude—that one should strive to achieve one's goals, even without evidence that these goals are attainable—is as important as her accomplishments.

After her retirement from amateur competition in 1988, Thomas returned to Stanford to complete her studies and also made professional figure skating appearances. In 1992, after winning several professional championships, she announced that she planned to retire from skating to realize her other ambition, going to medical school.

Thomas, Gerald Eustis (b. June 23, 1929, Natick, Mass.): U.S. Navy officer. Thomas joined the Naval Reserve Officers Training Corps (NROTC) while a student at Harvard University. He earned a B.A. in biochemical sciences in 1951 and was commissioned as an ensign. He studied Russian while serving with the cruiser USS *Worcester* and earned a certificate as an interpreter from the Defense Language Institute in 1957. He was assigned to the National Security Agency at Fort Meade, Md., from 1957 to 1960.

Thomas' first command was of the USS *Impervious*, in 1962 and 1963. In 1963, he became assistant head of the Navy's college training programs section. Thomas studied at the Naval War College for a year beginning in July, 1965, and was named as a distinguished graduate. He also earned an M.S. in international affairs from George Washington University in 1966. He commanded the USS *Bausell* for the next year, then went to the NROTC unit at Prairie View A&M College in Texas, where he was executive officer and later commanding officer. He also taught naval science.

Thomas earned a Ph.D. in diplomatic history from Yale University in 1975. He was also commander of Destroyer Squadron Nine from 1970 to 1973 and of Destroyer Group Five from 1974 to 1976. In 1974, he was designated as a rear admiral, only the second African American in U.S. Navy history to reach that rank.

Thomas began serving in the office of the assistant secretary of defense in 1976, as director of the Near East, Africa, and South Asia regions. He became commander of the training command of the U.S. Pacific Fleet at San Diego, Calif., in December, 1978, and retired in August, 1981. Among his service awards are a Meritorious Service Medal, the National Defense Service Medal, the Vietnam Service Medal, and the Republic of Vietnam Campaign Medal. He is a member of the Organization of American Historians.

Thomas, Isiah Lord, III (b. Apr. 30, 1961, Chicago, Ill.): Basketball player. Surviving the hunger, cold, and poverty of growing up in Chicago's tough West Side neighborhoods, Thomas was on a mission to succeed in BASKETBALL to help his family. In 1981, sophomore Thomas led Indiana University to a National Collegiate Athletic Association title, with his team defeating the University of North Carolina. Thomas was named as the most valuable player of the tournament, and he announced his intention to turn professional.

Thomas was the first-round draft pick of the Detroit Pistons in 1981 and was the second player chosen overall. Thomas thrived in the National Basketball Association (NBA), becoming the first player in league history to be selected to start on the All-Star team in each of his first five seasons in the league. His talent helped to revitalize an ailing franchise. In his first year, the team won nearly twice as many games as it had the year before, finishing 39-43, and in his third year the Pistons finished at 49-33, with their first winning season in seven years. By 1990, the Pistons had made three NBA championship appearances and had won back-to-back championships in 1989 and 1990. In 1988, Thomas scored a record twenty-five points in one quarter during the championship series. The 1989 victory marked the first championship won in the forty-one year history of the franchise. The 1990 championship was notable for Thomas' individual achievement, underscored when he was awarded the Most Valuable Player Award for the championship series.

Thomas, Rufus (b. Mar. 26, 1917, Casey, Miss.): Soul singer. A former minstrel-show dancer and comedian, Thomas became a soul music star for Memphis' Stax Records. Thomas is best known for his dance hits "The Dog" (1963), "Walking the Dog" (1963), and "Do the Funky Chicken" (1970).

Former Denver Nuggets forward David Thompson. (AP/Wide World Photos)

Thompson, David (b. July 13, 1954, Shelby, N.C.): Basketball player. Thompson was an All-American in three years of college BASKETBALL with North Carolina State University. He was drafted by teams in both the National Basketball Association (NBA) and the American Basketball Association (ABA), and he chose to play with the Denver Nuggets of the ABA. He was that league's Rookie of the Year in the 1975-1976 season. Denver and three other ABA teams joined the NBA the following year. Thompson was traded to the Seattle SuperSonics in 1982, and during the 1983-1984 season he injured a knee, ending his professional career.

Thompson, Era Bell (Aug. 10, 1906, Des Moines, Iowa—Dec. 30, 1986, Chicago, Ill.): Journalist. Thompson is best known as editor of *Negro Digest* and *Ebony* magazines. She grew up in Iowa and in an ethnically diverse farming community in North Dakota. At North Dakota State University, she wrote for the college paper and served as correspondent to the *Chicago Defender*, penning features on social issues as well as a lighthearted column under a cowboy pseudonym. After graduating from Iowa's Morningside College in 1933, Thompson moved to Chicago to work and study journalism at Northwestern University.

Between 1933 and 1945, Thompson worked for the Works Progress Administration, the Chicago Relief Administration, and many other public organizations. To combat discontent at work, Thompson utilized her tongue-in-cheek humor to write the *Giggle Sheet*, a one-page newspaper that poked fun at fellow employees.

In 1945, Thompson received the Newbery Fellowship to write her autobiography. Published a year later, *American Daughter* is an optimistic story of growing up that has been recognized for its warmhearted treatment of family relationships and rural life, as well as for its racial tolerance. The book earned Thompson the Patron Saints Award from the Society of Midland Authors in 1968. Thompson explored her African heritage in a second book, *Africa: Land of My Fathers* (1954), and coedited *White on Black: The Views of Twenty-two White Americans on the Negro* (1963) with Herbert Nipson.

In 1947, Thompson joined the Johnson Publishing Company as an associate editor of *Negro Digest* (later called *Black World*); in 1951, she was named comanaging editor of *Ebony*. She served in that position until 1964, when she became international editor for *Ebony*, specializing in on-the-spot coverage of foreign places and personalities. She traveled extensively, interviewing leaders in thatched huts and palaces and examining racial relations worldwide. Until her retirement in the 1980's, Thompson wrote features on such topics as Ugandan martyrs, Indian gurus, and problems facing the children of black soldiers in Asia. Thompson's honors include a Bread Loaf Writer's Fellowship in 1949 and a National Press Club citation in 1961. Her portrait was hung in the North Dakota Hall of Fame in 1977.

Thompson, John Robert, Jr. (b. Sept. 2, 1941, Washington, D.C.): Basketball coach. Thompson played for the Boston Celtics from 1964 to 1966. After coaching the BASKETBALL team at St. Anthony's High School in Washington, D.C. (1966-1972), he was named as the head coach for Georgetown University. He also was assistant coach (1976) and head coach (1988) of the United States Olympic basketball team.

Thompson, Robert "Bob" (June 26, 1937, Louisville, Ky.—1966, Rome, Italy): Painter. Thompson, a prolific painter, achieved greater fame after his death. A full-scale retrospective of his work was presented at the New School for Social Research in 1969. His paintings are characterized by areas of brilliant color, depicting inner feeling rather than objective form.

Thompson, William H. (b. Brooklyn, N.Y.—Aug. 6, 1950, Korea): One of two African American infantry soldiers to receive the Congressional Medal of Honor for service in the Korean War. Private, first class, Thompson was the first African American since the Spanish-American War to win this commendation, which was awarded posthumously. He remained at his machine-gun post while his fellow soldiers fled to safety.

Thornton, Willie Mae "Big Mama" (Dec. 11, 1926, Montgomery, Ala.—July 25, 1984, Los Angeles, Calif.): Singer. After winning an amateur talent contest at age fourteen, Thornton traveled to Atlanta, Ga., where she worked as a dancer and comedienne in a number of vaudeville shows. After successful stints with various show bands, she left for Houston, Tex., where she recorded for various labels and eventually began a long tenure with the Johnny Otis R&B Caravan shows. Her big break came when she met songwriters Mike Leiber and Jerry Stoller, who provided her with "Hound Dog," which she recorded in 1953 with the Johnny Otis Band as backup.

Thorpe, Jim (b. Feb. 1, 1949, Roxboro, N.C.): Golfer. Thorpe's father worked at a white golf club, enabling family members to master the sport. Thorpe's brother Charles (Chuck) entered the Professional Golf Association (PGA) Tour first. Thorpe turned pro in 1972, and by 1986, he had joined golf's exclusive million dollar club for career earnings. In the early 1990's, Thorpe emerged as the number-one African American golfer on the PGA Tour.

Thrash, Dox (b. 1893, Griffin, Ga.): Painter, printmaker, and coinventor of the carborundum print process. Thrash began studying art through a correspondence course. He went on to study at the Art Institute of Chicago (1919-1922). He also studied black and white media under Earl Horter of the Graphic Sketch Club in Philadelphia, Pa., and worked for the Pennsylvania Federal Art Project. His work is represented in the National Archives.

Thurman, Howard (Nov. 18, 1900, Daytona Beach, Fla.—Apr. 10, 1981, San Francisco, Calif.): Theologian and educator. Thurman received his B.A. degree from Morehouse College and the M.Div. degree from Colgate

Howard Thurman, prominent theologian and educator. (AP/Wide World Photos)

Rochester Divinity School. As a Kent Fellow at Haverford College, he studied under mystic scholar Rufus Jones. He began his career as a pastor in Oberlin, Ohio, in 1925. From 1929 to 1932, he was director of religious life and professor of religion at Morehouse and Spelman colleges in Atlanta, Ga. He was dean of Rankin Chapel and professor of theology at HOWARD UNIVERSITY from

1932 to 1944. In 1944, he cofounded the Church for the Fellowship of All Peoples in San Francisco. He served as pastor until 1953. From 1953 to 1964, Thurman was a professor in the school of religion and dean of Marsh Chapel at Boston University. He was that university's first full-time black professor. He established the Howard Thurman Educational Trust in San Francisco following his retirement.

Throughout his career, Thurman devoted himself intensely to meditation, study, reflection, and experience of the religious life and to sharing his findings with others for enhancement of their religious experiences. His life-long quest was for an inclusive community and "common ground" among people. He sought to fulfill this dream through pastoring, teaching, writing, lecturing, and other ventures. He attracted tremendous followings of students, professionals, and religious, social, and political leaders throughout the United States and in other parts of the world. Many graduate students, both black and white, in ethics, sociology, psychology, philosophy, theology, and literature have written dissertations and published books and articles on his life and teachings.

Thurman published more than twenty books and hundreds of journal articles. He held numerous guest and visiting lectureships at prestigious institutions, both in the United States and abroad. He addressed audiences at four hundred institutions in the United States and one hundred outside North America. Among his numerous awards are membership in Phi Beta Kappa and fourteen honorary doctorates from Ivy League colleges and universities.

Thurman, Wallace Henry (Aug. 16, 1902, Salt Lake City, Utah—Dec. 21, 1934, New York City): Novelist and editor. Thurman was a controversial figure associated with the HARLEM RENAISSANCE. He first gained attention with his literary quarterly *Fire!!*, which showcased younger black writers but gained little support from more-established African Americans. His novel *The Blacker the Berry* (1929) concerns the psychologically distorting effects of colorism and race-consciousness. *Infants of the Spring* (1932), one of his more controversial works, satirizes several writers of the Harlem Renaissance as "infants" who produced little of value. Thurman also wrote film scripts.

Thurmond, Nathaniel "Nate" (b. July 25, 1941, Akron, Ohio): BASKETBALL player. Thurmond attended Akron Central High School, then went to Bowling Green State University from 1959 to 1963. He was named All-American in his final two seasons. He averaged 17.8 points per game

at Bowling Green, amassing 1,356 career points. He was drafted by the San Francisco Warriors of the National Basketball Association (NBA) as the third pick in 1963.

A team-oriented player, Thurmond was forced to play at forward and as backup center to Wilt CHAMBERLAIN during his first seasons. Even so, he was named as an all-NBA rookie. He was allowed to play his natural

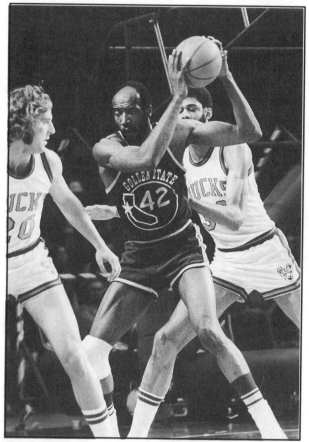

Former Golden State Warrior Nate Thurmond attempts to keep the ball out of the reach of Milwaukee players. (AP/ Wide World Photos)

position, center, in 1967, and developed into one of the great players of his time. He showed a remarkable offensive-defensive balance, scoring a career total of 14,437 points and making 14,464 total rebounds. He made 5,521 field goals (42 percent of his attempts) and 3,395 free throws (66.7 percent). He made the All-Star team in 1965, 1966, 1967, 1968, 1970, 1973, and 1974. Thurmond excelled as a defensive player, setting the NBA record for most rebounds (eighteen) in one quarter during a 1965 game and earning a place on the NBA All-Defensive team in 1969 and 1971-1974.

Thurmond was traded to the Chicago Bulls in 1974 and to the Cleveland Cavaliers in 1975. He retired in 1977 and was inducted into the Naismith Memorial Basketball Hall of Fame in 1984. Both the Cleveland Cavaliers and the Golden State (formerly San Francisco) Warriors retired Thurmond's number, making him the first NBA player to have a number retired by two teams. The Warriors hired Thurmond as director of community relations after his playing days were over.

Tiant, Luis (Luis Clemente Tiant y Vega; b. Nov. 23, 1940, Marianao, Cuba): Baseball pitcher. In nineteen seasons (1964-1982), Tiant won 229 games. He had four twenty-win seasons (1968, 1973, 1974, 1976) and twice led the American League in earned run average (1968, 1972). Tiant's best years were with the Boston Red Sox, whom he helped win the 1975 World Series. Tiant, at age thirty-four, won the hearts of BASEBALL fans around the country by twice beating the powerful Cincinnati Reds.

Luis Tiant. (National Baseball Library, Cooperstown, NY)

Tindley, Charles Albert (July 7, 1856, Berlin, Md.— July 26, 1933, Philadelphia, Pa.): Minister and gospel composer. Tindley was born to slave parents and taught himself to read and write. In 1873, he met and married Daisy Henry. Together they moved to Philadelphia, where Tindley worked as a hod carrier at Bainbridge Street Methodist Episcopal Church to support himself while in school. He studied at the Brandywine Institute in preparation to enter the Methodist ministry and took correspondence courses with Boston Theological Seminary. Tindley became a sexton of the Bainbridge Street church and passed his ministerial examinations in 1885.

After he was ordained a minister, Tindley spent seventeen years as an itinerant preacher, appointed to pastorates in New Jersey, Maryland, and Delaware. In 1902, he returned to Philadelphia as the pastor of the Bainbridge Street church. His popularity as a preacher helped increase the church's membership to more than ten thousand, and he made preaching tours throughout the United States. After his death, the Bainbridge Street congregation renamed the church Tindley Temple in his honor.

Tindley was well versed in the chorus and refrain tradition of black spirituals, and he began to compose gospel songs based on this tradition as early as 1901. He wrote more than fifty compositions, including "I'll Overcome Someday" (1901), "We'll Understand It Better By and By" (1905), "Stand By Me" (1905), and "Let Jesus Fix It for You" (1923). His songs were published in *Soul Echoes* (1905) and *Gospel Pearls* (1921), two compilations of gospel hymns that included Tindley's contemporary compositions along with older hymns and spirituals popular in both white and black churches. His own collection of gospel music was published in Philadelphia under the title *New Songs of Paradise* in 1916. In addition to being popular with black Methodist and Baptist congregations, Tindley's gospel hymns were adopted enthusiastically by fundamentalist black Pentecostal congregations of the early 1900's, which also were drawn to the songs' messages of comfort to the poor and oppressed who suffered hardships on earth but looked forward to the joys of the afterlife.

To Kill a Mockingbird (Universal, 1962): Film directed by Robert Mulligan. Adapted from Harper Lee's novel, this sensitive, powerful film tells the story of a southern town torn apart by an interracial rape trial. Gregory Peck received an Oscar for his performance as Atticus Finch, a widowed lawyer raising two children, who agrees to defend the young black man (played by Brock PETERS) a white girl has accused of rape. Estelle Evans appears as the Finch family's housekeeper, Calpurnia. Told through the eyes of Finch's young daughter, Scout, the film explores the complexities of life in a small southern town where warmth and hospitality exist side by side with racial hatred and violence.

To Sir with Love (Columbia, 1967): Film directed by James Clavell. Set in a London slum, the film centers on

Sidney Poitier starred in To Sir with Love, *a film about a teacher's efforts to reach a group of working-class students.* (Museum of Modern Art/Film Stills Archive, NY)

the efforts of a black teacher (Mark Thackeray, played by Sidney POITIER) to reach a class of troubled, economically disadvantaged students. Slowly earning their respect through a combination of humor, discipline, and understanding, Thackeray, whom the students call "Sir," manages to educate his students while instilling in them a sense of purpose and self-respect.

To Sleep with Anger (Samuel Goldwyn Company, 1990): Film written and directed by Charles Burnett. This original, offbeat film is set in Los Angeles, Calif., where a black family finds its life disrupted by the arrival of Harry Mention (Danny GLOVER), a friend from the South. Embraced by some members of the family and mistrusted by others, Mention is an enigmatic figure, by turns sinister and seemingly magical. Glover gives a memorable performance in the role.

tokenism: As applied to equal opportunity and desegregation efforts, it refers to efforts to show accommodation to a demand or principle without actually accommodating. The term also implies compliance with programs or requests in a visible but shallow manner. The term first surfaced in the early and mid-1960's, when school desegregation was being implemented. Token numbers of African American students were enrolled in predominantly white schools that wished to be perceived as implementing integration without actually doing so. The few African American students enrolled were tokens, or symbols, of integration efforts.

Tokenism is a result, in part, of the language used in defining equal opportunity and antidiscrimination programs. For example, the language used in legislating certain practices or kinds of conduct is frequently open to interpretation. "Representation" is one ambiguous term that is used commonly. When a community has a specific ethnic makeup, each ethnic group is supposed to be represented adequately in areas such as law enforcement agencies and public-sector employment, as well as in the political arena. It is not clear what form representation

Melba Tolliver, television broadcaster, won the Outstanding Woman in Media Award in 1975. (AP/Wide World Photos)

must take. Employment representation, for example, can be achieved by hiring members of targeted ethnic groups only at the lowest employment grades or categories. They are thus left unrepresented at higher levels. Tokenism might take place at those higher levels. An agency or firm may employ a member of a targeted ethnic group in a highly visible, but actually unimportant, capacity with the intention of conveying a false impression that it employs many minority-group members at high levels.

Political representation may take the form of single MINORITY-GROUP members in various political groups, as token members, or may take the form of officeholding by ethnic-group members who do not in fact hold the opinions of the majority of the group whom they supposedly represent. On the surface, however, minority groups are represented, because their members hold office.

Tokenism also can be found in the history of school integration in the United States, especially in the Deep South. Under court orders to desegregate, southern school districts often employed their own strategies of token desegregation. They spread the process of desegregation over many years or administered tests of dubious value as a means of denying or limiting admission. In ways such as these, districts made token efforts to desegregate but in fact had little intention of doing so.

Tolliver, Melba (b. 1939, Rome, Ga.): Television broadcaster. Before moving to an NBC affiliate as a newscaster in 1977, Tolliver worked at an ABC affiliate from 1968 to 1976 as a reporter for *Eyewitness News*, anchor and associate producer for *Sunday Hours News*, cohost for the show *Like It Is*, and host of her own show, *Melba Tolliver's New York*. She won the Outstanding Woman in Media award in 1975 and a National Endowment for the Humanities Fellowship in 1976.

Tolson, M(elvin) B(eaunorus) (Feb. 6, 1898, Moberly, Mo.—Aug. 29, 1966, Guthrie, Okla.): Poet. Known as a modernist, Tolson published *Rendezvous with America* in 1944. He was named poet laureate of LIBERIA in 1947 and was commissioned to write a poem for Liberia's centennial; he wrote *Libretto for the Republic of Liberia* (1953). In *Harlem Gallery: Book I, The Curator* (1965), Tolson explores the relationship of the artist with his community. In 1966, Tolson won the Arts and Letters Award in literature from the American Academy and Institute of Arts and Letters.

Toomer, Nathan Eugene "Jean" (Dec. 26, 1894, Washington, D.C.—Mar. 30, 1967, Doylestown, Pa.): Writer. Toomer earned his reputation as one of the major artists of the HARLEM RENAISSANCE with his book *CANE* (1923), a remarkable collection of short stories, poems, sketches, and drama that captured the poetic spirit of African Americans. He was the son of Nathan Toomer, a Georgia planter, and Nina Pinchback. Shortly after Toomer's birth, his father deserted the family, and Toomer was raised in the household of his maternal grandparents. His grandfather was the mulatto RECONSTRUCTION politician P. B. S. PINCHBACK, who had served as acting governor of Louisiana and was twice elected to, but denied a seat in, the U.S. Senate. In Washington, D.C., Jean lived in both white and black neighborhoods, and he came to consider himself neither white nor black, but rather as American. In a letter to *The Liberator* magazine, he wrote, "I am naturally and inevitably an American. I have strived for a spiritual fusion analogous to the fact of racial intermingling. Without denying a single element in me, with no desire to subdue one to the other, I have sought to let them function as complements." Resentful of his grandfather for allegedly driving his father away, Toomer turned to his uncle Bismarck for intellectual stimulation. His uncle encouraged his interest in science and in literature. Toomer enrolled in a variety of universities in several different majors, never staying long enough to earn a degree.

In 1921, as acting principal of an industrial and agricultural school in Sparta, Ga., Toomer at least temporarily found the harmony he sought. In the rural South, he learned to love the land, to admire the peasants' dignity in the face of oppression, and to value the songs they sang. His emotional response to the experience was *Cane*. In it, Toomer experimented with language and revealed his dissatisfaction with post-World War I society, typical attributes of American writing of the 1920's. In 1924, he became attracted to the philosophy of George Ivanovitch Gurdjieff, who sought to cure the division between body, mind, and soul that tormented modern man. Toomer's most famous work after *Cane*, the poem entitled "Blue Meridian" (1936), combines Gurdjieff's utopianism with Toomer's own long-standing conception of America as a new culture in which racial boundaries would be dissolved into a new spiritual synthesis.

In 1932, Toomer married Margery Latimer, a white member of a Gurdjieff group he had organized in Wisconsin. She died less than a year later, giving birth to their daughter. In 1934, he married Marjorie Content, another white woman, and moved to Doylestown, Pa. He was never again to achieve the literary success of *Cane*, despite attempts to have other works published. His prose and poetry were collected and edited by Darwin T. TURNER as *The Wayward and the Seeking* (1980).

Toote, Gloria E. A. (b. Nov. 8, 1931, New York, N.Y.): Businesswoman and political appointee. Toote received her J.D. degree from HOWARD UNIVERSITY School of Law in 1954 and earned her LL.M. degree from Columbia University Graduate School of Law in 1956. She wa an attorney in private practice in Englewood, N.J., from 1954 to 1971. In 1965, she helped open the Town Sound Recording Studios in Englewood with the aid of a Small Business Administration loan. Toote became president of Toote Town Publications, Inc., and was a member of the editorial staff of the national affairs section for *Time* magazine. In 1973, she was appointed assistant secretary of the DEPARTMENT OF HOUSING AND URBAN DEVELOPMENT (HUD), serving until 1975. After leaving HUD, she returned to private law practice and became an author and public lecturer.

Toussaint, Allen (b. Jan. 14, 1938, New Orleans, La.): Songwriter, producer, and arranger. Toussaint is an accomplished pianist and has written and produced songs and albums for artists such as Joe Cocker, Dr. John, and the POINTER SISTERS. Among the songs he has written are rock and soul classics from the 1960's such as "Mother-in-Law," "Workin' in a Coal Mine," and "Sea Cruise." His "Whipped Cream" was a hit for Herb Alpert. Tous-

saint made his own instrumental album for RCA, entitled *Wild Sounds of New Orleans* (1958) and released under the name of Al Tousan.

Towns, Edolphus "Ed" (b. July 21, 1934, Chadbourn, N.C.): Politician. Towns was graduated from North Carolina Agricultural and Technical University in 1956, then spent two years in the Army. He later settled in New York City. He earned a master's degree in social work from Adelphi University in 1973. He subsequently worked as a teacher, a hospital administrator, and a professor at Medgar EVERS College in Brooklyn.

Towns's political career grew out of his involvement in Democratic Party politics in Brooklyn. In 1976, he was named deputy borough president of Brooklyn. In 1982, he won his party's nomination for Congress on his first attempt and then was elected to represent New York's Eleventh District, a multicultural district in which African Americans and Hispanics were the two largest groups. Subsequently, he was reelected by large margins.

In Congress, Towns developed a low-key but effective style marked by strong ties to the Democratic leadership. His voting record has been characterized by liberal positions, party loyalty, and opposition to the Ronald Reagan and George Bush administrations, including a vote against the use of force against Iraq in 1991. Service on the House Energy and Commerce and Governmental Operations Committees as well as on the Select Committee on Narcotics Abuse and Control gave Towns the opportunity to deal with issues of vital importance to his urban constituents. Another issue on which Towns played a major role was his cosponsorship of legislation under which colleges were required to make available the graduation rates of scholarship athletes. He was also prominent on legislation that involved inner-city health care, having played a key role in keeping open federally funded community and migrant health centers.

In 1991, his quiet effectiveness was recognized by his election as chairman of the CONGRESSIONAL BLACK CAUCUS. In 1992, however, his congressional record was sullied by the House check-bouncing scandal. Towns, it was revealed, had written 408 checks on insufficient funds, and he was named by the House Ethics Committee as one of the abusers of the chamber's banking privileges.

Townsend, Robert (b. Feb. 6, 1957, Chicago, Ill.) Actor, comedian, director, producer, and writer. After graduation from high school in Chicago, Ill., in the mid-1970's, Townsend moved to New York City and began studying at Hunter College while commuting to acting classes. In 1982, he moved to Los Angeles, Calif. He landed small roles in several movies including *Streets of Fire* (1984), *American Flyers* (1985), and *A Soldier's Story* (1984). In 1987, he directed comedian Eddie MURPHY's concert film, *Raw*. That year, frustrated with the limited roles available to black actors in Hollywood, he cowrote, directed, and starred in the hit comedy *HOLLYWOOD SHUFFLE*, along with good friend Keenen Ivory WAYANS. Townsend's directorial debut was shot on a budget of only $100,000 and almost entirely financed with personal credit cards. *Hollywood Shuffle* took comic aim at the film industry's continued stereotyping of black actors, continually casting them as slaves, hookers, hustlers, or buffoons. The film's success established Townsend as one of the most talented, insightful directors of the time.

Robert Townsend starring in an HBO Comedy Hour special. (AP/Wide World Photos)

During the next few years, Townsend starred in *Uptown Comedy Express* on Home Box Office (HBO); wrote, directed, produced, and starred in a series of HBO comedy specials; appeared in the film *The Mighty Quinn* (1989); married his sweetheart, Cheri Jones; opened his own studio, Tinsel Townsend; and wrote, directed, and produced his next major film, *The Five Heartbeats* (1990). *The Five Heartbeats* tells the story of a group of talented young black men who learn about life, love, and friendship as they sing their way to stardom. The film was hailed as an old-fashioned love story that emphasized the strength and beauty of true friendship and love. It was

one of few films to show the tender, genuine bonds between black men. Townsend's inspirations for the film were the real-life singing groups the DELLS, the TEMPTATIONS, and the O'JAYS. The film was scored by jazz greats Stanley CLARKE and George Duke.

Townsend, Willard Saxby (Dec. 4, 1895, Cincinnati, Ohio—Feb. 3, 1957, Chicago, Ill.): Labor union official. Townsend served as president of the United Transport Service Employees of America (UTSEA) from 1940 to 1957. He, along with A. Philip RANDOLPH, was elected vice president of the American Federation of Labor-Congress of Industrial Organizations on Dec. 5, 1955.

After graduation from Walnut Hills High School in 1912, he took a railroad job as a "red cap." He served in the military during World War I, then returned to the railroads as a dining car waiter, based in Chicago. He wanted to escape the railroads' employment system, which closed the better jobs to black workers, so he entered the University of Toronto's premed course. After two years, he transferred to the Royal Academy of Science in Toronto, where he earned a degree in chemistry.

Townsend taught high school in Texas briefly but was unable to find work as a chemist. He reentered the railroad industry in 1932. Townsend was determined that black railroad workers, many of whom had college educations, would get the opportunities they deserved.

In 1936, Townsend was elected vice president of an American Federation of Labor (AFL) red cap local union. He had organized red cap workers at five Chicago train stations, in opposition to AFL practices of barring blacks from unions or attempting to remove them from the railroad industry. In 1937, he was elected president of the International Brotherhood of Red Caps.

After the Fair Labor Standards Act of 1937 was passed, white workers sought to have the red caps declared as independent contractors, and thus as ineligible for union organization, because they worked mainly for tips. The red caps won status as employees under the Railway Labor Act by appealing to the Interstate Commerce Commission. Railroad managements fought against granting bargaining rights, but Townsend's union continued to expand, bringing in train porters and Pullman laundry workers. The union was renamed the UTSEA in 1940, with Townsend still its president.

In 1942, Townsend led his union out of the AFL and into the CIO (Congress of Industrial Organizations). He joined the CIO executive board as its first black member. He was the only black leader of a national union that had white members. By 1944, his union's membership had reached about fifteen thousand. The union was successful in getting railroads to pay red caps a salary. Managements tried to count tips against salaries, finally settling on accepting a small "service charge" from each red cap for each bag handled.

Townsend continued to believe in the value of EDUCATION. He earned an LL.B. and a J.D. through correspondence and night courses at the Blackstone College of Law in Chicago. He lectured on human and industrial relations at the Seabury Western Theological Seminary in Evanston, Ill., and in 1942 won the Race Relation Leadership Award from the Arthur Schomburg Collection of the New York Public Library. He was part of numerous labor conferences and was commissioned by the State Department as a labor adviser to the International Labor Office Conference held in Mexico City, Mexico, in 1946.

The UTSEA declined after World War II as economic and technological changes affected the railroad industry and other modes of transportation competed. When the AFL merged with the CIO in 1955, Townsend was elected as a vice president of the new organization. By 1972, the UTSEA had a membership of less than two thousand. It then merged with a railway clerks union.

Track and Field: Contests in running, jumping, and throwing have a long and distinguished history. For centuries, these skills were part of a young African boy's passage into manhood, and slaves in early America engaged in physical contests during their brief recreational periods. In 1864, the first international competition in the one-mile run was held, and following the Civil War, track and field events began to be staged on college campuses across the United States. The commencement of the modern Olympic Games in 1896 in Athens, Greece, propelled the sport into prominence.

Track and field can be either an individual or a team effort. Even as a team sport, the requirements of speed, coordination, strength, stamina, and quick reflexes allow athletes to excel at their own levels. As a result, it was difficult for JIM CROW LAWS and racism to keep African American track and field athletes out of the sport.

Early Black Olympians. The first African American to win an Olympic medal was George POAGE, a hurdler and quarter-miler who had established a college record at the University of Wisconsin in the 440-yard dash and low hurdles. Poage won the bronze medal in the 400-meter hurdles and came in fourth in the 400-meter run at the 1904 Olympics in St. Louis.

On the national scene, African American athletes began to dominate in certain track and field events. In 1912, Howard P. Drew won national titles in the 100-yard dash and the 220-yard dash. Sol Butler won the Amateur

Athletic Union title in the broad jump in 1920, beginning the domination of African American men in the event.

Eddie Tolan won gold medals in the 1932 Olympics in the 100-meter dash and the 200-meter dash. Tolan went on to compete in more than three hundred meets, losing just seven times. One of Tolan's teammates on the 1932 American Olympic team was Ralph METCALFE. Metcalfe finished second to Tolan in the 100-meter race and third in the 200 meters. Four years later, Metcalfe placed second in the 100 meters again, this time to the legendary Jesse OWENS.

Jesse Owens. At the 1936 Olympics, Germany, under the leadership of Adolf Hitler, hoped to demonstrate the superiority of its people. The "Black Auxiliaries"—as the African American members of the U.S. Olympic team were called—performed with excellence, however, thus challenging Hitler's "master race" concept. Jesse Owens became the first athlete in modern Olympic history to win four gold medals at a single Olympics, setting three records and tying a fourth. Moreover, John Woodruff disproved the myth that African American runners could compete only in the sprints by winning the gold medal in the 800-meter run.

While the Olympics were interrupted by World War II, African American athletes continued to excel at domestic track meets. The Penn and Drake Relays, along with the Millrose Games, gave them the opportunities to display their talents. John Borican twice beat the legendary Glenn Cunningham in the 1,000-yard run, and Frank Dixon won the Millrose Mile.

The Olympic Games following World War II saw African American men begin to dominate in the dashes, short runs, hurdles, and long jump and as members of the 400- and 1,600-meter relay teams. In 1936, Tidye Ann Pickett, a hurdler, became the first African American woman to compete in the Olympics; Alice COACHMAN, however, was first to win a medal, a gold in the high jump in the 1948 Games. African American athletes won seventeen of the thirty-nine gold, silver, and bronze medals amassed by the United States team in the 1956 Summer Games.

For decades, African American colleges and universities had produced a number of exceptional track and field athletes. Ed Temple, track coach at Tennessee State College, helped to develop the talents of a number of young men and women, including long jumper Ralph Boston, who won a gold medal at the 1960 Olympics and a silver medal at the 1964 Games. A short time later, Boston set a world record with a jump of 27 feet 4¾ inches. Two other Temple protégés were Wilma RUDOLPH and Wyomia TYUS. In the 1960 Games, Rudolph became the first

Track-and-field star Jesse Owens took four gold medals at the 1936 Olympic Games. (AP/Wide World Photos)

American woman to win three gold medals in a single Olympics, winning in the 100- and 200-meter dashes and as the anchor of the 400-meter relay team.

The 1968 Olympics. The 1968 Olympics were held in Mexico City, and African Americans saw an opportunity to dramatize the Civil Rights movement on the international stage. A group was formed called the Olympic Committee for Human Rights that included such civil rights leaders as Martin Luther KING, JR., Louis Lomax, and Floyd McKISSICK, the director of the CONGRESS OF RACIAL EQUALITY. The committee's demands included calls for the removal of Avery Brundage—who was alleged to be antiblack and anti-Semitic—from the International Olympic Committee; for the banning of all-white teams from South Africa and Rhodesia from athletic competitions in the United States and the Olympics; for black U.S. Olympic coaches and for black members on the U.S. Olympic Committee; and for desegregation of the New York Athletic Club.

The demands were not met that year, but a threatened boycott of the games by African American athletes never materialized. The 1968 Olympics were a great triumph for African American athletes, both for the number of medals they won and for the records they set.

Two African American sprinters, Tommie SMITH and John CARLOS, made certain, however, that no one watching the Games would forget the struggle for racial equality and justice. After being presented with their medals—the gold and the bronze in the 200-meter dash—the two men raised their black-gloved fists in a Black Power salute as "The Star-Spangled Banner" was played. The two were immediately banned from the Olympic Village and ordered out of Mexico; most of the other African American athletes protested the exclusion of Smith and Carlos by wearing black-colored clothing either while competing in their respective events or when receiving their medals.

In the 1970's, African American athletes continued to dominate the shorter races—including the hurdles—and the long jump. They emerged as contenders in the decathlon, and began to win in the triple jump. Black men from the Caribbean island nations and from Africa had also established themselves as premier runners, with the latter excelling at the long distances, including the marathon.

Boycotts of the 1980's. The Olympics are the ultimate goal of most track and field athletes, but in 1980, international politics short-circuited the aspirations of athletes from the United States. Led by the United States, sixty-two countries boycotted the Moscow Games to protest the Soviet Union's invasion of Afghanistan.

Four years later, American athletes were able to compete in the Olympics in Los Angeles, but the Soviet Union and its allies pulled out of the competition in response to the 1980 boycott. Although African American athletes performed with distinction in the 1984 Games, it was not until 1988 that America's premier athletes were again able to compete in the Olympics against athletes from the Eastern Bloc countries.

Memorable Feats. As in other sports, whenever African American men and women were able to participate in track and field events, they aimed at excellence. Their individual feats are legendary: Jesse Owens' four gold medals in the 1936 Olympics, Carl LEWIS' matching four golds in the 1984 Games, and Wilma Rudolph's three gold medals in the 1960 Games are among the most memorable achievements in track and field history. Many other black athletes have set track and field records as well. Edwin MOSES dominated the 400-meter hurdles for more than a decade and set the world record at 47.02 seconds. Florence GRIFFITH-JOYNER set world records in both the 100- and 200-meter dashes. Bob BEAMON leaped two feet beyond the world long jump record in the 1968 Olympics, setting a new record of 29 feet 2½ inches, which was not surpassed until 1991, when Mike Powell jumped 29 feet 4½ inches. Willie Banks set the record in the triple jump at 58 feet 11½ inches, and Rafer JOHNSON's record 8,392 points amassed in the decathlon at the 1960 Olympics stood for twenty-four years.

African American athletes who have been inducted into the National Track and Field Hall of Fame include Dave Albritton, Bob Beamon, Ralph BOSTON, Lee Calhoun, Milt Campbell, Alice Coachman (Davis), Willie DAVENPORT, Harrison Dillard, Charles Dumas, Lee Evans, Barney Ewell, Mae Faggs (Starr), Bob HAYES, Jim Hines, DeHart HUBBARD, Edward Hurt, Nell C. JACKSON, Rafer Johnson, Hayes Jones, Ralph Metcalfe, Madeline Manning-Mims, Jesse Owens, Wilma Rudolph, Mel Sheppard, Tommie SMITH, Andy Stanfield, John Thomas, Eddie Tolan, Wyomia Tyus, LeRoy Walker, Willye WHITE, Mal Whitfield, and John Woodruff.—*Philip G. Smith*

SUGGESTED READINGS: • Archdeacon, H. C., and Kenneth G. Ellsworth, eds. *Track Cyclopedia.* 10th ed. Omaha, Neb.: Simmons-Boardman Books, 1985. • Ashe, Arthur. *A Hard Road To Glory: A History of the African American Athlete.* 3 vols. New York: Warner Books, 1988. • Henderson, Edwin B. *The Negro in Sports.* Washington, D.C.: Associated Press, Inc., 1939. • Matthews, Peter. *Track and Field Athletes: The Records.* Enfield, England: Guinness Superlative, 1985. • Rust, Art, Jr., and Edna Rust. *Art Rust's Illustrated History of the Black Athlete.* Garden City, N.Y.: Doubleday, 1985.

Traditional African Culture: The people that inhabit Africa, the world's second largest continent, have one of the richest and oldest traditional cultures in the world. Though the culture is as diverse as the people that inhabit the continent, it is possible to delineate the traditional way of life that Africans share.

Belief System. According to traditional African beliefs, all things in creation are accounted for in a chain of existence that stretches from a Supreme Being (God) in a descending order of importance through divinities (deities, gods), spirits, ancestors, humans, animate nature, and inanimate nature. The Supreme Being is all-seeing, all-knowing, all-powerful, ever-present, and immortal. The Supreme Being is the ultimate creator and sustainer of humans and the universe. Differences in human skin pigmentation are explained in African legend by the different shades of clay the Supreme Being used in molding people.

The divinities are the Supreme Being's associates and ministers. Some are dead national heroes and legendary figures who have been deified and who are associated with aspects of nature. They live in the spirit world with the Supreme Being; they have become timeless, and they serve as humankind's intermediaries to the Supreme Being.

Spirits are superhuman beings created as such by the Supreme Being to assist the divinities. Some of these were ancestors, but having been completely forgotten by the living over many generations, have risen to a position higher than the ancestors. Spirits appear mostly to priests, diviners, and medicine men to impart information, and they can possess mediums when solicited.

Ancestors (also called the living dead) are deceased family elders who are still fondly remembered by name and deed and to whom libations are given by living members of the family. From the spiritual world where they live, they still participate in the affairs of their earthly lineage. Ancestors are a traditional African vision of life after death. Ancestors are revered as part of the family; they protect it and are called upon as guardians of morality and as witnesses at the resolution of family feuds. They are humankind's closest link and intermediary to the spirit world.

Animals, plants, minerals, water, the sun, the moon, the stars, and other natural objects and phenomena round out this order of existence. There is harmony in the order; however, antisocial activities such as murder, incestuous relationships, wanton destruction of nature, irresponsible acts, and disrespect of the elderly can create disharmony in the chain of being. Such acts can result in epidemics, droughts, deaths, and natural disasters if not detected and corrected. Priests and priestesses, who may combine their religious calling with duties of rainmaking, divining, mediumship, and medicine, function to restore harmony.

Family Life. The traditional African family is an extended one in which grandparents, parents, uncles, aunts, brothers, sisters, nephews, nieces, and anyone related to them by blood or marriage may live in the same large house or houses in the same compound. Because family organization is mostly patriarchal and patrilineal, male children may grow up to marry and procreate and still live in the same house.

Many African American families are moving away from traditional roles, with fathers taking more of an active part in child rearing. (Cleo Freelance Photo)

Marriage and procreation go together; they account for one's personal immortality, as African parents see themselves reproduced in their children. Marriage involves the entire family, which must give its approval. Female virginity at time of marriage is highly prized and rewarded. To marry and not to procreate intentionally is forbidden, because it brings to an end the ancestral line. Monogamy and polygamy are legitimate; a widow may be remarried to a male adult member of the family of her deceased husband. Bride prices and dowries are acceptable parts of the marriage custom.

The husband, as the head of the family, is expected to provide food for the household; the wife is in charge of domestic responsibilities, especially cooking and child rearing. Members of the family eat at the same time, but not necessarily together in the same place. Rarely do men and women eat together. A visitor who meets a family at a meal is expected to eat with them without invitation if he is hungry.

Grandparents and great grandparents live in the general family home with their children, grandchildren, and relatives and are looked after by them. They are respected for their age and seen as sources of wisdom, experience, and love. Their words are believed to have spiritual force; their blessings are sought and their curses avoided. When they die, they are given elaborate funeral rites and ceremonies, since they go to live in the ancestral world and will possess spiritual powers that they may use to make their earthly families prosper or suffer. They may be reincarnated as future children of their families.

Social and Political Structure. It is customary in Africa for teenagers of the same age group to go through initiation rites before they are recognized as adults. Segregated according to gender, they spend a period together under the direction of elderly men and women. They develop strong group solidarity and receive traditional moral, social, and sex education. They are taught how to assume responsibilities to the community, family, and self and how to survive in a tough world. They graduate as adults and as defenders of traditions and customs. In times of crisis in the community, the age group is called upon by the ruler to restore law and order.

A chief usually rules a community; a paramount chief rules a clan, and a monarch rules a tribe. The monarchs have great powers over secular and spiritual affairs; they are considered God's mortal deputies. Rulers delegate some of their authority to subordinate chiefs, councils of elders, advisers, age groups, and heads of families. Where monarchy is absent, a class of hierarchically titled men rules the people.

Matters of dispute and justice are settled by the heads of the families involved. When disagreement occurs, the issue goes to the immediate higher authority until it reaches the monarch. The monarch invokes both his spiritual and temporal powers to give the final judgment.

Occupations. Farming is the principal occupation. Crops such as yams, rice, beans, maize, millet, and cassava are grown as staple foods. Tropical fruits grow abundantly. Onion, garlic, and a variety of peppers are the major spices. Animal husbandry, which is practiced especially by nomadic cattlemen, shepherds, and goatherds, is also important. Fishing and hunting are widely engaged in, and a hunter may earn a title by single-handedly killing a dangerous animal such as a lion. While both men and women cultivate crops, animal husbandry, palm-wine tapping, and hunting are exclusively masculine occupations.

Trading is an occupation that involves some men but it is mostly conducted by women. African markets are open markets where bargaining is the norm. Such markets have a festive aura; a woman selling cooked food may be flanked by butchers, snake charmers, soap sellers, music makers, and bicycle repairers. Africans compare life on earth to a market where people come to trade and then return home (to the spirit world of the ancestors).

Africans have medicine men (traditional doctors) whose occupation involves the exercise of spiritual and secular expertise. To obtain a healing that demands a spiritual touch, a medicine man may slaughter a bird or an animal and render an incantation to placate an invisible force that is held responsible for a particular illness. Medicine men are also considered knowledgeable in applied medicine and use herbs, minerals, barks, roots, leaves, and poultices to attempt cures. Their treatment of fractures, open wounds, fevers, skin diseases, aches, swells, snake bites, and scorpion stings endears them to their peoples.

The Arts. Fine and PERFORMING ARTS have always been central to traditional African culture. It is easy to recall the influence of Egyptian arts on Greece and the impact of African art on such twentieth century Western artists as Pablo Picasso, Henri Matisse, Alberto Giacometti, and Jean Mestach. In drama, a similar movement of pre-Islamic North African religious and dramatic practices influenced the origin of Greek theater.

Most traditional African arts have a utilitarian motive: to aid one's spiritual disposition, respect, and prayerful attitude toward the spirit world, especially the divinities and ancestors. The traditional arts respond to and support traditional beliefs and philosophies and include the creation masks of secret societies, ancestral figures, musical instruments, funerary art, personifications of fertility spirits, and costumes of masquerades. In Zaire, for example, a Ngata artist immortalizes a royal coffin by sculpting and painting it to look like the king whose corpse occupied it. The strength, beauty, and freshness of the art are a constant reminder of the immortality of the ancestor: Even in death, the ancestor is alive and present.

MUSIC and DANCE are also important arts in the cultural life of the African. People sing while they are working, and emotions of joy and sorrow are often expressed in songs. When the songs are accompanied by instruments, the music can move from simple to complex rhythms. Music is inevitably accompanied by dance. A dancer can simultaneously make different parts of the body respond to the different rhythms of music. The atmosphere of a dance is celebratory. Spectators can dance along with the principal performers without invitation; such participation is both allowed and encouraged. Even sacred music that accompanies rituals is danced to; some mediums require music and dance to arrive at a state of trance.—*I. Peter Ukpokodu*

SUGGESTED READINGS: • Ayittey, George B. N. *Indigenous African Institutions.* Ardsley-on-Hudson, N.Y.: Transnational Publishers, 1991. • Bohannan, Paul, and Philip Curtin. *Africa and Africans.* 3d ed. Prospect Heights, Ill.: Waveland Press, 1988. • Gibbs, James L., Jr., ed. *Peoples of Africa.* Prospect Heights, Ill.: Waveland Press, 1988. • July, Robert W. *A History of the African People.* 4th ed. Prospect Heights, Ill.: Waveland Press, 1992. • Mazrui, Ali Al'Amin. *The Africans: A Triple Heritage.* Boston: Little, Brown, 1986. • Mbiti, John S. *African Religions and Philosophy.* London: Heinemann, 1988.

TransAfrica: Pan-Africanist lobbying organization. In 1977, Randall ROBINSON, a Harvard Law School graduate and an assistant to Michigan Congressman Charles DIGGS, founded TransAfrica, an organization devoted to securing human and civil rights for black people worldwide. TransAfrica has been particularly successful in orchestrating American opposition to the apartheid regime of South Africa; by 1990, the group claimed to have about eighteen thousand members.

Objectives and Functions. From its inception, TransAfrica has had a simple but profound mandate: to advocate and pursue practices and activities designed to influence U.S. policies toward the continent of Africa and the Caribbean. TransAfrica thus epitomizes the efforts to strengthen the ties that bind African Americans to blacks around the globe.

TransAfrica is headquartered in Washington, D.C. It is headed by an executive director who conducts the daily business of the organization and is assisted by a legislative director and several legislative assistants; the executive director reports to a board of directors elected by the general membership. While much of its work is done in Washington, TransAfrica has chapters across the United States that work in conjunction with the national office.

Disseminating Information. Perhaps the most important function of TransAfrica has been advising the U.S. government on matters and issues affecting Africa and the Caribbean. The information generated by TransAfrica on Africa and the Caribbean has become relied on in Washington and beyond. TransAfrica's newsletter, *TransAfrica News,* and other news releases contain information for the general public and official Washington on political,

social, and economic conditions of the African world. The organization is able to obtain timely information on such matters in large part because of the strong and cordial ties that TransAfrica has fostered with the peoples and leaders of Africa and the Caribbean.

TransAfrica's reputation as a source of accurate, reliable information has done much to improve ways in which Africa has been portrayed. Recognizing the need for more accurate information, in 1981 TransAfrica created TransAfrica Forum, its educational and research-oriented arm. The forum, with its own board of directors, sponsors symposia on topics pertaining to Africa and the Caribbean and publishes *TransAfrica Forum: A Quarterly Journal of Opinion on Africa and the Caribbean.*

TransAfrica also incorporates a letter-writing system in its lobbying. The system allows TransAfrica to trigger a letter-writing campaign to produce quick mass mailings in selected congressional districts. Such shows of strength can be crucial when specific members of Congress are targeted on a particular issue or legislation.

TransAfrica is funded from sources that include membership dues, contributions from corporations, foundations, and individuals, and subscriptions to the journal. The organization sponsors a yearly dinner at which the Nelson Mandela Courage Award is bestowed.

Success and Challenges. As the premier African American lobby group for Africa and the Caribbean, TransAfrica has been quite successful. It has continually lobbied for increases in U.S. assistance to the African world; it was instrumental in getting Congress to pass the Clark Amendment, which barred the Central Intelligence Agency (CIA) from assisting any insurgency movement in Angola during that country's struggle for independence. TransAfrica was also active in prodding the U.S. government to work for black liberation in ZIMBABWE. TransAfrica continues to inform and update the world on human rights abuses on the African continent and has played the middleman role in many instances when leaders from Africa and the Caribbean have needed to be introduced to the American public.

Role in Abolishing Apartheid. Perhaps TransAfrica's biggest success has been in the role it has played in the transition to a postapartheid South Africa. TransAfrica has succeeded in mobilizing grass-roots American anti-apartheid efforts. In 1984, with the help of other anti-apartheid groups, TransAfrica established and coordinated the activities of the Free South Africa Movement (FSAM). The work of the FSAM eventually led to congressional action in 1986 placing U.S. economic sanctions on South Africa. The legislation, passed over the veto of President Ronald Reagan, played a major role in pushing the South African government into undertaking such far-reaching measures as releasing Nelson Mandela and other antiapartheid leaders from jail, repealing bans on major antiapartheid organizations, repealing the legal pillars of apartheid, and pledging to create a new, democratic South Africa in which all will be equal irrespective of race and ideology.

Above all, TransAfrica has raised, and continues to raise, the consciousness of African Americans about their heritage and calls the attention of Americans and the U.S. government to what they could contribute toward enhancing the quality of life in the African world. —*Akwasi Osei*

Suggested Readings: • Hadjor, Kofi Buenor. *Africa in an Era of Crisis.* Trenton, N.J.: Africa World Press, 1990. • Mazrui, Ali A., and Hasu H. Patel, eds. *Africa in World Affairs: The Next Thirty Years.* New York: Third Press, 1973 • Miller, Jake C. *The Black Presence in American Foreign Affairs.* Washington, D.C.: University Press of America, 1979. • Shepherd, George W., Jr., ed. *Racial Influences on American Foreign Policy.* New York: Basic Books, 1971.

Travis, Dempsey Jerome (b. Feb. 25, 1920, Chicago, Ill.): Business executive. Travis has owned numerous companies involved in the real estate, securities, and mortgage industries. As a piano player, he led his own orchestra at the age of fifteen, and he joined the musicians union at the age of sixteen. He was graduated from Chicago's Du Sable High School in 1939 and entered the U.S. Army, learning business skills while managing Post Exchanges. After his discharge, he tried to gain admission to Roosevelt University, but he failed the entrance examination. He realized how deficient his high school education had been, even though his grades were high. Travis attempted to get his high school music combo back together, but its members had scattered and the dime-a-dance establishments where he had played had gone out of style.

Travis decided to pursue his education, taking classes in accounting and social science at night at Englewood High School while working for the Veterans Administration. His efforts earned him admission to Wilson Junior College, where he earned an A.A. degree in 1948. He earned his B.A. from Roosevelt University in 1949 and a certificate from the Northwestern University School of Mortgage Banking in 1969. He enrolled in the Kent College of Law but dropped out when he realized that African Americans were limited almost entirely to practicing criminal law.

Travis formed the Sivart (Travis spelled backward)

Mortgage Company in 1945. At one time, it was the largest mortgage company owned by an African American, and in 1961, it was the first such company to be approved by the Federal Housing Administration and the Veterans Administration. This approval opened a large range of lending opportunities.

Travis founded the Travis Realty Company in 1949, even though he was struggling and had difficulty raising the $50 for a broker's license. He did not buy property for himself until he had been in the business for seven years. Although he advocated borrowing to buy property, paying off part of the mortgage, then using the property as collateral for more loans, he did not follow his own advice, preferring to pay substantial parts of the purchase price of his own properties in cash.

Dempsey Travis has owned numerous companies involved in the real estate, securities, and mortgage industries. (Urban Research Press, Inc.)

Travis founded the United Mortgage Bankers of America (UMBA) in 1960 and served as its president. The association of black mortgage bankers unfortunately brought in clients who were the least likely to qualify for loans and the worst prospects to repay them. Travis lost money on residential mortgages made through the group and sold the residential portfolio of Sivart Mortgage Company in 1974 at a loss. The UMBA already had dissolved. Travis remained interested in the problems of black property owners. He had testified in 1969 to the Senate Antitrust and Monopoly Subcommittee that insurance companies used the threat of RACE RIOTS as an excuse to deny coverage at standard rates to automobile and property owners in ghetto areas. He began serving on the advisory committee of the Federal National Mortgage Association in 1971 and was a director of the National Housing Conference, Inc.

Travis, who had to take remedial reading as a condition of college enrollment, is a published author. He has written books about black jazz, housing in Chicago, Chicago history, and former Chicago mayor Harold WASHINGTON, among other topics. He won the Society of Midland Authors Award in 1982 and was the group's president from 1988 to 1990.

Tresvant, Ralph (b. 1967 or 1968, Boston, Mass.): Soul vocalist. Tresvant began his singing career while still in junior high school, as a member of the group NEW EDITION. He often sang lead vocals. He left the group in 1990 and released his debut solo album, *Ralph Tresvant*, the same year. He cowrote several of the songs on that album.

Trimiar, Marian "Tyger" (b. 1953): Boxer. Trimiar, who began competing in the 1970's, weighed in at about 130 pounds. She believed that BOXING posed no greater danger to women than to men. Female boxers were required to wear special chest protectors and could not hit their opponents in the bust. Trimiar's trademark was her shaved head.

Troop: Rhythm-and-blues vocal group. The group signed a recording contract with Atlantic records, which released the debut album *Troop* as well as *Attitude* (1989) and *Deepa*. Troop is managed by Trevel Productions, run by Gerald Levert and Marc Gordon of the group Levert. Troop performed with QUEEN LATIFAH and LEVERT on the "For the Money/Living for the City" single on the sound track for *New Jack City* (1991).

Trotter, William Monroe (Apr. 7, 1872, Boston, Mass.—Apr. 7, 1934, Boston, Mass.): Civil rights activist. Trotter was one of the most outspoken critics of racial discrimination in the United States. He founded the militant newspaper the *Boston Guardian* in 1901 as his primary vehicle for advancing his views on the lack of socioeconomic and political rights for African Americans. He had little tolerance for groups and individuals he considered to be too moderate or accommodating to white society.

Trotter was one of the organizers of the NIAGARA MOVEMENT (1905), the forerunner of the NATIONAL ASSOCIATION FOR THE ADVANCEMENT OF COLORED PEOPLE (NAACP). Many of the Niagara movement proposals, such as equal educational and political rights for African Americans, were adopted at the founding of the NAACP. Trotter, however, refused to join the NAACP because he considered it to be moderate and incapable of advancing the real best interests of African Americans. He and his newspaper had always been critical of the accommodationist policies of NAACP organizer Booker T. WASHINGTON. This dissatisfaction led Trotter to found the National Equal Rights League, which adopted positions closer to Trotter's beliefs than those adopted by the NAACP, under Moorfield Storey and W. E. B. DU BOIS.

William Trotter started the Boston Guardian *newspaper as a forum for his views in favor of equal rights for African Americans.* (Schomburg Center, NY Public Library)

World leaders gathered in 1919 for the Paris Conference, at which they were to draft proposals designed to prevent further conflicts. Trotter took this opportunity to try to convince the conference to pass a law outlawing racial discrimination. The U.S. State Department denied him a passport, but he got to Paris by taking a job as a cook on a ship. Representing his National Equal Rights League, he supported an unsuccessful Japanese petition to include a prohibition against discrimination in the covenant of the League of Nations.

Trotter influenced the CIVIL RIGHTS movement of the 1950's and 1960's by his legacy of strategies, such as demonstrating against racist entertainment and getting arrested, to draw public attention to his cause. He urged nonviolent protest but was passionate in his beliefs. President Woodrow Wilson once dismissed him from a conference for use of insulting language. Trotter had shaken his finger at the president to emphasize a point.

Trouble in Mind (pr. 1955): Play by Alice CHILDRESS. This drama of revolt portrays the emotions and epiphanies of a group of black actors who must play stereotypical black roles and demean themselves in order to please their white director. It won the Obie Award for the best original Off-Broadway play of the 1955-1956 season.

Truth, Sojourner (Isabella Van Wagener; c. 1797, Ulster County, N.Y.—Nov. 26, 1883, Battle Creek, Mich.): Evangelist. Sojourner Truth, born a slave in rural New York state, emancipated herself in 1826, walking away from the farm of her master, John Dumont, early one morning. After a stay of some years in New York City as a freed woman, in June, 1843, she left New York, carrying a pillowcase stuffed with personal items and a basket of provisions, to begin her mission—preaching and lecturing on the promise of humanity.

Before leaving New York City, a place she described as the "second Sodom," Isabella stopped at the residence of a former employer to inform her that her name was now "Sojourner." She further reported that "the Spirit" had called her to the service of humanity. Later, she accounted for the name "Truth" by explaining that, during her travels, she would be declaring the truth to the people. The predominant image of Truth as recorded by her contemporaries is that of a deeply spiritual woman with great oratorical ability and immense energy for affecting change.

Her mission lasted for more than twenty-five years and included missionary efforts and calls for abolition, women's rights, temperance, civil rights, and the welfare of freed people. Among other activities, the former slave traveled thousands of miles, lectured and preached in many states, addressed Congress, visited President Abraham Lincoln, and stood fast in the face of mobs of bigots. Illiterate and poor, Truth succeeded in her endeavors at various reforms where many had failed. (She often stated that she had never determined to do anything and failed.) Her memory is celebrated by African American groups, women's groups, and others because her life is a testament to the boundless energy of the human spirit.

Early Life. The actual date of Truth's birth is unknown, but she was born to James Baumfree and Elizabeth, also affectionately known as "Mau-Mau Bett," who were both slaves of one Colonel Hardenbergh of Ulster County, N.Y. Elizabeth was the third wife of James Baumfree and was believed to have borne some ten or twelve children, most of whom were sold before Truth was old enough to retain any memory of them; Truth was the next to youngest child. Truth's recollections of her childhood, as dictated to various biographers, began at about age five. At that time, she lived with her father, mother, and the family's youngest child in a cellar beneath the hotel and home of then-master Charles Hardenbergh along with other slaves. The conditions of the cellar encouraged rheumatism, fever sores, and palsy, among other afflictions that would aggravate Truth throughout her later life.

Her family reportedly spoke only a form of Dutch, the language of the Hardenbergh family. In some accounts, Truth's parents and Truth herself were captured in Africa. Other accounts suggest that Truth's mother's parents came from the Coast of Guinea and that her paternal grandmother was a Mohawk Indian. Yet another account of Truth's life identifies her father as hailing from Africa, having received passage from the Gold Coast via an African trader.

Truth's religious awareness began with ideas related by her mother, Mau-Mau Bett. In the evening, after the completion of work on the estate, Truth's mother provided instruction in an open-air worship service. At such times, Truth learned something of the nature of God as Creator, transcendent, and immanent—ideas of traditional African origin. While both parents might have been instructed in some of the tenets of a Western religion, it is doubtful that theirs was a full-blown theological knowledge of any Western religion. Hence, whatever the truth of the origin of her parentage, her family retained traditional African beliefs that were communicated to Truth in her early life.

As human chattel, Truth passed from the hands of Colonel Hardenbergh to his son Charles, to John Neely, to Martin Scriver, to John Dumont. During her sojourn with Neely, an Englishman who did not understand her Dutch language, she was beaten severely. At the time, she began her petitions to God (as instructed by her mother) in earnest. With her next master, her biographers report, she all but abandoned the religious life in favor of the libertine, secular life led by Martin Scriver, a fisherman and tavern keeper. In 1810, at the age of thirteen, she was sold to John Dumont for the sum of seventy pounds.

Evangelist Sojourner Truth depicted here with Abraham Lincoln. (Library of Congress)

Marriage and Emancipation. During her service to Dumont, Truth married a man named Thomas with whom she reportedly bore five children. Their youngest child, Peter, is frequently mentioned in accounts of Truth because his illegal sale out of the state of New York gave occasion to the expression of Truth's demonstration of the power she appropriated as hers through her belief in God. Truth remained with Dumont until she was emancipated in 1827. She acquired the name Van Wagener from a Quaker who bought her services from Dumont in response to Dumont's threat to have Truth returned to him by force.

Thomas, much older than Truth, remained enslaved until freed in 1828. In poor health and advanced in age, he lived only a few years after his emancipation, leaving Truth with two children for whom to provide (the others had been sold away earlier). Truth was in her early thirties when she took the youngest child, Peter, with her to New York City, leaving the eldest child, Diana, in Ulster County.

Religious Instruction. Before her sojourn in New York City, Truth had contact with the Quakers who aided her endeavors to become reunited with her son Peter. With the Quakers, she was exposed to two of the sect's fundamental doctrines: the notion of an "inner light" (each individual was said to possess a spark of divinity) and the principle of mutual aid.

In New York City, she was witness to the Methodist moral reform movement within the city and aided women in their missionary efforts. Yet she insisted that she could develop no affinity for their prayer meetings, which she viewed as boisterous and exhausting.

Her experiences with various sects continued when in 1832 she met Robert Matthews (later Matthias), whom she mistook for Jesus Christ. Truth fell victim to Matthews' delusion, and subsequently contributed her earnings to his cause. Matthias declared that the spirit of God dwelt in him and preached the idea that the spirits of the former saints would enter the bodies of the present generation. Matthias' philosophies presumably proved attractive to Truth, insomuch as animism appeared to be an essential part of the traditional belief system embraced by her mother. After a scandal following the death of a former employer and benefactor of Matthias, and after Matthias' exoneration of the charge of murder and subsequent removal to the far West, Truth's liaison with Matthias ended.

Shortly thereafter, Truth felt her call to leave the city. On June 1, 1843, armed with an understanding of the principles of several sects and religions, Truth ordained herself as preacher—believing she needed no other authority—and left on her mission.

Her Legacy. Described by her contemporaries as in possession of "personal presence," "magnetism," and "magical influence," Truth is the prototype of the strong African American woman endowed with spiritual command. Hers was a strong belief in the power of God as being accessible to the individual. Anecdotes of her life experiences abound. She was able to reason to a group of anxious men at a women's rights convention that if the first woman God ever made was strong enough to turn the world upside down, then surely the group gathered was more than strong enough to turn it right side up. After Frederick DOUGLASS expressed his lack of hope in justice from whites, suggesting bloodshed as a means to freedom, Truth queried, "Frederick, is God dead?" Perhaps she is best remembered for her famous "Ain't I a Woman?" oration delivered at the Akron women's rights convention of 1851.

Charitable Work. In addition to the fame Truth garnered from her moving orations at antislavery and women's rights meetings, and in addition to the stirring sermons Truth delivered at camp meetings and churches, she also provided humanitarian aid to those in need, including efforts to provide shelter, food, and clothing to runaway slaves. With the commencement of the Civil War, Truth raised money to buy gifts for soldiers and frequented their camps. After the Civil War, she campaigned on behalf of education and improved conditions for the freed people.

Advanced age and poor health eventually forced her to retire to a Battle Creek, Mich., sanatorium, but by then, Truth had made a great impact on nineteenth century America. In a society that enslaved her and denied her humanity, Truth was able to forge a formidable identity owing to the supreme spirituality that empowered her missions. She died at about age 86.—*Adele S. Newson*

SUGGESTED READINGS: • Braxton, Joanne M. *Black Women Writing Autobiography.* Philadelphia: Temple University Press, 1989. • Joseph, Gloria I. "Sojourner Truth: Archetypal Black Feminist." In *Common Differences.* Edited by Gloria I. Joseph and Jill Lewis. New York: Anchor Press, 1981. • Ortiz, Victoria. *Sojourner Truth, a Self-Made Woman.* Philadelphia: J. B. Lippincott, 1974. • Pauli, Hertha Ernestine. *Her Name Was Sojourner Truth.* New York: Appleton-Century-Crofts, 1962. • Woodward, Helen Beal. "Aren't I a Woman?: Sojourner Truth and Harriet Tubman." In *The Bold Women.* Freeport, N.Y.: Books for Libraries Press, 1953.

tuberculosis: Disease caused by the mycobacterium tuberculosis, or tubercle bacillus. The disease which usually attacks the lungs, spreads on airborne droplets and usually enters the body through the air passages. Anyone sharing a poorly ventilated space with a victim can contract the disease. Once America's leading cause of death, the disease affected a disproportionately large number of African Americans, whose impoverished living conditions and inadequate health care made them its most likely targets.

From the post-Civil War era through the early decades of the twentieth century, public health officials, physicians, and black leaders cited pulmonary tuberculosis as the major threat to black health. Reports of health boards from urban centers repeatedly attributed high rates of morbidity and mortality among blacks to the ravages of tuberculosis. Moreover, sanitarians and reformers attending race conferences held at Atlanta University, HAMPTON INSTITUTE, and TUSKEGEE INSTITUTE at the turn of the century agreed that black mortality from tuberculosis posed a major threat to the well-being of African Americans. Many of these reformers believed that the excessive morbidity and mortality resulting from tuberculosis could be prevented.

Accordingly, during the early twentieth century, African Americans began a battle against tuberculosis. From 1907 to 1909, antituberculosis leagues were formed by black medical societies in Louisiana, Alabama, Virginia, and the District of Columbia. At its organizational meeting in 1908, the National Association of Colored Graduate Nurses discussed both the high incidence of black tuberculosis mortality and methods to control the disease. In addition, in 1910, the NATIONAL MEDICAL ASSOCIATION (composed primarily of blacks) appointed a special commission on tuberculosis which would attempt to educate African Americans about the disease. In 1915, Booker T. WASHINGTON of Tuskegee Institute initiated Negro National Health Week, focusing attention on tuberculosis and other health problems in the black community.

By the 1960's, tuberculosis was all but forgotten, as powerful drug therapy used during the 1950's had subdued it. The ACQUIRED IMMUNE DEFICIENCY SYNDROME (AIDS) epidemic beginning in the 1980's and the increasing number of homeless people caused a resurgence of the disease. AIDS victims, a disproportionate number of whom are African Americans, are also the most likely victims of tuberculosis. Homelessness is also disproportionately prevalent in the black community. The unsanitary conditions associated with homelessness put the homeless at special risk of contracting tuberculosis.

Tubman, Harriet (Araminta Ross; c. 1820, Bucktown, Dorchester County, Md.—Mar. 10, 1913, Auburn, N.Y.):

Civil rights activist. Dubbed "the greatest conductor of the UNDERGROUND RAILROAD" by abolitionists and sympathizers, "Moses" by fugitive slaves she led to freedom, and "General Tubman" by abolitionist John Brown, Harriet Tubman made a great impact on nineteenth century American life. Among other activities, the illiterate runaway slave made nineteen trips to the South, where she liberated more than three hundred people from SLAVERY, including all but one member of her own family. Tubman also served in the Union Army, without remuneration, as a spy, scout, and nurse. After the Civil War, she established a hospital for old and disabled freed people.

Like Sojourner TRUTH, Tubman forged an invincible persona with the aid of a belief that hers was an intimate and immediate relationship with God. The predominant image of Tubman as recorded by her contemporaries is that of a physically powerful woman, entirely African in features, possessing an abundance of spirituality. Sarah Bradford, Tubman's first biographer, described her as possessing "the strange familiarity of communion with God." She was given to premonitions (she called them "intimations"), which she believed warned her of impending dangers in her work as conductor of the Underground Railroad and as Union spy. Reasoning early in her life that she (as well as all people of African descent) had the right to liberty or death, she then proceeded to live her life of activism accordingly. At one point, slaveholders offered a reward of forty thousand dollars for her capture, dead or alive.

Early Life. Tubman's parents, Benjamin Ross and Harriet Green, were said to have been full-blooded Africans. Tubman's master named her Araminta, but Tubman later took her mother's first name. In addition to Tubman, her mother bore some ten other children. Beginning at age six, Tubman was subjected to a series of temporary masters, because her owner frequently hired her out to local planters and families. She was first taken away to learn the trade of weaving, and while in her early teens, she was hired out as a field hand. Tubman developed amazing strength and fortitude as she learned the tasks of the field hand. Additionally, her father taught her the medicinal value of roots derived from his understanding of his African past. Both apprenticeships would later serve her well in her endeavors to lead fugitive slaves to freedom. During Tubman's adolescence, an overseer struck her head with a two-pound weight; the effect of the blow was to plague Tubman for the rest of her life. She suffered from occasional lethargy and stupors. Once, she was made to work in the home of a woman who used her as a maid by day and a child's nurse by night, affording Tubman virtually no hours of rest. Her mistress often beat her savagely, and the discipline thus learned and hardship thus endured prepared Tubman for a life of activism that would involve enforced wakefulness and endurance. Eventually, Tubman was returned to her master battered and ill.

In 1844, she married John Tubman, but the couple had no children. By 1849, her young master died; aware of an impending sale, she then resolved, at the age of twenty-nine, to escape, and she convinced her two remaining brothers on the plantation to accompany her. After a while, the two brothers found the way north too foreign and fraught with dangers to continue. They abandoned the journey and returned to the plantation. With the North Star as her guide and with the good fortune of finding sympathetic blacks and whites alike, she continued alone.

Harriet Tubman, civil rights activist, was dubbed "the greatest conductor of the Underground Railroad." (Library of Congress)

The Underground Railroad. Tubman reached Philadelphia, where she worked for two years to save enough money to return to the South to liberate her family. Between 1850 and 1860, she made about twenty trips to the South and liberated some three hundred people,

among the last of whom were her aged parents. Because of the infirmity owing to their age, Tubman reasoned that they were in no immediate danger of being sold. Also, the journey with the aged parents proved most perilous, because they had to be transported much of the way by wagon. Tubman's efforts established her as the most able of those who led fugitive slaves to freedom via the Underground Railroad, a network of way stations that helped slaves to escape from the South to the free states.

Tubman effected escapes by traveling at night, hiding by day, drugging babies with opium to quiet their cries, and carrying a revolver for recalcitrant sojourners. In 1851, two years after her escape, Tubman returned for her husband, but she discovered that he had remarried and preferred to remain with his new wife. She then gathered a group of fugitives in the area and led them to Philadelphia. With the 1850 passage of the FUGITIVE SLAVE LAW, Tubman began to lead fugitive slaves to Canada. By 1852, famous abolitionists such as Thomas Garrett knew of Tubman; they often donated great sums of money to her cause. John Brown met with Tubman on many occasions, consulting and sharing with her, among other things, his plans for his attack on HARPERS FERRY, W.Va.

The late 1850's marked the beginning of Tubman's lecturing activity. Beginning with an appearance at an antislavery meeting in Boston, Tubman traveled the nation calling for the abolition of slavery and for women's rights.

The Civil War. During the early years of the Civil War, the governor of Massachusetts sent for Tubman to engage her services as a spy, scout, and nurse for the Union Army. At the time, Tubman lived in Auburn, N.Y., on a farm with her parents. Leaving her parents and farm to the care of charitable neighbors and friends, she went to war. Her labors included leading armies through swamps, gaining the confidence of recently liberated slaves (who often feared northern whites more than they feared their former owners), nursing soldiers, using the knowledge of roots and herbs acquired from her father, and passing through enemy lines as a spy. After the war, she returned to Auburn, where she found her farm being sold to satisfy delinquent mortgage payments.

Declining Years. By the war's end, Tubman was some forty-five years old and penniless. She also continued to suffer from the wound inflicted to her head during her youth. In 1867, Sarah Bradford wrote Tubman's biography, the proceeds from which Tubman used to aid aged freed slaves. In 1869, Tubman married Nelson Davis, a war veteran; her first husband had died shortly after the war.

Tubman continued to lobby for the establishment of a

home for the indigent aged blacks of Auburn. During the years that funds were insufficient for such a project, she converted her own home into a shelter for the aged. In 1897, more than thirty years after the end of the Civil War and after decades of asking the federal government, Tubman was awarded a pension of twenty dollars a month. Much of her pension she used to help shelter and care for the aged. The people of Auburn, moved by her selflessness, eventually rallied to her aid and established the Harriet Tubman Home for Aged and Indigent Negroes in 1908. After her death in 1913, Auburn erected a monument in her honor as a testament to her indomitable will.

Biographies and Writings About Tubman. During her long life, Tubman was well known to many famous personages, including statesmen, abolitionists, and literary figures. Records of her activities are found in the memoirs and writings of many famous people of the nineteenth century—William H. Seward, Gerrit Smith, Frederick Douglass, Elizabeth Stanton, Susan B. Anthony, and others. The first edition of Sarah Bradford's biography of Tubman appeared in 1869, and an expanded edition appeared in 1886; both were privately printed by Bradford, who donated the book's proceeds to Tubman.—*Adele S. Newson*

SUGGESTED READINGS: • Conrad, Earl. *Harriet Tubman: Negro Soldier and Abolitionist.* New York: International Publishers, 1942. • Heidish, Marcy. *A Woman Called Moses: A Novel Based on the Life of Harriet Tubman.* Boston: Houghton Mifflin, 1976. • Loewenberg, Bert James, and Ruth Bogin. *Black Women in Nineteenth-Century American Life.* University Park: Pennsylvania State University Press, 1976. • Scruggs, O. M. "The Meaning of Harriet Tubman." *In Remember the Ladies.* Edited by Carol V. R. George, Syracuse, N.Y.: Syracuse University Press, 1975. • Woodward, Helen Beal. "Aren't I a Woman?: Sojourner Truth and Harriet Tubman." In *The Bold Women.* Freeport, N.Y.: Books for Libraries Press, 1953.

Tucker, Cynthia DeLores Nottage (b. Oct. 4, 1927, Philadelphia, Pa.): Politician. Tucker served as vice chairperson of the Pennsylvania State Democratic Party and served on the executive committee of the Democratic National Committee. She was a member of the National Women's Political Caucus and a member of the Pennsylvania Commission on Women. Tucker was also the first African American woman to hold the office of secretary of state for Pennsylvania, serving from 1971 to 1977. During her term of office, Tucker was secretary of the National Association of Secretaries of State.

Cynthia Tucker became vice-president of the board of the NAACP in 1989. (Harlee Little)

As a result of her achievements, Tucker was named by *Ebony* magazine to its list of the one hundred most influential black Americans in 1973, 1974, and 1975. She served as president of the Federation of Democratic Women in 1977 and as chair of the Democratic National Committee Black Caucus in 1984.

Tucker was drafted as one of fourteen candidates to run for lieutenant governor of Pennsylvania in 1987—the first African American candidate ever selected—but she lost the primary election. In 1989, she became national vice president of the board of trustees of the NATIONAL ASSOCIATION FOR THE ADVANCEMENT OF COLORED PEOPLE and also was named vice president of the *Philadelphia Tribune.*

Tucker, Lemuel "Lem" (May 26, 1938, Saginaw, Mich.—Mar. 2, 1991, Washington, D.C.): Broadcaster. A broadcaster for decades, Tucker culminated his career as medical and science correspondent for *CBS Evening News with Dan Rather* from 1984 until his retirement in 1988. During his last years at CBS news, he garnered two Emmy Awards, for his reporting on black families in the 1981-1982 season and for coverage of the Iceland summit meeting in the 1986-1987 season. He also won an Emmy for a series on hunger in America for the 1968-1969 season.

Tucker, Walter, III (b. May 28, 1957, Los Angeles, Calif.): Politician. Tucker was reared in Compton, Calif. He was graduated as valedictorian of Compton Senior High School in 1974, attended Princeton University, and earned a B.A. with honors in political science from the University of Southern California in 1978. Tucker went on to earn his law degree at Georgetown University in Washington, D.C., in 1981. He worked for a law firm in Washington, then returned to California. Tucker passed the California bar exam and served as deputy district attorney for Los Angeles County from 1984 to 1986. He opened a law practice in 1986, specializing in criminal law.

Tucker was active in politics from an early age. Beginning in 1969, he worked on his father's campaigns for the school board and city council. He coordinated his father's last two campaigns for the mayoralty of Compton. Tucker had worked for the Los Angeles County district attorney's office, and at one time he pleaded no contest to misdemeanor charges connected to altering official documents.

Tucker's father died on Oct. 1, 1990, while serving his third term as mayor of Compton. Tucker won the special election to succeed his father on Apr. 16, 1991, and became Compton's youngest mayor. He immediately began campaigns to benefit to city's youth, improve police services and community involvement, and foster intracommunity cooperation. He organized the First Annual Unity Festival and Summit Conference in Compton. He is an ordained Christian minister and has taught Sunday school at his church, the Bread of Life Christian Center.

Tunnell, Emlen "Em" (Mar. 29, 1925, Bryn Mawr, Pa.— July 23, 1975, Pleasantville, N.Y.): FOOTBALL player. A 1967 inductee into the Pro Football Hall of Fame, Tunnell

New York Giants halfback Em Tunnell gains yardage against the Cleveland Browns. (AP/Wide World Photos)

began his career in 1948 by walking unannounced into the New York Giants office and asking for a job. He became the first black Giants player. He played in National Football League championship games in 1956, 1958, 1960, and 1961, and played in nine Pro Bowl games before retiring in 1961, after eleven seasons with the Giants and three with the Green Bay Packers.

Turner, Benjamin S. (Mar. 17, 1825, near Weldon, N.C.— Mar. 21, 1894, Selma, Ala.): Politician. Turner, born as a slave, was among the first African Americans to serve in Congress. He was a representative from Alabama in the 1871-1873 term. He was one of five African Americans to serve in Congress during that session. Following his defeat for the successive term, he retired from politics. Before becoming a congressman, he had served as a tax collector, a councilman in Selma, and an independent businessman.

Turner, Darwin Theodore Troy (May 7, 1931, Cincinnati, Ohio—1991, Iowa City, Iowa): Educator. Turner had a distinguished career as a university teacher, literary critic, anthologist, and pioneer of the study of African American history and culture within higher education. He began his academic career precociously, earning a B.A. in English from the University of Cincinnati in 1947 and an M.A. in 1949. From 1949 to 1951, he taught at Clark College in Atlanta, Ga., as an assistant professor of English. His Ph.D. in English and American drama was from the University of Chicago (1956).

His academic path involved several moves. He taught at Morgan State College in Baltimore, Md., from 1952 to 1957, then was chair of the English department at Florida A&M State University from 1957 to 1959. From 1959 to 1970, he was first chair of English then dean of the graduate school at North Carolina A&T University of Greensboro. His last positions were at the University of Iowa, where he was professor of English, chair of African American studies (1972-1991), and Iowa Foundation Distinguished Professor (1981).

Turner served on an array of national education committees, including those of the Modern Language Association, the National Committee of Teachers of English, the Rockefeller Committee on the Humanities, and Phi Beta Kappa. He built a deserved reputation as a kindly, committed educator and director of African American literary and cultural research. His own scholarly work equally made its mark.

Perhaps his best-acclaimed volume is *In a Minor Chord: Three Afro-American Writers and Their Search for Identity* (1971), a lucid critique of Jean TOOMER,

Countée CULLEN, and Zora Neale HURSTON. The Hurston chapters caused some controversy. For example, Turner described Hurston as superficial and shallow in her artistic and social judgments. Other representative publications include Turner's journal essays (he also served as a contributing editor to the *College Language Association Journal*), his own poetry in *Katharsis* (1964), the three-volume collection *Black American Literature: Essays, Poetry, Fiction, Drama* (1970), *Black Drama in America: An Anthology* (1971), and his edited works *The Wayward and the Seeking: A Collection of Writings by Jean Toomer* (1980) and *The Art of Slave Narrative: Original Essays in Criticism and Theory* (1982, with John Sekora).

Turner, Debbye (b. 1965, Ark.): Miss America 1990. Turner was the second African American woman to win the title, after Vanessa WILLIAMS in 1983. As a veterinary science student at the University of Missouri, she represented the state of Missouri in the pageant. Turner played the marimba in the talent competition. She created some controversy with the statement that "being black is the very least of who I am."

Debbye Turner, the second African American Miss America, gives the thumb's up sign at her coronation. (AP/Wide World Photos)

Turner, Henry McNeal (Feb. 1, 1834, Abbeville, S.C.—May 8, 1915, Windsor, Ontario, Canada): Religious leader and activist. Henry McNeal Turner's cry in response to the 1884 Democratic presidential victory was, "A man who loves a country that hates him is a human dog and not a man." In this speech, which ended with his famous slogan "Respect Black," Turner summarized the central tenets of his writings, works, and beliefs: that American blacks should act and think proudly for themselves and, if thwarted, should resist and protest or should find freedom in Africa. In a long life, Turner served as a preacher, organizer, and bishop for the AFRICAN METHODIST EPISCOPAL (AME) CHURCH, as a Georgia legislator, as a political critic, and as an active proponent of the AMERICAN COLONIZATION SOCIETY and its interests in LIBERIA. Above all, he was a crusader urging blacks to fight for their rights against the increasing inroads of Jim Crow legislation and racism at the turn of the twentieth century. While Booker T. WASHINGTON proposed harmonious cooperation between the races and W. E. B. DU BOIS argued the intellectual case for African American equality, Turner used a Biblical vision and rhetorical eloquence to appeal to a more popular audience.

Youth and Religious Training. Henry Turner was born to free parents in slave South Carolina, a society then in the process of constraining black opportunities in the wake of the Denmark VESEY and Nat TURNER uprisings. Despite the restrictions imposed on black education, Henry Turner learned reading, writing, and basic arithmetic in his adolescence while working at a variety of trades before pursuing his education while employed by a medical college in Baltimore. According to his first biographer, Mongo Ponton, Turner also believed himself descended from African royalty through his mother, Sarah Greer Turner, a belief that may have influenced his continuing interest in African colonization and study.

Turner joined the Methodist Episcopal Church, South, in 1851 and was licensed to preach in 1853. He relinquished his membership in this white-dominated denomination in the late 1850's after a dramatic meeting in New Orleans with Dr. Willis B. Revels of the African Methodist Episcopal church; the African church's black autonomy appealed more to Turner's temperament. Despite difficulties caused by his educational background, he was admitted to work in Baltimore with the support of Bishop Daniel A. PAYNE. Shortly thereafter, in 1862, Turner and his wife, Elizabeth Ann Peacher, moved to a church in Washington, D.C., where Turner's sermons and political views gained him more public attention.

Civil War and Political Work. In 1863, Abraham Lincoln commissioned Turner as chaplain of the First Regiment, U.S. Colored Troops, making Turner the first black U.S. Army chaplain. In 1865, he became a regular chaplain. He was also assigned to duty with the Georgia FREEDMEN'S BUREAU. In Georgia, he served the church by building AME churches and organizations; he claimed to have received more than fourteen thousand members into the church. Turner also spent five years in stormy political activities in the Georgia legislature and federal Republican patronage posts. His legislative career, for example, became embattled through white Georgians' 1868 rejection of black legislators and refusal to ratify the FIFTEENTH AMENDMENT. Turner also resigned federal posts in Macon and Savannah, Ga., after intense harassment. His speech arguing for political franchise, "On the Eligibility of Colored Members to Seats in the Georgia Legislature," circulated as a pamphlet, as did many of his later political and social arguments.

Church Publications and College Presidency. When not yet forty, Turner retired from politics to a pastorate in Savannah, and thereafter his political and critical base became the AME church. He became a bishop (1880-1892), general manager of the AME Book Concern, and a regular contributor to *The Christian Recorder.* He also served for twelve years as president of Morris Brown University. Turner proved active as a publicist and author for the church and as founder and editor of publications such as *The Southern Recorder* (1886-1888); *The Voice of Missions* (1893-1900); and *The Voice of the People* (1901-1907). Among his books were *The Negro in All Ages* (1873); *The Genius and Theory of Methodist Polity: Or, the Machinery of Methodism* (1885); *African Letters* (1893); and *Turner's Catechism* (c. 1917, also translated into French).

From the AME pulpit, Turner continued to criticize the political compromises that reconstituted segregation and black oppression in the South in the second half of the nineteenth century. He claimed in *The Christian Recorder*, for example, that the Supreme Court's 1883 reversal of the Civil Rights Act of 1875 "absolves the negro's allegiance to the general government" (Nov. 8, 1883) and attacked black leaders who adopted accommodationist positions. He also criticized the Republican Party's growing abandonment of black suffrage and civil rights.

Emigrationist Work. As early as the mid-1870's, Turner showed sympathy to those who felt the future of American blacks lay in a return to Africa. He argued in 1876 that "there is no instance mentioned in history where an enslaved people of an alien race rose to respectability upon the same territory of their enslavement and in the presence of their enslavers, without losing their identity or individuality by amalgamation. Can any result be hoped for the negro in the United States? I think not." Turner himself first visited Sierra Leone and LIBERIA in 1891, returning to Africa in 1893, 1895, and 1898. In the last trip, as senior bishop of the AME church, he arranged

affiliation for emergent black congregations in South Africa. His letters and editorials praised the opportunities of Liberia, although his critics noted that he himself never moved there. His vision was made clear in an 1880 letter to his son, John P. Turner, to whom he wrote: "If you want your name woven into song and history when you are dead, become an African explorer, geologist, mineralogist or something that will enlighten the world upon her resources, and make you her benefactor." Colonization, however, faced many practical problems and never proved a mass success.

As Turner's seniority and international fame grew, he received honorary doctorates from the University of Pennsylvania (1872), Wilberforce University (1873), and the College of Liberia (1894). A family man as well, he remarried twice in the 1890's and again before his death. His commentary on American life and politics grew ever more acid. In reference to the 1896 presidential election, for example, he wrote in *The Voice of the Missions*, "Vote any way in your power to overthrow, destroy, ruin, blot out, divide, crush, dissolve, wreck, consume, demolish, disorganize, suppress, subvert, smash, shipwreck, crumble, nullify, upset, uproot, expunge, and fragmentize this nation until it learns to deal justly with the black man." Turner opposed black participation in the Spanish-American War for the same reason. Moreover, in 1898, to the consternation of the white press, he declaimed that "God is a Negro."

Later Life. In the new century, Turner maintained his office and residence in Atlanta. His career, however, was tempered by health problems. He was accorded recognition for his service by the AME church in 1905. Still, in his final decade, he was quoted in the *Atlanta Constitution* of Feb. 16, 1906, as saying, "Without multiplying words, I wish to say that hell is an improvement upon the United States where the Negro is concerned."

After Turner's death in Canada, his body was brought back in state to Big Bethel Church in Atlanta for burial. More than fifteen thousand people attended the ceremony. Booker T. Washington died in the same year.

Turner's influence persisted in a variety of black movements, including the AME church. His Christian radicalism was influential on Marcus GARVEY and Garvey's UNIVERSAL NEGRO IMPROVEMENT ASSOCIATION as well as on others who demanded a radical reassessment of black opportunities in the United States. Although Turner's colonization projects failed, the congregations and spirit of the African Methodist Episcopal church that he spread along the Atlantic coast also became a bulwark for later nationalist identity. Thus Gayraud Wilmore, a prominent historian of African American religion and politics, considers Turner to have been the American black of his era of most lasting impact on the future of Africa, even beyond his rich legacy of actions and words in the United States.—*Gary W. McDonogh*

SUGGESTED READINGS: • Coulter, E. Merton. "Henry M. Turner: Georgia Negro Preacher-Politician During the Reconstruction Era." *Georgia Historical Quarterly* 48 (December, 1964): 371-410. • Perdue, Frank. *The Negro in Savannah, 1865-1900.* New York: Exposition Press, 1973. • Redkey, Edwin S. *Black Exodus: Black Nationalist and Back-to-Africa Movements, 1890-1910.* New Haven, Conn.: Yale University Press, 1969. • Redkey, Edwin S., ed. *Respect Black: The Writings and Speeches of Henry McNeal Turner.* New York: Arno, 1971. • Wilmore, Gayraud S. *Black Religion and Black Radicalism.* 2d rev. ed. Maryknoll, N.Y.: Orbis Books, 1983.

Turner, Ike (b. Nov. 5, 1931, Clarksdale, Miss.): Rhythm-and-blues pianist. Turner was playing piano by his mid-teens and working as a disc jockey on radio station WROX, which exposed him to the latest records by rhythm-and-blues (R&B) artists including Louis Jordan and Charles Brown. By 1951, he was playing with his own RHYTHM-AND-BLUES band, the Kings of Rhythm.

Turner's band toured the South, playing a fast, rough, and energetic style of rhythm and blues that prefigured early rock and roll. The Kings of Rhythm's "Rocket '88," a song recorded for Chess Records in 1951, is in fact regarded by many critics and musicians as the first identifiably rock-and-roll record. Although its sound was not significantly different from many other rhythm-and-blues records of the time, the popularity of "Rocket '88" with both white as well as black teenagers suggested a shift in the music's audience that predated the rock and roll from later in the decade.

Although Turner and the Kings of Rhythm recorded many records as backup musicians to Elmore JAMES, HOWLIN' WOLF, and others, and even though Turner himself was an accomplished talent scout for Modern Records and the Memphis Recording Studio, he is best known for his work with his former wife, Tina TURNER. Tina joined the Kings of Rhythm in 1956 and married Ike in 1958. By 1960, Turner had added a horn section and female backup singers (dubbed the Ikettes) to the group. Renamed "The Ike and Tina Turner Revue," the group attained a widespread following in Great Britain and opened for the Rolling Stones on their 1969 tour of the United States. Ike and Tina also recorded "River Deep, Mountain High" with producer Phil Spector in 1966. Their version of Creedence Clearwater Revival's "Proud Mary" (1971) remains their most recognized song.

Ike and Tina ended their personal and professional relationship in 1976, and Tina later alleged that Ike physically and emotionally abused her during their marriage. Additionally, Turner experienced legal trouble, including drug and battery arrests. He recorded two solo albums at his own studio.

Turner, James Milton (May 16, 1840, St. Louis County, Mo.—Nov. 1, 1915, Ardmore, Okla.): Educator and government official. Turner was born a slave. He and his mother were purchased from slavery by his father, John Turner, when he was four years old. Turner was largely self-educated but learned to read at a secret slave children's school conducted by nuns at the St. Louis Catholic Cathedral. In his early teen years, he attended a day school in Brooklyn, Ill., and at age fourteen he studied at the preparatory school at OBERLIN COLLEGE.

Turner served in the Civil War as valet to a northern officer. He was wounded in the hip during the Battle of Shiloh, causing a limp that he retained for the rest of his life. After the war, Turner became active in public life, promoting the cause of education for African Americans. In 1866, the Kansas City school board appointed him to teach in Missouri's first tax-supported school for black students. He helped to solicit money from black soldiers in the South for a new school. These funds, along with those collected by black infantry units, were the basis for Jefferson City's Lincoln Institute, which since 1921 has been known as Lincoln University. Turner joined Lincoln's board of trustees in 1868.

In view of the contributions of black soldiers, Turner in 1870 urged the Missouri state legislature to appropriate funds for schools based on the number of students enrolled, without regard to color. He was appointed as assistant state superintendent of schools, responsible for establishing free public schools for black students.

Turner emerged as Missouri's leading radical politician, largely as a result of his tours on behalf of Lincoln Institute and the Equal Rights League. He helped obtain the support of black voters for the election of Ulysses S. Grant to the U.S. presidency. Grant rewarded Turner by naming him as minister resident and consul-general at Monrovia, LIBERIA, on Mar. 1, 1871. This appointment made Turner the first black U.S. diplomat accredited to an African country. James W. Mason had been named as minister in March, 1870, but never traveled to his post.

Turner spent seven years in Liberia. Numerous tribal uprisings and changes in government there led him to oppose colonization by black people from the United States. He also thought that the equatorial climate of the country was unsuitable. He returned to the United States, and during the "Great Exodus" movement of 1879 he established a refuge depot in St. Louis for African Americans on their way to Kansas. As president of the Freedmen's Oklahoma Association of St. Louis, he circulated information about the free land that was available to homesteaders. During the 1880's, Turner worked as an attorney on behalf of black members of various Native American nations. Those members often were denied their share of money granted to the nations by the United States government in compensation for land taken from the nations.

Turner, Nat (Oct. 2, 1800, Southampton County, Va.— Nov. 11, 1831, Jerusalem, Va.): Slave revolt leader. Nat Turner was the leader of a slave revolt in Southampton County, Va., in 1831, variously known as "Nat's Fray," the "Southampton Insurrection," and the "First War" (the Civil War being regarded as the second war). Turner planned the insurrection, which involved between sixty and eighty slaves and free blacks and in which between fifty-five and sixty-five whites were killed. Turner's revolt was important because it disproved the myth of the happy slave, showed that slaves were willing to die for

Nat Turner was captured and eventually hanged after he launched a slave insurrection in Virginia in 1831; his capture is depicted in this woodcut. (Library of Congress)

freedom, and demonstrated that slaves were capable of organizing a movement themselves. It inspired many African Americans who would later strive for freedom and justice.

Early Influences. Nat Turner spent his entire life in Southampton County. The county is in the tidewater area of southeastern Virginia, near the North Carolina border. The county seat was the town of Jerusalem (now Court-land). The region underwent an economic depression in the 1820's; there was widespread white apprehension concerning possible slave revolts, as whites were out-numbered by blacks, and as the well-publicized abortive slave insurrection of GABRIEL Prosser had occurred near Richmond in 1800.

Nat Turner was born Oct. 2, 1800, to a slave called Nancy, who had been kidnapped from Africa in 1793 and purchased by Benjamin Turner. There is a legend that Nancy tried to kill Nat just after his birth to prevent him from being subjected to a life of SLAVERY. Nat Turner's father's name is unknown, but he was the son of another Turner farm slave and ran away when Nat was eight or nine.

During his boyhood, Nat Turner learned to read and write, an unusual accomplishment for a slave child. He also learned about Christianity. He came to associate RELIGION with freedom and to feel fervently about both. Turner had religious visions throughout his life. Once he reported hearing a voice tell him to seek the "Kingdom of Heaven," a phrase he interpreted to mean an end to servitude. He believed that it was his destiny to lead his fellow slaves to freedom.

Upon Benjamin Turner's death, Nat Turner was inherited by Benjamin's son, Samuel Turner. Samuel Turner hired a harsh overseer, and Nat Turner ran away. A month later, Nat returned and gave himself up. He reported having had a vision in which "the Spirit" chided him for being selfish. This may have caused him to see his destiny as the pursuit of freedom for his people, not merely himself.

Nat Turner was married in 1821 to a slave named Cherry. They had two sons and one daughter, but the family was split up as a result of the death of Samuel Turner in 1822. Nat was sold to Thomas Moore, whereas Cherry and the children were sold to Giles Reese, a neighbor of Moore.

Nat the Prophet. Between 1825 and 1830, Nat Turner became a popular preacher in a circuit of African American churches. His sermons were impassioned and poetic. He vividly described visions of conflict and liberation and said that the judgment day was at hand. His followers came to believe that he was a prophet. During these years,

he formulated a secret plan for insurrection.

In 1828, Thomas Moore died, and Turner was inherited by Moore's nine-year-old-son, Putnam Moore. Thomas Moore's widow, Sally Moore, married a carriage maker named Joseph Travis, who moved to the farm and supervised Nat and sixteen other slaves.

Plans for Revolt. Turner's travels as a preacher allowed him to learn things necessary to prepare an insurrection. He found out which slaves to trust and the location of roads and hiding places. He assembled a close group of followers, but he did not tell them his plans for rebellion until 1828, when he experienced a vision. A spirit told him he was soon to fight against "the serpent." His close followers included four other slaves and two free blacks.

Another sign came to Turner in February of 1831; he interpreted an eclipse of the sun as meaning that it was time to prepare his revolt. He assigned tasks to the members of his inner circle, who recruited followers, arranged for horses and mules, and prepared weapons. Turner chose July 4, 1831, for the revolt. When he became ill, though, the insurrection was postponed. Another vision came to him on Aug. 13, 1831, when Turner saw a dark spot moving on the sun and told his followers that blacks would pass over the earth just as the spot had passed across the sun. The insurrection was then set to begin in the early morning of Aug. 22, 1831. All whites, regardless of age or sex, were to be killed. As the rebels traveled from farm to farm, slaves would be recruited and weapons confiscated.

Insurrection. The revolt began with an attack on the Travis household by Turner and his close followers. Nat Turner drew the first blood, attacking Joseph Travis. Soon all the family were slain. Until the revolt was overcome by white resistance forty hours later, Turner directed his followers' actions. He reminded them to view themselves as soldiers rather than as outlaws and to keep liberation in mind.

The rebels used the cover of night to make surprise attacks on several farms. Whites were killed, and guns, horses, mules, and food were taken. There was no torture or rape. The rebels spared the home of Giles Reese, where Turner's wife and children were slaves, as well as the farm of a boyhood friend of Turner's. Also spared was a poor white family that did not own slaves.

When one member of the slave army urged the group to turn back because of the superior force of the whites, Turner pointed out that they could expect ruthless treatment if they gave up. He argued that death was acceptable because they had tasted freedom. Turner's view prevailed, and the group moved on. By noon, there were about sixty in the slave army, many mounted. Turner's goal was to take the town of Jerusalem, as it held a large store of ammunition.

Word of the revolt had spread throughout the area by mid-morning. Whites rushed to town for protection, and armed resistance was mobilized. The rebels and white militia clashed at the Battle of Parker's Field. After attack and counterattack, Turner led a retreat into a cover of woods. He rallied a force of twenty, which tried unsuccessfully to cross a bridge into Jerusalem from the south. Turner's force camped that night near a large plantation from which he hoped to recruit more slaves. At dawn, there was an ambush in which many of his men were wounded. The weakened slave army moved to another farm, where the militia waited. Only Turner and four others escaped, and soon only Turner was at large. All the coconspirators either died in the battles with militia or went to trial. Between fifteen and twenty men and a small number of women were hanged, and other Turner followers were sold to plantations in the Deep South or the Caribbean. There was a massive effort to find the missing leader, including the offer of a five-hundred-dollar reward.

Capture. After two months in hiding, Turner was captured and taken to the authorities by a poor white, Benjamin Phipps. Under heavy guard to prevent a LYNCHING, Turner was questioned by two judges in Jerusalem. He answered them calmly and frankly and did not repent; he said that he had done as God had commanded. He expressed no remorse over the killing of women and children, saying he thought such terror was necessary to win freedom from slavery. While in jail awaiting trial, he gave a statement to Thomas Gray, which Gray later published.

The trial began Nov. 5, 1831. Turner's lawyer, William Parker, entered a not-guilty plea, but Turner did not deny the deeds with which he was charged. His statement to Gray was read. Turner acknowledged the statement and said he had nothing to say beyond it. Turner was found guilty and sentenced to hang on Nov. 11, 1831. The hanging was a public spectacle; many in the crowd expected a show of cowardice, but Turner was calm. Eyewitnesses said he did not thrash about, as hanging victims often did.

Aftermath. There were more than one hundred lynchings of blacks in the area prompted by white anxiety and a desire for revenge. Thus, at least twice as many blacks as whites died as a result of the rebellion. Repressive laws were passed intended to suppress further rebellion, including rules against selling liquor to slaves and against allowing slaves to possess arms. Slaves, on the other hand, became still more restless and more determined to end their servitude.—*Nancy Conn Terjesen*

SUGGESTED READINGS: • Aptheker, Herbert. *Nat Turner's Slave Rebellion.* New York: Grove Press, 1966. • Foner, Eric, ed. *Nat Turner.* Englewood Cliffs, N.J.: Prentice-Hall, 1971. • Lindsay, Jack. *Turner.* Chicago: Academy Chicago Publishers, 1981. • Oates, Stephen B. *The Fires of Jubilee: Nat Turner's Fierce Rebellion.* New York: Harper & Row, 1975. • Tragle, Henry. *The Southampton Slave Revolt of 1831.* Amherst, Mass.: 1971.

Turner, Thomas Wyatt (Apr. 16, 1877, Hughesville, Md.—Apr. 21, 1978, Washington, D.C.): Scientist and religious activist. Turner had a distinguished career as a biologist and dean of HOWARD UNIVERSITY (1914-1920) and HAMPTON INSTITUTE (1924-1945). Primarily, however, Turner was the leading opponent of racism in the Catholic church. In 1924, he founded the Federation of Colored CATHOLICS. He bitterly fought its absorption in 1935 into the Catholic Interracial Council, which he regarded as white-dominated and passive. Turner remained a militant yet loyal Catholic. He was also a charter member of the NATIONAL ASSOCIATION FOR THE ADVANCEMENT OF COLORED PEOPLE.

Turner, Tina (Anna Mae Bullock; b. Nov. 26, 1939, Brownsville, Tenn.): Rock and soul singer. Turner was born in Brownsville's Haywood Memorial Hospital, at which African American patients were treated in the basement. Shortly after her birth, she was sent back to Nut Bush, Tenn., where the Bullock family lived. She was the second child of Floyd Richard Bullock, who worked as a manager for a cotton plantation and also served as a deacon of the Woodlawn Baptist Church, and Zelma Bullock. Her older sister, Alline, was nearly three years old at the time of Turner's birth. The Bullocks were divorced when Turner was eleven years old. After the divorce, the two girls moved in with their grandmother.

Turner began singing and dancing when she was a schoolgirl. In class talent shows, she would excel at singing ballads and operatic numbers. Normally a shy child, she found singing to be a wonderful outlet. In the church choir, she got a chance to sing gospel hymns, but it was the blues songs that she belted out at picnics that she really loved. After her grandmother died in the mid-1950's, Turner and her sister moved to St. Louis, Mo., to live with their mother. In St. Louis, they frequented nightclubs where RHYTHM AND BLUES was played. It was at one of these nightclubs in 1956 that Turner met guitarist Ike TURNER and his band, the Kings of Rhythm. It took almost a year of her pestering before Ike gave her a chance to sing. He was so impressed by her voice that he allowed her to sing with the band on occasional engagements.

When she did join the band, she used the name "Little Anna."

In 1958, the couple married. Shortly thereafter, Ike convinced Anna to change her name to Tina. Turner eventually got her chance to sing lead at a recording session when the scheduled vocalist failed to show up. The single that was recorded, "A Fool for Love," became a hit, selling eight hundred thousand copies. Ike decided to transform their band into the Ike and Tina Turner Revue, with Tina becoming the lead singer and the focal point of the group. Under Ike's supervision, the Revue blended gospel, rock, blues, and even country music into a powerful mix. During the 1960's, the Ike and Tina Turner Revue had a number of hits, including "It's Gonna Work Out Fine," "River Deep, Mountain High," and "Proud Mary." Tina Turner was an electrifying performer and in 1973 wrote the hit song "Nutbush City Limits." Ike and Tina separated in 1975 and were divorced in 1976. Tina Turner stated in her 1986 autobiography, *I, Tina*, that Ike was an abusive husband.

After a number of years of floundering, Turner, with the help of such friends as the Rolling Stones and Rod Stewart, began to rebuild her singing career in the early 1980's. In 1984, she released the album *Private Dancer*, which became a huge success. The album included the hit songs "Better Be Good to Me" and "What's Love Got to Do with It." Turner won a number of Grammy Awards for *Private Dancer*. Turner also has attempted to build an acting career, appearing in the Who's rock opera film *Tommy* (1975) and in *Mad Max Beyond Thunderdome* (1985). She also kept up the energetic and sexually provocative style of musical performance that made her an international star.

Tuskegee Airmen: African Americans trained at TUSKEGEE INSTITUTE during World War II to become pilots in the U.S. Air Force. In early 1941, responding to pressure from African American organizations, the Army established a special unit at Tuskegee to train African American pilots. Despite racism that hampered their training, the Tuskegee Airmen, who eventually served in the Ninety-ninth and three other fighter squadrons, became distinguished pilots during World War II.

Tuskegee Institute (Tuskegee, Ala.): School established in 1881 by Booker T. WASHINGTON. The institute, now a professional and technical school, evolved from a modest beginning as an industrial school with thirty students in one shanty room. The campus now encompasses five thousand acres. About three thousand students attended in 1992, and more than fifty-seven thousand had been graduated from the institute since its inception.

The school's history is significant to the understanding of the American dual system of EDUCATION. After the Civil War, the battle for control over the education of African Americans continued. In the 1880's, industrial philanthropists who realized the importance of shaping postsecondary training for African Americans expanded programs of industrial education. These curricula did not meet the educational aspirations of African Americans; black schools, however, could not afford to ignore the availability of philanthropic funds. This new focus represented a pragmatic move rather than a commitment to the social and educational philosophy of industrial training.

Industrial education was the core agenda at Tuskegee in its early years, consisting of masonry, carpentry, printing, skilled trades, domestic arts for women, and character development. Botanist George Washington CARVER joined the faculty in 1896 and stayed for forty-seven years, until his death. Christian dogma, moral sense, dignity of labor, self-reliance, thrift, and industry were among the middle-class values that Booker T. Washington tried to instill, hoping to achieve racial equality for his people. His accommodationist views explain why whites made him the spokesperson for African Americans and why his adversaries adamantly opposed him. W. E. B. Du Bois, his toughest critic, believed that "education makes men, not workers"; through a liberal arts curriculum, schools should articulate the sources of oppression, identify the aspirations and struggles of African Americans, and lead toward greater freedom and justice.

Tuskegee Institute was seen as a model by white southerners and philanthropic northerners. From RECONSTRUCTION to the Great Depression, HIGHER EDUCATION for

These young men wore uniforms reflecting their status as students of Tuskegee Institute. (Library of Congress)

African Americans took the form of training for industrial jobs rather than for changing social conditions. Two years of contention and unrest led to changes in the model in 1929. Students proclaimed that their "Du Bois ambition" could not be mixed with a "Washington education," and their demand for standard institutions of higher learning soon materialized.

The main emphasis at Tuskegee became science and technology. The school offered students a choice of forty-five undergraduate degrees in 1992, along with twenty-five master's degrees and a doctorate in veterinary medicine. Students could also gain experience and financial assistance by working in industry through a program of cooperative education.

Twenty-fifth Infantry: Black U.S. Army unit in service during the Indian wars, the Spanish-American War, and World War I. The unit first saw service in the Spanish-American War at Daiquiri, near Guantánamo Bay, in Cuba. On July 1, 1888, a battalion of the infantry attacked the El Caney garrison and won the position.

Twenty-fourth Infantry: Black U.S. Army unit in service during the Indian wars, the Spanish-American War, World War I, and World War II. The unit spent more than a month in combat in Cuba in 1888 before being ordered back to Siboney. Yellow fever had broken out there, and members of the Twenty-fourth Infantry responded to a call for volunteers to nurse the sick and dying and to bury the dead. More than 60 of the approximately 450 men volunteered. The regiment also helped capture the New Georgia Islands from Japan in May, 1942, and won one of the first victories in the Korean War. The unit was deactivated on Oct. 1, 1951. It was the last all-black unit in the U.S. Army and had been one of the first four such units created.

2 Live Crew: RAP group. The group's lead rapper, Luther Campbell, grew up as the youngest of four brothers in Liberty City, a GHETTO neighborhood in Miami, Fla. Campbell's father worked as a custodian, and his mother helped to support the family by working as a hairdresser. Campbell began his music career during his teens as a street deejay, using the name "Luke Skyywalker." He was graduated from Miami Beach High School in 1978 and played football as a linebacker on the school's team.

Campbell became involved as a rap promoter for shows at Miami area schools, parks, and recreational facilities that featured popular groups such as RUN-D.M.C. and the FAT BOYS. He started on the local rap circuit as the frontman for the group Ghetto Style DJs and made

his own solo recordings as a rapper before joining a Southern California crew called the 2 Live Crew in 1985. 2 Live Crew was one of the first to popularize the Miami rap sound. The group became known for its hard-core lyrics, often containing sexually explicit language and misogynistic themes. Its first hit, "Throw the D." (1986), was recorded on Campbell's own record label, called Skyywalker Records, and sold approximately 250,000 copies. *2 Live Is What We Are* (1986) and *Move Somethin'* (1987) sold almost one million copies each.

2 Live Crew's precedent-setting album, *As Nasty as They Wanna Be* (1989) sold nearly two million copies and was the first record declared legally obscene in an American court of law. Although some listeners accused the group of promoting serious hard-core pornography, most critics noted that 2 Live Crew's live performances—while crude and risqué—had the atmosphere of a raunchy stag party. As a result of the album's notoriety, *Star Wars* filmmaker George Lucas filed a $300 million lawsuit to prevent Campbell from using the name "Luke Skyy-walker" as his record label. Campbell changed the label's name to Luke Records and was able to settle the Lucas lawsuit out of court with a settlement of $300,000. The obscenity ruling against *As Nasty as They Wanna Be* was overturned by a federal appeals court in Florida in 1992.

The title single from the group's 1990 album, *Banned in the USA*, addressed the issue of the court battles. Bruce Springsteen gave his written consent for the group to use the melody from his hit song "Born in the USA." In an effort to protect musical artists from what it viewed as creeping censorship, Atlantic records agreed to release the group's single and negotiated a partnership deal to distribute new recordings by artists on Campbell's Luke Records label. Campbell had stated his concerns that his company had been singled out unfairly because of its independent status and reiterated his claim that he had always labeled the group's albums as containing explicit lyrics in accordance with guidelines proposed by parents' groups. By mid-1990, Campbell's corporation had grossed more than $17 million in record sales alone. 2 Live Crew's 1991 album, *Sports Weekend: As Nasty as They Wanna Be II*, was released with a warning label stating "Parental Advisory—Explicit Lyrics." The group also recorded the song "In the Dust" for the sound track of the film *New Jack City* (1991).

Two Trains Running (pr. 1990): Play by August WILSON. Set in Pittsburgh, Pa., this comical drama takes place in a restaurant. The interaction of the black customers and employees reveals fragments of their lives that mirror the concerns of African Americans in society at large.

227 (NBC, 1985-1990): Television sitcom. This was the Washington, D.C., address where Mary Jenkins (Marla Gibbs) lived with her husband, Lester (Hal Williams), and their daughter, Brenda (Regina King). Among their neighbors were sexy Sandra Clark (JACKÉE), Mary's best friend and landlady, Rose Lee Holloway (Alaina Reed), and elderly but still witty Pearl Shay (Helen Martin).

Track star Florence Griffith-Joyner (right) makes a guest appearance on Marla Gibb's television series 227. (AP/Wide World Photos)

Tyner, (Alfred) McCoy "Sulaimon Saud" (b. Dec. 11, 1938, Philadelphia, Pa.): Pianist. Tyner began studying music at an early age, starting his formal studies at the age of thirteen and then moving on to take theory lessons at the Granoff School of Music. He counts among his early influences the work of Richie and Bud POWELL, Art TATUM, and Thelonius MONK. Tyner joined the Benny Golson-Art FARMER Jazztet in 1959, then went on to play with John COLTRANE's quartet from 1960 to 1965. In addition to his work with Coltrane and others, he made a series of recordings under his own name for the Blue Note and Impulse labels, including *Inception* (1962) and *The Real McCoy* (1967). After a brief lull in the later 1960's, his career surged when he began to record for Milestone in 1972. He released *Sahara* in 1972, *Supertrio* in 1977, and *Four Times Four* in 1980. He toured and

Pianist McCoy Tyner played with John Coltrane's quartet from 1960 to 1965. (AP/Wide World Photos)

recorded with the Milestone Jazzstars in 1978, and in the mid-1980's, he led a quintet including Gary Bartz and John Blake. A volume of his transcriptions, *Inception to Now*, was published in 1983.

Tyson, Cicely (b. Dec. 19, 1939, New York, N.Y.): Actress. Cicely Tyson served as a symbol of black consciousness and pride as she earned acclaim as one of America's finest actresses in theater, film, and television.

Background. Tyson grew up in the Upper East Side of Manhattan, the youngest of three children of a West Indian couple who immigrated from Nevis, one of the Leeward Islands. The impoverished family sought various means to support itself. Cicely's father, William, worked as a carpenter and painter and, at times, sold fruit from a pushcart. Her mother, Theodosia, worked as a domestic. At age nine, Tyson also helped to support the family by selling shopping bags on the streets.

When Tyson was eleven, her parents were divorced, and her mother retained custody of the children. A fundamentalist religious woman, her mother forbade Tyson to date before the age of seventeen and prohibited her from attending films or the theater. Tyson spent most of her spare time at church, where she enjoyed the religious and social life of the congregation.

Upon graduating from Manhattan's Charles Evans Hughes High School, she obtained a secretarial position with the Red Cross but soon grew tired of the monotony of her work. One day, she has said, she decided that "I know God did not put me on the face of this earth to bang on a typewriter for the rest of my life!" Shortly afterward, she began working as a model, appearing in such magazines as *Vogue* and *Harper's Bazaar*. Her interest in acting was then encouraged by the producers of an independent film, *The Spectrum*, which was never completed. Tyson, however, decided she would seek training for her newfound career.

in a variety showcase on Broadway called *Talent '59*, she undertook roles in several television shows, including productions of *Between Yesterday and Today* in 1959 and *Brown Girl, Brownstones* in 1960. Her first film role was little more than a bit part in *Odds Against Tomorrow* (1959).

After a minor role in a 1960 production of *The Cool World*, Tyson played a prostitute, Virtue, in Jean Genet's controversial 1961 play *The Blacks*. The drama proved to be the biggest break of her career, as she was cast with such actors as James Earl JONES, Roscoe Lee BROWNE, and Godfrey CAMBRIDGE. Catching the notice of the crit-

Cicely Tyson was nominated for an Academy Award for her portrayal of Rebecca Morgan in the 1972 film Sounder. *(AP/Wide World Photos)*

Early Career. Tyson studied briefly at New York University and with director Lloyd RICHARDS. Director Vinnette CARROLL cast Tyson in her first starring role as Barbara Allen in a 1957 production of *Dark of the Moon*. After winning the position of understudy for Eartha KITT in a 1959 production of *Jolly's Progress* and performing

ics, she won the Vernon Rice Award for outstanding achievement in Off-Broadway theater. A year later, she won the award again for her portrayal of another prostitute, Mavis, in the 1962 production of Errol John's *Moon on a Rainbow Shawl*.

Impressed with her performance in *The Blacks*, George

C. Scott encouraged her casting in a role as his secretary on the critically acclaimed but short-lived television series *East Side/West Side*. Tyson became the first black actress with a continuing role in a dramatic television series. Moreover, the program introduced millions of viewers to Tyson's short-cropped, natural hairstyle. The style was widely imitated by black women, to the dismay of more conservatively minded individuals.

Throughout the 1960's, Tyson continued to hone her craft in such plays as *Tiger, Tiger Burning Bright* (1962), *Trumpets of the Lord* (1963), and *To Be Young, Gifted, and Black* (1969). She was one of the few black actresses to work regularly on television with guest appearances on such shows as *Slattery's People*, *I Spy*, *Medical Center*, and *The Courtship of Eddie's Father*. She won critical acclaim in her film roles in *A Man Called Adam* (1966), *The Comedians* (1967), and *The Heart Is a Lonely Hunter* (1968). Still, Tyson had to wait for four years after the release of the latter film before she found a project worthy of her talents that she felt was not demeaning to black women. She found that role in the character of Rebecca Morgan in the award-winning film SOUNDER (1972).

Sounder. Although the title refers to a dog, the film centers on a black Louisiana SHARECROPPING family and their struggle to survive and maintain their integrity amid the economic and racial hardships of the Depression. The film endeared itself to its audience, especially to blacks, who rarely saw themselves depicted in close and nurturing relationships.

Portraying the family's parents, Tyson and costar Paul WINFIELD received widespread praise for their talents, and both received Academy Award nominations. Tyson won best actress awards from the Atlanta Film Festival and the National Society of Film Critics.

The Autobiography of Miss Jane Pittman. In 1974, Tyson's triumph in *Sounder* was followed by one of the greatest challenges faced by an actor on television. *In THE AUTOBIOGRAPHY OF MISS JANE PITTMAN*, Tyson portrayed the life of a black woman from the age of nineteen to her 110th birthday. Through the life history of this woman, the film dramatized the social and political changes experienced by African Americans from the Civil War to the 1960's CIVIL RIGHTS movement. Critics and audiences agreed that Tyson met the challenge of the role with a performance that seemed inspired. Both the teleplay and Tyson's performance won the Critics Consensus Award for exceptional contributions to television. Her work also won Tyson an Emmy as best leading actress in a television special.

Other Roles. Since her role as Jane Pittman, Tyson has often appeared in theater, television, and film in works of uneven quality. Her performances in the drama *The Corn Is Green* (1983) and the films *The River Niger* (1976) and *Bustin' Loose* (1981) have been overshadowed by criticism of the production values of these works. Television seems to have provided her most noteworthy roles, showcasing her ability to portray strong, dignified women in such productions as ROOTS (1977), *A Woman Called Moses* (1978), *King* (1978), and THE WOMEN OF BREWSTER PLACE (1989).

Personal Life and Awards. Tyson keeps her personal life closely guarded. She is well known as a vegetarian who meditates daily and follows a routine of physical activity. Tyson and trumpeter Miles DAVIS were married in 1981 at the home of Bill COSBY. Former U.N. Ambassador and Atlanta mayor Andrew YOUNG married the couple, while Cosby served as best man. Tyson was later divorced from Davis, who died in 1991.

In addition to acting, Tyson has kept busy as one of the founders and board members of the DANCE THEATER OF HARLEM; by serving on the board of governors of Urban Gateways, an arts program for children; and as a trustee for the American Film Institute and Human Family Institute. For her accomplishments as an actress and humanitarian, Tyson received NATIONAL ASSOCIATION FOR THE ADVANCEMENT OF COLORED PEOPLE (NAACP) Image Awards in 1970, 1982, and 1986; honorary degrees from Atlanta, Loyola, and Lincoln universities; the Ladies Home Journal Woman of the Year Award (1978); the Wonder Woman Foundation's Roosevelt Women of Courage Award (1983); and in 1977 was inducted into the Black Filmmakers Hall of Fame. —*Addell Austin Anderson*

SUGGESTED READINGS: • Bogle, Donald. *Brown Sugar: Eighty Years of America's Black Female Superstars.* New York: Harmony Books, 1980. • Davis, Marianna W., ed. *Contributions of Black Women to America, Volume I: The Arts, Media, Business, Law, Sports.* Columbia, S.C.: Kendey Press, 1982. • Ebert, Alan. "Inside Cicely," *Essence* 4 (February, 1973) 40-41. • Robinson, Alice M., Vera Mowry Roberts, and Milly S. Barranger, eds. *Notable Women in the American Theatre.* New York: Greenwood Press, 1989. • Robinson, Louie. "Cicely Tyson, A Very Unlikely Movie Star," *Ebony* 29 (May, 1974) 33-36.

Tyson, Michael Gerard "Mike" (b. June 30, 1966, Brooklyn, N.Y.): Boxer. Tyson, the youngest of three children in a single-parent family, grew up in the impoverished Brownsville section of Brooklyn. After winding up in a reform school as a teenager, Tyson learned boxing skills and attracted the attention of the famous trainer Cus D'Amato. D'Amato became Tyson's legal guardian and worked closely with the young fighter to refine his talents.

In 1981 and 1982, Tyson won Junior Olympiad championships, and in 1983 and 1984 was a U.S. Junior Champion. Also in 1984, Tyson won the National Golden Gloves heavyweight championship, but he lost a spot on the 1984 U.S. Olympic Team when he was defeated by Henry Tillman at the Olympic trials (Tyson would later defeat Tillman as a professional).

In early 1985, Tyson turned professional, and he rapidly earned the attention of the boxing world. A stocky five-foot, eleven-inch fighter with explosive punching power, he won twenty-three of his first twenty-five professional fights by knockout. In November, 1986, Tyson knocked out Trevor Berbick to win the World Boxing Council (WBC) heavyweight title. At twenty years of age,

ing an acrimonious divorce from actress Robin Givens, did not seem to affect Tyson's performance in the ring, where he continued to awe fans and intimidate opponents with his ferocity and power. In February, 1990, however, Tyson was knocked out by James "Buster" Douglas, who was so lightly regarded that most oddsmakers refused to accept bets on the fight. While waiting for a match with Evander HOLYFIELD, who took the title from Douglas in October, 1990, Tyson was indicted by an Indiana grand jury on charges that he had raped a beauty-contest competitor. He was convicted of rape and other charges on Feb. 10, 1992, and was sentenced to several twenty-year prison terms. Tyson's attorneys have appealed the sentences; subsequent decisions have guaranteed that Tyson will remain in federal prison until at least 1995.

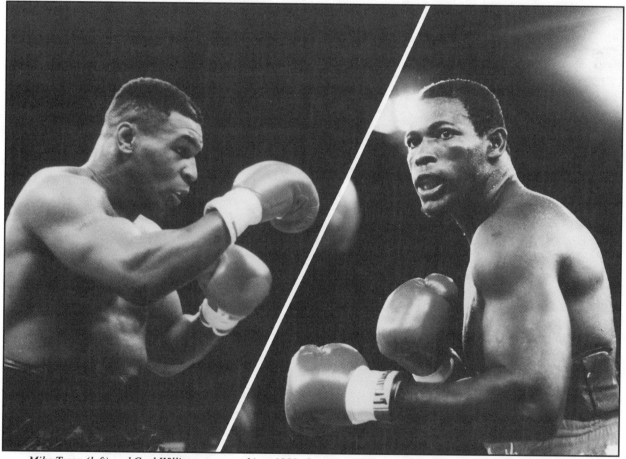

Mike Tyson (left) and Carl Williams competed in a 1989 championship bout in Atlantic City. (AP/Wide World Photos)

he was the youngest heavyweight champion in history. In 1987, he unified the heavyweight title by defeating the champions of the World Boxing Association (WBA) and the International Boxing Federation (IBF).

A series of widely publicized personal troubles, includ-

Tyus, Wyomia (b. Aug. 29, 1945, Griffin, Ga.): Sprinter. Tyus was the first athlete to win an Olympic sprint title twice. She won a gold medal in the 1964 Olympics for the 100-meter run with a world record time of 11.49 and a silver medal for the 4 × 100-meter relay with a time of

43.92. She won two gold medals in the 1968 Olympics, one for the 100-meter run with a world record time of 11.08 and one for the 4 × 100-meter relay with a time of 42.88, also a world record.

Tyus was undefeated in professional track events from 1974 to 1976. She was inducted into the Women's Sports Hall of Fame in 1981 and the U.S. Olympic Hall of Fame in 1985.

Wyomia Tyus hits the finish line to win a gold medal in the 100-meter dash at the Tokyo Olympic Games in 1964. (AP/Wide World Photos)

U

Uggams, Leslie (b. May 25, 1943, New York, N.Y.): Actor. Uggams began her professional career at the age of six. She gained prominence in the early 1960's as one of the few African American performers on a weekly variety television show, *Sing Along with Mitch*. Among her honors, Uggams won a 1968 Tony Award for her performance in the musical, *Hallelujah, Baby!*, and received an Emmy nomination for her portrayal of Kizzy in the television miniseries *Roots* (1977).

Leslie Uggams won a Tony Award for her performance in the musical Hallelujah, Baby! *(Courtesy of Leslie Uggams)*

Ujamaa: Term taken from the Swahili language. It refers to familyhood, communal life, or communal development and is often associated with the African concept of socialism. Ujamaa is also the fourth day of the week-long KWANZA holiday. It commemorates the goals of cooperative economics and of building and maintaining business enterprises to be profited from collectively.

Uncle Tom stereotype: Used disparagingly to denote an African American male who subordinates himself in order to achieve a more favorable status within the dominant society. Taken from the principal character in Harriet Beecher Stowe's *Uncle Tom's Cabin: or, Life Among the Lowly* (1853), who paradoxically refused to acquiesce, its modern use is a perversion of the author's original intent. Unlike many negative stereotypical images of African Americans, "Uncle Tom" is a label applied primarily within the African American community.

Underground Railroad: Although not an actual railroad of steel rails, locomotives, and steam engines, the Underground Railroad was real nevertheless; over time, it helped thousands of southern slaves reach freedom. A vast, informal network of paths through southern fields and woods, a network of fords across rivers, a network of safe houses where runaway slaves could hide, the Underground Railroad had many conductors—men and women, blacks and whites—some so famous that their names are still known, others whose names are lost in the past even though their work was heroic.

Runaways. Of all the heroes, the most heroic were the runaways themselves. William STILL, an underground agent in Philadelphia, wrote that "Guided by the north star alone . . . penniless, braving the perils of land and sea, eluding the keen scent of the blood-hound as well as the more dangerous pursuit of the savage slavehunter . . . [surviving] indescribable suffering from hunger and other privations, the fugitives made their way to freedom."

Although most slaves simply walked their way to freedom, a few concocted ingenious escapes. Henry "Box" BROWN, for example, had been a model slave in Richmond, but he grew resentful as his adult years slipped by. Then, disaster struck: Brown's wife and children were sold to North Carolina. Crushed, Brown decided to run away. He turned to a white Virginian, Samuel A. Smith, who was a conductor of the Underground Railroad. The two conspirators found a box big enough to hold a man. Brown got in; Smith handed him a few biscuits and a water bag before nailing down the box lid. Smith then shipped Brown to the Philadelphia Vigilance Committee, an abolitionist group. A short time later, the runaway arrived in the Quaker city safely, even though he had traveled upside down for part of his trip.

Men under thirty years of age were most likely to run away, although young women often joined them. Usually slaves ran alone or in small groups. Slaves were most likely to run during the warm months of late spring, summer, and early fall. The desire for freedom among slaves remained so strong that not only field hands but "faithful" domestics and artisans also left. As the Underground Railroad became more fully developed from the 1840's onward, entire families, including children, ran together.

quently roamed the South, trying to make contacts with potential runaways.

Development of the Underground Railroad. Despite hardships and a few failures, the "railroad" north became a network of "stations" located about a day's journey apart. Often, conductors told runaways how to reach the next station; sometimes they personally escorted the escapees. Further, as the Underground Railroad grew, so

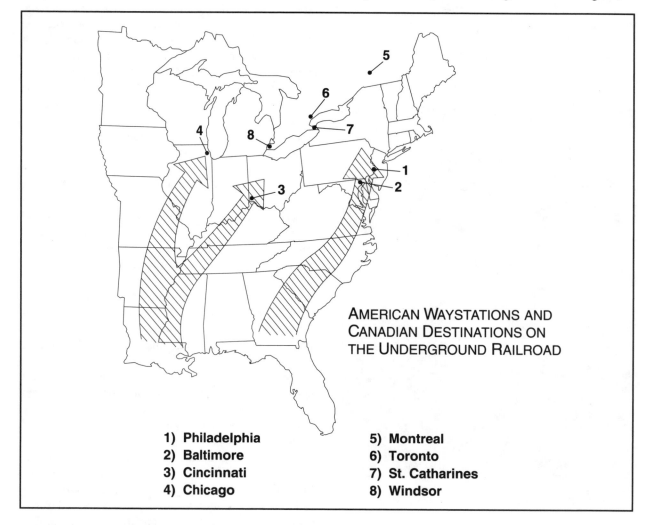

AMERICAN WAYSTATIONS AND
CANADIAN DESTINATIONS ON
THE UNDERGROUND RAILROAD

1) **Philadelphia**
2) **Baltimore**
3) **Cincinnati**
4) **Chicago**

5) **Montreal**
6) **Toronto**
7) **St. Catharines**
8) **Windsor**

Once slaves were on the run, typically, they would seek out other slaves along their route who seemed trustworthy and who would supply the runaways with food and with geographical information. Further, certain white groups were likely to aid escapees. In southern Texas, antislavery Germans of the hill country frequently helped runaways get to the Rio Grande, where Mexicans helped blacks cross into freedom. In the upper South, some Quakers became conductors for the Underground Railroad. Disguised as peddlers or census takers, abolitionists fre-

did the "grapevine telegraph"; word was passed from station to station to prepare transportation and safe hiding places for new fugitives. Using the railroad, from 1820 to 1860, approximately twenty-five hundred (possibly more) slaves each year reached freedom. The railroad had existed even earlier; as early as the mid-1780's, George Washington wrote that Quakers had organized the Abolition Society of Pennsylvania and that its members harbored runaways. The society's membership included such non-Quakers as Thomas Paine, Benjamin Franklin, and the Marquis de Lafayette, all heroes of the American Revolution.

Although records are sparse regarding the early work of the Underground Railroad, it is known that by 1787 Isaac T. Hopper, while still a teenager, had settled in Philadelphia, where he began a systematic, well-organized program to free slaves. Soon, he was contacting abolitionist leaders in other Pennsylvania towns, and he also included many New Jersey villages within his range. Hopper's work led to the liberation of hundreds of slaves even before the turn of the new century and well before the emergence of militant abolitionism in the 1820's.

Dramatic events occurred in 1804. General Thomas Boude, a veteran of the revolution, bought the slave Stephen Smith and took him to Columbia, Pa., the general's home, and freed him. Soon, Smith's mother arrived at the Boude home; she had escaped from slavery to find her son. A few weeks later, the owner of Stephen's mother came to Columbia, sought out Boude, and demanded her return. Boude refused the woman's demand, and the entire town resolved to support the general and to champion the cause of all fugitives who came their way. Slowly, the network grew; by 1815, conductors for the Underground Railroad were found as far west as Ohio. By 1831, all the northern states adjacent to the slave South had flourishing stations, conductors, and means for fast travel—farm wagons especially built to include closed compartments, covered wagons, and closed carriages. Passage of the FUGITIVE SLAVE LAW of 1850 made freedom in the North more precarious. As a result, Canada became the major destination of fugitives on the Underground Railroad.

Destinations. The paths of the Underground Railroad were several. Slaves in western Louisiana, Texas, and western territories usually headed south for Mexico. Those from eastern Louisiana, Mississippi, Alabama, and Tennessee usually moved west until they struck the Mississippi River, followed it to the Ohio River, and crossed into freedom in one of the states in the old Northwest; some continued on to Canada. Kentucky slaves also headed for the old Northwest and Canada. From Georgia and Florida, runaways most often headed for the Florida Keys; there, they hoped that they could find a ship captain to sail them to freedom. From the Carolinas northward to the Mason-Dixon line, escapees marched straight north, hoping to reach Pennsylvania, New Jersey, New England, and Canada.

The Conductors. Many former slaves who escaped became Underground Railroad conductors because they wished their family and friends could be free. In addition, many free African Americans so hated the South's "pe-

culiar institution" that they helped slaves escape. One former slave known only as Ben escaped from Kentucky by crossing the Ohio River and hiding in Ohio. Subsequently, he made several trips back to Kentucky in the 1830's to rescue others, but he was finally caught and reenslaved.

Harriet Tubman is probably the best known of the Underground Railroad "conductors." (AP/Wide World Photos)

The most famous conductor of the Underground Railroad was Harriet TUBMAN. Born a slave on Maryland's Eastern Shore in 1821, she was severely abused by her owner; once he almost killed her. In 1849, at the age of twenty-eight, she decided to run away. Traveling by night, she hid in caves and graveyards by day; she walked upstream in creeks and rivers to escape dog packs. She ultimately reached Philadelphia and freedom. Because she missed the friends and family that she had left behind the cotton curtain, she became a conductor. Between 1849 and 1861, she made nineteen trips back to the South and liberated more than three hundred slaves. Becoming a legendary figure and finally having a forty-thousand-dollar reward on her head, Tubman took pride that she never lost a single "passenger."

Although many conductors were black, others were white. One, Calvin Fairbanks, operated in Kentucky, where he assisted slaves trying to get to the Northwest; there, they could be placed in the hands of Levi Coffin, a Quaker who became known as the "president" of the railroad. Beginning in 1844, Fairbanks sent several slaves to Coffin, but Kentucky authorities caught him in 1845 and sentenced him to fifteen years' imprisonment. He received a pardon in 1849 on condition that he leave Kentucky. He ignored the warning and continued to work in the state, "liberating," as he said, "slaves from hell." Arrested again in 1852, Fairbanks again faced a fifteen-year sentence—this time at hard labor. Not pardoned until 1864, Fairbanks spent more than seventeen years of his life in prison as a consequence of his zeal.

Native Americans and Europeans also served as conductors. Ottawa Chief Kinjeino in western Ohio was among the earliest Indian friends of slave runaways. Seminoles in Florida harbored runaways, intermarried with them, and accepted them into their tribes. The Portuguese and other European fishermen sometimes allowed slaves living on the Atlantic Coast to come aboard ship and then took them to freedom.

Conclusion. In retrospect, it seems fair to say that the Underground Railroad was a tremendous success; at its peak in the 1850's, it had at least thirty-two hundred active conductors (and probably thousands more whose names and personal histories have been lost). Indirectly, conductors did much more than free thousands of slaves each year; they kept the issue of SLAVERY in the national focus, always condemning the institution as an abomination. The Underground Railroad and the conductors and slaves who "rode" it achieved final victory in 1865, when the THIRTEENTH AMENDMENT abolished slavery in the United States.—*James Smallwood*

SUGGESTED READINGS: • Breyfogle, William A. *Make Free: The Story of the Underground Railroad.* Philadelphia: J. B. Lippincott, 1958. • Buckmaster, Henrietta. *Let My People Go: The Story of the Underground Railroad and the Growth of the Abolition Movement.* New York: Harper & Brothers, 1941. • Franklin, John Hope, and Alfred A. Moss, Jr. *From Slavery to Freedom: A History of Negro Americans.* 6th ed. New York: Alfred A. Knopf, 1988. • Gara, Larry. *The Liberty Line: The Legend of the Underground Railroad.* Lexington: University of Kentucky Press, 1961. • Harding, Vincent. *There Is a River: The Black Struggle for Freedom in America.* New York: Vintage Books, 1983. • Still, William. *The Underground Rail Road: A Record of Facts, Authentic Narratives,* *Letters, &c, Narrating the Hardships, Hair-breadth Escapes and Death Struggles of the Slaves in Their Efforts for Freedom.* Phildelphia: Porter & Coates, 1872.

Underwood, Blair (b. 1964, Tacoma, Wash.): Actor. Underwood's father was a career officer in the Army and the family was transferred to numerous bases around the United States and in West Germany during Underwood's childhood. When Underwood was thirteen years old, his father retired from the Army, and the family settled in Petersburg, Va. After graduating from high school in Petersburg, Underwood was accepted at Carnegie-Mellon University in Pennsylvania, where he became a musical theater major. He left the university during his junior year to begin his acting career in New York.

Shortly after moving to New York City in 1985, Underwood appeared in guest spots on *THE COSBY SHOW* and landed a role as Bobby Blue on the daytime soap opera *One Life to Live.* Although the network offered him a contract after his first three months on the show, Underwood turned it down in order to accept a part on the CBS prime-time series *Downtown* (1986). On the short-lived show, Underwood was one of four young parolees who became involved in police work as a result of being supervised by a Los Angeles probation officer. Although the show was canceled after thirteen episodes were aired, Underwood was offered a role in 1987 on the hit NBC series *L.A. Law.* His character, Jonathan Rollins, was a young Harvard-educated attorney who negotiated a starting salary of $75,000 as the law firm's first African American associate. Underwood also appeared in a cameo role on *A DIFFERENT WORLD* and has been featured in a series of NBC public service announcements about education.

Union American Methodist Episcopal church: Church with early nineteenth century roots. In 1805, Peter Spencer, William Anderson, and forty other black members of the Asbury Methodist Church in Wilmington, Del., left that church after being denied full participation in church rites. The group established itself as the Ezion Methodist Episcopal church and held services under the direct supervision of the Asbury Church. When a white elder was appointed to preach in the Ezion church in 1812, Spencer, Anderson, and others left Ezion in protest and constructed another church building which was dedicated in 1813. They severed all ties with the AFRICAN METHODIST EPISCOPAL CHURCH in Philadelphia and established the Union Church of African Members. After 1816, thirty congregations of the Union Church split, eventually incorporating as the African Union American Methodist

Episcopal Church in the United States and Elsewhere. The church is Methodist in doctrine and Episcopal in governance, and it has a strong tradition of lay participation. The church also has a long-standing position in favor of licensing women to preach.

United Holy Church of America, Inc.: A Pentecostal group. It was founded in 1886 in Method, N.C., by Issac Cheshier. Most notable among early church organizers were the Reverend C. C. Craig and Mrs. E. E. Craig. The church was first known as the Holy Church of North

Many U.S. churches have maintained a tradition of integration while others have chosen to split, forming separate, all-black congregations. (AP/Wide World Photos)

United American Free Will Baptist Denomination, Inc.: Traces its origins to a general conference of Free Will BAPTISTS organized in 1827. In one of its first sessions, the general conference of Free Will Baptists decided to ordain African Americans to the ministry. The church also adopted a strong antislavery posture that attracted a number of African Americans to the organization in the nineteenth century. In 1901, African American members split from the Free Will Baptists and established their own denomination.

United Golfers Association: Sports group founded in the 1920's. The association was created to organize tournaments for African American golfers and to promote African Americans' rights to play golf.

Carolina, then as the Holy Church of North Carolina and Virginia. In 1916, the name of the church officially was changed to United Holy Church of America, Inc. Major rites include baptism, foot washing, communion, and divine healing. The church has a number of congregations in countries other than the United States.

United Negro College Fund: Provides financial support to HISTORICALLY BLACK COLLEGES and universities. The United Negro College Fund was the brainchild of TUSKEGEE INSTITUTE president Frederick D. Patterson. Like other heads of historically black colleges, Patterson understood the peculiar problems affecting these institutions, particularly fiscal problems. Located throughout the South, these schools educated the overwhelming majority of African American college students before the CIVIL RIGHTS movement of the 1960's and 1970's opened the doors of other schools. They relied upon limited state funds and contributions from alumni and philanthropists. During the Depression of the 1930's and its aftermath, these sources became inadequate as donors reduced their contributions.

Determined to maintain the Tuskegee Institute and other schools as viable centers for educating African American youth, Patterson devised a scheme that he introduced in his weekly column in the *Pittsburgh Courier*, a high-circulation black newspaper. He suggested that funds for black state and private colleges might be solicited from all segments of the population. He reasoned that everyone stood to gain if more African Americans received college degrees. Moreover, he was impressed with the American National Red Cross and the National Foundation for Infantile Paralysis, both of which raised funds through mass appeals.

Patterson convinced the majority of black college heads of the soundness of his plan. To raise money for operating costs, he used the John Price Jones consulting firm of New York City, which assisted him in securing $100,000. Half of that sum was provided by the Rosenwald Fund and the General Education Board, both of which had funded several black education projects. The United Negro College Fund held its opening fund-raiser at the Waldorf Astoria hotel. John D. Rockefeller, Jr.'s generous endorsement started the organization on a sound footing.

The fund selected New York City as the site of its headquarters. In 1944, William J. Trent, a Livingstone College alumnus and holder of an M.B.A. from the Wharton School at the University of Pennsylvania, became the first executive director. Patterson agreed to serve as the first president of the fund even though he was still president of Tuskegee. During its first year, the fund raised $760,000 of its one-million-dollar goal. By 1950, the fund had launched its first capital campaign, with a goal of $25 million. The first $5 million was given by the Rockefeller family.

Although significant numbers of African Americans were attending white colleges as early as the late 1970's, the United Negro College Fund continued to support black colleges and still relied on funding from all segments of the population. One of its most successful fund-raisers has been a series of telethons. The fund became even more successful in providing financial resources to about three dozen historically black institutions, mostly in the South. These institutions were then better able to provide financial aid to deserving students.

United Steelworkers of America v. Weber: U.S. Supreme Court discrimination case in 1979. The case involved a claim by a white employee, Brian Weber, who argued that Kaiser Aluminum and Chemical Corporation discriminated against him by initiating a training program for African Americans to which he was not admitted. Kaiser argued that the program was developed so that black employees could develop the necessary skills to compete for job positions within Kaiser that previously had been restricted to white employees. White employees were eligible for the voluntary training program, but its intent was to help African Americans to compete for the more desirable jobs within Kaiser. Such a voluntary AFFIRMATIVE ACTION plan, not ordered by legislation or by a court, did give preference to black employees, but Kaiser management believed that its own racial discrimination against African Americans in the past justified this preferential treatment. The United Steelworkers of America had agreed to the plan in collective bargaining with Kaiser.

The Court agreed with Kaiser and upheld the voluntary affirmative action plan in a 5-2 ruling that gave employers wide latitude in correcting past discrimination that had led to racial imbalances in their skilled craft work force. The Court's decision revolved around Title VII of the Civil Rights Act of 1964, which prohibited employment discrimination in the private sector, and the 1972 amendment which outlawed discrimination in the public sector as well. The 1964 act created the EQUAL EMPLOYMENT OPPORTUNITY COMMISSION to monitor compliance. Weber argued that Kaiser's plan had violated his rights under this legislation, since he was a contemporary "innocent victim" of past racial discrimination. Justice William Brennan, Jr., noted in his opinion that it would be ironic for the Civil Rights Act to be interpreted as prohibiting a good-faith effort to reverse the effects of past discrimination.

In the aftermath of this case, in a political atmosphere charged with anti-affirmative action protests, Assistant Attorney General William Bradford Reynolds called for test case litigation that would reverse the *Weber* ruling. Reynolds demonstrated his anti-affirmative action stance by forbidding preferential hiring with the Justice Department.

Universal Negro Improvement Association (UNIA): Organization founded by Marcus GARVEY. Garvey, one of the most important figures in African American history, founded the UNIA in 1917 in New York City. A Jamaican immigrant, Garvey intended the UNIA to be the vehicle for realizing his dream of a self-sufficient, powerful

African American community that would liberate Africans worldwide. With that in mind, the UNIA raised funds to establish small businesses in Harlem and elsewhere, started a newspaper, *The Negro World*, and built a huge assembly hall for its meetings and rallies. The UNIA also established the Black Cross Nurses, the AFRICAN ORTHODOX CHURCH, and the Black Star steamship line. At its height, according to Garvey, the UNIA had more than a million members. Although that figure was probably exaggerated, the UNIA unquestionably commanded an enormous amount of support from African American communities and was a major social, political, and economic force. The UNIA's message of race pride, love of Africa, and economic and political self-sufficiency struck a responsive chord among millions of African Americans in the early 1920's.

Unfortunately, the UNIA's reach exceeded its grasp. The organization was unable to gain a foothold on the African continent as a consequence of the hostility of the European powers that still controlled much of Africa. The UNIA was also the target of surveillance and harassment by law-enforcement agencies. Finally, the UNIA and Garvey fell victim to the failure of their major project, the Black Star steamship line. That firm's bankruptcy led to Garvey's prosecution on mail-fraud charges. With its leader convicted and sentenced to federal prison, the UNIA began to die. Its members were able to obtain a commutation of Garvey's sentence, but he was deported to Jamaica. With its charismatic leader gone, the UNIA faded into insignificance in the United States. Garvey was unable to continue the organization in Jamaica and died penniless in London in 1940. Still, during its heyday, the Universal Negro Improvement Association was a shining example of the potential power of the African American community.

Unseld, Westley Sissel "Wes" (b. Mar. 14, 1946, Louisville, Ky.): Basketball player and coach. Unseld began his BASKETBALL career at Louisville's Seneca High School, where he led his team to the Kentucky state championship in the 1962-1963 and 1963-1964 seasons. The first African American to be recruited by the University of Kentucky, he decided to turn that school down to play for its competitor, the University of Louisville, so that his father could watch him play. He set scoring and rebounding records for the Cardinals and was one of only three Louisville players to score more than a thousand points and make more than a thousand rebounds. His great commitment to athletics did not get in his way scholastically, and in 1968 he earned his bachelor's degree in physical education and history. Although he had

planned to become a teacher, Unseld was approached by the Baltimore Bullets of the National Basketball Association (NBA) in 1968 and decided to compete.

The Bullets made Unseld their first draft choice in 1968. For the 1968-1969 season, Unseld was named both Rookie of the Year and NBA Most Valuable Player. Only Wilt CHAMBERLAIN had earned both honors before Unseld. Additionally, Unseld made the All-Rookie Team and All-NBA First Team. A five-time All-Star, Unseld was the Bullets' all-time leader in rebounds and minutes played. He led the Bullets to the NBA championship in the 1977-1978 season, garnering honors as Most Valuable Player in the championship series. He received the first NBA Walter Kennedy Citizenship Award in 1975 for his public service activities in the Washington, D.C., and Baltimore, Md., areas. After his retirement in 1981, Un-

Wes Unseld (left) played thirteen seasons with the Baltimore Bullets. (AP/Wide World Photos)

seld served as vice president of the Capital Center and of the Washington Bullets. He became head coach in January, 1988, and guided the Bullets to the play-offs, where they were eliminated by the Detroit Pistons.

Up from Slavery (1901): Autobiography by Booker T. WASHINGTON. The author tells not only his story but also the story of oppressed people worldwide. He recounts in detail his miserable childhood, his emancipation, his work in a salt furnace and a coal mine at a young age, his longing to learn to read, his education at HAMPTON INSTITUTE, and his teaching there and at TUSKEGEE INSTITUTE. He also recalls his success in public speaking and his trip to Europe.

Uptown Saturday Night (Warner, 1974): Film directed by Sidney POITIER. This popular comedy stars Poitier and Bill COSBY as two friends out on the town for the night without their wives (Rosalind Cash and Kitty Lester). When thieves steal Poitier's wallet, and the valuable lottery ticket inside it, the two men enlist the aid of private eye Richard PRYOR. The film's strong supporting cast includes Harry BELAFONTE as a powerful mobster, Roscoe Lee BROWNE as a politician, Paula Kelly as his wife, and Flip WILSON as "The Reverend."

Upward Bound Program: Provides various forms of assistance to low-income high-school students so that they are able to attend college. The program emphasizes peer counseling and hands-on acquaintance with a college and its faculty and students. Students are selected from urban schools, usually from the inner city, or from rural areas, often very remote, and are then given weekly counseling and tutoring by student advisers at their intended colleges. They also participate in workshops and skill-development programs and are given assistance in

Sidney Poitier (second from right) and Bill Cosby (right) star in the film Uptown Saturday Night. *(The Museum of Modern Art/ Film Stills Archive, NY)*

career planning and counseling. These weekly sessions are conducted throughout the academic year.

For those students who have demonstrated a commitment to the program, the college becomes the site of residence for approximately six weeks during the summer. Students live on campus, usually in the dormitories, and attend classes for which they receive high school credit. Classes typically include writing, math, science, and preparation for the Scholastic Aptitude Test, as well as various electives. Sports and games play a large part in the program, as do field trips and explorations of the immediate and close environments of the campus.

The success of the Upward Bound Program can be measured perhaps by its endurance. Originating in 1964, out of the Economic Opportunity Act that was part of President Lyndon B. Johnson's Great Society, as Johnson's programs sometimes were called by those working to establish reform, it remained in the early

The Upward Bound program prepares low-income rural and inner-city high school students to attend college, with weekly peer counseling and tutoring sessions. (Cleo Freelance Photo)

1990's a popular and respected program. Because the groups of students at each campus tend to be small, usually less than one hundred, and because each campus program is autonomous, bureaucratic problems are avoided. The program is untainted by grandiose promises and unrealistic goals. Few can dispute the wisdom and integrity of a program that furnishes promising young people with a prospect of a future uncontaminated by POVERTY and that allows a glimpse of a life not ordinarily visualized in the inner city or within rural zones of poverty.

Urban Arts Corps: New York theater company. The company's objective is to develop the professional skills of minority writers, performers, and composers. Founded in 1967 by Vinnette CARROLL, the Corps uses a workshop format to create plays, using source material from folktales, the Bible, and Western classic and contemporary literature. The company is best known for its productions of Carroll's plays *DON'T BOTHER ME, I CAN'T COPE* (1972) and *YOUR ARMS TOO SHORT TO BOX WITH GOD* (1975).

Urban Bush Women: New York-based DANCE theater company established in 1984 by Jawole Willa Jo Zollar. The company performs "stage collages" using dance, narrative and imagistic texts, live music, and a cappella singing. Critics and audiences interpret the company's works variously, seeing them as spiritual, political, avant-garde, feminist, or as a fusion of modern and traditional African dance.

Usry, James L. (b. Feb. 2, 1922, Macon, Ga.): Politician. Usry earned the B.A. degree in 1946 from LINCOLN UNIVERSITY in Pennsylvania. He attended graduate school at Glassboro State University in New Jersey. After earning his master's degree, he did further studies at Temple University in Philadelphia.

Usry, a Vietnam veteran, was also a professional athlete who competed with the New York Rens and the HARLEM GLOBETROTTERS. After his basketball career, Usry became active in politics and education in Atlantic City, N.J. His career in education included positions as teacher, principal, and assistant superintendent of schools. He also joined the Board of Education. He was elected mayor of Atlantic City, serving from 1984 until 1990. He has served as a member of university boards and as an active member of political and educational organizations. His awards for public and professional service include the Omega Psi Phi Man of the Year (1986) and the Bob Douglas Hall of Fame (1984).

V

Van Der Zee, James Augustus Joseph (June 29, 1886, Lenox, Mass.—May 15, 1983, Washington, D.C.): Photographer. Van Der Zee is best known for his sensitive photographic portraits of both the celebrities and the common people who enjoyed the heyday of Harlem during its renaissance of the 1920's.

Van Der Zee taught himself the art of photography. He worked as a busboy, waiter, and musician. He married Kate Brown in 1906, and they were divorced in 1914. They had two children, Rachel, who died in 1923, and Emile, who died in 1911. Van Der Zee became a darkroom assistant for Gertz Department Store in Newark,

Highly regarded photographer James Van Der Zee captured a visual record of the Harlem Renaissance. (AP/Wide World Photos)

N.J., in 1915. In 1923, he remarried. He operated his own studio, Guarantee Photos (later GGG Photo Studio), in Harlem from 1916 to 1968. Often sought after to photograph weddings, funerals, and other auspicious occasions, Van Der Zee was the official photographer for Marcus GARVEY's Back to Africa movement. He became well known outside Harlem after his work was featured in the 1967 Metropolitan Museum of Art exhibition *Harlem on My Mind: Cultural Capital of Black America, 1900-1968.*

Van Der Zee's photographs are marked by warmth, grace, and dignity that reflect his sensitivity to his subjects. A man of Harlem himself, he found through his camera's lens the energy and pride of the black community in that city. His portraits are usually posed and capture the deeper, psychological character of his subjects, sometimes with the aid of his skillful air brush and double-printing techniques.

Among his many professional awards are the American Society of Magazine Photographers Award (1969), Life Fellowship at the Metropolitan Museum of Art (1970), the Pierre Toussaint Award for outstanding service to humanity (1978), the International Black Photographers Award (1979), and the Living Legacy Award (1979), presented by President Jimmy Carter. He received honorary doctorates from Seton Hall University in 1976 and from Haverford College (Pennsylvania) in 1980. He died while he was in Washington, D.C., to receive an honorary doctorate from HOWARD UNIVERSITY. The product of his long career as a professional photographer is a visual record of Harlem's most creatively energetic and prosperous era.

Van Peebles, Mario (b. Jan. 15, 1957, Mexico City, Mexico): Actor and director. Van Peebles is the son of Maria, a photographer, and Melvin, the acclaimed independent filmmaker and entrepreneur. During his childhood years, Van Peebles and his two siblings lived in Paris, Morocco, Denmark, San Francisco, and New York City. Besides English, he mastered the Spanish and French languages. Throughout his early life, he assisted his father on film projects, including a brief appearance in the controversial but influential *SWEET SWEETBACK'S BAADASSSSS SONG* (1971). After graduation from Columbia University with a B.A. in economics (1980), Van Peebles supported himself as a budget analyst, film crew assistant, Wall Street office worker, fashion model, and Off-Broadway actor.

Although he was cast as the lead in the low-budget film *Rappin'* (1985), Van Peebles most often played supporting roles in such movies as *Exterminator II* (1984), *Jaws: The Revenge* (1987), and *Heartbreak Ridge* (1986). On television, he achieved greater notice in the role of a pimp in the teleplay *Children of the Night* (1985), for which he won a Bronze Halo Award. He also appeared as attorney Andrew Taylor in *L.A. Law* (1986) and as the title character, a private detective who is a master of disguises, in SONNY SPOON (1988).

The talented actor, director, producer Mario Van Peebles showed Hollywood just how successful projects by African Americans can be. (AP/Wide World Photos)

In 1989, Van Peebles began his directing career in television for such series as *21 Jump Street, Wiseguy, Booker,* and *Gabriel's Fire.* In 1991, he directed his first feature-length film, *New Jack City.* The film, concerning the rise and fall of drug lord Nino Brown (Wesley SNIPES), grossed $23 million and had the distinction of being fifth on the list of all-time box-office hits by black directors.

Van Peebles, Melvin (b. Aug. 21, 1932, Chicago, Ill.): Director, producer, writer, actor, and composer. Van Peebles is credited with being one of the first African Americans to make Hollywood aware of the dollar potential and appeal that black films and filmmakers could have for a large African American audience. After graduating from Ohio Wesleyan University, Van Peebles spent time as a navigator in the United States Air Force. In 1959, while living in Hollywood, Calif., Van Peebles, frustrated because he could not break into the film business, decided to move his family to Holland, where he studied at the University of Amsterdam and acted with the Dutch National Theatre.

He then moved to France but found that breaking into filmmaking in France was no easier than in America. Van Peebles decided that the only way to get into filmmaking was to become a writer. With that determination, he wrote five novels. He used a screenplay adapted from his novel *Story of a Three Day Pass* as a vehicle to take the French Film Center's examination for directors, required for entry into the French directors' union.

Shot on a budget of $200,000, *Story of a Three Day Pass* debuted at the San Francisco International Film Festival in 1967. The film's success prompted critics and the press to call Van Peebles, inaccurately, America's first black film director. Van Peebles capitalized on this attention by directing 1970's WATERMELON MAN for Columbia Pictures.

In 1971, with no studio backing and a modest budget of $500,000, Van Peebles made the celebrated SWEET SWEETBACK'S BAADASSSSS SONG, a radical, political, sexually graphic, and violent picture. Van Peebles found it impossible to get publicity through the channels of the film industry, which had given the film an X rating. Van Peebles decided to market the film directly to the black public himself. He used the communication systems within the black community and word of mouth.

Sweet Sweetback's Baadasssss Song opened in sixty New York theaters and in one hundred fifty other film houses around the country. The extraordinary success of the film caught the interest of the press, and Van Peebles took advantage of the opportunity. He dressed in street styles and used street language to recount his problems as a black man trying to break into the film business and the obstacles he faced getting this particular picture made. The media loved this new black militant, and Hollywood realized that there was an audience of African Americans who would pay to see themselves on screen.

After the success of his film and his rise to fame, Van Peebles put together two Broadway plays, *Ain't Supposed to Die a Natural Death* in 1971 and *Don't Play Us Cheap* in 1972. He made an unsuccessful film version of his 1972 play, then vanished from public sight. In 1976, he surfaced in television as the writer of *Just an Old Sweet Song,* a mild family drama which was very different from his early works. In 1981, he wrote another television drama, *Sophisticated Gents,* which addressed the concerns of blacks trying to achieve in white society.

Vandross, Luther (b. Apr. 20, 1951, New York, N.Y.): Singer. Vandross was the champion of the love song for black America in the 1980's. No other male vocalist of the decade compiled such a wealth of achievements as a balladeer. As well as being a singer, Vandross wrote and produced some of the most moving vocal performances of the period.

Singer Luther Vandross displays his American Music Award. (AP/Wide World Photos)

Vandross grew up in the Alfred E. Smith housing projects at the Manhattan base of the Brooklyn Bridge. His mother, Mary Ida Vandross, started him on the piano at age three. Music surrounded him as a child, and he absorbed much of it. His sister Pat was a member of a DOO-WOP group, the Crests, in the late 1950's. In-house rehearsals formed much of the musical atmosphere that influenced Vandross. Along with the Crests, he cites Dionne WARWICK, Aretha FRANKLIN, and Diana ROSS as major early influences on his musical sensibilities.

Vandross spent one year at Western Michigan University but realized quickly that his calling was music. His earliest forays into the business were arranging music for *THE WIZ* and for David Bowie's *Young Americans*. After this informal introduction to the industry, he spent time singing jingles. Vandross was the voice for Kentucky Fried Chicken, Seven-Up, Burger King, and other large corporations. From jingles, he went to singing backup in studios, working with performers as diverse as the Average White Band, Chaka KAHN, Roberta FLACK, and Ringo Starr.

He took his material to Epic records in 1981. The result was two Grammy nominations and his first million seller, *Never Too Much*. Subsequent releases on Epic, *Forever, for Always, for Love*; *Busy Body*; and *The Night I Fell in Love*, brought more success and recognition. As a male performer with female influences, he attained the soft tone which is his signature. Known across the country simply as "Luther," he occupies his own space in the hearts of the African American music community.

Vanity (Denise Matthews; b. 1958, Niagara Falls, Ontario, Canada): Singer and actress. At the age of seventeen, Vanity left home to seek a career in the entertainment industry. In 1979, while serving as a model at the American Music Awards, Matthews met PRINCE Rogers Nelson, the young superstar-in-the-making, who was immediately taken with Matthews' beauty and charm. Shortly afterward, the roguish Prince passed her a note asking her to meet him in the ladies' room backstage. After some small talk and playful banter, they entered into an arrangement which would bring Matthews the fame she sought. Prince had Matthews change her name to Vanity because

Her mentor Prince introduced Vanity to the music world as a recording artist. (Oggie Ogburn)

he thought of her as the mirror in which he saw himself. He then surrounded her with two other beautiful and talented women, Susan Moonsie and Brenda Bennett, dressed the three in camisoles, and billed them as a vocal trio, Vanity 6.

Vanity 6 released its self-titled debut on Warner Bros. in 1982. The single "Nasty Girl," with its suggestive and provocative lyrics, peaked at number seven on the RHYTHM-AND-BLUES charts. In 1983, Vanity 6 toured the country with Prince during his "1999 Tour." They were backed musically by another of Prince's protégés, The Time.

Once the tour was over, Vanity, long rumored to have been a paramour of Prince, left the fold and began cultivating an acting career. She also became a solo act and signed with Motown Records, which released her first solo recording, *Wild Animal*. Two singles, "Pretty Mess" and "Mechanical Emotion," each reached the top twenty-five on the rhythm-and-blues charts in 1984. Another Motown release, *Skin on Skin*, produced the single "Under the Influence," which reached the number-nine spot in 1986.

Vanity has appeared in a number of motion pictures and television programs since her departure from Vanity 6. After her debut in 1985's *The Last Dragon*, Vanity was featured in *Fifty-two Pick-up* (1986) and *Never Too Young to Die* (1986). She costarred with Carl WEATHERS in *Action Jackson* in 1988. She has also appeared on the television serials *Miami Vice* and *The New Mike Hammer*.

Vaughan, Sarah (Mar. 27, 1924, Newark, N.J.—Apr. 3, 1990, Los Angeles, Calif.): Jazz singer. Vaughan received her first musical training as a choir member of Mount Zion Baptist Church, where, at the age of twelve, she became an organist. In 1942, she won an amateur contest at Harlem's famed APOLLO THEATER. This led to an engagement with Earl HINES's big band as a pianist and

Sarah Vaughan was described by singer Tony Bennett as "the greatest in the world." (AP/Wide World Photos)

singer. This affiliation led to her association with singer and bandleader Billy ECKSTINE, whose orchestra she joined. She first recorded with the orchestra in 1944.

Vaughan's associations with instrumentalists were not limited to big bands and orchestras. She frequently sang with BEBOP musicians of the era. Her recording of "Lover Man" established her as a jazz singer of the highest order. She recorded with Dizzy GILLESPIE and with John Kirby in the 1940's. Most of her subsequent work was as a soloist, performing and touring with small groups. She became known as a singer who used her voice as another instrument, not simply as a vehicle for words or sentiments. Her contralto voice, with its extraordinary range and timbre, seemed receptive to every kind of musical statement. She could, and did, record popular, more commercial tunes. She also performed and recorded jazz with such important musicians as trumpeter Clifford BROWN and saxophonist Cannonball ADDERLEY. She recorded numerous songs by Duke ELLINGTON and by George Gershwin. She won a 1982 Grammy Award for best female jazz vocal performance for her album *Gershwin Live!*

Vaughan's tours were always marked by enthusiastic audiences, with crowds cheering her splendid style and a musicianship that brought to each work a dynamic unsurpassed by other performers. Usually accompanied by a trio of piano, double bass, and drums, she unfolded to both new and experienced audiences the wonders of her versatility. Occasionally, she would perform with a symphony orchestra or a big band, but her preference seemed to reside in small combos, in which each musician is allowed the freest sort of range of expression.

Vereen, Ben (b. Oct. 10, 1946, Miami, Fla.): Singer, dancer, and actor. Vereen is best known for his singing and dancing career on stage and in nightclub appearances. Vereen, also a gifted actor, has garnered many awards for drama, including the Television Critics Award for his inspiring role of Chicken George in the landmark television miniseries *Roots* (1977).

Vereen's stage career began in 1965 with an appearance in the play *The Prodigal Son*. He went on to other performances in *Sweet Charity* (1966-1968), *Golden Boy* (1968), *Hair* (1968-1969), *Jesus Christ Superstar* (1971), *Pippin* (1972), and *Cabaret* and *Grind* (1975).

Vereen dazzled television audiences with his portrayal of Chicken George in the television adaptation of Alex HALEY's epic novel *Roots* (1976). He was given the Image Award by the NATIONAL ASSOCIATION FOR THE ADVANCEMENT OF COLORED PEOPLE in 1977 and 1978 for his portrayal of this character. Following *Roots*, Vereen had a

television special entitled *Ben Vereen: His Roots*, which aired in 1978. This entertaining show featured the many talents of Vereen as well as guest celebrities. It was honored with seven Emmy Awards in 1978. Other television appearances by Vereen included the role of Tenspeed in the ABC series *TENSPEED AND BROWN SHOE* in 1980 and appearances in the situation comedy *Webster* and the acclaimed children's series *Fairie Tale Theatre*. He was also featured in the television movie *Louis ARMSTRONG: Chicago Style* (1976).

All-around entertainer Ben Vereen portrayed Chicken George in the television miniseries Roots. *(AP/Wide World Photos)*

Vereen's influence extends beyond the entertainment arena, as evidenced by his involvement as celebrity spokesperson for the organizations Big Brothers and A Drug-Free America. He was the recipient of a Humanitarian Award from the state of Israel in 1975 and also received the Eleanor Roosevelt Humanitarian Award in 1978.

Honors for his entertainment talents include the Theatre World Award for *Jesus Christ Superstar* and a Tony Award, Drama Desk Award, and CLIO Award for *Pippin*. He was honored with a Cultural Award from Israel for his participation in *Roots*. Vereen has shared his talents worldwide through nightclub appearances in England, France, Monaco, Hong Kong, Portugal, and mainland China.

Verrett, Shirley (b. May 31, 1933, New Orleans, La.): Opera singer. This mezzo soprano studied at Ventura College in California and at the Juilliard School of Music. One of the most successful African Americans in opera, Verrett made her debut at the Metropolitan Opera House in 1968 in the role of Carmen. During the 1976-1977 season alone, she sang seventeen performances at the Met, including the opening night in *Il Travatore*. She has also sung in European opera houses, including Covent Garden (London) and Teatro Licero (Barcelona).

Vesey, Denmark (c. 1767—July 2, 1822, Charleston, S.C.): Slave insurrectionist. In 1822, Denmark Vesey, a free black carpenter, plotted a slave revolt in Charleston, S.C., that would have led to the largest such rebellion in American history. Local officials, uncovering and suppressing the conspiracy at the last moment, were deeply shaken by it and soon implemented policies that strengthened their commitment to preserve SLAVERY.

Biographical Background. Denmark Vesey was born about 1767, either in Africa or on the Caribbean island of St. Thomas. By 1781, he lived on St. Thomas, where he was purchased by a Bermuda slave trader named Joseph Vesey, who was impressed with Denmark's appearance and intelligence. Transported immediately to the booming French sugar colony of St. Domingue and sold to a planter, Denmark Vesey faced a short life of relentless labor in the cane fields and refineries. Denmark, though, was soon found unfit to labor because he showed signs of epilepsy, and Captain Vesey was required by law to buy him back a year later.

Denmark then became a hand on Vesey's ship and began a long relationship with the slavetrader. He worked alongside sailors of various nationalities and visited numerous ports in the West Indies, experiences that doubtless contributed to his facility with several languages, including English, French, Dutch, and Spanish. During this period, he also probably accompanied the captain to the west coast of Africa to buy Africans and became familiar with all aspects of the infamous Atlantic SLAVE TRADE. By 1783, when Captain Vesey decided to settle in Charleston as a slave merchant, there was little about the brutal slave world of the Caribbean to which the mobile Denmark had not been exposed.

Opportunities for slave merchandising, however, were not then good in South Carolina, as commerce slowed after the American Revolution and the state restricted trade in slaves. Captain Vesey soon shifted to the ship supply business, in which he appears to have remained for the balance of the century. Throughout this time, Denmark continued with him as his slave.

After a slave revolt exploded in St. Domingue in 1793 and led to the creation in 1804 of independent Haiti, many French colonials and their slaves fled the tumult and sought asylum at ports in the Caribbean and the southern United States. In Charleston, Joseph Vesey helped form a society to assist the beleaguered emigrants, giving Denmark many opportunities to talk with slaves who had witnessed or been directly involved in the uprising. The vision of slaves rising successfully against their overlords was vividly impressed upon him, and he would repeatedly use the example of Haiti to rally his recruits in 1822.

Depiction of Africans being held in stockades before shipment to the New World. After purchasing his own freedom, Denmark Vesey encouraged slave revolts. (The Associated Publishers, Inc.)

In 1800, Denmark's long servitude came to a startling end: He won fifteen hundred dollars in a local lottery, bought his freedom, and opened a carpenter's shop with the balance. Denmark then became one of the hundreds of free blacks in Charleston, and in the following years, his industriousness allowed him to become a homeowner, gain financial security, marry several times, and have numerous children.

Denmark Vesey's Conspiracy. Vesey's hatred of slavery and of the sway whites held over the lives of blacks appears only to have grown after his MANUMISSION. In 1817, Morris Brown and other black associates formed a Charleston branch of the AFRICAN METHODIST EPISCOPAL CHURCH after having become angered over local white METHODISTS' mounting efforts to curtail the black congregants' liberty to supervise their religious affairs. By late 1817, more than four thousand blacks had left the white churches and joined Brown's. Local authorities, threatened by this symbol of black autonomy, regularly harassed the church and intended to close it, but by early 1822 had still not succeeded.

First thoughts of revolt began with the bitter resentment this harassment engendered. Of the seventy-one individuals involved in the plot for whom trial transcripts remain, thirty-six were members of what was called the African church. Among the inner circle of conspirators, most members, including Vesey, had been class leaders in the church. The right to independence in churches and in biblical interpretations was critical to the members, and their church soon became a focal point of the conspiracy. In the latter stages of organizing, religious classes were used to disseminate information and biblical doctrines favorable to revolt. Vesey used his fervent faith in Christianity and its democratic tenets, such as the essential equality of all before God, to excoriate the slavery that prevented blacks from exercising freedom and dignity and to defend a revolt against such a devilish institution.

The most active phase of organizing for the rebellion began in late December, 1821, and continued through June, 1822. Fearing spies and traitors, Vesey gathered around him a small core of conspirators in whom he had complete trust: Peter Poyas; "Gullah" Jack Pritchard; Ned, Rolla, and Batteau Bennett; Mingo Harth; and Monday Gell. All were skilled slaves who were trusted by their owners and allowed to hire out their own time: So long as they regularly paid a large portion of their wages to their owners, they were at liberty to rent their own quarters and come and go as they chose. Vesey deliberately chose them because they had the mobility to recruit blacks throughout Charleston and the surrounding countryside without arousing the suspicions of their trusting masters. Some blacks whom Vesey believed could become zealous rebels at first feared joining the conspiracy, but he inspired them with rumors, threats, and his ferocious hatred of subservience.

Enlisting Black Support. It is difficult to estimate how many blacks may have been involved in the plot, but within Charleston itself, well more than one hundred probably figured into the scheme by its latter stages. Vesey enlisted teamsters and stablers who had access to large numbers of horses, blacksmiths who could make knives and swords, and others who worked in shops from which powder, shot, and guns could be stolen. A select few, including Vesey and "Gullah" Jack, recruited far into the countryside, where Jack claimed he had spoken to more than six thousand slaves. The date originally set for the uprising was the moonless night of Monday, July 15, by which time many whites had left town for summer homes on Sullivan's Island or in the cooler piedmont to the west. The date was moved forward to Sunday, June 16, by early June, after Vesey realized a slave had revealed the plot. Sunday was also selected because hundreds of slaves from the countryside routinely came into Charleston on that day to sell in the marketplace, and the conspirators thus would not create suspicion by concentrating themselves in the city.

Phalanxes of slaves—many from rural parishes—led by Vesey and his closest associates were to mass at various points around the city and attack it, some seizing strategic bridges, some setting fires, and others taking poorly guarded arsenals. Banking on surprise, the rebels planned to kill many whites as they emerged confused from their houses to battle fires. No whites were to be spared. The rebels believed that as they realized initial successes, many more blacks would take heart and assist them. Vesey also claimed that President Jean-Pierre Boyer of Haiti would send boats and troops to help the rebels and to evacuate them by sea if necessary. By early June, Vesey's plan was neatly in place and, if executed correctly, would have devastated Charleston.

Despite initial doubts about the rumored plot, however, white officials resumed suspicion after securing the confession of a lesser conspirator on June 8; the local militia was thus out in force on the planned evening of attack. Vesey had to cancel the attack, and within days, he and his closest allies were arrested. They were summarily tried and were hanged on July 2. Among them, only Monday Gell confessed; the balance died without saying anything of the plan. A proposed raid to rescue Vesey and the others from the gallows never occurred, but black mourners throughout Charleston risked wearing sackcloth and black crepe to show sympathy for the executed. Arrests, trials, and hangings extended into August and kept the town anxious for weeks. By the end, of the 131 suspected conspirators arrested and tried, thirty-five were executed, forty-three deported, and fifty-three acquitted.

Repercussions. The effects of the extensive conspiracy reverberated through Charleston and southern society for years to come. A rewritten slave code placed new restrictions on blacks, and the plot was used to justify razing the African church. Many whites, especially artisans, unsuccessfully demanded the removal or reduction of the free black population and their confinement to the most menial labor. The most foreboding action, however, was the passage in December, 1822, by the South Carolina legislature of the Negro Seamen's Act. The act was intended to prevent potentially subversive contact between local blacks and alien ones by requiring all ship captains entering Charleston's harbor to place any black mariners onboard in the local jail until the ship's departure. As many vessels, especially American and British, employed large numbers of black sailors, the act sparked an immediate controversy. Although the law violated Congress' right to regulate trade and was found unconstitutional in 1823, the act continued to be enforced by the state and became South Carolina's first act of nullification, setting it on its course toward civil war. The fear Denmark Vesey generated thus helped fuel the conflict between the states that led to the elimination of the slavery he detested so deeply.—*Peter P. Hinks*

SUGGESTED READINGS: • Freehling, William W. "Denmark Vesey's Peculiar Reality." In *New Perspectives on Race and Slavery in America: Essays in Honor of Kenneth M. Stampp*, edited by Robert H. Abzug and Stephen e. Maizlish. Lexington: University of Kentucky Press, 1986. • Freehling, William W. *Prelude to Civil War: The Nullification Controversy in South Carolina, 1818-1836*. New York: Harper & Row, 1966. • Lofton, John. *Insurrection in South Carolina: The Turbulent World of Denmark Vesey*. Yellow Springs, Ohio: Antioch Press, 1964. • Starobin, Robert S., ed. *Denmark Vesey: The Slave Conspiracy of 1822*. Englewood Cliffs, N.J.: Prentice-Hall, 1970. • Wade, Richard C. "The Vesey Plot: A Reconsideration." *Journal of Southern History* 30 (May, 1964): 148-161. • Wikramanayake, Marina. *A World in Shadow: The Free Black in Antebellum South Carolina*. Columbia: University of South Carolina Press, 1973.

Vietnam War and African Americans, The: The U.S. war in Vietnam officially began in August, 1964, and rapidly developed into extensive ground fighting with Viet Cong guerrillas, a contest that the U.S. forces and their South Vietnamese allies would eventually lose. During this period of heightened U.S. involvement in Southeast Asia, one out of seven U.S. troops stationed in the region was an African American.

Ultimately, Vietnam became the most unpopular war in U.S. history. Polls indicated that the majority of African Americans came to oppose the war by 1969, significantly earlier than the white majority.

Racism in the Vietnam-Era Military. African Americans serving in Vietnam worked under a military command structure that was disproportionately white and southern. Blacks were overrepresented in numbers among both enlisted and drafted soldiers, yet only 3 percent of the Army's officers were black. In 1967, blacks made up almost 10 percent of U.S. Marines but constituted less than 1 percent of Marine Corps officers. It was clear that, despite the official desegregation of the U.S. armed forces ordered in 1948, discriminatory structures remained. In Vietnam, this eventually produced destructive racial conflicts as well as profound changes in African American perceptions of the military.

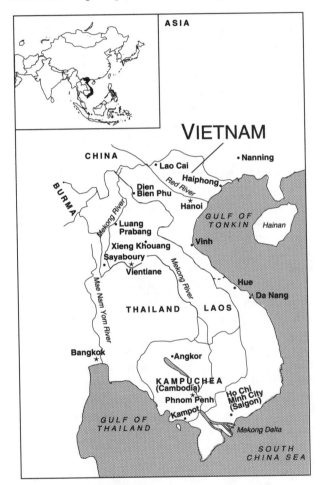

In mid-1966, the Defense Department devised "Project 100,000" to decrease the high rejection rate of African American enlistment applicants. Declaring that increased black enlistment would "rehabilitate" poor urban blacks and return them to society with socially useful skills, the military lowered induction standards and initiated special training programs.

This recruitment strategy, which coincided with the escalation of ground hostilities against the Vietnamese, succeeded in swelling the pool of recruits by approximately 340,000 during the 1966-1968 period. More than 40 percent of these recruits were African Americans. Many of the training programs envisioned by Project 100,000 subsequently folded under fiscal pressures, while the program's recruits became stigmatized as inferior, and many were given extensive combat duties.

By all accounts, black troops stationed in Southeast Asia achieved an extraordinary degree of racial consciousness. Some even formed underground organizations within the military dedicated to the defense of black troops against racist white officers.

Open Hostility. Open racial conflict was not uncommon in Vietnam, and many white officers accused blacks of disloyalty. By 1968, senior military officers were describing racial tensions as a serious and explosive problem. Field commanders frequently sought to restrict all symbols associated with BLACK NATIONALISM. Predictably, this only elevated tensions further, and by the late 1960's, virtual race riots were occurring in the Army. By 1972, the Navy experienced similar conditions.

At its worst, a fear developed among white officers that blacks would shoot at them instead of the enemy. The specter of "fragging,"—attacks on officers in the field by their own troops, usually by grenades—took on ominous racial overtones by 1972. Some 788 fully documented cases of fragging occurred during the war, a substantial percentage of which were suspected to be racially motivated. Official sources conceded that the actual number was probably much higher.

Discriminatory Practices. White officers, in turn, responded with behaviors ranging from verbal harassment and discrimination in military housing to unfair assignment in dangerous military missions. When ensuing disputes resulted in court martials, the military justice system mirrored its civilian counterpart by inflicting identifiable patterns of discrimination upon African Americans. An internal Defense Department study in 1972 concluded that blacks convicted of offenses during active service were receiving substantially harsher sentences than white offenders convicted of similar crimes.

A 1971 CONGRESSIONAL BLACK CAUCUS study found that more than half of those in military detention were African Americans. A NATIONAL ASSOCIATION FOR THE ADVANCEMENT OF COLORED PEOPLE (NAACP) report concluded that whites were twice as likely as blacks to be released without punishment for a first offense and that blacks received almost half of all dishonorable Army discharges. A separate study conducted by the NATIONAL URBAN LEAGUE uncovered similar discriminatory discharge patterns in the Air Force.

Many dishonorable discharges of African Americans were based on inconclusive evidence and yet went uncontested because of black distrust of white military lawyers and lack of legal awareness. The data was so conclusive on this point that by 1973 the EQUAL EMPLOYMENT OPPORTUNITY COMMISSION ruled that employers who required Vietnam veterans to have honorable discharges were engaging in racial discrimination.

Race and Casualties. In Vietnam, blacks died in numbers significantly higher than the black percentage of the U.S. population would have predicted. According to independent analyses of government sources, the "Black Belt" of the old plantation South and the coastal Carolinas stood among the areas with the highest relative percentages of black losses. Some analysts concluded that blacks constituted nearly one-quarter of all U.S. casualties in 1965; the percentage dropped after the disproportionate victimization of black troops became widely publicized.

Defense Department reporting procedures presented significant problems for constructing a precise racial analysis of Vietnam casualties. It has been established, however, that measures were eventually taken by the Pentagon to reduce combat exposure of black troops and to avert the potentially explosive implications of a high black casualty rate.

Far from ending with the war, this controversy became part of the "Vietnam syndrome" and returned to haunt the Defense Department during the subsequent 1991 Gulf War. As troops were sent to the Persian Gulf combat theater, blacks accounted for about one-fourth of the total forces. This produced a determined African American opposition to involvement in a bloody ground war like the fighting in Vietnam.

Black Opposition to the Vietnam War. Most African Americans initially supported the war, as did the majority of U.S. citizens as a whole. It was not until 1969 that a national poll appeared in *Newsweek* magazine indicating that 56 percent of African Americans opposed the war in Vietnam. A later Gallup Poll in the spring of 1971 showed that 83 percent of African Americans (compared to 67 percent of whites) believed that U.S. intervention in Vietnam was a mistake from the beginning.

As late as 1966, however, polls showed that only 35 percent of African Americans opposed U.S. involvement in Vietnam. While this total represented a substantial opposition relative to the larger population, it nevertheless created controversy within the African American community. The community's strong support for the war effort during the early years revealed the established tendency to see military participation as beneficial to career mobility. A 1965 survey indicated that approxi-

A youth burns his draft card during a Vietnam War protest near the Dallas draft board. (AP/Wide World Photos)

mately 40 percent of African Americans in the armed services had enlisted to increase their career opportunities, roughly twice the figure reported for whites. The growth of antiwar sentiment within the CIVIL RIGHTS movement, however, eventually helped to build a critical awareness toward U.S. interventionism.

By mid-1965, activists of the STUDENT NONVIOLENT COORDINATING COMMITTEE (SNCC) began vigorously opposing the "white man's war" in Vietnam, and in January, 1966, SNCC became the first civil rights organization to denounce the war officially. Later the same year, the Georgia legislature attempted to deny Julian BOND his elected seat as a state representative after he publicly declared his opposition to the war. Bond was later ordered seated by the courts.

Influential Pacifists. Martin Luther KING, JR., a committed pacifist, opposed U.S. military involvement in Vietnam on moral grounds. Throughout 1965, King attempted to convince the leadership of the Civil Rights movement to take a strong antiwar stand. Many movement leaders remained reluctant, however, believing that such a stand would seem unpatriotic and result in an uncontrollable backlash.

In January, 1966, King could no longer hold back his views, and he issued a scathing attack on the war, denouncing it as disastrous for the African American community. Although King was forced to declare his position strictly as an individual, his influence had a dramatic impact, and the SOUTHERN CHRISTIAN LEADERSHIP CONFERENCE issued its formal endorsement of King's antiwar stand later that spring. King made his most famous antiwar speech at New York's Riverside Church on Apr. 4, 1967, just days before he led a massive antiwar rally in New York City. His principled stand against military destruction in Vietnam had profound echoes throughout the African American community.

Also influential as a voice of African American dissent was heavyweight boxer Muhammad ALI, a member of the NATION OF ISLAM. Ali openly opposed the Vietnam War in 1966 and asserted that he "had no quarrel" with the Viet Cong. Following his public antiwar statements, Ali's draft status was reclassified, and he was ordered to report for active service.

Ali steadfastly refused induction, claiming exemption from the draft based on his Muslim beliefs. The courts rejected his case, and he was convicted of draft evasion, stripped of his championship title, and sentenced to five years' imprisonment (his conviction was later overturned by the U.S. Supreme Court). Ali's principled refusal to serve in the armed forces dramatically affected the African American community, and Ali emerged a hero to dissenting youth of all races who opposed the draft.—*Richard A. Dello Buono*

SUGGESTED READINGS: • Baskir, Lawrence M., and William A. Strauss. *Chance and Circumstances: The Draft, the War, and the Vietnam Generation.* New York: Alfred A. Knopf, 1978. • Harris, Norman. *Connecting Times: The Sixties in Afro-American Fiction.* Jackson: University Press of Mississippi, 1988. • Kolko, Gabriel. *Anatomy of a War: Vietnam, the United States, and the Modern Historical Experience.* New York: Pantheon Books, 1985. • Schuyler, Philippa. *Good Men Die.* New York: Twin Circle Publishing Company, 1969. • Taylor, Clyde, comp. *Vietnam and Black America: An Anthology of Protest and Resistance.* Garden City, N.Y.: Anchor Press, 1973.

Vincent, Edward (b. June 23, 1934, Stubenville, Ohio): Politician. Vincent received a B.A. in politics and government from the California State University at Los Angeles. His long-standing interest in civic and political affairs led to work with community organizations on a variety of issues. He entered local politics as a member of the school board and the city council of Inglewood, Calif., and was elected mayor in 1986.

Vincent, Marjorie (b. Nov. 21, 1964, Chicago, Ill.): Crowned Miss America in 1991. A third-year law student

Chicago's Marjorie Vincent was crowned Miss America in 1991. (AP/Wide World Photos)

at Duke University at the time, she competed as the Miss Illinois contestant. In addition to her academic achievements, Vincent is an accomplished classical pianist and is fluent in French and CREOLE. The focus during her reign was on issues of battered women.

Visions for Black Men (1991): Nonfiction work by Na'im Akbar. The book centers on the plight of African American males growing up in a racist society, their transition form boyhood to manhood, and their self-knowledge and self-mastery. Akbar stresses the importance of education, self-evaluation, and self-definition in order to achieve effective change, as well as the positive role that parents can play by taking charge of their children's lives.

Visual Arts: African Americans have made significant contributions to visual arts in areas such as painting, illustration, sculpture, photography, film direction/ cinematography, and fashion design. The long histories of African Americans in the various visual arts share some common attributes, including an Afrocentric orientation in black folk culture creations, use of African motifs and themes in modern styles, and adaptations of Eurocentric artistic ideals. A special relationship to ancestors, community, and nature as well as an affinity for decoration and design are some of the recurrent themes in African American visual arts.

During the slave years and into the postcolonial period, African Americans gave their personal signatures to a wide variety of utilitarian arts and crafts. In the eighteenth and nineteenth centuries, black people in the Americas established themselves in the more Eurocentric genres of portraiture and landscape painting. The HARLEM RENAISSANCE years and the 1960's showed a return to an Afrocentric emphasis amid social and political concerns. Achievements in the visual arts of film direction and cinematography began in the early part of the twentieth century, resurfaced strongly in the 1960's and 1970's, and exploded into mainstream prominence in the 1980's and 1990's, exposing African American culture and themes to a wider audience.

Retentions from Africa. Africans were first brought to the New World in the early sixteenth century. In 1619, a Dutch slave ship arrived in Jamestown, Va. The visual art creations of the first black people in the Americas expressed both a private and a public aspect. African retentions can be seen in the hoodoo fetishes, quilts, canes and staffs, dolls, pottery, shells, beads, bone carvings, and gravestones of this early colonial period. The use of woven and painted material in clothing and house decorations suggests West and Central African motifs as well

as establishing a unique fashion in adaptations of black dress that survived through the twentieth century world of fashion.

In the public sphere, African Americans were known to be excellent gold- and silversmiths, stoneware crafters, cabinetmakers, printers, engravers, and ironworkers who often incorporated aspects of African architectural and decorative techniques into their creations. The grotesque "monkey pots," or water jugs, created by slaves serve as one example. Many old buildings in Louisiana, South Carolina, and Georgia contain elements of African design. The African House (1750) on the Metoyer Estate in Louisiana reflects the architectural design found in a West African village. Likewise, Thomas Day, a free black slaveholder, was a noted cabinetmaker during the early 1800's who utilized African designs in his work. A slave named Henry Gudgell carved a number of walking sticks in the 1800's that boast designs closely linked to African creations.

Early Painters. The first professional African American artists, both free and slave, were portrait painters. Scipio MOORHEAD was a slave painter active in Boston, Mass., in the 1770's. There are no known survivals of his work. Phillis WHEATLEY, America's first black poet, dedicated a poem "to S.M., an African painter," probably referring to Moorhead. Neptune Thurston of Rhode Island was a slave known to have painted portraits around 1775. He may have influenced Gilbert Stuart, the famous painter of George Washington. The Reverend G. W. Hobbs, a former slave living in Baltimore, Md., painted the first known portrait pastel of another black person, in 1785.

The first authenticated African American artist was Joshua JOHNSTON. Born a slave in Baltimore, he is listed in that city's directories between 1796 and 1824 as a free householder who painted white society portraits such as *Young Lady on a Red Sofa* (c. 1810) in the style of Charles Peale. His *Portrait of a Cleric* (1805) depicts a black man. Julien Hudson was a free black portraitist active in the 1830's and 1840's whose *Self Portrait* (1839) is one of the first known self portraits by an African American.

Throughout the early and mid-1800's, a number of free black artists associated themselves with the abolitionist movement. Robert Douglas, Jr. (1809-1887) was the first black person to attend the Pennsylvania Academy of Fine Arts, America's oldest art school. He created a lithographic portrait of William Lloyd Garrison and was one of the first black artists to choose European exile. Patrick Henry Reason was a Philadelphia engraver who created the emblem of the British antislavery movement, depicting a chained slave in *Am I Not a Man and a Brother?*

His companion piece, *Am I Not a Woman and a Sister?*, shows his concern for the denial of rights of black women. His *Portrait of Henry Bibb* (1840) suggests a familiarity with photography, which had been brought to the United States from Europe only recently. One of the first Americans to use photography was Jules Lion, a mulatto artist who introduced the daguerreotype to New Orleans, La., in 1840 or earlier. Lion is noted for his portrait of the famous mulatto naturalist and artist John James Audubon, who was one of the greatest American painters of the natural world. Other painters of this era included David Bostill Bowser, who painted a portrait of Abraham Lincoln as well as marine landscapes that focus on personal impressions. A. B. Wilson was a self-taught painter who

canson was a master of atmospheric and pastoral elements. Listed in the Cincinnati, Ohio, directory as a daguerreotypist, Duncanson was associated with J. P. Ball, a black photographer who started taking pictures in 1845. His wide aerial perspective used in *View of Cincinnati* (c. 1852) suggests a camera angle and is one of the few surviving examples of an early American cityscape. Duncanson traveled to Europe a number of times and rendered several classical versions of the ruins of Pompeii. His painting *Uncle Tom and Little Eva* (1853) was inspired by the antislavery novel *Uncle Tom's Cabin: Or, Life Among the Lowly* (1852) and suggests his social conscience. Duncanson helped dispel the myth of black intellectual inferiority in the fine arts. His late landscapes

After Church, *by Romare Bearden.* (National Archives)

lived in Philadelphia and created a lithographic portrait of the Reverend John Cornish in 1840. William Simpson was listed in the Boston, Mass., directories (1860-1866) as a portrait painter. He is known for his Loguen portraits (1835) of Bishop Loguen and his wife Caroline, a fugitive slave.

Robert Duncanson was the first African American landscape painter to receive widespread recognition in the United States and abroad. Influenced by Thomas Cole and Asher B. Durand of the Hudson River school, Dun-

combined elements of naturalism with romantic fantasy, resulting in a unique style.

Edward Mitchell Bannister studied under noted sculptor William Rimmer. Considered to be the first black American regionalist painter, Bannister produced his first commissioned work, *The Ship Outward Bound*, in 1855. He won the bronze medal for painting at the Philadelphia Centennial Exposition (1876) for *Under the Oaks* (now lost) but was refused entry into the exhibit because of his color. Bannister painted atmospheric landscapes reminiscent of the Dutch masters and the Barbizon school, witnessed in such paintings as *Driving Home the Cows* (1881) and *Approaching Storm* (1886). It is reputed that Bannister painted to disprove a statement published in the *New York Herald* in 1867 that said "the Negro seems to have an appreciation for art, while being manifestly unable to produce it." Bannister was founder of the Providence Art Club, which later became the Rhode Island School of Design.

Early Sculptors. Eugene WARBOURG was a sculptor from New Orleans, La., who departed to Europe in the 1850's. His only existing sculpture is a portrait bust of John Young Mason (c. 1853). Edmonia LEWIS was one of the few women and the only black women represented at the Philadelphia Centennial Exposition. *The Dying Cleopatra* (c. 1876), a marble work in the neoclassical tradition, depicted the beauty of African people and won an award. As the first major African American woman sculptor, Lewis was also one of the first black women to attend OBERLIN COLLEGE. She strongly expressed African American and humanistic themes in her work. *Forever Free* (1867) shows two slave figures on the day of emancipation. Lewis, who was part Native American, was a visionary artist who foreshadowed many of the themes of racial injustice and black pride that were to reemerge in the 1920's, 1930's, and 1960's.

Painters of the Late 1800's. Grafton Tyler Brown was a lithographer, painter, and itinerant artist who probably was the first black artist to work in California, where he did many early views of San Francisco. As a member of a geological survey party in the West, Brown witnessed many natural wonders that he later depicted in paintings such as *Grand Canyon of the Yellowstone* (1891).

Henry Ossawa TANNER was the second black person to study at the Pennsylvania Academy of Fine Arts, where he worked under Thomas Eakins. Tanner taught at Clark College in Atlanta, Ga., and also was a photographer in that city. In 1891, Tanner studied with Benjamin Constant in Paris, painting landscapes before returning to the United States in 1892. His *The Banjo Lesson* (1893) is one of the most famous early African American genre paintings. Depicting an old man with a young boy on his knee strumming a banjo, the painting expresses a sense of continuity and tradition in African American culture. Tanner returned to Paris, where he painted a series of religious subjects such as *Two Disciples at the Tomb* (1906), *The Three Marys* (1910), and *Daniel in the Lions' Den* (c. 1916) that secured his reputation as a master of modern religious painting. Recognized both in the United States and abroad, Tanner was elected to the French National Academy. He remained an expatriate because

of racial prejudice. His romantic religious paintings, while extending an academic style, rejected modernism and failed to develop black themes in a distinctive African American way.

Other important artists of the period include William A. HARPER, a pupil of Tanner who died at the age of thirty-seven while traveling in Mexico, was primarily a landscape painter rooted in the Barbizon school, as witnessed in such paintings as *Autumn Landscape* (c. 1900-1910) and *Early Afternoon at Montigny* (1905). James V. Herring founded the art department at HOWARD UNIVERSITY in 1930 and organized the first major black-run art gallery. His work, for example *Campus Landscape* (1924), shows the influence of French Impressionism in line and color.

Sculptors of the Late 1800's and Early 1900's. Meta Vaux Warrick FULLER and May Howard JACKSON were two black female SCULPTORS who initiated black themes that pointed the way to the Harlem Renaissance. Fuller studied in Paris and was influenced by Rodin. Sculptures such as *The Wretched* (1903), *Waterboy* (1914), and *The Awakening of Ethiopia* (1914) were neoclassical in origin yet influenced by an emotional impressionism. Jackson rejected European themes and stressed in all of her work a deep concern with African American social problems. Her *Head of a Negro Child* (1916) is a fine example of her work, infused with dignity and hope.

Harlem Renaissance. During the 1920's in Harlem, a new awareness of black culture developed into an artistic movement known as the Harlem Renaissance. Critics such as Alain LOCKE in his *THE NEW NEGRO: An Interpretation* (1925), publishers and collectors such as James L. Coady and Albert C. Barnes, and organizations such as the Harmon Foundation stressed the positive attributes of African American cultural achievements. The first major exhibition of art by black Americans was held at the International House in New York City in 1928. The exhibition was one way of expressing those attributes to a wider audience. A sense of self-reliance, respect, and pride in African ancestry fostered the movement. White music critic, photographer, and novelist Carl Van Vechten helped popularize Harlem, and black photographers such as James VAN DER ZEE, Morgan and Marvin Smith, and Gordon PARKS, Sr., recorded the lively scene. Black female PHOTOGRAPHERS such as Elise Forrest Harleston and Jennie Louise Welcome, the sister of James Van Der Zee, also were active at this time.

The popularity of African American cultural expression in music, dance, and fashion led to an international awareness of black American creativity during the Jazz Age. Although a black American, Elizabeth Keckley, had designed a ball dress for Mary Todd Lincoln, it was megastars such as the black performer Josephine BAKER who helped transform the Parisian fashion world. Eventually the clothes, dances, and speaking styles of black musicians, actors, and actresses would influence whole segments of the American fashion and social worlds.

At the same time, African American interest in cinema generated an independent FILM movement, establishing a tradition that continued through the twentieth century. The first black film, *Darktown Jubilee* starring Bert WILLIAMS, was made in 1914. Oscar MICHEAUX is the best-known early black director. He made his first film, *The Homesteader*, in 1918. His *Within Our Gates* (1920) and *Body and Soul* (1925), the latter starring Paul ROBE-SON, were silent films influenced by Hollywood productions but with black actors and actresses. Micheaux's *The Exile* (1931) was the first black talking picture, and *God's Step Children* (1937) tackles black social issues such as PASSING. Micheaux made more than thirty films between 1918 and 1948.

Emmett J. Scott, in collaboration with the NATIONAL ASSOCIATION FOR THE ADVANCEMENT OF COLORED PEOPLE (NAACP), made a film called *The Birth of a Race* (1918) that stands as a counterstatement to D. W. Griffith's racist *The Birth of a Nation* (1915). The Ebony Film Company's *Spyin' the Spy* (1915) and the LINCOLN MOTION PICTURE COMPANY's *the Realization of a Negro's Ambition* (1916) are other early silent films. The Colored Players Film Corporation was responsible for *Ten Nights in a Barroom* (1926) with Charles GILPIN and *Scar of Shame* (1927). FOLKLORE inspired films such as *Georgia Rose* (1930), *Absent* (1928), a black Western titled *Bronze Buckaroo* (1938), a black horror movie titled *Son of Ingagi* (1940), and straightforward folktales such as *The Blood of Jesus* (1941) and *Go Down Death* (1944). World War II inspired Carlton Moss's *The Negro Soldier* (1943), made for the Department of the Army.

Painters of the Harlem Renaissance and 1930's. As a painter, illustrator, and muralist in the forefront of the Harlem Renaissance, Aaron DOUGLAS studied with Winold Reiss in New York and Othon Frieze in Paris (1931). Douglas illustrated James Weldon JOHNSON's *God's Trombones: Seven Negro Sermons in Verse* (1927) and painted a series of murals that combined an inspirational vision of African American nobility with proletarian themes. His angular silhouettes offset by jagged intrusions, wavy lines, and pastel circles transformed Art Deco conventions with African art motifs and African American themes. His murals entitled *Aspects of Negro Life* (1934) are displayed at the Schomburg Center in the New York Public Library. In them, he traces the course of African

Americans from Africa through slavery to an enlightened future. Douglas depicted the dignity, courage, and hope of African Americans on an epic scale.

Archibald J. MOTLEY, Jr., and Palmer C. HAYDEN brought new attention to black genre painting. Motley did a series of canvases between 1933 and 1936 that includes *The Barbecue, Saturday Night*, and *The Chicken Shack*. The paintings render in vivid detail the raucous nightlife of Harlem. Hayden combined African sculpture with a modern setting in his still life *Fetiche et Fleurs* (1926) and depicted street life in Harlem in pictures such as *Midsummer Night in Harlem* (c. 1934). Both artists based their art on black life in the United States. Many other artists, including Hale Woodruff, Charles ALSTON, DOX THRASH, Eldzier CORTOR, and Joseph DELANEY, participated in or were influenced by the Harlem Renaissance and went on to work for the Federal Art Project, a Depression-era government program for artists.

Artists such as Charles SEBREE, Charles WHITE, John WILSON, and John BIGGERS developed their own variations on the social realist style. Many artists worked in a social-protest style. Hale WOODRUFF visited with Henry Ossawa Tanner in 1927 and soon after painted the *Card Players* (1930), which shows the influence of cubism. His *Amistad* (1939) murals are large works commemorating the Amistad Mutiny (1839). Malvin Gray JOHNSON also experimented with American cubism and African themes in such paintings as *Negro Masks* (1932).

William Edouard SCOTT was a painter and muralist who attended the Art Institute of Chicago and who helped define a new African American tradition in painting. Traveling to Haiti in 1931 on a Rosenwald Grant, Scott executed a series of paintings on folk themes. *Haitian Fisherman* (c. 1931) and *When the Tide is Out* (c. 1931) are examples of rich coloring and expressive brush stroke applied to indigenous motifs. Ellis WILSON is another black artist who traveled to Haiti and painted local subjects, in *Funeral Procession* (1940) and *Field Workers* (1941), using an expressionistic style. Laura Wheeler WARING and Edwin A. Harleston are best known for their realistic figure portraits. In Waring's *Frankie, Portrait of a Child* (1937) and Harleston's *The Old Servant* (1930), genre scenes are executed with impressionistic coloring that contributed much to the tradition of American portraiture.

Sculptors and Photographers. A stonemason named William EDMUNSON started sculpting in stone when he was fifty years old. His direct yet unique figures (among them the undated *Eve* and *Nude Woman Seated on a Stool*) show a distinctive style reminiscent of African totem sculpture. Selma BURKE also stylized sculptures, as in

Temptation (1938). Two other sculptors, Sargent JOHNSON and Richmond BARTHÉ, were concerned with African American themes in their work. Johnson's *Forever Free* (1933) and Barthé's *Blackberry Woman* (1932) and *African Dancer* (1933) depict black subjects with Afrocentric stylizations. Many photographers were working in the early part of the century, including Addison Scurlock, P. H. Polk, and Ellis L. Weems, who was active in the early 1920's.

Primitive Painters. Artists including Bill Traylor, Clementine HUNTER, Horace PIPPIN, Minnie EVANS, and Edward

Near the end of his life, he turned to spiritual themes, as in *the Holy Mountain II* (1945).

Traylor and Hunter were self-taught artists who concentrated on American scenes handled with a naïve folk quality. Hunter's *The Funeral on Cane River (1948)* and *Cotton Ginning* (1975) are good examples of her art. Evans was born in a log cabin in North Carolina. Her paintings, many influenced by the Book of Revelations, are filled with designs and arcane imagery. *Design Made at Airlie Garden* (1967) expresses her style well. Edward Webster, who worked as a postal carrier, also shows the

From Jacob Lawrence's Frederick Douglass *series of paintings. Douglass argued against John Brown's plan to attack the arsenal at Harpers Ferry.* (National Archives)

Webster can be grouped together as "primitives." Their approach relies in part on intuition and an independent, nonacademic attitude that results in unique work combining naïve experimentation with folk elements. Pippin in some ways exemplifies this group. His style suggests the limners of early Americana, but his content depicts African American culture. His devastating experiences fighting in the trenches during World War I are expressed in his painting *The End of the War: Starting Home* (c. 1931). Pippin painted genre scenes such as *Domino Players* (1943) and *Cabin in the Cotton III* (1944) as well as still-life interiors such as *Victorian Interior* (1946).

influence of religion in his paintings. A good example is *The Nativity* (1957).

Black Modernists. A connection might be made in the use of color, perspective, and design between the "primitive" African American painters and the black modernists, who were influenced by European movements such as fauvism, expressionism, and cubism as well as by African art. Artists such as William H. JOHNSON, Romare BEARDEN, Thomas Sills, Jacob LAWRENCE, Claude Clark, and Beauford DELANEY heightened their colors and utilized abstract design qualities to produce high emotion in their work. Hughie Lee Smith retained elements of Surrealism in his work. James PORTER, the author of *Modern Negro Art* (1943), Margaret BURROUGHS, Augusta SAVAGE, and James LEWIS were educators as well as artists successful in the modernist tradition.

Artists in other areas also developed along modernist lines. Sculptors in this style include William Artis, Marion PERKINS, Elizabeth CATLETT, John Rhoden, Ed Wilson, Earl Hooks, and William Taylor. Allan Rohan Crite, Wilmer Jennings, Walter Williams, Richard MAYHEW, George Ridley, Jr., and Sam Middleton were successful illustrators, printmakers, and painters. Photographers such as Austin Hansen and Roy DeCarava were active in Harlem during and after World War II. Female photographers working in this period included Louise MARTIN, Wilhelmina Pearl Selena ROBERTS.

William H. Johnson worked his way through the National Academy of Design in New York. In 1924, he traveled to Europe, where he lived and painted for twenty years. Influenced by African art as well as by German expressionism, Johnson returned to the United States. In paintings such as *Harbour Under the Midnight Sun* (c. 1935-1938) and *Mt. Calvary* (1939), he produced work that expressed his personal vision of the world.

Jacob Lawrence is perhaps the best-known African American postwar painter and illustrator. He used African American themes of history and culture in a number of series of paintings, such as the Frederick DOUGLASS series (1937-1938). These series may have been influenced by the historical antecedents of Egyptian wall painting and Mexican murals. Lawrence was a master craftsman able to merge narration, figuration, and abstract design into striking statements. He illustrated poet Langston Hughes's *One-Way Ticket* (1948). Concerned with African American history, culture, and social injustice, Lawrence depicts historical figures and black communal life with harsh angular movement and explosive colors. His distorted but highly intuitive paintings combine elements of expressionism and cubism with African American themes. In paintings such as *Street Scene #1* (1936) and *3 Family Toilet* (1943), Lawrence affirmed his commitment to the bitter struggle of black people for personal dignity and freedom.

Romare Bearden was a member of the American Academy of Arts and Letters and received the President's National Medal of Arts in 1987. As a painter, scholar, and curator, Bearden added to as well as preserved the traditions of African American art. Bearden studied with the German social satirist painter George Grosz. He is recognized as one of America's finest collagists. He sometimes used the *dechirage* technique, in which paper is torn away to reveal underlying areas. He juxtaposed dynamic colors and distorted images to create a unified iconography that was particularly American but influenced by the Dada and Surrealist movements. *Conjur Woman* (1964) suggests a fascination with African American religious traditions. He used photomontage images of masks and textiles from Africa in combination with black vernacular themes and saw a connection between his methods and jazz improvisation. Bearden organized "Contemporary Art of the American Negro" (1966) as the first major show in Harlem since the 1930's. He wrote *The Painters Mind: The Relations of Structure and Space in Painting* (1969) with Carl Holty. Bearden was working on a history of African American artists with Harry Henderson when he died in New York City in 1988, at the age of seventy-six.

The Black Arts Movement. The Black Arts movement of the 1960's and 1970's demanded that art and politics be interconnected, and that African American arts be given public access and recognition. Numerous museums and galleries were founded in response to the movement, and others began showing a greater interest in African American art. The Studio Museum of Harlem had a long history of presenting black artists. Community workshops and galleries sprang up in many major cities, such as the Cinque gallery in Manhattan and the Black Man's Art Gallery in San Francisco. Benny Andrews and Cliff Joseph were cofounders of the Black Emergency Cultural Coalition, which supported black artists. After the 1963 MARCH ON WASHINGTON, Alvin Hollingsworth and Norman Lewis founded Spiral, a group of black artists organized around the black aesthetic. In 1968, Jeff Donaldson and Frederic Jon Eversley, among others, founded AFRICOBRA, or the African Commune of Bad Relevant Artists. Weusi ("black" in Swahili) was founded in Harlem in 1965. In 1971, Kay Brown and Faith RINGGOLD helped found a group of black women artists called Where We At. The Black Arts movement also resulted in a return to public art, as witnessed by the many politically inspired murals collectively painted on buildings in major cities. Among them is the *Wall of Respect* (1967) in Chicago. During the late 1960's and 1970's, street art in mural form was created by artists such as William Walker and Mitchell Caton in Chicago and Dana CHANDLER in Boston.

Paintings with themes encompassing civil rights and the Vietnam War, many of which depicted the American flag, were produced by Reginald Gammon, Herman "Kofi" Bailey, David Braford, Bertrand Phillips, Manuel Hughes, Phillip Lindsay Mason, William Henderson, and David Hammon, among many others. A number of artists were inspired by visits to Africa. Among them were

A Decorative Head, *by William Artis*. (National Archives)

Ademola Olugebefola, Raymond Saunders, Lucile Malkia Roberts, Floyd Coleman, and David Driskell. Other artists, such as Paul Keene, Arthur Carraway, and Mikelle Fletcher, were influenced by voodoo and a synthesis of Pan-African and American themes.

Painters such as Thomas Sills, Richard MAYHEW, Daniel Johnson, Xenobia Smith, Milton Young, Emilio CRUZ, and Bernie CASEY worked in abstract and geometric symbolist styles. Charles Young, Teixeira Nash, Edward Sowells, and particularly Robert Thompson extended the expressionist experimentation in figurative paintings.

Artists Using Other Forms. Assemblage and painted constructions offered other avenues of expression for black artists such as Noah Purifoy, Sam GILLIAM, Christopher Shelton, Joe OVERSTREET, Alvin Loving, Bing Davis, Ron Griffin, Marie Johnson, Edward Bural, and Betye Saar. Contemporary sculptors made important contributions in the post-World War II years. Among them are Juan Logan, John Riddle, Mel Edwards, Houston Conwill, and particularly Richard HUNT, whose welded steel forms pushed sculpture in a new direction. Tom Lloyd, who edited *Black Art Notes*, Ed Love, Mel Edwards, Walter Johnson, Evangeline Montgomery, and P'lla Mills also were known for steel and welding construction. Earl Hooks, Mahler Ryder, Daniel Johnson, Walter Jackson, Larry Urbina, and Ben Hazard used plastics and resins to create sculptures. Barbara CHASE-RIBOUD used the lost wax technique and fiber-wrapped art that recalled weaving, while Allen Fannin used yarns, and Maven Hassinger and Napoleon Jones Henderson used pottery and carvings. Ruth Waddy, Margo Humphrey, Carol Ward, Devoice Berry, Marion Epting, and Cleveland Bellow worked in silkscreen and lithography. Mikki FERRILL and Phillda Ragland-Njau are two of the better-known female photographers from this civil rights period.

The Fashion Industry and Crafts. African Americans also were active in the fashion industry in the 1960's and 1970's, designing clothes and influencing the international market. Among them were Willi SMITH, Patrick Kelley, Jay Smith, and Ann LOWE, who designed dresses for movie stars as well as making Jacqueline Kennedy's wedding dress. Lois Alexander had her own boutique in Washington, D.C., for more than thirty years, and in 1979 she opened the Black Fashion Museum in Harlem.

Many black artists of this period turned to traditional crafts. Bill Maxwell, Camille BILLOPS, and Doyle Lane worked in clay and ceramics. Art Smith, Bob Jefferson, Joanne Lee, and Margaret Collins used jewelry and beads. Douglass Phillips used stained glass. Other artists, recalling an Afrocentric tradition of tree and yard decoration,

used found objects and other devices to create provocative sculptures and constructions. Among these artists were Sultan Rogers, Bessie Harvey, Ibibio Fundi, Derek Webster, Mr. Imagination, and John Outerbridge. Ben Jones and Lovett Thompson used African sculpture forms to create modern sculpture in *The Junkie* (1970). Robert Reid and Makam Bailey combined elements of street art, graffiti, and other black iconographies into their works. Finally, a number of artists used nature and animal symbology combined with the traditions of Surrealism to express African American themes. These include Irene Clark, Norma Morgan, Gary Rickson, Suzanne Jackson, and Leslie Price.

Black Filmmaking. A second important phase of filmmaking occurred during this period. Black directors worked with limited budgets on films starring black actors and featuring African American themes. Melvin VAN PEEBLES directed *WATERMELON MAN* (1970) and *SWEET SWEETBACK'S BAADASSSSS SONG* (1971) and wrote the screenplay for *The Sophisticated Gents* (1981). Ossie DAVIS directed *COTTON COMES TO HARLEM* (1970). Gordon Parks, Sr., made *THE LEARNING TREE* (1969) and *SHAFT* (1971), and his son, Gordon Parks, Jr., directed *SUPER FLY* (1972). These last two films were part of the BLAXPLOITATION trend in filmmaking, which used themes of black militancy and urban unrest in urban crime dramas. Sexual themes were common in Blaxploitation films. Other notable directors and films from this period are Hugh A. Robertson's *Melinda* (1972); Robert Downey's satiric comedy about a black takeover of an advertising agency, titled *Putney Swope* (1969); Charles Burnett's *Killer of Sheep* (1977); Larry Clark's *Passing Through* (1977); and Haile Gerima's *Bush Mama* (1977).

The 1980's and 1990's. The 1980's and 1990's witnessed the blossoming of a new interest in African American culture and its influence on mainstream American culture as a whole. Black fashion designers such as Carl Jones, Thomas Walker, C. D. Greene, Eric Gaskins, and Bryon Lars created distinctive styles influenced by urban street fashion as well as by old films. Others, such as Arthur McGee, had been creating original clothes since the 1950's. Once again, as in the 1920's and 1930's, celebrities from sports and films, as well as from television, created new fashion styles.

Black directors created films with black actors and black themes that have been seen by culturally diverse audiences. Among these directors is Spike LEE, with *SHE'S GOTTA HAVE IT* (1986), *SCHOOL DAZE* (1988), *DO THE RIGHT THING* (1989), *MO' BETTER BLUES* (1990), *JUNGLE FEVER* (1991), and *MALCOLM X* (1992). Other directors contributing to this movement are Robert TOWNSEND with *HOL-*

LYWOOD SHUFFLE (1987), Reginald and Warrington HUDLIN with *HOUSE PARTY* (1990), Mario VAN PEEBLES with *New Jack City* (1991), and John SINGLETON with *BOYZ 'N THE HOOD* (1991). Julie DASH's *DAUGHTERS OF THE DUST* (1992) concerns a South Sea Island GULLAH family and resonates with the themes of community, ancestor worship, and African retentions in clothing, food, and language.

African Americans continued to use the visual arts to redefine their culture through a revitalization of spirit that draws from African and African American sources. Some artists, such as Alma Thomas and Lois Mailou Jones, created important art for much of the twentieth century. Other female artists, such as Bessie Harvey, Betye Saar, Jean Lacy, Varnette Honeywood, and Renee Stout, used painting and various types of assemblage to express Afrocentric themes of community and religion in new ways. Women contributed strongly to the tradition of African American photography. Among them are Coreen SIMPSON, Marilyn Nance, Lorna SIMPSON, and Carrie Mae WEEMS. A number of photographers, such as Anthony Barboza, Billy (Fundi) Abernathy, Dawoud Bey, Todd Gray, and Wendell White, used African American figures and themes in their pictures. Moneta SLEET, Jr., was the first black photographer to win the Pulitzer Prize, in 1969. Chuck Stewart took pictures of jazz stars, and Dick Saunders was a famous photojournalist.

Multicultural awareness has influenced such painters as Emma Amos, Howardena Pindell, Vernell DeSilva, Larry Rivers, and Jean Michel Basquiat. Ancestral arts and trips to Africa affected other painters, such as Roosevelt "Rip" Woods, Jr., Charles Searles, Leon Refro, Jack Whitten, Vusumuzi Maduna, William T. Williams, Matthew Thomas, Kofi Kayiga, James Phillips, and Marion Brown. They express, through their use of design, color, and geometries, a renewed interest in Afrocentric music and movement. They and other artists continued to express the essential spirit of African American culture.—*Stephen Soitos*

SUGGESTED READINGS:

- Bogle, Donald. *Toms, Coons, Mulattoes, Mammies, and Bucks: An Interpretive History of Blacks in American Films*. New York: Viking Press, 1973. A comprehensive survey of American film and African American participation in the industry. Devotes a short chapter to black independent filmmaking.
- Dallas Museum of Art. *Black Art Ancestral Legacy: The African Impulse in African-American Art*. New York: Harry Abrams, 1989. Contains a number of excellent essays concerning postmodern African American artists' use of ancestral arts and Afrocentric inspiration in their creations.
- Driskell, David C. *Two Centuries of Black American Art*. New York: Alfred A. Knopf, 1976. An excellent introduction to African American art by a noted scholar and painter. Traces African American art from its beginning into the 1960's, with many full color reproductions.
- Fine, Elsa Honig. *The Afro-American Artist: A Search for Identity*. New York: Hacker Art Books, 1982. An informative introduction to African American art that covers individual artists and movements up to the postmodern period.
- Lewis, Samella S. *Art: African American*. New York: Harcourt Brace Jovanovich, 1969. A valuable survey of African American art from its beginnings until the 1960's. Illustrates its points well with color reproductions of many important paintings.
- Locke, Alain. *The Negro in Art: A Pictorial Record of the Negro Artist and of the Negro Theme in Art*. New York: Hacker Art Books, 1971. One of the first and most important surveys of African American artists, by the seminal art historian and critic of the Harlem Renaissance.
- Moutoussamy-Ashe, Jeanne. *Viewfinders: Black Women Photographers*. New York: Dodd, Mead, 1986. First detailed survey of black female photographers. Includes many fine photographs.
- Porter, James A. *Modern Negro Art*. New York: Dryden Press, 1943. One of the earliest comprehensive explorations of African American art, providing an essential survey of the artists and an intelligent analysis.
- Thompson, Robert F. *Flash of the Spirit: African and Afro-American Art and Philosophy*. New York: Vintage, 1984. An extremely important book that helps explain Afrocentrism and African retentions in terms of African American art.
- Willis-Thomas, Deborah. *Black Photographers, 1940-1988: An Illustrated Bio-Bibliography*. New York: Garland, 1989. An extensive survey of African American photographers that picks up where Willis-Thomas' work on earlier black photography (1840-1940) left off.

Voter Education Project: Attempt to register African American voters in the South. The Voter Education Project (VEP) was started by the Southern Regional Council (SRC) in March of 1962. The idea for the VEP evolved from discussions started by officials of the Justice Department and SRC leaders after the CONGRESS OF RACIAL EQUALITY (CORE) had sponsored its "FREEDOM RIDES" through the South. The VEP was conceived as a nonpartisan voter registration drive and provided financial support for voter registration campaigns throughout the South. The VEP at first was financed by the Taconic Foundation, the Field Foundation, the Edgar Stern Family Fund, and the National Association of Intergroup Relations Officers.

The VEP voter registration activities were executed through the leading civil rights organizations, including the NATIONAL ASSOCIATION FOR THE ADVANCEMENT OF COLORED PEOPLE (NAACP), STUDENT NONVIOLENT COORDINATING COMMITTEE (SNCC), and SOUTHERN CHRISTIAN LEADERSHIP CONFERENCE (SCLC). In Mississippi, an umbrella organization known as the Council of Federated Organizations (COFO) was the conduit for the VEP voter registration efforts. In the mid-1960's through a part of the 1970's, the VEP provided leadership and assistance to

Vernon E. JORDAN, Jr. (1965-1970), and John LEWIS (1970-1977). After the main burst of voter registration, the SRC conformed to a 1969 tax reform law which stated that any tax-exempt organization engaged in voter-registration activities was not allowed to receive more than 25 percent of its financial support from one source. To comply, the SRC decided in 1970 to separate from the VEP, and the VEP organized itself as an independent body. The VEP was granted a charter and tax-exempt status as an independent voter-registration organization. It also began a program of informing black officeholders about issues and about techniques of achieving the goals held by black voters.

1958 class for African Americans preparing to take the voter registration test. (Library of Congress)

the MISSISSIPPI FREEDOM DEMOCRATIC PARTY.

The VEP registered approximately 688,000 African Americans as voters in eleven southern states between April of 1962 and November of 1964. The VEP registration drive resulted in one of the largest and most significant increases in African American voters since the Supreme Court had outlawed all-white primaries in *SMITH V. ALWRIGHT* in 1944.

The VEP provided strategy and administration. Its first executive directors were Wiley A. Branton (1962-1965),

Voters: African Americans have long recognized that the ballot box is one of the most effective instruments that can be used to achieve equality. With the right to vote comes political power, with political power comes the ability to effect real and lasting changes within American society and to allow the voices of minority groups to be heard.

History. Although some blacks were permitted to vote in each of the original thirteen colonies, African American suffrage was not established as a national policy until the ratification of the FIFTEENTH AMENDMENT in 1870. Before that time, the U.S. Constitution left the question of electoral qualifications up to the states. Since slaves were not recognized as American citizens, they were not given the right to vote, and only a few states permitted free blacks to vote. For purposes of congressional representation, however, which is determined by a state's population, the Constitution stated that "all other persons" (for example, black slaves) were to be counted as three-fifths of a person. Thus, those states with large slave populations procured a relatively large number of representatives in Congress on the basis of possessing a large body of slaves who could not vote.

Even before the American Revolution began, several states began restricting the black vote: South Carolina in 1716, Virginia in 1723, and Georgia in 1761. As the slave population grew, and with it the fear of SLAVE INSURRECTIONS, state after state began restricting suffrage to white males. Delaware prohibited black voting in 1792, Kentucky in 1799, Ohio in 1803, New Jersey in 1807, Maryland in 1810, Louisiana in 1812, Connecticut in 1814, Tennessee in 1834, North Carolina in 1835, Pennsylvania in 1838, and Florida in 1845. New York allowed only those blacks who owned property to vote, a qualification not required of white voters, and the new states coming into the Union all banned black voting. Thus, in the pre-Civil War United States, free blacks were permitted to vote without restriction only in five New England states.

The Fifteenth Amendment. Resistance to black suffrage continued throughout the Civil War and into RECONSTRUCTION. Even after SLAVERY was formally abolished by the THIRTEENTH AMENDMENT in 1865, the defeated southern states continued to oppose the recognition of the free status of African Americans. Blacks legally received the right to vote in 1867 with the passage of the first Reconstruction Act, which granted African Americans voting rights as part of the price paid by rebellious southern states for readmission to the Union. Yet in the lower North, where most northern blacks lived, white voters in referendum after referendum rejected black suffrage. In 1869, adult black males could vote in only twenty states.

During this time, congressional Republicans pressed for a constitutional amendment to secure the right of blacks to vote in every state, thus avoiding the risk of possible rejection by state referenda. The Fifteenth Amendment finally became law on March 30, 1870, after thirteen months of debate and a number of compromises. To ensure passage, its sponsors were forced to omit a clause outlawing literacy tests and another banning racial discrimination in determining qualifications for holding political office. Nevertheless, most African Americans celebrated its ratification, believing it to be a solemn written pledge by the U.S. government that their right to vote was now guaranteed. Subsequent events would make a mockery of the law, however, as blacks would continue to be denied full voting rights for almost a century thereafter.

At first, the white South did not challenge the legality of black suffrage. Instead, southern racists resorted to terror, intimidation, and economic pressure. Polling places were mysteriously moved the night before elections, blacks were required to produce registration certificates, and those accused of even minor crimes based on flimsy evidence were stripped of their voting privileges. These and other devious tactics succeeded in drastically reducing the number of black voters. By 1900, the African American vote had practically disappeared in the South.

Attempts at Reform. On May 31, 1870, the Enforcement Act was passed, which directed that all citizens otherwise qualified to vote in any election should not be denied that privilege because of race. States were allowed to establish certain qualifications for voter eligibility but were prohibited from obstructing any person from casting a vote. The act was amended in 1871 to eliminate fraudulent voter-registration practices. The U.S. circuit courts could, upon petition, commission election supervisors to oversee both registration and voting in any state.

Poll Taxes and Literacy Tests. In direct defiance of the Enforcement Act, many states, especially in the South, continued to frustrate African Americans' attempts at voting as the twentieth century dawned. The most effective weapon used against black voters was the poll tax. Payment of the tax was required several months before the election, at which time a tax receipt had to be presented. In addition, only property owners were allowed to vote, and voters were required to read, understand, and interpret the state or federal constitution to the satisfaction of election officials. In addition, some states, such as Oklahoma, exempted any voters whose ancestors had been registered to vote in 1866, which in effect meant that only black registrants were required to take literacy tests. In states such as Louisiana, these tactics were almost 100 percent effective in keeping blacks away from the polls, even though the state contained more than 130,000 eligible black voters. The results were equally devastating in other states.

The Civil Rights Years. In the 1950's, many Americans believed that the problems of racism and discrimination would not be solved until blacks had secured the right to vote; however, a majority of African Americans of voting age in the South had yet to cast a single ballot in an election. Although poll taxes had been outlawed in most state and local elections, southern whites continued to utilize comprehension and literacy tests, as well as intimidation, to keep blacks from voting.

In 1957, after much pressure by civil rights advocates, Congress passed the first civil rights act since 1875, which also provided for the creation of a COMMISSION ON CIVIL RIGHTS that empowered the government, through the federal courts, to file lawsuits on behalf of any person who was denied the right to vote. Unfortunately, the new law contained many loopholes, and proved to be largely ineffective in guaranteeing voting rights. As a result, a new civil rights act was passed in 1960 that required that all registration and voting records be made available for public inspection. The act required state election officials to preserve records for at least twenty-two months for inspection by the U.S. attorney general and made it a federal crime to obstruct or ignore any federal court order pertaining to voting rights.

The Civil Rights Act of 1964 contained a section that served to strengthen the provisions of the two previous acts, and guaranteed protection against the use of different standards for black voters. Following the passage of this act, the Twenty-fourth Amendment to the Constitution was ratified, abolishing the poll tax as a prerequisite for voting in federal elections

The most important and far-reaching piece of voting-rights legislation was the VOTING RIGHTS ACT of 1965, which provided for direct federal examination of voter registration. The act outlawed all knowledge, character, and literacy tests and greatly strengthened the existing laws. As a result, the percentage of registered black voters began to increase dramatically. By 1968, more than 50 percent of the black voting-age population in the South was registered, a development that greatly increased the numbers of African Americans elected to public office. In 1966, there were ninety-seven black members of state legislatures and nine members of Congress; by 1973, there were more than two hundred blacks serving in thirty-seven state legislatures and sixteen black members of Congress. Soon, African Americans would also be elected to serve as mayors of several large American cities, including Chicago, Los Angeles, Newark, New Orleans, and New York.

The large numbers of registered African American voters began to show their influence among the major political parties as well. In the 1960 presidential election, one of the closest in American history, black voters in several key states delivered decisive votes to John F. Kennedy. In the 1968 presidential election, 20 percent of the Democratic vote came from African Americans. Such large and influential numbers prompted black leaders to demand a greater voice in party affairs. In 1984, the Reverend Jesse JACKSON, during the announcement of his candidacy for the Democratic presidential nomination, made it clear that his main goal was to induce more African Americans and other disfranchised people to vote. The surge of black registration and voting in the 1980's was largely the result of Jackson's strong showing in the 1984 presidential primary.

The newly found strength of the African American voter has come as a result of the changes within the Civil Rights movement. The coalitions that were formed to push for the passage of civil rights legislation in the 1960's have been replaced by ever-increasing numbers of black elected officials in local, state, and federal government and by the increased participation of black American citizens in the political process. Thus, the large number of actively participating black voters has become the new mechanism for future social, political, and economic change.—*Raymond Frey*

SUGGESTED READINGS: • Keech, William R. *The Impact of Negro Voting: The Role of the Vote in the Quest for Equality.* Chicago: Rand McNally, 1968. • Moon, Henry Lee. *Balance of Power: The Negro Vote.* Westport, Conn.: Greenwood Press, 1977. • Walters, Ronald W. *Black Presidential Politics in America: A Strategic Approach.* Albany: State University of New York Press, 1988. • Walton, Hanes Jr. *Invisible Politics: Black Political Behavior.* Albany: State University of New York Press, 1985. • Watters, Pat, and Reese Cleghorn. *Climbing Jacob's Ladder: The Arrival of Negroes in Southern Politics.* New York: Harcourt, Brace & World, 1967.

Voting Rights Act of 1965: Legislation signed on August 6, intended to eliminate discriminatory voting restrictions and expand registration of black voters. The act mobilized the most significant change in the politics of the South since the RECONSTRUCTION ACT OF 1867. This law made voting booths and polling stations that effectively had been closed for nearly one hundred years accessible to more than 2.5 million African Americans. The potential impact of this act lies in the fact that there were numerous counties in the South where the African American vote could carry an election. For example, the act effectively removed all-white city councils from southern cities with African American majorities. The impact of this legislation was such that white southerners tried to prevent the law from taking effect. Massive voter-registration projects, confrontations between African Americans and local officials, and federal assistance were necessary before any actual headway was made.

In the election following passage of the Voting Rights Act, the Reverend Channing Phillips was nominated for president. (The Associated Publishers, Inc.)

The Voting Rights Act abolished poll taxes, grandfather clauses, literacy tests, and other rules that were employed to disqualify African American voters. The act also empowered the United States attorney general to send federal registrars into counties where evidence of discrimination was present. The signing of the Voting Rights Act by President Lyndon Johnson followed demonstrations in Selma, Ala. Selma exemplified many southern cities, in that half of its population was African American, but only 2 percent of eligible African American voters were registered.

The Voting Rights Act had an immediate impact. Through the efforts of the SOUTHERN CHRISTIAN LEADERSHIP CONFERENCE, the STUDENT NONVIOLENT COORDINATING COMMITTEE, the federal government, and grass-roots organizations, more than three hundred thousand African Americans were registered in the South for the first time. Most southern states registered more than half of their eligible African American voters. Four African Americans were elected to county and state legislative offices. White candidates such as moderate Wilson Baker, who defeated Jim Clark, a staunch foe of civil rights activists and integration, for sheriff, also benefited from African American votes. Over the subsequent months and years, African American voters helped elect African American officials to numerous positions at the local, state, and federal levels, as well as electing white and other officials who were sympathetic and responsive to their needs.

W

WAACs and WAVES: Female members of the armed forces. The WAVES (Women Accepted for Volunteer Emergency Service) were authorized on a trial basis by a congressional bill signed by President Franklin Roosevelt on July 30, 1942. The WAVES were to be a temporary auxiliary to the U.S. Naval Reserve, with members having no permanent military status. African American women were not admitted until December, 1944, and then only under public pressure. Among the first black WAVES were Harriet Ida Pickens, Francis

WAVES provided a variety of support services during World War II. (National Archives)

Ellis, and Francis Eliza Willis. During all of World War II, only seventy-two black women were enlisted and only two more became officers. In contrast, by August of 1945 there were more than eighty thousand WAVES serving in their noncombat positions. Most WAVES were discharged at the end of World War II, but their numbers increased during the 1950's and 1960's. By 1970, black representation had improved considerably, and about fifty out of a total of about two thousand officers were black. The WAVES no longer exist. Their members and functions were integrated into the regular Navy.

The Women's Auxiliary Army Corps (WAACs) were created by congressional legislation signed by Roosevelt on May 14, 1942. Black women were among those eager to volunteer, but just as for black males in the MILITARY, their participation was limited to 10 percent of the total. Also as was the case for black males, various black organizations and the black press objected to this limit. The actual percentage of black WAACs did not rise above 6 percent, however, between 1943 and 1946. Of the first 440 women to report to Fort Des Moines, Iowa, for training, 40 were black.

The WAAC organization, renamed as the Women's Army Corps (WACs), became an official part of the Army in July, 1943. Members still had only temporary status in the military. During World War II, black WAC officers trained and commanded black units and performed other noncombat tasks. As was the case for WAVES, all WAACs (and later WACs) were volunteers. About one hundred black women served as WAAC or WAC officers during World War II, and about three hundred had been officers by 1970.

In July, 1943, black WAC recruiting officers were withdrawn from the field. This withdrawal, along with charges that the War Department was failing to give technical training to black women, led to complaints in the black press. Eventually, black WACs found themselves assigned to more technical tasks.

Political pressure from the black community also led to the creation of the 6888th Central Postal Battalion, the only black WAC battalion to serve overseas. Its eight hundred members, all black, were commanded by Major Charity Adams. The battalion's mission was to establish a central postal directory in Europe. The battalion arrived in England in February, 1945, and shortly thereafter moved to France.

In June, 1948, the Women's Armed Forces Integration Act gave women permanent status in the regular and reserve components of the armed forces. The minimum age and educational requirements for enlistment, however, were higher for women then for men. With the creation of an all-volunteer military in the 1970's, more positions opened to women. Women were allowed to hold positions in 90 percent of all occupational specialties. The WAC was disestablished in April, 1978, with its members reassigned to regular Army or other positions.

Waddles, Mrs. Payton "Mother" (Charleszetta Lina; b. Oct. 7, 1913, St. Louis, Mo.): Mission director and charity leader. Waddles has been called "Detroit's Black Angel" in recognition of her charity work in that city. Along with being the biological mother of ten children,

Mother Waddles dedicated her life to charitable work. (AP/Wide World Photos)

she served as mission director and founder of the nonprofit, nondenominational, charitable organization "Waddles' Perpetual Mission for Saving Souls of All Nations, Inc.," which began operation in 1956. She is also an ordained Pentecostal minister. The mission's Emergency Service Program provides food, clothing, shelter, medicine, and transportation to the needy, maintaining kitchens on Detroit's skid row. Mother Waddles had her own radio and television programs and is a life member of the NATIONAL ASSOCIATION FOR THE ADVANCEMENT OF COLORED PEOPLE. She served on the Mayor's Task Force Committees and was honorary chair of the Women's Conference of Concern. In the course of her long career, she received more than 150 awards, including the 1988 Humanitarian Award from the NATIONAL URBAN LEAGUE. She was featured in the traveling Smithsonian exhibit, "Black Women of Courage."

Waddy, Joseph C. (b. 1911, Louisa, Va.): Judge. Waddy received his LL.B. degree from HOWARD UNIVERSITY in 1938. He pursued his legal career mainly in the District of Columbia. Between 1939 and 1962, he practiced for a law firm before being appointed as an associate judge of the domestic relations municipal court. In 1967, he became a judge on the U.S. District Court for the District of Columbia.

Wade-Davis Bill: Legislation sponsored by Senator Benjamin F. Wade and Representative Henry W. Davis. The bill, introduced in 1864, unsuccessfully attempted to set RECONSTRUCTION policy. President Abraham Lincoln allowed the bill to expire at the end of the congressional session without signing it. The battle over the bill presaged the struggles to set Reconstruction policy at the conclusion of the war.

Walcott, "Jersey Joe" (Arnold Raymond Cream; b. Jan. 31, 1914, Merchantville, N.J.): Boxer. A late starter in BOXING, Walcott did not attain the heavyweight championship until 1951. He surprised the boxing world by knocking out Ezzard CHARLES in the seventh round of their bout. Over his career, Walcott scored thirty knockouts, won twenty decisions, lost six fights by knockouts and twelve by decision, and had one draw. After retiring, Walcott served as a referee and was sheriff of Camden County, N.J., from 1972 to 1975.

Waldon, Alton Ronald, Jr. (b. Dec. 31, 1936, Lakeland, Fla.): U.S. representative from New York. Waldon served in the U.S. Army from 1956 to 1959 and was discharged at the rank of specialist fourth class. He was graduated from John Jay College with his bachelor of science degree in 1968. He attended law school at New York University and earned his J.D. degree in 1973. From 1962 to 1975, Waldon was a captain with the New York City Housing Authority Police Department. In 1975, he became deputy commissioner of the New York State Division of Human Rights, serving until 1981. In that year, Waldon became an assistant counsel to the County Service Group of the New York State Office of Mental Retardation and Developmental Disabilities. In 1982, he was elected to the New York State House of Representatives as a representative from the Thirty-third Assembly District. He served as an assemblyman until 1986.

When Congressman Joseph Addabbo died in 1986, the Democratic leaders of New York's Sixth Congressional District were authorized to select a candidate to fill the remainder of Addabbo's term. In May of 1986, they nominated Waldon to run in the special election. Absentee ballots gave Waldon a narrow victory over Floyd H. FLAKE for the congressional seat. Waldon took office on July 29, 1986, and was appointed to serve on the House Committee on Education and Labor and the House Committee on Small Business.

During his term on Capitol Hill, Waldon supported legislation to halt the illegal traffic in crack cocaine and sponsored a resolution to create a national task force to address the problem of functional illiteracy. He also called on the House to override President Ronald Reagan's veto of legislative sanctions against South Africa and introduced a resolution proposing that the president attend a summit with African leaders whose countries bordered on South Africa. Waldon opposed the U.S. government's covert aid to rebel forces in Angola who were supported by South Africa's white minority government.

Waldon ran for reelection as the Democratic candidate for the Sixth Congressional District but lost the primary in September of 1986 to Floyd H. Flake, who went on to win in the general election. Waldon completed his congressional term and returned to New York, where he was appointed to serve as a commissioner on the New York State Investigation Committee from 1987 to 1990. In 1991, he was elected to the New York State Senate from the Tenth Senate District.

Walker, Aaron Thibeaux "T-Bone" (May 28, 1910, Linden, Tex.—Mar. 16, 1975, Los Angeles, Calif.): Blues singer and guitarist. Walker was the only son of Movelia Jimerson and Rance Walker, both musicians. The Walker family moved to Dallas in 1912, where Aaron was soon imbued with his parents' passion for music. He sang with his stepfather, Marco Washington, at local drive-ins and, at age ten, was lead-boy for the legendary bluesman Blind Lemon JEFFERSON, a family friend. By 1923, Walker had taught himself to play guitar and had begun to play at private parties in the Dallas area. In the late 1920's, Walker traveled throughout the South with a road show headed by Ida COX. Walker also made his first recordings on the Columbia label and achieved some local notoriety by winning first prize at Cab CALLOWAY's Amateur Show in Dallas.

Walker moved to Los Angeles in 1934. He spent the next several years working at the Little Harlem Club in Los Angeles and the Trocadero in Hollywood. He is credited with being the first blues guitarist to use electric amplification. In the late 1930's and early 1940's, Walker toured and recorded with the Les Hite Orchestra. During the war years, he toured army bases throughout the United States but also continued to play clubs in the Los Angeles area. From 1946 until the early 1950's, Walker toured the country with his own band and recorded on the Capitol and Imperial record labels. He then solidified his West Coast reputation with an extended engagement at the Blue Mirror Club in San Francisco and frequent appearances on local television shows.

In the 1960's, blues music enjoyed a dramatic rise in popularity, in part as a result of its acknowledged formative influence on rock music. Consequently, T-Bone Walker became something of an international celebrity. Having first played in England and Europe with a package tour called Rhythm & Blues USA in 1962, he criss-crossed North America and Europe in the late 1960's and early 1970's, appearing at dozens of folk, blues, and jazz festivals, including the 1967 Monterey Jazz Festival and the 1972 Montreux Jazz Festival. In 1970, Walker won a Grammy Award for an album on the Polydor label entitled *Good Feelin'*. Walker is generally acknowledged to have been one of the great modern blues guitarists. Billed as "Daddy of the Blues," he influenced such diverse talents as Chuck BERRY, Eric Clapton, Jimi HENDRIX, Albert Collins, and B. B. KING.

Walker, Alice Malsenior (b. Feb. 9, 1944, Eatonton, Ga.): Novelist, essayist, and poet. Alice Walker was born the eighth of eight children to SHARECROPPING parents in Eatonton, Ga. Walker believes that her family's name belonged to the white man who owned and fathered a child by her then eleven-year-old great-great-grandmother. She has kept her maiden name for quite another reason: Her great-great-great-grandmother, a slave with two babies, walked from Virginia to Eatonton, Ga. Allied to her pride in her family is the excitement and pride she felt upon the realization that she shared her name with her spiritual ancestor, Sojourner TRUTH ("Sojourner" translating to "Walker"; "Alice," in old Greek, meaning "Truth"). Another ancestor in whom Walker, in her work, often expresses pride is her mother's Cherokee grandmother.

Youth and Education. Because her mother could no longer carry Alice to the fields where she worked alongside her husband, Alice entered first grade at the early age of four. Always precocious, Alice was successful and happy in school until an accident (a brother shot her with a BB gun) blinded her in one eye and made her feel ugly. Her family moved shortly after the accident, and Alice entered a school that had formerly been a penitentiary.

Alice Walker's writing focuses on changing people's lives. (Jeff Reinking/Picture Group)

The site of the electric chair frightened Alice, and the children tormented her; Alice was sent back to live with her grandparents and to her old school. Her grades and disposition were not to return to near their former heights, however, until she was fourteen, at which time her brother Bill and his wife took her to their local Boston hospital, where the "glob" on her eye was removed. Soon her self-confidence and grades improved and she eventually graduated as valedictorian of her class.

Her three-year-old daughter Rebecca, years later, finally freed her from her self-consciousness (a blue scar remained on her eye): Rebecca told Alice that she had the world in her eye; and Alice, who realized the beauty and the necessity of having the world in her eye, was once again buoyant and whole.

Walker left for Spelman College in Atlanta when she was seventeen. She remained at Spelman for two and one-half years; she found the school opposed to change, however, and left to attend Sarah Lawrence College in New York. During her final college year, she wrote her first book, *Once: Poems* (1968), and published her first short story, "To Hell with Dying."

Activism and Teaching Career. Walker went to the South in the mid-1960's with her husband, Mel Leventhal, a civil rights activist, to educate and assist prospective voters. Her trips to and through college gave her the impetus for what was to become her life's work. She deliberately sat in the front section of a Greyhound bus on her way to Atlanta. When asked to move to the back, she vowed to change the social order of the world that humiliated her. (It was Martin Luther KING, JR., who gave her her first hope that such change was possible.) When she realized that even in a college course in southern writers she had not been presented with the works of African American writers, Walker vowed to correct her "miseducation." In researching a story on voodoo, she discovered the work of Zora Neale HURSTON, the writer of what she came to consider one of the greatest American novels, *THEIR EYES WERE WATCHING GOD* (1937). Walker included Hurston's work in her course (which she believed to be the first of its kind) on black women writers, which she taught first at Wellesley College and later at the University of Massachusetts.

Walker's devotion to Hurston did not stop with her courses or with Walker's essays, in which Hurston's influence is often evident. Walker, posing as Hurston's niece, sought out her spiritual aunt's burial site in Florida. The search was difficult; Hurston was not remembered in her own town, and her grave, in the middle of an overgrown field, was not marked. Walker scouted and found what she believed to be the burial site and purchased the marker that she felt was owed the great writer.

Essays. Words are the weapons of Walker's political arsenal. What her conscience would not allow her in the physical arena she transferred to the mental, the literary, and the oral: She has studied the peoples of the world and has taken her ideas to them. She is both a prolific writer and a much-sought-after speaker. Her ideas are spelled out in her collections of essays *In Search of Our Mothers' Gardens: Womanist Prose* (1983) and *Living by the Word: Selected Writings, 1973-1987* (1988).

"I am preoccupied," she has said, "with the spiritual survival, the survival *whole* of my people. But beyond that, I am committed to exploring the oppressions, the insanities, the loyalties, and the triumphs of black WOMEN." She shows, further, her commitment to the "survival *whole*" of the earth and its creatures. "Earth itself," she says, "has become the nigger of the world. It is perceived, ironically, as other, alien, evil, and threatening by those who are finding they cannot draw a healthful breath without its cooperation." Walker argues that people must, rather, hold themselves accountable for the planet's well-being and their own.

Her overriding feeling of kinship with all living things has caused her anxiety, because she has not been able to physically strike out against those she has called "Hitlers" who "murdered our children, called us chimpanzees from their judges' benches and made life a daily ordeal for us." In Cuba, she studied the effects of the Cuban Revolution, because she "still needed to know that the use of violence did not necessarily destroy humanity." While others fought physically, she feared that her mere words might not change anything. She has remained, however, a peaceful revolutionary, with change the constant focus of her work.

Novels. Her novels illustrate the ideas of her essays. *THE THIRD LIFE OF GRANGE COPELAND* (1970) explores conditions in the South that contribute to the mistreatment of women. Grange Copeland's struggle to survive as a sharecropper for a white man who degrades him causes him to turn his own abuse upon his wife, who commits suicide. His son Brownfield's life is a repetition and a magnification of his own: Brownfield serves and hates his servitude, and he finally fires a gun into the face of his wife. Grange, however, finds redemption through Brownfield's daughter, Ruth. He allows his unhappy life to inform hers, but he bestows upon her all the love he would like to have given his own wife and children. Grange dies saving Ruth.

MERIDIAN (1976) begins where *The Third Life of Grange Copeland* ends, in the turbulent 1960's. In college, the title character becomes a part of a radical group that her pacifist beliefs force her to abandon. She does not, however, abandon their common goals: She goes South to help oppressed blacks to vote and to achieve their everyday rights peacefully.

Celie in *THE COLOR PURPLE* (1982) undergoes physical and mental abuse from her stepfather and husband, but she is saved by a woman who teaches and loves her. Whereas Grange teaches Ruth the caution necessary to the young black girl's survival in a world that does not see her as significant, Shug teaches the mature Celie to surrender herself to the earth, to its creatures, and to their informing spiritual force, all of which are ready to serve and to love her. Learning that God is everything and that she is a part of everything frees Celie from her hatred of her abusive husband and brings, finally, all of what has troubled her life to happy resolution.

Lissie, the informing spirit of *The Temple of My Familiar* (1989) remembers as her earliest incarnation one of the earliest humans, who learned her lessons from the beasts. The peaceful lesson that Lissie teaches the novel's other principals brings them from their bestiality to a perfect union with the Earth, with their loved ones, and with their own no-longer-abused bodies.

Conclusion. Walker is best known for her Pulitzer

Prize-winning novel *The Color Purple*, which was made into a major motion picture. Her poetry, collected in *Once, Revolutionary Petunias and Other Poems* (1973), *Goodnight, Willie Lee, I'll See You in the Morning: Poems* (1979), *Horses Make a Landscape Look More Beautiful* (1984), and *Her Blue Body Everything We Know: Earthling Poems, 1965-1990 Complete* (1991), and her short stories, collected in *In Love and in Trouble: Stories of Black Women* (1973) and *You Can't Keep a Good Woman Down* (1981), contain unique pieces of writing, most of which nevertheless offer some aspect of the corrective vision for humankind set forth in her essays and in her novels. Her children's biography *Langston HUGHES: American Poet* (1974) and her edition of Hurston's works, *I Love Myself When I Am Laughing . . . And Then Again When I Am Looking Mean and Impressive: A Zora Neale Hurston Reader* (1979), afford this same view.— *Judith K. Taylor*

Oprah Winfrey played Sofia in the film adaptation of Walker's prize-winning novel The Color Purple. *(AP/Wide World Photos)*

SUGGESTED READINGS: • Christian, Barbara. "Novel for Everyday Use: The Novels of Alice Walker." In *Black Women Novelists: The Development of a Tradition, 1896-1976*. Westport, Conn.: Greenwood Press, 1980. • De Veaux, Alice. "Alice Walker." *Essence* 20 (September, 1989): 56-62. • De Weever, Jacqueline. *Mythmaking and Metaphor in Black Women's Fiction*. New York: St. Martin's Press, 1992. • Parker-Smith, Bettye J. "Alice Walker's Women: In Search of Some Peace of Mind." In *Black Women Writers (1950-1980): A Critical Evaluation*, edited by Mari Evans. Garden City, N.Y.: Anchor, 1984. • Tate, Claudia. *Black Women Writers at Work*. New York: Continuum, 1983.

Walker, Chester "Chet" (b. Feb. 22, 1940, Benton Harbor, Mich.): Basketball player. After a notable college BASKETBALL career at Bradley University, where he averaged 24.4 points per game, Walker spent the years 1962-1975 as a forward in the National Basketball Association (NBA). Regardless of the team he played on, Walker reached the play-offs in each of his thirteen seasons as a professional. Known for his well-rounded playing skills that managed to combine considerable power with smoothness, Walker's one-on-one game was especially strong. The six-foot, seven-inch, 220-pound forward was part of the Philadelphia 76ers front court trio that included Luke Jackson and Wilt CHAMBERLAIN and won the 1966-1967 championship. In addition to his perennial play-off performances, he left the game with a scoring average of 18.2 points per game, seven All-Star appearances, and playing time logged with the Syracuse Nationals (transferred to Philadelphia and renamed the 76ers in 1963) and the Chicago Bulls. He had the highest free throw completion percentage in the NBA in 1971.

Walker, David (Sept. 28, 1785, Wilmington, N.C.—1830, Boston, Mass.): Abolitionist author. In 1829, Walker wrote one of the most significant documents in African American history, a pamphlet called *Walker's Appeal, in Four Articles: Together with a Preamble to the Colored Citizens of the World*. A stinging indictment of SLAVERY, Walker's pamphlet called for free northern blacks to make common cause with southern slaves in a violent overthrow of slavery. Condemning slavery as a violation of God's and nature's laws, Walker's *Appeal* fired the first shot in the ABOLITIONIST MOVEMENT's war against slavery.

Walker himself was a runaway slave who escaped to Pennsylvania. A tailor by trade, Walker operated a used-clothing shop in Philadelphia and sold clothing and cloth door-to-door. Although prosperous, Walker burned with bitter memories of his slave experience and vowed to fight the institution of slavery in any way he could. His pamphlet raised a storm of controversy throughout the United States, especially in the South, where attempts were made to ban its circulation. Walker's advocacy of violent revolution to overthrow slavery touched a nerve in a nation fearful of its slaves. His violent prophecies almost came true two years later, with the bloody Nat TURNER rebellion in Southhampton County, Va. Walker himself died in suspicious circumstances, perhaps the victim of a backlash against his pamphlet, shortly after the *Appeal*'s publication.

Walker, George (1873, Lawrence, Kans.—1911, Lawrence, Kans.): Singer and comedian. Walker was attracted to show business at an early age. He left Lawrence High School to follow a minstrel group of African Americans. From performing in minstrel shows, he graduated to performing in circuses and musical shows. In 1893, he met Bert WILLIAMS in California. Williams was a singer, an instrumental musician, and a comedian whose parents had migrated from Nassau, in the Bahamas Islands of the Caribbean, to California. By 1895, Walker and Williams had put together their talents to form a team that would make a great impact on American show business.

Success did not come until Walker and Williams advertised themselves in theaters as "Two Real Coons," an idea that came to them after observing Caucasian performers in BLACKFACE billing themselves as "coons." Walker and Williams began to enjoy popularity in Californian theaters. In 1896, they started performing in New York City, appearing first in *The Gold Bug*. It was during their stay in New York that they brought into vogue the CAKEWALK, a type of dance invented by African Americans for competitions in which a cake traditionally was awarded as prize.

Walker and Williams made history when, in 1902, they teamed up with Jesse Shipp (director) and Will Marion Cook (playwright) to produce a musical play, *IN DAHOMEY*. It was the first African American production ever to open on Broadway, in 1903. Its success attained international proportions when Walker and Williams performed it at the Shaftesbury Theatre and at a command performance at Buckingham Palace in London in 1903. It was followed by another successful production, *Abyssinia*, at the Majestic Theatre in New York City in 1906. These two plays are important in the annals of African American theater history because they boldly introduced African settings, characters, and songs into American show business. Walker last teamed with Williams in 1908, when they produced *Bandanna Land* with much success. Walker fell ill while the production was still running in 1909.

Walker, Herschel (b. Mar. 3, 1962, Wrightsville, Ga.): FOOTBALL player. Winner of the 1982 Heisman Trophy for his play with the University of Georgia, Walker set ten National Collegiate Athletic Association records, in-

cluding most carries (994) and most yards gained rushing (5,259) over his three years there. He left college in 1983 to play for the New Jersey Generals of the United States Football League. He led the league in rushing in 1983 and was third in 1984. In 1985, he set a single-season record for rushing with 2,411 yards gained. Additionally, he has been in the top five nationally in track and field for the sixty-yard dash and competed in the 1992 Winter Olympics as pusher for the U.S. bobsled team. He played several seasons in the National Football League, for the Dallas Cowboys and Minnesota Vikings, leading the league in rushing in 1988.

Cutting around defenders, Herschel Walker manages to gain yardage against the Dolphins. (AP/Wide World Photos)

Walker, James Carter "Jimmie" (b. June 25, 1948, New York, N.Y.): Comedian and actor. Originally a stand-up comedian, Walker was cast in the role of J. J. Evans on the CBS television series *GOOD TIMES*. As played by Walker, J. J. was a jive-talking teen who was fond of the phrase "Dy-No-Mite" and was constantly involved in get-rich-quick schemes to help finance his family's escape from the GHETTO. He eventually became more responsible and used his drawing abilities to gain employment as a graphic artist and later as a syndicated cartoonist. After the series was canceled, Walker returned to stand-up comedy and also became a television scriptwriter.

Walker, Madam C. J. (Sarah Breedlove; Dec. 23, 1867, Delta, La.—May 25, 1919, Irvington, N.Y.): Entrepreneur. Born to ex-slaves and sharecroppers Owen and Minerva Breedlove, Madam C. J. Walker became the first African American woman millionaire and a pioneer in the cosmetics industry. She was one of the best-known African American women of the early twentieth century.

Early Years. Walker was orphaned by age seven and was reared by Louvenia, her married sister, in Vicksburg, Miss. She married a man named McWilliams at age fourteen in order to escape the cruelties of Louvenia's husband; however, McWilliams was killed when Walker was twenty, leaving her alone to rear Lelia, their two-year-old daughter. Shortly thereafter, Walker moved to St. Louis, where she worked as a washerwoman for eighteen years; she put Lelia through public schools and Knoxville College, a private black school in Tennessee.

Manufacturer and philanthropist, Madam Walker succeeded in her business ventures of the early twentieth century. (The Associated Publishers, Inc.)

Madam C. J. Walker Manufacturing Company. Suffering from thinning hair, Walker began experimenting with patent medicines and hair-care products. In 1905, she dreamed that a black man appeared to her with a formula for a new hair preparation. She mixed these ingredients and, pleased with the results, began selling the preparation to friends and neighbors. In July, she moved to

Denver to be with her brother's wife, who had been recently widowed, but she continued to peddle her product to local African American women.

Six months later, she married Charles J. Walker, a newspaperman who brought his understanding of advertising and mail-order operations to the business. The relationship was of short duration, however, because Charles Walker was satisfied with only a local market. Madam C. J. Walker had larger plans.

In 1906, she put twenty-one-year-old Lelia in charge while she traveled throughout the country, giving demonstrations in homes, churches, and clubs. Two years later, they moved to Pittsburgh, where Lelia ran both the manufacturing operation and Lelia College, which trained African American women to be cosmetologists. Walker continued to travel.

Impressed with the transportation facilities in Indianapolis in 1910, she decided to build a plant and relocate her headquarters there, and she placed both under the leadership of Freeman B. Ransom. She had met Ransom when he was working as a train porter during his vacations from Columbia University Law School. This arrangement freed Walker and her daughter to move to New York in 1913; there, she established a second Lelia College in her expensively furnished Harlem brownstone. Walker continued her travels, often using Lelia's adopted daughter, Mae, as a model to demonstrate the Walker System.

Walker System. "Kinky" and "nappy" hair, rather than being simply descriptive terms, were considered to be badges of slavery. Walker developed a system—consisting of a shampoo, the application of a pomade "hair grower," vigorous brushing, and the use of hot-iron combs—that resulted in a shiny, smooth coiffure. She called her beauticians "hair culturists," "scalp specialists," or "beauty culturists" to distinguish them from "hair straighteners." Walker insisted that her purpose was not to straighten hair but to encourage hair growth and cures for common scalp problems.

The Walker System offended some preachers who objected to attempts by black women to make themselves "look white," but popular songs sung by black men praised "long-haired babes." The Walker System's popularity rested on its ability to provide the versatility in styling African American women desired. Even the internationally renowned entertainer Josephine BAKER used the Walker System, and the French developed their own pomade called the "Baker-Fix."

Walker's method differed from earlier hair-care practices, which often involved dividing hair into sections that were tightly wrapped with string and twisted. This process left the hair straighter when it was brushed out, but the strain could lead to balding. Walker's early efforts were an attempt to stimulate hair growth to overcome this problem.

She also used her "miracle ingredient," sulphur, to address common scalp infections caused by poor nutrition and other problems associated with a low standard of living. In addition, she developed a steel comb with wide teeth to accommodate thicker hair.

Walker advertised her products widely in African American newspapers and magazines. Her primary competition came from Annie M. Turnbo Malone's "Poro System"; "Poro Colleges" were located in St. Louis and Chicago. Other African American owned beauty-product companies of the time included Madame Sarah Spencer Washington's "Apex System" of Atlantic City and the Boston company of W. A. Johnson and his wife, M. L. Johnson. Some white-owned companies such as Ozono and Kinkilla also competed in the black hair-care market.

Madam C. J. Walker's Hair Grower, a pomade sold in tins embellished with her portrait, remained her best-selling product. Despite the argument over "looking white," Walker emphasized the view that being well groomed instilled pride. More important than her success in the cosmetics industry, however, was the opportunity she afforded to African American women. Few had the education to succeed in most professions, but Walker offered many the opportunity of leaving domestic service to become economically independent entrepreneurs.

Walker Agents. On her travels, Walker recruited agents who signed contracts to sell her products exclusively and also to follow her hygienic system, which was a regimen antedating similar practices later put into law by most states. A 1919 editorial in *The Crisis* magazine suggested that Walker had revolutionized the personal habits of millions of women. Walker agents, dressed in white shirts and long black skirts and carrying black satchels of hair-care products, were a common sight making house calls throughout the United States and in the Caribbean. Walker's assistants taught women how to set up beauty parlors in their homes, keep business records, and become financially independent. Speaking before Booker T. WASHINGTON'S NATIONAL NEGRO BUSINESS LEAGUE in 1913, Walker presented herself as a role model to other women. Starting with only one dollar and fifty cents eight years earlier, she had come to own her own factory and employ more than one thousand women.

Madam C. J. Walker Hair Culturists' Union of America. About the time Mary Kay Ash of Mary Kay Cosmetics was born, Walker organized local and state clubs of women selling her hair-care products. In 1917, members of more than two hundred clubs met in Philadelphia for their first convention. They learned new techniques, shared business experiences, and heard Walker address them on "Women's Duty to Women." In addition to showing others how to be independent, Walker encouraged philanthropy by giving prizes to the clubs with the best charitable records. She also encouraged political and social involvement. For example, at her suggestion, the convention wired President Woodrow Wilson to urge passage of legislation making lynching a federal crime.

Club Women and Philanthropies. Walker compensated for her lack of formal education by hiring tutors and becoming an avid reader. She joined the National Association of Colored Women (NACW), the organization of the nation's most educated and progressive African American women, and was introduced to the membership along with Mary McLeod BETHUNE at the group's 1912 convention. Through the NACW, she associated with Bethune, Ida B. WELLS-Barnett, Mary Talbert, and others. At the NACW's 1918 convention, she was given the honor of burning the mortgage to Frederick DOUGLASS' Washington home, having made the largest contribution to pay off the loan and refurbish the house as a memorial and museum.

Her interest in women's education was strong. She contributed women's scholarships to TUSKEGEE INSTITUTE and to Charlotte Hawkins' Palmer Memorial Institute and bequeathed five thousand dollars each to Bethune's Daytona Normal and Industrial Institute for Negro Girls and Lucy LANEY's Haynes Institute in Augusta, Ga. She also contributed to homes for the aged in St. Louis and Indianapolis and to the Young Women's Christian Association, and she was a strong supporter of the NATIONAL ASSOCIATION FOR THE ADVANCEMENT OF COLORED PEOPLE (NAACP).

Final Years. Walker remained president and sole owner of the business and continued to travel throughout her life, despite problems with hypertension. She found time to enjoy an electric car. Her mansion in Harlem became famous as "Dark Tower" when her daughter, now known as A'Lelia, presided over a salon of talented African Americans. Called the "joy goddess" of the HARLEM RENAISSANCE by poet Langston HUGHES, A'Lelia introduced authors, artists, and musicians to white publishers, critics, and patrons of the arts.

Walker also built a thirty-four-room mansion designed by African American architect Vertner Tandy, at Irvington, N.Y. Internationally renowned tenor Enrico Caruso named the estate "Villa Lewaro" by combining the initial syllables of Walker's daughter's name, which had become A'Lelia Walker Robinson.

Walker died in 1919 at Villa Lewaro of chronic nephritis. Funeral services were conducted there, with interment in Woodlawn Cemetery in The Bronx. She left her company to her daughter, stipulating that the presidency always be held by a woman.

A'Lelia was succeeded as the company president by her daughter, Mae Walker Perry; Perry was followed in turn by her daughter, A'Lelia Mae Perry Bundles. The manufacturing plant planned by Walker was completed in 1927 and renovated in the 1980's. Known as the Madam Walker Urban Life Center, it serves as a cultural center in downtown Indianapolis.—*Christie Farnham*

SUGGESTED READINGS: • Bundles, A'Lelia Perry. *Madam C. J. Walker*. New York: Chelsea House, 1991. • Bundles, A'Lelia Perry. "Madam C. J. Walker—Cosmetics Tycoon." *Ms.* 12 (July, 1983): 91-94. • Davis, Marianna W., ed. *Contributions of Black Women to America, Volume 1: The Arts, Media, Business, Law, Sports*. Columbia, S.C.: Kenday Press, 1982. • Giddings, Paula. *When and Where I Enter: The Impact of Black Women on Race and Sex in America*. New York: William Morrow, 1984. • Haskins, Jim. *One More River to Cross: The Stories of Twelve Black Americans*. New York: Scholastic, 1992. • James, Edward T. et al., eds. *Notable American Women, 1607-1950: A Biographical Dictionary*. Vol. 3. Cambridge, Mass.: The Belknap Press of Harvard University Press, 1971.

Walker, Maggie Lena Draper (July 15, 1867, Richmond, Va.—Dec. 15, 1934, Richmond, Va.): Banker and organizer. After her father's death, she helped her mother support the family, working as a washerwoman while she attended school. She was graduated from Richmond's Colored Normal School in 1883, and she taught until her marriage to Armstead Walker in 1886.

At the age of fourteen, Walker joined the Independent Order of St. Luke. She became its Right Worthy Grand Secretary in 1899 and served until her death, as the order grew from one thousand to more than eighty thousand members in twenty-three states. Walker founded youth branches, published a weekly newspaper, the *St. Luke Herald*, created an educational loan fund, and ran a department store. The order was a mutual benefit society, providing insurance, economic, social, and political services for its members.

The Saint Luke Penny Savings Bank, which Walker established in 1903, was her best-known achievement. Walker was the first female bank president in the United States. She ran the bank, reorganizing it as the Consolidated Bank and Trust Company in 1934. By the 1990's, it was the oldest continually black-owned and black-run bank in the nation. The bank was an outgrowth of the

As the first female bank president in the United States, Maggie Walker provided various social services. (The Associated Publishers, Inc.)

Independent Order of St. Luke.

Walker also founded and led other organizations to benefit African Americans. Believing that education and employment of black women would benefit the whole race, Walker was active in the Richmond Council of Colored Women, Virginia State Federation of Colored Women, National Association of Wage Earners, International Council of Women of the Darker Races, National Training School for Girls, and Virginia Industrial School for Colored Girls. She worked in the NATIONAL ASSOCIATION FOR THE ADVANCEMENT OF COLORED PEOPLE, Richmond Urban League, Negro Organization Society of Virginia, and Virginia Interracial Commission. Supporting women's suffrage, she worked for voter registration and belonged to the Virginia Lily Black Republican Party, running on its ticket for state superintendent of schools. She also managed the finances of the National League of Republican Colored Women.

Maggie and Armstead Walker had two sons, Russell and Melvin. In 1904, the family moved into the home in Richmond's Jackson Ward that was later purchased and operated by the National Park Service as the Maggie Lena Walker National Historic Site. After her husband's death in 1915, Walker expanded her household to include her mother, her sons, and their wives and children. By 1928, health problems had confined her to a wheelchair. Walker died of diabetic gangrene at her home.

Walker, Margaret Abigail (b. July 7, 1915, Birmingham, Ala.): Author and educator. Walker received a B.A. from Northwestern University in 1935, an M.A. from the University of Iowa in 1940, and a Ph.D. from Iowa in 1965. She also holds several honorary doctorates. She is the daughter of a Jamaican-born Methodist minister and a music teacher.

Walker's academic career is multifaceted. She taught at Livingstone College in North Carolina and at West Virginia State College before joining the faculty at Jackson State University in 1949. She taught there until her retirement in 1979. She is the recipient of many awards, including a Yale Younger Poets Award, a Rosenwald Fellowship, a Ford Fellowship, and a Houghton Mifflin literary fellowship.

Walker's literary career soared with the publication of a collection of poetry, *For My People*, in 1942. She received a Yale Younger Poets Series Award for that volume. She did not publish another volume of poetry for more than twenty years. In 1966, Walker's acclaimed novel of the African American experiences of the Civil War, *Jubilee*, was published. The Houghton Mifflin Award novel was written as her doctoral dissertation. *Jubilee* is noted for its historical accuracy and its authenticity of folk material. It spans the antebellum period through RECONSTRUCTION. The central character is Vyry, one of the most complex and admirable examples of an African American heroine to appear in an American novel. Vyry is intelligent, brave, daring, loyal, persistent, and indefatigable. *Jubilee* often is compared favorably with THE AUTOBIOGRAPHY OF MISS JANE PITTMAN (1971) by Ernest J. GAINES.

After receiving critical acclaim for *Jubilee*, Walker returned to writing poetry, conducting research, teaching, and promoting the causes of African Americans. An excellent example of generational views is available in Nikki GIOVANNI's *A Poetic Equation: Conversations Between Nikki Giovanni and Margaret Walker* (1974). A biography by Walker, *Richard WRIGHT, Daemonic Genius: A Portrait of the Man, a Critical Look at His Work*, appeared in 1988.

Walker, Moses Fleetwood (Oct. 7, 1857, Mt. Pleasant, Ohio—May 11, 1924, Cleveland, Ohio): First African American to play major league BASEBALL. Walker played forty-two games in 1884 with the Toledo Blue Stockings of the American Association, which is considered a major league. The Blue Stockings disbanded after 1884, and

Walker never again reached the major leagues, although he played for several seasons at the minor league level. His brother, Welday, also played for Toledo in 1884.

Moses Fleetwood Walker was the first African American to play major league baseball. (National Baseball Library, Cooperstown, NY)

Wallace, Beulah "Sippie" (Nov. 11, 1898, Houston, Tex.—Nov. 1, 1986, Detroit, Mich.): Blues singer and musician. Wallace traveled with a number of tent shows during World War I, then migrated to Chicago, Ill. She cut a number of sides with OKeh Records. She is most remembered as a blues singer with strong ties to gospel music, having served as director of the National Convention of Gospel Choirs and Choruses for most of the 1930's. Wallace influenced many later singers. In 1976, she recorded a duet of her own classic "Women Be Wise" with Bonnie Raitt.

Wallace, C. Everett (b. Aug. 16, 1951, Chicago, Ill.): Attorney and political appointee. Wallace was graduated from Northwestern University, receiving his bachelor's degree in 1973 and his J.D. degree in 1976. Upon graduation, Wallace worked as a staff attorney for Memphis Light, Gas, and Water from 1976 to 1977, when he was admitted to the Tennessee State Bar. He was cofounder and legal counsel to the Shelby County Black Republican Council in Tennessee.

He first served in Washington, D.C., as a legal assistant to Senator Howard Baker of Tennessee between 1977 and 1980. While serving on Baker's staff, Wallace became cofounder and vice chairman of the Black Republican Congressional Staffers Association and served as counsel secretary of the 1980 Republican National Convention. In 1980, he became a senior analyst and energy counsel to the U.S. Senate Budget Committee. President Ronald Reagan appointed Wallace as deputy assistant secretary of Fair Housing for the DEPARTMENT OF HOUSING AND URBAN DEVELOPMENT.

Wallace, George (b. Atlanta, Ga.): Comedian. Wallace's club appearances have included Caroline's in 1983 and Happy Days at Kew Gardens in 1985. Television appearances include the *Mike Douglas Show* in 1980, *Late Night with David Letterman in 1983 and 1985, and the Tonight Show* in 1986.

Wallace, Michele (b. Jan. 4, 1952, New York, N.Y.): Journalist, cultural critic, and feminist. Wallace's chief subject is the lack of respect black women have received in American society. Wallace has described her Harlem childhood as sheltered and middle-class. Her mother, Faith RINGGOLD Wallace, was an artist. Her father, Robert Earl Wallace, was a jazz pianist who died of a heroin overdose when she was thirteen.

Wallace attended the City University of New York, from which she received a B.A. in 1974. She was a book review researcher for *Newsweek* in 1974 and 1975 and was an instructor in journalism at New York University beginning in 1976. Her most influential work, *Black Macho and the Myth of the Superwoman*, was published in 1979. She taught in the black studies department at the University of Oklahoma and, in 1987, took a position at the State University of New York at Buffalo. A collection of her essays entitled *Invisibility Blues: From Pop to Theory* was published in 1990.

Wallace achieved notoriety with *Black Macho and the Myth of the Superwoman*, her probing analysis of the sexism and racism that relegated black women to second-class citizenship in American society and, more particularly, in the CIVIL RIGHTS and Black Power movements of the 1960's. She notes that black women were denied a voice because of two misconceptions: the belief that the black woman was a "superwoman" who emasculated the black man and took over his role as head of the household and as chief breadwinner; and that the black man, in order to be liberated, had to prove that he was "macho" by suppressing the black woman to gain his own self-respect. In support of her position, Wallace cites, among other

sources, the MOYNIHAN REPORT on the black family, which deplored black female dominance, and Stokely CAR-MICHAEL's infamous remark that the proper position of the black woman in the BLACK POWER MOVEMENT was "prone"— that is, in a position to satisfy the black male's sexual appetite but with no voice in political decisions.

Wallace's essays are often commentaries on those works she feels will have the greatest potential influence on popular attitudes toward race and gender. She has written essays about Alice Walker's novel *THE COLOR PURPLE* (1982), Ntozake SHANGE's choreopoem *FOR COLORED GIRLS WHO HAVE CONSIDERED SUICIDE/ WHEN THE RAINBOW IS ENUF* (1976), and the films of Spike LEE, among other works.

Waller, Calvin Augustine Hoffman (b. Dec. 17, 1937, Baton Rouge, La.): Military officer. Waller retired from the United States Army on Nov. 30, 1991, with the rank of lieutenant general. His combat experience included a year in Vietnam as a chemical operations officer and

Calvin Waller served as deputy commander in chief of the U.S. Central Command during Operation Desert Storm. (Dept. of Defense)

service from November, 1989, to January, 1991, as deputy commander in chief with the United States Central Command (Forward) during Operation Desert Storm in Saudi Arabia. He was criticized for expressing his opinion that U.S. forces would not be ready by the Jan. 15, 1991, the date given as a deadline by the United Nations for Iraq to withdraw from Kuwait.

Waller is a graduate of Prairie View A&M College (B.S., 1959, agriculture) and of Shippensburg State University (M.S., 1978, public administration). He attended the Army's chemical school advanced course and infantry school basic course in addition to graduating from the Command and General Staff College and the War College.

After taking the infantry officer basic course in 1959, Waller was stationed at Fort Lewis, Wash. He was advanced from platoon leader to executive officer to commander of a chemical platoon. After taking the associate chemical career course in 1963, he was made chief of the chemical, biological, and radiological center for the Seventh Logistics Command of the Eighth Army in Korea. Later, he was made an operations officer for the Eighth United States Army Support Command in Korea.

Waller returned to the United States in 1965 to serve at Fort Bragg, N.C. His positions there included chemical officer (later brigade chemical officer) and assistant training officer (later training officer) in the office of the assistant chief of staff for the Eighty-second Airborne Division. After attending the Army Command and General Staff College, Waller was assigned to Vietnam from May, 1969, to May, 1970. Upon his return to the United States, Waller was stationed in Washington, D.C., serving as personnel management officer in the chemical branch of the office of personnel operations, then as training staff officer in the office of the deputy chief of staff for personnel. Waller served in Europe from July, 1972, to August, 1975, as S-3 (later executive officer) in an infantry battalion and as deputy assistant chief of staff with the Eighth Infantry Division.

Waller returned to the United States to command a mechanized infantry battalion at Fort Carson, Colo. After a year at the Army War College, he returned to Fort Carson for two years, serving as deputy G-3 and later assistant chief of staff for the Fourth Infantry Division. In July, 1980, he became senior military assistant to the assistant secretary of defense. Waller commanded a mechanized infantry brigade in Europe from July, 1981, to July, 1983. Later positions included chief of staff for the Eighteenth Airborne Corps and assistant division commander of the Eighty-second Airborne Division, both at Fort Bragg, N.C. He was deputy commanding general of I Corps and Fort Lewis, Wash., for a year, then became commanding general of the Eighth Infantry Division of the United States Army Europe and Seventh Army. He returned to Fort Lewis for a year, as commanding general, before his

service in Operation Desert Storm. Waller resumed his position at Fort Lewis to finish his military career. His awards and commendations include the Distinguished Service Medal with oak leaf cluster, the Defense Superior Service Medal, the Bronze Star with oak leaf cluster, and the Meritorious Service Medal with three oak leaf clusters.

Waller, Thomas Wright "Fats" (May 21, 1904, Waverley, N.Y.—Dec. 15, 1937, Kansas City, Mo.): Composer and pianist. A legendary performer of New York stride piano, Waller was active in nightclubs, theaters, and recording studios. Known for such solo recordings of his own works as "Handful of Keys" (1929), Waller was heard on so-called "race records" during the 1920's. Born to Edward Waller, a Baptist clergyman, and his wife, Adeline, young Fats Waller played organ for church services. Waller received his training from the equally legendary James P. JOHNSON.

In the early 1920's, Waller began to be heard on recordings, and sheet music publications of his compositions were released. His 1922 recordings of "Birmingham Blues" and "Muscle Shoals Blues," both for OKeh Records, were followed by the publication of "Wild Cat Blues" and "Squeeze Me." Waller also made an impact in the broadcasting field; he could be heard as both pianist and singer on WHN in New York City. In New York, Waller performed on organ and piano at the Lafayette and Lincoln theaters in Harlem. He coauthored, with Andy Razaf, the music for *Keep Shufflin'* (1928) and *Hot Chocolates* (1929), both of which were Broadway productions. With Razaf, he also composed the music for *Load of Coal*. As a recording artist, Waller performed in the late 1920's with McKinney's Cotton Pickers, Morris's Hot Babes, and Fats Waller's Buddies, an early integrated ensemble.

By the 1930's, Waller's recording career had expanded, and the formation of the sextet Fats Waller and his Rhythm resulted in numerous recordings. Waller ventured to the West Coast in the mid-1930's to work with Les Hite's band. He also made Hollywood film appearances, which included *King of Burlesque* and *Hooray for Love!*, both in 1935. In 1943, Waller appeared in *STORMY WEATHER* with Lena HORNE. Waller's international reputation was launched with two European tours, in 1938 and in 1939. "London Suite" (1939), an extended work, displayed Waller's solo piano skills. Waller died of pneumonia after an arduous touring schedule.

Walls, Josiah Thomas (1842, Winchester, Va.—May 15, 1905, Tallahassee, Fla.): Politician. Walls was the first

African American state representative from Florida, serving in the Forty-second through Forty-fourth Congresses. He served in the Third Infantry Regiment of the United States Colored Troops until 1865 and was elected to the Florida state assembly in 1868. Later that year, he was elected to the state senate from the Thirteenth District. After serving in the U.S. Congress, he was elected to the state senate in 1876. Walls became a champion of mandatory public education and, in 1895, was placed in charge of the farm at Florida Normal College.

Walrond, Eric (1898, Georgetown, British Guiana—1966, London, England): Author. Walrond was one of the most important figures associated with the HARLEM RENAISSANCE. He became a journalist upon arrival in New York, writing for *Opportunity*, the publication of the NATIONAL URBAN LEAGUE. His short stories discuss discrimination and racial prejudice; his collection of ten stories, *Tropic Death* (1926), has a tropical setting (the Barbados, Panama, and British Guiana) and deals with POVERTY, famine, racial prejudice, and imperialism. His work is noted for its experimental, impressionistic qualities.

Walters, Alexander (Aug. 1, 1858, Bardstown, Ky.—Feb. 2, 1917, New York, N.Y.): Religious leader and civil rights activist. Both of Walters' parents, Henry Walters and Harriet Mathers Walters, were slaves. He was the sixth of eight children, four of whom died as infants. He studied at private schools and was educated for the ministry in the AFRICAN METHODIST EPISCOPAL ZION (AMEZ) CHURCH. He was graduated in 1875 as class valedictorian, ending his formal education.

In 1876, he and his brother Isaac took jobs as waiters in Indianapolis, Ind. He was licensed to preach by the Quarterly Conference of the AMEZ church in March, 1977, and was appointed pastor of a newly organized church in Indianapolis. On Aug. 28, 1877, he married Kate Knox, with whom he had five children.

Walters was ordained a deacon on July 8, 1879. In 1881, he was elected assistant secretary of the Kentucky Conference, beginning a rapid rise within his church. He held pastorates in Louisville, Ky., San Francisco, Calif., and Portland, Oreg., between 1881 and 1886. He was elected to represent California at the General Conference held in May, 1884. The conference elected him as first assistant secretary.

Between 1886 and 1888, Walters pastored in Chattanooga and Knoxville, Tenn. He then became pastor at the historic Mother Zion Church in New York, N.Y. On May 4, 1892, he was elected bishop of the Seventh District by the General Conference of the AMEZ church.

Walters joined with the publisher T. Thomas FORTUNE in the National Afro-American League, which disbanded after two years because of a lack of interest. Walters noted how the United States Congress had retreated from its commitment to civil rights, how state legislatures had begun barring African Americans from the polls, and how the Supreme Court had legitimated the policy of "SEPARATE BUT EQUAL" in the 1896 case of *PLESSY V. FERGUSON*. He asked Fortune to call a meeting of black leaders. On Sept. 15, 1898, the National Afro-American Council was formed in Rochester, N.Y., with Walters as president. He would be elected to the office of president seven times.

On Dec. 29, 1898, at its second meeting, the council drew up what was probably the most comprehensive program to date to address the problems of African Americans. Walters addressed the council, opposing Booker T. WASHINGTON's policy of separation. At the Aug. 18, 1899, national meeting in Chicago, Ill., he opposed the idea of emigration to LIBERIA and presented a defense of equal rights for black people in the United States. He also was elected president of the Pan-African Association at the Pan-African Congress held July 23-25, 1900, in London.

Washington gained control of the National Afro-American Council, which became a forerunner of the NIAGARA MOVEMENT. Walters joined the District of Columbia branch of the Niagara movement in 1908. He also joined the NATIONAL ASSOCIATION FOR THE ADVANCEMENT OF COLORED PEOPLE soon after its founding. In 1909, he and other black leaders including W. E. B. DU BOIS signed a document calling for a national conference on the race problem, in the wake of the Springfield Massacre, in which white people killed and wounded scores of African Americans and drove hundreds of others from that Illinois city.

Walters traveled to West Africa in 1910 to reorganize the Cape Coast, West Gold Coast, and Liberian conferences of the AMEZ church. He thought that the church's priority should be to lay the basis for education and let churches be natural outgrowths of schools. He was offered the post of minister to Liberia by President Woodrow Wilson in 1915, but he declined because of his duties in the United States. His autobiography, *My Life and Work*, was published in 1917.

Walters, Ricky "Slick Rick" (b. England): Rap vocalist. Walters was one of the early RAP acts to be managed by Russell SIMMONS, who signed him as Slick Rick to his Def Jam rap label. Walters appeared as a guest vocalist on DOUG E. FRESH's hit "The Show." In 1988, Columbia

Records released a compilation of his singles on the album *The Great Adventures of Slick Rick*. Walters was charged with attempted murder for a shooting that occurred in July of 1990. As his manager, Simmons put up a huge bail bond in order to keep Walters out of jail before the case went to trial. During this period, Walters recorded several singles and accompanying videos. The murder trial was held in the fall of 1991. Walters received a three- to nine-year sentence for attempted murder and was incarcerated at Attica. He released the album *The Ruler's Back* in 1991. The first single, released from the album after he went to prison, had the ironic title "Shouldn'a Done It," although the song's lyrics did not specifically refer to Walters' murder charge.

Walters, Ronald (b. July 20, 1938, Wichita, Kans.): Educator, writer, and activist. Walters earned a bachelor's degree at FISK UNIVERSITY and a master's and doctorate at American University. He taught at Syracuse and Brandeis universities prior to joining the faculty at HOWARD UNIVERSITY. He became chairman of the political science department at Howard.

Educator Ronald Walters provided policy analysis to Jesse Jackson and Charles Diggs. (Harlee Little)

Walters has been an active leader and member in numerous civic and scholarly organizations, including the African Heritage Association (president), Social Science Research Council, National Conference of Black Political Scientists, National Black Leadership Roundtable (secretary), National Congress of Black Faculty (vice president), TRANSAFRICA, American Political Science Association, Overseas Development Council, and African Political Science Association. In 1991, he was a member of the board of trustees of Howard University.

Walters served as senior foreign affairs consultant for Congressman Charles DIGGS in 1976 and for Congressman William GRAY from 1977 to 1979. He was deputy campaign manager for issues for Jesse JACKSON's 1984 presidential campaign and consultant for platform and convention operations for the 1988 campaign. He has also served as a consultant to the United Nations' Special Committee Against Apartheid of the Security Council.

Walters' more than eighty-five publications have appeared in the United States and abroad. He is the author of four research monographs on the subjects of African affairs and American black politics. He authored several books, including *South Africa and the Bomb: Responsibility and Deterrence* (1987), *Black Presidential Politics in America* (1988), and *Jesse Jackson's 1984 Presidential Campaign: Challenge and Change in American Politics* (1989, with Lucius Barker).

Among Walters' awards are the Distinguished Community Service Award from Howard University (1982), Distinguished Scholar/Activist Award from *Black Scholar Magazine* (1984), Ida WELLS Barnett Award from the National Alliance of Black School Educators (1985), and Congressional Black Associates Award (1986). In 1985, he was the recipient of a Rockefeller Foundation research grant which provided for a visiting professorship at Princeton University. In 1989, Walters was a member of the delegation of African American leaders that went to Beirut, Lebanon, and in 1986 he was an invited guest at the World Conference on Sanctions Against South Africa in Paris, France.

War: Funk music group. The members of War included Thomas Sylvester "Papa Dee" Allen, percussion; Harold Ray Brown, drums; Morris Dewayne "B.B." Dickerson, bass; Lonnie Lee Jordan, keyboards and vocals; Charles William Miller, reeds; and Howard E. Scott, guitar and vocals. The band originally performed under the name Night Shift in various Los Angeles nightclubs and served as a backup group for football star Deacon Jones, who aspired to a career in music. The members were discovered by Danish harmonica player Lee Oskar and British rock vocalist Eric Burdon. The group, augmented by Oskar, was renamed War by Burdon and recorded two albums as his backup band. One of the albums produced the hit single " Spill the Wine" (1970).

Burdon left the band during a 1971 European tour. Upon their return to the United States, the remaining members released a self-titled debut album, *War*, on the United Artists record label. Their 1973 album, *Deliver the World*, contained the hit single "The Cisco Kid," which reached number two on the pop chart and number five on the rhythm-and-blues chart. The title cut from their album *Why Can't We Be Friends?* (1975) reached number six on the pop chart and number seven on the RHYTHM-AND-BLUES chart. The follow-up single, "Low Rider," was even more successful, reaching number one on the pop chart. The band developed an ensemble sound that provided feel-good funk dance tracks.

After releasing a greatest hits album with United Artists, War signed with MCA Records in 1977. The group's first MCA album, *Galaxy*, produced a disco hit with the title single. The group's trademark sound did not translate into other disco hits, however, and its subsequent albums with MCA were not commercially successful. RCA Records signed War to a new contract in 1982, and the group released a modestly successful comeback album entitled *Outlaw*.

War of 1812 and African Americans, The: The War of 1812 was fought between the United States and Great Britain from June, 1812, through the spring of 1815. In part a continuation of hostilities and resentments between the two nations in the aftermath of the American Revolution, the War of 1812 began with a declaration of war by the U.S. Congress on June 18, 1812, and officially closed with the signing of the Treaty of Ghent on Dec. 14, 1814 (although word of the treaty was slow to reach battlefronts, and fighting continued into 1815).

Historical Background. As a fledgling nation, the United States profited considerably during the first thirty years of its existence from the European wars in which Great Britain and France were primary antagonists. These were the French Revolutionary Wars (1792-1802) and the Napoleonic Wars (1803-1815). The British navy drove French and Spanish ships from major trade routes, allowing American shippers the opportunity to carry merchandise between France and Spain and between French and Spanish Caribbean colonies. Despite America's previously paltry shipping power, U.S. businessmen looked to a newly robust shipping industry to expand trade and fill a gap left by the preoccupation of France and England. Between the early 1790's and 1807, the American merchant marine was able to increase its number of vessels by 300 percent.

Increasingly, though, Great Britain, a legendary maritime power, sought to cripple American commerce and shipping. By 1805, the British sought to block American ships from the North Sea coast of France. The resentment expressed in response by the United States, a neutral power, was exacerbated by other long-standing grievances against the British, who had a history of refusing to sign trade agreements favorable to the United States. The British had neglected to withdraw from American territory along the Great Lakes, and on American frontiers, British support for Native Americans in conflicts with European-American settlers had consistently rankled the U.S. government.

In 1807, the British government attempted to channel all neutral trade through Great Britain, where a duty would be charged. British naval officers also claimed the right to come aboard American merchant ships and to take into custody any personnel whom they considered British sailors. On certain occasions, British officers claimed that U.S. citizens were British and removed them from American ships. This practice, known as impressment, allowed American resentment of the British to come to a focus over specific incidents in which citizenship rights were flagrantly violated.

The Prelude to War and African Americans. Of the many confrontations and conflicts between the United States and Great Britain during the several years prior to war, the most notorious incident involved three African American sailors. On June 22, 1807, the American frigate *Chesapeake*, commanded by Commodore James Barron, was approached by the British ship *Leopard* and requested to stop. When Barron refused, the *Leopard* fired several broadsides into the *Chesapeake*. Barron then stopped, allowing his ship to be boarded and four sailors to be removed, of whom only one proved to be a British subject. The other three—William Ware, Daniel Martin, and John Strachan—were African Americans with full U.S. citizenship. The incident was widely publicized in the United States, arousing considerable indignation against the British. Shortly thereafter, President Thomas Jefferson interdicted all American harbors and waters to vessels of the British navy. The United States, however, lacked sufficient naval power to declare immediate war.

African Americans in the U.S. Navy. African Americans fought in every sea engagement of the War of 1812. During the war, free African Americans of the northern states enlisted in the Navy in great numbers, while in the South, many slaves were offered their freedom in exchange for service in the Navy. It is estimated that one-sixth of the U.S. Navy servicemen during the war were African Americans.

The most memorable naval battle of the war was fought

on Lake Erie. Captain Oliver Hazard Perry, in anticipation of the battle, had sent word from Lake Erie requesting that his superior, Commodore Isaac Chauncey, send reinforcements. When Chauncey sent a company of African Americans, Perry sent back a message complaining bitterly about the prospect of leading "inferior" men into battle. Chauncey replied with a scathing letter that rebuked the captain's prejudice: "I have yet to learn that the color of the skin . . . can affect a man's qualifications or usefulness. I have fifty blacks on board this ship and many of them are my best men." Between fifty and one hundred of Perry's 432 men at Lake Erie were African Americans. By the time the battle was won, Perry had amended his views; he was known to have marveled over the bravery of the black sailors.

At the Battle of Lake Champlain, as well, many of the gunners who contributed to the American victory were African Americans, including John Day, who served on board the *Viper*, and Charles Black, whose father had fought at Bunker Hill. Nathaniel Shaler, the captain of the privateer *Governor Tompkins*, reported on the bravery of John Johnson and John Davis, African Americans who, though mortally wounded, implored their shipmates to fight.

The Battle of New Orleans. Late in 1814, the British turned their attention to the South, seeking to gain control of the logistically crucial port of New Orleans, through which nearly half of U.S. produce passed en route to various markets. The British began assembling an armada in the Caribbean, intercepting merchant ships and bringing trade in the South to a standstill. Major General Andrew Jackson, charged with defending the Gulf Coast and the southern states, issued a proclamation calling upon free African Americans to join the fight against the British. While African American participation in the Navy was widespread, the U.S. government had refused African Americans enlistment in the Army until that point.

Jackson's opinion of African Americans had been influenced in 1813 at the Battle of Fort Boyer near Mobile, Ala. An African American named Jeffrey had mounted a horse and rallied American troops to fight off a British charge. The rally had succeeded, and Jackson had given Jeffrey the rank of major.

Jackson's proclamation addressed African Americans as citizens of the nation; its first words were: "Through a mistaken policy, you have heretofore been deprived of a participation in the glorious struggle for national rights, in which *our* country is engaged. This no longer shall exist."

The Battle of New Orleans was the greatest land battle of the war. Two battalions made up of approximately six hundred African Americans, with African American line officers, fought under Jackson. On Dec. 23, 1814, Jackson and his men met a British army on the Gulf Coast near the mouth of the Mississippi. For more than two weeks, they skirmished to within a few miles of New Orleans. The fighting came to a climax in a ferocious struggle on Jan. 8, 1815. Within twenty-five minutes, more than two thousand British soldiers were killed, wounded, or taken prisoner; American losses were tiny in comparison. The Treaty of Ghent had been signed several weeks previously, but the Battle of New Orleans, along with other impressive American victories during the final six months of the war, established the United States in the popular mind as having triumphed.

"King Dick." Throughout the war, the British used their naval might to enforce blockades of the coasts of America and to capture American prisoners of war in large numbers. More than five thousand of these men were kept at Dartmoor prison in the west of England. American sailors who had entered the British Navy but who refused to fight against the United States were also confined there; one such was Richard Seavers, an African American from Massachusetts.

Seavers, reportedly the largest and strongest man in the prison, stood at six feet five inches and carried himself with a regal bearing. He demonstrated a natural leadership in prison block four, to which all black prisoners were assigned. A former teacher of boxing, Seavers was known to stride imperially through the prison, carrying a large club, attended by two white boys, and wearing a great bearskin cap. He came to be known as "King Dick," a renowned figure who is described in various memoirs of life at Dartmoor prison. King Dick zealously governed block four, dispensing beatings if prisoners were caught stealing. Yet his rule was accepted by the majority of the inmates, and he presided over organized gambling, boxing and fencing events, musical performances, and productions of Shakespeare. The more respectable prisoners in other blocks requested transfers to block four because of its superior order.

Results of the War. The War of 1812 established American rights as a neutral nation and won recognition of the United States from the maritime powers of the world. As has been the case with nearly all wars in U.S. history, the participation and sacrifices of African Americans raised hopes that racist practices would be considerably diminished at war's end. The Treaty of Ghent, however, declared that all slaves captured by the British during the war would be returned to American SLAVERY. In 1820, the U.S. Army adjutant general's office ordered that African

Americans were not to be received as recruits in the Army.—*James Knippling*

SUGGESTED READINGS: • Carter, Samuel. *Blaze of Glory: The Fight for New Orleans. New York: St. Martin's Press, 1971.* • Hickey, Donald R. *The War of 1812: A Forgotten Conflict.* Urbana: University of Illinois Press, 1989. • Horsman, Reginald. The War of 1812. New York: Alfred A. Knopf, 1969. • Nell, William C. *Services of Colored Americans in the Wars of 1776 and 1812.* Boston: Prentiss & Sawyer, 1851. Reprint. New York: AMS Press, 1976. • Wilson, Joseph Thomas. *The Black Phalanx: A History of Negro Soldiers of the U.S. in the Wars of 1775-1812 and 1861-1865.* Hartford, Conn.: American, 1888. Reprint. New York: Arno Press, 1968.

effectiveness of earlier welfare programs, focused on health, nutrition, and income maintenance, in meeting the needs of the poor. A third force was the organized protests of African Americans during the CIVIL RIGHTS movement for jobs and new programs to lift them out of poverty.

The principal programs in the War on Poverty focused on employment and EDUCATION, food and nutrition, and health care. In the areas of job training and employment, the following initiatives were developed or expanded: the Neighborhood Youth Corps, the Job Corps, the 1964 Economic Opportunity Act, and the Manpower Development and Training Act. Educational initiatives included HEAD START, the UPWARD BOUND program, Follow Through, and Title I of the Aid to Education Act. The

Many of the War on Poverty programs provided aid to children. (AP/Wide World Photos)

War on Poverty: Government programs for the poor initiated in the 1960's. By 1961, several forces had created a need for programs to reduce POVERTY in the United States. One was the paradox of extreme poverty in the midst of a wealthy nation. In these pockets of poverty there was starvation, poor sanitation, joblessness, poor health, and illiteracy. A second force was the limited

FOOD STAMP program, Emergency Food Aid, and the school lunch program were expanded during this period. Finally, the Neighborhood Health Centers program and the Medicaid program were implemented as part of the WAR ON POVERTY.

These programs were supplemented by the implementation of a community action program (a political action program that attempted to empower the poor) and a legal services program that was geared toward improving the access of the poor to affordable legal representation. Although cash assistance programs originated before the War on Poverty, between 1965 and 1975 they were expanded significantly. The AID TO FAMILIES WITH DEPENDENT CHILDREN (AFDC) and the Aid to the Aged, Blind, and Disabled were the primary targets of expansion in cash assistance programs. As a result of these programs, there was a significant decrease in the percentage of poor Americans between 1965 and 1975, to less than 10 percent of all families but still more than 25 percent of African American families. The community action programs also helped to increase the level of participation of African Americans in the political process.

Warbourg, Eugene (c. 1825, New Orleans, La.—1867): Sculptor. Warbourg's most famous sculpture is a portrait bust of John Young Mason, a United States minister to France. Warbourg, who was trained as a stonemason, shared a studio with his brother, Daniel, in New Orleans. The jealousy of local white artists allegedly prompted Warbourg to leave the United States for Europe, where he resided until his death.

Ward, Clara (Apr. 21, 1924, Philadelphia, Pa.—Jan. 16, 1973, Los Angeles, Calif.): Gospel singer and composer.

Gospel singer Clara Ward. (AP/Wide World Photos)

Ward began her career as a gospel singer and pianist at the age of six. In 1934, she was an accompanist for the Ward Trio, a family group that included her mother, Gertrude, and her sister, Willa. The group received national recognition in 1943 when it sang at the National Baptist Convention. After this appearance, the group began touring throughout the United States.

In 1949, the group joined with composer W. Herbert Brewsters. Their association lasted fifteen years and produced "Surely God Is Able," the song that made the group one of the most popular female gospel groups of the time.

Ward was highly regarded for her ability to express drama in slow gospel ballads and nonmetrical hymns such as Thomas Dorsey's "When I've Done the Best I Can." Later, Ward improved on her style by incorporating techniques such as shrieks and growls, turning her style to what is known as "hard" gospel. An example of this is her 1957 release "Packing Up."

During the 1960's, Ward turned increasingly toward secular music, even though her gospel music had attracted wide audiences. The move to secular music cost her much of her gospel following. In 1963, she performed in the first gospel musical written by Langston HUGHES, entitled *TAMBOURINES TO GLORY*. She made several successful tours abroad and appeared at major U.S. venues, including the Newport Jazz Festival.

Ward, Douglas Turner (b. May 5, 1930, Burnside, La.): Actor, director, and playwright. Ward cofounded the Negro Ensemble Company (NEC) in 1967 and was its artistic director. He first won recognition as author of the one-act plays *Happy Ending* and *Day of Absence*, both produced in 1965. Among his many notable roles with the NEC were that of Russell B. Parker in *CEREMONIES IN DARK OLD MEN* (1969) and Johnny Williams in *River Niger* (1973).

Ward, Samuel Ringgold (Oct. 17, 1817, eastern shore of Maryland—1866, St. George Parish, Jamaica): Congregational minister, orator, and abolitionist. Ward served two pastorates, neither to a black congregation. He was cofounder of the LIBERTY PARTY and helped to organize the FREE SOIL PARTY in New York State. He was a friend of abolitionist Frederick DOUGLASS. In 1851, Ward left the United States for Canada. The bulk of his 1855 *Autobiography of a Fugitive Negro: His Anti-Slavery Labours in the United States, Canada, and England* is devoted to his experiences in Canada and the British Isles (1853-1855). Ward spent his final years farming in Jamaica.

Ward, Theodore (Sept. 15, 1902, Thibodaux, La.—May 8, 1983, Chicago, Ill.): Dramatist. Ward was one of the earliest African Americans to have a play produced on Broadway, *Our Lan'* (1947). Ward's first acclaimed work, *BIG WHITE FOG* (pr. 1938), was produced by the Chicago unit of the FEDERAL THEATRE PROJECT. Among his awards, he received a Guggenheim Fellowship for creative writing (1947) and the AUDELCO Outstanding Pioneer Award for his contribution to the growth and development of black theater (1975). His works often portrayed American heroes for African Americans.

Warfield, Paul D. (b. Nov. 28, 1942, Warren, Ohio): FOOTBALL player. Considered to be a premier wide receiver of the National Football League (NFL), Warfield was a first-round draft choice for the Cleveland Browns when he was graduated from Ohio State University in 1964. He played in four NFL championships with Cleveland before being traded to the Miami Dolphins in 1969.

Warfield helped the Dolphins reach the play-offs five years in a row. He was named All-Pro with the Browns in 1968 and 1969 and with the Dolphins from 1971 through 1973. He signed with the Memphis Southmen of the World Football League in 1974 and retired in 1977. He was elected to the Pro Football Hall of Fame in 1983 and named to the AFL-NFL 1960-1984 All-Star Team.

Warfield, William (b. Jan. 22, 1920, West Helena, Ark.): Singer. Warfield trained at the Eastman School, with his study interrupted by service in the Army. He made his recital debut in New York City in 1950. This was followed by recordings and tours of the United States, Europe, Africa, the Middle East, and Central and South America, performing with major orchestras. He is highly regarded for his interpretations of spirituals and for his performances of Porgy in George Gershwin's *PORGY AND BESS*. He joined the faculty of the University of Illinois in 1974 and has been president of the National Association of Negro Musicians.

William Warfield played "De Lawd" in a 1957 television presentation of The Green Pastures. *(AP/Wide World Photos)*

Waring, Laura Wheeler (1887, Hartford, Conn.—Feb. 3, 1948, Philadelphia, Pa.): Artist. Waring studied at the Pennsylvania Academy of Fine Arts in Philadelphia and in Europe. Primarily known as a portrait painter of well-to-do Americans, Waring painted several famous African Americans, including W. E. B. Du Bois and James Weldon Johnson. Her works were exhibited at the Corcoran, the Brooklyn Museum, and other galleries. For more than thirty years, Waring directed the art and music department at Cheyney State College in Pennsylvania.

Laura Wheeler Waring painted this portrait of religious leader George Edmund Hayes. (National Archives)

Warren, Michael (b. Mar. 5, 1946, South Bend, Ind.): Actor. Best known for his role on the television series *Hill Street Blues* from 1981 to 1987, Warren was an All-American basketball player at UCLA before going on to a career in acting. He was named an Academic All-American by the National Collegiate Athletic Association in 1966. Warren appeared in the films *Fast Break* (1979), *Norman, Is That You?* (1976), and *Drive He Said* (1970). He appeared in the television movies *The Child Saver* in 1989 and *The Kid Who Loved Christmas* in 1990. He produced and acted in the television pilot *Home Free* in 1988. Warren's work on *Hill Street Blues* garnered him an Emmy nomination.

Warwick, Dionne (b. Dec. 12, 1941, East Orange, N.J.): Singer. Warwick's parents valued music, especially gospel singing, and saw to it that their daughter received musical training at an early age. At the age of six, she began singing gospel music in her church choir. Later, as a college student at the Hartt College of Music in Hartford, Conn., she was able to supplement tuition costs by singing in a trio, the Gospelaires, comprising herself, her sister Dee Dee, and her cousin Cissy Houston, who later became the mother of singer Whitney Houston.

It was through the songs of composer Burt Bacharach that Warwick became well known. Recordings of his songs, many of which reached the top ten, led to greater public exposure. In 1963, she went on an international tour that culminated in Paris, where she was received ecstatically. Critic Jean Monteaux endowed her with the name, "Paris's Black Pearl," a symbolic assessment of her tremendous audience appeal. Warwicks's first number one-hit, "Then Came You" (1974), was recorded with the Spinners.

Dionne Warwick. (AP/ Wide World Photos)

Eventually, antagonism within the Bacharach team and dissension among associates created a rift that caused Warwick to dissociate herself as collaborator. The conflicts were not resolved until 1986. Warwick had a number of successful albums in the late 1970's and early 1980's, and recorded the hit "I'll Never Love This Way Again" in 1979. As an active participant in the USA for Africa project, Warwick joined with forty-four other singers to record "We Are the World," a smash hit worldwide whose proceeds were donated for African relief.

Washington, Booker T(aliaferro): (Apr. 5, 1856, near Hale's Ford, Va.—Nov. 14, 1915, Tuskegee, Ala.): Social reformer. Booker T. Washington was born a slave on a Virginia farm. Booker's father was said to be white, but his mother Jane apparently never told Booker or his older brother John anything about their paternity. By 1860, Jane had married a slave named Washington from a nearby farm and had borne a daughter named Amanda by him.

Youth and Education. After emancipation in 1865, Jane and her three children followed her husband to Malden, W. Va. There, Booker joined his stepfather working in the town's salt furnaces, but after much begging, the boy was also allowed to attend school. Known only by his first name until he began going to school, he told his teacher his full name was Booker Washington. Sometime later, he added the middle name Taliaferro.

Never happy with his stepfather, Washington moved out of the family cabin sometime within his first two years in Malden. He became the houseboy of General Lewis Ruffner and his wife Viola. Viola Ruffner took a motherly interest in Washington and encouraged his education. She also taught him the virtues of rigorous cleanliness and hard work.

In 1872, Washington decided to further his education by traveling to Hampton Normal and Agricultural Institute in Virginia. He arrived dirty and practically penniless. There, he met two more whites who played important roles in the development of his personality. Mary F. Mackie admitted Washington and hired him as a janitor after an entrance exam that consisted of his sweeping a room. The head of the school, General Samuel Chapman Armstrong, was a New Englander who became a father figure to Washington. At Hampton, Washington was taught the dignity of labor and the benefits of discipline and self-improvement.

After graduating from Hampton in 1875, Washington returned to Malden to teach. Three years later, he entered Wayland Seminary in Washington, D.C. In 1879, Washington returned to Hampton to teach night school. During the 1880-1881 school year, he became supervisor of the dormitory for Native American students. In May, 1881, Armstrong received a letter from Tuskegee, Ala., asking him to recommend a white man to head a new school for African Americans. Instead, Armstrong recommended Washington.

The Tuskegee Institute. When Washington arrived in Tuskegee on June 24, 1881, he expected to find a school to head. All that existed, however, was an uncertain two

thousand-dollar appropriation from the state legislature. Utilizing the industrial education format of Hampton and currying the favor of prominent whites, he was able to create Tuskegee Normal and Industrial Institute. All students were required to work, and they made bricks, built buildings, and raised food for the school. They were taught a trade as well as academic subjects. Soon, Washington reached out to surrounding farmers through yearly conferences and educational outreach programs. By 1915, Tuskegee had an endowment of nearly two million dollars.

To raise money for his school, Washington embarked on many speaking tours and became well known. In 1895, he was asked to speak at the Cotton States Industrial Exposition in Atlanta, in the middle of a decade of bloody racial violence. Washington had the difficult task of addressing an audience composed of white and black northerners and southerners without offending anyone. Incredibly, he succeeded.

His speech became known as the ATLANTA COMPROMISE ADDRESS and spelled out a basis for interracial cooperation. From whites, Washington asked for economic and educational opportunities for African Americans. Appealing to white self-interest, he noted that black southerners made up one-third of the region's population. Kept ignorant and poor, they would drag the South down; through industrial education, they could help to bring the dawning of a richer "New South." In return for educational and economic opportunity, Washington asked black southerners to forego temporarily agitation for civil and political rights. He argued that if African Americans made themselves indispensable to the South, they would soon be granted all the rights they desired.

One reason his speech was so popular was that almost everyone who heard it interpreted the speech differently. When it became apparent that white southerners interpreted Washington's comments as an endorsement of segregation, black support for the Atlanta Compromise began to erode. Washington's popularity, however, remained high among whites. Prominent Americans such as Andrew Carnegie and John D. Rockefeller supported Tuskegee, and in 1901 Washington dined with President Theodore Roosevelt at the White House. The publication of Washington's immensely popular *Up from Slavery: An Autobiography* (1901) further enhanced his status.

National Prominence. Washington belittled the importance of politics and civil rights in speeches but became one of the most powerful men in the South. Presidents consulted him on political appointments, philanthropists sought his advice on charitable contributions, and much of the black press became financially dependent on his

Booker T. Washington promoted education as a means of advancement. (Library of Congress)

support. He sought to control such organizations as the Afro-American Council to increase the power of his "Tuskegee Machine." He also practiced in secret what he preached against in public. Behind the scenes, he challenged segregation and DISFRANCHISEMENT through quiet diplomacy and secret financial contributions. Nevertheless, conditions continued to deteriorate for African Americans.

Rights that had been won for blacks during RECONSTRUCTION were being increasingly denied, and some black leaders challenged both the conciliatory nature of Washington's accommodationism and his emphasis on industrial education at the expense of higher education. Under the leadership of William Monroe Trotter and W. E. B. DU BOIS, several dozen black intellectuals founded the NIAGARA MOVEMENT in 1905 as an alternative to Washington's leadership. The movement was largely unsuccessful, but a number of its members joined with white liberals four years later to organize the NATIONAL ASSOCIATION FOR THE ADVANCEMENT OF COLORED PEOPLE (NAACP). Probably because of the group's links with Du Bois, Washington continued to have a strained relationship with the organization until his death.

Last Years. During his last two decades at TUSKEGEE INSTITUTE, Washington gave many speeches, published books and articles, received numerous honors, and was asked to serve on boards of trustees and to join dozens of organizations. He retained the support of prominent white politicians in the North and the South as well of the majority of African Americans. At the same time, he expanded the influence of Tuskegee by founding the NATIONAL NEGRO BUSINESS LEAGUE in 1900 and beginning National Negro Health Week in 1914. When Washington died on Nov. 14, 1915, he was survived by his wife Margaret and three children. He had been predeceased by two wives, Fanny and Olivia.

Historical Assessment. Few African American leaders have been more controversial than Booker T. Washington. Some scholars have depicted him as a power-hungry politician who bartered away the rights of his people. Others have denounced his bourgeois capitalism and deification of white middle-class values. A few assert that Washington was a dedicated, practical realist who accomplished as much as was possible in an age of escalating racism. Still others have seen seeds of BLACK NATIONALISM in his self-help ideology and his organization of all-black institutions. Many believe Washington was a complex man who played so many different roles that the real Washington is virtually impossible to know. All agree that his legacy was mixed, with both positive and negative consequences.—*Linda O. McMurry*

SUGGESTED READINGS: • Du Bois, W. E. B. *The Souls of Black Folk.* Chicago: A. C. McClurg, 1903. • Harlan, Louis R. *Booker T. Washington: The Making of a Black Leader, 1856-1901.* New York: Oxford University Press, 1972. • Harlan, Louis R. *Booker T. Washington: The Wizard of Tuskegee, 1901-1915.* New York: Oxford University Press, 1983. • Harlan, Louis R. *Booker T. Washington in Perspective: Essays of Louis R. Harlan.* Edited by Raymond W. Smock. Jackson: University Press of Mississippi, 1986. • Meier, August. *Negro Thought in America, 1880-1915.* Ann Arbor: University of Michigan Press, 1963. • Washington, Booker T. *The Booker T. Washington Papers.* 13 vols. Edited by Louis R. Harlan et al. Urbana: University of Illinois Press, 1972-1984.

Washington, Craig Anthony (b. Oct. 12, 1941, Longview, Tex.): U.S. representative from Texas. Washington received his bachelor of science degree from Prairie View A&M University in Texas in 1966. He attended Thurgood MARSHALL School of Law at Texas Southern University and was graduated cum laude with a J.D. degree in 1969. From 1969 to 1970, Washington served as assistant dean of the law school at Texas Southern University. In 1970, he went into private practice as a criminal defense attorney.

Washington became involved in state politics when he was elected to serve in the Texas State House of Representatives. He and George "Mickey" LELAND served as freshman members of the legislature in 1973. When Leland went on to serve in Congress in 1978, Washington continued to serve in the Texas House of Representatives until he was elected to the Texas State Senate in 1983. During his time in the House, Washington served as chairman of the committees on criminal jurisprudence, human services, and social services, and he was chairman of the Texas Legislative Black Caucus. He led efforts to increase the participation of women and minorities in Texas state government, coordinated the state's fight against ACQUIRED IMMUNE DEFICIENCY SYNDROME (AIDS) and focused attention on the state's poverty programs.

When Congressman Leland died in a plane crash in ETHIOPIA on Aug. 7, 1989, during a famine relief trip to Africa, Washington became the leading candidate to succeed his friend and former colleague as representative from Texas' Eighteenth Congressional District. He received the most votes in the nonpartisan primary election and was victorious in the special election on Dec. 9, 1989. Washington took office on Jan. 23, 1990.

Washington, D.C.: Site of HOWARD UNIVERSITY and Martin Luther KING, JR.'s "I Have a Dream" speech. Washington is the nation's capital. The site was developed by Pierre Charles L'Enfant in a tightly controlled grid pattern radiating from the White House and Capitol. Largely destroyed by fire during the War of 1812, it was restored and continued its phenomenal growth. Graced with parks, reflecting pools, gardens, and the country's most imposing statuary and architectural treasures, including the Washington Monument, the Lincoln, Jefferson, and Vietnam memorials, the Pentagon, and the Library of Congress, the city hosts tourists from all nations.

WOODSON, the National Arboretum, the National Geographic Museum, and the National Zoo.

Washington's residents, 66 percent of whom were African Americans according to the 1990 census, epitomize the sharply divided interests and culture created by middle-class white flight. Run-down buildings and housing projects, permeated with drug dealers and criminals, reduce the quality of life for families. Martin Luther King, Jr., climaxed his 1963 MARCH ON WASHINGTON with his "I Have a Dream" speech in front of the Lincoln Memorial

A Washington, D.C., neighborhood following rioting in 1968. (Library of Congress)

As an educational and cultural center, the small, compact city leads the nation in opportunity. Paramount among its offerings are the Kennedy Center for the Performing Arts, Folger Library, National Museum of African Art, Smithsonian Institution, Howard, Georgetown, American, and George Washington universities, and Catholic University of America. A focus of historical interest is Ford's Theatre, a restored nineteenth century stage and museum dedicated to Abraham Lincoln, who was shot while attending a performance and died at a private residence across the street. Other important sites include the homes of Frederick DOUGLASS and Carter G.

on August 28. The POOR PEOPLE'S CAMPAIGN, another attempt to gain rights for African Americans, also ended there. Washington residents have been served by African Americans Walter E. WASHINGTON, who was Washington's first mayor, and Marion BARRY, Jr., who was mayor for three terms before announcing that he would not run again. At the time of the announcement, the former civil rights activist was on trial on charges related to possession of cocaine. His predicament was seen by some as indicative of the problems pervasive in Washington. Sharon Pratt DIXON Kelly was elected in 1990 as the city's first black woman mayor.

Washington, Denzel, Jr. (b. Dec. 28, 1954, Mt. Vernon, N.Y.): Actor. Denzel Washington is one of America's most dynamic actors. His work runs the gamut of styles from romance to serious drama, from action-adventure to comedy. Some critics have credited him with helping to redefine the portrayal of African Americans in the film industry. In his personal life, Washington is a happily married father of two (John David, born in 1984, and Katia, born in 1987). His process for choosing a role is to consider whether he would want his children or his parents to see him as that character; this luxury, not afforded to many black performers, has been obtained by Washington as the result of years of hard work and a clear dedication to his craft.

Family Life. Washington is the son of a Pentecostal minister, after whom he was named, and a beautician who had been a gospel singer prior to her marriage. Reared in a strict, religious household, neither he nor his two sib-lings were allowed to watch much television or go to many films. Instead, they spent much of their time at church or in one of the beauty parlors their mother owned. His parents, very industrious people, worked several jobs in order to give their children a decent home. Washington's parents, though, separated when he was twelve, finally getting a divorce when he was fourteen. After Washington's mother received custody of the children, she removed Washington from public school and enrolled him in Oakland Academy in upstate New York, a private school primarily attended by white children of wealthy families.

Collegiate Years. In 1972, after graduating from Oakland, Washington entered Fordham University with aspirations of becoming a medical student. While still an undergraduate, Washington received his first exposure to acting while working as a camp counselor one summer in Lakeville, Conn. Persuaded to participate in a talent

Denzel Washington, shown here with presenter Geena Davis, won an Oscar in 1990 for Best Supporting Actor for his role in Glory. (AP/Wide World Photos)

show by the other staff members, Washington found himself quite comfortable on stage, where he enjoyed the audience response. In his junior year, he signed up for an acting workshop with film actor and professor Robinson Stone, whom Washington credits as being directly responsible for his success. Stone recognized talent in Washington and encouraged him to audition for university productions. After winning the title role in productions of Eugene O'Neill's *THE EMPEROR JONES* and William Shakespeare's *Othello* from several theater majors, Washington decided to commit himself to the acting profession.

First Professional Roles. Prior to his graduation from Fordham in 1977 with a bachelor's degree in journalism, Washington acquired an agent. Washington obtained a role in the NBC teleplay *Wilma*, based on the life of track star Wilma RUDOLPH. On the last day of filming the teleplay, Washington was introduced to his future wife, Pauletta Pearson, a singer and pianist.

With the exception of the teleplay *Flesh and Blood* in 1978 and a few theater roles, Washington found the early part of his new career to be financially frustrating. He entered a three-year acting program at the American Conservatory Theater in San Francisco with the assistance of Stone, but he left after the first year and returned to New York. Unable to find work, he reluctantly accepted a position in a New York recreation center. Prompted by Pauletta to continue auditioning, Washington tried out for the role of MALCOLM X in *When the Chickens Come Home to Roost* (1980) at the New Federal Theater. Upon being cast as the legendary Black Muslim leader, Washington resigned the recreation center job. Critics and audiences alike were stunned at how Washington seemed to become Malcolm X. Not only did he dye his hair red to match that of the slain activist, but Washington also studied Malcolm's life in an attempt to understand his motivations. His performance garnered him an AUDELCO Recognition Award. Within the next two years, he would have several major turns to his career.

Washington received his first film role in *Carbon Copy* (1981), playing a jive-talking black teenager. Although the role secured him financially for a period, critics were unappreciative.

Major Stage Roles. Returning to the stage, Washington drew the interest of prominent Off-Broadway theater companies, including the New York Shakespeare Festival and the National Black Touring Circuit. He appeared in productions of *CEREMONIES IN DARK OLD MEN*, *Coriolanus*, *Every Goodbye Ain't Gone*, *Spell #7*, and *The Mighty Gents*. In 1981, Washington won the role that would be his major break. Hired by the Negro Ensemble Company

as a last-minute replacement, he originated the role of Private Melvin Peterson in Charles FULLER's Pulitzer-Prize winning drama *A SOLDIER'S PLAY*. His performance garnered him that year's Obie Award as best supporting actor.

Fame in Television and Film. While performing in *A Soldier's Play* in Los Angeles, Washington landed the part of Dr. Phillip Chandler on the television series *St. Elsewhere*. Although he remained on the show for five seasons, his first two years were frustrating. Little was done to make his character anything more than a token black doctor. To remedy this dilemma, he was given sabbaticals to do other projects, and the show's writers began to give him more interesting stories. After marrying Pauletta Pearson in 1983, Washington appeared in the teleplay *License to Kill* (1983) and reprised the character of Peterson in *A Soldier's Story* (1984), the film version of Fuller's play.

Wanting to work with Gene Hackman and director Sidney Lumet, Washington petitioned and won the role of a media lobbyist—a part originally written for a white actor—in the film *Power* (1986). After starring in the title role of the teleplay *The George McKenna Story* (1986), Washington was asked to play martyred South African leader Steven Biko in Richard Attenborough's film *Cry Freedom* (1987). Although critics heralded his performance as the slain activist, and although he received an Oscar nomination, *Cry Freedom* stands as a bittersweet experience for Washington. He felt Biko's struggle against South Africa's apartheid system was compromised by Attenborough's attempt to focus the film on Donald Woods, Biko's white friend and the author of the book upon which the film was based.

After receiving numerous film offers, Washington left *St. Elsewhere* in 1987. Immediately, he found himself involved in several projects at once. After playing a former paratrooper returning home to Thatcherite England from the Falklands War in *For Queen and Country* (1988), he returned to the stage with his first Broadway role as Sylvester Cooper in the Ron Milner comedy *Checkmates*. Directly after the close of the *Checkmates* New York production, Washington went to the Caribbean to shoot *The Mighty Quinn* (1989). Washington then journeyed to Georgia to film *GLORY* (1989), in which he portrayed a former slave named Trip. Always an avid researcher, Washington immersed himself in historical records and slave diaries to bring authenticity to the film. Again, critics praised his performance for its intensity. Washington won an Oscar as best supporting actor, joining the small ranks of black Oscar winners.

Post-Oscar Work. In 1990, Washington switched from

serious drama to comedy with the film *Heart Condition*, playing a hip black lawyer who dies and haunts a bigoted white cop (Bob Hoskins) after the attorney's heart is transplanted into the officer's body. The movie reminded many critics of *Carbon Copy*, another ill-fated comedy about black-white relationships.

this film again earned for him recognition by Academy members at the Academy Awards.

Not one to be typecast—he resents comparisons to Sidney POITIER—Denzel Washington has had a rich career presenting his audiences with a diverse group of engaging characters. Ironically, contrary to the views of many of

Washington played the lead in Spike Lee's sweeping biographical film, Malcolm X; *Angela Bassett played his wife, Betty.* (AP/Wide World Photos)

Washington then returned to drama, starring in Spike LEE's jazz film *MO' BETTER BLUES* (1990) as trumpeter Bleek Gilliam. Lee stated that he wanted Washington for the role after seeing the effect he had on women during a performance of *Checkmates*. Washington has said that Lee's improvisational style of directing made the film one of his most enjoyable working experiences. Afterward, Washington performed the title role in Shakespeare's *Richard III* for the New York Shakespeare Festival. Many critics, however, found Washington's Richard weak and somewhat unfinished.

Washington's only 1991 release was the action-adventure film, *Ricochet*, in which he played framed police officer Nick Styles. In 1992, Washington appeared as the romantic lead in *Mississippi Masala*, a film about interracial love and prejudice. He also reprised the role of Malcolm X, this time in Spike Lee's controversial film about the Black Muslim leader. His outstanding work in

those characters, Washington has no political agenda he wishes to express. He is, rather, content to render, with skill and intelligence, the versatility and complexity of African Americans.—*Gary Anderson*

SUGGESTED READINGS: • Bogle, Donald. *Blacks in American Films and Television: An Illustrated Encyclopedia.* New York: Garland, 1988. • Davis, Thulani. "Denzel in the Swing." *American Film* 15 (August, 1990): 26-31. • Hoban, Phoebe. "Days of Glory: Denzel Washington—From Spike Lee's Blues to Richard III." *New York Magazine* 23 (August 13, 1990): 34-38. • Randolph, Laura B. "The Glory Days of Denzel Washington." *Ebony* 45 (September, 1990): 80-82. • Shah, Diane K. "Soldier, Healer, Seller of Rye." *GQ* 58 (October, 1988): 312-317.

Washington, Dinah (Ruth Lee Jones; Aug. 29, 1924, Tuscaloosa, Ala.—Dec. 14, 1963, Detroit, Mich.): Jazz, blues, and soul singer. "The Mother of Soul" influenced many artists, including "The Lady of Soul," Aretha FRANKLIN. Washington first sang gospel in the church, later joining the Lionel Hampton band as lead singer in 1943. This hardworking performer died from an overdose of sleeping pills.

Washington, Fredricka Carolyn "Fredi" (b. Dec. 23, 1903, Savannah, Ga.): Stage and film actress. Washington began her career as a dancer, performing in nightclubs and in the touring production of *SHUFFLE ALONG* (1922-1926). In her first dramatic stage role, she appeared opposite Paul ROBESON in the play *Black Boy* (1926). Her most notable performance came in the role of Peola in the popular film *IMITATION OF LIFE* (1934). In 1937, she cofounded the Negro Actors Guild and served as its executive secretary.

Washington, George (1817, Frederick County, Va.— 1905): Pioneer, The son of a white mother and a slave father, Washington was given to a white family that he accompanied to Ohio and later to Missouri. He ran businesses as a sawmill operator and a tailor but moved to what is now Washington State to escape discriminatory laws. He bought land and established the town now known as Centralia by offering free lots to people willing to settle there, along the Northern Pacific Railroad.

Washington, Grover, Jr. (b. Dec. 12, 1943, Buffalo, N.Y.): Jazz saxophonist. Washington's father played saxophone and was a jazz fan, his mother sang in church choirs, one brother is an organist, and another plays drums. As a boy, he played with a blues band as well as with a rhythm-and-blues group. He also received formal training in music that later served him well as a composer.

After graduating from high school at the age of sixteen, Washington formed, with friends, a group called the Four Clefs. The group was based in Ohio but performed wherever it could find engagements. Members, especially

Grover Washington experiments with different types of music. (Oggie Ogburn)

Washington, frequently performed on a number of instruments, from sax to bass to piano. Washington was drafted into the Army and sent to radio school at Fort Dix, N.J., where he also was accepted into the Nineteenth Army Band. The proximity of Fort Dix to New York City and Philadelphia enabled him to moonlight as a musician. He also was able to meet and play with many of the important musicians of the time.

After his discharge from the Army, Washington moved to Philadelphia. He continued to play in clubs there and in New York, and he also was in great demand as a recording artist. In 1971, he fronted his own recording group, resulting in his debut album, *Inner City Blues*. Reviewers were quick to praise his virtuoso saxophone work. He became much in demand on the jazz concert circuit and earned various awards and honors, including three *Ebony* Music Awards, England's Top Instrumentalist of the Year (1978), and Philadelphia's Citation of Merit for Community Service.

Long recognized as one of the leading reed players in the world of jazz, he attempted to break out of conventional jazz molds through increasing experimentation and use of nontraditional jazz forms such as rock and RHYTHM AND BLUES. For his efforts, he was awarded a Grammy for best jazz fusion performance in 1981. Washington's musical career has encompassed roles as composer, producer, sound track artist, and video performer, as well as instrumentalist.

Washington, Harold (Apr. 15, 1922, Chicago, Ill.—Nov. 25, 1987, Chicago, Ill.): Politician. Harold Washington's father, Roy, was a practicing attorney and an African Methodist Episcopal minister; his mother was a homemaker. As a child, Washington was known for his slender build, his interest in sports, and his ferocious appetite for books. For example, while playing for his neighborhood baseball team, he was often found with a glove in one hand and a book in one of his pockets. Washington read a wide range of books and magazines, but he found himself particularly drawn to his father's large collection of books on power and self-determination. His reading was diverse; from books, he taught himself how to run the hurdles as part of his stint as a track runner in high school.

Washington's early development was also supplemented by open discussions of politics and religion, conducted by his father at the dinner table almost every night. Washington wrote that "before I reached my teens, I was aware of presidents, MAYORS, governors, aldermen, and people of that nature." When Washington turned seventeen, he dropped out of high school to enter the

Civilian Conservation Corps, for which he planted trees and quarried limestone in Bitely, Mich. Once he returned to Chicago, he married his childhood sweetheart, Nancy Dorothy Finch.

Between the completion of high school in 1939 and his 1942 enlistment in the armed forces in World War II, Washington was employed in a variety of jobs that ranged from selling snacks at a bus station in Chicago to working as a laborer in the Chicago stockyards and operating data-processing machines in the Chicago Merchandise Mart. While serving in the Pacific between 1942 and 1946, Washington completed his high school training by taking correspondence courses in history, literature, chemistry, and English literature. After World War II, Washington took advantage of the G.I. Bill to complete his undergraduate studies as a political science major at Roosevelt University. After his graduation from Roosevelt, he studied law at Northwestern University's law school, where he was the only African American admitted out of an incoming freshman class of 185.

In 1952, Washington received his law degree from Northwestern, and in 1953 he was admitted to the Illinois bar. In 1954, he became active in local politics, succeeding his late father as the Chicago Democratic Party's Third Ward precinct captain. In 1954, too, he joined the Chicago city corporation counsel's office as an assistant prosecutor, a post he occupied until 1958. In 1960, he began a four-year term as an arbitrator for the Illinois State Industrial Commission.

Entry into Politics. In 1964, Washington ran for and won election to the Illinois House of Representatives. From the start of his legislative career in 1965, Washington was a persuasive speaker and a fighter for the concerns of his constituents. In 1965, he was at the forefront of a fight to reform consumer credit. In 1969, Washington organized an African American caucus in the Illinois House of Representatives. He was also responsible for helping make Martin Luther KING, JR.'s birthday a commemorative day in Illinois. Although Washington was seen as an initiator at the legislature in Springfield, Ill., he ran his precinct as an integral part of the Democratic machine in Chicago. During his tenure in the state legislature, Washington was involved in legislation ranging from the Fair Employment Practices Act to saving Provident Hospital, a beleaguered African American hospital on Chicago's South Side.

First Race for Mayor. Pressure for the election of an African American mayor in the city of Chicago escalated in the 1970's. Washington's first attempt to pursue candidacy for the mayor's office came in 1977, in a special election that occurred after the death of Mayor Richard

Harold Washington addresses supporters after his 1987 victory in the Chicago mayoral primary election; he is flanked by running mates Cecil A. Partee (left) and Gloria Chevere. (AP/Wide World Photos)

J. Daley in December, 1976. Although Washington was picked as a potential candidate for mayor by two separate committees, he withdrew his candidacy after Congressman Ralph METCALFE stated that he would not support Washington because of Washington's early 1970's troubles with the Internal Revenue Service; he had been convicted of having failed to file income-tax returns for four years and had served a month in jail. Washington nevertheless was unofficially submitted as a candidate in the 1978 race, but he lost. Yet even though Washington lost the 1978 race, the effort helped bring more African American representatives to the city council and helped Washington to become a U.S. Congressman in 1980 following Metcalfe's death.

Second Campaign for Mayor. Several forces led Washington to again seek the mayor's office in 1982. First, Chicago's African American community was disappointed with the lack of concern that Mayor Jane Byrne had shown for their needs. Second, several grass-roots coalitions developed to raise the consciousness of African American Chicagoans regarding the possibility of the election of an African American mayor in 1983. These organizations contributed to the movement to elect Washington by placing welfare recipients, the poor, the elderly, African Americans, and Hispanics on the voting rolls as well as by coordinating fund-raisers across the city. Third, the African American business community provided financial support for his campaign. Fourth, more than 250 African American ministers showed their support for Washington's candidacy by urging their congregations to register to vote. In the wake of this overwhelming current of mobilization in the African American community, Washington again entered the race for mayor.

While it was the activity of the coalitions that solidified Washington's support in the African American and Hispanic communities, it was a series of debates and public speaking events in January, 1983, that broadened his appeal to the rest of the city. Washington captured the votes of the masses in a televised debate with incumbent Jane Byrne and candidate Richard M. Daley (son of the late mayor, Richard J. Daley) as well as through public appearances with prominent supporters. As a result of these efforts, Washington narrowly defeated Byrne and Daley in the Democratic primary and captured the party's nomination.

Following Washington's primary victory, the Republican primary winner, Bernard Epton, attempted to use Washington's earlier tax conviction and conducted a campaign of race-based politics in an effort to win the general election. In spite of such tactics, Washington became Chicago's first African American mayor, receiv-

ing 640,738 votes to Epton's 599,144 votes.

Washington the Mayor. Washington was elected mayor on a reform platform; he promised to eliminate patronage jobs, increase the ethnic diversity of city government, and promote the growth of industry in Chicago. His main obstacle to these objectives was a bloc of twenty-nine city councilmen organized to oppose Washington's programs. The coalition attempted to stop Washington's appointments of agency officials, the passage of the city budget, and the funding of capital improvements for the city. They also used the media in an attempt to draw Washington into conflict with Hispanics, Jews, and the gay community to dilute his political base. Washington's opponents hoped that, as a result of these efforts, Washington would be seen as an ineffective mayor and would lose in the 1987 election.

In spite of such opposition, Washington was able to oversee a number of important changes. He reduced the number of discretionary (patronage) jobs in Chicago from more than forty thousand to fewer than a thousand; he used AFFIRMATIVE ACTION policies to boost the percentage of city contracts for minority- and women-owned businesses; and he obtained bonds for sorely needed capital improvements to the infrastructure of the city of Chicago. Furthermore, following twenty years of decline in industry and employment, the number of jobs in Chicago increased. Retail sales and manufacturing investment also increased during the same period.

Washington's battles with the twenty-nine councilmen ended after a court ruling ordered the reconfiguration of council wards drawn by Mayor Jane Byrne in 1981. The reconfiguration created seven new wards and changed the power balance between the mayor and his enemies on the council. After special elections were held in 1986 to fill the new seats, an even balance was achieved between Washington's supporters and his foes, leaving the final vote to the mayor on issues affecting his political agenda.

Final Campaign. In the 1987 election Washington faced and beat Byrne in the primary and won the general election by a wide margin. In his second term, Washington moved his fights from the local to the national level, fighting the attempted takeover of the Chicago Housing Authority by the U.S. DEPARTMENT OF HOUSING AND URBAN DEVELOPMENT and by supporting Jesse JACKSON in his candidacy for president. On Nov. 25, 1987, however, not long after his reelection, Washington died of a heart attack.—*Llewellyn Cornelius*

SUGGESTED READINGS: • Holli, Melvin G., and Paul M. Green, eds. *The Making of the Mayor, Chicago, 1983*. Grand Rapids, Mich.: Eerdmans, 1984. • Miller, Alton.

Harold Washington: The Mayor, the Man. Chicago: Bonus Books, 1989. • Royko, Mike. *Boss: Richard J. Daley of Chicago*. New York: E. P. Dutton, 1971. • Travis, Dempsey. *An Autobiography of Black Politics*. Chicago: Urban Research Institute, 1987. • Young, Henry J., ed. *The Black Church and the Harold Washington Story: The Man, the Message, the Movement*. Bristol, Ind.: Wyndham Hall Press, 1988.

Washington, Kenneth S. "Kenny" (Aug. 31, 1918, Los Angeles, Calif.—June 24, 1971, Los Angeles, Calif.): FOOTBALL player. Washington starred at halfback for the UCLA Bruins from 1937 to 1939, gaining All-American honors in his last year and breaking the all-time Bruin rushing record with 1,915 yards. Washington and UCLA teammate Woody Strode became the first post-World War II black players in the National Football League (NFL). Washington played for the Los Angeles Rams from 1946 until 1948, and in 1947 he led the NFL in rushing average with 7.4 yards per attempt, gaining 444 yards in sixty carries.

Kenny Washington was a star halfback for UCLA. (AP/Wide World Photos)

Washington, Lula (b. c. 1951): Dancer and choreographer. Washington is artistic director of the Los Angeles Contemporary Dance Theater, which performs modern dance. It is part of the Lula Washington Contemporary Dance Foundation, which also operates the Children's Jazz Dance Ensemble. Washington founded her company in 1980, created and ran the Rainbow Outta This World Dance Festival in 1981, danced in the opening ceremonies of the Olympic Games in 1984, and choreographed the 1989 film *The Little Mermaid*. Her own works include "Urban Man," "Reggae Suite," and "Lift Every Voice." Washington grew up in South Central Los Angeles and WATTS and holds a master's degree in dance from UCLA. She has taught at numerous Southern California colleges and universities and at her own studio school. In addition to her live performances, she has appeared in several television shows and films, including *Sgt. Pepper's Lonely Hearts Club Band* (1978).

Washington, Mary Helen (b. Jan. 21, 1941, Cleveland, Ohio): Educator. Washington taught English in Cleveland's public schools (1962-1964) before becoming an instructor in English at St. John College in that city. She moved to the University of Detroit in 1972, becoming director of its Center for Black Studies in 1975. She won the Richard WRIGHT Award for Literary Criticism in 1974.

Washington, Ora (b. c. 1900, Philadelphia, Pa.): Tennis and BASKETBALL player. Washington's tennis career began in 1924, when she defeated Dorothy Radcliff in her first tournament. Washington remained undefeated until 1936. Suffering form sunstroke, she was beaten by Lulu Ballard. Washington also starred for eighteen years as the center on the *Philadelphia Tribune* women's basketball team and later played for the Germantown Hornets. She was the top scorer for both teams. Washington's dream of playing the top-rated white tennis player of the day, Helen Wills Moody, was never realized because Moody refused to play against her.

Washington, Walter E. (b. Apr. 15, 1915, Dawson, Ga.): First mayor of Washington, D.C. Washington earned an undergraduate degree and a law degree at HOWARD UNIVERSITY, then did further studies at American University. He served on the National Capital Housing Authority from 1941 to 1966, then briefly served as chairman of the New York City Housing Authority. He was appointed as commissioner of the District of Columbia by President Lyndon Johnson on Sept. 21, 1967. That post, in effect, was that of mayor of Washington, D.C., the nation's largest predominantly black city. Washington had also been a member of the National Advisory Commission on Civil Disorders, which was formed to investigate the causes of rioting during the 1960's. Washington served

Walter Washington was the first person to hold the office of mayor of Washington, D.C. (Library of Congress)

as appointed mayor until 1975, when he won an election for the post. He served until 1979, then went into law practice.

Watermelon Man (Columbia, 1970): Film directed by Melvin VAN PEEBLES. Comedian Godfrey CAMBRIDGE stars as Jeff Gerber, a white insurance salesman whose comfortable suburban life is shattered when he wakes up one morning to find that he has become black. The film's humor lies both in Gerber's own reaction to his situation and the ways in which his family, friends, and coworkers respond to the change. Van Peebles also composed the film's musical score.

Waters, Ethel (Oct. 31, 1900, Chester, Pa.—Sept. 1, 1977, Chatsworth, Calif.): Singer and actress. Waters grew up very interested in theatrical activities such as singing, dancing, and acting. Because of her poverty, she could not obtain formal training in the PERFORMING ARTS. She compensated for this by watching people perform and imitating them in the privacy of her home. At any

opportunity, she would sing, dance, and perform before an audience.

Her career in vaudeville began when, during one of her performances at a party in 1917, some vaudeville performers noticed her theatrical ability and gave her a singing and dancing role in their company. That year, she toured with the Braxton and Nugent circuit. She was particularly successful in her singing of the St. Louis blues. Waters was engaged to perform at a New York City club called Edmond Johnson's Cellar until 1925, when she got a better opportunity at the famous Plantation Club.

Waters debuted as a Broadway star after successfully performing in *Africana*, a revue she put together with the assistance of Donald Hayward and Earl Dancer. Broadway roles in *Blackbirds* and *Rhapsody in Blue* followed in quick succession, but the shows were more successful on tour than on Broadway. In a production of *As Thousands Cheer*, Waters became the first African American since Egbert (Bert) WILLIAMS to star in an otherwise all-Caucasian performance on Broadway. Waters was in demand for radio performances and on Broadway, where she performed in the musical *At Home Abroad* in 1935.

During the FEDERAL THEATRE PROJECT era, Waters took a break from singing to give an excellent performance of Shaw's *Androcles and the Lion*. She also played success-

Ethel Waters was a popular stage actress. (AP/Wide World Photos)

fully the difficult role of Hagar in DuBose and Dorothy Heyward's *Mamba's Daughters*. With that performance she established herself as a full-range actress. In 1950, she put on a brilliant performance of the character Berenice Sadie Brown in Carson McCullers' play, *The Member of the Wedding*, at the Empire Theatre. Her unforgettable performance helped the play win the Drama Critics Circle Award for best American play of the year (1950). Waters also starred in Hollywood films such as *PINKY* (1949), *Tales of Manhattan* (1942), and *CABIN IN THE SKY* (1943) and in the television show *BEULAH*.

Waters, Maxine (b. 1938, St. Louis, Mo.): Politician. Waters received a B.A. degree from California State University, Los Angeles. She has been honored with doctoral degrees by Spelman College and North Carolina A&T University. She was a member of the California State Assembly before her election to the U.S. House of Representatives in 1990. She became the first nonlawyer to serve on the House Judiciary Committee. Her main legislative interests are in foreign policy issues and social issues such as civil rights. She is particularly concerned with disarmament, opportunities for women, ACQUIRED

Congresswoman Maxine Waters focuses on social issues and foreign relations. (Roy Lewis Photography)

IMMUNE DEFICIENCY SYNDROME, tenant protection, and small business protection. She introduced a bill to limit police authority to strip and search persons arrested for minor offenses.

Watkins, Bruce R., Sr. (1933?—Sept.13, 1980, Kansas City, Mo.): Politician and civil rights activist. A World War II Air Force veteran, Watkins cofounded a civil rights group in Kansas City called Freedom, Inc., in 1962. He first was elected to the city council in 1963. Watkins served as clerk for Jackson county from 1969 to 1974 and later was reelected to the city council. He left the council in 1979 to run for mayor of Kansas City. As the first African American candidate for the city's top post, Watkins defeated the incumbent mayor in the Democratic primary. After losing the election to Richard Berkley, Watkins served as an executive assistant to the regional director for the DEPARTMENT OF HOUSING AND URBAN DEVELOPMENT (HUD). Soon after, he was diagnosed with cancer. He died at Kansas City's Research Medical Center at the age of fifty-seven.

Watkins, Joseph Philip (b. Aug. 24, 1953, New York, N.Y.): Minister, journalist, and political appointee. Watkins was graduated from the University of Pennsylvania with a bachelor of arts degree in history in 1975. He earned his master of arts degree in religious education from Princeton Theological Seminary in 1979. He was chaplain and religion instructor at Talladega College from 1978 to 1979. Watkins moved to Indiana to serve as campus minister at Indiana University-Purdue University at Fort Wayne between 1979 and 1981.

Watkins first worked in Washington, D.C., as an aide to Senator Dan Quayle of Indiana between 1981 and 1984, serving as the senator's assistant state director. During his time on Capitol Hill, Watkins was named to *Ebony* magazine's 1983 list of 50 Young Leaders of the Future. Watkins campaigned against incumbent congressman Andy Jacobs, Jr., for Indiana's Tenth District Seat in 1984 but was unsuccessful. He returned to Indiana to take the position of vice president and director of missions for *The Saturday Evening Post* in 1984. He was serving as an assistant to the president of the University of Pennsylvania when President George Bush appointed him to serve as associate director of the White House Office of Public Liaison.

Watkins, Perry (1907—1974, Newburgh, N.Y.): Theater scenic designer, costume designer, producer, and film director. Watkins was the first African American to break the color barrier in scenic designing, by becoming a member of the United Scenic Artists in the 1930's. He became famous with his production designs for the Harlem Unit of the FEDERAL THEATRE PROJECT.

Watley, Jody (b. Jan. 30, 1961, Chicago, Ill.): Singer and dancer. A former Soul Train dancer, Watley joined up with her dancing partner Jeffrey Daniels and Howard HEWETT to form the group SHALAMAR. They enjoyed great success in the late 1970's and early 1980's before Watley left the group in 1983 to pursue her solo career. Her second album, *Larger than Life*, produced six top-ten singles, and she won a 1988 Grammy as best new artist. Her album *Affairs of the Heart* came out in 1991 and soon went platinum. She released an exercise video, *Dance to Fitness*, the same year.

Watson, Barbara M. (b. Nov. 5, 1918, New York, N.Y.): Political appointee. Watson received her bachelor of arts degree from Barnard College and went on to earn her LL.B. from New York University School of Law. She served as a special assistant to the U.S. deputy undersec-

Barbara M. Watson served in a variety of diplomatic positions. (AP/Wide World Photos)

retary of state for administration during the Lyndon B. Johnson Administration. She later served as deputy and acting administrator of the Bureau of Security and Consular Affairs of the U.S. State Department before being appointed as administrator of the bureau in 1968, serving until 1974. Watson was the first woman to attain the rank of assistant secretary of state at the State Department, in 1977. She served until 1980 and was appointed as ambassador to Malaysia that same year.

Watson, James L. (b. May 21, 1922, New York, N.Y.): Federal judge. Watson served with the 92d Infantry Division of the U.S. Army during World War II. He was wounded in active duty in Italy and received the Purple Heart and other medals and commendations for his actions. After his discharge, Watson attended New York University and was graduated with his B.A. degree in 1947. He was graduated from Brooklyn Law School with his LL.B. degree in 1951. In that same year, he was admitted to the New York State Bar and was admitted to practice in the U.S. District Court for the Southern District of New York.

Watson's first political appointment came when he served on the Board of Immigrations Appeals in New York City in 1952. In 1954, Watson was elected to the New York State Senate as a representative from the Twenty-first Senatorial District. He served until 1963, when he was elected to the post of judge of the Civil Court of New York City and became the first African American judge to be elected in the history of New York State. In 1966, President Lyndon B. Johnson appointed Watson to serve as judge on the U.S. Customs Court, which later was renamed the U.S. Court of International Trade.

Wattleton, (Alyce) Faye (b. July 8, 1943, St. Louis, Mo.): Reproductive rights advocate. Having observed the results of "back alley" abortions during her career as a nurse, Wattleton vicariously experienced the hardship, and sometimes death, of women who tried to terminate unwanted pregnancies. Appointed president of the Planned Parenthood Federation of America (PPFA) in 1978, she managed the nation's oldest and largest voluntary reproductive health organization in its crusade to safeguard individual rights concerning pregnancy and pregnancy termination. As president of Planned Parenthood, she played a major role in defining the national debate over reproductive rights and the shaping of family planning policies of governments worldwide. Her unprecedented vision and courage projected the PPFA into the forefront of the battle to preserve women's fundamental rights.

Attacks by antichoice, or prolife, factions in the White House, Supreme Court, Congress, and state legislatures seriously jeopardized Americans' reproductive rights and threatened federally funded family planning programs

that served millions of low-income families in the United States and in the developing world. Articulate leadership, endless energy, and high visibility have characterized Wattleton's strategies for bolstering an uncompromising prochoice position.

Wattleton has a bachelor's degree from Ohio State University and a master's degree in maternal and infant care, with certification as a nurse-midwife, from Columbia University. In 1970, she became executive director of Planned Parenthood in Dayton, Ohio. She has also served as chairwoman of the National Executive Directors' Council of PPFA.

Having witnessed the results of illegal abortions as a nurse, Faye Wattleton fought to keep abortion legal. (Library of Congress)

Wattleton is the recipient of the 1989 American Public Health Association Award of Excellence, the Better World Society 1989 Population Medal, the 1989 CONGRESSIONAL BLACK CAUCUS Foundation Humanitarian Award, and numerous other citations and several honorary degrees. She was recognized by *Money* magazine as one of five outstanding Americans who project the forces that would shape American lives by the year 2000. In 1992, she made the decision to leave the presidency of the PPFA, but she planned to continue to fight for all individuals' right to take charge of their lives and fight reproduction victimization.

Watts: District in the southern portion of Los Angeles, Calif. Watts originally was a middle-class district of white-collar workers, but World War II and the times immediately after it changed Watts into a community with a preponderance of African American residents. Those who had migrated to Los Angeles during the war years, usually from the rural South, to work in shipyards and other government-related industries experienced great difficulty in finding housing. Blatant discrimination, as well as more subtle economic forms of discrimination, kept black residents out of most of Los Angeles. Prohibitively high rents, along with then-legal restrictive covenants, effectively served to retain the whites-only composition of most of the districts in the city. Thus it was economic necessity that precipitated the enormous increase of population, especially of African Americans, in Watts during the immediate postwar years.

The newly arrived residents were by no means assured of jobs, nor of job security once they had found employment. Unstable employment was perhaps the most important factor in maintaining POVERTY and deprivation in Watts. Critical community services, such as decent schools, transportation, and medical care, as well as adequate housing, became severely deficient. Even for those people who found jobs in defense-related industries, work was low-paying and often seasonal. Because of the lack of public transportation, expensive commutes often were involved.

The WATTS RIOTS that began on Aug. 11, 1965, called attention, on a nationwide scale, to the deplorable GHETTO conditions and provided to the public graphic illustrations of the horrors of life for Watts' approximately ninety thousand residents. Six days of rioting left thirty-four people dead and more than a thousand wounded. Out of

National Guard troops patrol the streets of Watts following the rioting in 1965. (AP/Wide World Photos)

the horrors of the riots emerged a new identity, one that stressed black pride and emphasized a sense of community and solidarity. Groups and projects formed, sponsored both by the government and by the community. Theater projects were spawned, and day-care and HEAD START educational programs were developed. More attention was paid to job training and procurement, and housing conditions were improved through new projects. Residents achieved political representation, and through the legislative process sought employment and contracts for minority-owned and -operated businesses.

Watts as a community possessed a unique emblem, the towers built by an Italian immigrant, Sebastiano Rodia, known more commonly as Simon. Created between 1921 and 1954 out of discarded materials—bottles and bottle caps, broken tiles and pottery, seashells, and old shoes, to name but a few of the found objects—and rising some fifty-five, ninety-seven, and ninety-nine feet, they served as reminders that art can reside in environments normally considered hostile or unsympathetic, and that creativity can occur despite the most appalling of circumstances.

Watts, Andre (b. June 20, 1946, Nuremberg, Germany): Concert pianist. Watts was introduced to the piano at age seven by his mother. He studied at the Philadelphia Musical Academy and at the Peabody Institute in Baltimore. He came to national prominence at age sixteen, when he flawlessly played, under conductor Leonard Bernstein, with the New York Philharmonic. He performed at President Nixon's inaugural in 1969. He has played for other international leaders, including President Mobutu Sese Seko of Zaire, who gave Watts the country's highest honor, the Order of the Zaire.

Watts riots: Widespread disturbance in the WATTS district of Los Angeles, Calif., in August, 1965. The Watts district was an overcrowded GHETTO area whose residents predominantly were African American. The Watts riots brought the POVERTY-stricken area to the attention of the United States public.

The riots stemmed from an incident on August 11 involving a Los Angeles police officer and an intoxicated African American driver, Marquette Frye. The officer stopped the twenty-one-year-old man for reckless driving in a Watts neighborhood after Frye swerved across adjacent lanes on a busy street. Area residents, including the suspect's relatives, began gathering at the scene to observe the arrest.

At first, the incident was void of tension and anger, and observers joked with the police officer. The suspect's mother even scolded her son publicly for his behavior and urged him to cooperate with the officer. When Frye became angry and resisted the arrest, while shouting obscenities at the police officer, the mood of the crowd gradually changed to one of anger.

An altercation developed between the officer, Frye, and members of the crowd. As it intensified, a second officer arrived, carrying his riot baton to assist the arresting officer. When the second officer began hitting bystanders with his baton in an attempt to disperse them, the scene became more chaotic, resulting in several arrests.

Rumors later abounded regarding the incident, replete with embellished details of the arrests and police brutality. This incident further increased the already existing tensions between the African American Watts community and the Los Angeles police force. The Watts area exploded into violence the next day, following a meeting intended to ease tensions.

Rioting, rock throwing, looting, sniper shooting, and arson occurred in the midst of tension, bitterness, and anger. Approximately five thousand African Americans rioted, targeting white-owned businesses to loot and destroy. More than twelve thousand National Guards and several thousand local police officers were called into Watts.

Order eventually was restored on August 16, after six days of rioting that resulted in more than thirty deaths, about one thousand injuries, and nearly four thousand arrests. Hundreds of families were left homeless. Property damage was estimated by various observers at $40 million to more than $200 million.

Wayans, Damon (b. 1960, New York, N.Y.): Comedian. Wayans, the brother of Keenen Ivory WAYANS, was on the original cast of television's *IN LIVING COLOR*, which began airing in 1990. He also appeared on *Saturday Night Live* in 1985 and 1986. Among his film appearances are roles in *BEVERLY HILLS COP* (1984), *The Last Boy Scout* (1991), and *Mo' Money* (1992), for which he also wrote the screenplay.

Wayans, Keenen Ivory (b. June 8, 1958, New York, N.Y.): Writer, director, producer, and actor. Wayans grew up in the Fulton housing projects in New York City. Wayans, the second of ten children, began performing comedy at an early age. He dropped out of TUSKEGEE INSTITUTE in Alabama and returned to New York City to pursue a career in stand-up comedy. Wayans then moved to Los Angeles, Calif., and began an acting career, appearing in such television hits as *BENSON, Cheers,* and *A DIFFERENT WORLD.*

He began collaborating with his good friend and colleague, the actor, director, producer, and writer Robert TOWNSEND. Wayans cowrote and starred in several Townsend productions. These included 1982's hit film HOLLYWOOD SHUFFLE, and *Robert Townsend's Partners in Crime*, produced for Home Box Office. Wayans also worked with Townsend as coproducer and cowriter on *Eddie Murphy Raw*, a 1987 concert film. In 1989, he branched out on his own, serving as executive producer, writer, director, and star of *I'M GONNA GIT YOU SUCKA*, a comedy spoof of the BLAXPLOITATION films of the 1970's. The film, which was made on a very small budget, grossed more than $19 million. These phenomenal successes found Wayans emerging as one of the prominent young black directors of the 1980's.

Keenen Ivory Wayans succeeded in ventures into film and television. (AP/Wide World Photos)

Using his keen imagination and business sense, Wayans capitalized on his newfound popularity to launch the Fox Broadcasting Network's hit comedy series *IN LIVING COLOR*. In addition to being the show's creator, Wayans served as executive producer, writer, host, and cast member. The controversial comedy series satirizes current events, racial attitudes, celebrities, history, movies, and more. Anything and everything is fair game for Wayans. The show, which includes two Wayans brothers and a sister as cast members, also hosts dance numbers by the *In Living Color* dance group, The Fly Girls.

In 1990, Wayans received the prestigious American Black Achievement Award for his contributions to dramatic arts. That same year, *In Living Color* won an Emmy Award as the most outstanding variety, music, and comedy series and a NATIONAL ASSOCIATION FOR THE ADVANCEMENT OF COLORED PEOPLE Image Award as best variety show. The show was nominated for Emmy Awards in five categories in 1991, including music, writing, and costume design. *In Living Color* won the People's Choice Award as favorite new television comedy series in 1991. Wayans' other projects include creating and serving as executive producer of a comedy-adventure pilot for ABC television entitled "Hammer, Slammer, and Slade," based on *I'm Gonna Git You Sucka.*

Weary Blues, The (1926): Poetry collection by Langston HUGHES. The work, with its wide range of subject matter, illustrates the author's love for and devotion to black American life. The poems, in which Hughes made use of the blues style, celebrate black life in all of its forms, including dialect, heritage, spiritual growth, Harlem cabaret life, jazz and blues, sad and joyous moments, ties with the motherland, and hope.

Weathers, Carl (b. Jan. 14, 1948, New Orleans, La.): Film and television actor. He is best known as boxer Apollo Creed in the first four films of the series that began with *Rocky* (1976). In 1986, he starred as the title character in the television series *FORTUNE DANE*.

Weaver, George Leon-Paul (b. June 18, 1912, Pittsburgh, Pa.): Political appointee and business consultant. Weaver attended Roosevelt University from 1940 to 1942 and attended law school at HOWARD UNIVERSITY from 1942 to 1943. From 1941 to 1942, Weaver was a member of the Congress of Industrial Organizations (CIO) War and Relief Commission, and he served as assistant to the secretary-treasurer of the CIO from 1942 to 1955. When the American Federation of Labor and the CIO were reconciled in 1955, Weaver became executive secretary of the AFL-CIO, serving in this position until 1958.

In 1961, President John F. Kennedy appointed Weaver to serve as special assistant to the secretary of labor. Weaver served as assistant secretary of labor international affairs and special assistant to the director general of the International Labor Organization in Geneva from 1969 until his retirement. In 1975, he became a consultant to the World ORT Union. Among his other activities, Weaver served as a member of the board of the UNITED NEGRO COLLEGE FUND.

Weaver, Robert Clipton (b. Dec. 29, 1907, Washington, D.C.): Government official. Weaver was the first African American to be named as a cabinet member when Lyndon Johnson made him the secretary of housing and urban development in 1966. Previously, Weaver had served in several high-ranking federal posts and was a member of Franklin D. Roosevelt's "black cabinet." Weaver earned a Ph.D. in economics at Harvard University and wrote several books analyzing the plight of African American workers. He was an adviser to several fellowship funds and served as a director of the John Hay Whitney Foundation.

The first African American in the cabinet, Robert Weaver previously had served in Franklin D. Roosevelt's unofficial "black cabinet." (Harlee Little)

Webb, Clifton (b. Aug. 7, 1950, New Orleans, La.): Painter and sculptor. Webb's work synthesizes African and Central American approaches to the senses along with conveying a sense of musical order. His work, which often combines painting and sculpture, gains kinetic energy from the raw materials used while emphasizing the individuality of each element.

Webb, Spud (b. July 13, 1963, Dallas, Tex.): Basketball player. Small by professional BASKETBALL standards, the five-foot, seven-inch, 135-pound guard played basketball

for North Carolina State University until 1985. After college, Webb was signed by the Atlanta Hawks after being waived by the Detroit Pistons. He is recognized for his pesky and effective defensive play and for his surprising slam dunk capability.

Webb, William Henry "Chick" (Feb. 10, 1909, Baltimore, Md.—June 16, 1939, Baltimore, Md.): Drummer, bandleader, and composer. Webb was forced to endure and overcome the physical deformity of being hunchbacked. His deformity was the result of tuberculosis of the spine. Webb began playing the drums when he was three years old. Six years later, he was performing on pleasure steamers in Sheepshead Bay. As a teenager, Webb played with the Jazzola Orchestra and began his long association with guitarist John Trueheart. In 1926, he formed his own band in New York. The band performed at such clubs as the Black Bottom and the Paddock. Eventually, Webb became the resident bandleader, with his Harlem Stompers, at the SAVOY BALLROOM in Harlem. He would remain at the Savoy for approximately ten years.

Although his deformity could be very painful, Webb was a dynamic drummer. According to most jazz experts, he is considered to be one of the great drummers of his time. As a bandleader, Webb was very competitive. He always wanted to have the best possible band in town. During this time, Webb heard the teenager Ella FITZGERALD sing, and he instantly knew that she would be a major talent. In 1935, she became part of his band, and it was not long before the band's show was built around Fitzgerald's singing. Webb continued to play the drums as forcefully as ever, even though playing was becoming extremely painful. His drum equipment always had to be specially constructed in order for him to perform.

Webb was admired greatly by his fellow drummers for his swing style and his solid technique. The legendary drummer Gene Krupa referred to Webb as "the little giant of the drums." In 1938, Fitzgerald sang the hit song "A-tisket, A-tasket." Both Fitzgerald and Webb became immensely popular because of the song. During the summer of 1938, Webb's band broke a number of attendance records at various ballrooms and theaters. Webb's health was not very good, yet he continued to perform as often as he could. In late 1938, he had to be hospitalized because of pleurisy. Webb remained in the hospital until January of 1939. He went back to leading his band until he was forced to return to the hospital. Webb finally died shortly after undergoing major urological surgery. In addition to his spectacular drumming and impressive bandleading, Webb cowrote several memorable songs, including "Stompin' at the Savoy," "Lonesome Moments," "Holiday in Harlem," and "Heart of Mine." In 1947, a recreation center in memory of Webb was opened in Baltimore.

Webster (ABC, 1983-1987): Television sitcom. As a result of his tiny size, twelve-year-old Emmanuel Lewis was able to portray the title character as a six-year-old. In a standard sitcom premise for uniting unlikely families, Webster was an orphan taken in by a friend and colleague of his dead father. Webster's new dad, George Papadapolis (Alex Karras), knew almost as little about rearing a child as did his socialite wife, Katherine (Susan Clark), but the adorable Webster brought out the best in them.

Emmanuel Lewis as the title character in Webster. (Capital Cities/ABC, Inc.)

Webster, Ben (Mar. 27, 1909, Kansas City, Mo.—Sept. 20, 1973, Amsterdam, The Netherlands): Jazz tenor saxophonist. By the time he joined pianist Duke ELLINGTON's band on a permanent basis in 1939, Webster was a veteran musician who, although he had not led a recording session, had played and recorded with such significant musicians as singer Billie HOLIDAY, trumpeter Roy ELDRIDGE, saxophonist Benny CARTER, and pianist Teddy WILSON. Webster had an accomplished career highlighted by his four years with Ellington, probably the best years of the Ellington band. Webster was part of the reason why the band was so good. His solos on "Cotton Tail" (1940) and "All too Soon" (1940) demonstrated his fiery potential and his more rhapsodic side, respectively.

Webster made some of his greatest recordings in the 1950's, particularly on an album with pianist Art TATUM (1956), on his own *Soulville* (1957), and on singer Jimmy Witherspoon's *At the Renaissance* (1959). In the mid-1960's, he moved permanently to Europe, where he performed frequently with his own groups.

Always a master ballad player, late in his life Webster turned to ballads with increased frequency and with added poignancy. His playing became more intimate. Occasionally, he would conclude a performance by emitting a barely audible breath through his saxophone, as if to blur the boundary between sound and silence. This practice can be heard on "Deep River" (1970) and "The Man I Love" (1972), to cite but two examples. Originally influenced by saxophonist Coleman HAWKINS, Webster developed his own breathy style, perfectly suited to the material he played.

Wedding Band (pr. 1966): Play by Alice CHILDRESS. Subtitled *A Love/Hate Story in Black and White*, the work portrays emotionally scarred characters who find themselves drawn into a dramatic interracial romance. It delicately examines their daily struggle and the effects their relationship has on them.

Weems, Carrie Mae: Photographer. In addition to her photography, Weems has worked in video. She was a Smithsonian Fellow and has organized various exhibitions and conferences related to photography, black PHOTOGRAPHERS, and women photographers. Her work concentrates on showing African American culture from an insider's perspective.

Wells, Ida B(ell) (July 16, 1862, Holly Springs, Miss.—Mar. 25, 1931, Chicago, Ill.): Civil rights activist. One of the nation's leading equal-rights crusaders around the turn of the twentieth century was Ida B. Wells. This African American woman journalist, whose career spanned more than forty years, was a pioneer in the area of investigative reporting, specializing in cases where civil rights of black Americans had been violated in the most extreme way—by LYNCHING. Her investigations entailed using records from the white press to uncover the reasons underlying large-scale mob executions of blacks during the turbulent years following the Civil War. What Wells uncovered corroborated her theory that race hatred, and not the common cry of "rape," was the real motivation behind the rising menace to African Americans of her day.

Study on Lynching. In 1895, she published *The Red Record*, which contained her findings. Wells's seminal report covered a three-year period, 1892-1894. It sacrificed breadth in order to achieve more depth than the *Chicago Tribune's* 1892 report, which had revealed that, in 728 cases in which blacks had been lynched over an eight-year period, rape or attempted rape was mentioned in only one-third of the cases. In her study, Wells analyzed the evidence for the relatively small number of lynchings ostensibly carried out to punish rapists. She found that many of the so-called rapists were not guilty of any crime for a variety of reasons, a common one being that the sex act had been consensual. Wells also reported that in the vast majority of lynchings, the reasons advanced by lynching perpetrators in justification of their crimes ranged from charges of sassiness or drunkenness to thievery and murderous assault by blacks.

Not only did Wells use her journalistic talent to get across her antilynching message, but she also utilized other platforms. As an orator, she was commanding and convincing; as the organizer of a powerful crusade against lynching in America and in England, she was dynamic and effective.

Early Life and Education. Ida B. Wells was born in Holly Springs, Miss., the first of eight children born to Jim and Lizzie Wells. Jim Wells, the son of his white master and a slave woman, had been favored by his father, who had him apprenticed in his youth to a carpenter. Later, the consummate skill Jim Wells acquired in carpentry allowed him to support his wife and children after the Civil War ended in 1865.

From the ruins of the postwar South, Jim Wells carved out a relatively comfortable living for himself and his family. Choosing to stay close to his roots after the emancipation of the slaves, Jim Wells left his master's farm and settled his family closer to the center of town. In those days, Holly Springs was a beautiful town of rolling hills, cotton plantations, and stately architecture. Although little actual fighting had occurred in the town, it had been hit in the war's scathing aftermath when Union soldiers had passed through, destroying the main street and many beautiful homes. In helping to restore the town, Jim Wells had all the work he could handle. His skill and ambition gave him and his family status in the larger community among both whites and blacks.

While she was growing up, Ida, like all the Wells children, attended school. Mother Lizzie joined the children in the classroom and also learned how to read. Ida B. Wells first attended Tiny Schools and later Rust University, both in Holly Springs. From the beginning, she distinguished herself as an apt student.

The peaceful quality of Ida's world was abruptly shattered the year she turned sixteen. In 1878, a terrible yellow-fever epidemic claimed the lives of both her parents on the same day. Her ten-month-old brother also died of the fever.

Supporting Her Family. Calling upon a reserve of inner strength and fortified by the Christian foundation her parents had given her, Ida steeled herself to become head of a household of six. (Another brother had died before the epidemic.) Ida quit school and began teaching six miles from home to support the family. Several years later, when her two brothers could fend for themselves, Ida moved to Tennessee with her two sisters to secure a higher-paying teaching position. (One sister who was paralyzed was taken in by an aunt.)

In May, 1884, while on her way to her job in Woodstock, Tenn., Wells boarded the Chesapeake and Ohio Railroad in Memphis. Having a first-class ticket, she sat in a first-class car and refused to move to the dingy smoking car, where blacks were expected to sit. She stubbornly defied the conductor, who had to enlist the assistance of two other white men to throw Wells from the train. Afterward, Wells, a much-offended young woman, sued for justice. Justice came in 1885, when a federal court judge ruled in her favor and awarded her five hundred dollars in damages. After the judgment, which was widely reported across the country, the state of Tennessee petitioned to have the trial moved to the state supreme court. The state's appeal was granted. In the second trial, Wells lost her claim and was assessed a two-hundred-dollar fine.

When the second railroad verdict was handed down, Wells had already started to teach in Memphis. She had also joined a literary group; by 1887, she was regularly contributing to a church newspaper. That same year, she purchased a part interest in the local black newspaper, *The Free Speech and Headlight.*

Journalism Career. As an independent journalist, Wells placed in her paper several articles critical of the Memphis school board. Finally, one article pointing to an illicit affair between a prominent white man and a black female teacher got her into serious trouble. The exposé cost Wells her teaching job in 1891.

Theretofore, journalism had been something of a hobby for Wells; but with the turn of events, journalism became the only available professional work to which she could turn. Wells vigorously took on the challenge of making her newspaper profitable enough to provide her with a livelihood. She set about increasing *The Free*

Ida B. Wells

"I'D RATHER GO DOWN IN HISTORY AS ONE LONE NEGRO WHO DARED TO TELL THE GOVERNMENT THAT IT HAD DONE A DASTARDLY THING THAN TO SAVE MY SKIN BY TAKING BACK WHAT I HAVE SAID." --1917

Speech and Headlight's circulation, drumming up new subscribers across the state. She was so successful in her efforts that soon her income from the newspaper surpassed the salary she had received as a teacher.

Fight Against Lynching. Wells's journalistic battle against lynch mobs began on Mar. 9, 1892, when her friend Thomas Moss, a young black entrepreneur, and two of his partners were brutally murdered for protecting their store against a band of white men. Their store, located just outside Memphis city limits in a section popularly called the Curve, sat in a spot unprotected by city law. Therefore, when a group of strange white men who were rumored to be raiders sent to close down the successful black business approached the store, the black men took an armed stand. In a quick volley of fire, several of the whites were injured. Although the black grocers surrendered and submitted to arrest immediately after the whites identified themselves as agents of the law, a lynch mob formed. In the middle of the night, the mob mutilated and killed the blacks.

After the black store owners were lynched, Wells set aside the official version of events reported in the white press and made her own analysis. She connected the grocers' case to others that had been explained by what she now believed were lies told by whites to justify crimes against blacks. Her startling reinterpretation of the facts greatly alarmed the white community. On Mar. 21, 1892, *The Free Speech and Headlight* published an editorial that stated:

"Nobody in this section of the country believes the old threadbare lie that Negro men rape white women. If the Southern white men are not careful, they will over-reach themselves and public sentiment will have a reaction; a conclusion will then be reached which will be very damaging to the moral reputation of their women."

Several days later, Wells's entire editorial, along with castigations of it, was reprinted in a leading white Memphis paper. The white paper not only flayed Wells's column but also ended its criticism with a call for group revenge on the black person who had written the offending piece. Luckily, while a mob gathered, Wells (who then owned 50 percent of *The Free Speech and Headlight*) was in Philadelphia; fortunately, too, her partner in the business was forewarned of the impending mob attack and managed to escape. Consequently, when the would-be lynchers finally descended upon the office of the black newspaper, they found the building empty. They vented their anger by destroying the entire operation. They then sent forth the warning that if Wells reappeared in the city within the next twenty years, she, too, would be lynched.

Wells was convinced by her friends to stay in the North

for her own safety. T. Thomas FORTUNE gave her a one-fourth interest in his paper, *The New York Age*, in exchange for her subscription lists and her promise to write a weekly column covering news from the black South.

Public Lectures and Lobbying Efforts. Soon after Wells resigned herself to her exile status in 1892, she embarked upon an antilynching campaign that remained in high gear for the next three years. Wells started the movement by lecturing in northeastern cities, sharing her opinions about the underlying causes of lynching. She journeyed to England in 1893 and again in 1894, staying for several months each time, arousing the sympathies of the English and pushing them to exert pressure on American lawmakers to do something about lynching. During her antilynching campaign, Wells stirred people and electrified audiences wherever she went. Although white American legislators expressed disdain for Wells and her work, they realized she was placing them under national and world scrutiny. By the end of Wells's campaign in 1895, some southern governors and legislative bodies were issuing antilynching proclamations and trying to adopt measures to stop lynch mobs.

In 1895, Wells decided to retire from the public stage and leave the fight for justice for others ready to take up the banner. On June 27 of that year, she married Ferdinand Lee BARNETT, the founder of the *Conservator*, the first black-owned newspaper in Chicago. Although Wells stuck to her plan of rearing a family, she found it impossible to turn her back on the black struggle for civil rights. Whenever she felt she was needed in a difficult case, she sallied forth to do battle; with her fiery pen, she continued to expose the flaws in whites' accounts of alleged crimes committed by blacks for which lynchings were ostensibly carried out as punishments.

Later Years. After settling in Chicago in 1895, Wells became greatly concerned about the plight of urban blacks. Her concern led her into the field of social work. Over the next thirty-five years, she worked as a probation officer, a woman's club organizer, and the founder and director of the Negro Fellowship League, which provided assistance to homeless young black men. After many years of service, following a brief illness, Ida B. Wells died on Mar. 25, 1931. For her work on behalf of Chicago's most downtrodden citizens, in 1940 a Chicago housing project was dedicated to her memory; in 1950, the city of Chicago honored her as one of its most illustrious women.

More than any other person of her day, Ida B. Wells opened the eyes of many people, black and white, who had believed the old propaganda supporting lynching; more than anyone else, she helped to undermine the spirit of vigilantism in the United States. Her crusade for justice helped to awaken Americans to the need for social change.—*Sarah Smith Ducksworth*

SUGGESTED READINGS: • Duster, Alfreda M., ed. *Crusade for Justice: The Autobiography of Ida B. Wells.* Chicago: University of Chicago Press, 1970. • Giddens, Paula. *When and Where I Enter: The Impact of Black Women on Race and Sex in America.* New York: William Morrow, 1984. • Harris, Trudier, comp. *The Selected Works of Ida B. Wells-Barnett.* New York: Oxford University Press, 1991. • Sterling, Dorothy. *Black Foremothers: Three Lives.* Old Westbury, N.Y.: Feminist Press, 1979. • Thompson, Mildred I. *Ida B. Wells-Barnett: Exploratory Study of an American Black Woman, 1893-1930.* Vol. 15 in *Black Women in American History.* Washington, D.C.: George Washington University Press, 1979.

Wells, Junior (Amos Blackmore; b. Dec. 9, 1934, Memphis, Tenn.): Blues harmonica player and singer. Raised in West Memphis, Ark., Wells learned to play harmonica at an early age and was playing on the streets for tips by the time he was seven years old. In 1946, Wells joined the ongoing black exodus from the rural South to northern cities in search of work. He settled in Chicago, Ill.

Wells's professional career began in 1948, when he sat in with TAMPA RED at Chicago's C & T Lounge. He was also befriended by MUDDY WATERS, who acted as the boy's "guardian," as Wells was still too young to frequent clubs alone. Shortly thereafter, Wells teamed up with David and Louis Myers, guitar-playing brothers from Byhalia, Miss., to form a group called the Little Boys, later called the Three Deuces and the Three Aces. The group worked the C & T Lounge and other local clubs over the next several years.

In 1952, Muddy Waters' harmonica player, LITTLE WALTER, scored a major rhythm-and-blues hit with an instrumental entitled "Juke." Anxious to capitalize on his success, he quit the Waters band, deposed Wells as leader of the Aces, added a fourth musician, drummer Fred Below, Jr., and took the group on a national tour. Wells, in turn, took Little Walter's place with the Muddy Waters band. He toured with Waters for about a year, until he was inducted into the U.S. Army. During this period, Wells made some of his best recordings, for the States label. These include "Eagle Rock" (1953), "Hoodoo Man" (1953), "Lawdy, Lawdy" (1954), and "So All Alone" (1954). Discharged from military service in 1955, Wells formed a new version of the Three Aces, which recorded for CHICAGO BLUES labels and played club dates throughout the United States in the late 1950's.

In the 1960's, Wells's career was bolstered by a tremendous upswing in the popularity of the Chicago blues style. Often teaming with guitarist Buddy GUY, he alternated tours of the American college circuit with trips to Europe, Africa, and the Far East for the U.S. State Department. In 1966, a Wells album, *Hoodoo Man Blues*, won the JAY Award from *Jazz* magazine for best blues album of the year. Increasingly influenced by soul, FUNK, and RHYTHM AND BLUES in the 1970's and 1980's, Wells veered away from the traditional Chicago blues idiom to a style of playing and vocal delivery that some critics have called similar to that of James BROWN.

Wells, Mary (May 13, 1943, Detroit, Mich.—July 26, 1991, Los Angeles, Calif.): Pop and soul singer. As one of Motown's first stars in the 1960's, Wells brought black music to the radio, popularized the Motown sound among white as well as African American audiences, and helped break down the musical segregation of her era.

Wells began singing in clubs and talent contests at the age of ten. During her teens, she was a soloist in her church and high school choirs; inspired by gospel music, she also wrote songs. In 1960, the sixteen-year-old Wells sang an original composition, "Bye Bye Baby," for Berry GORDY, Jr., the founder of Motown Records. Wells hoped Gordy would buy the song, but Gordy insisted that Wells record the tune herself and signed her to a contract. The slow rock ballad became a 1961 national hit, and Wells quit school to tour with the Motortown Revue.

From 1961 to 1964, Wells made such top-ten records as "You Beat Me to the Punch" (1962), "Two Lovers" (1962), and "My Guy" (1964), which became her signature song. These and most of Wells's Motown recordings were written or co-composed by Smokey Robinson, a black singer-songwriter-producer whose tales of love held universal appeal.

In 1964, Wells recorded two hit duets with singer Marvin GAYE, toured with the Beatles, and was voted top female singer in the *Melody Maker* readers' poll. She left Motown Records for Twentieth Century-Fox and later recorded for Atlantic-Atco and Jubilee, although none of her subsequent releases was as successful as her Motown recordings. In the late 1970's, she performed in revues and clubs across America.

Wells had no medical insurance when she was diagnosed with cancer of the larynx. The Rhythm and Blues Foundation, with contributions from singers Diana ROSS, Rod Stewart, Bruce Springsteen, and the TEMPTATIONS, raised money to pay her medical bills. Wells underwent surgery in 1990 but died later at the age of forty-nine. Wells's early work retains its appeal, and the songs she made famous in the 1960's have been the subject of periodic revivals. Actress Whoopi GOLDBERG's 1992 film *Sister Act* highlighted "My Guy."

Welsing, Frances Cress (b. Mar. 18, 1935, Chicago, Ill.): Psychiatrist. Welsing, whose father and grandfather were doctors, received her training at Antioch College (B.S., 1957) and the HOWARD UNIVERSITY School of Medicine (M.D., 1962). She is the author of *The Cress Theory of Color-Confrontation and Racism* (1970) and *The Isis Papers* (1991). She has taught pediatrics at Howard University.

Psychiatrist Frances Cress Welsing also taught pediatrics. (Roy Lewis Photography)

Wesley, Charles Harris (Dec. 2, 1895, Louisville, Ky.—Aug. 16, 1987, Washington, D.C.): Historian. Wesley studied at several prestigious universities, including Howard, Harvard, Yale, and Fisk. He won a Guggenheim Fellowship in 1930 and was president of Central State University in Arkansas from 1942 until the mid-1960's. He was also a professor and dean at HOWARD UNIVERSITY and published numerous books. He directed the Association for the Study of Afro-American Life and History for several years.

West, Cornel (b. June 2, 1953, Tulsa, Okla.): Educator and philosopher. West's parents met at FISK UNIVERSITY and reared their family on the various Air Force bases where West's father was employed as a civilian administrator. The family eventually settled in a black neighborhood in Sacramento, Calif.

West was a bright child who excelled in school despite bouts with asthma. At the age of eight, he became determined to enroll at Harvard University after reading a juvenile biography of Teddy Roosevelt. His family attended a Baptist church in Sacramento that was next door to the local office of the BLACK PANTHER PARTY. West's contact with the Black Panthers shaped his political views about the second-class status of African Americans, and he refused to participate in the flag salute at school in protest. After striking a teacher who forced him to salute the flag, West was suspended from elementary school for six months and eventually was transferred to an accelerated school across town.

He was accepted at Harvard when he was seventeen years old, and he took odd jobs as a dishwasher and janitor to earn money to pay his tuition. West took eight courses per semester during his junior year in order to graduate early. He was graduated magna cum laude with a bachelor's degree in Near Eastern languages and was accepted into a doctoral program in philosophy at Princeton University. After receiving his Ph.D. from Princeton, West returned to Harvard as a W. E. B. Du Bois Fellow. West next took an academic post at Union Theological Seminary, teaching there until 1984.

In 1984, he was appointed to teach at Yale Divinity School. The Yale appointment eventually became a joint professorship with the American Studies department. While at Yale, West was active in the campus movement to force the university to divest itself of its South African investments, and he was arrested during a protest. The university administration expressed its disapproval of West's actions by canceling his scheduled leave to teach at the University of Paris and requiring him to teach a full course load at Yale. Although West managed to meet both teaching commitments by commuting between Paris and New Haven, Conn., he left Yale at the end of the academic year to resume teaching at Union Theological Seminary. Princeton hired West to revive its struggling program in Afro-American studies. Joined by novelist Toni MORRISON, historian Nell PAINTER, and biographer Arthur Rampersad, West began to serve as director of Afro-American studies at Princeton in 1986.

In 1982, West published the book *Prophesy Deliverance!: An Afro-American Revolutionary Christianity*, which was based on a series of lectures he gave at a black church in Brooklyn, N.Y. *Prophetic Fragments* (1988) and *The American Evasion of Philosophy: A Genealogy of Pragmatism* (1989) followed. In 1991, he returned to his interests in political philosophy and published *The Ethical Dimensions of Marxist Thought*. In 1992, West published *Breaking Bread: Insurgent Black Intellectual Life* a series of conversations he had with black feminist and social critic Bell HOOKS.

West Indian Heritage: West Indian immigration to the United States began in the early nineteenth century and accelerated after the Civil War. Caribbean natives sought to leave the West Indies to escape overcrowding, an unequal distribution of wealth and land, limited educational opportunities, and poor economic conditions. The Caribbean is often spoken of as having a "culture of migration" because of the continued flight of its residents from economic and political problems, and the United States (along with Canada and Great Britain) has been one of the key destinations of West Indian immigrants during the twentieth century.

Waves of Immigration. Between 1911 and 1920, the United States experienced the first wave of immigration by West Indians, most of whom settled in New York City. During the HARLEM RENAISSANCE of the 1920's, 25 percent of the population of Harlem consisted of foreign-born blacks, the majority of whom were from the Caribbean islands. In the 1930's, West Indian immigrants encountered resentment and hostility, because their arrival coincided with the northward migration of southern African Americans, and the two groups were frequently in competition for the same jobs. Nevertheless, there was a steady trickle of immigration from the West Indies until the late 1960's, when a large jump in the number of immigrants occurred once more. This increase resulted partly because of the 1965 amendments to the Immigration Act of 1921 and a similar act in 1924 that had set ethnic quotas on immigration, and partly because of Great Britain's concurrent ban on West Indian immigration.

The primary areas of settlement by West Indian immigrants in the United States are New York and New Jersey, particularly New York City. In 1977, West Indians made up about twenty percent of New York City's black population. Smaller numbers of West Indian immigrants, but larger numbers of part-time migrant laborers, also reside in Florida. The loss of skilled professional and technical workers from the West Indies to the United States has been termed a "brain drain" by West Indian governments, but many unskilled workers have also immigrated to the United States to work as domestic workers or farm laborers.

The Culture of West Indian African Americans. The slave trade linked Africa, the West Indies, and the United States in a triangle of oppression; their peoples thus share a common history, but they do not necessarily share the same culture. African Americans and West Indians have much in common: their African ancestry, their slave pasts, and the racism and segregation that both groups suffered after the emancipation of slaves. Yet the relations between West Indian immigrants and native black Americans have not always been harmonious.

Whether they are skilled or unskilled immigrants, West Indians in the United States tend to place great emphasis on a few key goals: education for themselves and their children, social and economic betterment, family unity, and home ownership. This strong desire for upward mobility, sometimes at the cost of racial solidarity, has tended to alienate the West Indian community from other African Americans. This factor, together with the perception, strongest during the Depression of the 1930's, that West Indians were taking jobs from American-born blacks, has caused some friction between West Indian Americans and other American blacks.

In contrast with African Americans, many British West Indians have tended to identify with England as the

West Indian educated Sidney Poitier won a best actor Oscar for his portrayal of Homer Smith in Lilies of the Field. *(AP/ Wide World Photos)*

"mother" country rather than with Africa, and this British perspective has often alienated these immigrants from other African Americans. Many West Indian immigrants and their descendants celebrate British holidays and ceremonial events, play cricket and soccer, and place British culture and customs above their American counterparts. A large number of West Indian immigrants also speak nostalgically of the islands, intending to return there to retire. This identification with a Caribbean heritage has led to tightly knit (and often closed) community structures evident in the many nationalistic West Indian benevolent societies. These differences have naturally tended to estrange the West Indians from native African Americans and sometimes have led to antagonism and misunderstandings between the groups.

Yet there are also many West Indians who have immersed themselves in African American culture and taken on the causes of their fellows. These immigrants, many of whom have been attracted to the United States by its democratic ideals, have united with other African Americans in the fight for equality and against racism. Brooklyn, which has the largest concentration of Caribbean people outside the Caribbean, has hosted the West Indian-American Day Parade on Labor Day for more than thirty years. This massive carnival celebrates the best aspects of West Indian and African American unity with music, dance, and food of the West Indies drawing everyone into celebration and harmony.

Some Prominent African Americans of West Indian Descent. Many West Indian immigrants and their descendants have played important roles in the development and diversity of African American culture. African Americans of West Indian descent have been leaders in a variety of spheres, including politics, education, art, and literature. John Brown RUSSWURM, a former slave from Jamaica, was one of the first African Americans to graduate from college and went on to coedit the first African American newspaper, *Freedom's Journal*. Sidney POITIER, who was educated in the West Indies, in 1963 became the first African American to be awarded an Oscar as best actor. Shirley CHISHOLM, a well-known feminist and political activist, is a second-generation Barbadian who was born in Brooklyn. She was the first African American woman to serve in Congress.

Claude McKAY, a prominent poet and novelist, was born in Jamaica and moved to the United States in 1912 to further his studies. After a few years, he gave up studying to live in New York City and pursue a writing career. He lived in England and elsewhere from 1922 to 1934, during which time he published three novels, among them HOME TO HARLEM (1928), based on Harlem

life in the 1920's. McKay returned to live and write in the United States until he died in 1948. His interest in African American culture and Harlem in particular is clear in some of his later writings: articles on the Harlem labor movement and a journalistic work entitled *Harlem: Negro Metropolis* (1940). McKay is perhaps best remembered for his poetry; his ironic protest poems are characteristic of much of the writing of the Harlem Renaissance. He believed that black folk culture could become a central, energizing factor in the revitalization of a degenerate Western civilization.

Marcus GARVEY, a powerful political organizer and supporter of BLACK NATIONALISM, was born in Jamaica. In 1912, he studied in England, where he met several African nationalists and read Booker T. WASHINGTON's *Up from Slavery* (1901). These new influences inspired Garvey to return to Jamaica and form a self-help organization to foster racial pride, education, and AFROCENTRISM as a philosophy. In 1916, Garvey went to the United States to gain support for his organization, the UNIVERSAL NEGRO IMPROVEMENT ASSOCIATION (UNIA), and he founded many branches of the group in New York City and elsewhere. Initially, support for Garvey came from the West Indian immigrant community, but gradually Garvey won African Americans over to his black nationalist ideals. In 1918, he founded a newspaper, *The Negro World*, which helped to spread his message worldwide. By 1919, Garvey had formed two African American companies, the Black Star Line, which operated a steamship line to Africa, and the Negro Factories Corporation, which provided loans and advice to African Americans starting small businesses. Garvey also negotiated with the government of LIBERIA to start a UNIA-led back-to-Africa project. Unfortunately, the financial collapse of the Black Star Line brought Garvey into legal trouble, and he was imprisoned for mail fraud. In 1927, he was deported to Jamaica, where his political career was short-lived. He died in 1940 in England. Despite his personal failings, Marcus Garvey was one of the forefathers of the black pride and black nationalist movements, and he demonstrated that African Americans of all backgrounds could be united in a mass movement built on worldwide black solidarity.

Paule MARSHALL, a novelist originally from Barbados, has written many powerful novels about the West Indian experience and particularly about the acculturation experiences of African Americans of West Indian descent. Her most celebrated novel, *Brown Girl, Brownstones* (1959), is set in Brooklyn and tells the story of Selina Boyce, a second-generation Barbadian growing up in Brooklyn. Selina's struggle to live between two cultures and two lands is powerfully portrayed by Marshall, and the novel stresses the value of community, but it offers no easy answers to the issues it raises about assimilation and biculturalism.—*Fiona R. Barnes*

SUGGESTED READINGS: • Diaz-Briquets, Sergio, and Sidney Weintraub, eds. *Determinants of Emigration from Mexico, Central America, and the Caribbean.* Boulder, Colo.: Westview Press, 1991. • Marr, Warren, II, and Maybelle Ward, eds. *Minorities and the American Dream: A Bicentennial Perspective.* New York: Arno Press, 1976. • Parrillo, Vincent N. *Strangers to These Shores: Race and Ethnic Relations in the U.S.* Boston: Houghton-Mifflin, 1980. • Raphael, Lennox. "West Indians and Afro-Americans." *Freedomways* 4, no. 3 (Summer, 1964): 438-445. • Samuels, Wilfred David. *Five Afro-Caribbean Voices in American Culture: 1917-1929.* Ann Arbor, Mich.: University Microfilm International, 1977. • Stengel, Richard. "Resentment Tinged with Envy." *Time* 126 (July 8, 1985): 56-57. • Traub, James, "You Can Get It if You Really Want." *Harper's* 264 (June, 1982): 27-31.

West, Lightfoot Allen (?-1942): Physician. West was president of the NATIONAL MEDICAL ASSOCIATION from 1929 to 1930 and was one of the founders of the National Hospital Association. He also founded Mercy Hospital in Memphis, Tenn., in 1917.

Lightfoot Allen West founded Mercy Hospital. (Schomburg Center, NY Public Library)

West, Roy A.: Mayor of Richmond, Va. West was elected to serve as a member of the city council from Richmond's Third District. He was elected by his fellow councilmembers as the city's mayor and concurrently served from 1985 through June of 1986. He was reelected to an additional term on the council through June of 1990 but was not chosen to serve as mayor.

Westerfield, Samuel Z. (b. 1919, Chicago, Ill.): Political appointee and economist. Westerfield was graduated from HOWARD UNIVERSITY in 1939 with his A.B. in economics and political science. He later earned his M.A. and Ph.D. degrees from Harvard University in economics. Westerfield continued in academia as a professor and research associate from 1940 to 1961 and served as a faculty member at Howard University, West Virginia State University, LINCOLN UNIVERSITY, and Atlanta University. In 1961, he was appointed to serve in the Department of the Treasury as associate director of the debt analysis staff. His expertise in the areas of African and Latin American economics led him to serve as senior adviser to the Treasury Department's Office of International Affairs. In 1964, President Lyndon Johnson appointed Westerfield to serve on the staff of the Bureau of African Affairs of the U.S. Department of State as deputy assistant secretary for economic affairs. Westerfield was appointed to serve as U.S. ambassador to LIBERIA in 1969.

We've Come a Long, Long Way (Negro Marches On, 1945): Film directed by Jack Goldberg. Piecing together newsreel footage and photographs, the film traces the achievements of African Americans in a variety of fields, illustrating their contributions to American life. A lively score helps offset mediocre production values.

Wharton, Clifton Reginald, Jr. (b. Sept. 13, 1926, Boston, Mass.): Educator. Wharton worked as an economic researcher, beginning in 1948, for various university and private groups. He was elected as the president of Michigan State University in 1969, the first African American to lead a major, predominantly white university. He was appointed chancellor of the State University of New York in Albany in 1978 and was appointed to the President's Commission on World Hunger by Jimmy Carter in 1975. In 1992, President-elect Bill Clinton chose Wharton to serve in his cabinet as deputy secretary of state.

Wharton, Clifton Reginald, Sr. (May 11, 1899, Baltimore, Md.—Apr. 23, 1990, Phoenix, Ariz.): Diplomat. Wharton entered the foreign service of the U.S. government in 1925. He served in several countries and was the first black diplomat to head a U.S. delegation to a European country (Romania), in 1958. He was named as ambassador to Norway in 1961 and resigned from that post in 1964.

What's Happening!! (ABC, 1976-1979): Television sitcom. Raj (Ernest Thomas), Rerun (Freddie Berry), and Dwayne (Haywood Nelson) were friends and schoolmates who hung out at the local diner where another friend, Shirley (Shirley Hemphill), worked as waitress. Raj's mother (Mabel King) was a loving but strict woman who worked hard to hold her family together, which often meant stopping fights between Raj and his little sister, Dee (Danielle Spencer). Six years after leaving ABC, the series appeared in syndication as *What's Happening Now!!* (1985-1988). By this time, Dee was in college, Dwayne and Rerun shared an apartment and struggled with careers, and Raj had become a writer and married Nadine (Anne-Marie Johnson), with whom he cared for a foster child named Carolyn (Reina King).

Wheat, Alan Dupree (b. Oct. 16, 1951, San Antonio, Tex): U.S. representative from Missouri. Wheat received his bachelor's degree in economics from Grinnell College in 1972. Upon graduation, Wheat took a position as an economist with the DEPARTMENT OF HOUSING AND URBAN DEVELOPMENT. He was hired in 1973 as an economist for the Mid-America Regional Council in Kansas City and worked in that capacity until 1975. Between 1975 and 1976, Wheat worked as an aide to Missouri legislator Mike White and was later elected to the Missouri general assembly, serving from 1977 to 1982. Wheat was chairman of the urban affairs committee during his time in the Missouri assembly.

Wheat declared his candidacy in the race to succeed retiring U.S. congressman Richard W. Bolling and was elected on Nov. 2, 1982; he took his seat as U.S. representative from Missouri's Fifth District. Wheat was selected as a member of the House Committee on Rules during his freshman term, one of only three congressmen to achieve this distinction. He has also been a member of

What's Happening!! stars *(from left)* Fred Berry, Ernest Thomas, Haywood Nelson, and Shirley Hemphill. (Capital Cities/ABC, Inc.)

the House Select Committee on Children, Youth, and Families; the House Committee on the District of Columbia; the House Select Committee on Hunger; and the Martin Luther KING, JR., Federal Holiday Commission. He was appointed chairman of the House Subcommittee on Judiciary and Education and vice chairman of the CONGRESSIONAL BLACK CAUCUS, serving in Congress into the 1990's.

Wheatley, Phillis (1753?, Gambia, Africa—Dec. 5, 1784, Boston, Mass.): Poet. Frederick DOUGLASS, the famed runaway slave, writer, and abolitionist leader of the antebellum United States, angrily recalls in the opening of his *Narrative of the Life of Frederick Douglass: An American Slave* (1845) that nobody bothered to record the exact date of his birth. Yet at least Douglass, like most American-born slaves, knew he was born on a plantation in Talbot County, Md. Phillis Wheatley, an African-born slave who became famous as an eighteenth century child-prodigy poet and as a model of early African American achievement, knew neither when nor where she was born.

Early Life. In 1761, an African girl who was estimated to be about seven years old (because she was then just losing her baby teeth) was kidnapped, probably from somewhere in the area of West Africa that in the twentieth century became the independent African states of Gambia and Senegal. The little girl was transported to Boston, where she was bought by a rich tailor, John Wheatley, probably with the intention of providing some company for his wife, Susanna. The girl's owners renamed her Phillis Wheatley.

Phillis Wheatley was comparatively lucky in that, unlike most slaves, she was bought for relatively light housework, rather than for grueling fieldwork; she was even more unusual in that, unlike virtually all house slaves, she was taught to read and to write. She was not educated primarily to raise her social, political, economic, or gender status, however, or to cultivate her personal gifts—which were evidently extraordinary, and which were quickly appreciated by her owners—but rather to help save her soul. Literacy and Christianity were closely connected in eighteenth century New England, and the single text that was most widely used to teach reading and writing was the Bible.

Thus, a primary way in which Phillis Wheatley's precocity was measured during her childhood was the rapidity with which she managed to learn to parse complicated verses from the Bible. Many of her most popular published poems, which began appearing in New England newspapers when she was only about thirteen years old (her earliest known published poem appeared in the *Rhode Island Mercury* on Dec. 21, 1767), were conventional eighteenth century Christian elegies.

Literary Fame. The publication that made her famous was her elegy "On the Death of the Rev. Mr. George Whitefield, 1770," a broadside commemorating a famous itinerant Christian preacher who had helped to inspire the mass Christian revivals of the eighteenth century that came to be known as The Great Awakening. After having been celebrated in the Colonies as America's "sooty prodigy," Phillis Wheatley was taken to England to meet many dignitaries, including the Countess of Huntington, the Lord Mayor of London, and America's colonial agent in Britain, Benjamin Franklin. A major condition of her fame under the new, English, and somewhat less demeaning sobriquet of "the Sable Muse" was her Christian piety; among the sponsors of Phillis' visit to England was a Christian missionary group, and the title of the volume of her poetry that was published in London during the year of her visit was *Poems on Various Subjects, Religious and Moral* (1773).

Later Years. News of the illness of her mistress called Phillis Wheatley back early from London—to which she had gone in part because of her own ill health. Susanna Wheatley died, John Wheatley died, the Wheatley family circle broke up, and the slave Phillis Wheatley, at around the same time that the British colonies of North America were beginning to rebel against the colonial power of Great Britain, was granted her freedom. In 1778, Phillis Wheatley married John Peters, an African American freedman about whom little is known other than that Phillis' owners had disapproved of him, that he had to change jobs often and was once imprisoned for debt, and that he might have been an early proponent of African American rights. With him, Phillis bore three children. The first two died in infancy; the third shared a deathbed with its mother, whose life ended when she was about thirty, alone—her husband may have been in prison for debt at the time—poor, and in a cheap boardinghouse where she had been forced to work during the final months of her life. Phillis Wheatley, the first African American known to have published a volume of poetry, was buried together with her dead baby in an unmarked grave someplace in Boston in 1784.

Literary Reputation. That Phillis Wheatley was largely forgotten soon after she died in obscurity suggests that she functioned in eighteenth century literary and religious culture largely as a curiosity, and that interest in her then was condescending at best. When interest in her was revived by abolitionist culture in the 1830's, she was cited primarily as evidence of the humanity of African American slaves, in particular to help prove that eloquence and righteousness could survive even the brutal inhumanities of slavery.

Wheatley's poetry did not begin to be read for its strictly literary merits, as well as for its peculiarly African American characteristics, until interest in the African American cultural heritage became widespread in the twentieth century. Such aesthetic and ethnic appreciations of Wheatley's verse have little use for its Christian religiosity, which had been deemed the prime condition "America," "On the Arrival of the Ships of War, and Landing of the Troops," and "On the Affray in King-Street"—an early name for what would later be known as the Boston Massacre. It has been noted, moreover, that in several of her letters, Wheatley emphatically and explicitly states her opposition to the institution of slavery.

Criticism of Her Work. Unfortunately, demands that Wheatley's poetry reflect modern aesthetic standards and modern ethnic and feminist pride seem to have yielded

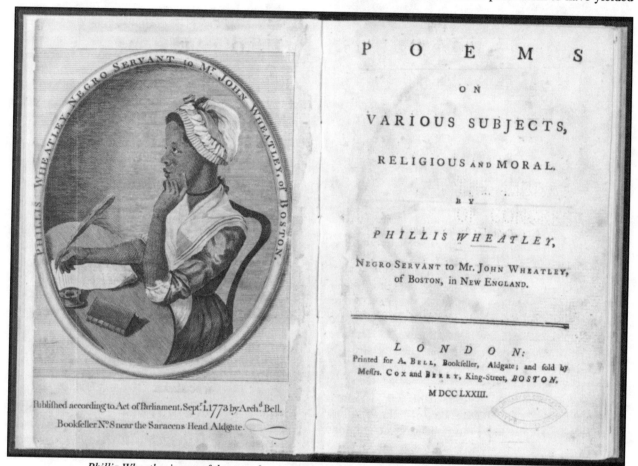

Phillis Wheatley is one of the most famous early African American poets. (Library of Congress)

of its excellence while it was being written. Twentieth century readers have accordingly searched Wheatley's life and work for secular and humanist elements. It has been noted that the prodigiousness of her literary gifts included knowledge not only of English and the Bible, but also of Latin and the pagan lyric poets of Roman antiquity; such knowledge suggests the possibility that Wheatley was influenced also by pre- and non-Christian traditions. It has been noted also that she was called upon, both before and during the revolution, to write poems on American patriotic subjects and occasions: on the repeal of the Stamp Act, on the pardoning of a deserter, on to more widespread, and more forceful, criticism. Scholars continue to try to find evidence of abolitionist sentiment in her poetry, and to find in it also some subtle indications of AFROCENTRISM, feminism, and resentment over her forced conversion to dominant European cultural norms, but these efforts still seem weak. In contrast, critics have noted how often in her poems Wheatley passes over opportunities to champion herself, her race, or her gender, and how often she expressly substitutes transcendent, theist values for immediate, humanist ones. Wheatley's work is often included in modern anthologies of American literature, but always with the same kinds

Richard Pryor starred in Which Way Is Up? *(Museum of Modern Art/Film Stills Archive, NY)*

of reservations: "Phillis Wheatley was the first important Afro-American poet, but only rarely does her poetry reveal an awareness of the problems of blackness"; "The only hint of injustice found in her poetry is in the line 'Some view our sable race with scornful eye'"; "Hers was a thoroughly conventional poetic talent, tied too strongly to Miltonic cadences and the balanced couplets of Alexander Pope."

Modern aesthetic and ethnic standards would seem in their own ways to have condescended to Phillis Wheatley as much as did eighteenth century literary and religious ones. Perhaps a better way to kindle continuing interest in her writing would be to encourage wonder at its incredible lack of emphasis on the personal, especially given the painful facts of Wheatley's life. How astonishing that Phillis Wheatley could have foregone making personal witness the dominant mode of her poetry, and how astonishing that she could have taken comfort in the preservation of a soul that somehow remained separate from, and superior to, her individuality, ethnicity, and gender.—*R. C. De Prospo*

SUGGESTED READINGS: • Fuller, Miriam M. *Phillis Wheatley: America's First Black Poetess*. Champaign, Ill.: Garrard Publishing Company, 1971. • Richmond, Merle A. *Bid the Vassal Soar: Interpretive Essays on the Life and Poetry of Phillis Wheatley and George Moses Horton*. Washington, D.C.: Howard University Press, 1974. • Richmond, Merle A. *Phillis Wheatley*. New York: Chelsea House, 1988. • Robinson, William H. *Phillis Wheatley: A Bio-Bibliography*. Boston: G. K. Hall, 1981. • Robinson, William H. *Phillis Wheatley and Her Writings*. New York: Garland, 1984. • Robinson, William H. *Phillis Wheatley in the Black American Beginnings*. Detroit: Broadside Press, 1975.

Which Way Is Up? (Universal, 1977): Film directed by Michael Schultz. Based on the Italian film *The Seduction of Mimi* (1974), this comedy follows the fortunes of a farm worker (played by Richard PRYOR) who becomes a labor leader and is then co-opted by management as part of a quota hiring program. Lonette McKEE and Margaret AVERY are the women in his life, and Pryor himself plays three roles: the farm worker, his father, and a corrupt minister.

Whipple, Prince: Revolutionary War soldier. Whipple's original name and date of birth are unknown. He is believed to have been born in Amabou, Africa. Legend says that his parents sent him to America to obtain an education. Like most Africans in the Colonies, Whipple became a slave. He was enlisted into the Continental Army either by Maryland or by his owner, to fill Maryland's quota for soldiers. Whipple served as an aid to a General Whipple from New Hampshire, and from him obtained his American name. He was with George Washington at the general's famous crossing of the Delaware River, and he is depicted in Emanuel Leutze's painting of this event. Whipple died at the age of thirty-two in Portsmouth, N.H.

Whispers, The: Singing group. Although this highly polished group began performing in the 1960's, it was not until the late 1970's and 1980's that it found much popularity. The group formed in Los Angeles under the leadership of twin brothers Wallace ("Scotty") and Walter Scott. They had dreamed of careers in music since they were children and had some experience under the name of the Scott Brothers before forming the Whispers.

The first incarnation of the group formed while the boys were still in high school. The Scotts joined Nicholas Caldwell, Gordy Harmon, and Marcus Hutson, patterning their group after jazz vocal stylists of the 1950's such as the Hi-Los and Four Freshmen. By the late 1960's, the Whispers had begun to build a following, and Wallace Scott had made a name for himself as a songwriter. Ray CHARLES, Isaac HAYES, and Aretha FRANKLIN recorded songs penned by Scott.

The group's only personnel change came in 1973, when Gordy Harmon left the group. The group recorded albums for the small record companies Soul Clock and Chess/Janus up until the mid-1970's, with only marginal success. The best of these efforts was its Janus album *The Whispers' Greatest Hits*. The group signed to Soul Train Records (which soon became Solar records) in 1976, and its career picked up speed. The album *One for the Money* came out in 1976 and was followed by *Open Up Your Love* in 1977. It was the 1978 release *Headlights*, however, that was the turning point. One single, "Olivia," nearly went gold. The group's next album, *Whisper in Your Ear* (1979), went platinum and featured several gold singles. Another 1979 release, *Happy Holidays to You*, was followed by *Imagination* in 1980, *This Kind of Lovin'* in 1981, and *Best of the Whispers* in 1982. All produced hit singles and were heavy sellers. The group became a member of Solar's elite and began to travel around the world, including appearances in Africa. *Love Is Where You Find It* came out in late 1981 and turned gold, producing two 1982 hit singles, "In the Raw" and "Emergency." *Love for Love* (1983) and *So Good* (1985) added to the group's list of hit albums. *Just Gets Better with Time* (1987) seems to sum up the career of this amazing vocal group. Its mixture of up-tempo soul songs and low-key romantic ballads kept listeners coming back.

Whitaker, Forest (b. July 15, 1961, Longview, Tex.): Actor. Whitaker's father, an insurance man, and his mother, a special education teacher for the Los Angeles school system, raised him and his three siblings in Carson and South Central Los Angeles, Calif. While in high school, Whitaker sang with the choir and was named All League defensive back for his football talents. He attended California State University at Pomona before transferring to the University of Southern California for classical voice training and drama studies.

Although featured in a small role in *Fast Times at Ridgemont High* (1982), Whitaker did not catch the attention of critics until four years later. In supporting roles, he played Amos, the pool hustler in *The Color of Money* (1986); Big Harold, a Vietnam soldier in *Platoon* (1986); and Private Edward Garlick, Robin Williams' companion in *Good Morning, Vietnam* (1987). His most acclaimed role came when Clint Eastwood cast him as legendary jazz saxophonist Charlie PARKER in *Bird* (1988). For his performance, Whitaker won the Best Actor Award at the Cannes Film Festival.

After *Bird*, Whitaker appeared as Dr. Resher in *Johnny Handsome* (1990), police officer Dennis Curren in *Downtown*, (1990), and as an ex-convict in the Home Box

Forest Whitaker won the Best Actor Award at the Cannes Film Festival for his portrayal of Charlie Parker in the biographical film Bird. *(AP/Wide World Photos)*

Office movie *Criminal Justice* (1990). In 1991, the large-framed actor starred as Jackson, a mortician's accountant and love interest to Robin Givens, in the film *A Rage in Harlem*. Whitaker also served as coproducer of this film, which drew mixed reviews from critics. In 1992, he was featured in the critically acclaimed *The Crying Game*.

Whitaker, Louis Rodman (b. May 12, 1957, Brooklyn, N.Y.): BASEBALL player. Whitaker began as second baseman for the Detroit Tigers in 1977. A solid hitter and reliable fielder, Whitaker enjoyed his best season in 1983, when he batted .320 and garnered 206 hits. He helped the Tigers win the World Series in 1984.

white backlash: Negative response of some white people to gains made by African Americans. These opponents of equality or of what they perceived as unfair special dispensations for African Americans acted out their hostilities in a variety of ways, from direct violence to voting for politicians who shared their views. An example of white backlash occurred in 1964, when Senator Barry Goldwater's campaign for the presidency attracted many white people opposed to the CIVIL RIGHTS movement.

White, Barry (b. Sept. 12, 1944, Galveston, Tex.): Singer, songwriter, and record producer. In 1963, White wrote "The Harlem Shuffle," a rhythm-and-blues hit recorded by Bob and Earl the same year. White began a solo recording career in 1973, becoming known for his deep, husky voice and lush orchestral arrangements, reminiscent of the recordings of Isaac HAYES. White was also a pioneering disco record producer and songwriter. "Love's Theme" (1973), written for the Love Unlimited Orchestra, reached the top position on the pop music charts. White had several more hits, alone and with that group, in the mid-1970's.

White, Charles (b. 1918, Chicago, Ill.): Painter. White attended the Art Institute of Chicago and the Art Students League in New York City. A Rosenwald Fellowship awarded to him at the age of twenty-three enabled him to work in the South for two years. That work resulted in his renowned mural *The Contribution of the Negro to American Democracy*. He is considered to be an eminent leader in social art, and his paintings often depict achievements of famous African Americans.

White, Cheryl (b. 1954, Rome, Ohio): Jockey. On June 15, 1971, White rode her first mount in an organized race and became the first recognized female JOCKEY.

White Citizens Council: White segregationist group centered in MONTGOMERY, ALA. The council became very active in attempts to weaken the MONTGOMERY BUS BOYCOTT of 1955. As African American resistance to segregation on buses grew, the council increased its membership to counter that resistance. It became the largest organized white group in Montgomery.

The council held large rallies to express racist propaganda. The council often held meetings in union halls and became allied with the labor movement in the South. The group vowed to fight desegregation efforts at all costs. It went after anybody or any group, black or white, that supported the bus boycott or desegregation. The members' tactics included violence. Several bombings and bomb threats were made against the organizers of the bus boycott, including Martin Luther KING, JR.

white flight: As most commonly used, migration of white people from an area into which African Americans

are moving. White flight occurs as a result of direct or indirect prejudice. White people themselves may be unwilling to have African American neighbors. Others believe that migration of African Americans into an area will reduce property values, so move out as a precaution.

This type of behavior is not confined to whites. The same scenario can occur when a group that is perceived to be from a lower social or economic level tries to move into a new area. The term "white flight" therefore can be misleading. African Americans also have been known to leave a neighborhood when other ethnic groups move in. During the nineteenth century, African Americans fled from a number of New York City neighborhoods when Italian immigrants moved in. They also left Detroit neighborhoods when Polish immigrants moved in. In recent years, African Americans have left some Southern California neighborhoods in response to an increasing presence of Central American and Asian immigrants.

White, George Henry (Dec. 18, 1852, Rosindale, N.C.—Dec. 28, 1918, Philadelphia, Pa.): U.S. representative from North Carolina. White was born into slavery, but after emancipation he attended public schools in North Carolina. He entered HOWARD UNIVERSITY in 1873 to pursue the study of medicine but soon switched to the

As a representative from North Carolina, George Henry White was the only African American member of the Fifty-fifth Congress. (The Associated Publisher, Inc.)

study of law and returned to North Carolina. After his graduation in 1877, White began to teach and, in 1879, he was admitted to the North Carolina bar.

White was elected as a state representative in 1880 and lobbied for legislation to establish normal schools to train black teachers. He became the principal of the normal school that was established in New Bern, N.C. White was elected to the state senate in 1884 and then became prosecuting attorney and solicitor for North Carolina's second judicial district in 1886. His first venture into congressional politics occurred in 1894, when he ran for the Republican nomination for North Carolina's Second Congressional District. He lost the nomination to Henry P. Cheatham, his brother-in-law and a former congressman. White defeated Cheatham for the nomination in 1896 and won the election against a Democrat and a Populist candidate.

White took office on Mar. 15, 1897, and was the only black representative to serve during the Fifty-fifth Congress. He was a member of the House Committee on Agriculture and introduced legislation to make LYNCHING a federal crime. Although the bill did not succeed, it was the first such legislation to be brought before Congress. White was reelected in 1898, but editorial attacks in North Carolina papers and the intimidation tactics of white supremacy groups convinced him that running for a third term would be grueling and dangerous. In his final speech before Congress, White noted that his departure would leave no black representatives in the House or the Senate. He predicted that black exclusion from Congress would not continue indefinitely. After his term ended, White opened a law office in Washington, D.C., and began development of a black township on land that he and five partners had acquired in New Jersey. The town, named Whitesboro in honor of its organizer, had a population of more than eight hundred black residents by 1906. White moved from Washington to Philadelphia in 1905 and began a new legal practice. In addition, he founded People's Savings Bank, a financial institution dedicated to assisting black home buyers and business entrepreneurs. White also worked with numerous black organizations, including the Frederick Douglass Hospital and the NATIONAL ASSOCIATION FOR THE ADVANCEMENT OF COLORED PEOPLE. White's ill health forced him to close the People's Savings Bank shortly before his death.

White, Maurice (b. Dec. 19, 1941, Memphis, Tenn.): Singer, percussionist, songwriter, and leader of EARTH, WIND, AND FIRE. White's first exposure to music was singing in the church. He began playing the drums as a teenager through the influence of his father, a physician

who had played saxophone alongside jazz saxophonist Illinois Jacquet in the 1940's.

After moving with his family to Chicago, Ill., in the mid-1950's, White attended the Chicago Conservatory of Music. He gained valuable experience working as a sideman. In addition to being a session drummer for Chess Records in Chicago, White worked with musicians such as saxophonist John COLTRANE, singer Jackie WILSON, and pianist Ramsey LEWIS, who tabbed White as the successor to drummer Red Holt after Holt left the Ramsey Lewis Trio.

Maurice White led the band Earth, Wind, and Fire. (AP/ Wide World Photos)

Before the end of 1969, White left Lewis' trio and formed the first edition of Earth, Wind, and Fire with the aid of his brother Verdine on bass, vocals, and percussion. This incarnation of the group, featuring Don Myrick on tenor sax and Louis Satterfield on trombone, released a single on Capitol Records and two albums for Warner Bros. in the early 1970's that had moderate success. While touring the United States with another outfit, Friends and Love, White struck up a friendship with that band's vocalist, Philip Baily, pianist Larry Dunn, and saxophonist Andrew Woolfolk. White persuaded them to join his band. With an expanded roster that also included saxophonist Ronnie Laws, and a new deal with CBS Records, the group released *Last Days and Time* in 1972. It was the band's first charted effort and the beginning of a string of successful releases.

Through White's leadership, the band managed to remain among the elite of the period, although it experienced a significant number of lineup changes. Its first certified gold record, 1973's *Head to the Sky*, was followed by another gold in 1974, *Open Our Eyes*. In 1975, the group released the sound track to *That's the Way of the World*, an album that featured White's compositions. The film itself featured the group as a rock and soul band. In the remainder of the 1970's and into the early 1980's, the band would accumulate sixteen Grammy nominations, six Grammy Awards, and a number of certified gold and platinum releases. The group appeared in the 1978 film *Sgt. Pepper's Lonely Hearts Club Band*. It also became a unique and memorable live act with a flair for space-age lighting and effects.

The middle and late 1980's brought stylistic changes in the band's sound, changes for which White, as the group's spokesperson, has been criticized. Although the band continued to record into the 1990's—*Heritage* was released in February of 1990—its appeal lay less within popular circles and increasingly with music critics.

White, Melvin "Slappy" (b. 1921): Comedian. White, a comedy partner of Redd Foxx in the 1950's, is a popular performer both live and on the big and small screens. He has appeared in the film *Amazing Grace* (1974) and on television shows such as SANFORD AND SON, THE FLIP WILSON SHOW, and *Double Trouble*. He also has recorded comedy albums.

White, Ruth (b. 1951 or 1952): Fencer. In 1969, at seventeen years of age, White became the youngest national fencing champion and the first African American to win a major American fencing title. She also was one of the first black Americans to compete on an Olympic fencing team, taking part in the 1972 Olympics.

White Shadow, The (CBS, 1978-1981): Television school drama. Ken Howard played a white retired Chicago Bulls forward who derived professional and personal fulfillment coaching basketball at an inner-city Los Angeles high school. Unafraid to confront difficult issues, such as drugs, gangs, and crime (including the shooting of one of the characters while he witnessed a liquor-store robbery), the series depicted its characters' lives with care and realism.

white supremacy: Attitude, ideology, or policy that claims superiority of Euro-American peoples over "non-white" populations. White supremacy is a conscious effort to make "race" a qualification for membership in civil society. The perceived inferiority of a particular skin pigmentation, ancestry, religion, or physical characteristic can be the foundation of white supremacist views.

White, Walter Francis (July 1, 1893, Atlanta, Ga.— Mar. 21, 1955, New York, N.Y.): Civil rights leader. White was one of the United States' foremost spokespeople for African Americans' rights for almost a quarter of a century, as executive secretary of the NATIONAL ASSOCIATION FOR THE ADVANCEMENT OF COLORED PEOPLE from 1931 to 1955. Although he had blond hair and blue eyes and only partial African ancestry, he chose to be recognized as a black person. He campaigned against LYNCHING and fought unsuccessfully for passage of a federal antilynching law. He wrote two fictional accounts of lynchings as well as an autobiography and a report on African Americans who served in the American armed forces during World War II.

Although of only partial African ancestry, NAACP leader Walter White chose to be recognized as an African American. (Schomburg Center, NY Public Library)

White, William DeKova "Bill" (b. Jan. 28, 1934, Lakewood, Fla.): Baseball player and president of the National League. White became the first African American to serve as president of one of the major leagues, in 1989. He began his BASEBALL career in the New York Giants system in 1953, playing for Danville in the Carolina League.

Bill White became president of the National League in 1989. (National Baseball Library, Cooperstown, NY)

White first reached the majors in 1956, but then lost most of the next two seasons to military service. When he returned late in the 1958 season, the Giants had moved to San Francisco. He did not hit well in his late-season return and was traded to the St. Louis Cardinals in March, 1959. The trade proved a great success for St. Louis, as White established himself as one of baseball's premier first basemen, starring with St. Louis through the 1965 season.

An exceptional defensive player, White also hit consistently and for power. He four times batted above .300 for the Cardinals, five times hit twenty or more home runs, and for three straight years batted in more than one hundred runners. He also helped St. Louis win the World Series in 1964. A quietly consistent player, White was somewhat overshadowed by more famous teammates such as the aging Stan Musial, third baseman Ken Boyer, center fielder Curt FLOOD, and pitcher Bob GIBSON.

White, Willye B. (b. Jan. 1, 1939, Money, Mich.): Long jumper and runner. White won a silver medal in the 1956 Olympics in the long jump, with a jump of nineteen feet, eleven and three-quarters inches. She went on to become the first female TRACK AND FIELD athlete to represent the United States in five Olympics, from 1956 to 1972. A member of the Black Sports Hall of Fame and of the President's Commission on Olympic Sports, White was awarded the Pierre de Coubertin International Fair Play Trophy in 1965, the first individual to receive the award.

Whitfield, Lynn (b. Baton Rouge, La.): Film and television actress. Best known for her work in television, she won an Emmy Award for her portrayal of the title character in the Home Box Office film *The Josephine BAKER Story* (1991). She was also featured in such television films as *Johnnie Mae Gibson: FBI* (1986) and *THE WOMEN OF BREWSTER PLACE* (1989), and in the series *Heartbeat*, in 1989, and *Equal Justice*, beginning in 1990.

Whitfield, Norman (b. 1943, New York, N.Y.): Songwriter and producer. In addition to being the coauthor of one of Motown Records' most successful tracks, "I Heard it Through the Grapevine" (1968), a top-ten single for Marvin GAYE, Whitfield, along with his collaborator Barrett Strong, pioneered Motown's shift from the lyrical purity of Motown's first writing team, HOLLAND-DOZIER-HOLLAND, to the "psychedelic soul" sound. After he left Motown in the mid-1970's, Whitfield involved himself in a number of different endeavors, including writing for and producing acts such as Rose Royce and the Undisputed Truth and completing the sound track for the disco movie *Car Wash* (1976).

Whitman Sisters, The: Dancers. As one of the leading family acts of African American vaudeville, these four sisters ran their own musical revue and maintained a successful touring company for more than forty years. The four Whitman sisters—Mabel, Essie, Alberta ("Bert"), and Alice—were daughters of a southern Methodist minister. Mabel and Essie first performed as harmony singers to raise money for their father's church. In 1904, they teamed with Alberta in New Orleans to become the Whitman Sisters' New Orleans Troubadours, traveling and sharing business responsibilities. Mabel handled bookings, Essie made costumes, and Alberta composed music and served as financial secretary. In 1909, Alice joined the troupe and became a favorite with audiences.

Mabel left the company for a while to tour abroad with her own show. When she returned, the original, four-person act was renamed the Whitman Sisters and subsequently landed top billing with the THEATRE OWNERS BOOKING ASSOCIATION, a black vaudeville circuit stretching from New York to Florida and from Chicago to New Orleans.

Mabel eventually retired from the stage to become the troupe's full-time manager. The remaining Whitman sisters developed special stage talents. Essie was featured as a comedienne with a drunk act, Alberta did a male impersonation, and Alice was billed as "the queen of the taps." With a jazz ensemble and a cast of some thirty singers, dancers, and comedians, the show included novelty acts, production numbers with a chorus line, and a boy-girl song and dance. When silent films became popular, the Whitman Sisters shortened their act to fit between screenings, and business continued to thrive.

Alice's son Albert, who performed at the age of four, was the last family member to join the show. Mabel died in 1942, and the show closed the following year. The Whitman Sisters provided an enduring example of success for other African American performers. They gave hundreds of dancers their first break in show business and launched the careers of many who later became notable entertainers. The Whitman Sisters helped black dancers shed slave dance stereotypes and earn respect for their talents.

Whitten, Jack (b. 1939, Bessemer, Ala.): Painter. Whitten studied at TUSKEGEE INSTITUTE, Southern University in Baton Rouge, La., Cooper Union in New York (where he earned his B.F.A.), the Art Students League, and the Brooklyn Museum School of Art. He exhibited at a one-man show at the Allan Stone Gallery in 1970 and received a John Hay Whitney Fellowship in 1964. He has taught at the Pratt Institute.

Whodini (Jalil Hutchins, Ecstasy, and DJ Grandmaster Dee): RAP trio. Whodini was one of the early rap crews and gained popularity based on its funky, danceable rhythms and spooky, horror-film sound. The group signed a record deal with Jive records, which was distributed by Arista, and worked closely with producer Larry Smith. Its best known hit was the single "The Freaks Come Out at Night," released from its second album, *Escape* (1985), and featured on the sound track of *The Jewel of the Nile* (1985). The group's third album, *Back in Black* (1986), was somewhat less popular but did contain a rock-style guitar solo on the single "Fugitive" that seemed to echo the heavy metal-rap blend being popularized by RUN-D.M.C.

Wideman, John Edgar (b. June 14, 1941, Washington, D.C.): Novelist, short-story writer, and scholar. Wideman spent most of his early childhood and youth in Homewood, Pa., which is a predominantly African American subdivision of Pittsburgh, and in Shadyside, Pa., which

was predominantly white. Wideman was a gifted athlete and secured an athletic grant to attend the University of Pennsylvania as a member of the varsity basketball team. He excelled both on the court and in the classroom. He was graduated Phi Beta Kappa in 1963, with a B.A. in English. He won a prestigious Rhodes Scholarship, the second African American to win that honor. (The first African American recipient of a Rhodes Scholarship was Alain LOCKE, of HARLEM RENAISSANCE fame.) Wideman was awarded a bachelor's degree in philosophy from the University of Oxford in 1966.

Writer John Edgar Wideman is most famous for his Homewood *trilogy.* (Photo by Fred Vuich)

Wideman continued his education by attending the famed Creative Writing Workshop at the University of Iowa during the 1966-1967 academic year. It was there that Wideman began to expand his literary talent. With these solid academic credentials, Wideman returned to the University of Pennsylvania, where he began a distinguished career as an educator, lecturer, and author.

Wideman has extensive publications, including *A Glance Away* (1967), written when he was twenty-six years old, and *Philadelphia Fire* (1990). In between these novels, Wideman's most acclaimed works are *Sent for You Yesterday* (1983), which won the 1984 Faulkner Award for Fiction, and *Fever* (1989), a collection of twelve loosely related short stories.

Hiding Place (1981) is the first novel of the *Homewood* trilogy, followed by *Damballah* (1981), which is a collection, and *Sent for You Yesterday*. *Hiding Place* features the relationship of Sybela Owens and Charles Bell, both early settlers of Homewood. Their lineage proceeds downward to Tommy, a child of the 1940's facing false charges of armed robbery and murder. He hides with Mother Bess Owens, herself a recluse since the death of her husband and son. The bulk of the novel is devoted to the efforts of Bess and Tommy to end their different forms of hiding.

Wideman's acclaimed novel *Philadelphia Fire* is based on the actual 1985 fire bombing of a West Philadelphia row house which purportedly housed the Afrocentric cult called MOVE. Narrated from the point of view of Cudjoe, a gifted but tortured African American writer, the novel explores contemporary race relations and examines the role of authority in contemporary society.

Wilder, L(awrence) Douglas (b. Jan. 17, 1931, Richmond, Va.): Politician. L. Douglas Wilder grew up in an era of widespread segregation and discrimination, yet by the 1990's he attained the status of a major national Democratic Party spokesman. After receiving his early education in the segregated schools in his hometown, he enrolled at Virginia Union University, where he took his bachelor's degree in 1951. After graduation, he served in the Korean War, and became a bona fide hero. He fought in the battle for Pork Chop Hill, an epic struggle that became the topic of a 1950's Hollywood film. In that battle, Wilder won a Bronze Star for carrying injured comrades off the field while enemy fire peppered the entire hill. Once behind the lines, he did not rest; he made return trips until he had carried most of the wounded to safety. By the time he was in Korea, Wilder apparently already had a nose for politics. Using the leverage that a Bronze Star gave him, he complained to his white commanders that many African Americans had been passed over for promotions. The command listened, and blacks began, belatedly, receiving their due.

Early Career. After his return to the United States, Wilder decided to attend Howard Law School in Washington, D.C., and received his J.D. in 1959. Unlike many African Americans who left the South to escape the harsher aspects of segregation and discrimination, Wilder stayed in Richmond and was soon admitted to the Virginia bar. In time, he became one of the best trial lawyers in the South. The son of an insurance agent and a domestic worker, Wilder disappointed his parents with his career choice. They did not believe that he could buck the

Virginia establishment of white judges and white juries; they wanted him in a "safe" occupation in which he could develop an African American clientele within the black community, a trade that would insulate him from the discrimination of the white world. Nevertheless, as Wilder began to achieve career goals, his parents realized that they had a special child, even if he was sometimes seen as too much a fun-loving free spirit.

As a youngster growing up in Richmond's Church Hill neighborhood, Wilder loved to play pranks, one of which ran Arthur Ashe, another neighborhood child, off the tennis courts. Later, in law school, classmates knew that he subordinated good grades to good times. He enjoyed the once-thriving U Street clubs of Washington, D.C., places where he could soak up jazz music along with generous doses of alcohol. At one club, however, he had his comeuppance. One of his professors saw him and gave him a strongly worded lecture that had a decided effect. Wilder settled down, studied hard, and pulled his grades up.

In the 1950's and 1960's, Wilder participated in the Civil Rights movement, always acting as a pacifist and as a believer in nonviolence. He joined the Richmond branch of the National Urban League, eventually becoming a director of the board. A member of the National Association for the Advancement of Colored People (NAACP), he volunteered his time to the association's legal defense fund, handling test cases without demanding a fee. He joined other civic groups, including the Red Shield Boys Club, for which he eventually became chairman of the board, the Masons, and the Shriners.

Entry into Politics. Riding the crest of the Civil Rights movement, Wilder sought political office in 1969. He wanted a seat in the state senate. The thirty-eight-year-old was unorthodox in his first campaign; he thought that he had to be, since whites held the majority in his district. He ran as a healer who could bring the races together. He located his headquarters in the white section of town, but he did not cater to whites on most issues. In one campaign speech, for example, delivered on the steps of the state capitol, he criticized the state song, "Carry Me Back to Old Virginny," because it glorified slave times and the master-slave relationship.

Wilder won his 1969 race and became the first African American elected to the Virginia senate since the Reconstruction era. In the following years, he became a consummate legislative leader as a compromiser and healer. Furthermore, he was a staunch fiscal conservative, and he took other positions that pleased the conservative leaders within the Democratic Party and the conservative voters around the state. Yet Wilder could play hardball with conservatives; he proved that in 1982, when he threatened to run for the U.S. Senate, thus dooming his party's chances for success, unless an archconservative dropped out of the race. The conservative candidate complied with Wilder's demand. Wilder achieved another political first in 1985, when he sought and won the lieutenant governorship. Four years later, he was elected Virginia's governor. As his political star rose, the only apparent blemish on his record was a messy divorce in which his wife had accused him of abuse.

drug scandal at the University of Virginia. Others, too, criticized his management of the state's $2.2 billion shortfall. He closed that gap without increasing taxes, but his methods drew frowns from many people. His methods included applying state lottery money—cash that was once spent on roads—to the shortfalls. Further, with his budget slashing, he doomed some programs while consolidating others. For example, former Governor Gerald Baliles had created a Department of World Trade to spur

Douglas Wilder being sworn in as governor of Virginia in 1990. (AP/Wide World Photos)

Record as Governor. Despite his admirable service to Virginia, Wilder had critics. For example, some leaders labeled him as an opportunist, citing his record on at least two issues. First, critics noted that Wilder had reversed his stand against capital punishment. For years its strongest foe in Virginia, Wilder had embraced it once he had to appeal to the state's entire constituency. Second, although for years he had been a strong believer in privacy rights, in the late 1980's he advocated mandatory drug tests for college students; that reversal came after a major

the state's economic development. As Baliles left office, the Corporation for Enterprise Development, a think tank, ranked Virginia as the eighth state in international marketing; under Wilder, Virginia fell to twenty-second.

Wilder alienated other Virginia leaders in several ways. In 1991, he backed a state senate redistricting plan just because it diluted the power of a region in which many of his in-state conservative critics resided. Yet he also upset some among his African American constituency. For example, he publicly stated that poor, ghetto-dwelling urban African Americans had caused many of their own problems. He argued that many had a great aversion to good, honest, hard work but had no aversion at all to making illegitimate babies. Even as Wilder's thoughts seemed to go in one political direction, however, his next policy statement appeared to swing in another. For example, he suggested that Virginia restrict its college tuition-aid program to those in poverty. He also argued that the affluent in the United States should be excluded from such federal entitlement programs as Medicare and agricultural subsidies. Such money, he argued, should be spent on the truly needy, not on the middle and upper classes.

Presidential Campaign. In 1991, Virginia's governor began a campaign for the presidency. In his strategic planning, Wilder hoped that the electorate would perceive him as a new kind of Democrat. According to Wilder, whereas traditional Democrats believed in taxing and spending, he did not; whereas other Democrats were soft on military spending, he was not; and whereas traditional Democrats were also soft on crime, he was not. Further, he promised to lower the national deficit without raising taxes by pursuing policies similar to the "cures" that he had developed in Virginia. He argued that he could reduce military spending by $10 billion without weakening the American military machine. He said that he could trim $25 billion out of the federal bureaucracy alone. Further, he promised to give more federal money to states and cities for education, for roads, and for a war on crime.

Although Wilder withdrew from the presidential race and therefore failed in his presidential bid, his campaign—indeed, his entire political career—may have benefited the whole country. The white electorate in the 1980's had proven to be afraid of Jesse JACKSON, a national leader of the African American community. Many whites perceived him as too radical, even though he fit the liberal Democratic mold. By contrast, Wilder appeared more moderate than Jackson. Wilder appealed to more white voters than Jackson; Wilder's career in Virginia alone proved that. After the efforts of Jackson and Wilder, it was no longer farfetched to believe that an African American could one day win nomination for the presidency or the vice presidency from one of the major American political parties.—*James Smallwood*

SUGGESTED READINGS: • Barnes, Frank. "The Wilder Side." *The New Republic* 201 (November 13, 1989): 9-10. • Barone, Michael, and Gloria Borger. "The End of the Civil War." *U.S. News & World Report*, November 20, 1989, 45-48. • Bennett, Lerone. "Inaugurating the Future." *Ebony* 45 (April, 1990): 8-12. • Dingle, D. T. "Governor Wilder: Champion of the 'New Mainstream.'"

Black Enterprise 20 (March, 1990): 17. • Haywood, R. L. "Inside Look as First Black Governor of Virginia Takes Charge." *Jet* 77 (February 5, 1990): 8-11. • Williams, Michael. "Putting a New Face on Virginia's Future." *Black Enterprise* 21 (June, 1991): 284-294.

Wiley, George (Feb. 26, 1931, Bayonne, N.J.—Aug. 9, 1973, off Chesapeake Beach, Md.): Welfare rights activist. Wiley, a soft-spoken organic chemistry professor from Syracuse University, gave up an academic career to become a social activist. He left Syracuse University to serve as associate director of the CONGRESS OF RACIAL EQUALITY (CORE) from 1964 to 1966, when he resigned to establish the National Welfare Rights Organization (NWRO). Created to "provide for bread, justice, dignity, and democracy of welfare recipients," the NWRO consisted at its greatest strength of some eight hundred local

As leader of the NWRO, George Wiley fought for increased rights for people on welfare. (Library of Congress)

groups of welfare recipients and low-income people across the United States. As leader of the organization, Wiley led marches and filed lawsuits on behalf of increased rights and respect for those on welfare. In founding the NWRO, Wiley provided the first forum for welfare recipients to speak out on their own behalf, and he encouraged local chapters to develop spokespeople and become skilled at organizing.

During the 1960's, much of Wiley's work with the

NWRO involved lobbying and demonstrations. In 1969, he and other NWRO members met with Robert Finch, then secretary of health, education and welfare, to discuss the needs of welfare mothers and lobby for increased public assistance to the poor. In an attempt to secure emergency aid for an American hunger crisis, he tried to stage a sit-in at President Richard Nixon's 1969 conference on food, nutrition, and health. At a Vietnam moratorium in Washington, D.C., in the late 1960's, Wiley gave an urgent speech describing the enormous toll the Vietnam War was taking on the poor and on African Americans in particular. Wiley approved rent strikes to protest low welfare allowances and demonstrations against retail stores that denied credit to welfare recipients. Wiley's crusade has been credited with quadrupling family assistance for the poor in the United States, increasing welfare eligibility by eliminating residency requirements, and ensuring welfare recipients' right to privacy. After a rift developed between Wiley and other members of the NWRO, he resigned early in 1973. That same year, he founded a new organization, the Movement for Economic Justice, just before his death in a boating accident on Chesapeake Bay. The NWRO closed its national office in 1975, but several local chapters remained active.

Wilkens, Leonard Randolph "Lenny" (b. Oct. 28, 1937, Brooklyn, N.Y.): Basketball player and coach. After a successful career as an All-American BASKETBALL player at Providence College, the six-foot one-inch Wilkens became the St. Louis Hawks' first-round draft choice in 1960. Small by basketball standards, he proved himself by averaging 15.9 points and more than three assists per game during his eight seasons with the Hawks. Traded to the Seattle Supersonics after the 1967-1968 season, Wilkens achieved a career-high 22.4 points per game scoring average and became the Sonics' player-coach. The Cleveland Cavaliers traded for Wilkens in 1972. After two seasons with the Cavaliers, he became player-coach for the Portland Trail Blazers. Retiring as a player in 1975 after a fifteen-year career Wilkens had compiled 17,772 points and 7,211 assists, averaging 16.5 points per game. He had played in nine All-Star games.

Wilkens continued his career as a coach, working for Portland, Seattle, and Cleveland. He coached the 1978-1979 Seattle Supersonics team to National Basketball Association (NBA) Championship. He was inducted into the Naismith Memorial Basketball Hall of Fame in 1989.

Wilkins, (Jacques) Dominique (b. Jan. 12, 1960, Paris, France): BASKETBALL player. After playing at the college level for the University of Georgia, Wilkins signed with the Atlanta Hawks. In his first year of play, the six-foot eight-inch, 200-pound Wilkins was named to the 1982-1983 All-Rookie team. He was the top scorer in the National Basketball Association (NBA) for the 1985-1986 season, averaging 30.3 points per game. He was on the NBA All-Star team every season from 1983 to 1991, except for 1984-1985.

Dominique Wilkins led the NBA in scoring for the 1985-1986 season. (Atlanta Hawks)

Wilkins, Roy (Aug. 30, 1901, St. Louis, Mo.—Sept. 8, 1981, New York, N.Y.): Civil rights leader. Sometimes called "Mr. Civil Rights", Roy Wilkins played a major role in the Civil Rights movement of the 1950's and 1960's, working with other activists including Martin Luther KING, JR., Whitney YOUNG, and A. Philip RANDOLPH. Wilkins, who spent his life working to improve conditions for African Americans, was best known for

his work with the NATIONAL ASSOCIATION FOR THE ADVANCE-
MENT OF COLORED PEOPLE (NAACP).

Early Life. Roy Wilkins' parents, who were originally
from Mississippi, fled to St. Louis for safety in 1900 after
Wilkins' father defended himself from a white man who
had attempted to order him out of the road. He left to
escape being beaten and lynched, a practice commonly
used to punish African Americans who were considered
disrespectful toward whites.

earn money for college. He worked as a caddy, a red cap,
a slaughterhouse worker, and eventually as a waiter on a
dining car for the Northern Pacific Railroad.

In 1920, when an African American man was accused
of raping a white girl, three African American men were
lynched by a mob of five thousand whites in Duluth,
Minn. The incident had a profound effect on the eighteen-
year-old Wilkins, making him more aware of the strength
of racial hatred. As a result, Wilkins became more inter-

Roy Wilkins, soon after taking over as executive secretary of the NAACP. (AP/Wide World Photos)

Wilkins' mother died in 1906, leaving behind three
young children. Their father eventually took them to St.
Paul, Minn., to be reared by an aunt. Even though Wilkins
lived in poverty, life in St. Paul provided him his first
experience of living in a racially integrated community
and attending integrated schools. Although he experienced bouts with racial prejudice, it was this experience
that shaped his later belief that racial integration was an
achievable and necessary goal.

During Wilkins' teen years, he worked various jobs to

ested in learning about the goals and work of the NAACP.
He later won a prize of twenty-five dollars in a college
oratorical contest; Wilkins' entry, entitled "Democracy
or Demoncracy?," focused on the Duluth lynching.

Wilkins attended the University of Minnesota in St.
Paul, where he joined the NAACP. His love for journal-
ism led to his working on the campus newspaper, *The
Minnesota Daily*; he eventually became the paper's night
editor. Wilkins also worked on the staff of two African
American newspapers in the St. Paul community. He was

graduated in 1923 with a degree in sociology and a minor in journalism.

Early Career. Despite Wilkins' journalistic talent and experience, upon his graduation, the white-owned newspapers of St. Paul were not interested in hiring him. He found his first job in Kansas City, working for the *Kansas City Call*, an African American weekly newspaper. While living in Kansas City for eight years, Wilkins observed and experienced the blatant racial prejudice of the city's Jim Crow policies.

In Kansas City, for example, African Americans were not allowed to try on clothing in white-owned stores. Schools, parks, theaters, and other public facilities were either off-limits to African Americans or segregated. Wilkins' lifelong fight for civil rights began when he organized a boycott of the segregated theaters and campaigned for voters to reject bonds that upheld segregation. While in Kansas, Wilkins married Aminda (Minnie) Badeau on Sept. 15, 1929.

W. E. B. DU BOIS, the editor of the NAACP's *The Crisis*, offered Wilkins a position as the magazine's business manager, but Wilkins declined the offer; he was more interested in the journalism and writing of *The Crisis* than in its business aspects. In 1931, Walter WHITE, the acting executive secretary of the NAACP, invited Wilkins to serve as the organization's assistant secretary. Impressed by White's leadership and his work for civil rights, Wilkins accepted the position. His work as a journalist continued during his early career in the NAACP; he investigated discriminatory pay practices directed against African American workers involved in dam and levee construction projects in the Mississippi Delta.

In 1934, Wilkins was arrested for the first time when he demonstrated to protest the refusal of Attorney General Homer Cummings to include the issue of LYNCHING on the agenda of a major conference on crime. That same year, he was appointed editor of *The Crisis* when Du Bois resigned. Wilkins also continued to serve as an assistant secretary and administrator in the NAACP. In 1949, he was appointed the NAACP's acting executive secretary when White took a leave of absence.

Leading the NAACP. In 1955, following the death of Walter White, Wilkins was named the NAACP's executive secretary; in 1964, his title was officially changed to executive director. Under his leadership, the NAACP undertook the legal battle of school desegregation; court cases were necessary to ensure that states implemented and enforced the landmark Supreme Court decision of *BROWN V. BOARD OF EDUCATION*, which had outlawed school segregation in 1954. Wilkins' administration also fought

to integrate the Army, planned and sponsored events to end discrimination, and pressured presidents to implement civil rights legislation. Wilkins and Clarence MITCHELL, an NAACP lobbyist, worked relentlessly together to secure the passage of much of the civil rights legislation of the 1950's.

In the 1960's during Wilkins' leadership of the NAACP, the Civil Rights movement reached its pinnacle: the era of SIT-INS, FREEDOM RIDES, protest marches, and emergence of radical organizations. In 1963, while Congress debated civil rights legislation, the MARCH ON WASHINGTON for jobs and freedom occurred on August 23. Roy Wilkins was one of the key speakers, along with other civil rights giants such as A. Philip Randolph and Martin Luther King, Jr. After the March on Washington, President John Kennedy met with King, Wilkins, and other leaders to pledge his support for black efforts to achieve equality.

Division Within the Movement. With the emergence of the BLACK POWER MOVEMENT, radical activists increasingly criticized Wilkins and the NAACP for being too old-fashioned and conservative. Young radicals argued that the social climate of the Civil Rights movement had changed to a more volatile one, and that the advocacy of nonviolence and integration had become anachronistic. Wilkins responded by denouncing the Black Power movement as fanatical.

In 1972, the first National Black Political Convention was held in Gary, Ind. The leaders from the convention met later to draft a document, referred to as the National Black Political Agenda, that voiced their platforms on social, economic, and political issues pertaining to African Americans, U.S. foreign policy, school BUSING, and other issues. Because the positions outlined in the document were not a consensus of views, Roy Wilkins withdrew the NAACP's support from the paper. Again, he was criticized for his conservative views by various other leaders, including Mayor Richard HATCHER of Gary.

Despite growing criticism of his leadership, however, Wilkins remained widely respected as a civil rights leader. He continued to serve as the executive director of the NAACP until his retirement in 1977.

Achievements. Wilkins received numerous awards, including the prestigious Spingarn Medal in 1964. While he was primarily active in the Civil Rights movement, he was appointed to other positions in which he was influential in working to achieve equality for all. He served as the chairman of the Leadership Conference on Civil Rights, and he was appointed to serve as a trustee member of the Eleanor Roosevelt Foundation, the Kennedy Memorial Library Foundation, and the Estes Kefauver Memorial Foundation. Wilkins was also a member of the board of directors of the Riverdale Children's Association, the John LaFarge Institute, the Stockbridge School, and the Peace with Freedom organization.

Declining health in the last years of his life forced Wilkins to cut back on his busy schedule. He died in New York City in 1981 at the age of eighty.—*Kibibi Mack-Williams*

SUGGESTED READINGS: • Bennett, Lerone, Jr. *Before the Mayflower: A History of Black America*. New York: Penguin Books, 1984. • Franklin, John Hope, and Alfred A. Moss, Jr. *From Slavery to Freedom: A History of Negro Americans*. 6th ed. New York: Alfred A. Knopf, 1988. • Kellogg, Charles Flint. *NAACP: A History of the National Association of the Advancement of Colored People*. Baltimore, Md: John Hopkins University Press, 1967. • Weisbrot, Robert. *Freedom Bound: A History of America's Civil Rights Movement*. New York: Plume Books, 1991. • Wilkins, Roy. *Standing Fast: The Autobiography of Roy Wilkins*. New York: Viking Press, 1982.

Wilkinson, Frederick D., Jr. (b. Jan. 25, 1921, Washington, D.C.): Business executive. After being graduated from HOWARD UNIVERSITY with an A.B. degree earned magna cum laude, Wilkinson entered the U.S. Army. He earned a certificate in business law and accounting from the Army University Center of Oahu in 1946. In 1948, he earned his M.B.A. from Harvard University.

Wilkinson began working for Macy's department store in New York City in 1949, as a junior assistant buyer. He became senior assistant buyer in 1950 and buyer in 1952. He stayed in that position until 1968, when he was named as a company vice president. The New York City Transit Authority hired Wilkinson in 1974 as its executive officer for passenger service. He held that position until 1976, then was executive officer for surface transit. American Express Company made Wilkinson its vice president for travel in 1977. He became vice president for consumer cards in 1979 and senior vice president in 1985. Wilkinson also has served as trustee of Jamaica Hospital in New York State and of the NATIONAL URBAN LEAGUE, for which he was national treasurer at one time. He also was on the board of directors of the Jamaica Chamber of Commerce and of Freedom National Bank.

Williams, Albert P. (b. Savannah, Ga.): Judge. Williams was graduated from LINCOLN UNIVERSITY with his A.B. degree in 1940. After serving in World War II, he attended Brooklyn Law School and earned his J.D. degree in 1952. Williams passed the New York State bar examination and entered private practice as an attorney.

Williams' public legal career began in 1962, when he served as chief trial attorney in the torts division of the Queens County Civil Court in New York. He continued in this post until 1969, then served as assistant corporate counsel for the City of New York. Williams accepted his first judicial appointment in 1970, when he became judge of the Civil Court of New York City. He was selected to serve as an associate justice on the New York State Supreme Court in 1978.

Williams, Ann Claire (b. Aug. 16, 1949, Detroit, Mich.): Federal judge. Williams grew up in Detroit and was graduated with her B.A. in education from Wayne State University in 1970. She worked as an elementary school music teacher and earned her M.A. in counseling from the University of Michigan in 1972. Williams then entered law school at the University of Notre Dame, earning her J.D. degree in 1975.

She worked as a judicial clerk for Judge Robert A. Sprecher in Chicago from 1975 to 1976. Williams then served as an assistant U.S. attorney in the U.S. attorney's office in Chicago, attaining the position of deputy chief attorney before serving as the chief attorney on the Organized Crime Drug Enforcement Task Force for the North Central Region from 1983 to 1985. In addition to her work as a U.S. attorney, Williams was an adjunct professor at Northwestern University and served on the faculty of the National Institute for Trial Advocacy beginning in 1979. President Ronald Reagan appointed Williams to a lifetime post as U.S. district judge for the Northern District of Illinois in June of 1985. Upon taking her post, Williams became the first African American woman appointed to the federal bench by Reagan.

Williams, Billy Dee (b. Apr. 6, 1937, New York, N.Y.): Actor. Billy Dee Williams is best known for his cultivation of the image of a debonair and handsome leading man. More than merely a sex symbol, he has undertaken a variety of challenging roles in theater, television, and film.

Early Years. Born in Harlem with a twin sister to Loretta Anne and William December Williams, Billy Dee was named after his father. His mother, a native of the Caribbean island of Montserrat, had aspired to the operatic stage but gave up her dream to raise a family. His father, formerly of Texas, worked three jobs as a cook, janitor, and maintenance man to support his family.

Overweight and shy as a child, Williams endured the teasing of his neighborhood peers. At an early age, he became interested in drawing and, later, painting. He studied art at the New York High School of Music and

Popular leading actor for stage, screen, and television Billy Dee Williams. (AP/Wide World Photos)

Art and the National Academy of Fine Arts and Design and briefly took acting classes at the Actors Workshop in Harlem under the tutelage of Sidney POITIER. Williams says he became involved in acting as a way of earning money to pay for his art supplies.

Theatrical Career. Williams made his professional stage debut at the age of seven as a page in the musical *The Firebrand of Florence* (1945). He garnered the walk-on role when, while visiting his mother at the theater, where she worked as an elevator operator, he came to the attention of the show's producer.

Eleven years later, Williams again performed on the stage, this time in the revival of *TAKE A GIANT STEP* (1956). His painting, although important to him, became a hobby as he accepted more stage roles. A critically acclaimed supporting role in *A Taste of Honey* (1960) brought him greater notice and earned for him a spot on a *Holiday* magazine list as one of the most promising young men of Manhattan. After he moved to California to seek work in television and film, he occasionally returned to New York to star in such plays as *Slow Dance on the Killing* (1970), *I Have a Dream* (1976), and *FENCES* (1988).

Television Career. During the 1960's and 1970's, Williams served as a guest star on many television series, including *The Defenders*, *Hawk*, *The F.B.I.*, *Mission: Impossible*, and *THE MOD SQUAD*, and starred in a number of made-for-television movies, including *Carter's Army* (1969). During this phase of his career, he often played an angry young black man with a tough exterior hiding a sensitive and, at times, vulnerable nature.

The turning point in his career came with his starring role as famed football player Gayle SAYERS in the popular made-for-television film *Brian's Song* (1970). Based on Sayers' autobiography, the film depicted the close relationship between Sayers and his Chicago Bears teammate Brian Piccolo, who had been stricken with cancer. Williams earned widespread acclaim and an Emmy nomination in one of the most highly rated television programs of the decade.

Film Career. Berry GORDY, Jr., the president of MOTOWN INDUSTRIES, signed Williams to a seven-year contract with the company's young film production unit before the initial showing of *Brian's Song*. Gordy teamed Williams with Diana ROSS in a film treatment of the life of Billie HOLIDAY, *LADY SINGS THE BLUES* (1972). Starring as Holiday's third husband, Louis McKay, Williams created an enduring screen persona as a suave, romantic leading man. After the film's release, critics began to call Williams "the black Clark Gable." Despite the film's success, Gordy began to lose interest in the film unit and used the actor in only three other projects: *MAHOGANY*

(1975), in which Williams again teamed with Ross; *THE BINGO LONG TRAVELING ALL-STARS AND MOTOR KINGS* (1976), a film about barnstorming black baseball players in which Williams costarred with Richard PRYOR and James Earl JONES; and the made-for-television film *Scott JOPLIN*, a biography of the famous ragtime composer in which Williams was cast as the lead.

Motown's contract did not prohibit Williams from accepting roles in other studios' projects. He appeared in such films as *The Final Comedown* (1972), *Hit!* (1973), and *The Take* (1974). After his Motown contract expired, Williams undertook a part that became one of his personal favorites, the role of a roguish space pirate, Lando Calrissian, in the second film of the *Star Wars* series, *The Empire Strikes Back* (1980). He reprised the role in the third film of the series, *Return of the Jedi* (1983). Increasingly, though, Williams found himself offered nondescript supporting roles, such as the role of District Attorney Harvey Dent in *Batman* (1989), instead of leading parts.

The 1980's and 1990's. Occasionally appearing in films, Williams also had a brief cameo role on the prime-time television soap opera, *Dynasty*, broadcast on the ABC network. On the series, he portrayed Diahann CARROLL's record-mogul husband, Brady Lloyd. Williams costarred on the short-lived drama *Double Dare* (1985). Television audiences also frequently saw him on commercials. He also endorsed a signature perfume manufactured by Avon cosmetics.

His acting talents received recognition with the addition of his star on the Hollywood Walk of Fame in 1982. In 1984, Williams was the recipient of a Black Achievement Award and was also inducted into the Black Filmmakers Hall of Fame. He received a Black American Cinema Society Phoenix Award in 1988.

During this period, Williams' painting garnered wider public notice. While not working as an actor, he had continued to pursue his other artistic talents and had created more than 150 paintings by 1990. His works have been exhibited in galleries in Beverly Hills and New York at prices as high as $35,000.

Personal Life. In his early twenties, Williams married Audrey Sellers. Their union lasted five years and produced a son, Corey Dee. After a brief second marriage to model Marlene Clark, Williams was married for a third time in 1973. His third wife, Teruko Nakagami, brought to their family a daughter, Miyako, from a previous marriage to musician Wayne SHORTER. In 1974, Teruko gave birth to another daughter, Hanako.—*Addell Austin Anderson*

SUGGESTED READINGS: • Bogle, Donald. *Blacks in*

American Films and Television: An Illustrated Encyclopedia. New York: Garland, 1988. • Campbell, Bebe Moore. "Spotlight: Billy Dee Williams." *Essence* 16 (July, 1985): 61. • Leab, Daniel J. *From Sambo to Superspade: The Black Experience in Motion Pictures.* Boston: Houghton Mifflin, 1975. • Norment, Lynn. "Ebony Interview: Billy Dee Williams." *Ebony* 36 (January, 1981): 31-34. • Sanders, Charles L. "Billy Dee Williams: The Serious Side of a Sex Symbol." *Ebony* 38 (June, 1983): 126-128.

Williams, Chancellor (b. Dec. 22, 1905, Bennettsville, S.C.): Historian. Williams completed his elementary education at the Marlboro Academy in Bennettsville before his family moved to Washington, D.C. He attended Dunbar High School and Armstrong High School in Washington. His B.A. in education and M.A. in history are from HOWARD UNIVERSITY. Williams did postgraduate nonresident studies at the University of Chicago and the University of Iowa, then earned his Ph.D. from The American University in 1949.

Williams spent a year as a visiting research scholar at the University of Oxford in England and at the University of London. He began direct field studies in African history in 1956, using University College (later called the University of GHANA) as a base. He attempted to determine the independent achievements of African people and the nature of civilization in Africa before Asian and European influence. His final field studies, covering twenty-six countries and more than one hundred language groups, were completed in 1964.

Williams has been president of a baking company, editor of *The New Challenge*, organizer of a cooperative, an economist with the United States government, a high-school teacher, a school principal, a historical novelist, and a university professor in addition to his career as a historian. His *The Destruction of Black Civilization: Great Issues of a Race from 4500 B.C. to 2000 A.D.* (1971) won the 1971 Book Award from the Black Academy of Arts and Letters. It is an overview of the history of black nations and various black cultural ideas.

Williams, Charles Edward (b. Aug. 8, 1938, Wedgeworth, Ala.): Military officer. Williams retired from the United States Army on July 31, 1989, as a major general with more than twenty-eight years of active commissioned service. His combat experience included two stints in Vietnam. The first, from August, 1966, to August, 1967, involved service in an assault helicopter company as platoon leader, then as administrative officer, and later as executive officer. The second, from July, 1968, to May,

1969, saw Williams as an aviation officer at the headquarters of the Eighteenth Engineer Brigade.

Williams earned a Distinguished Flying Cross on Apr. 7, 1967, by entering a landing zone and using his landing lights as a beacon to guide a helicopter team. His own helicopter was exposed to heavy ground fire, but he flew over the hostile position so that his crew could fire on the enemy and allow the other helicopter to land. He earned an Army Commendation Medal with V device on Oct. 10, 1967, when he assisted those wounded during a mortar and rocket attack. Among his other commendations and awards are the Distinguished Service Medal with oak leaf cluster, the Legion of Merit with two oak leaf clusters, and the Bronze Star with oak leaf cluster.

Williams is a graduate of TUSKEGEE INSTITUTE (B.S., biology) and Atlanta University (M.B.A.) as well as the United States Army Command and General Staff College and the War College. He also took the basic and advanced courses at the Army's engineer school. After taking the basic course for engineer officers in 1960, he was stationed at Fort Campbell, Ky., rising to the position of commander of the headquarters company of the Seventieth Engineer Battalion. In 1962 and 1963, he took the fixed wing aviator course for officers and was assigned to the United States Army Europe as a fixed wing aviator (later platoon leader) with the Thirty-seventh Engineer Corps. He took the rotary wing aviation qualification course in 1966, then used that training in Vietnam.

Williams' service in Vietnam was interrupted by a year taking the engineer officer advanced course. Following his second tour of duty in Vietnam, Williams attended Atlanta University and the Army Command and General Staff College. In June, 1972, he was made a management analyst at the Army Materiel Command in Alexandria, Va. From 1974 to 1977, he served with the comptroller of the Army in various administrative positions. He transferred to Fort Belvoir, Va., in 1977 and served as commander of the Third Battalion and later executive officer of the Training Brigade at the Army engineer center there. Williams' last decade of service included positions as chief of the installations planning division in the office of the chief of engineers, commander of the Eighteenth Engineer Brigade for the United States Army Europe, director of operations and maintenance in the office of the comptroller of the Army, commanding general of the Army Engineer Division for the North Atlantic area, and director of management in the office of the chief of staff of the Army.

Williams, Clarence, III (b. Aug. 21, 1939, New York, N.Y.): Actor. Best known for his role as Linc Hayes on the television series THE MOD SQUAD from 1968 to 1973, Williams has also appeared on the television shows *Daktari* (1967) and *Miami Vice* (1985), among others. His film credits include *PURPLE RAIN* (1984) and *Deep Cover* (1992).

Williams, Daniel Hale (Jan. 18, 1858, Hollidaysburg, Pa.—Aug. 4, 1931, Idlewild, Mich.): Surgeon. One of the best-known physicians of his day, Daniel Hale Williams was the fifth child of Daniel Williams, Jr., a barber, and Sara Price Williams. As a youngster, Williams moved to Wisconsin, where in 1878 he was graduated from Haire's Classical Academy in Janesville. Having decided to become a physician, he apprenticed himself to Henry Palmer, a prominent physician who had served as surgeon general of Wisconsin. Under Palmer's guidance, Williams prepared himself to enter the Chicago Medical College, an affiliate institution of Northwestern University, from which he received a medical degree in 1883.

Early Professional Career. After serving an internship at Mercy Hospital in Chicago, Williams established a private practice in an integrated Chicago neighborhood. Despite the restrictions and limitations that often affected black doctors, Williams, an ambitious, hardworking man, assumed many responsibilities. He became attending physician at the Protestant Orphan Asylum and a member of the surgical staff of the South Side Dispensary. In 1885, two years after having earned his medical degree, he became a demonstrator of anatomy at his alma mater. During the same period, he accepted a position as a surgeon with the City Railway Company. Williams' reputation as a physician also earned him an appointment to the Illinois State Board of Health. As one of the few black sanitarians of the era, he served on the board for four years and helped to draft public health legislation.

As a public health official, Williams was anxious to provide additional hospital facilities for residents of Chicago. Moreover, as a black surgeon, he was also aware of the dire need to establish an institution where African Americans could secure medical internships and nurse's training. His hopes were realized in 1891 with the opening of the Provident Hospital in Chicago, which had an interracial staff and which eventually opened a school for nurses. Beginning with practically no resources, this hospital, under Williams' guidance, made a significant contribution to training black health-care professionals. Its nurse's training program was the first of its kind for black women in the United States. Williams served on the surgical staff of Provident from its beginning until 1912, save for short periods of time he spent at Freedmen's Hospital in Washington, D.C., and at MEHARRY MEDICAL COLLEGE in Nashville, Tenn.

Successful Heart Surgery. It was during Provident's early history that "Dr. Dan," as he came to be known, became the first surgeon to perform a heart operation. In July of 1893, James Cornish, a black expressman, was admitted to the hospital with a stab wound in the region of his heart. At first, the wound appeared superficial, but the patient's distress soon indicated that his condition was more serious than originally thought. Medical opinion of the day did not recommend surgery in cases of this type. Williams, however, was convinced that the patient would die if the wound was ignored. He entered the thoracic cavity and sutured Cornish's pericardial sac. The patient not only survived but also fully recovered. Williams, who was only thirty-seven at the time, had performed an astonishing operation. Claims were made that a St. Louis surgeon had performed a successful heart operation in 1891, but the *New York Medical Record* reported in 1897 that Williams' surgical procedure was the first recorded case of suture of the pericardium.

Reorganizing Freedmen's Hospital. In February of 1894, Williams accepted an appointment at the Freedmen's Hospital in Washington, D.C. As surgeon-in-chief, he viewed this institution as having a special mission: to provide training for black interns and nurses who were denied access to other institutions and to provide decent health care for its patients, the majority of whom were black. Accordingly, Williams implemented a system in which young medical-school graduates could secure temporary residence within the hospital and could also perform practical work on the wards. This system, Williams argued, would cut expenses, as fewer practicing physicians would be hired; at the same time, the young graduates could take advantage of opportunities that many hospitals had denied them on the basis of race. In 1894, Williams implemented the nurse's training program at Freedmen's, thereby permitting black women to secure professional training.

In his 1897 annual report, Williams complained about the condition of the hospital buildings at Freedmen's, describing them as old frame buildings built on army barracks. In order to render better services to patients, he argued, the hospital needed new buildings with adequate heat, light, and ventilation. Although he did not realize all of his ambitions for Freedmen's, Williams was able to organize the hospital into seven departments: medical, surgical, gynecological, obstetrical, dermatological, genito-urinary, and throat and chest. He also established more internships and was able to acquire a serviceable horse-drawn ambulance. Williams resigned his position at Freedmen's in 1897, having become disgusted with the internal politics and other problems associated with the institution.

Williams returned to Chicago after he left Freedmen's, with plans of resuming his work at Provident. Unfortu-nately, things had changed at the hospital during his absence; Dr. George C. Hall had become a powerful force at Provident. An intense rivalry developed between the two men, with Hall emerging as the winner.

Daniel Hale Williams, surgeon, was the first physician to perform a heart operation. (National Library of Medicine)

Eventually, Williams severed his ties with Provident. Throughout the painful ordeal, however, he continued to be a significant influence in the medical profession in Chicago and the nation. In 1899, for example, he became a professor of clinical surgery at Meharry Medical College. As one of the two successful medical colleges for blacks, Meharry had a unique mission, and Williams was determined to make it a first-rate institution; he was responsible for establishing the first surgical clinics at the college. Upon his return to Chicago, he served as a member of the surgical staff of the Cook County Hospital, a white-administered institution.

Other Medical Appointments and Activities. In 1913, Williams became an associate attending surgeon at St. Luke's, a white Chicago hospital. For a black practitioner of the day, the appointment was an unusual honor, and it enabled Williams to become influential in running one of the largest gynecological services in the city. That same year, when the American College of Surgeons was organized, Williams was invited to become a charter member, the only African American so honored. For many years, he was the only black who held membership in the organization.

Despite his acceptance into the mainstream of American medicine—the white medical community—Williams continued his efforts to improve the status of and to promote professionalism among black physicians. In 1895, when a group of black doctors attending the Cotton States and International Exposition in Atlanta met to organize a medical association for black physicians, dentists, and pharmacists, Williams was present. He became a charter member of the body known as the NATIONAL MEDICAL ASSOCIATION, the black counterpart of the American Medical Association. At a meeting of the group held in New York City in 1908, Williams performed surgery at Lincoln Hospital as a part of "Negro Doctor's Clinic Day." At an evening session, he lectured on "Crushing Injuries to the Extremities." At another early National Medical Association meeting in St. Louis, he again demonstrated his surgical skills before fellow members.

Research. In addition to his commitment to improving the training of black health-care professionals, his involvement in medical and surgical societies, and his private practice, Williams was a researcher who contributed to medical journals and presented papers at professional meetings. He was intent upon promoting sound surgical knowledge and correcting errors that had crept into medical thinking, including erroneous ideas about black health. American practitioners had long pointed to certain physiological differences between the races, many of which were unfounded. One such misconception, according to Williams, was that certain gynecological problems occurred only in whites. Accordingly, many physicians held that black women were not at risk for ovarian cysts, as this condition allegedly occurred only among whites. In a paper entitled "Ovarian Cysts in Colored Women, with Notes on the Relative Frequency of Fibromata in Both Races," published in *The Chicago Medical Recorder*, he noted that, despite the literature and the information imparted in the best medical colleges regarding the incidence of ovarian cysts, the condition did affect blacks. As proof of his position, he stated that between 1886 and 1893 he had surgically removed ovarian cysts from blacks in Chicago; moreover, he had seen the condition among black women at the Washington, D.C., morgue and also in the wards at Freedmen's Hospital. As further evidence, Williams cited the findings of the prominent New Orleans surgeon Rudolph Matas, who had also observed the condition in several blacks at that city's Charity Hospital. A longtime proponent of better health care for African Americans, Williams cautioned that generalizations regarding the absence or presence of certain conditions among blacks were likely to be incorrect, as many blacks received neither proper diagnosis nor treatment.

Final Years. In 1924, Williams' wife, the former Alice Johnson, died. Two years later, Williams suffered a stroke and went into semiretirement at his home in Michigan. He died there on Aug. 4, 1931.—*Betty L. Plummer*

SUGGESTED READINGS: • Buckler, Helen. *Daniel Hale Williams, Negro Surgeon.* New York: Pitman, 1968. • Buckler, Helen. Doctor Dan, Pioneer in American Surgery. Boston: Little, Brown, 1954. • Fenderson, Lewis R. *Daniel Hale Williams: Open-Heart Doctor.* New York: McGraw-Hill, 1971. • Morais, Herbert M. *The History of the Negro in Medicine.* New York: Publishers Company, 1967. • Patterson, Lillie. *Sure Hands, Strong Heart: The Life of Daniel Hale Williams.* Nashville: Abingdon Press, 1981.

Williams, David Welford (b. Mar. 20, 1910, Atlanta, Ga.): Attorney and jurist. Williams received his education from Los Angeles Junior College, UCLA (A.B., 1934), and the University of Southern California Law School (LL.B., 1937). He became a judge on the Los Angeles Municipal Court in 1956 and joined the Superior Court in 1962. In 1969, he was elevated to the federal bench.

Williams, Deniece (b. June 3, 1951, Gary, Ind.): Singer. While working in a record shop, the young Williams and her singing talents were discovered by the store owner, who got her an audition with a record company. She produced a single, "Love Is Tears," then went on to enroll in college. In 1969, Stevie WONDER approached her to travel on the road with him, singing backup with his group Wonderlove. She took her eighteen-month-old son with her on tour but took time off to have a second child. After a short break she returned, appearing on every Stevie Wonder album between 1972 and 1976 as well as appearing on albums by Roberta FLACK, Minnie RIPERTON, D. J. Rogers, and Weather Report.

Williams left Wonderlove in 1975 to focus on a solo career. Her first album, *This Is Niecey*, was released in 1977 and spawned a worldwide hit single, "Free." The follow-up single, "That's What Friends Are For," also was an enormous hit. Meanwhile, Williams' considerable songwriting talents were paying off, with Frankie Valli, the Soul Train Gang, Stanley Turrentine, and Nancy Wilson recording her songs. In 1978, after releasing another album and touring with EARTH, WIND, AND FIRE, she released a duet with Johnny MATHIS, "Too Much, Too Little, Too Late," which became a number-one hit. Two more albums were produced in 1980 and 1981. Her 1984 single "Let's Hear It for the Boy," also was a hit. She went on to produce several gospel records before returning to pop. Her gospel work garnered her three Grammy Awards. Her album *I Can't Wait* was released in 1988, and a duet album featuring Williams, *Better Together*, appeared in 1992.

Williams, Douglas Lee (b. Aug. 9, 1955, Zachary, La.): Football player. Williams was one of six children born to Laura and Robert, Sr. A sports star in high school who competed in baseball, basketball, and FOOTBALL, Williams credits his oldest brother, Robert, Jr., as giving him his inspiration to succeed in athletics. Williams attended college at Grambling State University in Louisiana, where he played football for the legendary coach Eddie Robinson. After a difficult beginning, Williams settled into the role of team leader and was rewarded for his efforts by being named All-American quarterback his senior year and finishing fourth in the balloting for the Heisman Trophy, given each year to college football's dominant player. He earned his B.S. in education from Grambling in 1978.

He was chosen in the first round of the 1978 National Football League draft by the woeful Tampa Bay Buccaneers, an expansion team which continued to struggle through each of its years in the league. Williams was only the second African American quarterback to be drafted in the first round, the first being Eldridge Dickey in 1968. Williams, whose incredibly strong throwing arm was both his blessing and his curse—in his younger days,

Williams threw everything as hard as he could—adapted to his new surroundings admirably and led the Buccaneers to their first three playoff appearances.

After a heated contract dispute following the 1982 season, Williams reluctantly signed with the Oklahoma Outlaws of the fledgling United States Football League. By the next season, the franchise had merged with the Arizona team. The league itself was doomed and folded in 1985, leaving Williams and scores of other talented ballplayers out of work.

Washington Redskins quarterback Doug Williams looks for his receiver in a 1988 game against the Green Bay Packers. (AP/Wide World Photos)

In 1986, Williams signed with the Washington Redskins as a backup quarterback, seeing action in only one play that season, an incomplete pass attempt. In November, 1987, he came off the bench following an injury to the starter and led Washington to a come-from-behind victory. That earned him a start, but a minor injury kept him sidelined. By the end of the 1987-1988 season, Williams was Washington's starting quarterback, and he led the team to a resounding Super Bowl victory over the Denver Broncos despite having undergone an emergency root canal the previous day and spraining his knee in the first half of the game. He was the first African American ever to have started at quarterback in Super Bowl history, and for his part in Washington's victory, he was named Most Valuable Player.

For all his professional success, Williams endured much personal adversity. In 1977, his first wife, Janice, died of a brain tumor three months after the birth of their daughter and ten days short of their first anniversary. He subsequently remarried.

After his Super Bowl victory, Williams became increasingly inconsistent as a result of a chronic back injury. Relegated to the role of injured superstar, Williams, an eleven-year veteran of pro football, announced his retirement from the game at the end of the 1989 season.

Williams, Eddie Nathan (b. Aug. 18, 1932, Memphis, Tenn.): Political scientist. Williams became president of the Joint Center for Political Studies in 1972. The center, cosponsored by HOWARD UNIVERSITY, tries to meet the information and technical needs of minority elected officials associated with the National Black Caucus. It provides information on voting patterns and on proposed legislation, among other data.

Williams holds a B.S. degree from the University of Illinois at Urbana (1954). He did postgraduate work at Atlanta University in 1957 and at Howard University in 1958. From 1955 to 1957, he was a radar officer in the United States Army. Following his discharge, he became a reporter for the *Atlanta Daily World* newspaper. He was a fellow of the American Political Science Association in 1958, then became staff assistant for the U.S. Senate Committee on Foreign Relations. From 1961 to 1968, Williams was a foreign service officer with the State Department. He became vice president for public affairs at the University of Chicago in 1968 and served until 1972, when he joined the Joint Center for Political Studies.

Williams joined the Black Leadership Forum in 1977. He chaired an advisory commission on black population and advised the United States Census Bureau on the 1980 census. From 1970 to 1972, he was an editorial columnist for the *Chicago Sun-Times*. Williams also has been the vice chair of the board of trustees of the National Children's Television Workshop and chair of the National Coalition on Black Voter Participation.

Williams, Egbert Austin "Bert" (Nov. 12, 1874, Antigua, West Indies—Mar. 4, 1922, New York, N.Y.): Vaudeville star. Bert Williams is considered one of the finest comedians in the history of American show busi-

ness. He appeared in two films, *Darktown Jubliee* (1914) and *A Natural Born Gambler* (1916), and recorded such hit songs as "It's Nobody's Business but My Own," "Oh Death Where Is Thy Sting," and "It's Getting So You Can't Trust Nobody." He is best known, however, for his partnership with song-and-dance man George WALKER and for his work with the Ziegfeld Follies.

Early Years. Born in the West Indies as Egbert Austin Williams, he migrated as a young child with his family to Riverside, Calif. His father, a railroad worker, wanted Williams to earn a degree at Stanford University; however, three of Williams' white friends persuaded him to join their theatrical troupe. Often, he could not stay in the same hotels or eat in the same restaurants as his white peers. When the group finally reached San Francisco, their clothes were so filled with lice that they had to be burned. The hardships led to the disbanding of the quartet, and only Williams decided to pursue a career as an entertainer. Musically gifted, he could play almost any instrument and had a fine singing voice. As a solo act, he first performed with Lew Johnson's Minstrels for two dollars a week and later played San Francisco vaudeville houses for seven dollars a week.

Partnership with Walker. Growing tired of working alone, Williams agreed to form a partnership with George Walker, a former minstrel- and medicine-show entertainer from Lawrence, Kans. Initially, Williams played a straight man to Walker's fool, but it was not long before the roles were reversed. During this early period in their career, the team was often unemployed, so they spent many nights watching other vaudevillians work their craft. After studying white comedians who performed in BLACKFACE, the team felt they had to conform to tradition and portray stereotypical black characters in order to achieve success. They billed themselves as the "Real Coons" and toured across the nation.

In 1896, while Williams and Walker were playing at a second-rate vaudeville house in Chicago, a Broadway theater manager named George Lederer heard of the team and sent for them to perk up a faltering Victor Herbert musical called *The Gold Bug.* Although they could not stop the ill-fated show from closing, the experience served to boost Williams and Walker's career. For forty weeks, they played in first-rate vaudeville houses along the East Coast. Their act also popularized the CAKEWALK among New York's high society.

Enthused by their East Coast popularity, the team set sail for London, where they unexpectedly met with a cool reception. Back in New York, they garnered modest success in 1900 with the shows *The Policy Players* and *The Sons of Ham.* Like other musicals of the day, these

Vaudeville star Bert Williams was partnered with George Walker in many popular musical stage productions at the turn of the century. (Library of Congress)

shows featured improvised routines that were changed nightly. Music and dance were of utmost importance. Termed "coon shows" by contemporaries, these musicals did not differ greatly from minstrel entertainments. *The Sons of Ham* featured a song that would become one of Williams' trademark numbers, "I'm A Jonah Man."

Most Significant Productions. Williams and Walker might not be well remembered today if it were not for their next three musical shows, created in collaboration with some of the era's most talented black artists: director Jesse Shipp, composer Will Marion Cook, lyricist-comedian Alex Rogers, and actress-singer-dancer Ada Overton Walker (George's wife). Williams and Walker had long wanted to perform in the first-rate Broadway houses that had traditionally prohibited black musicals. In contrast to their former musicals, the company sought to devise a show with an African setting and a more formal structure. The result was IN DAHOMEY (1903), which featured two detectives from Boston, Shylock Homestead (Williams) and Rareback Pinkerton (Walker), who are hired to find a lost silver casket. The show did little to enlighten audiences about African culture, and actually spent only one of three acts in an African setting. The team's old vaudeville routines, humorous tunes, and popular cake-walk numbers were the real draws for the musical.

Following a successful Broadway run, the show sailed to England for a London engagement. *In Dahomey* was greeted by a lukewarm reception until the show gave a command performance in honor of the ninth birthday of the Prince of Wales. Afterward, not only did ticket sales pick up considerably, but the musical also initiated a cakewalk craze that swept England and France. Upon its return to the United States, the show had a successful tour in 1904 and 1905. The musical returned 400 percent profit to its producers and quelled the belief that all-black-cast shows lost money. Moreover, the team, especially Williams, became the talk of the entertainment world. Stories circulated about Williams, who off-stage was the antithesis of his onstage persona and who had married a demure former Chicago showgirl named Lottie. Williams was light skinned and broad shouldered, and his manners were correct and elegant; his library contained works by Charles Darwin, Thomas Paine, Arthur Schopenhauer, Oscar Wilde, Voltaire, Immanuel Kant, Johann von Goethe, and Mark Twain.

In 1906, the next Williams and Walker show, *Abyssinia*, followed the adventures of African Americans Rastus Johnson (Walker) and Jasmine Jenkins (Williams) on the African continent. Unlike its predecessor, the show strayed from minstrel stereotypes and depicted a more complimentary image of African life.

The production of *Bandana Land* (1908) marked the end of the partnership. In the play, Bud Jenkins (Walker) attempts to swindle a railway company in a land-speculation deal and tries to trick Skunkton Bowser (Williams) out of his inheritance. Like the two previous shows, *Bandana Land* proved to be a profitable investment for its producers. Walker's philandering, however, had made him susceptible to SYPHILIS, a debilitating disease that had no cure at that time. Early in the run of the show, Walker began to show symptoms of syphilitic infection: He lisped, stuttered, and forgot his lines. He continued his role as long as he was physically able, but by February, 1909, Walker had become bedridden. For the final weeks of the run, his wife Ada wore his costume to perform his role. Walker died two years later at the age of thirty-eight.

Ziegfeld Follies. Williams once again performed a solo act. In 1909, he starred in his last all-black-cast show, *Mr. Lode of Koal.* For the next ten years, he became a headliner with the famed previously all-white cast of the Ziegfeld Follies. Initially, other Follies entertainers threatened to strike if Williams was hired. The producer called their bluff, and predictably, the cast relented; some, however, insisted they would not appear on stage with a black man. This threat remained until Williams proved much too popular with audiences for other cast members to ignore. During this period, "Nobody" appropriately became Williams' theme song, as he endured racial slurs from his white colleagues and from society at large. He was also one of the few black entertainers of the decade given the opportunity to perform on Broadway. Follies comedian W. C. Fields would say of Williams, "He is the funniest man I ever saw and the saddest man I ever knew." Williams left the Follies in 1919 and signed to star in the revue *Broadway Brevities of 1920.* The show became his last; he was struck down by pneumonia and died at the age of forty-seven.

Career Assessment. The Williams and Walker team was not without its detractors. While the black press lauded their talents, it criticized the duo for playing in Jim Crow houses where ushers were the only blacks allowed on the main floor. Critics also accused them of not overtly challenging black stereotypes; their shows included demeaning material, and Williams donned a blackface mask throughout his career. Moreover, the financial and critical success of their shows had little lasting impact on encouraging managers to book black acts in first-rate Broadway houses.

Nevertheless, the team is remembered for its more praiseworthy accomplishments. They introduced many of the most popular songs of their era, such as "Dora

Dean," "I Don't Like No Cheap Man," and "When It's All Goin' out and Nothin's Comin' In." Many of Williams' trademark songs—"Jonah Man," "I Must Be Crazy but I Ain't No Fool," "Nobody," and "Why Adam Sinned"— were written by the comedian in collaboration with lyricist Alex Rogers. The team's shows were written and staged by some of the era's most talented black artists. They employed numerous black actors, some of whom, such as Charles GILPIN and Abbie MITCHELL, went on to star in dramatic roles on Broadway. The legacy of the team, especially of Williams, will continue to be acknowledged with admiration.—*Gary Anderson*

SUGGESTED READINGS: • Charters, Ann. *Nobody: The Story of Bert Williams.* New York: Macmillan, 1970. • Haskins, James. *Black Theater in America.* New York: Thomas Y. Crowell, 1982. • Riis, Thomas L. *Just Before Jazz: Black Musical Theater in New York: 1890-1915.* Washington, D.C.: Smithsonian Institution Press, 1989. • Stein, Charles W., ed. *American Vaudeville as Seen by Its Contemporaries.* New York: Alfred A. Knopf, 1984. • Woll, Allen L. *Black Musical Theatre.* Baton Rouge: Louisiana State University Press, 1989.

Williams, Franklin H. (b. Oct. 22, 1917, Flushing, N.Y.): Political appointee and association executive. Williams was graduated from LINCOLN UNIVERSITY with his A.B. degree in 1941 and attended law school at Fordham University, earning his J.D. degree in 1945. Upon graduation, Williams served as assistant special counsel for the NATIONAL ASSOCIATION FOR THE ADVANCEMENT OF COLORED PEOPLE (NAACP) national office from 1945 to 1950. He was sent to California to serve as the director of the NAACP's West Coast office from 1950 to 1959.

Williams' political career began in 1959, when he was appointed to serve as assistant attorney general for the state of California. He left that post in 1960 to become African regional director for the United States Peace Corps. In 1963, Williams was appointed to serve as U.S. representative to the United Nations Economic and Social Council. Williams left the U.N. in 1965 to accept an appointment as U.S. ambassador to GHANA, a post he held until 1968. While in the foreign service, Williams was chairman of the Association of Black Ambassadors and served as vice chairman of the Council of American Ambassadors.

He left public office to become director of Columbia University's Urban Center, also serving as president of the Phelps-Stokes Fund. In addition, Williams served as director on the boards of various corporations including Chemical Bank, Consolidated Edison of New York, and Borden, Inc.

Williams, George Washington (Oct. 16, 1849, Bedford Springs, Pa.—Aug. 4, 1891, Blackpool, England): Historian, soldier, legislator, and diplomat. Williams joined the Union Army at the age of fourteen. He served as a state representative in the Ohio legislature from 1879 to 1881. His *History of the Negro Race in America from 1619 to 1880* (1882) and *A History of the Negro Troops in the War of the Rebellion, 1861-1865* (1888) were important early histories of African Americans. After visiting the Congo, he protested the oppression of Africans by the Belgian colonial government.

Williams, Harvey Dean (b. Whiteville, N.C.): Military officer. Williams retired from the United States Army in 1982 with the rank of major general. At that time, he was commanding general of the United States Army Readiness and Mobilization Region III and deputy commanding general of the First United States Army at Fort Mead, Md.

Williams received his commission through the Reserve Officers' Training Corps program and was made a second lieutenant on Jan. 16, 1951. He was graduated

Franklin Williams served as U.S. ambassador to Ghana. (Harlee Little)

from West Virginia State College with a B.A. in political science and an M.S. in international relations. He also was graduated from the Armed Forces Staff College and the United States Naval War College.

Among Williams' assignments were positions as assistant G-4 and deputy G-4 for logistics, as well as commander of the First Battalion of the Ninety-second Artillery, all for the First Field Force in Vietnam. Williams also has been chief of the security division in the office of the assistant chief of staff for intelligence and a military adviser to the United States Arms Control and Disarmament Agency. Among his command positions were those as head of the Seventy-fifth Field Artillery Group at Fort Sill, Okla.; the United States Military District of Washington, D.C.; and the Seventh Corps Artillery of the United States Army Europe. He also has served as a member of the Special Review Board in the office of the deputy chief of staff for personnel and as deputy for inspections and compliance for the inspector general.

Among Williams' awards and decorations are the Legion of Merit, the Bronze Star with oak leaf cluster, and the Army Commendation Medal with three oak leaf clusters.

Williams, Hosea (b. Jan. 5, 1926, Attapulgus, Ga.): Civil rights activist and clergyman. A lifetime civil rights crusader, Williams is an ordained minister, pastor, businessman, and politician who came to fame in the CIVIL RIGHTS movement of the 1960's. An integral part of the SOUTHERN CHRISTIAN LEADERSHIP CONFERENCE (SCLC), begun in Atlanta, Ga., under the direction of Martin Luther KING, JR., Williams was a vigorous participant in the marches, demonstrations, boycotts, SIT-INS, strikes, and other nonviolent direct action protects of the movement. He was arrested more than one hundred times for his involvement activities.

Williams has been a unique voice and a controversial figure in national, state, and local politics, as well as in the religious ministry. Serving as pastor of the Martin Luther King, Jr., People's Church of Love, Incorporated, beginning in 1972, he simultaneously functioned as a successful businessman and holder of a number of organizational leadership positions and political offices in the state, city, and country. He began publishing the *Crusador Newspaper* in 1961 and continued to publish it for decades. He served as organizer and president of the Atlanta chapter of the SCLC from 1967 to 1969, as SCLC national executive director from 1969 to 1971, and as regional vice president from 1970 to 1971. His business experience includes the presidency of Kingwell Chemical Corporation (1975-1976) and founding Southeastern Chemi-

cal Manufacturing and Distribution Corporation in 1976. He was elected as representative to the Georgia state legislature in 1974. After his tenure as representative, he was elected to the Atlanta City Council. Later, he was elected to the De Kaib County Commission. Williams claims to be an independent but runs in elections as a Democrat because of African American preference for that party. In 1980, he served as an adviser to Ronald Reagan.

Williams, Joe (b. Dec. 12, 1918, Cordele, Ga.): Singer. Williams is best known for his years with the Count BASIE band (1954-1961). His first Basie recording session resulted in the hit, "All Right, Okay, You Win" (1955). His album *Nothin' but the Blues* won a Grammy Award in 1984.

Vocalist Joe Williams won a Grammy Award in 1984 for his album Nothin' but the Blues. *(AP/Wide World Photos)*

Williams, John Alfred (b. Dec. 5, 1925, Jackson, Miss.): Novelist, journalist, social critic, and educator. In his early career, Williams wrote for several newspapers, including *The National Leader*, *Progressive Herald*, *The Age*, and *The Defender*, and worked for *Newsweek* magazine as a correspondent in Africa (1964-1965). Previously, he had written for *Ebony* and *Jet* as a correspondent based in Spain (1958-1959). In 1961, Williams was awarded a fellowship by the American Academy of Arts and Letters, but the fellowship was rejected by the American Academy in Rome in what many observers at the time believed was an act of blatant racial discrimination. Williams later traveled extensively in Africa. In addition to his journalistic work there for *Newsweek*, he published a nonfiction book entitled *Africa: Her History, Lands, and People* (1962). Williams has also written *The King God Didn't Save: Reflections on the Life and Death of Martin Luther King, Jr.* (1970). He served the Black Academy of Arts and Letters as director in the early 1970's. He has taught English and creative writing at several prestigious American universities, including Rutgers, whose faculty he joined in 1979.

Williams is best known as a novelist, and has written several complex and highly regarded novels. Beginning with his first novel, *The Angry Ones* (1961), he followed with *Night Song* (1961), *Sissie* (1963), *The Man Who Cried I Am* (1967), *Sons of Darkness, Sons of Light* (1969), *CAPTAIN BLACKMAN* (1972), *Mothersill and the Foxes* (1975), *The Junior Bachelor Society* (1976), *!Click Song* (1982), and *Jacob's Ladder* (1987).

His novels directly confront both racial and class tensions in American society. Williams has, in several interviews, compared his style and artistic design to the patterns of jazz music. In his fiction, he experiments with the motions of time, multiple voices, and variations of form. Additionally, many of Williams' works deal with the challenges his African American characters face in reconciling the legacy of collective African American history with their own experience as individuals in American society. In this sense, his novels critique the dynamics of American culture as well as particular aspects of African American experience.

Williams, Mary Lou (Mary Elfrieda Scruggs; May 8, 1910, Atlanta, Ga.—May 28, 1981, Durham, N.C.): Jazz pianist and composer. Williams was one of the first African American female jazz pianists, composers, and arrangers to achieve national recognition. In the later stages of her career, she composed and performed pieces which were inspired by her religious faith. Although she was born in the South, she was reared in Pittsburgh, Pa., having been part of a family that included her stepfather, whose last name, Burley, Williams assumed in her youth. Her professional career developed rapidly, and by 1925 she was performing with John Williams, whom she married.

Williams' recognition as a pianist during a time when most ensembles contained only male instrumentalists was highlighted by her joining, in 1930, the Andy Kirk ensemble, which became known as Andy Kirk and the TWELVE CLOUDS OF JOY. Williams eventually served as both arranger and pianist for the ensemble during the 1930's. Williams' skills as an arranger were also evident in her writing for the orchestras of Benny Goodman, Earl

HINES, and Duke ELLINGTON. In 1942, Williams formed her own ensemble, which included Shorty Baker. As part of the emerging bop movement, Williams was associated with Dizzy GILLESPIE, for whom she also wrote arrangements. Her international reputation was furthered by a two-year European tour beginning in 1952.

Jazz pianist and composer Mary Lou Williams wrote music for Dizzy Gillespie, Duke Ellington, Benny Goodman, and other greats. (AP/Wide World Photos)

A major transition occurred in Williams' professional career in the mid-1950's, when she embarked on religiously inspired activities. She reemerged in the 1970's, working in her later years as a soloist or in trio format, performing both ragtime and avant-garde music. One of the culminating recordings of her career was *The History of Jazz* (1970), which contained solo piano work as well as narrative history. She became artist-in-residence at Duke University in 1977. Among her noted recordings as a leader are "Zodiac Suite" (1945), "In London" (1953), "Black Christ of the Andes" (1963), and "My Mama Pinned a Rose on Me" (1977).

Williams, Paul Revere (Feb. 1894, Los Angeles, Calif.—Jan. 23, 1980, Los Angeles, Calif.): Architect. Williams won a Spingarn Medal in 1953 for his contributions as an architect and designer. He designed homes for such celebrities as Frank Sinatra, Lon Chaney, and Julie London as well as a Young Men's Christian Association building in Los Angeles and several fraternity and sorority houses at UCLA.

Williams, Robert Franklin (b. 1925): Political activist. Williams became one of the most notorious figures of the CIVIL RIGHTS movement of the 1960's. Williams was the president of the NATIONAL ASSOCIATION FOR THE ADVANCEMENT OF COLORED PEOPLE (NAACP) chapter in Monroe, N.C., in the late 1950's. The NAACP was hated by southern white racists and was the target of numerous acts of racial harassment and terror. Williams' chapter was no exception; what he did about this harassment was exceptional, though.

Williams organized a rifle club of fifty black men and drilled them in self-defense tactics. The group violently repelled a KU KLUX KLAN attack on the home of a local NAACP official. Williams then called on other southern NAACP chapters threatened by racial terrorists to emulate his chapter by forming gun clubs. Williams' actions disconcerted the national office of the NAACP, and at the annual convention of the NAACP in 1959, Williams and his chapter were expelled.

For the next few years, Williams spoke out in favor of armed resistance to southern racism. In 1962, he published *Negroes with Guns*, which outlined his strategy of using armed force to achieve racial equality. That year, he fled the country to escape prosecution on charges of kidnapping. Traveling to Cuba and then to China, Williams continued to advocate armed revolution as a way for African Americans to achieve freedom in the United States.

Williams, Stanley R. "Fess" (Apr. 10, 1894, Danville, Ky.—Dec. 17, 1975, New York, N.Y.): Jazz clarinetist and bandleader. After graduation from TUSKEGEE INSTITUTE in 1914, he taught music for several years in Kentucky public schools, where he received his nickname, an abbreviation of "professor." From 1919 to the mid-1940's, Williams regularly led dance bands. His Royal Flush Orchestra played long engagements in New York City's Harlem neighborhood and attracted a national following through recordings, tours, and radio broadcasts.

Williams, Vanessa (b. Mar. 18, 1963, Millwood, N.Y.): Former Miss America. Williams was the first African American to win the title of Miss America, in 1983. She

Vanessa Williams was the first African American to win the title Miss America. (AP/Wide World Photos)

relinquished the title on July 23, 1984, after the publisher of *Penthouse* magazine revealed that he would print nude photos of her in the September issue. Suzette Charles served the remaining months of Williams' term as Miss America. Williams went on to launch a successful singing and acting career.

Williams, Vesta: Pop vocalist. Williams records on the A&M Records label. Her 1986 album *Vesta* contained the hit single "Once Bitten Twice Shy," and her follow-up album, *Special* (1991), was a best-seller. Williams is active in charitable causes, and in 1991 she served as honorary chairperson of the NATIONAL ASSOCIATION FOR THE ADVANCEMENT OF COLORED PEOPLE (NAACP) Radio-thon.

Williams, Wayne Bertram (b. May 27, 1958): Accused serial killer. On June 28, 1981, Williams, an African American, was arrested for the murder of two young men, Jimmy Ray Payne and Nathaniel Cater. Williams was soon linked to an unsolved series of murders of twenty-eight African American children in Atlanta, Ga., between July, 1979, and 1981. He was tried and sentenced to two consecutive life sentences in prison for the murder of Payne and Cater. Evidence presented at his trial also suggested that he was guilty of the slaying of the twenty-eight children.

President Ronald Reagan had committed $1.5 million in federal funds as well as scores of Federal Bureau of Investigation agents to solving what were known as the "Atlanta Child Murder Cases." Boxer Muhammad ALI pledged $400,000, and hundreds of thousands of dollars were raised from other sources, including benefit concerts. Although he was not convicted of the child murder cases, Williams is widely believed to have been guilty of them and to be the first major African American serial killer.

African American author James BALDWIN wrote a book dealing with Williams' case entitled *The Evidence of Things Not Seen* (1985). He discovered many irregularities in Williams' trial and was not convinced that Williams was guilty of the child murders. The murders, however, stopped after Williams was arrested.

Williamson, Fred (b. Mar. 5, 1938, Gary, Ind.): Actor, director, and producer. Williamson is best known for his starring roles as the hero of action movies during the BLAXPLOITATION era of the 1970's. His athletic talents earned him a track scholarship to Northwestern University. He majored in architectural engineering while participating in track and field events and playing flanker on the football team. After graduation, in 1959, he signed a professional football contract with the San Francisco 49ers. During his football career, he played as a defensive back and earned the nickname of "The Hammer" for the way he tackled his opponents. After playing for three other teams in addition to the 49ers, Williamson retired from football in 1968.

Williamson decided to go into show business and obtained the role of Steve Bruce, one of Diahann CARROLL's suitors in the television series *JULIA* (1970-1971). In 1970, he also played small roles in the films *M*A*S*H* and *Tell Me That You Love Me, Junie Moon* before his first starring roles as the title characters in *Hammer* (1972) and *The Legend of Nigger Charley* (1972). In these and such films as *Black Caesar* (1973), *Black Eye* (1974), *Three the Hard Way* (1974), and *Bucktown* (1975), Williamson cultivated an image as a confident, sexy, and indestructible black man.

Fred Williamson starred in many television and film productions after retiring from professional football. (AP/Wide World Photos)

By the mid-1970's, Williamson had formed his own production company, Po' Boy Productions, which afforded him the opportunity to produce and direct while, at times, writing and starring in his own films. These included *Adios Amigo* (1975), *No Way Back* (1976), *Mr. Mean* (1978), and *One Down, Two to Go* (1983), the last of which starred Williamson and three other action heroes of the 1970's, Jim Kelly, Richard ROUNDTREE, and Jim Brown.

Williamson appeared in guest spots on television throughout the 1970's and 1980's in such shows as *The Rookies* (1974) *Fantasy Island* (1980), *Lou Grant* (1981), and *The Equalizer* (1986). In 1974, he served briefly as a commentator for *NFL Monday Night Football*.

Williamson, John Lee "Sonny Boy" (Mar. 30, 1914, Jackson, Tenn.—June 1, 1948, Chicago, Ill.): Blues harmonica player. Williamson learned the harmonica as a child and left home in 1929 to join a jug band comprised of James "Yank" Rachel (mandolin), Sleepy John Estes (guitar), John "Homesick James" Williamson (fiddle), and Hammie Nixon (harmonica and jug). Over the next year, the five traveled throughout western Tennessee and into eastern Arkansas, playing at taverns, juke joints, picnics, and parties. Thereafter, Williamson gravitated to Memphis, Tenn., where he spent the next few years working local clubs with Sunnyland Slim and with Yank Rachel.

Blues harmonica player Sonny Boy Williamson perfected the Chicago sound with his band. (AP/Wide World Photos)

In 1937, Williamson married his childhood sweetheart, Lacey Belle, who collaborated with him on many of his songs. The couple then relocated to Chicago, Ill., where

Williamson began to play local clubs and started a five-year recording stint with Lester Melrose's Bluebird label. Musicians on these sessions—which produced such blues classics as "Good Morning, Little Schoolgirl" and "Stop Breakin' Down"—included guitarists Big Joe Williams and Big Bill BROONZY, Robert Nighthawk on bass, and at least in one instance, Yank Rachel. An innovative musician, Williamson experimented with the traditional string band sound by adding a piano player. he then further expanded his rhythm section by including drums and two more bass players. What resulted was a richer sound, with a decidedly more forceful backbeat. In essence, Williamson was transforming the rural blues into an urban idiom. Williamson's recording career was interrupted by World War II. The shellac used to make records was rationed, and commercial recordings were banned from 1942 until 1944.

In the last years of his life, Williamson perfected the CHICAGO BLUES sound. In 1946, he added electric guitarist Willie Lacie to a band that included himself on harmonica and lead vocals, Eddie Boyd on piano, Ransome Knowling on bass, and Judge Riley on percussion. This popular group played the local clubs and recorded for the Victor label.

In the early morning hours of June 1, 1948, Williamson was attacked and severely beaten by muggers after leaving Chicago's Plantation Club after a playing date. He died of a fractured skull.

Williamson, Sonny Boy, II (Aleck Ford, later Rice Miller; Dec. 5, 1899, Glendora, Miss.—May 25, 1965, Helena, Ark.): Blues musician. Also known as Willie Miller, Willie Williams, "Sib," and " Little Boy Blue," Sonny Boy Williamson II was born Aleck Ford, the illegitimate son of Millie Ford. He later assumed his stepfather's surname, Miller, and the nickname "Rice." Self-taught on the harmonica at a very young age, he left home in his early twenties to wander the Mississippi delta region as an itinerant blues musician.

In the early 1930's, Rice Miller transformed himself into a "one-man band" by adding drums and a zoothorn to his performance. He worked carnivals, dance halls, ball parks, and lumber camps from Missouri to Arkansas. In the latter part of the decade, Miller returned to the harmonica and vocals and teamed up with such blues legends as Arthur "Big Boy" CRUDUP, Elmore JAMES, HOWLIN' WOLF, and Robert JOHNSON to play juke joints throughout the South.

In 1941, his career took a decisive turn when he and Robert Lockwood, Jr., were hired to appear regularly on "King Biscuit Time," an afternoon radio show broadcast daily on KFFA in Helena, Ark. It was probably for the show that Miller adopted the name "Sonny Boy Williamson," even though John Lee WILLIAMSON, a Chicago-based blues harmonica player, was already using that name. The show, which ran throughout the war years, made Sonny Boy Williamson II famous throughout the delta region.

Williamson married Mattie Jones in 1948. The couple lived in Little Rock, Ark., and later in Belzoni, Miss. In 1951, he made his first recordings, for the Trumpet label in Jackson, Miss. Among them were such classics as "Eyesight to the Blind" (later recorded by the Who on the album *Tommy*), "Mighty Long Time," "Pontiac Blues," and "Nine Below Zero."

In 1955, Williamson and his wife moved north to settle in Milwaukee, Wis. He began an eight-year recording stint for the Checker-Chess label and played club dates in East St. Louis, Chicago, and Milwaukee during this period. The last phase of his life began in 1963, when he was invited to tour Europe with the American Folk Blues Festival. In 1964, after a long succession of playing dates in England and on the continent, Williamson returned to the United States as an international celebrity.

Willie, Charles Vert (b. Oct. 8, 1927, Dallas, Tex.): Researcher, writer, and social scientist. Willie was graduated from Morehouse College in 1948. He received a master's degree from Atlanta University in 1949 and a doctorate from Syracuse University in 1957. He began teaching at the State University of New York, Upstate Medical Center, followed by appointments at Harvard Medical School, Syracuse University, and Harvard University's graduate school of education. He has taught in various fields, primarily sociology, education, and urban studies.

A noted writer, Willie has authored or edited more than a dozen books, including *The Family Life of Black People* (1970); *Black Students at White Colleges* (1972); *A New Look at Black Families* (1976); *Five Black Scholars: An Analysis of Family Life, Education, and Career* (1986); *African Americans and the Doctoral Experience: Implications for Policy* (1991 with Michael Grady and Richard Hope), and *The Education of African Americans* (1990 with Antoine Garibaldi and Wornie Reed).

Willie has researched the educational system and its impact on students at every level, from elementary to graduate. Recognizing that the philosophy of black colleges is to emphasize and legitimate public and community service, he noted the benefits this philosophy has brought to African American students. He further advocated this kind of education for white students, so that they could liberate themselves from a sense of racial superiority and the need always to be in the majority.

In *Five Black Scholars: An Analysis of Family Life, Education, and Career*, Willie explores the backgrounds and lives of five noted scholars in an effort to determine how they achieved eminence. He found that the education, career, and family systems were interrelated and contributed to achievement in each area. Willie's groundbreaking writings on the African American family provided evidence of previously unexplored characteristics that offered a better understanding of it. He provided comparisons of adaptations made by different social classes which revealed both strengths and weaknesses that are associated with status levels.

Willie has received several honorary degrees and numerous awards. He is past president of the Eastern Sociological Society, served on the executive committee of the Social Science Research Council, and was a fellow of the American Sociological Society. He served on the National Advisory Committee of the Maxwell School of Citizenship and Public Affairs, Syracuse University, and hosted *Inner City*, a weekly public affairs television program. He has contributed to numerous publications, including the *American Sociological Review*, *American Journal of Public Health*, *Journal of Negro Education*, and *Psychology Today*. He has served on several government commissions and was master of the Boston, Mass., school desegregation case in the federal district court in 1975.

Wills, Frank: Security guard. Wills was working as a security guard at the Watergate office complex in June, 1972, when he detained a group of men who were installing surveillance equipment in the offices occupied by the Democratic Party National Headquarters. Wills summoned the Washington, D.C., police, who arrested the intruders. In 1974, the SOUTHERN CHRISTIAN LEADERSHIP CONFERENCE honored Wills with the Martin Luther KING, JR., Award for his role in uncovering the break-in.

Wills, Harry (May 15, 1892, New Orleans, La.—Dec. 21, 1958, New York, N.Y.): Boxer. Nicknamed "The Brown Panther" because of his grace, Wills was one of the top heavyweight contenders through much of the 1920's. Racism prevented him from fighting Jack Dempsey, as promoters feared the repercussions should Wills defeat the white Dempsey. Wills retired in 1932 after losing only 8 of 102 official fights. He was elected to *Ring*'s Boxing Hall of Fame in 1970.

Wills, Maurice Morning "Maury" (b. Oct. 2, 1932, Washington, D.C.): Baseball player. Wills revolutionized baseball through his revival of the stolen base as an offensive weapon. An All-Star shortstop for the Los Angeles Dodgers for five years in the 1960's, he set the single-season record for stolen bases with 104 in 1962 and led the National League in stolen bases for six consecutive seasons. Wills was voted the Most Valuable Player for the National League in 1962.

Wilson, August (b. Apr. 27, 1945, Pittsburgh, Pa.): Playwright. One of six children, Wilson dropped out of school in the ninth grade. He educated himself and began writing poetry as he worked at odd jobs. During the 1960's, Wilson involved himself in the BLACK ARTS MOVEMENT, and in 1968, he founded the Black Horizon Theatre, where he directed and produced plays. In 1978, he moved to St. Paul, Minn., where he saw some of his own plays performed. The quality of *MA RAINEY'S BLACK BOTTOM* (pr. 1984) led to an invitation to participate in the Eugene O'Neill National Playwrights Conference at Yale Univer-

sity. Subsequently, the Yale Repertory Theater produced both *Ma Rainey's Black Bottom* and *FENCES* (1985).

Ma Rainey's Black Bottom, regarded as the best play of 1986 by the Drama Critics Circle, is set in a Chicago recording studio in the 1920's and focuses on the legendary blues singer and her band as they resist attempts by the recording industry to exploit their talent. *Fences* is the story of the strong-willed Troy Maxson, who swallows his disappointment over his thwarted baseball career and accepts responsibility for his family in an urban neighborhood of the 1950's. It won the Pulitzer Prize for drama in 1987. It also won four Tony Awards, including one for James Earl JONES, who played Troy. Wilson's other important plays include *JOE TURNER'S COME AND GONE* (pr. 1986) and *THE PIANO LESSON* (pr. 1988).

Wilson has called writing a play "walking down the landscape of the self, unattended, unadorned." At the same time, he believed that as an African American playwright, he was "a representative of a culture and the

Playwright August Wilson discusses his Broadway play Ma Rainey's Black Bottom. (AP/Wide World Photos)

carrier of some very valuable antecedents." Aided by the black cultural nationalism articulated by Amiri BARAKA and Larry NEAL in the 1960's, he developed a blues aesthetic. Like them, he committed himself to reclaiming black culture and strengthening it. His plays embody the central symbols and history of African Americans, from Ma RAINEY's blues to Troy Maxson's legendary baseball playing ability. Mixed with the bitterness of oppression is the joy of accomplishment and cultural self-assertion.

Wilson, Clerow "Flip" (b. Dec. 8, 1933, Jersey City, N.J.): Comedian. Perhaps the most visible black comic of the 1970's, Wilson grew up in disadvantaged surroundings. He was tenth in a family of twenty-four children, eighteen of whom survived. He struggled to get out of his poverty, running away several times. His talents were first discovered while he served in the Air Force from 1950 to 1954. After the Air Force, he struggled to make

ends meet until opportunity struck in 1959, when a Miami businessman gave him $50 a week for one year. This enabled him to focus on his career and develop his style without having to struggle quite so hard.

Wilson went on to be a regular at the APOLLO THEATER for a number of years. In 1965, he began appearing on *The Tonight Show*, speeding his ascent into the top echelons of comedy. With THE FLIP WILSON SHOW, he became the first African American after Nat "King" COLE to have a weekly prime-time television show with his own name. The show, which ran on NBC from 1970 to 1974, spawned his famous character Geraldine and garnered Wilson an Emmy in 1971. He appeared on the Jan. 31, 1972 cover of *Time*, and in 1976 he made his television dramatic debut on the ABC series *The Six Million Dollar Man*. He hosted the show *People Are Funny* in 1984 and had the title role in the series CHARLIE AND CO. in 1985 and 1986. He has appeared in several films, including UPTOWN

Flip Wilson accepts a Peabody Award for his 1971 television comedy show. (AP/Wide World Photos)

SATURDAY NIGHT (1974), *Skatetown, U.S.A.* (1979), and *The Fish That Saved Pittsburgh* (1979). Wilson also has recorded his comedy on records, releasing *Cowboys and Colored People* in 1967, *Flippin'* in 1968, and *Flip Wilson, You Devil, You* in 1968. A past national president of the American Cancer Society, he spends much of his time doing nightclub acts and television specials.

Wilson, Demond (b. Oct. 13, 1946, Valdosta, Ga.): Actor and evangelist. Best known for his role as Lamont on the television series *SANFORD AND SON*, costarring Redd FOXX, from 1972 to 1977; he also starred in *THE NEW ODD COUPLE* from 1982 to 1983. Wilson's theater credits include his acting debut in *GREEN PASTURES* in 1951 and *Five on the Black Hand Side* in 1970. He became an evangelist in Southern California.

Wilson, Ellis (b. 1899, Mayfield, Ky.): Painter. Wilson attended the Art Institute of Chicago. He has been awarded the Charles S. Peterson Prize for Fine Arts, for an African poster, and a Guggenheim Fellowship (1944). His work is represented in many museums and private collections, including the Schomburg Collection of the New York Public Library.

Wilson, Jack "Jackie" (Jan. 17, 1918, Spencer, N.C.— Mar. 10, 1956): Boxer. Wilson retired from amateur BOXING with only one defeat in fifty-one bouts. That defeat came in the finals of the 1936 Olympics, where he came away with a silver medal in bantamweight competition. During his thirteen-year professional career, Wilson never competed for a championship, but he fought such boxing greats as Ray Robinson and Jake LaMotta. He retired in 1949 with a professional record of 69 wins, 19 losses, and 5 draws.

Wilson, Jackie (June 9, 1934, Detroit, Mich.—Jan. 21, 1984, Mount Holly, N.J.): Singer nicknamed "Mr. Excitement," Wilson played a major role in the continuing development of rhythm and blues and pop music in the 1950's and 1960's. As a child, Wilson had shown promise as a boxer, winning the eighteen-year-old division of the Golden Gloves competition at age sixteen, but his mother discovered his avocation and encouraged him to change directions.

Wilson started his musical career after high school with a vocal group called the Royals, a group that evolved into Hank Ballard and the Midnighters and which also featured Levi Stubbs, who would later perform with the FOUR TOPS. In 1953, when Clyde McPHATTER left the DOMINOES, Wilson was asked to take his place. Wilson stayed with

the Dominoes until his first solo recording, "Reet Petite," cowritten by Berry GORDY, Jr., was released in 1957 on the Brunswick label. Wilson's next four singles, "Lonely Teardrops," "That's Why (I Love You So)," "I'll Be Satisfied," and "Talk That Talk," all cowritten by Gordy, appeared on *Billboard's* top-forty song charts.

Wilson's big breakthrough occurred in 1960, when "Doggin' Around" (backed by a successful B side, "Night") and "A Woman, A Lover, A Friend" both spent time at number one on the *Billboard* rhythm-and-blues charts. His success was halted temporarily in 1961, however, when he was shot accidentally by a female fan who

Singer Jackie Wilson appeared on the pop charts for many years. (AP/Wide World Photos)

actually was attempting to shoot herself.

After he recovered from his wounds, Wilson made further ventures into both the RHYTHM-AND-BLUES and the pop charts throughout much of the 1960's. These songs included the top-ten single "Alone at Last" and the top-forty release "Am I the Man." After 1968, he appeared only on the rhythm-and-blues charts, but he could boast of fifty-four national hits.

Through the early 1970's, Wilson was still very much in demand as a concert artist, even though his chart success had waned significantly. In 1975, however, while performing at the Latin Casino in Cherry Hill, N.J., Wilson suffered a debilitating heart attack which left him hospitalized until his death. He was elected to the Rock and Roll Hall of Fame in 1987.

Wilson, John (b. Apr. 14, 1922, Boston, Mass.): Painter, printmaker, illustrator, and educator. Wilson attended the Boston Museum School, Fernand Leger's school in Paris, France, the Institute Politécnico in Mexico City, Mexico, and others. He earned a B.S. in education at Tufts University in 1947 and has taught at the Boston Museum School and Boston University, among other schools. His work, which has won numerous prizes, is represented in many collections in the United States and abroad, including those held by the Bezalel Museum in Jerusalem and by the department of fine arts of the French government.

Wilson, Lance Henry (b. July 5, 1948, New York, N.Y.): Political appointee and attorney. Wilson attended Hunter College in New York and was graduated with his A.B. degree in 1969. He entered law school at the University of Pennsylvania and received his J.D. degree in 1972. After passing the bar, Wilson worked as an attorney with the law firm of Mudge, Rose, Guthrie, and Alexander from 1972 to 1977. He left the firm to work as an associate counsel for the Equitable Life Assurance Company until 1981. Wilson's first political appointment came in 1981, when President Ronald Reagan appointed him to serve as executive assistant to Secretary Samuel R. Pierce, Jr., of the Department of Housing and Urban Development (HUD). While in office, Wilson received leadership awards from the New York State Council of Black Republicans and the National Black Republican Council. Wilson also received the Secretary's Award for Excellence in 1984 for his work at HUD. Wilson held his post until 1984, when he left to serve as president of the New York City Housing Development Corporation. Before stepping down as president, Wilson was the recipient of a Private Sector Initiative Commendation from President Ronald Reagan in 1986. Wilson left the post as president to accept a corporate position as first vice president of Paine Webber, Inc., in New York City.

Wilson, Lionel J. (b. Mar. 14, 1915, New Orleans, La.): Mayor of Oakland, Calif. Although born in New Orleans, Wilson moved to Oakland with his family when he was four years old. The oldest of eight children, Wilson was

In the aftermath of the 1989 Loma Prieta earthquake, Oakland mayor Lionel Wilson reports that rescuers have found a man in a collapsed section of the freeway. (AP/Wide World Photos)

graduated from high school in Oakland and attended the University of California at Berkeley. He received his bachelor of arts degree in economics in 1939. Wilson served in the U.S. Army overseas during World War II, reaching the rank of first sergeant by war's end. Wilson received his discharge in 1945 and earned a law degree from Hastings College of Law in 1949. Upon graduation, he entered private practice and worked as an attorney in Oakland from 1950 to 1960.

Governor Edmund "Pat" Brown appointed Wilson to the Oakland Piedmont Municipal Court in 1960, making him the first African American judge to preside in Alameda County. Governor Brown later appointed him to the Superior Court, in 1964. Wilson became presiding judge of the Alameda County Superior Court in 1973 and was elected as mayor of Oakland in 1977, becoming the first African American mayor of Oakland. Governor Jerry Brown appointed him to the California State COMPREHEN-SIVE EMPLOYMENT TRAINING ACT Board. Wilson was reelected as mayor of Oakland in 1981 and served until 1990. Wilson served on various committees of the U.S. Conference of Mayors and on the board of directors of the League of California Cities. During his tenure as mayor, Wilson was appointed by President Jimmy Carter to serve on the U.S. Committee on the Selection of Federal Judicial Officers for the U.S. Court of Patents and Appeals.

Wilson, Margaret Bush (b. Jan. 30, 1919, St. Louis, Mo.): Civil rights leader. Wilson was the first African American woman to be named as national chair of the NATIONAL ASSOCIATION FOR THE ADVANCEMENT OF COLORED PEOPLE (NAACP), in 1975. She previously had served as the first female president of the St. Louis NAACP branch and on the national NAACP board of directors. Wilson was active in civil rights throughout her professional life as a lawyer in St. Louis, Mo., where she had a private practice for eighteen years and worked with a law firm. She served with numerous community organizations, including the St. Louis Model City Agency, the Missouri Council on Criminal Justice, and St. Louis Lawyers for Housing.

Wilson, Mary (b. Mar. 6, 1944, Greenville, Miss.): Singer. Wilson was reared in the Brewster-Douglass housing projects in Detroit, Mich., after 1955. She was one-third of one of history's most successful vocal groups, the Supremes. Wilson and her childhood friend Florence Ballard had been singing together since they first met in the Brewster-Douglass projects while both were in elementary school. They once performed the

FRANKIE LYMON AND THE TEENAGERS tune "I'm Not a Juvenile Delinquent" for a school talent show. By the time they were teenagers, they were part of an all-female vocal group called the Primettes, the female counterparts to the Primes, which consisted of future TEMPTATIONS Eddie KENDRICKS and Paul Williams. After one of the members of the Primettes left the group and was replaced by Diana ROSS, also of Brewster-Douglass, the group destined to become the SUPREMES was synthesized.

While still in high school, the Primettes were signed to the Lupine label, where they sang backing for, among others, singers Eddie Floyd and the then-unknown Wilson PICKETT. They released their own single, "Pretty Baby," which saw limited success. Shortly thereafter, the Primettes, now a trio, were signed by Berry GORDY, Jr., to his fledgling Motown label. They were renamed as the Supremes at that time.

Once it became evident that Gordy's objective was to focus the group around Diana Ross, Wilson reluctantly accepted her role as backup singer by justifying it as vital. She did, however, express her dismay at what she believed to be the shallow and sophomoric material provided to the group by Gordy's writers. The Supremes enjoyed a phenomenal run of successful recording and performance ventures, and, along with the FOUR TOPS and the Temptations, they helped elevate Motown Records from the status of fledgling independent to that of successful label.

Through her willingness to compromise, Wilson became the group's spiritual leader, staying with the group long after Ballard's firing and subsequent death and Ross's departure for a solo career. After the group officially disbanded, Wilson toured with Ballard's replacement, Cindy Birdsong, as a Supremes-type act, often resorting to the name "Mary Wilson and Cindy Birdsong of the Supremes" for promoting their shows as a way of circumventing Motown's burdensome restrictions over the group's rights and controls.

In 1977, Wilson sued Motown for its unwillingness to release her from the management contract she had signed as a teenager in 1961. She was awarded half of the rights to the Supremes' revenue but was barred from using the group's name in subsequent appearances. In 1990, Wilson (with coauthor Patricia Romanowski) published her account of the Supremes' legacy, an often unflattering behind-the-scenes look at the group and the Motown empire entitled *Supreme Faith: Someday We'll Be Together*.

Wilson, Nancy (b. Feb. 20, 1937, Chillicothe, Ohio): Jazz singer. Discovered by bandleader and saxophonist

Julian "Cannonball" ADDERLEY during a scheduled performance in 1959 in Columbus, Ohio, Wilson subsequently was signed by Capitol Records. Capitol released her first hit record, "Guess Who I Saw Yesterday," shortly thereafter. With an amazing string of recordings and performances since the late 1950's, Wilson, along with her husband and manager, Kenny Dennis, also heads Wil-Den Enterprises, an organization that manages and publishes the works of a variety of entertainers in various media.

Wilson, Olly (b. Sept. 7, 1937, St. Louis, Mo.): Composer. In 1968, Wilson's electronic music composition *Cetus* (1967) won first prize in the first International Electronic Music Competition. In 1970, he became a professor at the University of California at Berkeley. His major works include *Structure for Orchestra* (1960), *Sextet* (1963), *In Memoriam—Martin Luther King, Jr.* (1969), *Voices* (1970), and *Akwan* (1974).

Wilson, Shanice (b. 1973): Pop vocalist. Wilson grew up in Southern California. Her precocious RHYTHM-AND-BLUES singing style brought her to the attention of A&M Records, which signed her to her first recording contract at the age of fourteen. Her debut album, *Discovery*, was praised by critics but failed to achieve commercial success because of management controversies at A&M. Wilson left A&M to sign with Motown Records. Her second album, *Inner Child* (1991), was produced by Narada Michael Walden, who had produced records for Aretha FRANKLIN and Whitney HOUSTON. Wilson cowrote eight songs on the album, mostly with Walden.

Wilson, Theodore Shaw "Teddy" (Nov. 24, 1912, Austin, Tex.—July 31, 1986, New Britain, Conn.): Pianist. Wilson was a major swing-era pianist. His early years were spent in Tuskegee, Ala., where he studied violin and piano. He later pursued music studies at Talladega College in Alabama. In 1929, Wilson migrated to

Jazz pianist Teddy Wilson performs during his daily radio broadcast in 1950. (AP/Wide World Photos)

Detroit, Mich., to perform in local bands. He later joined the Milton Senior band in Toledo, Ohio. Wilson migrated to Chicago, and between 1931 and 1933 he performed with Jimmie NOONE, Louis ARMSTRONG, and Erskine Tate. Wilson's move to New York in 1933 to join the Benny CARTER band led to Wilson's recognition for his performances on *Once Upon a Time* and *Blue Interlude* (1933), recordings by the Chocolate Dandies. With Carter, Wilson also recorded *Symphony in Riffs* (1933).

After a year-long association with Willie Bryant's band in 1934, Wilson was part of the integration of jazz bands when he joined the Benny Goodman Trio. He stayed with Goodman's band from 1935 to 1939. With Goodman, Wilson recorded *Body and Soul* (1935) and *Sweet Sue, Just You* (1936). In the 1930's, Wilson's solo releases included *Liza* (1935) and *Between the Devil and the Deep Blue Sea* (1937). Wilson, who won the *Down Beat* poll from 1936 to 1938, performed and recorded with Lester YOUNG and Billie HOLIDAY and briefly led his own big band, for which he composed and arranged, at the close of the 1930's. He appeared in the film *Hollywood Hotel* in 1938. His collaboration with Billie Holiday led to the recording *Jim* (1941).

During the 1940's, Wilson often was heard in sextet format at Cafe Society. In 1945, the year he received the Esquire Gold Award, Wilson appeared with Benny Goodman in the Broadway production *The Seven Lively Arts* (1945). Wilson taught a summer course at Juilliard from 1945 to 1952 and played in concert in Europe in 1952 and 1953. He appeared at the Brussels World Fair in 1958 and in the film *The Benny Goodman Story* (1955). His recordings include *Pres and Teddy* (1956 with Lester Young), *Three Little Words* (1976), *With Billie in Mind* (1972), *Striding After Fats* (1974), and *Cole Porter Classics* (1977).

Wilson, William Julius (b. Dec. 20, 1935, Derry Township, Pa.): Sociologist. Wilson taught at the University of Massachusetts at Amherst (1965-1971) and at the University of Chicago beginning in 1971. He became chair of that university's department of sociology in 1981. His *The Declining Significance of Race: Blacks and Changing American Institutions* (1979) postulated a wider gap for African Americans between the middle and lower class than existed between African Americans and whites as a whole.

Wiltshire, George: Comedian. He is known for his work as a straight man for other comedians from the 1920's through the 1950's. In the early 1920's, he received his initial training as a member of the Sandy Burns stock company at the Standard Theater in Philadelphia, Pa. In 1926, he performed in Noble SISSLE and Eubie BLAKE's musical *SHUFFLE ALONG*. Wiltshire's most fruitful partnership was with comedian Dewey "Pigmeat" MARKHAM. The team played the Alhambra Theater in the late 1920's and the APOLLO THEATER beginning in the 1930's. Wiltshire and Markham were featured with singer Edith Wilson in the Broadway cast of *Hot Rhythm* (1930).

Winans, Benjamin "BeBe" and Cecelia "CeCe": Gospel singers. Part of the enormously talented gospel-singing WINANS clan, BeBe and CeCe often sing separately from the rest of the family during the lengthy Winans shows. Known for their soulful, sophisticated style, the duo often produces the most spine-tingling portions of the shows. CeCe's powerful voice is considered to be one of the best in the music business, both gospel and secular.

Winans, The: Gospel singing group. Twins Marvin and Carvin and their brothers Michael and Ronald were initiated into gospel music apprenticing in church choirs in their hometown of Detroit, Mich. Gospel legend Andrae CROUCH helped them to record their first single, the hit "The Quest Is." The quartet then recorded a number of albums for the gospel label Light records including the Grammy-nominated *Introducing the Winans, Tomorrow*, and *Long Time Comin'*. The brothers signed with producer Quincy JONES's label Qwest records in 1984 and burst into national prominence with *Let My People Go*, the 1985 Grammy Award-winning recording in the Best Gospel Album category.

Winbush, Angela (b. 195?): Pop vocalist, songwriter, and producer. Winbush's four-octave soprano range was much in demand after she received attention as a singer on Stevie WONDER's hit album *Songs in the Key of Life* (1976). While pursuing a solo career as a vocalist, she used her connections in the music business to carve out another career as a music producer. As a testament to her success, Winbush has written, arranged, and produced songs for stars such as the ISLEY BROTHERS, Stephanie MILLS, and Janet JACKSON. Winbush recorded with Polydor/Mercury records, and her solo albums include *Sharp* and *The Real Thing*. She and singer Ronald Isley, her boyfriend and personal manager, formed Angela Winbush Productions in order to promote her performing and producing talents and to help guide other young African Americans into the production side of the music business. Their production company signed a six-figure publishing deal with Warner Bros. in the early 1990's.

Winfield, David Mark "Dave" (b. Oct. 3, 1951, St. Paul, Minn.): BASEBALL player. Winfield, a versatile six-foot, six-inch athlete, starred in both baseball and BASKETBALL for the University of Minnesota and was subsequently drafted by four professional teams in three different sports. Winfield signed to play baseball with the San Diego Padres of the National League (NL), and he made his major league debut with the Padres in 1973 without playing any minor-league baseball.

Dave Winfield, a power-hitting outfielder with a tremendous throwing arm. (National Baseball Library, Cooperstown, NY)

A power-hitting outfielder with a tremendous throwing arm, Winfield was chosen to NL All-Star teams in 1977, 1978, 1979, and 1980 and earned NL Gold Glove awards in 1979 and 1980. In 1980, Winfield, a free agent, signed a ten-year contract with the New York Yankees of the American League (AL). With the Yankees, Winfield was chosen to AL All-Star teams every year from 1981 to 1988 and won AL Gold Gloves in 1982, 1983, 1984, 1985, and 1987. Winfield moved to the California Angels in 1990 and to the Toronto Blue Jays in 1991; in 1992, he helped lead the Blue Jays to the World Series title. He signed with the Minnesota Twins for the 1993 season.

Winfield, Hemsley (1907, Yonkers, N.Y.—1934): Dancer and choreographer. As the founder of the New Negro Art Theater Dance Group, Winfield brought tribal African dance forms and African American themes to the stage in a serious dance format. He made history as a pioneer of black concert dance.

Winfield began his career as an actor in the Broadway plays *Lulu Belle* (1926) and *Harlem* (1929). In 1927, he organized a group of dancers to perform in *Wade in the Water*, a play his mother had written for Greenwich Village's Cherry Lane Theater. Although he had had little dance training, Winfield later filled in for the actress playing the title role in *Salome*, performing the required "dance of the seven veils." As a result, Winfield decided to become a professional dancer. At the age of twenty-five, he formed the Negro Art Theater in Harlem. Later renamed the New Negro Art Theater Dance Group, the company consisted of eighteen members dedicated to expanding the frontiers of black dance beyond the limitations of vaudeville and musical comedy.

Billed as the "first Negro dance recital in America," the initial performance by Winfield's company was given in 1931 at the Theater in the Clouds in New York City. The program included primitive ritual numbers, dances performed to black spirituals, and Winfield's own solo, "Bronze Study." In 1932, the company danced in *Let Freedom Ring* at the Roxy Theater. In 1933, it appeared in the black musical drama *RUN LITTLE CHILLUN*.

Winfield participated in the first of a 1933 series of "forum-recitals" sponsored in Harlem by the Workers' Dance League. After his company performed dances from its repertory, he led a discussion on the purposes of African American dance. The highlights of Winfield's career was the New York Metropolitan Opera's 1933 presentation of *THE EMPEROR JONES*. Winfield danced the role of the witch doctor, becoming the first African American to appear at the Metropolitan Opera. His company took the place of the Metropolitan Opera's corps de ballet.

Winfield, Paul (b. May 22, 1940, Los Angeles, Calif.): Actor. Winfield's first screen appearance was in Stanley Kramer's daring *RPM* (1970). Since then he has had a distinguished film career that includes roles in *SOUNDER* (1972), *THE GREATEST* (1977), *A HERO AIN'T NOTHIN' BUT A SANDWICH* (1977), *Star Trek II: The Wrath of Khan* (1982), *The Serpent and the Rainbow* (1988), and *Presumed Innocent* (1990). His television credits include *The Sophisticated Gents*, *Backstairs at the Whitehouse*, *ROOTS: THE NEXT GENERATIONS* and *Roots: The Gift*, and *THE WOMEN OF BREWSTER PLACE*. In the theater, he has acted in *Enemy of the People* and *Richard III*.

Winfrey, Oprah Gail (b. Jan. 29, 1954, Kosciusko, Miss.): Television talk-show host and actress. One of the most captivating television and film personalities in the United States since the mid-1980's has been Oprah Winfrey. The first African American female to host a successful nationally syndicated weekday talk show, Winfrey was also the first African American female proprietor of a production company for film and television in the United States.

Early Childhood. Born out of wedlock, Winfrey got her name from a misspelling of the biblical name "Orpah." Her mother, Vernita Lee, was a farm girl and a housemaid, and her father, Vernon Winfrey, was a soldier who later became a council official, a Baptist deacon, a grocer, and a barber. The burden of bringing up the baby Winfrey was on her paternal grandmother, who lived on a small pig farm on the outskirts of Kosciusko.

School Days. Winfrey's elementary education was one of disruptive school changes, from Kosciusko to Milwaukee to Nashville and back to Milwaukee. Because of her intelligence, Winfrey was awarded a scholarship to attend the prestigious Nicolet High School in the suburbs of Milwaukee. Moving to Nashville, she attended East High School; her father and stepmother kept her under strict discipline in behavior, attitude, and schoolwork. They implanted in her the view that education is the key to success in life.

While maintaining excellent grades at East High School, Winfrey was voted the most popular girl in her class at age sixteen. In 1970, she was elected president of the student council of her school and was invited to Washington, D.C., to participate in the White House

Oprah Winfrey joined comedians Robin Williams, Billy Crystal, Dudley Moore and John Laroquette to promote the 1987 Comic Relief benefit concert to aid the homeless. (AP/Wide World Photos)

Winfrey later went to live with her mother and stepfather in Milwaukee. The living conditions of the family were so cramped and terrible that Winfrey, at nine years of age, was made to share her bed with a nineteen-year-old male relative. He raped her; it was the beginning of what would be a streak of sexual encounters for the next five years with trusted family members and friends. This early sexual abuse made her angry and rebellious toward her mother and the people around her. She even attempted running away from home. It was her mother's sending her away to Vernon Winfrey that saved Oprah from being institutionalized as a troubled child.

Conference on Youth. She also became a member of the drama club to develop her oratory, for which she had won an award, and her acting skills. On a trip to Hollywood, Winfrey was so impressed by the names of the performing stars she saw carved in concrete in front of Grauman's Chinese Theater that she promised her father her name would be among them some day as an actress.

With the help of an Elks Club four-year scholarship she won at a beauty contest, Winfrey attended the Tennessee State University in Nashville, a predominantly African American college. Winfrey was graduated from Tennessee State University in 1976 with a bachelor of arts degree in speech and drama.

Broadcasting Career. Winfrey's career as a broadcaster began in 1971, when, after winning a beauty contest for which she had been sponsored by a Nashville radio station, WVOL, she was invited by the station to try out for a part-time position in newscasting. She got the job. In 1973, a CBS television outlet in Nashville, WTVF-TV, offered her a position as reporter and news anchor. Winfrey was able to carry on her college studies with her exciting new job, which paid her fifteen thousand dollars a year. Not only was she the first African American television newscaster in Nashville, she was also the first female newscaster in that city.

To escape the strict discipline imposed on her by her father, Winfrey left Nashville and WTVF-TV in 1976 to become a news coanchor at the ABC affiliate WJZ-TV in Baltimore. She was not happy in Baltimore, however, and she failed to deliver the news objectively, much to the anger of the television management. Looking for ways to remove her, the station humiliated Winfrey by sending her to New York to a beautician for cosmetic improvements. Winfrey returned to Baltimore with a bald head and a shattered ego. Next, she was sent back to New York to be coached by a specialist who was to teach her how to communicate well on television. The specialist found nothing wrong with Winfrey and encouraged her to stand up for her rights.

WJZ-TV made Winfrey the cohost of an early-morning talk show called *People Are Talking*. The show was very successful, but in 1984, Winfrey left Baltimore to work for WLS-TV, an ABC affiliate in Chicago. She became the host of the talk show *A.M. Chicago* and handled the show with such expertise that within one year it was extended from thirty minutes to a full hour. Her success at *A.M. Chicago* was such that in 1985 WLS-TV decided to change the program's name to *The Oprah Winfrey Show*. A marketing campaign for national syndication of the show began that same year; in 1986, *The Oprah Winfrey Show* was successfully syndicated, and it grossed about $125 million the following season. 1986 was also eventful for Winfrey because it was the year she formed her own production company, Harpo Studios. ("Harpo" is "Oprah" spelled backward.)

Winfrey's talk show highlights her confidence, empathy, humor, frankness, intelligence, and curiosity. She is capable of reaching every segment of American society and of making people of all backgrounds feel comfortable with her. She exudes honesty and draws respect even when she is engaged in discussing such sensitive and diverse subjects as the KU KLUX KLAN, nudism, or rape.

Acting on Film and Television. Winfrey's childhood interest in being an actress—an interest that led her to participate in church pageants, visit Hollywood, become a member of a drama club, and study for a degree in speech and drama—was finally realized when she was cast in the role of Sofia in the 1985 film *THE COLOR PURPLE*, an adaptation of Alice Walker's book directed by Steven Spielberg. Winfrey played her role remarkably well alongside such other African American stars as Whoopi GOLDBERG and Margaret AVERY. Though the film was nominated for an Academy Award as best picture and Winfrey was nominated as best supporting actress, *The Color Purple* was criticized by some African Americans and African American organizations for allegedly portraying only the bad side of the African American male and family. In defense, Winfrey argued that the film was about women, not for or against men, and that it should be seen as a work of art.

Determined to act in more films, Winfrey starred in *NATIVE SON* (1986), a movie based on Richard WRIGHT's novel. In 1989, she began producing and acting in the television miniseries *THE WOMEN OF BREWSTER PLACE* and later the series *Brewster Place*. She has also appeared on numerous other television shows, including *Dolly, Saturday Night Live, The Tonight Show*, and *60 Minutes.*

Philosophy of Life. Winfrey's attitude toward life and her optimistic ideas about it have contributed to her success. She believes that education is power; she has provided scholarships to students and improved standards of education by donating generously to academic institutions. She frequently talks to students about pregnancy and education and has spoken before lawmakers on the topic of child abuse.

She has been influenced by Jesse JACKSON's philosophy that personal excellence is the best deterrent to sexist and racial prejudices. Guided by this philosophy, Winfrey pays tribute to those African American women who have made it possible for her to achieve her success. Winfrey believes that people have the same basic desires and hopes, and she directs her talk show to give people the feeling that they are not alone.

Honors and Awards. What would become a lifetime of awards and honors for Oprah Winfrey began in 1971, when she became the first African American to win a local Nashville beauty pageant. That year, she also won another beauty contest and was named Miss Black Tennessee. She has also won numerous awards for her television and acting career, including a Woman of Achievement Award from the National Organization of Women, an Emmy Award as best daytime talk-show host, and a Broadcaster of the Year Award from the International Radio and Television Society.

Conclusion. Winfrey is a source of inspiration to many Americans. Not one to forget her humble beginnings, she has used her power and generosity to help the less fortunate. Warm and caring, industrious and charismatic, she has used her productions to transcend racial and gender confines, and her achievements have helped to pave the way for the success of other women and minorities as talk-show personalities.—*I. Peter Ukpokodu*

SUGGESTED READINGS: • Edwards, Audrey. "Oprah Winfrey: Stealing the Show!" Essence 17 (October, 1986): 50-52. • King, Norman. Everybody Loves Oprah! Her Remarkable Life Story. New York: William Morrow, 1987. • Noel, Pamela. "Lights! Camera! Oprah!" *Ebony* 40 (April, 1985): 100-105. • Waldron, Robert, *Oprah!* New York: St. Martin's Press, 1987. • Waters, Harry F., and Patricia King. "Chicago's Grand New Oprah." *Newsweek*, December 31, 1984, 51. • Zoglin, Richard. "Lady with a Calling." *Time*, August 8, 1988, 62-64.

Wingate, Henry T.: Federal judge. Wingate was appointed to serve as a judge on the U.S. District Court in Mississippi in 1985 by President Ronald Reagan.

Winkfield, Jimmy: JOCKEY. Winkfield was victorious in consecutive Kentucky Derbys, with His Eminence in 1901 and Alan-a-Dale in 1902. He continued his career in France, becoming a successful jockey and trainer there.

Wiz, The (pr. 1975): Musical comedy by William F. Brown; music and lyrics by Charlie Smalls. This is a black version of L. Frank Baum's *The Wonderful Wizard of Oz* (1900), about Dorothy, a girl from Kansas, who is blown by a cyclone to the land of Oz, where she befriends some strange characters. Producers made use of soft rock music and theater magic to their advantage in order to replace film special effects, made famous in Metro-Goldwyn-Mayer's 1939 motion picture. The musical won six Tony Awards in 1975: for best musical director (Geoffrey HOLDER); for best musical composer and lyricist (Charlie Smalls); for best musical production (Ken Harper); for best choreography (George Faison); and for stars Ted Rose and Dee Dee Bridgewater. A 1978 film version by Sydney Lumet stars Diana Ross, Richard PRYOR, Michael JACKSON, and Lena HORNE.

Womack, Bobby (b. Mar. 4, 1944, Cleveland, Ohio): Singer, guitarist, and one of the most prolific songwriters in rock-and-roll history. Womack, one of the five boys in his family, learned to sing in the church, and while still a teenager he helped to form a gospel group with his siblings called the Womack Brothers. It was through the

success of this group that he met singer Sam COOKE, leader of the famed gospel group the SOUL STIRRERS, who recommended him for the opening in his group's band. Still a teenager, Womack accepted the job with the Soul Stirrers while he continued to sing with the Womack Brothers, now called the Valentinos at Cooke's suggestion.

Bobby Womack, one of the most prolific songwriters in rock-and-roll history. (AP/Wide World Photos)

In 1964, Womack embarked upon a solo career, moved to Memphis, Tenn., and became a much-heralded songwriter and session musician. While in Memphis, he wrote the song that would become the second U.S. hit for the Rolling Stones, "It's All Over Now." It was also during this time that he collaborated on projects with saxophonist King CURTIS, pianist Ray CHARLES, singers Joe Tex and Aretha FRANKLIN, and emerging rhythm-and-blues star Wilson PICKETT. Womack was forging a reputation as a major force within the popular music circles, but he had yet to enjoy any of the popular acclaim often recorded to talents such as his.

In an effort to boost his own career, he released eight singles and a number of albums for the United Artist, CBS, and Arista labels from the late 1960's through the early 1980'S. Through these efforts, he managed to secure a faithful following in Europe. He never enjoyed the popular status he sought in the United States, though his 1981 Beverly Glen Music release, *The Poet*, garnered him some acclaim within the African American community. The 1982 single from this album, "If You Think You're Lonely," reached the top twenty on the rhythm-and-blues charts, but popular appeal still eluded him.

Tragedy struck the Womack family in 1982 when a brother was murdered by a jealous girlfriend. Womack temporarily abandoned his music, but he came back with strong releases in 1984 with *The Poet II* and in 1985 with *Someday We'll All Be Free*. He continued to record and write prolifically but with the same lack of popular appeal. He made several ventures into the pop markets, performing duets with singer Patti LaBelle and with Mick Jagger, on "The Harlem Shuffle" from the Rolling Stones' 1986 release *Dirty Work*.

Women: Mother. Daughter. Sister. Lover. Friend. Worker. Fighter. African American women have assumed many roles since they were brought to the North American continent more than three hundred years ago. Although there is no monolithic concept of the African American woman, one common truth does apply: The history of African American women has been characterized by oppression and struggle. They have struggled against the oppression that has deemed their culture as substandard and illegitimate; they have also struggled against the oppression that has relegated them to second-class citizenship because of their gender. This double burden of racism and sexism has made it difficult for the African American woman to develop, not only in her own right but also for her family. Yet African American women have not only survived but have also managed to flourish, often in the face of seemingly insurmountable odds. Their tenacity, their strength, their will, and their spirit to provide for self, family, and community have contributed to the strides that have been made by the African American community throughout history.

African Background. In order to understand African American women, it is necessary to examine not only their contemporary experiences but also those characteristics that were brought to America from Africa.

The role of the woman in West Africa, where it is agreed that most of the enslaved Africans brought to America came from, was different from the roles those women would encounter in American society. African women came to America with behaviors, expectations, and value systems based on well-established patterns of culture that were not modeled on European traditions. They came from highly complex civilizations that prepared them to function in African societies.

In African society, the family unit was very important. The extended family was highly structured, and women had well-defined roles within it. The African woman was primarily responsible for caring for her children and her husband, and often lived in a polygamous situation, rotating with the other wives in serving a single husband.

Beyond functioning as mother and wife, the African woman was also active in the economics of the family and community. Many women were traders in the marketplace and were often in control of the making and selling of cloth, pottery, and other goods. They were also in charge of providing food for the family.

Affirmative action programs have enabled many highly qualified women to enter managerial positions. (D & I MacDonald, Unicorn Stock Photos)

The Enslaved African American Woman. African women, along with their husbands and children, were forcibly taken from their homes and brought to an alien culture in North America. Whites made systematic attempts to strip Africans of their dignity and to define them as less than human. Blacks were treated with contempt, and their cultural values and traditions were disregarded.

Some aspects of this new experience were familiar to African women; they were used to hard work and to caring for children. Yet they were also taught to expect some amount of independence and some control over their own lives and over the affairs of their families. Slavery presented a harsh and demeaning environment in which they, like African American men, had little, if any, power.

During slavery, the worth of the African American woman became defined by her breeding capacity. She was expected by her owner to have many children, often one a year, and was given little time to regain her strength or to take care of her children. This was probably the most devastating aspect of slavery, psychologically, for the African American woman, given the importance played on the mother-child bond in traditional African cultures. As an added insult, a slave woman was often expected to nurse and care for her owners's children while neglecting her own. Like the rest of her family, she was often whipped and physically abused by slaveowners. She also had to endure the sexual assaults of white men and the jealous rage of white women. She was blamed and punished for situations in which she was the victim.

with other African Americans that the values, traditions, and knowledge remembered from Africa were passed down from adults to children. Family ties were nurtured, lessons on survival were given; many Africanisms remained with African Americans in spite of attempts to strip such customs away. The traditions and culture were modified to accommodate the demands of slavery.

African American Women After Slavery. The Civil War brought an end to slavery in 1865, but the situation for the African American woman did not change greatly. She still managed multiple roles: wife, mother, and worker. She still had to deal with poverty and economic hardship. Although she did not have to worry about her children or husband being sold away, she and her family still had far fewer opportunities than whites did.

Florence Griffith-Joyner races toward her second record-breaking gold medal of the 1980 Olympics; she is a good example of a highly motivated, highly successful woman. (AP/Wide World Photos)

In spite of all these hardships, African American women managed to have some time with their families away from the slaveowners. It was during this time shared

These same conditions persisted in the experience of many African American women. In 1990, according to the Bureau of the Census, 51.2 percent of African American families were headed by single women, many of them in their twenties; these women were also among the lowest income earners in American society. In 1987, 5.6 million African American women were in the work force, up from 3.7 million in 1970. Seventy percent of married African American mothers worked, while 62 percent of single African American female heads of households worked. Married and single African American mothers were also found to be more likely to live in POVERTY than their white counterparts were.

There are also growing African American working, middle, and upper classes composed of blacks who have been able to escape the poverty that affects much of the black community. Often through education and employment in skilled occupations, they have been able to improve their quality of life and to move up the socioeconomic ladder. In spite of such strides, however, African American women who are relatively higher in socioeconomic status are still affected by oppression and discrimination. For example, although African American women are moving into more white-collar and professional positions, they are still, by and large, segregated into the lowest-paying jobs, often with little possibility of further advancement. African American women's salaries are, on average, 61 percent of the earnings of white male professionals.

African American women have also had to deal with detrimental stereotypes about their womanhood; they have been described as domineering and emasculating. The MOYNIHAN REPORT, a government-sponsored study published in 1965, asserted that the African American family had deteriorated because of the preponderance of female-headed households, although at the time, only 21 percent of African American families were female-headed. Many of these female-headed families were the result of divorce, separation, death, or common-law arrangements that were not considered legitimate.

By 1990, however, female-headed households constituted 51.2 percent of all African American families; only 37.7 percent of all African American families had both parents present. The situation reflects problems for the African American community at large, including the marginalization of African American men as the result of unemployment, underemployment, and incarceration, and added responsibilities and less support for often overburdened African American women.

The image of the superhuman African American woman has implied that she is stronger than other women and stronger than African American men. This stereotype of the woman who is always in charge has raised expectations of the African American woman, leading to more responsibilities placed on her. The stereotype of her dominance has also interfered in her relationships with African American men, and has been used to suggest that black men cannot fulfill their responsibilities to their families.

It must be kept in mind that many of the roles filled by African American women are undertaken out of necessity in a society that historically has not allowed blacks to participate in it. For example, for low-income families receiving public assistance, the presence of a man in a household has often resulted in the loss of a family's food, housing, and medical benefits. Such restrictions do not always prevent men from remaining involved with such families, as sociologists have pointed out.

The African American woman has also long been held to a white standard of womanhood that has defined female beauty as exemplified by white skin, long, flowing, straight hair, and narrow noses and lips. This attitude has led many black women to attempt to change their appearance in order to conform to the white standard. The BLACK POWER MOVEMENT introduced a trend toward Afro hairstyles and acceptance of natural beauty. The 1980's and 1990's have also found growing numbers of African American women rejecting white definitions of beauty and becoming increasingly willing to embrace and celebrate their natural beauty.

Conclusion. In the face of the double burden of racism and sexism, African American women, in a variety of roles, continue their struggle to make a way for themselves, their families, and their community. The legacy and the spirit of their African ancestors continue to strengthen them.—*Derise E. Tolliver*

SUGGESTED READINGS: • Caraway, Nancie. *Segregated Sisterhood: Racism and the Politics of American Feminism.* Knoxville: University of Tennessee Press, 1991. • Davis, Angela Yvonne. *Women, Culture, and Politics.* New York: Random House, 1989. • Hine, Darlene Clark, ed. *Black Women in United States History.* 16 vols. Brooklyn, N.Y.: Carlson Publishing, 1990. • Jones, Jacqueline. *Labor of Love, Labor of Sorrow: Black Women, Work, and Family from Slavery to the Present.* New York: Basic Books, 1985. • Malson, Micheline R., et al., eds. *Black Women in America: Social Science Perspectives.* Chicago: University of Chicago Press, 1990. • Morton, Patricia. *Disfigured Images: The Historical Assault on Afro-American Women.* New York: Greenwood Press, 1991.

Women of Brewster Place, The (1982): Novel by Gloria NAYLOR. Aptly subtitled *A Novel in Seven Stories,* the work deals with the lives of seven dauntless black women who live in an urban ghetto in a northern American city. It accurately depicts the reality of African American women in the United States who are victims of emotional and physical abuse by men. It won the American Book Award and was made into a television miniseries.

Women's Health: Although nineteenth century medical writings contained few references to the health of black women, it is evident that certain ideas of the time were based upon race rather than upon scientific findings. First, some physicians were convinced that black and white people of both sexes were physiologically different. Second, they believed that race was a factor affecting the incidence of life-threatening diseases among women. Some physicians speculated that women of color were physically stronger than whites, more capable of enduring pain and less at risk for neurological disorders.

High blood pressure is 82 percent more common among black women than white women. (Cleo Freelance Photo)

Reproductive Systems. Nineteenth century physicians believed that the female sexual organs significantly affected women's overall health and well-being. Accordingly, much of the literature on female health focused on the reproductive system. Practitioners cited differences in the genitalia of blacks and whites. Some doctors

thought that black women had larger clitorides, and that this physical difference caused lasciviousness and had led to the practice of female circumcision in Africa. Others maintained that African Americans had a thicker hymen which was more difficult to penetrate and which was positioned differently in the vagina. The black woman, according to the literature, also had a narrower pelvis, designed to accommodate her offspring's narrower, more elongated head.

Physicians also speculated that whites and blacks were affected differently by common female complaints, for example, problems associated with pregnancy. One Washington, D.C., practitioner who witnessed more than two thousand black women in labor noted that African Americans had shorter periods of labor, briefer periods of confinement, and a relative rarity of breech births.

The notion of race as a factor influencing the incidence of malignant and benign growths in the reproductive site was also popular in nineteenth century medical writings. Most doctors believed that ovarian cysts were rare among African Americans. One Alabama doctor, C. H. Mastin, attributed the absence of ovarian cysts in African Americans to the failure of the race to evolve to the same position as whites. A few surgeons argued that ovarian cysts were not unknown among African Americans. Daniel Hale WILLIAMS, a prominent black surgeon, observed the condition in both fair-skinned and dark-skinned women.

Physicians also disagreed regarding the incidence of uterine fibroids among blacks and whites. The majority believed that black people were more at risk, and that fibroids rarely ever occurred in white women. Middleton Michel of Charleston, S.C., disputed this notion, arguing that he had observed the condition in several whites. Daniel Hale Williams noted that he had removed these growths from both races, but he thought that they occurred more frequently among African Americans.

In addition to arguments relative to fibroids and ovarian cysts, physicians disagreed over the incidence of malignant growths or CANCER in the reproductive system among blacks and whites. They agreed that cancer in this site was the most prevalent cause of cancer mortality among females. They were certain that lower-class women were more at risk for the disease, but ironically, many doctors believed that African Americans had some immunity from cancer. According to the literature, the belief that black women were virtually free of cancer of the uterus was widespread. Some surgeons, including Michel, used vital statistics and case histories to show that uterine cancer did affect black women.

Physicians also were convinced that blacks and whites

exhibited noticeable differences in strength and endurance. Gaillard T. Hunt, a respected physician, marveled that refined white women and "powerful negresses" in the South could belong to the same species. Moreover, Joseph T. Johnson, a Washington, D.C., gynecologist, observed that the stresses of childbirth posed few problems for African Americans. Postpartum hemorrhage, he noted, affected few black women. He had also attended black women in very unwholesome environments and could not recall having seen a single case of puerperal fever, an indication that the women were not affected by stale air and noxious odors while giving birth.

Anatomical differences between black and white women were not confined to the reproductive system. Like the men of their race, black women were thought to have smaller, tropical lungs that placed them at greater risk for respiratory ailments. Neurological disorders were less likely to affect African American women since, according to the literature, they were "strong nerved" and less sensitive than whites.

Evidence of Health Differences. It is difficult to find accurate or extensive vital statistics for nineteenth century black women, but medical services rendered to them in Washington, D.C., an area with a sizable black population and a black medical community, suggest that many of these views were inaccurate. Dispensaries provided treatment for many of the urban poor. In the District of Columbia, these clinics treated and prescribed medication for thousands of black women during the late nineteenth century. Not surprisingly, women of all classes and races had their share of female complaints. African Americans were no different. They sought medical care for pregnancy more than any other gynecological condition, but they were treated for a variety of female problems. Black women were also diagnosed and treated for bronchitis, which accounted for more visits to dispensaries than did any other nongynecological ailment.

Although the upper classes of nineteenth century Americans avoided hospitals, the poor had little choice. In Washington, D.C., the largest number of black women who were hospitalized were there to give birth. Pulmonary TUBERCULOSIS ranked second, rheumatism third, and bronchitis fourth as reasons for the hospitalization of African American women. If the evidence from the nation's capital is indicative of black women's health, clearly they were not immune from the ailments that affected whites. Dispensary, hospital, and mortality reports from that city also indicate that African Americans were treated for ovarian cysts, neurological disorders, fibroids, and uterine cancer. Moreover, black women in the nation's capital often had the highest mortality rates for pulmonary tuberculosis throughout the nineteenth century.

The Twentieth Century. During the early decades of the twentieth century, black health conditions differed slightly from those of the nineteenth century. Tuberculosis remained the major killer of African Americans of both sexes. This situation changed, however, as a result of education, better housing, better health care, and the use of antibiotics. Tuberculosis ceased to be the major killer of black Americans. During the post-World War II era, other diseases became major killers in America, affecting a disproportionate number of African Americans.

Unlike nineteenth century physicians and sanitarians, the twentieth century medical community used a more sophisticated approach to epidemiology and had access to better reporting techniques. Racial differences were used far less often to explain the incidence of disease among various segments of the population. Greater emphasis was placed on environmental factors. Poor health among African Americans, including women, has been attributed to poverty, which is acknowledged as a major cause of sickness and death in the United States. Low income is a recognized risk factor for all of the chronic diseases that cause the greatest mortality. One-third of the black population was impoverished in the late decades of the century, and women accounted for a large number of those who were black and poor. Accordingly, it is not surprising that black women had generally poorer health than white women.

Heart diseases became the leading cause of death for Americans, but the risk of heart diseases was 25 percent higher for low-income persons. HIGH BLOOD PRESSURE, an important factor in many of these deaths, was 82 percent more common among black women than whites. In addition, one study showed that 44 percent of black women over the age of twenty and 37 percent of all women below the poverty level were overweight, putting them at greater risk of hypertension.

Cancer became the second-leading cause of death among African Americans. Since the late 1970's, the age-adjusted cancer mortality rates has been higher for blacks than whites. By the early 1990's, the cancer mortality rate was 11 percent higher for black than white women. Among black women, the major sites for cancer were the breast, lung, colon, rectum, uterus/cervix, and pancreas. The incidence of cervical cancer was twice as high for black women as compared to white women. The incidence of breast cancer, the major source of cancer mortality for women, continued to be lower than the rate for whites.

Diabetes, cited as another leading cause of death among Americans, was 33 percent more common among blacks than whites. Black women had higher rates of diabetes than whites, with higher rates of being overweight as part of the explanation.

Black women became victims of two epidemics that posed special problems in the United States during the 1980's and 1990's. First, the outbreak of homicides in much of urban America claimed a disproportionate number of African Americans. It was estimated that black women were four times more likely to become victims of homicide than were whites. Second, ACQUIRED IMMUNE DEFICIENCY SYNDROME (AIDS) became widespread. Black women were more likely to contract the disease than whites, and 52 percent of those women diagnosed with AIDS were black, according to one measurement. Poverty and its ramifications—poor health maintenance, drug use, and a high incidence of sexually transmitted diseases among them—have placed African American women at greater risk for the disease.

Lesser-Known Diseases. In addition to the better-known disorders that have posed greater problems for black women, some lesser-known diseases seem to strike more African Americans. Systematic lupus erythematosus is a potentially fatal disorder that tends to strike women between the ages of twenty and thirty-five. Although not an exclusively "female" disease, lupus strikes black women, for reasons not fully understood, twice as often as whites.

That black women are at great risk for depression and other mental disorders comes as no surprise. By the 1980's, 65 percent of African American women over the age of sixteen were single. A large number of them were impoverished, were mothers, or were heads of households. Each of these circumstances can engender stress, which, if not resolved in a positive way, makes depression and other forms of mental disease more likely.

Although twentieth century African American women were at greater risk than white women for many diseases, the medical community no longer attributed their relatively poor health to any peculiar racial characteristics. Instead, the blame went to poverty and all of its ramifications, including diet and life-style.—*Betty L. Plummer*

SUGGESTED READINGS: • Boston Women's Health Book Collective. *The New Our Bodies, Ourselves: A Book by and for Women.* New York: Simon & Schuster, 1984. • United States Department of Health and Human Services. *Healthy People 2000: National Health Promotion and Disease Prevention Objectives.* Washington, D.C.: Government Printing Office, 1991. • United States Department of Health and Human Services. *Secretary's Task Force on Black and Minority Health.* Washington, D.C.: Author, 1985. • Willis, David P., ed. *Health Policies and Black Americans.* New Brunswick, N.J.: Transaction Books, 1989.

Wonder, Stevie (Steveland Judkins or Steveland Morris; b. May 13, 1950, Saginaw, Mich.): Musician. Stevie Wonder is one of the enduring talents of twentieth century popular music. His voice is recognized throughout the world, and his influence on Western music and the music industry has been great. With more top-ten records to his credit than anyone except the Beatles and Elvis Presley, he has toured the world and collaborated with artists as diverse as Spike LEE and Julio Iglesias. Since making his first record in 1963 at the age of twelve, Stevie Wonder has never slacked his tremendous pace nor compromised his artistic vision.

Biographical Background. The name on Wonder's birth certificate is Steveland Morris. His father's name, and the name by which he signed his first recording contract, is Judkins. Because he was born prematurely, he spent his first hours in an incubator. An excess of oxygen in the incubator caused him to contract a condition called retrolental fibroplasia; as a result, his sight was lost.

From the age of two, Steveland showed a propensity for music, or at least for making noise, by banging on pots and pans. He received toy drum kits, which he quickly demolished, year after year until he was given a snare drum at the age of nine. He quickly became proficient on his first harmonica, a four-hole cardboard toy. When Stevie was seven, a neighbor leaving the housing project in which Stevie lived offered her piano to the musical little boy.

His family moved to Detroit when he was still quite young, and the relocation was traumatic. His blindness made it more than ordinarily difficult for him to adjust to a new home in a new city. It was in Detroit, however, that he met Ronnie White of the Miracles, the older cousin of one of Stevie's new friends. White, impressed with the ten-year-old's abilities, introduced him to Berry GORDY, Jr., who promptly signed him on with his company Tamla Motown (then known as Hitsville, U.S.A.) and gave the boy the name Little Stevie Wonder. Stevie had a five-year contract and a musical paradise to play in. Hitsville already boasted the talents of the MIRACLES, the MARVELLETTES, and the TEMPTATIONS. In a few years, the Motown sound would make the recording company the industry's most successful label featuring only black artists.

Early Hit Song. Little Stevie, Hitsville's boy wonder,

Stevie Wonder has more top-ten records to his credit than anyone except Elvis Presley and The Beatles. (Steveland Morris, Co.)

was sent on the road with the Motown Revue. His energetic performances were enthusiastically received, but his first two records did not sell particularly well. Gordy decided to try to capture some of Little Stevie Wonder's electricity by recording his third single live—a first in the industry. "Fingertips" went straight up the pop charts to number one and remained there for fifteen weeks. The record was the first in an impressive history of hits; throughout his career, Wonder has never gone long without a song on the charts.

At the age of twenty, he was married to singer SYREETA Wright, but the marriage was dissolved amicably eighteen months later. He has three children: a daughter, Aisha Zakia, and two sons, Kieta Sawandi and Mumtaz.

Wonder's growing concern about issues of race and poverty became apparent in the early 1970's, especially with the release of "Living for the City" and "You Haven't Done Nothing." His social concerns persisted in the following decades. He participated in recording the 1985 single "We Are the World" to aid famine victims in Africa, and in 1991, he received the Nelson Mandela Courage Award for his part in the struggle to overthrow apartheid in South Africa.

Wonder has consistently given of his time and talent to benefit a wide variety of people and organizations. He has donated concert earnings and participated in telethons. He was a leading figure in the effort to make the birthday of Martin Luther KING, JR., a national holiday. He was even featured on a poster as part of a campaign against drunk driving. The poster's caption read: "Before I ride with a drunk, I'll drive myself." Stevie has done much for the blind, raising funds and helping to develop technological devices to assist the sight-impaired.

In addition to the titles in his own lengthy discography, he has produced albums for other artists, including his former wife Syreeta Wright, and collaborated with such stars as Paul McCartney and Michael JACKSON. He also wrote and recorded the sound tracks to the films *The Woman in Red* (1984) and *JUNGLE FEVER* (1991).

Musical Achievements. "Fingertips" sold more than a million copies. Stevie's first album, *Little Stevie Wonder, The Twelve-Year-Old Genius*, followed a few months later in 1963. Wonder's first big hit did more than make him a young star; it helped establish Motown as a prominent force in the music industry. Nevertheless, Wonder's own sound was distinct from Gordy's formula and remained distinct from any other musical trend.

Another album and a number of singles followed but did not receive much attention. In 1965, though, Stevie recorded "Uptight (Everything's All Right)," which reached number three on the pop charts. The song is

credited to two Motown songwriters and "S. Judkins." Wonder, at fifteen, was already gaining a remarkable measure of control over his recordings. His influence and independence were demonstrated when Motown reluctantly agreed to let him record Bob Dylan's protest anthem "Blowin' in the Wind." The record was not a great success, but it was something Wonder wanted to do.

In 1967, "I Was Made to Love Her," a song Wonder had written with his mother, remained at number two on the pop charts for fifteen weeks. Within the next two years, he wrote and recorded "Shoo-Be-Doo-Be-Doo-Da-Day," "My Cherie Amour," and "Yester-Me, Yester-You, Yesterday," all major hits. He acted as his own producer for the first time on the 1970 album *Signed, Sealed and Delivered.*

Distinct Musical Vision. Wonder had always disliked being categorized, and his ambivalence toward being labeled a "soul" artist had been increasing. He wanted his music to be appreciated for its universality, rather than restricted by the assumption that, since he was black, he had to be making soul music. He received that recognition in 1973 for Talking Book (1972) and *Innervisions* (1973) and again in 1974 for *Fulfillingness' First Finale* (1974). In each of those years, he won five Grammy Awards, including the best album award. In 1975, Paul Simon, in his acceptance speech for his best album Grammy Award, thanked Wonder for not releasing an album that year. In 1976, however, *Songs in the Key of Life*, a double album and what many consider Wonder's masterpiece, went to the top and brought his total to fourteen Grammys.

Much of what makes Wonder's music distinct is his use of electronic instrumentation. He was a pioneer in 1972 when he recorded *Music of My Mind* using Arp and Moog synthesizers and a clavinet. The record was his second album and his first significant work after his initial break with Motown. Wonder had canceled his contract with the label when he turned twenty-one; his first million dollars had been held in trust until that time, and when it became available to him he started his own production company, Taurus Productions, and publishing company, Black Bull Music. He negotiated a distribution deal with Motown—another precedent—but the control, as well as the sound, was all Wonder's.

Near-Fatal Accident. On Aug. 6, 1973, Wonder was being driven to a concert in South Carolina when a log from a truck crashed through the windshield of his car and struck him in the head. Wonder spent four days in a coma and another week in a semiconscious state. According to publicist Ira Tucker, it was the words to Wonder's 1973 hit "Higher Ground" sung into his ear that brought him out of his coma. The albums for which he received his fourteen Grammys reflect his renewed appreciation for life.

Journey Through the Secret Life of Plants (1979), the experimental sound track to the documentary film *The Secret Life of Plants* (1978), followed *Songs in the Key of Life*. The album was largely instrumental, though, and did not meet with popular success. *Hotter Than July*, however, Stevie's 1980 album, featured four hit singles, including "Happy Birthday," written in honor of Martin Luther King, Jr., and "Master Blaster (Jammin')," a homage to Bob Marley.

The 1980's. Five years passed before Wonder released another album of entirely new material. He was not idle during this time, spending much of his time writing songs and recording. A compilation album, *Original Musiquarium I* (1982) was released with some new material; he recorded "Ebony and Ivory" (1982) with Paul McCartney, and he wrote "I Just Called to Say I Love You," the Oscar-winning theme to the film *The Woman in Red. In Square Circle*, released in 1985, featured another big hit, "Overjoyed." His next album *Characters* (1986), contained much material critical of the Ronald Reagan era. The dance remix of the single "Skeletons" featured snatches of Oliver North's Iran-Contra Senate hearings testimony.

Through the years, Wonder's professional output has never let up, and his popularity has remained strong. He tours frequently, drawing enormous crowds. His recordings continue to demonstrate his personal style and progressiveness while garnering awards. In 1989, he was inducted into the Rock and Roll Hall of Fame. —*Ivy Potts*

SUGGESTED READINGS: • Elsner, Constanze. Steve Wonder. New York: Popular Library, 1980. • George, Nelson. The Death of Rhythm and Blues. New York: E. P. Dutton, 1985. • Jacobs, Linda. *Stevie Wonder: Sunshine in the Shadow*. St. Paul, Minn.: EMC, 1976. • Peisch, Jeffrey. *Stevie Wonder*. New York: Ballantine Books, 1985. • Singleton, Raynoma Gordy, with Bryan Brown and Mim Eichler. *Berry, Me, & Motown: The Untold Story*. Chicago: Contemporary Books, 1990. • Swenson, John. *Stevie Wonder*. London: Plexus, 1986.

Wood, Thomas Alexander (b. Jan. 26, 1926, New York, N.Y.): Business executive. Wood holds an A.B. from Columbia University (1949) and a B.S. in electrical engineering from the University of Michigan (1951). He did postgraduate work at Wayne State University (1953-1954) and at the Massachusetts Institute of Technology (1958).

During the 1950's, Wood worked at the U.S. Ordnance Tank Automotive Center in Detroit, Mich. He specialized in electronics and computer development, and by the time he left the center in 1959, he was chief of the research and development computer laboratory. Wood worked briefly for International Telephone and Telegraph Corporation, but he and three coworkers left in 1960 to form Decision Systems, Inc. They built the computer firm to be worth millions of dollars. Its stock sold publicly, and Wood sold his shares in 1966, using the money to establish TAW Development Corporation that year and TAW International Leasing Corporation in 1968.

The leasing company was owned principally by African Americans, though Prudential Insurance Company at one time owned about one-fourth of it. The company was based in New York City but operated principally in Africa, leasing capital equipment. It was the first leasing company to get a guarantee from the Agency for International Development, protecting the company from losses associated with political disturbances.

Wood was elected to the board of directors of Chase Manhattan Bank and of its parent company, Chase Manhattan Corporation, in 1970. This made him the first African American director of a major U.S. bank not owned by African Americans. He also has served as a trustee of the NATIONAL URBAN LEAGUE.

Woodard, Lynette (b. Aug. 12, 1959, Wichita, Kans.): BASKETBALL player. The youngest of five children, Woodard first became interested in basketball as a child while watching her cousin, Geese Ausbie, a member of the Harlem Globetrotters, perform ball-handling tricks. Woodard played on two state championship teams while attending Wichita North High School, and she was recruited by many colleges. She chose to stay close to home, and in 1977 she enrolled at the University of Kansas.

In college, Woodard rapidly emerged as one of the top players in the nation. In her freshman season, she led the National Collegiate Athletic Association (NCAA) in rebounding and was chosen by *Street and Smith's*, a well-known basketball publication, as the top freshman female Player of the Year. The next season, she led the NCAA in scoring with a 31.7 points-per-game average. In three of her four college seasons, Woodard led the NCAA in steals, and she earned numerous All-America and All-Conference selections. In 1981, she became the NCAA's all-time women's scoring leader and won the Wade Trophy as the outstanding female college player in the nation.

While in college, Woodard also represented the United States in international competition. In 1979, she was a member of the U.S. team that won the gold medal at the World University Games, and she was selected for the 1980 U.S. Olympic team, though she did not play because of the U.S.-led boycott of the Moscow Olympics. After playing for a year in a women's professional league in Italy, she returned to the United States. In 1983, she played for U.S. teams that won the gold medal in the Pan-American Games and the silver medal in the World University Games. In 1984, Woodard again was chosen for the U.S. Olympic team. She was named the captain of the squad that won the gold medal at the Los Angeles Olympics.

After her Olympic triumph, Woodard made history as the first woman to play for the HARLEM GLOBETROTTERS. After two years and hundreds of performances, she retired from the team to concentrate on a teaching and coaching career.

Woodruff, Hale (Aug. 26, 1900, Cairo, Ill.—Sept. 15, 1980, New York, N.Y.): Painter. Woodruff studied at the Herron Institute in Indianapolis, Ind., Harvard University, and art institutes in France. Acclaimed as one of the masters of modernist painting, Woodruff taught at Atlanta and New York universities.

Among his works are *Ancestral Remedies, The Amistad Mutiny, The Art of the Negro, Founding of Talladega,* and *Summer Landscape.* His *Shantytown* and *Mudhill Row,* done in connection with the Depression-era Work

Hale Woodruff was recognized as one of the masters of modernist painting. (Library of Congress)

Projects Administration, helped to focus attention on African American POVERTY and slums.

Woods, Granville T. (Apr. 23, 1856, Columbus, Ohio—Jan. 30, 1910, New York, N.Y.): Inventor. In 1872, Woods's family settled in Missouri. Although his early education ended when he was ten years old, he later took college-level electrical and mechanical engineering courses between 1876 and 1878. He worked as a machinist, blacksmith, railroad fireman and engineer, and engineer on a British steamer, *Ironsides.* When he was in his mid-twenties, he moved to Cincinnati, Ohio, where he started Woods Electric Company, which manufactured telephones, telegraphs, and other electrical equipments.

Woods is best known as the inventor of more than fifty patented devices. His first patent was granted in 1884, for a steam boiler system. Among his other inventions are a telephone transmitter, a system for pulling electricity from overhead power lines into the motor of a train or trolley, a dimmer switch for theater lights that used 40 percent less electricity than its forerunners, an egg incubating system, an automatic air brake for trains, a regulation device for electric motors that conserved electricity because it used smaller resistances, and a third-rail system for trains which is still in use today in New York City's subway system. Possibly his most important invention was the synchronous multiplex railway telegraph, which permitted members of train crews to send messages to each other and to railroad stations, thus decreasing the chance of collisions. He sold some of his inventions to the American Bell Telephone Company, Westinghouse Air Brake, and General Electric. He kept the rights to other inventions and sold the products through his own company.

In 1888, the *American Catholic Tribune* termed him "the greatest electrician in the world." He won two patent suits filed against him by the Edison and Phelp companies by proving that he had invented the devices in question before Edison had. After he won the suits, Edison offered him a job, but he refused, choosing to remain his own boss. He moved to New York in 1890. In 1907, the *New York Sun* included Woods in an article titled "Negroes Who Have Made Good."

Woods, Howard B. (b. 1917, Perry, Okla.): Journalist, public official, and publisher. Woods founded, edited, and published the *St. Louis Sentinel.* He was St. Louis bureau chief for the *Chicago Defender* from 1942 until 1949 and executive editor of the *St. Louis Argus* in 1954. He was a member of the Committee on Equal Employment Opportunity from 1961 until 1965. President Lyndon B.

Johnson appointed him to the Community Relations Service established under the 1964 Civil Rights Act, and he was appointed associate of the United States Information Agency in 1965. He also served as chair of the Board of Commissioners of the St. Louis Housing Authority.

Woodson, Carter G(odwin) (Dec. 19, 1875, New Canton, Va.—Apr. 3, 1950, Washington, D.C.): Historian. Carter G. Woodson was responsible for helping to research, collect, write, and disseminate African American history through his organization, the Association for the Study of Negro Life and History (later the Association for the Study of Afro-American Life and History). From his headquarters in Washington, D.C., he founded and edited *The Journal of Negro History* and the *Negro History Bulletin*. Most important, he was the creator of Negro History Week, a celebration of black achievement that later became Black History Month.

Youth and Education. Woodson's parents, James Henry Woodson and Eliza Riddle Woodson, both former slaves, had nine children. During the Civil War, James had, in fact, run away to join the Union forces and was involved in action against the Confederacy. In his youth, Carter worked on the family farm but later moved to West Virginia (near Huntington) to work on a railroad and in coal mines. He attended the only African American high school in the area, Frederick Douglass High School, before enrolling in Berea College in Kentucky. The college was interracial, having been a center of learning for abolitionists.

Prior to graduating in 1903 from Berea College, which he attended on and off, Woodson obtained a teaching position in Winona, W.Va. In 1901, he began teaching at his former high school and, for a short while, served as principal. The United States War Department engaged Woodson to provide instruction in English to Spanish-speaking students on the Philippine Islands in 1903. At the same time, in order to make himself more proficient in his new job, Woodson began to take correspondence courses, particularly in Spanish, from the University of Chicago.

Upon leaving the Philippines in 1907, Woodson made his way to Europe, where for one semester he was a student at the University of Paris. This proved to be a fruitful trip, as he gained a deeper appreciation for history and expanded his vision while traveling throughout Europe and Asia.

Arriving back in the United States, Woodson soon completed requirements in history and romance languages at the University of Chicago and, in 1908, received both a bachelor's and master's degree. During his

studies for these degrees, his interest in history was piqued; he was accepted into a doctoral program in history at Harvard University in the same year that he received his master's degree. After completing his course work at Harvard in one year, he took a teaching position at Dunbar High School in Washington, D.C., in 1909, remaining at this post until 1919.

Achievements. The period from 1909 to 1919 was extremely productive for Woodson. Not only was he a full-time high school instructor, but he was also able to complete his doctoral dissertation in 1912 and to research, write, and publish his first book, *The Education of the Negro Prior to 1861: A History of the Education of the Colored People of the United States from the Beginning of Slavery to the Civil War* (1915), which some historians believe to be Woodson's most important work. The book was the first of nineteen authored or coauthored by Woodson.

Historian Carter Woodson started the tradition of Negro History Week in 1926. (The Associated Publishers, Inc.)

Additionally, during these years, his concern for the preservation of African American history led him to establish the Association for the Study of Negro Life and History (ASNLH). The organization was formed in September, 1915, when Woodson and several others met in Chicago; headquarters of the ASNLH was soon shifted to Washington, D.C. Woodson had lamented the fact that virtually nothing had been done regarding the preservation and publishing of records about African Americans, and as a result, the image of blacks had been warped. The ASNLH's aim was to promote historical research and writing about the black experience, to see that these efforts were published, to encourage the study of the African American past, and to raise funds in order to employ investigators to collect historical and sociological material relating to black Americans.

A significant outgrowth of the ASNLH was the publication of *The Journal of Negro History*, which commenced in 1916. Woodson was the editor of the journal, which was published four times each year. The journal has profoundly affected the discipline of history by providing primary sources for use by scholars and by serving as a forum for scholarly articles; many historians and experts from other disciplines have been given an opportunity to publish their research in the journal's pages. To publicize *The Journal of Negro History*, Woodson sent copies to such prominent academics as Edward Channing and Frederick Jackson Turner, both of Harvard, and F. W. Shepardson at the University of Chicago, and the journal received very favorable reviews.

In 1919, Woodson went to work at HOWARD UNIVERSITY as dean of the school's college of liberal arts. Remaining at Howard for only one year, he was then appointed as a dean at West Virginia Collegiate Institute. Woodson remained at the institute for two years, but responsibilities at the ASNLH demanded his return to Washington, D.C.

To further disseminate knowledge about African Americans, Woodson organized Associated Publishers in 1921. This publishing firm enabled him to publish full-length manuscripts and to publish studies from various authors. For example, the foremost textbook on black history at the time was *The Negro in Our History* (1917), an Associated Publishers book written by Woodson. Another popular Associated Publishers volume by Woodson was *The Miseducation of the Negro* (1933). *The African Background Outlined: Or, Handbook for the Study of the Negro* (1936), another Woodson study published by Associated Publishers, surveyed African history and societies.

Woodson is perhaps best remembered for inaugurating the first Negro History Week in 1926. This celebration of the African American experience, another outgrowth of the ASNLH, occurred during the second week of each February and later became a month-long commemoration. The 1926 celebration was orchestrated by Woodson, who offered general themes and circulars explaining the purpose for the observations, celebration kits containing pictures of African Americans, stories about notable blacks, and study guides for adult groups.

Woodson did not stop at the pageantry of Negro History Week. He desired to reach a still wider audience, and in 1937, he began the *Negro History Bulletin*, a publication directed at elementary and secondary schools. Woodson also initiated correspondence courses through the ASNLH in order to bring the study of African American history into the home.

Woodson's life was so intertwined with the ASNLH that they became almost one and the same. He never married; all of his time and energy were directed to raising funds for the ASNLH's activities and to investigating, recording, collecting, and publishing material on African American history. A constant irritant for Woodson was the chronic lack of funds to maintain the ASNLH. His efforts to collect funds proved taxing and frustrating, as he was unable to obtain sustaining grants from various foundations and philanthropists despite his courting of Julius Rosenwald, George Peabody, the Phelps-Stokes Fund, and the Rockefeller Foundation. He did receive small contributions here and there, however, such as a Social Science Research Council grant in 1929.

Fear of losing his independence and his control over the ASNLH forced Woodson to spurn requests to align his organization with a university in order to ease the financial stress. As a result, Woodson turned toward the African American community. He sought funds from local groups, schools, and organizations and drew up several ways for blacks to help the ASNLH, including subscribing to *The Journal of Negro History*, becoming a member of the ASNLH, and contributing to the group's research fund. W. E. B. DU BOIS summarized Woodson's efforts at obtaining financial assistance by stating that Woodson was not adept at begging and that begging was a necessity for the promotion of scholarly material concerning African Americans. Additionally, Du Bois candidly stated that philanthropic organizations ostracized Woodson, believing him to be overly self-centered and too self-assertive.

Throughout his life, Woodson worked and associated with such noted scholars as Du Bois, Rayford Logan, Charles Wesley, E. Franklin Frazier, Lorenzo Greene, Luther P. Jackson, and John Hope FRANKLIN, but relations between these men and Woodson were not always pleasant. Colleagues often described Woodson as arrogant, cantankerous, and domineering; Du Bois claimed that Woodson found it difficult to sympathize with people. When Woodson proposed a merger between *The Journal of Negro History* and the NATIONAL ASSOCIATION FOR THE ADVANCEMENT OF COLORED PEOPLE (NAACP), Du Bois, the NAACP's leader, believed that it would be too difficult to work with Woodson, and the negotiations collapsed. Relations between Woodson and his disciples were rocky at times, too. Protégés Lorenzo Greene and Rayford Logan were fired by Woodson from the ASNLH, although their association with him continued. Another disciple, Charles Wesley, often overlooked ill-treatment from Woodson and continued to work for the ASNLH.

Conclusion. Woodson, more than any other person, was responsible for developing African American history into a recognized and respected academic discipline. He also was instrumental in getting the United States to celebrate the contributions of African Americans to American history and to the history of the world. A fiercely independent workaholic who demanded complete control of the ASNLH, Woodson dedicated his life to the collection and dissemination of knowledge about the African American experience.—*Lester S. Brooks*

SUGGESTED READINGS: • Franklin, John Hope. "The Place of Carter G. Woodson in American Historiography." *Negro History Bulletin* 13, no. 8 (1950): 174-176. • Greene, Lorenzo J. *Working with Carter G. Woodson, the Father of Black History: A Diary, 1928-1930*. Baton Rouge: Louisiana State University Press, 1989. • Meier, August, and Elliott Rudwick. *Black History and the Historical Profession, 1915-1980*. Urbana: University of Illinois Press, 1986. • Scally, M. Anthony, ed. *Carter G. Woodson: A Bio-Bibliography*. Westport, Conn.: Greenwood Press, 1985. • Thorpe, Earl E. *Black Historians: A Critique*. New York: William Morrow, 1971.

Woodson, Lewis (b. c. 1805, Virginia): Reformer. Woodson moved to Ohio as a young boy. In the early 1830's, he moved to Pittsburgh, Pa., with his wife and two children. Over the following decades, he worked in that city as a teacher to black youth, a minister in the African Methodist Episcopal church, and a barber. Woodson was an early and ardent supporter of William Lloyd Garrison and the white-led abolitionist movement of the 1830's. He became controversial among both black and white abolitionists by arguing that the oppressive conditions under which African Americans had existed for generations had rendered them a distinct class and that they must be responsible for the uplift of their race.

In a series of letters published under the pseudonym "Augustine" in the *Colored American* in the late 1830's, Woodson called for the creation of separate black moral reform societies and black agricultural communities in the West, where African Americans could begin their reformation unmolested. Although some have designated Woodson as "the father of BLACK NATIONALISM," he believed that whites and blacks varied only in condition—which could be equalized over time—and that they actually shared an interest in advancing American economic prosperity and political ideals.

Woodson, Robert L. (b. Apr. 8, 1937, Philadelphia, Pa.): Public servant. Woodson has held high posts in various agencies. He was director of the NATIONAL URBAN LEAGUE, director of the American Enterprise Institute Neighborhood Revitalization Project, a fellow at the American Enterprise Institute for Public Policy Research, chair of the Council for a Black Economic Agenda, and president of the National Center for Neighborhood Enterprise, which he founded in 1981. He also has advised various governmental agencies and written a number of books outlining self-help plans for African American communities.

Robert Woodson was director of the National Urban League. (Harlee Little)

World Saxophone Quartet: Group founded in 1976 by David Murray. This revolutionary all-saxophone jazz group has included from the beginning Murray, Oliver Lake, Julius Hemphill, and Hamiet Bluiett. Among the group's recordings is a 1986 album of compositions associated with Duke ELLINGTON and composed by Ellington or Billy STRAYHORN.

World War I and African Americans: In April, 1917, the United States entered World War I "to make the world safe for democracy." Although African Americans were denied democratic rights in the United States, the majority of them supported the war effort. African American spokesmen were more eager to secure combat and officer training for African Americans than to challenge segregation in the Army. W. E. B. DU BOIS, editor of *The Crisis*, called on African Americans to "close ranks" despite segregation, hoping that military participation would earn African Americans civil rights after the war. Yet African American military and home-front support during World War I did not end Jim Crowism. Upon demobilization, African American soldiers returned to their homes to face continued segregation and discrimination and increased racial violence.

Military Experience. On the eve of World War I, the United States Army limited African Americans to service in four segregated regiments. Approximately ten thousand African American soldiers served in the TWENTY-FOURTH AND TWENTY-FIFTH INFANTRY and the NINTH AND TENTH CAVALRY. An additional ten thousand African Americans served in segregated National Guard units in Tennessee, Maryland, Ohio, Illinois, Connecticut, New York, and the District of Columbia. After the United States entered World War I, Congress passed the Selective Service Act, which ended the Army's policy of voluntary enlistment and initiated a draft system. Under the Selective Service Act, more than 2.2 million African Americans registered, and of those, 367,710 were inducted into the Army. Although the Selective Service Act made no provision for racial distinctions, local draft boards were composed almost entirely of whites and often discriminated against African Americans.

As a result, African American spokesmen feared that African Americans would be utilized only in labor troops and not as combat soldiers. The NATIONAL ASSOCIATION FOR THE ADVANCEMENT OF COLORED PEOPLE (NAACP) tried

The 367th Infantry, 77th Division. (National Archives)

to ensure that African Americans would have the opportunity to serve their country in arms as well as under the command of African American officers. In May, 1917, the NAACP convened with seven hundred African American representatives in Washington, D.C., to pressure the government into training African American combat soldiers and officers.

African American officers received their commissions at Des Moines.

Despite the successful recruitment of officer candidates, African Americans feared that the Army had little interest in the training of African American officers as combat soldiers. The retirement of Colonel Charles D. YOUNG, the highest-ranking African American officer,

Troops waiting to be shipped to Europe. (National Archives)

Training Black Officers. Concerned about home-front unity, the government offered to establish a segregated officers' training camp if the group secured two hundred African American college men willing to sign up for training. A group of HOWARD UNIVERSITY students organized the Central Committee of Negro College Men and recruited approximately fifteen hundred officer candidates at African American colleges throughout the country. In September, 1917, the officers' training camp for African Americans opened at Des Moines, Iowa. The recruits were trained by whites and African American noncommissioned officers. In the following month, 639

seemed to indicate to them that their concerns were justified. In the summer of 1917, the Army retired Young, who allegedly suffered from high blood pressure but who was apparently fit for active service, on the grounds of physical disability. Young tried to convince the War Department of his fitness and rode on horseback from Ohio to the nation's capital. Only in November, 1918, after the war was virtually over, was Young reinstated.

Racial Violence. Furthermore, African Americans were concerned that the Army was not committed to the training of African American combat soldiers, especially after racial violence erupted in Houston in August, 1917.

Soldiers of the African American Twenty-fourth Infantry stationed near Houston attacked members of the local police force in retaliation for alleged discriminatory treatment. The Houston disturbance led to the court-martial of 156 African American soldiers and the execution of thirteen of them.

Following the Houston incident, Secretary of War Newton D. Baker convened with several African American spokesmen. In order to avert further racial violence, Baker appointed Emmett J. Scott as a special assistant to the secretary of war. Scott, who had been Booker T. WASHINGTON's secretary for eighteen years, was made responsible for all matters involving African American troops.

Ninety-second Division served in France under the command of white American officers, while the Ninety-third Division was assigned to the French Army and served throughout the war under French command. By the end of the war, nearly 380,000 African Americans had served with the U.S. Army. Of those, approximately 140,000 served abroad in labor battalions, while 42,000 African American soldiers fought in combat units. Throughout the war, the U.S. Marine Corps excluded African Americans, and the U.S. Navy accepted them only in menial positions.

Home Front. World War I also brought about economic and demographic changes for African Americans on the home front. The outbreak of war in Europe reduced the

The First Army Post Band, an all-black unit, served in France during World War I. (National Archives)

Another result of Baker's meeting with African American spokesmen was the creation of two African American combat divisions, the Ninety-second Division, made up of draftees, and the Ninety-third Division, composed largely of African American National Guard units. The

number of immigrants to the United States. At the same time, American industries expanded in response to increased wartime production. The resulting labor shortage opened new employment opportunities for African Americans in the North. Northern industries that had previously excluded African Americans sent labor agents to the South to recruit African American workers. Between 1916 and 1919, more than 400,000 African Americans left the South during the so-called Great Migration. African Americans went north for a variety of reasons; they hoped to improve their economic conditions, they tried to escape racial violence, and they sought to provide their children with better educational opportunities.

The arrival of large numbers of African American migrants from the South created numerous problems for northern communities. The Great Migration contributed to the deterioration of ghettos into slums and triggered intraracial as well as interracial tensions. The influx of large numbers of African Americans into a few select cities in the North led to overcrowding and resulted in health and sanitation problems. In some cities, the migrants shook the foundations of the existing African American communities because of the large number of single male migrants. Moreover, intraracial tensions developed because the majority of migrants came from the rural South. African Americans from the urban North often looked down on the migrants, who were usually less educated than northern blacks and who had different values, standards, behavior patterns, and dress codes.

The Great Migration also contributed to increased interracial tensions. African American workers from the South were often willing to work for lower wages than whites. Thus, white workers feared that African Americans from the South were going to compete for their jobs, lower their wages, or serve as strikebreakers. Some local politicians exploited the theme of white economic insecurity and facilitated outbreaks of racial violence. In the summer of 1917, interracial tensions caused by the Great Migration resulted in a race riot in East St. Louis that left at least forty African Americans dead. The federal government was concerned about the impact of racial tensions on the nation's wartime productivity and created within the Department of Labor a Division of Negro Economics under the directorship of George E. Haynes.

Conclusions. World War I did not radically alter the status and conditions of African Americans in the United States. Throughout the war, the Army remained segregated, the majority of African American soldiers served in labor battalions, and African American workers continued to be at the bottom of the wage scale. Nevertheless, African Americans made modest gains during World War I. They successfully lobbied for combat troops, and African American soldiers participated on an unprecedented scale in the nation's military. Moreover, the training and commission of large numbers of African American officers signaled the opening of higher military ranks

for African Americans. In addition, the southern exodus improved the working conditions and wages of many African Americans, and increased wartime demand created new employment opportunities. African Americans in the North remained largely unskilled or semiskilled; however, they did experience a significant shift from domestic service to industrial employment. Finally, military participation and home-front support raised the hopes and expectations of many African Americans. Following the war, however, African Americans did not receive civil rights in exchange for their patriotism. Nevertheless, the disillusionment many African Americans experienced after their support of World War I paved the way for the more militant rhetoric of African Americans in World War II.—*Nina Mjagkij*

SUGGESTED READINGS: • Barbeau, Arthur E., and Florette Henri. *The Unknown Soldiers: Black American Troops in World War I.* Philadelphia: Temple University Press, 1974. • Giffin, William W. "Mobilization of Black Militiamen in World War I: Ohio's Ninth Battalion." *Historian* 40 (August, 1978): 686-703. • Kornweibel, Theodore, Jr. "Apathy and Dissent: Black America's Negative Responses to World War I." *South Atlantic Quarterly* 80, no. 3 (1981): 322-338. • Murray, Paul Thom, Jr. "Blacks and the Draft: A History of Institutional Racism." *Journal of Black Studies* 2, no. 1 (1971): 57-76. • Nalty, Bernard C. *Strength for the Fight: A History of Black Americans in the Military.* New York: Free Press, 1986. • Patton, Gerald W. *War and Race: The Black Officer in the American Military, 1915-1941.* Westport, Conn.: Greenwood Press, 1981.

World War II and African Americans: World War II was a watershed for African Americans. During the war years, African Americans planted the seeds of the CIVIL RIGHTS movement of the 1950's and 1960's. Stimulated by the democratic ideology and rhetoric of World War II, African Americans reexamined their position in American society. They challenged racism, discrimination, and segregation and insisted that America live up to its democratic ideals. African Americans adopted the slogan "Double V" and proclaimed that they were fighting for victory on two fronts: They were defending democracy overseas and fighting for democracy in the United States. In their struggle against segregation, African Americans focused on two issues. They challenged the government to desegregate the armed forces and to end discrimination in defense-industry employment.

Military Experience. African Americans who joined the ranks of the armed forces encountered numerous obstacles. Many military officials believed that African

This band unit is shown before a performance in New York City during World War II. (National Archives)

Americans were inferior and not suited for combat. Thus, they tried to limit the number of African American soldiers. On the eve of World War II, African Americans constituted 1.5 percent of the U.S. Army. Moreover, whenever possible, the Army assigned white commanders to African American troops, and some branches of the armed forces confined African Americans to menial tasks; others excluded them altogether. Throughout World War II, the Army maintained its traditional policy of segregation, the Navy confined African Americans largely to service in the messmate branch, and the Army Air Corps excluded them.

Although the military tried to limit the participation of African American soldiers, African Americans joined the Army in large numbers. Approximately one million African Americans served in the various branches of the armed forces, nearly 500,000 of them overseas. During the war, approximately 800,000 African Americans served in the Army, 164,942 joined the Navy, more than 5,000 enlisted in the Coast Guard, and 19,168 entered the Marine Corps. In addition, approximately 24,000 served in the Merchant Marine, and four African American captains commanded Liberty Ships. The Army Air Corps excluded African Americans but established a special training school for them at TUSKEGEE INSTITUTE. By the end of the war, approximately six hundred African American pilots had received their wings.

Roles for Women. African American women also participated in the military defense of the country. More than four thousand African American women entered segregated units of the Women's Auxiliary Army Corps (WAACs), later known as the Women's Army Corps (WACs); seventy-two served with the Navy Women Accepted for Volunteer Emergency Services (WAVES); and five became SPARS (members of the women's reserve of the Coast Guard). By the end of the war, five hundred African American nurses had joined the Army Nurse Corps.

Despite their support of the war effort, African Americans continued to protest against discrimination and segregation in the armed forces. Numerous individuals challenged discriminatory practices, and several race riots erupted at Army bases throughout the country. A particularly troublesome issue for African American soldiers was the Red Cross policy of segregating blood donations for the Army by the race of the donors. African Americans were outraged, especially because Dr. Charles R. DREW, an African American surgeon, had been instrumental in developing the process of storing blood plasma.

Government Response. The War Department tried to counter the low morale of African Americans with the

In addition, the government tried to neutralize African American criticism by appointing several African Americans to high positions in federal wartime agencies. William H. HASTIE and Truman K. Gibson, Jr., successively served as civilian aides to the secretary of war. Campbell C. Johnson held the office of executive assistant to the director of the Selective Service, Crystal Bird Fauset was appointed race-relations adviser to the Office of Civilian Defense, and Ted Poston served as racial adviser in the Office of War Information.

New women's branches were created to support the military effort. (National Archives)

production of several propaganda films. The documentaries *The Negro Soldier*, *The Negro Sailor*, *Wings for this Man*, and *Teamwork* emphasized the important contributions African Americans had made to the war effort. The films offered a positive portrayal of African Americans in the various branches of the armed forces, but they omitted any discussion of racism and segregation. Nevertheless, the films were well received by African American soldiers and civilians.

Home Front. World War II also had an important impact on African Americans on the home front. The expansion of the defense industry ended the Depression and created new employment opportunities. African Americans benefited from the growth in industry; however, discriminatory hiring practices kept them out of the best-paying jobs, and African American workers continued to receive lower wages than white workers. In January, 1941, A. Philip RANDOLPH, president of the BROTHER-

HOOD OF SLEEPING CAR PORTERS, urged African American workers to challenge discrimination in defense industries. In an article in the African American weekly the *Pittsburgh Courier*, Randolph called on African Americans to march on Washington to demand the desegregation of the armed forces as well as the elimination of discriminatory employment practices. The ensuing March on Washington Movement (MOWM) threatened to march tens of thousands of African Americans to the Capitol to embarrass the government. President Franklin D. Roosevelt

and a measure of economic security.

Along with increased employment opportunities, World War II also triggered demographic shifts. African Americans left the South in large numbers to move to the industrial centers of the North and West. On the West Coast, African Americans frequently moved into neighborhoods vacated by Japanese Americans. In Los Angeles, for example, African American defense workers turned "Little Tokyo" into "Bronzeville." In many other cities, the large influx of African Americans resulted in

Many jobs vacated by draftees or enlistees were filled by women such as these railroad workers. (National Archives)

averted the march, scheduled for July 1, 1941, by signing EXECUTIVE ORDER 8802 on June 25, 1941. The order created the Fair Employment Practices Committee (FEPC), which investigated charges of discrimination in defense industries. The creation of the FEPC was a partial victory for African Americans, but the committee was slow to respond to charges and thus did not end discrimination in employment. Nevertheless, World War II did bring African Americans increased employment opportunities

severe housing shortages and racial tensions. In Detroit, a major defense-production center, racial violence erupted in February, 1942. The federal government had provided funds for the construction of public housing for defense workers. When African American families tried to move into one such housing project, the Sojourner Truth Homes, a group of whites met them with violence. City officials called in state militia troops to restore order and to ensure the safety of the African American tenants.

Race Riots in Detroit. The racial violence surrounding Detroit's public housing project was merely the beginning. On June 20, 1943, Detroit became the site of the most severe race riot of World War II. Rumors that whites had killed several African Americans sparked a full-scale riot. Unable to handle the mobs, the governor of Michigan turned to President Roosevelt, who proclaimed a state of emergency and sent six thousand federal troops to restore order in Detroit. After less than two days of rioting, seven hundred people had been injured, and twenty-five African Americans and nine whites had been killed. Detroit was the city most affected by racial violence, but wartime migration triggered similar incidents in numerous other cities in 1943.

Racial Cooperation. In addition to such interracial violence, however, the war years also brought about some degree of interracial cooperation. In Chicago, African American and white pacifists established the CONGRESS OF RACIAL EQUALITY (CORE) in 1942. CORE utilized direct, nonviolent action to expose racism and to challenge Jim Crow practices. CORE members successfully staged SIT-INS in restaurants and picketed movie theaters in cities in the North and West.

The American government was afraid that racial divisions on the home front would reflect poorly upon the nation's fight against Adolf Hitler's racial ideology. Thus, the Office of War Information (OWI) tried to create an image of racial harmony and unity. The OWI asked Hollywood to break with the portrayal of stereotypical "Mammies" and "Uncle Toms" and suggested positive images of African Americans. The results could be seen in such films as *Casablanca* (1942), *Sahara* (1943), *Bataan* (1943), and *Lifeboat* (1944). Although these films continued to reflect aspects of traditional stereotypes, they nevertheless represented an important turning point. Instead of portraying the war as exclusively white, these films included African Americans in important supporting roles and thus introduced cultural pluralism to the screen.

Conclusions. World War II did not end discrimination and segregation in the United States, but the war years created new opportunities for African Americans and accelerated the breakdown of Jim Crow practices. Despite discrimination and segregation in the military, World War II provided African Americans with increased opportunities to serve their country. African American workers continued to earn less than their white counterparts, but growing economic demands and labor shortages triggered by the war created new employment opportunities. Moreover, protest strategies initiated by MOWM and CORE during the war years were success-fully applied by civil rights activists during the 1950's and 1960's.—*Nina Mjagkij*

SUGGESTED READINGS: • Garfinkel, Herbert. When Negroes March: The March on Washington Movement in the Organizational Politics of FEPC. Glencoe, Ill.: Free Press, 1959. • Koppes, Clayton R., and Gregory D. Black. "Blacks, Loyalty and Motion-Picture Propaganda in World War II." The Journal of American History 73 (September, 1986): 383-406. • Nalty, Bernard C. *Strength for the Fight: A History of Black Americans in the Military.* New York: Free Press, 1986. • Osur, Alan M. *Blacks in the Army Air Forces During World War II: The Problem of Race Relations.* Washington, D.C.: Office of Air Force History, 1977. • Potter, Lou, with William Miles and Nina Rosenblum. *Liberators: Fighting on Two Fronts in World War II.* New York: Harcourt Brace Jovanovich, 1992. • Wynn, Neil A. *The Afro-American and the Second World War.* New York: Holmes & Meier, 1975.

Wormley, James (Jan. 16, 1819, Washington, D.C.—Oct. 18, 1884, Boston, Mass.): Hotel proprietor. Both of Wormley's parents were born free. While Wormley was a child, his family lived on E Street in Washington, D.C., near 14th Street NW. His father kept a livery stable, and at an early age, Wormley began driving his own hack.

Wormley traveled to California in 1849, during the gold rush. Later, he worked as a steward on a Mississippi River steamboat, on ocean-going vessels, and at the Metropolitan Club in Washington, D.C. Shortly before the Civil War, he opened a catering business in Washington, next door to a candy store operated by his wife, the former Anna Thompson, whom he had married in 1841.

Even though he had a wife, three sons, and a daughter, Wormley took a job as steward to Reverdy Johnson, a newly appointed minister to England. He impressed Johnson's guests with his cooking, earning praise from them. After visiting Paris on his own, he returned to Washington and bought a building on the corner of H Street and 15th Street. In 1871, he opened what came to be known as Wormley's Hotel.

Wormley was unable to make mortgage payments on the building, so he transferred the property to Representative Samuel Hooper of Massachusetts, who leased it back to him. The hotel came to be known for its excellent menu offerings and its maintenance. Numerous congressmen and other notables were guests there. Rutherford B. Hayes and Samuel Tilden met at the hotel in February, 1877, to forge the "Compromise of 1877," which settled a controversy in the electoral college and gave Hayes the presidency of the United States.

When Wormley died, he left an estate worth in excess of $100,000, a sizable fortune at the time. His children and grandchildren were among the elite of Washington, D.C. His son, James T. Wormley, ran Wormley's Hotel until 1893. He sold it to Charles E. Gibbs, another hotel owner, who operated it as Wormley's Hotel until 1897, when he changed the name to the Colonial House. The building was torn down in 1906 to allow the Union Trust Company Building to be erected.

Worthy, James Ager (b. Feb. 27, 1961, Gastonia, N.C.): BASKETBALL player. In 1982, as a junior, playing for the University of North Carolina, Worthy and freshman Michael JORDAN led the Tar Heels to a regular-season number-one ranking and their first National Collegiate Athletic Association (NCAA) championship in twenty-five years. Named the outstanding player of the NCAA tournament, Worthy declared himself eligible for the National Basketball Association (NBA) draft shortly after the tournament and went to the Los Angeles Lakers as their first overall pick. The six-foot, nine-inch, 225-pound forward is respected for his footwork and quickness. His illustrious career for the Lakers includes a Most Valuable Player Award from the 1988 NBA play-offs.

Wright, Betty (b. Dec. 21, 1953, Miami, Fla.): Rhythm-and-blues singer. Wright began her career as a gospel singer in her native Miami. She switched to RHYTHM AND BLUES and recorded the single "Paralyzed" for a local Florida record label when she was thirteen years old. Her first hit single, "Girls Can't Do What the Guys Do," was released on the Alston label of Miami's T.K. Records in 1968. The single, which appeared on her debut album *My First Time Around*, reached number fifteen on the rhythm-and-blues chart and number thirty-three on the pop chart. In 1971, the single "Clean Up Woman" was released from Wright's album *I Love the Way You Love Me*. The single went gold and reached number two on the rhythm-and-blues chart and number six on the pop chart. Wright's biggest success came when she won a Grammy Award for her 1975 hit single, "Where Is the Love." In addition to her solo career, Wright worked as a guest vocalist on disco hits with other T.K. Records artists such as K.C. and the Sunshine Band. After T.K. Records filed for bankruptcy, Wright signed a record deal with Epic Records and released the album *Betty Wright* in 1981. The album contained the single she recorded with Stevie WONDER, "What Are You Going to Do with It."

Wright, Jay (b. May 25, 1934 or 1935, Albuquerque, N.Mex.): Poet. Wright was educated at the University of California at Berkeley, Union Theological Seminary, and Rutgers. His intellectually demanding poetry is informed by his studies in history, anthropology, and primitive religions and is also infused with allusions to early Christian and Renaissance writers such as St. Augustine and Dante. His publications include *The Homecoming Singer* (1971), *Dimensions of History* (1976), and *The Double Invention of Komo* (1980).

Wright, Louis Tompkins (July 23, 1981, La Grange, Ga.—Oct. 8, 1952, New York, N.Y.): Medical researcher. Wright was graduated fourth in his class from Harvard Medical College in 1915. For more than thirty years, he had a private practice in New York City, and he directed the surgery department and cancer research at Harlem Hospital. Wright also served as chairman of the NATIONAL ASSOCIATION FOR THE ADVANCEMENT OF COLORED PEOPLE's national board of directors. He is known for his studies of the intradermal method of smallpox vaccination and for being the first to use chlortetracycline, an antibiotic, on humans.

Louis Tompkins Wright directed the surgery department and cancer research at Harlem Hospital. (Schomburg Center, NY Public Library)

Wright, Nathan, Jr. (b. Aug. 5, 1923, Shreveport, La.): Educator. Wright began teaching urban affairs at the State

University of New York in 1969 and was chair of the department of Afro-American studies. His work, much of it relating to urban unrest, has resulted in more than three hundred published articles and several books. He chaired the 1967 National Conference on Black Power in Newark, N.J., and the 1968 International Conference on Black Power in Philadelphia, Pa.

Wright, Richard (Sept. 4, 1908, Natchez, Miss.—Nov. 28, 1960, Paris, France): Novelist and essayist. African American author Richard Wright is known primarily for three important books. *Uncle Tom's Children* (1938), his first major indictment of racist America, set the tone for the protest literature of generations to follow. NATIVE SON (1940) and BLACK BOY: *A Record of Childhood and Youth* (1945), now considered American classics, won Wright international renown. They established him not only as a perceptive social critic but also as a spiritual mentor of almost every important African American writer since the end of World War II.

Wright's contribution, however, was not confined to his three most popular books. He published eleven more in addition, including *Twelve Million Black Voices* (1941), a pictorial history of black American life. He published poetry and as a journalist wrote numerous essays, articles, and reviews. He cowrote a successful Broadway play, starred in the film adaptation of *Native Son*, helped compose blues songs, and produced drama for radio. Whatever his choice of medium, Wright, an activist until his death in 1960, never flinched from his concern to examine and challenge oppression.

Early Life. Wright was born on a plantation outside Natchez, Miss., to Nathan and Ella Wright. Not long after the family moved to Memphis, Wright's father deserted the family, leaving them hungry and broke. Over the next fifteen years, Wright helped support his mother, whose crippling strokes left her paralyzed for months at a time, and his younger brother. When Wright's Grandmother Wilson took control of the household, conditions grew worse. A strict Seventh-day Adventist, she ran a harsh "religious regime" and often blamed her daughter Ella's illnesses on Wright's lack of faith. These unhappy childhood experiences made Wright realize early in life the meaning of suffering.

Racial hatred, however, was the determining factor in shaping Wright's vision. A Jim Crow education, characteristic of the Deep South of the day, taught him his place beneath whites. In the South, he witnessed insult and false accusation, police brutality, castration, rape, and LYNCHING. Determined from an early age to overcome his

background, Wright explained in *Black Boy* that his southern oppressors had never really known him, nor had they given him the chance to learn his true potential. So as to seize that opportunity, Wright, like thousands of blacks in the 1920's, fled north.

Racism in the North. In many ways, the move proved unsuccessful, and it often plunged Wright into deeper despair. Confronting the more subtle racism of Chicago and New York, he discovered that even after he had earned fame as a writer he was still denied entry into many public places. Both cities, however, did offer relief from the more brutal, overt antagonism of the South, and they proved fertile ground for thought and action, giving Wright for the first time a sense of solidarity with other politically committed writers. He soon attached himself to the American Communist Party, believing that, as a writer with an agenda, he could effect social change. Although they helped publish his earliest writings, Wright soon grew wary of the Communists and argued that they exploited blacks merely to further their cause. By 1947, Wright was thoroughly disillusioned with his country, which he felt had given him false hope and empty values. With his wife and daughter, he sailed for Paris, never to move back to his native land.

Exile in Paris. Paris offered intellectual freedom and the chance for Wright to involve himself in international affairs. Befriending Jean-Paul Sartre, he quickly became aligned with the French existentialists, who convinced him to broaden his perspective and transcend seeing the world strictly in terms of black and white Americans. Wright also attached himself to African writers and intellectuals residing in Paris. These "outsiders" exposed Wright to the global dimensions of oppression. They also encouraged him to travel outside the West. Wright explored parts of Africa and Asia, where he recorded some of his most insightful and provocative literature. By the time of his death, he had declared that oppressed peoples throughout the world suffered the same hopeless fate.

Literary Career. Although Wright had already begun his reading of H. L. Mencken and the Naturalists while living in Memphis, the John Reed circle in Chicago provided Wright entry into the literary world. Aside from generating a feeling of community, the circle also helped Wright publish his earliest poetry in *New Masses, Left Front,* and other radical journals. Reflecting on his southern heritage, he had secured a theme that would dominate much of his writing: the apparently hopeless plight of the individual trapped in an environment of oppression. Each tale in *Uncle Tom's Children,* Wright's first collection of short stories, pits its protagonist against harsh Mississippi surroundings; by the end of the stories, these strugglers

Richard Wright, the noted author of Native Son. (Library of Congress)

have either lost their lives or been scarred by the countless hardships they have suffered.

An equally disturbing statement—perhaps Wright's most important—came two years later with the publication of *Native Son*. Tired of writing stories that "even bankers' daughters could read and weep over," Wright delivered a damning narrative that put to rest the myth that America confined its racism to the Deep South. Set in Chicago, the novel renders the drama of nineteen-year-old Bigger Thomas, who kills a young white woman and burns her body in a furnace to cover up his crime. Before he is apprehended, Bigger smashes his girlfriend's face with a brick and throws her out a window to die. The white girl's death was partly accidental, but Bigger concludes that his crimes had been "creative acts." By the end of the novel, he rejects his family, religion, and the Communist Party, which had acted in his defense. He exclaims to his horrified attorney: "What I killed for must've been good! . . . When a man kills, it's for something . . . I didn't know I was really alive in this world until I felt things hard enough to kill for 'em." These startling words echoed worldwide and provoked a vehement national reaction.

Exploring the Past. Fascinated by his roots, Wright published *Twelve Million Black Voices* the following year. Based on James Agee's and Walker Evans' *Let Us Now Praise Famous Men* (1941), it celebrated African American folk tradition and foretold the coming CIVIL RIGHTS movement. It also helped gain Wright recognition as one of the nation's most important black thinkers. He lectured frequently, declaiming against discrimination and racism; he also appeared on panels with noted literary figures, including Alain LOCKE and Langston HUGHES. Wright was barely thirty-two when he was approached about writing his autobiography. Convinced by his editors that a remembrance specifically of his youth would be more engaging, Wright published *Black Boy*, which ended with his journey by train out of the South. The book attacked both the oppressive religious practices that pervaded the black community and the racism that ran rampant in the South. Like his early journalism, the autobiography placed Wright beside writers concerned with individual freedom and equal rights.

Wright read more than he wrote during his first six years in exile. Instead of contributing to his growth as an artist, however, the hiatus merely ostracized him from the reading public. Critics dismissed *The Outsider* (1953), Wright's eagerly anticipated second novel, as too heady and claimed that Wright had been misled by his existentialist friends. Actually, the book stands as one of Wright's edgiest and most noteworthy achievements. Unlike Bigger Thomas, *The Outsider*'s Cross Damon is a prisoner of his own intellect. Adhering too desperately to nihilism, he flees into irrational behavior that eventually destroys him.

Return to Nonfiction. Such a negative public reception convinced Wright to temporarily abandon fiction and return to journalism. He turned to travel writing, a form he had experimented with while still living in the United States. In 1954, he published *Black Power*, an account of his journey through GHANA, the first African nation to wrest independence from imperial Great Britain. The book accused the British of barring the country's entry into the modern age and blocking its attempt to catch up with the industrialized West. That same year, Wright traveled to Spain, where he witnessed Francisco Franco's exploitation of the Spanish people. In *Pagan Spain* (1957), Wright not only assailed the Franco regime but also chided the pro-Franco Catholic hierarchy for shackling the peasantry to a religious tradition Wright saw as devoid of meaning and hope. In 1955, Wright traveled to the historic Bandung Conference and recorded in his last travel book, *The Color Curtain* (1956), his thoughts on speeches by African and Asian leaders who decried Western racist policies and called for an allegiance of emergent powers. He managed one last book of nonfiction, *White Man, Listen!* (1957), which attacked racism on an international scale.

Later Works and Life. While the dramatic narrative of *Native Son* and *Uncle Tom's Children* might have been more provocative than the travel literature and essays, these later works contain some of Wright's most perceptive writing. Over thirty years, Wright proved that he could move with ease across formal restrictions and work fiction and reportage with equal skills. The posthumous publications of *Eight Men* (1961), a collection of short stories, *Lawd Today* (1963), a first novel, and *American Hunger* (1977), the second volume of his autobiography, contributed to Wright's diverse repertoire.

Yet the measure of his growth was more than an artistic one. By 1953, Wright was no longer an American citizen but an international citizen interested in global affairs. He devoted himself to formulating answers that would deliver all nations from hate. His quest was cut short by a heart attack, but not before he had discerned the rhythms for future generations committed to making the world a safer, more tolerant place for all people, regardless of color.—*Bruce Dick*

SUGGESTED READINGS: • Fabre, Michel. *Richard Wright: Books and Writers*. Jackson: University Press of Mississippi, 1990. • Fabre, Michel. *The Unfinished Quest of*

Richard Wright. Translated by Isabel Barzun. New York: William Morrow, 1973. • Fabre, Michel. *The World of Richard Wright.* Jackson: University Press of Mississippi, 1985. • Miller, Eugene E. *Voice of a Native Son: The Poetics of Richard Wright.* Jackson: University Press of Mississippi, 1990. • Walker, Margaret. *Richard Wright, Daemonic Genius: A Portrait of the Man, a Critical Look at His Work.* New York: Warner Books, 1988. • Williams, John A. *The Most Native of Sons: A Biography of Richard Wright.* New York: Doubleday, 1971.

Wright, Robert Courtlant (b. Nov. 5, 1944, Chester, Pa.): State politician and attorney. Wright's father was an attorney who served as a judge on the Pennsylvania Court of Common Pleas. Wright enrolled at George Washington University and was graduated with a bachelor of arts degree in political science in 1966. He attended law school at Villanova University and received his law degree in 1969. After passing the bar exam, Wright went into private practice as an attorney in 1970.

Wright became active in local politics in Pennsylvania and served as president of the Republican Council of Delaware County in 1977. He began his political career in 1981, when he was elected to the Pennsylvania state legislature as a representative from District 159 for Chester County. In addition to his legislative duties, Wright served as treasurer of the Pennsylvania Legislative Black Caucus and served on the executive boards of the National Black Caucus of State Legislators and the Pennsylvania Minority Business Development Authority.

Wright-Jones, Jane Cooke (b. Nov. 30, 1919, New York, N.Y.): Surgeon and educator. She earned a bachelor's degree from Smith College in 1942 and received a medical degree from New York Medical College in 1945. She has served as associate dean and professor of surgery at New York Medical College, and has been a member of the board of trustees at Smith College. She was a member of the President's Commission on Heart Disease, and succeeded her father, Louis Tompkins Wright, as director of the Harlem Hospital Cancer Research Foundation.

Y

Yancey, James Edward "Jimmy" (b. Feb. 20, 1889, Chicago, Ill.—Sept. 17, 1951, Chicago, Ill.): Piano player. Yancey was one of the true pioneers of the rock-and-roll sound and is regarded as the father of the BOOGIE-WOOGIE piano style. A child prodigy, Yancey learned about music from his father, a singer and guitarist. He began touring with various vaudeville troupes as a singer and a dancer through the early 1900's. A highlight of his early career was a 1913 command performance at Buckingham Palace before King George V.

He returned to Chicago in 1915 and spent most of the 1920's playing piano at various nightclubs and for the popular rent parties around town. He also began a long affiliation as a groundskeeper at Comiskey Park, home of the Chicago White Sox. That job occupied his time until the late 1930's, and he was musically inactive. He had not recorded at this point, but there was a resurgence of popularity in the rollicking piano style that came about through Meade "Lux" Lewis' recording of "The Yancey Special" in 1936. The subsequent appearances of Lewis and fellow pianists Albert AMMONS and Pete Johnson at the remarkably successful "From Spirituals to Swing" concert at Carnegie Hall in 1939 brought Yancey to the forefront as the founding father of this piano style.

Yancey's newfound celebrity status finally brought him opportunities to record, of which he quickly took advantage. His brief recording career included some fine performances with his wife, singer Estella "Mama" Yancey, on the Solo Art, Victor, Session, and Atlantic labels. His career was cut short in 1948 by chronic illnesses which haunted him for the remainder of his life. He suffered from a debilitating stroke and years of diabetes before his death. He was elected to the Rock and Roll Hall of Fame in 1986.

Yellow Back Radio Broke-Down (1969): Novel by Ishmael REED. The work is a parody of the Western dime novel. It portrays, in a mixture of epic, fantasy, and myth, the supernatural characters of the Loop Garoo Kid, a black circus cowboy who is the hero of the story, and Drag Gibson, a wealthy rancher and Loop's nemesis.

Yerby, Frank (b. Sept. 5, 1916, Augusta, Ga.): Author. Yerby was educated at Paine College and FISK UNIVERSITY, where he received a master's degree in 1938. Although he has written critically acclaimed short stories

and novels on racial themes, Yerby's popularity as a novelist rests on a series of Old South plantation romances that began with *The Foxes of Harrow* in 1946.

Frank Yerby wrote plantation romances in addition to his works on racial themes; early photographs were often retouched to give everyone more Anglo features. (AP/Wide World Photos)

York (c. 1770—c. 1806): Explorer. York was a slave in the household of William Clark. He accompanied the 1804-1806 Lewis and Clark expedition beginning in Louisville, Ky. York, who was a curiosity to the Plains Indians, allowed them to touch his black skin and made up stories about being a wild animal that ate young children. Freed and set up in the freight business on his return from the expedition, York later died of cholera.

Young, Al (b. May 31, 1939, Ocean Springs, Miss.): Short-story writer, poet, novelist, and editor. Young moved to Detroit, Mich., after the end of World War II. He attended the University of Michigan from 1957 to 1961. Shortly thereafter, he moved to California and attended the University of California at Berkeley. He continued to reside in California after being graduated.

During his early writing career, Young published four volumes of poetry, the most successful being *The Blues Don't Change: New and Selected Poems* (1982). His style is characterized by examinations of the human condition. He is a satirist and a keen observer of the frailties of so-called civilized society. A clear example of Young's poetic gifts is "The Old O. O. Blues," a parody of the black nationalistic rhetoric of the 1960's which resurfaces periodically. The poet is O. O. Gabugah, who decides to "Blow some funky rhyme on [my] mental saxophone."

"Chicken Hawk's Dream" is a prime example of Young's talent with short fiction. First published in 1968, it is similar to Henry James's "The Beast in the Jungle." Each is concerned with a protagonist who waits for fame. Chicken Hawk thinks that one day he will be a revered artist, but he never puts forth any effort to become one. Predictably, he fails.

Young's novel *Who Is Angelina?* (1975) is the story of Angelina Green, a bright young Berkeleyite who goes through a rapid series of experiences, each designed to test and, simultaneously, to inform her of her real self—her best self. Written while Young enjoyed a Guggenheim Fellowship and taught at Stanford University, the novel represents a significant stretch into long fiction for Young.

Young has also enjoyed success as an editor, working with Ishmael REED on *Yardbird Lives!* (1978) and other projects. Young contributed "Chicken Hawk's Dream" to Abraham Chapman's *New Black Voices: An Anthology of Afro-American Literature (1972).* In his autobiographical sketch, Young writes that he was "born under Gemini at the outset of World War II. . . . For some time earned a precarious living as a musician and FM disc jockey, but also worked in less glamorous fields." Another contribution to *New Black Voices* was the provocative essay "Statement on Aesthetics, Poetics, Kinetics."

Young, Andrew Jackson, Jr. (b. Mar 12, 1932, New Orleans, La.): Politician and diplomat. Andrew Young was born to Andrew J. and Daisy (Fuller) Young. His father was a prosperous light-skinned dentist who stressed the family's "Indian" blood and who provided well for his family. Part of the black bourgeoisie, Andrew's family lived in a racially mixed, middle-class neighborhood where apparent racial tolerance existed; in such an environment, as the mature Young later explained, he learned to talk to and to deal with white people. Yet Andrew and his brother eventually heard the taunt "nigger"; in re-

sponse, their father hired a professional boxer to teach both boys how to fight. As an adult, Young had no fear of the white community and could not be intimidated.

Andrew attended local schools, including Dillard University (1947-1948); he then transferred to HOWARD UNIVERSITY, from which he was graduated in 1951. Four years later, he was graduated from Hartford Theological Seminary in Connecticut and was ordained as a minister. Thwarted in an early attempt to become a church missionary in Africa, he nevertheless began his career as a religious and civil leader. On June 7, 1954, he married Jean Childs; the couple eventually had four children.

From 1955 to 1957, Young served as pastor of two churches in Thomasville, Ga., not far from the Florida state line. Always adaptable, Young, brought up on classical music, educated himself about jazz and the blues to prepare for the rural Georgia job. The Youngs lived in a segregated area in a shotgun house on a dirt street.

Civil Rights Work. In Thomasville, Young surprised many local whites by quietly and peacefully joining the local Civil Rights movement. Young had, of course, heard of the movement that Martin Luther KING, JR., was leading and wanted to contribute. Young first attracted Thomasville's white community's attention because he refused to use side and rear entries to white businesses and homes as segregation customs dictated.

Soon, Young launched the first black voter-registration drive to occur in southern Georgia, an act that earned him the animosity of a KU KLUX KLAN group from the nearby town of Albany. Rumors flew that the group would soon be coming to Thomasville to stop the voter drive. Before that could happen, Young talked to many of the white business leaders of the town; shortly thereafter, a white group announced that they would not tolerate the Klan in Thomasville.

In 1959, Young left the South and resettled in New York City to become associate director of the Youth Department for the National Council of Churches, a post he held until 1961. Because he had become increasingly dedicated to the CIVIL RIGHTS movement, in 1961 he became a staff member of the SOUTHERN CHRISTIAN LEADERSHIP CONFERENCE (SCLC), which had been founded in 1957 by King and other clergymen. Bringing with him a grant from the Marshall Field Foundation to establish literacy programs for African Americans, Young served as the SCLC's administrator for its citizens' education program until 1964, when he became executive director of the organization, a post he held until 1970. In 1967, he was also named as the executive vice president of the SCLC. While remaining on the SCLC's board of directors from 1970 until 1972, Young served as chairman of

Atlanta's Community Relations Commission.

Entry into Politics. In 1970, Young entered a congressional race and was narrowly beaten by an ultraconservative white Republican. In 1972, however, Young ran again, and after running an impressive campaign emerged as victor and claimed a seat in the U.S. House of Representatives. Young served on the House's banking committee, where he learned much about both national and international investment markets and made many contacts in the international world of business. In 1976, Young became more involved in national politics when he began working for Georgian Jimmy Carter's presidential campaign. Young helped to convince northern liberals, blacks and whites alike, that Carter, a white southerner, was a proponent of integration.

to improve U.S. relations with Third World nations. He was forced to resign his post in 1979, however, after it was disclosed that he had met secretly with representatives of the Palestine Liberation Organization (PLO), an act forbidden by U.S. policy. Young did not remain out of politics for long, however; in 1980, he supported Carter's failed reelection bid, and in 1984 he worked for Walter Mondale's unsuccessful presidential campaign. In 1982, he ran for the office of mayor of Atlanta and won in another impressive campaign; he held the post until 1989.

Tenure as Mayor. Young's eight-year stint as mayor was marked by both successes and failures. During his administration, one thousand new companies established themselves in Atlanta (three hundred from abroad); those companies invested $70 billion in central Georgia

Andrew Young served as mayor of Atlanta, Ga., as part of a long political career; he is seen here speaking at the Foreign Correspondents Club in Tokyo. (AP/Wide World Photos)

After serving three terms in Congress, Young accepted an appointment from President Carter as U.S. ambassador to the United Nations. As a diplomat, Young helped

($11 billion from overseas) and created 700,000 new jobs. Yet some of Young's critics said that he reigned in "Crime City" because Atlanta saw a 50 percent increase in crime during Young's tenure. Additionally, critics also talked about his absenteeism during his mayoralty and called him "Globetrotter Andy." Defending himself against such charges in 1990, Young mentioned his trip to Barbados, Trinidad, and Jamaica in the summer of 1989; he took thirty small businessmen from Atlanta with him on the trip, and the group came away with $134 million in new contracts.

Clearly, Young's previous networking in the international arena paid dividends for Atlanta. As Young was ending his mayoralty, it was noted that he had met with more than 189 foreign business delegations, had been interviewed by at least 105 international media organizations, and had spent a yearly average of eighty-five days on the road attending to city business. One of Young's biggest coups was winning the 1996 Summer Olympics for Atlanta. Backed by such powerful business concerns as Coca-Cola and Turner Broadcasting, Young waged a long publicity campaign, finally seeing his city beat such contenders as Montreal and Athens for the chance to host the Games.

Campaigning for Governor. Young next mounted a campaign for the governorship of Georgia and secured the endorsement of many of Georgia's politicians, both white and African American. For example, the Georgia congressman John LEWIS, himself a hero of the early Civil Rights movement, gave Young his full support, arguing that Young could show potential voters a record of real achievements. To orchestrate his campaign, Young hired Frank Greer, a media specialist who had earlier masterminded L. Douglas WILDER's successful quest for Virginia's governorship.

Still, Young's high visibility through the years and some of his controversial words and actions had alienated some potential voters, including some in the African American community. For example, during his term as mayor, more low-income housing had been torn down than had been built. Further, he had spearheaded a drive for a domed sports stadium even though several black preachers fumed that their churches were being torn down to create the space for the "Andy Dome." On another occasion, he visited a bar in a suburb that catered to a mostly white clientele; one record in the bar's jukebox was entitled "My Wife Ran Off with a Nigger." Again, some among Young's African American constituency were outraged, but Young justified his visit by saying that he would go anywhere and talk to anyone if it could help Atlanta and the state of Georgia.

Always outspoken, Young ran a spirited, if controversial, campaign for the governorship. For example, as he tried to court conservatives, he once gave a discourse on the Georgia state flag, with its Confederate stars and bars. He could live with the flag, he said, because it was really patterned after the flag of Saint Andrew and was of Scottish origin. Moreover, Young concluded, the flag stood for unity and family—at least among the Scots. Yet although he had an early lead in public opinion polls, Young was defeated in the Democratic primary by Zell Miller, a white politician.

Awards and Honors. In his long career, Young has held many civic posts and received many awards of merit. He was a long-time chairman of the board for the Delta Ministry of Mississippi. He also served on the boards of the Martin Luther King, Jr., Center for Social Change, the Robert F. Kennedy Memorial Foundation, and the Field Foundation.

Young holds honorary degrees from a host of schools, including Wesleyan University (1970), Wilberforce University (1970), Clark College (1973), and Yale University (1973). He received the Pax-Christi Award from St. John's University in 1970, the Spingarn Medal from the NATIONAL ASSOCIATION FOR THE ADVANCEMENT OF COLORED PEOPLE in 1980, and the Legion of Honor from France in 1982. In 1989, he was named by *American City and County* magazine as municipal leader of the year.

In addition to continuing his busy career as a civic and civil rights leader, in the 1990's Young continued to preach every Sunday and to devote time to his congregation. The jobs were really the same, he maintained. His whole life's purpose, he said, was to get food for the hungry, to give clothes to the naked, and to find decent living space for the poverty-stricken.—*James Smallwood*

SUGGESTED READINGS: • Forman, James. *The Making of Black Revolutionaries.* New York: Macmillan, 1972. • Gardner, Carl. *Andrew Young.* New York: Sterling, 1980. • Garrow, David J. *We Shall Overcome: The Civil Rights Movement in the United States in the 1950's and 1960's.* 3 vols. New York: Carlson Publishing, 1989. • Powledge, Fred. *Free At Last? The Civil Rights Movement and the People Who Made It.* Boston: Little, Brown, 1991. • Wills, Garry. "Georgia Is Much on His Mind." *Time,* July 16, 1990, pp. 66-68.

Young, Charles (Mar. 12, 1864, Mayslick, Ky.—Jan. 18, 1922, Lagos, Nigeria): Military figure. Young was one of three African Americans to be graduated from the U.S. Military Academy in the late 1880's. He served in the all-black Tenth Cavalry and fought in the Spanish-American War and in the Mexican military campaign in 1915. The War Department declared him medically unfit as an excuse to keep him from serving in World War I. Colonel Young protested by riding his horse from Ohio to Washington, D.C., to prove his fitness, but he was not reinstated. He is buried in Arlington National Cemetery, and his home in Wilberforce, Ohio, was declared a national historical landmark.

Young, Claude Henry "Buddy" (Jan. 5, 1926, Chicago, Ill.—Sept, 4, 1983, Terrell, Tex.): Football player. After a successful college career in track and football, the short (5 feet 4 inches) and speedy Young went on to play professional football with the New York Yankees from 1947 to 1949, then played in the National Football League with the New York Yanks from 1950 to 1951 and the Dallas Texans in 1952 (both franchises failed). The Baltimore Colts had Young from 1953 to 1955. He compiled 9,601 total yards and scored 44 touchdowns in nine seasons, retiring with a record 27.7-yard average on kickoff returns.

Young, Coleman Alexander (b. May 24, 1918, Tuscaloosa, Ala.): Mayor of Detroit, Mich. Young grew up in Huntsville, Ala., but Ku Klux Klan harassment and poor employment opportunities convinced his father to move the family to Detroit in the late 1920's. They settled in the Black Bottom section of the city, and Young's father began his own dry cleaning business. After graduating from high school with excellent grades, Young was denied financial aid to attend the University of Michigan because of his race. Unable to raise the funds to enroll at the university, Young had to go to work to help support the rest of his family.

In the late 1930's, Young was trained in an apprentice electrician program sponsored by Ford Motor Company. Although he finished first in the course, he was passed over for the next available opening as an electrician in favor of a white candidate. In the early 1940's, Young went to work on the assembly line at Ford and became a union activist. Although he was fired from his job at Ford because of a fistfight provoked by racial tension and name-calling, Young continued his union activism in his next job, with the postal service. Young was drafted during World War II and served with the Tuskegee Airmen, becoming a second lieutenant and flying missions as a bombardier-navigator. Near the war's end, he was one of several black officers who were arrested for demanding service at a segregated officers' club. The incident was highly publicized and resulted in the eventual integration of the Army officers' club.

Young returned to Detroit after the war ended and went back to work with the U.S. postal service. He resumed his union activities and campaigned vigorously for the Progressive Party. During the 1950's, he founded the National Negro Labor Council, an organization designed to promote civil rights in the workplace. Young's activities caused him to be investigated by the House Committee on Un-American Activities for possible Communist involvement. When summoned to Washington, D.C., Young refused to testify and chose to disband the Labor Council rather than release its membership list to the U.S. attorney general. His resulting notoriety made it difficult for Young to remain employed in Detroit. He finally began to achieve financial success as an insurance salesman in the late 1950's.

After more than a decade of involvement in Michigan politics, Coleman Young was elected mayor of Detroit. (Library of Congress)

Young became active in the Democratic Party and was elected as a delegate to the Michigan Constitutional Convention in 1960. His political popularity grew, and he was elected to the Michigan state senate in 1964. His efforts on behalf of open housing legislation and school desegregation, as well as his support for labor unions, won him wide support in Detroit. In 1973, he declared his candidacy for the office of mayor. He finished second in the nonpartisan primary election, then campaigned vigorously against his opponent, John F. Nicholls, a white police commissioner who focused on his law-and-order record. Young's margin of victory was approximately seventeen thousand votes and was achieved by his strong appeal among Detroit's black citizens.

As mayor, Young focused on reforming the police department, increasing the number of African Americans on its staff, and combating crime by opening small police stations in high-crime neighborhoods. He also brought labor and big business together to work out a plan to encourage local industries to remain and to attract new industries to Detroit. Young fought efforts to reduce Detroit's share of federal funds and worked on increasing Detroit's tax revenues in the face of a declining population. He was selected to four subsequent terms as mayor and turned down a possible cabinet appointment from Jimmy Carter in order to continue his efforts in Detroit. Although his administration was investigated on a variety of charges, ranging from improper awarding of city contracts and illegal use of civic funds by the police department, Young himself never was personally implicated, and his popularity remained high among the city's voters.

Young, Lester "Pres" or "Prez" (Aug. 27, 1909, Woodville, Miss.—Mar. 15, 1959, New York, N.Y.): Tenor saxophonist. Young began his musical career playing drums in the family band in the 1920's. Bandleader Art Bronson, with whom he played in the late 1920's, persuaded him to take up the tenor saxophone. Young performed extensively with singer Billie HOLIDAY, who gave him his nickname (short for "president") in admiration of his playing, with all-star groups, with Count BASIE's band, and at jazz concerts. His tender, suavely lyrical style significantly influenced many outstanding bebop saxophonists, including Charlie PARKER and Dexter GORDON.

Young M.C. (Marvin Young; b. 1968, London, England): RAP music artist. Young M.C., who was born to Jamaican parents and grew up in Queens, N.Y., performs in an easygoing rap style. He had a million-selling single with "Bust a Move." His albums include *Stone Cold Rhymin'* (1989) and *Brainstorm* (1991). In 1990, he won both an American Music Award and a Grammy Award.

Young, Nathan Benjamin (Sept. 15, 1862, Newbern, Ala.—1933): Educator. Young served as president of Florida A&M University for twenty-two years. In 1915, he proposed creation of a graduate school for African Americans. He was the first president (1921-1927, 1929-1931) of LINCOLN UNIVERSITY after its conversion to a university from its previous form as Lincoln Institute. He is known for advancing the ideal of liberal arts education

for African Americans rather than only vocational training.

Young, Whitney Moore, Jr. (July 31, 1921, Lincoln Ridge, Ky.—Mar. 11, 1971, Lagos, Nigeria): CIVIL RIGHTS leader. Young earned a B.S. degree at the historically black Kentucky State College in 1941. He attended the Massachusetts Institute of Technology for graduate work but actually received an M.A. in social work from the University of Minnesota in 1947.

Between 1954 and 1961, Young was dean of the school of social work at Atlanta University. The Rockefeller Foundation awarded him a grant to spend the 1960-1961 academic year as a visiting scholar at Harvard University. He published two books, *To Be Equal* (1964) and *Beyond Racism: Building an Open Society* (1969).

Whitney Young saw cooperation with white community leaders as beneficial to achieving goals set by black leaders. (Library of Congress)

Young became a prominent lecturer, serving as president of the National Association of Social Workers and the National Conference on Social Welfare, and as board member and adviser to the Rockefeller Foundation, Urban Coalition, and Urban Institute. He also became a part of seven presidential commissions during the Kennedy and Johnson administrations. President Lyndon B. Johnson recognized him in 1969 as one of twenty Americans to receive the Medal of Freedom, America's highest civilian award.

Young is best remembered for serving as executive director of the NATIONAL URBAN LEAGUE between 1961 and 1971. Under his leadership, the league began to emerge as a force in the civil rights struggle. He forged friendships with American business and political leaders that led to criticism from within the black community. Regardless of racial tensions, he saw communication

Tank Younger was the first NFL player to come from a black college. (National Football Foundation Hall of Fame)

with prominent white leaders as an avenue to educate them about the needs of his people. He saw his efforts as necessary to achieve the league's goal of greater job opportunities for blacks. Although he urged cooperation with the white business world, he was outspoken in his criticism of the pace of reforms. He attempted to make African Americans part of the decision-making process, and he allied the National Urban League with some of its more militant counterparts.

Younger, Paul "Tank" (b. 1925?) FOOTBALL player. Considered to be one of the best players in the black college system, Younger scored sixty touchdowns and was a two-time All-American while at Grambling University. Younger joined the Los Angeles Rams in 1949 as the first player from a black college to be signed by a National Football League team. In 1951, he was named All-Pro outside linebacker, the first African American to receive the award. An intense competitor with a reputed mean streak, he once was jailed for five days for hitting his mother-in-law.

Your Arms Too Short to Box with God (pr. 1976): Gospel musical by Vinette CARROLL; music and lyrics by Alex Bradford and Micki GRANT. The work, a black version of the Book of Matthew told in black idiom, was developed by Carroll and the URBAN ARTS CORPS for presentation at the Festival of Two Worlds in Spoleto, Italy. Delores Hall won a Tony Award as best featured actress for her performance.

Z

Zimbabwe: Massive ancient monument, probably built in the ninth century A.D., located in the present-day country of Zimbabwe. An oval enclosure with walls more than thirty feet high and fifteen feet thick formed what served as both a sacred space and a center for royal activity. Little is known of the Zimbabwe culture, made up of Shona peoples, but there are artifacts indicating trade with China, Persia, and Arabia. The last Shona federation was broken by the Ngoni in the 1930's. The ruins demonstrate the high level of technology developed by the people of the region.

zydeco: Music style. Zydeco is the fast, syncopated dance music of Louisiana's CREOLE population. Influenced by Cajun, African American, and African Caribbean musical styles, zydeco is a form which has evolved since the mid-eighteenth century. Modern zydeco tends toward fewer traditional waltzes and more blues and up-tempo two-steps. A zydeco band generally consists of a lead accordion, guitars, and various percussion instruments, including the washboard.

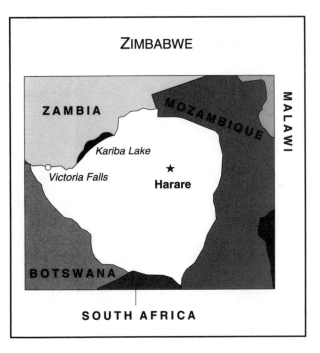

100 Most Profitable Black-Owned Businesses, 1992

1. **TLC Beatrice International Holdings, Inc.** (Food products). Founded: 1987. Headquarters: New York, N.Y. Chief Executive Officer: Reginald F. Lewis. 1991 sales figures: $1,542,000,000.

2. **Johnson Publishing Company, Inc.** Founded: 1942. Headquarters: Chicago, Ill. Chief Executive Officer: John H. Johnson. 1991 sales figures: $261,364,000.

3. **Philadelphia Coca-Cola Bottling Company, Inc.** Founded: 1985. Headquarters: Philadelphia, Pa. Chief Executive Officer: J. Bruce Llewellyn. 1991 sales figures: $256,000,000.

4. **H. J. Russell & Company** (Construction and development; food services). Founded: 1952. Headquarters: Atlanta, Ga. Chief Executive Officer: Herman J. Russell. 1991 sales figures: $143,590,000.

5. **Barden Communications, Inc.** (Communications and real estate; development). Founded: 1981. Headquarters: Detroit, Mich. Chief Executive Officer: Don H. Barden. 1991 sales figures: $91,200,000.

6. **Garden State Cable Television.** Founded: 1989. Headquarters: Cherry Hill, N.J. Chief Executive Officer: J. Bruce Llewellyn. 1991 sales figures: $88,000,000.

7. **Soft Sheen Products, Inc.** (Hair care products). Founded: 1964. Headquarters: Chicago, Ill. Chief Executive Officer: Edward G. Gardner. 1991 sales figures: $87,900,000.

8. **RMS Technologies, Inc.** (Computer and technical services). Founded: 1977. Headquarters: Marlton, N.J. Chief Executive Officer: David W. Huggins. 1991 sales figures: $79,856,000.

9. **Stop Shop and Save** (Supermarket chain). Founded: 1978. Headquarters: Baltimore, Md. Chief Executive Officers: Henry T. Baines and Edward Hunt. 1991 sales figures: $66,000,000.

10. **The Bing Group** (Steel processing and metal stamping distribution). Founded: 1980. Headquarters: Detroit, Mich. Chief Executive Officer: David Bing. 1991 sales figures: $64,898,000.

11. **Technology Applications, Inc.** (Information systems integration). Founded: 1977. Headquarters: Alexandria, Va. Chief Executive Officer: James I. Chatman. 1991 sales figures: $64,000,000.

12. **Trans Jones, Inc. and Jones Transfer Company** (Transportation services). Founded: 1986. Headquarters: Monroe, Mich. Chief Executive Officer: Gary L. White. 1991 sales figures: $61,200,000.

13. **Mays Chemical Company, Inc.** (Industrial chemical distributors). Founded: 1980. Headquarters: Indianapolis, Ind. Chief Executive Officer: William G. Mays. 1991 sales figures: $56,700,000.

14. **Pulsar Data Systems, Inc.** (Systems integration; office automation; computer resaler). Founded: 1982. Headquarters: Lanham, Md. Chief Executive Officer: William W. Davis, Sr. 1991 sales figures: $53,000,000.

15. **Black Entertainment Television (BET) Holdings, Inc.** Founded: 1980. Headquarters: Washington, D.C. Chief Executive Officer: Robert L. Johnson. 1991 sales figures: $50,809,000.

16. **The Maxima Group** (Systems engineering and computer facilities management). Founded: 1978. Headquarters: Lanham, Md. Chief Executive Officer: Joshua I. Smith. 1991 sales figures: $49,824,000.

17. **Network Solutions, Inc.** (Systems integration). Founded: 1979. Headquarters: Herndon, Va. Chief Executive Officer: Emmit J. McHenry. 1991 sales figures: $48,800,000.

18. **Community Foods, Inc.** (Supermarkets). Founded: 1970. Headquarters: Baltimore, Md. Chief Executive Officer: Oscar A. Smith, Jr. 1991 sales figures: $47,500,000.

19. **Pepsi-Cola of Washington, D.C., L.P.** Founded: 1990. Headquarters: Washington, D.C. Chief Executive Officer: Earl G. Graves. 1991 sales figures: $44,112,000.

20. **Johnson Products Company, Inc.** (Hair and personal care products manufacturer). Founded: 1954. Headquarters: Chicago, Ill. Chief Executive Officer: Eric G. Johnson. 1991 sales figures: $44,000,000.

21. **Luster Products Company** (Hair care products manufacturer and distributor). Founded: 1957. Headquarters: Chicago, Ill. Chief Executive Officer: Jory Luster. 1991 sales figures: $44,000,000.

22. **Surface Protection Industries, Inc.** (Paint and specialty coatings manufacturer). Founded: 1978. Headquarters: Los Angeles, Calif. Chief Executive Officer: Robert C. Davidson, Jr. 1991 sales figures: $44,000,000.

23. **Essence Communications, Inc.** Founded: 1969. Headquarters: New York, N.Y. Chief Executive Officer: Edward Lewis. 1991 sales figures: $43,254,000.

24. **Granite Broadcasting Corporation** (Television). Founded: 1988. Headquarters: New York, N.Y. Chief Executive Officer: W. Don Cornwell. 1991 sales figures: $39,986,000.

25. **Westside Distributors** (Beer and snack foods distributor). Founded: 1974. Headquarters: South Gate, Calif. Chief Executive Officer: Edison R. Lara, Sr. 1991 sales figures: $39,000,000.

26. **Grimes Oil Company, Inc.** (Petroleum products distributor). Founded: 1940. Headquarters: Boston, Mass. Chief Executive Officer: Calvin M. Grimes. 1991 sales figures: $36,000,000.

27. **Calhoun Enterprises** (Supermarkets). Founded: 1984. Headquarters: Montgomery, Ala. Chief Executive Officer: Greg Calhoun. 1991 sales figures: $35,800,000.

28. **Gold Line Refining, Ltd.** (Oil refinery). Founded: 1990. Headquarters: Houston, Tex. Chief Executive Officer: Earl Thomas. 1991 sales figures: $35,720,000.

29. **Beauchamp Distributing Company** (Beer distributor). Founded: 1971. Headquarters: Compton, Calif. Chief Executive Officer: Patrick L. Beauchamp. 1991 sales figures: $34,500,000.

30. **The Gourmet Companies** (Food service; golf facilities management). Founded: 1975. Headquarters: Atlanta, Ga. Chief Executive Officer: Nathaniel R. Goldston III. 1991 sales figures: $34,300,000.

31. **Am-Pro Protective Agency, Inc.** (Security guard services). Founded: 1982. Headquarters: Columbia, S.C. Chief Executive Officer: John E. Brown. 1991 sales figures: $34,300,000.

32. **Rush Communications** (Music publishing; television/film/radio production and artist management). Founded: 1990. Headquarters: New York, N.Y. Chief Executive Officer: Russell Simmons. 1991 sales figures: $34,000,000.

33. **Pro-Line Corporation** (Hair care products manufacturer and distributor). Founded: 1970. Headquarters: Dallas, Tex. Chief Executive Officer: Isabel P. Cottrell. 1991 sales figures: $33,826,000.

34. **Integrated Systems Analysts, Inc.** (Engineering; technical support; electronic repair). Founded: 1980. Headquarters: Ar-

lington, Va. Chief Executive Officer: C. Michael Gooden. 1991 sales figures: $33,500,000.

35. Wesley Industries, Inc. (Industrial coatings and grey iron foundry products). Founded: 1983. Headquarters: Flint, Mich. Chief Executive Officer: Delbert W. Mullens. 1991 sales figures: $32,500,000.

36. The Thacker Organization (Construction; construction management; engineering). Founded: 1970. Headquarters: Decatur, Ga. Chief Executive Officer: Floyd G. Thacker. 1991 sales figures: $30,800,000.

37. Automated Sciences Group, Inc. (Information and sensor technology). Founded: 1974. Headquarters: Silver Spring, Md. Chief Executive Officer: Conrad Hipkins. 1991 sales figures: $30,000,000.

38. Input Output Computer Services, Inc. (Computer software and systems integration). Founded: 1969. Headquarters: Waltham, Mass. Chief Executive Officer: Thomas A. Farrington. 1991 sales figures: $30,000,000.

39. Brooks Sausage Company, Inc. Founded: 1985. Headquarters: Chicago, Ill. Chief Executive Officer: Frank B. Brooks. 1991 sales figures: $29,750,000.

40. Orchem, Inc. (Specialty chemicals manufacturer). Founded: 1981. Headquarters: Cincinnati, Ohio. Chief Executive Officer: Oscar Robertson. 1991 sales figures: $28,500,000.

41. Crest Computer Supply (Computer hardware and software supplier). Founded: 1984. Headquarters: Skokie, Ill. Chief Executive Officer: Gale Sayers. 1991 sales figures: $28,000,000.

42. Yancy Minerals (Industrial metals, minerals, and coal distributors). Founded: 1977. Headquarters: Woodbridge, Conn. Chief Executive Officer: Earl J. Yancy. 1991 sales figures: $27,000,000.

43. Metters Industries, Inc. (Systems engineering; computer science; telecommunications). Founded: 1981. Headquarters: McLean, Va. Chief Executive Officer: Samuel Metters. 1991 sales figures: $26,829,000.

44. Trumark, Inc. (Metal stamping; manufacturing; welding). Founded: 1985. Headquarters: Lansing, Mich. Chief Executive Officer: Carlton L. Guthrie. 1991 sales figures: $26,500,000.

45. Inner City Broadcasting Corporation (Radio, television, and cable television franchise). Founded: 1972. Headquarters: New York, N.Y. Chief Executive Officer: Pierre Sutton. 1991 sales figures: $26,000,000.

46. Premium Distributors, Inc., of Washington, D.C. (Beer distributors). Founded: 1984. Headquarters: Washington, D.C.

Chief Executive Officer: Henry Neloms. 1991 sales figures: $26,000,000.

47. Restoration Supermarket Corporation (Supermarkets and drugstores). Founded: 1977. Headquarters: Brooklyn, N.Y. Chief Executive Officer: Roderick B. Mitchell. 1991 sales figures: $25,300,000.

48. Queen City Broadcasting, Inc. (Network television affiliates). Founded: 1985. Headquarters: New York, N.Y. Chief Executive Officer: J. Bruce Llewellyn. 1991 sales figures: $25,200,000.

49. Parks Sausage Company. Founded: 1951. Headquarters: Baltimore, Md. Chief Executive Officer: Raymond V. Haysbert, Sr. 1991 sales figures: $25,002,000.

50. American Development Corporation (Manufacturing and sheet metal fabrication). Founded: 1972. Headquarters: North Charleston, S.C. Chief Executive Officer: W. Melvin Brown, Jr. 1991 sales figures: $25,000,000.

51. Superb Manufacturing, Inc. (Automotive parts supplier). Founded: 1985. Headquarters: Detroit, Mich. Chief Executive Officer: Dave Bing. 1991 sales figures: $25,000,000.

52. Systems Management American Corporation (Computer systems integration). Founded: 1970. Headquarters: Norfolk, Va. Chief Executive Officer: Herman E. Valentine. 1991 sales figures: $24,000,000.

53. African Development Public Investment Corporation (African commodities and air charter service). Founded: 1985. Headquarters: Hollywood, Calif. Chief Executive Officer: Dick Griffey. 1991 sales figures: $23,000,000.

54. Regal Plastics Company, Inc. (Custom plastic; ejection molding). Founded: 1985. Headquarters: Roseville, Mich. Chief Executive Officer: William F. Pickard. 1991 sales figures: $22,857,000.

55. Dick Griffey Productions (Entertainment). Founded: 1975. Headquarters: Hollywood, Calif. Chief Executive Officer: Dick Griffey. 1991 sales figures: $22,000,000.

56. R.O.W. Sciences, Inc. (Biomedical and health services; research and information systems). Founded: 1983. Headquarters: Rockville, Md. Chief Executive Officer: Ralph O. Williams. 1991 sales figures: $22,000,000.

57. Powers and Sons Construction Company, Inc. Founded: 1967. Headquarters: Gary, Ind. Chief Executive Officer: Mamon Powers, Sr. 1991 sales figures: $21,663,000.

58. Orpack-Stone Corporation (Corrugated containers manufacturers). Founded: 1990. Headquarters: Herrin, Ill. Chief Executive Officer: Oscar Robertson. 1991 sales figures: $21,000,000.

59. Advanced Consumer Marketing Corporation (Information systems integration; mail-order products). Founded: 1984. Headquarters: Burlingame, Calif. Chief Executive Officer: Harry W. Brooks, Jr. 1991 sales figures: $20,704,000.

60. Summa-Harrison Metal Products, Inc. (Engineering and metal stampings). Founded: 1978. Headquarters: Mt. Clemens, Mich. Chief Executive Officer: Charlie J. Harrison, Jr. 1991 sales figures: $20,390,000.

61. Burns Enterprises (Janitorial services; light manufacturing; supermarkets). Founded: 1969. Headquarters: Louisville, Ky. Chief Executive Officer: Tommie Burns, Jr. 1991 sales figures: $20,000,000.

62. V-Tech, Inc. (Biomedical test products manufacturer). Founded: 1982. Headquarters: Pomona, Calif. Chief Executive Officer: James E. Parker. 1991 sales figures: $20,000,000.

63. Stephens Engineering Company, Inc. (System integration, facility and computer maintenance). Founded: 1979. Headquarters: Lanham, Md. Chief Executive Officer: Wallace O. Stephens. 1991 sales figures: $20,000,000.

64. Navcom Systems, Inc. (Electronic engineering system design and integration). Founded: 1986. Headquarters: Manassas, Va. Chief Executive Officer: Elijah "Zeke" Jackson. 1991 sales figures: $20,000,000.

65. Simmons Enterprises, Inc. (Aerospace engineering and trucking). Founded: 1970. Headquarters: Cincinnati, Ohio. Chief Executive Officer: Carvel E. Simmons. 1991 sales figures: $19,620,000.

66. H. F. Henderson Industries, Inc. (Industrial process controls and defense electronics). Founded: 1954. Headquarters: West Caldwell, N.J. Chief Executive Officer: Henry F. Henderson, Jr. 1991 sales figures: $19,200,000.

67. Bronner Brothers (Hair care products manufacturer). Founded: 1947. Headquarters: Atlanta, Ga. Chief Executive Officer: Nathaniel Bronner, Sr. 1991 sales figures: $19,000,000.

68. Best Foam Fabricators, Inc. (Corrugated boxes and cushioning materials manufacturer). Founded: 1981. Headquarters: Chicago, Ill. Chief Executive Officer: Keith A. Hasty. 1991 sales figures: $19,000,000.

69. Dual & Associates, Inc. (Engineering and technical services). Founded: 1983. Headquarters: Arlington, Va. Chief Executive Officer: J. Fred Dual, Jr. 1991 sales figures: $18,725,000.

70. Telephone Advertising Corporation of America, Inc. (Public telephone kiosks). Founded: 1988. Headquarters: Atlanta, Ga.

Chief Executive Officer: Herbert H. Hamlett, Sr. 1991 sales figures: $18,605,000.

71. Viking Enterprises Corporation (Color separation and commercial printing). Founded: 1990. Headquarters: Chicago, Ill. Chief Executive Officer: Fletcher E. Allen. 1991 sales figures: $18,500,000.

72. C. H. James & Company (Wholesale food distribution). Founded: 1883. Headquarters: Charleston, W.Va. Chief Executive Officer: Charles H. James III. 1991 sales figures: $18,004,000.

73. Earl G. Graves Ltd. (Magazine publishing). Founded: 1970. Headquarters: New York, N.Y. Chief Executive Officer: Earl G. Graves. 1991 sales figures: $17,450,000.

74. Sylvest Management Systems Corporation (Computer systems and engineering). Founded: 1987. Headquarters: Lanham, Md. Chief Executive Officer: Gary S. Murray. 1991 sales figures: $16,800,000.

75. Accurate Information Systems, Inc. (Software development and systems integration). Founded: 1983. Headquarters: South Plainfield, N.J. Chief Executive Officer: Stephen Yelity. 1991 sales figures: $16,500,000.

76. Terry Manufacturing Company, Inc. (Apparel manufacturing). Founded: 1963. Headquarters: Roanoke, Va. Chief Executive Officer: Roy D. Terry. 1991 sales figures: $16,000,000.

77. A. L. Eastmond & Sons, Inc. (Boilers and storage tanks manufacturer). Founded: 1925. Headquarters: Bronx, N.Y. Chief Executive Officer: Leon Eastmond. 1991 sales figures: $15,402,000.

78. A Minority Entity, Inc. (Janitorial and food services). Founded: 1978. Headquarters: Norco, La. Chief Executive Officer: Burnell K. Moliere. 1991 sales figures: $15,225,000.

79. Drew Pearson Companies (Sports licensing and sportswear manufacturer). Founded: 1985. Headquarters: Addison, Tex. Chief Executive Officers: Drew Pearson and Ken Shead. 1991 sales figures: $15,002,000.

80. Systems Engineering & Management Associates, Inc. (Computer technical support services). Founded: 1985. Headquarters: Falls Church, Va. Chief Executive Officer: James C. Smith. 1991 sales figures: $15,000,000.

81. Solo Joint, Inc. (Cross Colours; apparel manufacturer). Founded: 1990. Headquarters: Los Angeles, Calif. Chief Executive Officer: Carl Jones. 1991 sales figures: $15,000,000.

82. Consolidated Beverage Corporation (Soft drink bottler and distributor). Founded: 1978. Headquarters: New York, N.Y. Chief Executive Officer: Albert N. Thompson. 1991 sales figures: $14,600,000.

83. American Urban Radio Networks. Founded: 1973. Headquarters: New York, N.Y. Chief Executive Officer: Sydney L. Small. 1991 sales figures: $14,000,000.

84. Walker International Transportation, Inc. Founded: 1989. Headquarters: Jamaica, N.Y. Chief Executive Officer: Emmett F. Walker, Jr. 1991 sales figures: $13,600,000.

85. Delta Enterprises, Inc. (Electronics, railroad products, apparel, and wood products). Founded: 1969. Headquarters: Greenville, Miss. Chief Executive Officer: Harold L. Hall. 1991 sales figures: $13,500,000.

86. Carter Industrial Services, Inc. (Shipping container repair and trucking). Founded: 1976. Headquarters: Anderson, Ind. Chief Executive Officer: Will J. Carter. 1991 sales figures: $13,125,000.

87. Watiker & Son, Inc. (Highways, bridges, paving, drainage, and mine reclamation). Founded: 1973. Headquarters: Zanesville, Ohio. Chief Executive Officer: Al Watiker, Jr. 1991 sales figures: $13,000,000.

88. Ozanne Construction Company, Inc. Founded: 1956. Headquarters: Cleveland, Ohio. Chief Executive Officer: Leroy Ozanne. 1991 sales figures: $12,900,000.

89. Specialized Packaging International, Inc. (Packaging design and engineering). Founded: 1983. Headquarters: Hamden, Conn. Chief Executive Officer: Carlton L. Highsmith. 1991 sales figures: $12,774,000.

90. James T. Heard Management Corporation (Fast foods). Founded: 1971. Headquarters: Cerritos, Calif. Chief Executive Officer: Lonear Heard. 1991 sales figures: $12,700,000.

91. Advance, Inc. (Computer systems integration; telecommunications). Founded: 1980. Headquarters: Arlington, Va. Chief Executive Officer: Dennis J. Brownlee. 1991 sales figures: $12,500,000.

92. Michael Alan Lewis Company (Auto parts manufacturer). Founded: 1978. Headquarters: Union, Ill. Chief Executive Officer: Wayne Embry, Sr. 1991 sales figures: $12,376,000.

93. Eltrex Industries (Officer furniture manufacturer fulfillment services; direct mail). Founded: 1968. Headquarters: Rochester, N.Y. Chief Executive Officer: Matthew Augustine. 1991 sales figures: $12,250,000.

94. Tresp Associates, Inc. (Military logistics; systems engineering; computer integration). Founded: 1981. Headquarters: Alexandria, Va. Chief Executive Officer: Lillian B. Handy. 1991 sales figures: $12,000,000.

95. Williams-Russell and Johnson, Inc. (Engineering, architecture, and construction management). Founded: 1976. Headquarters: Atlanta, Ga. Chief Executive Officer: Pelham C. Williams. 1991 sales figures: $11,300,000.

96. Black River Manufacturing, Inc. (Auto parts manufacturer). Founded: 1977. Headquarters: Port Huron, Mich. Chief Executive Officer: Isaac Lang, Jr. 1991 sales figures: $11,200,000.

97. Mandex, Inc. (Telecommunications; computer engineering services). Founded: 1974. Headquarters: Springfield, Va. Chief Executive Officer: Carl A. Brown. 1991 sales figures: $11,040,000.

98. William Cargile Contractor, Inc. Founded: 1956. Headquarters: Cincinnati, Ohio. Chief Executive Officer: William Cargile III. 1991 sales figures: 11,000,000.

99. RPM Supply Company, Inc. (Electrical and electric components distributor). Founded: 1977. Headquarters: Philadelphia, Pa. Chief Executive Officer: Robert P. Mapp. 1991 sales figures: $10,828,000.

100. Burrell Communications Group (Advertising and public relations). Founded: 1971. Headquarters: Chicago, Ill. Chief Executive Officer: Thomas J. Burrell. 1991 sales figures: $10,510,000.

Source: "The Nation's Largest Black Businesses." *Black Enterprise* 22 (June, 1992): 115-122.

Research Centers and Libraries

The following research centers and libraries are dedicated to gathering, recording, and preserving a wide range of materials related to African American history and culture. Some contain a wealth of material on African heritage and survivals in America. While many university, government, and urban public libraries also have substantial collections, this list has been limited to research centers and libraries whose primary focus is to support the study of African American life.

Amistad Research Center, Tilton Hall, Tulane University, 6823 St. Charles Ave., New Orleans, LA 70118. Telephone: (504) 865-5535. Founded: 1966. Director: Clifton H. Johnson.

Association for the Study of Afro-American Life and History, 1407 14th St., NW, Washington, DC 20005. Telephone: (202) 667-2822. Founded: 1915. Director: Karen Robinson.

Atlanta University, Trevor Arnett Library, 273 Chestnut St., SW, Atlanta, GA 30314. Telephone: (404) 681-0251, ext. 335.

Black Music Archives, 1130 S. Michigan Ave. #3204, Chicago, IL 60605-2322. Founded: 1976. Director: Dominique-René de Lerma.

Black Periodical Literature Project, 1827-1940, Department of English, Duke University, Durham, NC 27706. Telephone: (919) 684-3769. Founded: 1981. Director: Henry Louis Gates, Jr.

Black Research and Resource Center, 253 W. 72nd St., Suite 211A, New York, NY 10023. Telephone: (212) 496-2234. Founded: 1986. Director: Robert Hess.

Boston University, African Studies Library, 771 Commonwealth Ave., Boston, MA 02215. Telephone: (617) 353-3726.

Boston University, African Studies Center, 125 Bay State Rd., Boston, MA 02215. Telephone: (617) 353-3674. Founded: 1953. Director: Allan Hoben.

Brooklyn College, City University of New York, Africana Research Center, 3105 James Hall Building, Brooklyn, NY 11210. Telephone: (718) 780-5597. Founded: 1968. Director: George Cunningham.

Clark Atlanta University, Southern Center for Studies in Public Policy, Brawley and Fair Sts., SW, Atlanta, GA 30314. Telephone: (404) 880-8085. Founded: 1968. Director: Robert A. Holmes.

Clemson University, Center for the Study of the Black Experience in Higher Education, E-103 Martin Hall, Clemson, SC 29634-5404. Telephone: (803) 656-0313 Founded: 1988. Director: Herman G. Green.

College of Staten Island, City University of New York, Institute for African American Studies, 130 Stuyvesant Pl., Staten Island, New York, NY 10301. Telephone: (718) 390-7990. Founded: 1969. Director: Calvin B. Holder.

Columbia University, Institute of African Studies, 420 W. 118th St., New York, NY 10027. Telephone: (212) 854-4633. Founded: 1982. Director: George Bond.

Cornell University, Africana Studies and Research Center, 310 Triphammer Rd., Ithaca, NY 14853. Telephone: (607) 255-5218. Founded: 1969. Director: Robert Harris.

Fisk University Library, Special Collections, Fisk University, Nashville, TN 37203. Telephone: (615) 329-8730.

Florida State University, Black Abolitionists Papers Project, Department of History, Tallahassee, FL 32306. Telephone: (904) 644-4527. Founded: 1976. Director: C. Peter Ripley.

Hampton Institute, Collis P. Huntington Memorial Library, Hampton, VA 23668. Telephone: (804) 727-5371.

Harvard University, W. E. B. Du Bois Institute for Afro-American Research, 44 Brattle St., Cambridge, MA 02138. Telephone: (617) 495-4192. Founded: 1975. Director: Peter J. Gomes (Acting).

Hoover Institution, Africa Collection, Stanford, CA 94305. Telephone: (415) 725-3505.

Howard University, African Studies and Research Program, Washington, DC 20059. Telephone: (202) 806-7115. Founded: 1953. Director: Sulayman S. Nyang.

Howard University, Institute for Urban Affairs and Research, 2900 Van Ness St., NW, Washington, DC 20008. Telephone: (202) 686-6770. Founded: 1972. Director: Lawrence E. Gary.

Howard University, Moorland-Spingarn Research Center, 500 Howard Pl., NW, Washington, DC 20059. Telephone: (202) 806-7239. Founded: 1914. Director: Elinor DesVerney Sinette (Chief Librarian).

Indiana University, African Studies Program, Bloomington, IN 47405. Telephone: (812) 855-6825. Founded: 1961. Director: Patrick O'Meara.

Indiana University, Afro-American Arts Institute, 109 N. Jordan Ave., Bloomington, IN 47405. Telephone: (812) 855-9501.

Founded: 1974. Director: Charles Sukes (Executive).

Institute for the Preservation and Study of African-American Writing, P.O. Box 50172, Washington, DC 20004. Telephone: (202) 628-0454. Founded: 1978. Director: Joseph Jordan.

Joint Center for Political and Economic Studies, 1301 Pennsylvania Ave., NW, Suite 400, Washington, DC 20004. Telephone: (202) 626-3500. Founded: 1970. Director: Milton Morris (V. Pres. of Research).

Kent State University, Institute for African American Affairs, 18 Ritchie Hall, Kent, OH 44240. Telephone: (216) 672-2300. Founded: 1969. Director: Mohan Kaul.

Library of Congress, African Section, African and Middle Eastern Division, Adams Building, Room 1026A, Washington, DC 20540. Telephone: (202) 707-5528.

Martin Luther King, Jr., Center for Nonviolent Social Change, Inc., 449 Auburn Ave., NE, Atlanta, GA 30312. Telephone: (404) 524-1956. Director: Coretta Scott King (President).

Michigan State University, African Studies Center, East Lansing, MI 48824-1035. Telephone: (517) 353-1700. Founded: 1960. Director: David Wiley.

National Black Child Development Institute, 1463 Rhode Island Ave., NW, Washington, DC 20005. Telephone: (202) 387-1281. Founded: 1970. Director: Evelyn K. Moore.

National Caucus and Center on Black Aged, 1424 K St., NW, Suite 500, Washington, DC 20005. Telephone: (202) 637-8400. Founded: 1970. Director: Samuel J. Simmons (President).

National Institute for Women of Color, 1301-20th St., NW, Suite 202, Washington, DC 20036. Telephone: (202) 296-2661. Founded: 1981. Director: Sharon Parker (Chair, Bd. of Directors).

National Urban Coalition, 8601 Georgia Ave., Suite 500, Silver Spring, MD 20910. Telephone: (301) 495-4999. Founded: 1967. Director: Ramona H. Edelin (President).

National Urban League Research Department, 1111 14th St., NW, 6th Floor, Washington, DC 20005. Telephone: (202) 898-1604. Director: Billy J. Tidwell (Dir. of Research).

New York Public Library, Schomburg Center for Research in Black Culture, 515 Malcolm X Blvd., New York, NY 10037-1801. Telephone: (212) 491-2200. Founded: 1925. Director: Howard Dodson (Chief).

Niagara University, Center for the Study and Stabilization of the Black Family, P.O. Box 367, Niagara Falls, NY 14109. Telephone: (716) 285-1212. Director: Umeme Sababu.

North Carolina Central University, Institute on Desegregation, 214 Taylor Education Building, Durham, NC 27707. Telephone: (919) 560-6367. Founded: 1972. Director: Beverly W. Jones.

Northern Illinois University, Center for Black Studies, DeKalb, IL 60115. Telephone: (815) 753-1709. Founded: 1970. Director: Admasu Zike.

Northwestern University Library, Melville J. Herskovits Library of African Studies, Evanston, IL 60208-2300. Telephone: (708) 491-7684.

Northwestern University, Program of African Studies, 620 Library Pl., Evanston, IL 60208. Telephone: (708) 491-7323. Founded: 1948. Director: David William-Cohen.

Ohio University, African Studies Program, 56 E. Union St., Athens, OH 45701. Telephone: (614) 593-1834. Founded: 1964. Director: Gifford Doxsee.

Ohio University, Center for Afro-American Studies, 300 Lindley Hall, Athens, OH 45701. Telephone: (614) 593-4546. Founded: 1969. Director: Vattel T. Rose.

Purdue University, Afro-American Studies Center, 326 Stone Hall, West Lafayette, IN 47907. Telephone: (317) 494-5680. Founded: 1974. Director: Carolyn E. Johnson.

Queens College, City University of New York, Africana Studies and Research Institute, 65-30 Kissena Blvd., Flushing, NY 11367. Telephone: (718) 520-7545. Founded: 1973. Director: Omayemi Agbeyebe.

Seton Hall University, Center for African American Studies, 400 S. Orange Ave., South Orange, NJ 07079. Telephone: (201) 761-9411. Founded: 1970. Director: Julia A. Miller.

Spelman College, Women's Research and Resource Center, Box 115, Atlanta, GA 30314. Telephone: (404) 681-3643. Founded: 1981. Director: Beverly Guy-Sheftall.

Tuskegee Institute, Division of Behavioral Science Research, 1506 Franklin Rd., Tuskegee, AL 36088. Telephone: (205) 727-8575. Founded: 1967. Director: Paul L. Wall.

University of California at Los Angeles, African Studies Center, 405 Hilgard Ave., Los Angeles, CA 90024-1310. Telephone: (310) 825-3779. Founded: 1959. Director: Merrick Posnansky.

University of California at Los Angeles, Center for Afro-American Studies, 160 Haines Hall, 405 Hilgard Ave., Los Angeles, CA 90024-1545. Telephone: (310) 825-7403. Founded: 1969. Director: M. Belinda Tucker (Acting).

University of California at Los Angeles, National Study of Black College Students, Department of Sociology, 405 Hilgard Ave., Los Angeles, CA 90024-1551. Telephone: (310) 206-7107. Director: Walter R. Allen.

University of California at Santa Barbara, Center for Black Studies, Santa Barbara, CA 93106. Telephone: (805) 893-3914. Founded: 1969. Director: Gerald C. Horne (Acting).

University of Chicago, Committee on African and African-American Studies, 5828 S. University Ave., Chicago, IL 60637. Telephone: (312) 702-8344. Director: Jean Conaroff (Chair).

University of Florida, Center for African Studies, 470 Grinter Hall, Gainesville, FL 32611. Telephone: (904) 392-2183. Founded: 1964. Director: Peter R. Schmidt.

University of Houston, African and Afro-American Studies Program, College of Humanities and Fine Arts, Agnes Arnold Hall, Houston, TX 77204-3784. Telephone: (713) 749-2900. Founded: 1969. Director: Lawrence Currey (Assoc. Dean).

University of Illinois, Afro-American Studies and Research Program, 1204 W. Oregon, Urbana, IL 61801. Telephone: (217) 333-7781. Founded: 1969. Director: Alice A. Deck (Acting).

University of Illinois, Center for African Studies, 1208 W. California, Room 101, Urbana, IL 61801. Telephone: (217) 333-6335. Founded: 1970. Director: D. E. Crummey.

University of Massachusetts at Boston, William Monroe Trotter Institute for the Study of Black Culture, Harbor Campus, Boston, MA 02125-3393. Telephone: (617) 287-5880. Founded: 1984. Director: Wornie L. Reed.

University of Michigan, Center for Afro-American and African Studies, Room 200 W. Engineering Building, 550 E. University, Ann Arbor, MI 48109-1092. Telephone: (313) 764-5514. Founded: 1970. Director: Earl Lewis (Interim).

University of Michigan, Program for Research on Black Americans, 5118 Institute for Social Research, 426 Thompson St., P.O. Box 1248, Ann Arbor, MI 48106. Telephone: (313) 763-0045. Founded: 1976. Director: James S. Jackson.

University of Texas at Austin, African and Afro-American Studies & Research Center, Jester A232A, Austin, TX 78705. Telephone: (512) 471-1784. Founded: 1969. Director: John Sibley Butler (Acting).

University of Virginia, Carter G. Woodson Institute for Afro-American and African Studies, 1512 Jefferson Park Ave., Charlottesville, VA 22903. Telephone: (804) 924-3109. Founded: 1981. Director: Armstead L. Robinson.

University of Wisconsin—Madison, African Studies Program, 1454 Van Hise Hall, 1220 Linden Dr., Madison, WI 53706. Telephone: (608) 262-2380. Founded: 1961. Director: Edris Makward.

Washington, D.C., Public Library, Black Studies Reference Division, 901 G St., NW, Washington, DC 20001. Telephone: (202) 727-1211.

Western Michigan University, Black Americana Studies Center, 814 Sprau Tower, Kalamazoo, MI 49008. Telephone: (616) 387-2661. Director: Leroi Ray, Jr.

Yale University Library, African Collection, James Weldon Johnson Memorial Collection of Negro Arts and Letters, Beinecke Rare Book and Manuscript Library, New Haven, CT 06520. Telephone: (203) 432-1882.

Colleges and Universities

The following colleges and universities either were founded as institutes of higher learning for African Americans or have predominantly African American student bodies as a result of serving communities where African Americans constitute a substantial proportion of the population. In order to reflect their regional distribution, the schools have been listed under the state or federal district in which they are located. Schools in the District of Columbia and the Virgin Islands have been included. The date in parentheses indicates the year that the institution was founded.

ALABAMA
Alabama A&M University (1875)
Alabama State University (1874)
Bishop State Community College (1927)
Concordia College (1922)
Lawson State Community College (1973)
Miles College (1905)
Oakwood College (1896)
Selma University (1878)
Stillman College (1876)
Talladega College (1867)
Tuskegee Institute (1881)

ARKANSAS
Arkansas Baptist College (1884)
Philander-Smith College (1877)
Shorter College (1886)
University of Arkansas, Pine Bluff (1873)

CALIFORNIA
Charles R. Drew University of Medicine and Science (1978)
Compton Community College (1927)

DELAWARE
Delaware State College (1891)

DISTRICT OF COLUMBIA
Howard University (1867)
University of the District of Columbia (1976)

FLORIDA
Bethune-Cookman College (1904)
Edward Waters College (1866)
Florida A&M University (1887)
Florida Memorial College (1879)

GEORGIA
Albany State College (1903)
Atlanta Metropolitan College (1974)
Clark Atlanta University (1869)
Fort Valley State College (1895)
Interdenominational Theological Center (1958)
Morehouse College (1867)
Morehouse School of Medicine (1975)
Morris Brown College (1881)
Paine College (1882)
Savannah State College (1890)
Spelman College (1881)

ILLINOIS
Chicago State University (1867)

KENTUCKY
Kentucky State University (1886)
Simmons Bible College (1879)

LOUISIANA
Dillard University (1869)

Grambling State University (1901)
Southern University and A&M College (1880)
Southern University—New Orleans (1959)
Southern University—Shreveport (1964)
Xavier University of Louisiana (1915)

MARYLAND
Bowie State University (1865)
Coppin State College (1900)
Morgan State University (1867)
Sojourner-Douglass College (1972)
University of Maryland, Eastern Shore (1886)

MASSACHUSETTS
Roxbury Community College (1973)

MICHIGAN
Highland Park Community College (1918)
Lewis College of Business (1929)
Wayne County Community College (1968)

MISSISSIPPI
Alcorn State University (1871)
Coahoma Community College (1949)
Hinds Community College—Utica Campus (1903)
Jackson State University (1877)
Mary Holmes Junior College (1892)
Mississippi Valley State University (1946)
Natchez Junior College (1885)
Prentiss Normal & Industrial Institute (1907)
Rust College (1866)
Tougaloo College (1869)

MISSOURI
Harris-Stowe State College (1857)
Lincoln University of Missouri (1866)

NEW YORK
Medgar Evers College of the City University of New York (1969)

NORTH CAROLINA
Barber-Scotia College (1867)
Bennett College (1873)
Elizabeth City State University (1891)
Fayetteville State University (1867)
Johnson C. Smith University (1867)
Livingstone College, Hood Theological Seminary (1879)
North Carolina A&T State University (1891)
North Carolina Central University (1910)
St. Augustine's College (1867)

Shaw University (1865)
Winston-Salem State University (1892)

OHIO
Central State University (1887)
Cuyahoga Community College (1963)
Wilberforce University (1856)

OKLAHOMA
Langston University (1897)

PENNSYLVANIA
Cheyney State University (1837)
Lincoln University of Pennsylvania (1854)

SOUTH CAROLINA
Allen University (1870)
Benedict College (1870)
Claflin College (1869)
Clinton Junior College (1894)
Denmark Technical College (1948)
Morris College (1908)
South Carolina State College (1896)
Voorhees College (1897)

TENNESSEE
Fisk University (1866)
Knoxville College (1875)
Lane College (1882)
LeMoyne-Owen College (1870)
Meharry Medical College (1876)
Morristown College (1881)
Tennessee State University (1912)

TEXAS
Bishop College (1881)
Huston-Tillotson College (1875)
Jarvis Christian College (1912)
Paul Quinn College (1872)
Prairie View A&M University (1876)
Southwestern Christian College (1949)
Texas College (1894)
Texas Southern University (1947)
Wiley College (1873)

VIRGIN ISLANDS
College of the Virgin Islands (1963)

VIRGINIA
Hampton University (1868)
Norfolk State University (1935)
St. Paul's College (1888)
Virginia State University (1882)
Virginia Union University (1865)

WEST VIRGINIA
West Virginia State College (1891)

Newspapers, Magazines, Journals, and Other Periodicals

The following list includes publications that are oriented toward African American readers—primarily as a result of the communities they serve or the subjects they address. Many are owned and operated by African Americans. In order to reflect their regional distribution, African American newspapers have been listed under the state or federal district in which they appear. The date in parentheses indicates the year that the publication was founded.

NEWSPAPERS

Alabama
Birmingham Times (1964)
Birmingham World (1930)
Greene County Democrat (Eutaw, 1890)
Inner City News (Mobile, 1977)
Mobile Beacon (1943)
Montgomery-Tuskegee Times (1977)
New Times, The (Mobile, 1981)
Shoals News Leader (Florence, 1980)
Speakin' Out News (Huntsville, 1980)

Arizona
Arizona Informant (Phoenix, 1958)

Arkansas
Arkansas State Press (Little Rock, 1941)

California
Bakersfield News Observer
Bayou Talk (Moreno Valley)
Berkeley Tri City Post (1963)
Black Voice News (Riverside, 1972)
California Advocate (Fresno, 1967)
California Voice (Sacramento, 1919)
Carson Bulletin
Central Star/Journal Wave (Los Angeles, 1919)
Compton Bulletin
Compton/Carson Wave
Culver City/Westchester Wave (1980)
Firestone Park News/Southeast News Press (1924)
Herald Dispatch (Los Angeles, 1952)
Inglewood/Hawthorne Wave (1978)
Inglewood Tribune
Los Angeles Sentinel (1934)
Lynwood Journal
Lynwood Wave (1919)
Mesa Tribune Wave (Los Angeles, 1919)
Metro Reporter (San Francisco, 1973)
Metro Star (Quartz Hill)
Metropolitan Gazette (Pasadena, 1966)
New Bayview (San Francisco, 1976)
Oakland Post (1963)
Precinct Reporter (San Bernardino, 1965)
Richmond Post (1963)
Sacramento Observer (1962)
San Bernardino American News, The (1969)
San Diego Voice and Viewpoint (1960)

San Francisco Post (1963)
Seaside Post News-Sentinel (1947)
Southwest News Wave (Los Angeles, 1919)
Southwest Topics/Sun Wave (Los Angeles, 1919)
Sun-Reporter (San Francisco, 1943)
Watts Star Review (1875)
Wilmington Beacon

Colorado
Denver Weekly News

Connecticut
Hartford Inquirer (1975)

Delaware
Defender, The (Wilmington, 1962)

District of Columbia
Metro Chronicle
New Observer
Washington Afro-American Tribune (1933)
Washington Capital Spotlight Newspaper, The (1953)
Washington Informer, The (1964)
Washington New Observer, The (1957)

Florida
Black Miami Weekly
Bulletin, The (Sarasota, 1959)
Capital Outlook (Tallahassee, 1964)
Daytona Times (1978)
Florida Sentinel-Bulletin (Tampa, 1945)
Florida Star Times (Jacksonville)
Florida Sun Review (Orlando, 1931)
Fort Pierce Chronicle (1957)
Miami Times, The (1923)
News Reporter (Tampa)
Orlando Times, The (1975)
Pensacola Voice (1966)
Weekly Challenger, The (St. Petersburg, 1967)
Westside Gazette (Fort Lauderdale, 1971)

Georgia
Atlanta Daily World (1928)
Atlanta Inquirer, The (1960)
Atlanta Tribune, The (1986)
Atlanta Voice, The (1966)
Columbus Times, The (1970)
Fort Valley Herald (1986)
Herald, The (Savannah, 1945)

Metro County Courier (Augusta, 1983)
Savannah Tribune, The (1875)
Southeastern News (Cordele)

Illinois
Chatham-Southeast Citizen (Chicago, 1965)
Chicago Citizen (1965)
Chicago Crusader (1940)
Chicago Independent Bulletin (1958)
Chicago Metro News (1965)
Chicago Shoreland News (1974)
Chicago South Shore Scene (1959)
Chicago Standard News (1984)
Chicago Weekend (1974)
Decatur Voice (1968)
East St. Louis Crusader
East St. Louis Monitor (1963)
Hyde Park Citizen (1987)
Mississippi Enterprise, The (Chicago, 1933)
Nightmoves (Chicago, 1980)
Observer (Chicago, 1964)
South End Citizen (Chicago, 1966)
South Suburban Citizen (Chicago, 1983)
South Suburban Standard (Chicago Heights, 1979)
Tri-City Journal (Chicago, 1978)

Indiana
Frost Illustrated (Fort Wayne, 1968)
Gary American (1927)
Gary New Crusader (1961)
Indianapolis Recorder, The (1895)
Info (Gary, 1963)

Iowa
New Iowa Bystander, The (Des Moines, 1893)

Kansas
Kansas City Voice, The
Miami Republican (Paola, 1866)
Western Spirit (Paola, 1871)

Kentucky
Louisville Defender (1933)
Suspension Press, The (Covington, 1982)

Louisiana
Alexandria News Weekly, The (1975)
Baton Rouge Community Leader (1952)
Community Leader (Baton Rouge)
Louisiana Weekly (New Orleans)

New Orleans Data News Weekly (1966)
Shreveport Sun, The (1920)
Maryland
Afro American, The (Baltimore, 1892)
Baltimore Afro-American (1892)
Every Wednesday (Baltimore, 1984)
Massachusetts
Bay State Banner (Dorchester, 1965)
Boston Greater News (1983)
Michigan
Citizen (Benton Harbor)
Ecorse Telegram (1945)
Grand Rapids Times, The (1959)
Jackson Blazer (1963)
Michigan Chronicle (Detroit, 1936)
Michigan Citizen (Highland Park, 1978)
Minnesota
Minneapolis Spokesman (1934)
St. Paul Recorder
Twin Cities Courier (Minneapolis)
Mississippi
Jackson Advocate (1937)
Mississippi Memo Digest (Meridian, 1961)
Missouri
Call (Kansas City, 1919)
Evening Whirl, The (St. Louis, 1938)
Kansas City Globe (1972)
St. Louis American, The (1928)
St. Louis Argus
St. Louis Crusader
St. Louis Sentinel Newspaper (1968)
New Jersey
Afro-American (East Orange)
New Jersey Afro-American (Newark, 1892)
New York
Afro-American Times (Brooklyn)
Amsterdam News (New York City, 1909)
Big Red News (Brooklyn, 1976)
Black American (New York City, 1960)
Brooklyn New York Recorder
Buffalo Criterion (1925)
Challenger, The (Buffalo, 1963)
City Sun, The (Brooklyn, 1984)
Communicade (Rochester, 1972)
Daily Challenge (Brooklyn)
Fine Print News (Buffalo)
Hudson Valley Black Press (Newburgh, 1983)
New York Voice, The (Flushing, 1959)
NY Carib News (New York City, 1982)
Westchester County Press (White Plains, 1928)
Westchester Observer (Mount Vernon)
North Carolina
Carolina Peacemaker (Greensboro, 1967)
Carolina Times, The (Durham, 1926)
Carolinian, The (Raleigh, 1940)
Charlotte Post, The (1887)
Fayetteville Black Times, The
Iredell County News (Statesville, 1980)

Metro Times Newspaper (Goldsboro, 1978)
Public Post, The (Laurinburg, 1981)
Wilmington Journal, The (1927)
Winston-Salem Chronicle (1974)
Ohio
Akron Reporter, The (1969)
Buckeye Review, The (Youngstown, 1937)
Call and Post (Cleveland, 1919)
Cincinnati Herald (1955)
South East Times (Cleveland)
Toledo Journal, The (1975)
Oklahoma
Black Chronicle, The (Oklahoma City, 1979)
Oklahoma Eagle, The (Tulsa, 1921)
Oregon
Portland Observer
Portland Skanner, The (1975)
Pennsylvania
New Pittsburgh Courier (1910)
Philadelphia New Observer (1975)
Philadelphia Tribune, The (1884)
Rhode Island
Ocean State Grapevine (Providence)
South Carolina
Charleston Black Times (1970)
Charleston Chronicle, The (1971)
Coastal Times, The (Charleston, 1983)
Columbia Black News (1970)
Florence Black Sun (1970)
Greenville Black Star
Orangeburg Black Voice (1970)
Rock Hill Black View (1970)
Sumter Black Post (1970)
View South News (Orangeburg, 1979)
Tennessee
Memphis Silver Star News
Tri-State Defender (Memphis, 1951)
Texas
Dallas Examiner (1986)
Dallas Post Tribune (1962)
Dallas Weekly Newspaper, The (1955)
Houston Defender (1930)
Houston Forward Times (1960)
Houston Informer (1893)
Houston Sun (1983)
Lubbock Southwest Digest
Villager, The (Austin, 1973)
Waco Messenger, The (1929)
Virginia
Journal & Guide (Richmond, 1900)
Richmond Afro-American (1882)
Roanoke Tribune (1938)
Washington
Facts News (Seattle, 1961)
Northwest Dispatch, The (Tacoma, 1982)
Seattle Medium (1970)
Tacoma True Citizen
West Virginia
West Virginia Beacon Digest (South Charleston, 1957)

Wisconsin
Milwaukee Community Journal (1976)
Milwaukee Courier (1964)
Milwaukee Star (1961)
Milwaukee Times

COLLEGE NEWSPAPERS
Campus Digest (Tuskegee Institute, Ala., 1931)
Famuan, The (Florida A&M University)
Fisk News (Fisk University, Tenn., 1950)
Herald, The (Texas Southern University, 1947)
Lincolnian, The (Lincoln University of Pennsylvania, 1929)
Voice of the Wildcats (Bethune-Cookman College, Fla., 1974)

MAGAZINES
A&T Register (North Carolina A&T University, 1892)
About... Time (1972)
Aim—America's Intercultural Magazine (1974)
American Visions: The Magazine of Afro-American Culture (1986)
AUC Digest (Atlanta University Center, 1973)
BLACK CAREERS (1965)
Black College Sports Review
Black Collegian, The (1970)
Black Enterprise (1970)
Black Family (1980)
Black Health (1988)
Black News Digest (U.S. Department of Labor)
Black Tennis Magazine (1977)
Black Writer, The (1974)
Caribbean Review (1969)
Chocolate Singles
Class Magazine (1979)
Clubdate Magazine (1979)
CORPORATE HEADQUARTERS (1985)
Crisis, The (National Association for the Advancement of Colored People, 1910)
Dollars & Sense Magazine (1973)
Ebony (1945)
EM: Ebony Man
Emerge (1989)
Essence (1970)
Gladiator (1989)
Impartial Citizen (1980)
In a Word (Black Catholics, 1983)
Ivy Leaf (Alpha Kappa Alpha Sorority, 1921)
Jet (1951)
Living Blues (Center for Study of Southern Culture, University of Mississippi, 1970)
Message Magazine (1898)

Minorities and Women in Business
(1984)
Minority Business Entrepreneur (1984)
Minority Engineer (1980)
National Scene Magazine
Network Africa (1982)
New Research Traveler &
Conventioneer (1942)
New Visions (1989)
Northwest Ethnic News (1984)
NSBE Magazine (National Society of
Black Engineers, 1985)
PHYLON (Atlanta University, 1940)
Players (1973)
Right On! (1971)
SISTERS (National Council of Negro
Women, 1988)
Sophisticate's Black Hairstyles and Care
Guide (1984)
U.S. Black Engineer (1980)
Washington View (1989)

RELIGIOUS NEWSPAPERS AND MAGAZINES

Catholic Mentor, The (1986)
Christian Index, The (Christian
Methodist Episcopal Church, 1868)
Final Call, The (Nation of Islam, 197?)
Muslim Journal (Islamic international
paper, 1961)
Star of Zion (African Methodist
Episcopal Zion church, 1876)
Voice of Missions (Black Methodist
Episcopal church, 1898)

JOURNALS

Africa Today (1954)
Black American Literature Forum (1967)
Black Scholar, The (1969)
Botswana Review (1989)
Callaloo (1978)
Cultural Survival Quarterly (1976)
International Journal on Intercultural
Relations

International Review of African
American Art
Interracial Books for Children Bulletin
(1967)
Journal of Black Studies (1970)
Journal of Ethnic Stuides (1973)
Journal of Intergroup Relations (1960)
Journal of Modern African Studies
Journal of Negro Education, The (1932)
Journal of Negro History (1916)
Journal of the National Medical
Association (1909)
Journal of the National Technical
Association (1926)
Lincoln Review (1979)
Negro Educational Review (1950)
Negro History Bulletin, The (1937)
Review of Black Political Economy
(1970)
Western Journal of Black Studies, The
(1977)

Radio and Television Stations

The following list includes radio and television stations that are owned and operated by African Americans. Many have come under black ownership as a result of changes in Federal Communications Commission (FCC) regulations that encouraged the transfer of broadcasting licenses to owners who are members of a minority group. Many of the radio stations are affiliated with two New York-based African American broadcasting networks, the National Black Network and the Sheridan Broadcasting Network, and some of the television stations broadcast programs produced by Black Entertainment Television (BET). In order to reflect their regional distribution, the stations have been listed under the state or federal district in which they broadcast.

Alabama
WAGG-AM
WAPZ-AM
WATV-AM
WAYE-AM
WBIL-FM
WBTG-FM
WENN-FM
WMMV-FM
WNPT-FM
WTQX-AM
WTSK-AM
WTUG-FM
WZZA-AM

Arizona
KJZZ-FM

Arkansas
KCAT-AM
KELD-AM
KITA-AM
KJWH-AM
KLRC-FM
KMTL-AM
KMZX-FM
KNEA-AM
KXAR-FM
WJAK-AM

California
KACE-FM
KBFN-AM
KBLX-FM
KDAY-AM
KDIA-AM
KEST-AM
KGFJ-AM
KJAZ-FM
KJLH-FM
KKAM-AM
KKBT-FM
KKGO-FM
KMJC-AM
KMYX-FM
KNTV-TV Channel 11 San Jose
KRML-AM
KSDS-FM
KSOL-FM
KUOR-FM

Connecticut
WKND-AM
WNHC-AM

WQQQ-FM
WYBC-FM

District of Columbia
WDCU-FM
WHMM-TV Channel 32
WHUR-FM
WKYS-FM
WMMJ-FM
WOL-AM
WUST-AM
WYCB-AM

Florida
WAMF-FM
WANM-AM
WAVS-AM
WCGL-AM
WEDR-FM
WEXY-AM
WHJX-FM
WHOG-AM
WHQT-FM
WIQI-FM
WJHM-FM
WJST-FM
WLIT-AM
WLOQ-FM
WLQY-AM
WLTG-AM
WLVJ-AM
WMBM-AM
WPOM-AM
WPUL-AM
WRBD-AM
WRFA-AM
WRXB-AM
WSVE-AM
WSWN-AM
WTMP-AM
WTOT-AM
WTVT-TV Channel 13 Tampa
WTWB-AM
WVIJ-FM
WWAB-AM
WYFX-AM
WZAZ-AM

Georgia
WCLK-FM
WDCY-AM
WDDO-AM
WFXA-AM

WFXM-FM
WGML-AM
WGOV-AM
WGUN-AM
WGXA-TV Channel 24 Macon
WHCJ-FM
WHGH-AM
WIGO-AM
WIQN-AM
WJGA-FM
WKIG-AM
WKZK-AM
WLOV-AM & WLOV-FM
WPGA-FM
WQVE-FM
WRDW-AM
WROM-AM
WSNT-AM & WSNT-FM
WSOK-AM
WTJH-AM
WVEE-FM
WXAG-AM
WXKO-AM
WXRS-AM
WYZE-AM

Illinois
WBEE-AM
WCFJ-AM
WEEK-TV Channel 25 Peoria
WESL-AM
WGCI-FM
WJPC-AM
WKDC-AM
WKRO-AM
WLNR-FM
WLUV-FM
WPNA-AM
WSBC-AM
WSIE-FM
WVON-AM
WXAN-FM

Indiana
WPTA-TV Channel 21 Fort Wayne
WPZZ-FM
WRTV-TV Channel 6 Indianapolis
WSLM-FM
WTLC-FM
WWCA-AM

Iowa
KBBG-FM

KCCK-FM
KIGC-FM
KTFC-FM
Kentucky
WCKU-FM
WLLV-AM
WLOU-AM
WQKS-AM
WRLV-AM
WTCV-AM
WWXL-AM
Louisiana
KBCE-FM
KDKS-FM
KFXZ-FM
KJCB-AM
KOKA-AM
KRUS-AM
KSLU-FM
KXZZ-AM
KYEA-FM
WABL-AM
WNOL-TV Channel 38 New Orleans
WQUE-AM & WQUE-FM
WXOK-AM
WYLD-AM
Maine
WVII-TV Channel 7 Bangor
Maryland
WANN-AM
WBGR-AM
WBZE-AM
WEAA-FM
WEBB-AM
WESM-FM
WJDY-AM
WWIN-AM & WWIN-FM
Massachusetts
WILD-AM
WJJW-FM
WLVG-AM
WMLN-FM
WWKX-FM
Michigan
WCHB-AM
WDZZ-FM
WFLT-AM
WGPR-FM
WGPR-TV Channel 62 Detroit
WGVU-FM
WILS-AM
WJLB-FM
WJZZ-FM
WKWM-AM
WLLJ-AM
WNMC-FM
WQBH-AM
WTLZ-FM
WXLA-AM
WYCE-FM
Minnesota
KBEM-FM

KBJR-TV Channel 6 Duluth
KTCJ-AM
Mississippi
WACR-AM
WALT-AM
WAML-AM
WBAD-FM
WESY-AM
WJMG-FM
WKKY-FM
WKRA-AM
WKXG-AM
WKXI-AM
WLBM-TV Channel 30 Meridian
WLBT-TV Channel 3 Jackson
WLTD-FM
WMIS-AM
WMLC-AM
WNBN-AM
WOAD-AM
WORV-AM
WQIC-AM
WQIS-AM
WRDC-AM
WRJH-FM
WRKN-AM
WTYJ-FM
Missouri
KATZ-AM & KATZ-FM
KCXL-AM
KIRL-AM
KMJM-FM
KPRS-FM
KPRT-AM
KSTL-AM
Nevada
KCEP-FM
New Jersey
WBJB-FM
WNJR-AM
WUSS-AM
New York
WAER-FM
WBLK-FM
WBLS-FM
WDKX-FM
WGMC-FM
WHEC-TV Channel 10 Rochester
WKBW-TV Channel 7 Buffalo
WLKA-FM
WRKS-FM
WUFO-AM
WWRL-AM
North Carolina
WAAA-AM
WARR-AM
WBCG-FM
WBMS-AM
WBTE-AM
WCKB-AM
WDRV-AM
WDUR-AM

WEAL-AM
WEGG-AM
WFXC-FM
WGCR-AM
WGIV-AM
WGSP-AM
WGTM-AM
WIKS-FM
WJMH-FM
WJOS-AM
WLLE-AM
WNAA-FM
WOKN-FM
WOOW-AM
WPEG-FM
WQOK-FM
WRCS-AM
WRRZ-AM
WRSV-FM
WRVS-FM
WSMX-AM
WSMY-AM
WSNC-FM
WSRC-AM
WTNC-AM
WVCB-AM
WWIL-AM
WYZD-AM
WZFX-FM
WZOO-AM
Ohio
WABQ-AM
WBBY-FM
WCKX-FM
WCPN-FM
WIZF-FM
WJMO-AM & WJMO-FM
WJTB-AM
WMMX-AM
WNOP-AM
WNRB-AM
WVKO-AM
WVOI-AM
WXTS-FM
WZAK-FM
Oklahoma
KPWR-AM
KTOW-FM
KXOJ-AM
Oregon
KBSP-TV Channel 22 Salem
KMHD-FM
Pennsylvania
WADV-AM
WAMO-AM & WAMO-FM
WCXJ-AM
WDAS-AM & WDAS-FM
WIBF-FM
WIMG-AM
WJSM-AM & WJSM-FM
WKDU-FM
WLIU-FM

WPLW-AM
WSAJ-AM
WTEL-AM
WUSL-FM
Rhode Island
WOTB-FM
WRIB-AM
South Carolina
WASC-AM
WCIG-FM
WDOG-FM
WFXA-FM
WHYZ-AM
WJKI-AM
WLBG-AM
WLGI-FM
WLWZ-FM
WMCJ-AM
WMNY-AM & WMNY-FM
WMTY-AM & WMTY-FM
WPAL-AM
WQIZ-AM
WQKI-AM
WSSB-FM
WTGH-AM
WUJM-AM & WUJM-FM
WVGB-AM
WWDM-FM
WWWZ-FM
WYNN-AM & WYNN-FM
WZJY-AM
Tennessee
KHUL-FM
KWAM-AM
WABD-AM
WBCV-AM
WBOL-AM

WDIA-AM
WETB-AM
WFKX-FM
WHRK-FM
WJTT-FM
WKJQ-AM
WLOK-AM
WMOT-FM
WNAH-AM
WNOO-AM
WRKM-AM
WSMS-FM
WSVT-AM
WVOL-AM
WWGR-AM
WXSS-AM
Texas
KALO-AM
KBUK-AM
KBWC-FM
KCHL-AM
KCOH-AM
KDLF-AM
KHRN-FM
KHVN-AM
KIIZ-AM
KJBX-AM
KJMZ-FM
KKDA-FM
KMHT-FM
KMJQ-FM
KMXO-AM
KNBO-AM
KNTU-FM
KPVU-FM
KRBA-AM
KRZI-AM

KSAU-FM
KSGB-AM
KSKY-AM
KTSU-FM
KTXS-TV Channel 12 Abilene
KZEY-AM
Utah
KMGR-AM
Virginia
WANT-AM
WBTX-AM
WCDX-FM
WGCV-AM
WILA-AM
WJCB-TV Channel 49 Hampton
WJJS-AM
WKBY-AM
WMYK-AM & WMYK-FM
WOWI-FM
WPLZ-FM
WRAP-AM
WTOY-AM
WVST-FM
Washington
KARI-AM
KEWU-FM
KKFX-AM
KRIZ-AM
West Virginia
WVKV-AM
Wisconsin
WJFW-TV Channel 12 Rhinelander
WMVP-AM
WNOV-AM
WYMS-FM

Bibliography

AFRICAN HERITAGE

Asante, Molefi K. *Afrocentricity*. Rev. ed. Trenton, N.J.: Africa World Press, 1988.

_____. Kemet, Afrocentricity, and Knowledge. Trenton, N.J.: Africa World Press, 1990.

Balandier, Georges, et al., eds. *Dictionary of Black African Civilization*. New York: Leon Amiel, 1974.

Barrett, Leonard E. *Soul Force: African Heritage in Afro-American Religion*. Garden City, N.J.: Anchor Press, 1974.

Bascom, William. *African Folktales in the New World*. Bloomington: Indiana University Press, 1992.

Beyan, Amos J. *The American Colonization Society and the Creation of the Liberian State: A Historical Perspective, 1822-1900*. Lanham, Md.: University Press of America, 1991.

Blassingame, John W. *The Slave Community: Plantation Life in the Antebellum South*. Rev. ed. New York: Oxford University Press, 1979.

Burkett, Randall K. *Garveyism as a Religious Movement*. Metuchen, N.J.: Scarecrow Press, 1978.

Campbell, Penelope. *Maryland in Africa: The Maryland Colonization Society, 1831-1857*. Urbana: University of Illinois Press, 1971.

Crowley, Daniel J. "Negro Folklore: An Africanist's View." *Texas Quarterly* 5 (Fall, 1962): 65-71.

Davidson, Basil. *Africa in History: Themes and Outlines*. Rev. ed. New York: Collier Books, 1991.

_____. *African Kingdoms*. Alexandria, Va.: Time-Life Books, 1978.

_____. *The Black Man's Burden: Africa and the Curse of the Nation-State*. New York: Times Books, 1993.

_____. *Discovering Our African Heritage*. Boston: Ginn, 1972.

Diop, Cheikh Anta. *The African Origin of Civilization: Myth or Reality*. Translated by Mercer Cook. New York: Lawrence Hill, 1974.

Drake, St. Clair. *Black Folk Here and There*. Vol. 1. Los Angeles: Center for Afro-American Studies, University of California Press, 1987.

_____. *Redemption of Africa and Black Religion*. Chicago: Third World Press, 1970.

Ellis, A. B. "Evolution in Folklore: Some West African Prototypes of the Uncle Remus Stories." *Popular Science Monthly* 48 (November, 1895): 93-104.

Franklin, John Hope, and Alfred A. Moss, Jr. *From Slavery to Freedom: A History of Negro Americans*. 6th ed. New York: Alfred A. Knopf, 1988.

Gerber, A. J. "Uncle Remus Traced to the Old World." *Journal of American Folklore* 6 (December, 1893): 245-257.

Harris, Joseph E., ed. *Global Dimensions of the African Diaspora*. Washington, D.C.: Howard University Press, 1982.

Harris, Katherine. *African and American Values: Liberia and West Africa*. Lanham, Md.: University Press of America, 1985.

Hodges, Norman E. W. *Breaking the Chains of Bondage: Black History from Its Origins in Africa to the Present*. New York: Simon & Schuster, 1972.

Holloway, Joseph E., and Winifred K. Vass. *The African Heritage of American English*. Bloomington: Indiana University Press, 1993.

Hutchinson, Louise Daniel. *Out of Africa: From West African Kingdoms to Civilizations*. Washington, D.C.: Smithsonian Institution Press, 1979.

Jackson, John G. *Introduction to African Civilizations*. New York: University Books, 1970.

Jones, Edward L. *Profiles in African Heritage*. Seattle: Frayn, 1972.

Kinshasa, Kwando M. *Emigration vs. Assimilation*. Jefferson, N.C.: McFarland, 1988.

Martin, Tony. *Race First: The Ideological and Organizational Struggles of Marcus Garvey and the Universal Negro Improvement Association*. Westport, Conn.: Greenwood Press, 1976.

Moses, Wilson J. *The Golden Age of Black Nationalism, 1850-1925*. Hamden, Conn.: Archon Books, 1978.

Mufwene, Salikoko S., ed. *Africanisms in Afro-American Language Varieties*. Athens: University of Georgia Press, 1993.

Owens, William. "Folklore of the Southern Negroes." *Lippincott's Magazine* 20 (December, 1877): 748-755.

Scruggs, Otey M. "We the Children of Africa in This Land: Alexander Crummell." In *Africa and the Afro-American Experience: Eight Essays*. Edited by Lorraine A. Williams. Washington, D.C.: Howard University Press, 1977.

Shick, Tom W. *Behold the Promised Land: A History of Afro-American Settler Society in Nineteenth Century Liberia*. Baltimore: The Johns Hopkins University Press, 1980.

Straudenraus, P. J. *The African Colonization Movement, 1816-1865*. New York: Columbia University Press, 1861.

Stuckey, Sterling, ed. *The Ideological Origins of Black Nationalism*. Boston: Beacon Press, 1972.

Van Sertima, Ivan. *They Came Before Columbus*. New York: Random House, 1976.

Wilmore, Gayraud S. *Black Religion and Black Radicalism: An Interpretation of the Religious History of Afro-American People*. 2d rev. ed. Maryknoll, N.Y.: Orbis Books, 1983.

BLACK NATIONALISM

Asante, S. K. B. *Pan African Protest: West Africa and the Italo-Ethiopian Crisis, 1934-41*. London: Longman, 1977.

Bracey, John H., Jr., August Meier, and Elliott Rudwick. *Black Nationalism in America*. The American Heritage series. Indianapolis: Bobbs-Merrill, 1970.

Carlisle, Rodney. *The Roots of Black Nationalism*. Port Washington, N.Y.: Kennikat Press, 1975.

Clarke, John Henrik, ed. *Marcus Garvey and the Vision of Africa*. New York: Vintage Books, 1974.

Cronon, Edmund David. *Black Moses: The Story of Marcus Garvey and the Universal Negro Improvement Association*. Madison: University of Wisconsin Press, 1955.

Esedebe, Peter Olisanwuche. *Pan Africanism: The Idea and the Movement, 1776-1963*. Washington, D.C.: Howard University Press, 1982.

Essien-Udom, Essien U. *Black Nationalism: A Search for an Identity in America*. New York: Dell Publishing Company, 1964.

"Farrakhan, Louis." *Contemporary Biography* 53 (April, 1992): 14-18.

Garvey, Marcus. *Philosophy and Opinions of Marcus Garvey*. 2 vols. Edited by Amy Jacques Garvey. New York: The Universal Publishing House, 1923-1925. Reprint. New York: Arno Press, 1968-1969.

Geiss, Imanuel. *The Pan-African Movement*. New York: Africana Publishing Company, 1974.

Griffith, Cyril E. *The American Dream: Martin R. Delany and the Emergence of Pan-African Thought*. University Park: Pennsylvania State University Press, 1975.

Hill, Robert A., ed. *The Marcus Garvey and Universal Negro Improvement Association Papers*. 7 vols. Berkeley: University of

California Press, 1983-1990.

Lewis, Rupert. *Marcus Garvey, Anti-Colonial Champion*. Trenton, N.J.: Africa World Press, 1988.

Lincoln, C. Eric. *The Black Muslims in America*. Boston: Beacon Press, 1961.

Martin, Tony. *The Pan-African Connection*. Dover, Mass.: Majority Press, 1963.

_____. *Race First: The Ideological and Organizational Struggles of Marcus Garvey and the Universal Negro Improvement Association*. Westport, Conn.: Greenwood Press, 1976.

Moses, Wilson J. *The Golden Age of Black Nationalism, 1850-1925*. Hamden, Conn.: Archon Books, 1978.

Muhammad, Elijah. *Message to the Blackman in America*. Chicago: Muhammad Mosque of Islam Number 2, 1965.

Padmore, George. *Pan-Africanism or Communism?* New York: Roy Publishers, 1956.

Perry, Bruce. *Malcolm: The Life of a Man Who Changed Black America*. Barrytown, N.Y.: Station Hill Press, 1991.

Rigsby, Gregory U. *Alexander Crummell: Pioneer in Nineteenth Century Pan-African Thought*. New York: Greenwood Press, 1987.

Rollin, Frank A. *Life and Public Services of Martin R. Delany*. Reprint. New York: Arno Press, 1969.

Scruggs, Otey M. "We the Children of Africa in This Land: Alexander Crummell." In *Africa and the Afro-American Experience: Eight Essays*. Edited by Lorraine A. Williams. Washington, D.C.: Howard University Press, 1977.

Stein, Judith. *The World of Marcus Garvey: Race and Class in Modern Society*. Baton Rouge: Louisiana State University Press, 1986.

Sterling, Dorothy. *The Making of an Afro-American: Martin Robison Delany, 1812-1885*. Garden City, N.Y.: Doubleday, 1971.

Stuckey, Sterling, ed. *The Ideological Origins of Black Nationalism*. Boston: Beacon Press, 1972.

Tate, Gayle T. "Black Nationalism: An Angle of Vision." *Western Journal of Black Studies* 12 (Spring, 1988): 40-48.

Ullman, Victor. *Martin R. Delany: The Beginnings of Black Nationalism*. Boston: Beacon Press, 1971.

Wiltse, Charles M., ed. *David Walker's Appeal to the Colored Citizens of the World*. New York: Hill & Wang, 1965.

BUSINESS, COMMERCE, AND ECONOMIC LIFE

Alexander, Lois K. *Blacks in the History of Fashion*. New York: Harlem Institute of Fashion, 1982.

Altschiller, Donald, ed. *Affirmative Action*. New York: H. W. Wilson Co., 1991.

Anderson, Jervis. *A. Philip Randolph: A Biographical Portrait*. New York: Harcourt Brace Jovanovich, 1973.

Bailey, Ronald W., ed. *Black Business Enterprise: Historical and Contemporary Perspectives*. New York: Basic Books, 1971.

Banks, Vera J. *Black Farmers and Their Farms*. Washington, D.C.: U.S. Department of Agriculture, Economic Research Service, 1986.

Becker, Gary Stanley. *The Economics of Discrimination*. Chicago: University of Chicago Press, 1957.

Berry, Mary Frances, and John W. Blassingame. *Long Memory: The Black Experience in America*. New York: Oxford University Press, 1982.

Berry, Wendell. *The Unsettling of America: Culture and Agriculture*. San Francisco, Calif.: Sierra Club Books, 1977.

Blackwell, James E. *The Black Community: Diversity and Unity*. 3d ed. New York: HarperCollins, 1991.

Bracey, John H., Jr., August Meier, and Elliott Rudwick, eds. *Black Workers and Organized Labor*. Belmont, Calif.: Wadsworth Publishing Company, 1971.

Bremner, Robert H. *The Discovery of Poverty in the United States*. New Brunswick, N.J.: Transaction Books, 1992.

Bundles, A'Lelia Perry. *Madam C. J. Walker*. New York: Chelsea House, 1991.

_____. "Madam C. J. Walker—Cosmetics Tycoon." *Ms.* 12 (July, 1983): 91-94.

Castellblanch, Ramon. *Union Support Among Women and Minority Workers*. Berkeley: Center for Labor Research and Education, Institute of Industrial Relations, University of California, Berkeley, 1990.

Claypool, Jane. *The Worker in America*. New York: Franklin Watts, 1985.

Daniel, Pete. *The Shadow of Slavery: Peonage in the South, 1901-1969*. Urbana: University of Illinois Press, 1972.

Danziger, Sheldon. *The War on Income Poverty: Achievements and Failures*. Madison: Institute for Research on Poverty, University of Wisconsin, 1981.

Davis, Marianna W., ed. *Contributions of Black Women to America*. 2 vols. Columbia, S.C.: Kenday Press, 1982.

Detweiler, Frederick G. *The Negro Press in the United States*. Chicago: University of Chicago Press, 1922.

Edwards, Audrey. "Oprah Winfrey: Stealing the Show!" *Essence* 17 (October, 1986): 50-52.

Fields, Mike. *Getting It Together: The Black Man's Guide to Good Grooming and Fashion*. New York: Dodd, Mead, 1983.

Fisher, Walter. "Sarah Breedlove Walker." In *Notable American Women, 1607-1950: A Biographical Dictionary*. Vol. 3. Edited by Edward T. James et al. Cambridge, Mass.: The Belknap Press of Harvard University Press, 1971.

Foner, Philip S. *History of Black Americans*. Westport, Conn.: Greenwood Press, 1983.

Franklin, John Hope, and Alfred A. Moss, Jr. *From Slavery to Freedom: A History of Negro Americans*. 6th ed. New York: Alfred A. Knopf, 1988.

Frazier, E. Franklin. "The Negro Press and Wish-Fulfillment." In *Black Bourgeoisie: The Rise of a New Middle Class*. Glencoe, Ill.: Free Press, 1957.

Giddings, Paula. *When and Where I Enter: The Impact of Black Women on Race and Sex in America*. New York: William Morrow, 1984.

Hageney, Wolfgang, ed. *Black Africa Impressions: Graphic and Color and Fashion and Design*. 2d ed. Rome, Italy: Belvedere, 1983.

Harding, Vincent. *There Is a River: The Black Struggle for Freedom in America*. 2d ed. New York: Harcourt Brace Jovanovich, 1993.

Harris, William H. *Keeping the Faith: A. Philip Randolph, Milton P. Webster, and the Brotherhood of Sleeping Car Porters, 1925-1937*. Urbana: University of Illinois Press, 1977.

Haskins, Jim. *One More River to Cross: The Stories of Twelve Black Americans*. New York: Scholastic, 1992.

Heady, Earl Orel, et al. *Roots of the Farm Problem: Changing Technology, Changing Capital Use, Changing Labor Needs*. Ames: Iowa State University Center for Agricultural and Economic Development, 1965.

Hill, Herbert. *The AFL-CIO and the Black Worker: Twenty-five Years After the Merger*. Madison: Industrial Relations Research Institute, University of Wisconsin-Madison, 1982.

Jencks, Christopher. *Rethinking Social Policy: Race, Poverty, and the Underclass*. Cambridge, Mass.: Harvard University Press, 1992.

Johnson, John H., with Lerone Bennett, Jr. *Succeeding Against the Odds: The Inspiring Autobiography of One of America's Wealthiest Entrepreneurs*. New York: Warner Books, 1989.

Kester, Howard. *Revolt Among the Share-croppers*. New York: Arno Press, 1969.

King, Norman. *Everybody Loves Oprah! Her Remarkable Life Story*. New York: William Morrow, 1987.

Kornweibel, Theodore, Jr. *No Crystal Stair: Black Life and the Messenger, 1917-1928*. Westport, Conn.: Greenwood Press, 1975.

Leonard, Jonathan S. "The Effect of Unions

on the Employment of Blacks, Hispanics, and Women." *Industrial and Labor Relations Review* 39 (October, 1985): 115-132.

Lipton, Michael. *Demography and Poverty.* Washington, D.C.: Work Bank, 1983.

Long, Robert Emmet, ed. *The Farm Crisis.* New York: H. W. Wilson, 1987.

Mangum, Garth L., and Stephen F. Seninger. *Coming of Age in the Ghetto: A Dilemma of Youth Unemployment.* Baltimore: Johns Hopkins University Press, 1978.

Myers, Walter Dean. *Crystal.* New York: Viking Kestrel, 1987.

Noel, Pamela. "Lights! Camera! Oprah!" *Ebony* 40 (April, 1985): 100-105.

Pfeffer, Paula F. *A. Philip Randolph, Pioneer of the Civil Rights Movement.* Baton Rouge: Louisiana State University Press, 1990.

Salley, Columbus, ed. *Accent African Fashions.* New York: Col-Bob Associates, 1975.

Santino, Jack. *Miles of Smiles, Years of Struggle: Stories of Black Pullman Porters.* Urbana: University of Illinois Press, 1989.

Starke, Barbara M., Lillian O. Holloman, and Barbara K. Nordquist. *African American Dress and Adornment: A Cultural Perspective.* Dubuque, Iowa: Kendall/Hunt, 1990.

Suggs, Henry Lewis. *The Black Press in the South, 1865-1979.* Westport, Conn.: Greenwood Press, 1983.

Swinton, David H. "The Economic Status of African Americans: Limited Ownership and Persistent Inequality." In *The State of Black America 1992.* Edited by Janet Dewart. New York: Urban League, 1992.

U.S. Commission on Civil Rights. *Affirmative Action in the 1980s: Dismantling the Process of Discrimination.* Washington, D.C.: U.S. Government Printing Office, 1981.

_____. *Nonreferral Unions and Equal Employment Opportunity: A Report of the United States Commission on Civil Rights.* Washington, D.C.: U.S. Government Printing Office, 1982.

_____. *Promises and Perceptions.* Washington, D.C.: Government Printing Office, 1981.

Waldron, Robert. *Oprah!* New York: St. Martin's Press, 1987.

Waters, Harry F., and Patricia King. "Chicago's Grand New Oprah." *Newsweek*, December 31, 1984, 51.

Weare, Walter B. *Black Business in the New South: A Social History of the North Carolina Mutual Life Insurance Company.* Durham, N.C.: Duke University Press, 1992.

Williams, James D., ed. *The State of Black America, 1986.* New York: National Urban League, 1986.

Wolseley, Roland E. *The Black Press, U.S.A.* Ames: Iowa State University Press, 1971.

Woodward, Comer Vann. *The Origins of the New South, 1877-1913.* Baton Rouge: Louisiana State University Press, 1951.

Zarefsky, David. *President Johnson's War on Poverty: Rhetoric and History.* University: University of Alabama Press, 1986.

Zoglin, Richard. "Lady with a Calling." *Time*, August 8, 1988, 62-64.

CIVIL RIGHTS

Albert, Peter J., and Ronald Hoffman, eds. *We Shall Overcome: Martin Luther King and the Black Freedom Struggle.* New York: Pantheon Books, 1990.

Anderson, Jervis. *A. Philip Randolph: A Biographical Portrait.* New York: Harcourt Brace Jovanovich, 1973.

Altschiller, Donald, ed. *Affirmative Action.* New York: H. W. Wilson Co., 1991.

Aptheker, Herbert, ed. *From the Colonial Times Through the Civil War.* Volume 1 in *A Documentary History of the Negro People of The United States.* New York: Citadel Press, 1951.

Baum, Lawrence. *The Supreme Court.* 4th ed. Washington, D.C.: Congressional Quarterly Press, 1992.

Becker, Gary Stanley. *The Economics of Discrimination.* Chicago: University of Chicago Press, 1957.

Bell, Derrick A., Jr. *Race, Racism, and American Law.* 2d ed. Boston: Little, Brown and Co., 1980.

Bell, Malcolm. *The Turkey Shoot: Tracking the Attica Cover-up.* New York: Grove Press, 1985.

Bennett, Lerone, Jr. *Before the Mayflower: A History of Black America.* 6th ed. Chicago: Johnson Publishing Company, 1987.

Bond, Julian. *A Time to Speak, A Time to Act: The Movement in Politics.* New York: Simon & Schuster, 1972.

Branch, Taylor. *Parting the Waters: America in the King Years, 1954-63.* New York: Simon & Schuster, 1988.

Bruce, Dickson D., Jr. *Archibald Grimké: Portrait of a Black Independent.* Baton Rouge: Louisiana State University Press, 1993.

Bullard, Sara, et al., eds. *The Ku Klux Klan: A History of Racism and Violence.* 3d ed. Montgomery, Ala.: Klanwatch, 1988.

Burstein, Paul. *Discrimination, Jobs, Politics.* Chicago: University of Chicago Press, 1985.

Carson, Clayborne. *In Struggle: SNCC and the Black Awakening of the 1960's.* Cambridge, Mass.: Harvard University Press, 1981.

Carson, Clayborne, David J. Garrow, Gerald Gill, Vincent Harding, and Darlene Clark Hine, eds. "A Nation of Law?" In *The Eyes on the Prize: Civil Rights Reader.* New York: Penguin, 1991.

Chalmers, David M. *Hooded Americanism: The History of the Ku Klux Klan.* 3d ed. Durham, N.C.: Duke University Press, 1987.

Claypool, Jane. *The Worker in America.* New York: Franklin Watts, 1985.

Coons, William R. *Attica Diary.* New York: Stein & Day, 1972.

Dann, Martin E., ed. *The Black Press: 1827-1890.* New York: Putnam, 1971.

Davis, Marianna W., ed. *Contributions of Black Women to America.* 2 vols. Columbia, S.C.: Kenday Press, 1982.

DeMarco, Joseph P. *The Social Thought of W. E. B. Du Bois.* Lanham, Md.: University Press of America, 1983.

Du Bois, Shirley Graham. *Du Bois: A Pictorial Biography.* Chicago: Johnson Publishing, 1978.

Du Bois, W. E. B. *The Autobiography of W. E. B. Du Bois: A Soliloquy on Viewing My Life from the Last Decade of Its First Century.* New York: International Publishing Co., 1968.

_____. *The Souls of Black Folk: Essays and Sketches.* Chicago: A. C. McClurg, 1903.

Duster, Alfreda M., ed. *Crusade for Justice: The Autobiography of Ida B. Wells.* Chicago: University of Chicago Press, 1970.

Evers, Mrs. Medgar, with William Peters. *For Us, The Living.* Garden City, N.Y.: Doubleday, 1967.

Forman, James. *The Making of Black Revolutionaries.* New York: Macmillan, 1972.

Franklin, John Hope, and Alfred A. Moss, Jr. *From Slavery to Freedom: A History of Negro Americans.* 6th ed. New York: Alfred A. Knopf, 1988.

Gardner, Carl. *Andrew Young.* New York: Sterling, 1980.

Garrow, David J. *Bearing the Cross: Martin Luther King, Jr., and the Southern Christian Leadership Conference, 1955-1968.* New York: William Morrow, 1986.

_____, ed. *We Shall Overcome: The Civil Rights Movement in the United States in the 1950's and 1960's.* 3 vols. New York: Carlson Publishing, 1989.

Gest, Ted. "Affirmative Verdict on Racial Hiring." *U.S. News & World Report* 101 (July 14, 1986): 17-18.

_____. "Why Drive on Job Bias Is Still Going Strong." *U.S. News & World Report* 98 (June 17, 1985): 67-68.

Giddings, Paula. *When and Where I Enter: The Impact of Black Women on Race and Sex in America.* New York: William Morrow, 1984.

Ginger, Ann Fagan. *The Law, the Supreme Court and the People's Rights.* Rev. ed. Woodbury, N.Y.: Barron's, 1977.

Goode, Stephen. *The Controversial Court.*

New York: J. Messner, 1982.

Graham, Hugh Davis. *The Civil Rights Era.* New York: Oxford University Press, 1990.

Gross, Barry, ed. *Reverse Discrimination.* Buffalo, N.Y.: Prometheus Books, 1977.

Harding, Vincent. *Hope and History: Why We Must Share the Story of the Movement.* Maryknoll. N.Y.: Orbis Books, 1990.

_____. *There Is a River: The Black Struggle for Freedom in America.* 2d ed. New York: Harcourt Brace Jovanovich, 1993.

Harlan, Louis R. *Booker T. Washington in Perspective: Essays of Louis R. Harlan.* Edited by Raymond W. Smock. Jackson: University Press of Mississippi, 1986.

_____. *Booker T. Washington: The Making of a Black Leader, 1856-1901.* New York: Oxford University Press, 1972.

_____. *Booker T. Washington: The Wizard of Tuskegee, 1901-1915.* New York: Oxford University Press, 1983.

Harris, Trudier, comp. *The Selected Works of Ida B. Wells-Barnett.* New York: Oxford University Press, 1991.

Harris, William H. *Keeping the Faith: A. Philip Randolph, Milton P. Webster, and the Brotherhood of Sleeping Car Porters, 1925-1937.* Urbana: University of Illinois Press, 1977.

Horne, Gerald. *Black and Red: W. E. B. Du Bois and the Afro-American Response to the Cold War, 1944-1963.* Albany: State University of New York Press, 1986.

Jordan, June. *Fannie Lou Hamer.* New York: Thomas Y. Crowell, 1972.

Katz, William Loren. *The Invisible Empire: The Ku Klux Klan Impact on History.* Washington, D.C.: Open Hand Publishers, 1986.

Kellogg, Charles Flint. *NAACP: A History of the National Association for the Advancement of Colored People.* Baltimore, Md: The Johns Hopkins University Press, 1967.

Kluger, Richard. *Simple Justice: The History of Brown v. Board of Education and Black America's Struggle for Equality.* New York: Alfred A. Knopf, 1976.

Kornweibel, Theodore, Jr. *No Crystal Stair: Black Life and the Messenger, 1917-1928.* Westport, Conn.: Greenwood Press, 1975.

Lester, J. C., and D. L. Wilson. *Ku Klux Klan: Its Origin, Growth, and Disbandment.* Reprint. New York: Da Capo Press, 1973.

Lincoln, Charles Eric. *Race, Religion, and the Continuing American Dilemma.* New York: Hill & Wang, 1984.

Logan, Rayford W. *The Betrayal of the Negro.* Enlarged ed. New York: Collier Books, 1965.

_____, ed. *W. E. B. Du Bois: A Profile.* New York: Hill & Wang, 1971.

McEvoy, James, and Abraham Miller, eds. *Black Power and Student Rebellion.* Belmont, Calif.: Wadsworth Publishing Company, 1969.

Manly, Howard. "Gregory Buys Hotel and Fattens His Diet Empire." *Black Enterprise* 19 (March, 1989): 22.

Mann, Coramae Richey. *Unequal Justice: A Question of Color.* Bloomington: Indiana University Press, 1993.

Marable, Manning. *Race, Reform, and Rebellion: The Second Reconstruction in Black America, 1945-1990.* 2d ed. Jackson: University Press of Mississippi, 1984.

Meier, August. *Negro Thought in America, 1880-1915.* Ann Arbor: University of Michigan Press, 1963.

Mendelson, Wallace. *The American Constitution and the Judicial Process.* Homewood, Ill.: Dorsey Press, 1980.

Mills, Kay. *This Little Light of Mine: The Life of Fannie Lou Hamer.* New York: E. P. Dutton, 1993.

Moody, Anne. *Coming of Age in Mississippi.* New York: Dell Books, 1968.

Morris, Aldon D. *The Origins of the Civil Rights Movement: Black Communities Organizing for Change.* New York: Free Press, 1984.

Neary, John. *Julian Bond: Black Rebel.* New York: William Morrow, 1971.

New York (State) Special Commission on Attica. *Attica: The Official Report of the New York State Special Commission on Attica.* New York: Praeger, 1972.

Newby, Idus A. *The Development of Segregationist Thought.* Homewood, Ill.: Dorsey Press, 1969.

Noble, Jeanne L. *Beautiful, Also, Are the Souls of My Black Sisters.* Englewood Cliffs, N.J.: Prentice-Hall, 1978.

Norton, Eleanor Holmes. "Woman Who Changed the South." *Ms.* 6 (July, 1977): 51.

Oates, Stephen B. *Let the Trumpet Sound: The Life of Martin Luther King, Jr.* New York: Harper & Row, 1982.

Persico, Joseph E. *The Imperial Rockefeller.* New York: Simon & Schuster, 1982.

Pfeffer, Paula F. *A. Philip Randolph, Pioneer of the Civil Rights Movement.* Baton Rouge: Louisiana State University Press, 1990.

Powledge, Fred. *Free At Last? The Civil Rights Movement and the People Who Made It.* Boston: Little, Brown, 1991.

Quarles, Benjamin. *Black Abolitionists.* London: Oxford University Press, 1969.

Rampersad, Arnold. *The Art and Imagination of W. E. B. Du Bois.* Cambridge, Mass.: Harvard University Press, 1976.

Ripley, C. Peter, et al., eds. *The Black Abolitionist Papers.* 5 vols. Chapel Hill: University of North Carolina Press, 1985-1992.

Rose, Thomas. *Black Leaders, Then and Now: A Personal History of Students Who Led the Civil Rights Movement in the 1960's—and What Happened to Them.* Garrett Park, Md.: Garrett Park Press, 1984.

Rubel, David. *Fannie Lou Hamer: From Sharecropping to Politics.* Englewood Cliffs, N.J.: Silver Burdett Press, 1990.

Salter, John R., Jr. *Jackson, Mississippi: An American Chronicle of Struggle and Schism.* Hicksville, N.Y.: Exposition Press, 1979.

Santino, Jack. *Miles of Smiles, Years of Struggle: Stories of Black Pullman Porters.* Urbana: University of Illinois Press, 1989.

Sewell, George Alexander. *Mississippi Black History Makers.* Jackson: University Press of Mississippi, 1977.

Sitkoff, Harvard. *The Struggle for Black Equality, 1954-1980.* New York: Hill & Wang, 1981.

Stephan, Walter G., and Joe R. Feagin. *School Desegregation: Past, Present, and Future.* New York: Plenum Press, 1980.

Sterling, Dorothy. *Black Foremothers: Three Lives.* Old Westbury, N.Y.: Feminist Press, 1979.

Thompson, Mildred I. *Ida B. Wells-Barnett: Exploratory Study of an American Black Woman, 1893-1930.* Vol. 15 in *Black Women in American History.* Washington, D.C.: George Washington University Press, 1979.

Tyack, David B., ed. *Turning Points in American Educational History.* Waltham, Mass: Blaisdell, 1967.

U.S. Commission on Civil Rights. *Nonreferral Unions and Equal Employment Opportunity: A Report of the United States Commission on Civil Rights.* Washington, D.C.: U.S. Government Printing Office, 1982.

_____. *Twenty Years After Brown: The Shadows of the Past.* Washington, D.C.: U.S. Government Printing Office, 1974.

Washington, Booker T. *The Booker T. Washington Papers.* 13 vols. Edited by Louis R. Harlan et al. Urbana: University of Illinois Press, 1972-1984.

Watson, Denton L. *Lion in the Lobby.* New York: William Morrow, 1990.

Weisbrot, Robert. *Freedom Bound: A History of America's Civil Rights Movement.* New York: Plume Books, 1991.

Wells, Dean Faulkner, and Hunter Cole, eds. *Mississippi Heroes.* Jackson: University Press of Mississippi, 1980.

Wilkins, Roy. *Standing Fast: The Autobiography of Roy Wilkins.* New York: Viking Press, 1982.

Wills, Garry. "Georgia Is Much on His Mind." *Time,* July 16, 1990, pp. 66-68.

Woods, Geraldine. *Affirmative Action.* New York: Franklin Watts, 1989.

COMMUNITY AND CULTURE

Anderson, Talmadge, ed. *Black Studies: Theory, Method, and Cultural Perspectives.* Pullman: Washington State University Press, 1990.

Asante, Molefi K. *The Afrocentric Idea.* Philadelphia: Temple University Press, 1987.

_____. *Afrocentricity.* Rev. ed. Trenton, N.J.: Africa World Press, 1988.

_____. *Kemet, Afrocentricity, and Knowledge.* Trenton, N.J.: Africa World Press, 1990.

Athearn, Robert G. *In Search of Canaan: Black Migration to Kansas, 1879-80.* Lawrence: Regents Press of Kansas, 1978.

Banks, Vera J. *Black Farmers and Their Farms.* Washington, D.C.: U.S. Department of Agriculture, Economic Research Service, 1986.

Berry, Wendell. *The Unsettling of America: Culture and Agriculture.* San Francisco, Calif.: Sierra Club Books, 1977.

Blackwell, James E. *The Black Community: Diversity and Unity.* 3d ed. New York: HarperCollins, 1991.

Blassingame, John W. *The Slave Community: Plantation Life in the Antebellum South.* Rev. ed. New York: Oxford University Press, 1979.

Brown, Claude. *Manchild in the Promised Land.* New York: Macmillan, 1965.

Carter, Keith. *Mojo.* Houston, Tex.: Rice University Press, 1992.

Cone, James H. *A Black Theology of Liberation.* New York: J. B. Lippincott, 1970.

Crowley, Daniel J., ed. *African Folktales in the New World.* Austin: University of Texas Press, 1979.

Daniel, Pete. *The Shadow of Slavery: Peonage in the South, 1901-1969.* Urbana: University of Illinois Press, 1972.

Davis, Marianna W., ed. *Contributions of Black Women to America.* 2 vols. Columbia, S.C.: Kenday Press, 1982.

Diaz-Briquets, Sergio, and Sidney Weintraub, eds. *Determinants of Emigration from Mexico, Central America, and the Caribbean.* Boulder, Colo.: Westview Press, 1991.

Diop, Cheikh Anta. *The African Origin of Civilization: Myth or Reality.* Translated by Mercer Cook. New York: Lawrence Hill, 1974.

Drake, St. Clair, and Horace R. Cayton. *Black Metropolis: A Study of Negro Life in a Northern City.* 2d ed. Chicago: University of Chicago Press, 1993.

Du Bois, W. E. B. *The Souls of Black Folk: Essays and Sketches.* Chicago: A. C. McClurg, 1903.

Dundes, Alan, ed. *Mother Wit from the Laughing Barrel: Readings in the Interpretation of Afro-American Folklore.* Jackson: University Press of Mississippi, 1990.

Fanon, Frantz. *The Wretched of the Earth.* New York: Grove Press, 1963.

Farley, Reynolds. *Growth of the Black Population.* Chicago: Markham Publishing Company, 1970.

Frazier, E. Franklin. *Black Bourgeoisie: The Rise of a New Middle Class.* Glencoe, Ill.: Free Press, 1957.

Garwood, Alfred N., ed. *Black Americans: A Statistical Sourcebook.* Boulder, Colo.: Numbers & Concepts, 1991.

George, Lynell. *No Crystal Stair: African-Americans in the City of Angels.* New York: Verso, 1993.

Hamilton, Virginia. *Many Thousand Gone: African-Americans from Slavery to Freedom.* New York: Alfred A. Knopf, 1993.

_____. *The People Could Fly: American Black Folktales.* New York: Alfred A. Knopf, 1985.

Harding, Vincent. *Hope and History: Why We Must Share the Story of the Movement.* Maryknoll, N.Y.: Orbis Books, 1990.

Harris, Robert L., Jr., Darlene Clark Hine, and Nellie McKay. *Black Studies in the United States: Three Essays.* New York: Ford Foundation, 1990.

Heady, Earl Orel, et al. *Roots of the Farm Problem: Changing Technology, Changing Capital Use, Changing Labor Needs.* Ames: Iowa State University Center for Agricultural and Economic Development, 1965.

Hine, Darlene Clark, ed. *The State of Afro-American History: Past, Present, and Future.* Baton Rouge: Louisiana State University Press, 1986.

Horton, Carrell Peterson, and Jessie Carney Smith, eds. *Statistical Record of Black America.* Detroit: Gale Research, 1990.

James, G. M. *Stolen Legacy.* San Francisco: Julian Richardson Associates, 1976.

Jones, Edward L. *Profiles in African Heritage.* Seattle: Frayn, 1972.

Kamau-Collier, M. A. Z. *Phoenix Arising: A Psycho-cultural Perspective on African American Issues up to the Twenty-first Century.* Baltimore: TransPress, 1990.

Karenga, Maulana. *Introduction to Black Studies.* Inglewood, Calif.: Kawaida Publications, 1982.

Kester, Howard. *Revolt Among the Sharecroppers.* New York: Arno Press, 1969.

Kremer, Gary R., and Antonio F. Holland. *Missouri's Black Heritage.* Rev. ed. Columbia: University of Missouri Press, 1993.

Locke, Alain, ed. *The New Negro: An Interpretation.* New York: A. and C. Boni, 1925. Reprint. New York: Atheneum, 1968.

Long, Robert Emmet, ed. *The Farm Crisis.* New York: H. W. Wilson, 1987.

McDonogh, Gary W., ed. *The Florida Negro: A Federal Writers' Project Legacy.* Jackson: University Press of Mississippi, 1993.

Magubane, Bernard Makhosezwe. *The Ties That Bind: African-American Consciousness of Africa.* Trenton, N.J.: Africa World Press, 1987.

Morton, Patricia. *Disfigured Images: The Historical Assault on Afro-American Women.* New York: Greenwood Press, 1991.

Muhammad, Elijah. *Message to the Blackman in America.* Chicago: Muhammad Mosque of Islam Number 2, 1965.

Myrdal, Gunnar. *An American Dilemma: The Negro Problem and Modern Democracy.* New York: Harper & Brothers, 1944.

Painter, Nell Irvin. *Exodusters: Black Migration to Kansas After Reconstruction.* Lawrence: University Press of Kansas, 1986.

Pemberton, Gayle. *The Hottest Water in Chicago: On Family, Race, Time, and American Culture.* Boston: Faber & Faber, 1992.

Raphael, Lennox. "West Indians and Afro-Americans." *Freedomways* 4, no. 3 (Summer, 1964): 438-445.

Roberts, John Storm. *Black Music of Two Worlds.* New York: Praeger, 1972.

Samuels, Wilfred David. *Five Afro-Caribbean Voices in American Culture: 1917-1929.* Ann Arbor, Mich.: University Microfilm International, 1977.

Schoener, Allon, ed. *Harlem on My Mind: Cultural Capital of Black America, 1900-1968.* Rev. ed. New York: Dell, 1979.

Studio Museum in Harlem, The. *Harlem Renaissance: Art of Black America.* New York: Harry N. Abrams, 1987.

Traub, James, "You Can Get It if You Really Want." *Harper's* 264 (June, 1982): 27-31.

Van Sertima, Ivan. *They Came Before Columbus.* New York: Random House, 1976.

Vlach, John Michael. *By the Work of Their Hands: Studies in Afro-American Folklife.* Charlottesville: University Press of Virginia, 1991.

Weisbord, Robert G. *Ebony Kinship: Africa, Africans, and the Afro-American.* Westport, Conn.: Greenwood Press, 1974.

Westmacott, Richard. *African-American Gardens and Yards in the Rural South.* Knoxville: University of Tennessee Press, 1993.

Wheeler, B. Gordon. *Black California: A History of African-Americans in the Gold State.* New York: Hippocrene Books, 1993.

Woodward, Comer Vann. *The Origins of the New South, 1877-1913.* Baton Rouge: Louisiana State University Press, 1951.

EDUCATION

Adams, Russell L. *Great Negroes, Past and*

Present. 3d ed. Chicago: Afro-American Publishing Co., 1969.

Adler, Jerry, and Donna Foote. "The Marva Collins Story." *Newsweek*, March 8, 1982, 64-65.

Allen, Walter R., Edgar G. Epps, and Nesha Z. Haniff, eds. *College in Black and White.* Albany: State University of New York Press, 1991.

Anderson, Talmadge, ed. *Black Studies: Theory, Method, and Cultural Perspective.* Pullman: Washington State University Press, 1990.

Arnez, N. L. "Implementation of Desegregation as a Discriminatory Process." *Journal of Negro Education* 47 (Winter, 1978): 28-45.

Bennett, Lerone, Jr. *Before the Mayflower: A History of Black America.* 6th ed. Chicago: Johnson Publishing Company, 1987.

Berman, Daniel Marvin. *It Is So Ordered.* New York: W. W. Norton, 1966.

Berry, Gordon LaVern, and Joy Keiko Asamen, eds. *Black Students: Psychosocial Issues and Academic Achievement.* Newbury Park, Calif.: Sage Publications, 1989.

Blackwell, James E. *The Black Community: Diversity and Unity.* 3d ed. New York: HarperCollins, 1991.

Bracey, John H., Jr., August Meier, and Elliott Rudwick. *Black Nationalism in America.* The American Heritage series. Indianapolis: Bobbs-Merrill, 1970.

Bullock, Henry Allen. *A History of Negro Education in the South.* Cambridge, Mass.: Harvard University Press, 1967.

Clarke, John Henrik. "The Origin and Growth of Afro-American Literature." In *Black Voices: An Anthology of Afro-American Literature.* Edited by Abraham Chapman. New York: Mentor Books, 1968.

Collins, Marva, and Civia Tamarkin. *Marva Collins' Way.* Los Angeles: Jeremy P. Tarcher, 1990.

Cruse, Harold. *The Crisis of the Negro Intellectual.* New York: Quill, 1984.

Davis, Marianna W., ed. *Contributions of Black Women to America.* 2 vols. Columbia, S.C.: Kenday Press, 1982.

Du Bois, W. E. B. *The Souls of Black Folk: Essays and Sketches.* Chicago: A. C. McClurg, 1903.

Eyler, J., V. J. Cook, and L. E. Ward. "Resegregation: Segregation Within Desegregated Schools." In *The Consequences of School Desegregation,* edited by Christine H. Rossell and Willis D. Hawley. Philadelphia: Temple University Press, 1983.

Fine, Michelle. *Framing Dropouts.* Albany: State University of New York Press, 1991.

Ford, Nick A. *Black Studies: Threat or Challenge?* Port Washington, N.Y.: Kennikat Press, 1973.

Franklin, John Hope. "The Place of Carter G. Woodson in American Historiography." *Negro History Bulletin* 13, no. 8 (1950): 174-176.

_____. *Race and History: Selected Essays, 1938-1988.* Baton Rouge: Louisiana State University Press, 1989.

Franklin, John Hope, and Alfred A. Moss, Jr. *From Slavery to Freedom: A History of Negro Americans.* 6th ed. New York: Alfred A. Knopf, 1988.

Frazier, E. Franklin. *Black Bourgeoisie: The Rise of a New Middle Class.* Glencoe, Ill.: Free Press, 1957.

_____. *The Negro Family in the United States.* Chicago: University of Chicago Press, 1939.

_____. *On Race Relations: Selected Writings.* Chicago: University of Chicago Press, 1968.

Goggin, Jacqueline. *Carter G. Woodson: A Life in Black History.* Baton Rouge: Louisiana State University Press, 1993.

Graglia, Lino A. *Disaster by Decree: The Supreme Court Decisions on Race and the Schools.* Ithaca, N.Y.: Cornell University Press, 1976.

Greene, Lorenzo J. *Working with Carter G. Woodson, the Father of Black History: A Diary, 1928-1930.* Baton Rouge: Louisiana State University Press, 1989.

Hale-Benson, Janice E. *Black Children: Their Roots, Culture, and Learning Styles* Rev. ed. Baltimore: The Johns Hopkins University Press, 1986.

Harris, Joseph E., ed. *Global Dimensions of the African Diaspora.* Washington, D.C.: Howard University Press, 1982.

Hine, Darlene Clark, ed. *The State of Afro-American History: Past, Present, and Future.* Baton Rouge: Louisiana State University Press, 1986.

Kinshasa, Kwando M. *Emigration vs. Assimilation.* Jefferson, N.C.: McFarland, 1988.

Kluger, Richard. *Simple Justice: The History of Brown v. Board of Education and Black America's Struggle for Equality.* New York: Alfred A. Knopf, 1976.

Kunjufu, Jawanza. *Developing Positive Self-Images and Discipline in Black Children.* Chicago: African-American Images, 1984.

Kusmer, Kenneth L. "The Black Urban Experience in American History." In *The State of Afro-American History: Past, Present, and Future.* Edited by Darlene Clark Hine. Baton Rouge: Louisiana State University Press, 1986.

Lincoln, Charles Eric. *Race, Religion, and the Continuing American Dilemma.* New York: Hill & Wang, 1984.

Lukas, J. Anthony. *Common Ground: A Turbulent Decade in the Lives of Three American Families.* New York: Alfred A. Knopf, 1985.

Lupo, Alan. *Liberty's Chosen Home: The Politics of Violence in Boston.* 2d ed. Boston: Beacon Press, 1988.

Mangum, Garth L., and Stephen F. Seninger. *Coming of Age in the Ghetto: A Dilemma of Youth Unemployment.* Baltimore: The Johns Hopkins University Press, 1978.

"Marva Collins." In *Contemporary Heroes and Heroines.* Edited by Ray B. Browne. Detroit: Gale Research, 1990.

Meier, August, and Elliott Rudwick. *Black History and the Historical Profession, 1915-1980.* Urbana: University of Illinois Press, 1986.

Meier, Kenneth J., Joseph Stewart, Jr., and Robert E. England. *Race, Class, and Education: The Politics of Second-Generation Discrimination.* Madison: University of Wisconsin Press, 1989.

National Center for Education Statistics. *Elementary and Secondary Education.* Vol. 1 in *The Condition of Education, 1991.* Washington, D.C.: Government Printing Office, 1991.

Newby, Idus A. *The Development of Segregationist Thought.* Homewood, Ill.: Dorsey Press, 1969.

O'Neil, Timothy J. *Bakke and the Politics of Equality: Friends and Foes in the Classroom of Litigation.* Middletown, Conn.: Wesleyan University Press, 1985.

Pallas, Aaron M., Gary Natriello, and Edward L. McDill. "The Changing Nature of the Disadvantaged Population: Current Dimensions and Future Trends." *Educational Researcher* 18 (1989): 16-22.

Persell, Caroline Hodges. *Education and Inequality.* New York: Free Press, 1977.

Platt, Anthony M. *E. Franklin Frazier Reconsidered.* New Brunswick, N.J.: Rutgers University Press, 1991.

Pratt, Robert A. *The Color of Their Skin: Education and Race in Richmond, Virginia, 1954-89.* Charlottesville: University Press of Virginia, 1992.

Reed, S. "Marva Collins: 'I Take the Kids No One Else Wants!'" *Instructor* 91 (January, 1982): 18-19.

Rigsby, Gregory U. *Alexander Crummell: Pioneer in Nineteenth Century Pan-African Thought.* New York: Greenwood Press, 1987.

Sachar, Emily. *Shut Up and Let the Lady Teach: A Teacher's Year in a Public School.* New York: Poseidon Press, 1991.

Scally, M. Anthony, ed. *Carter G. Woodson: A Bio-Bibliography.* Westport, Conn.: Greenwood Press, 1985.

Schofield, Janet Ward. *Black and White in School.* New York: Teachers College Press, 1989.

"Schooling of Black Americans, The." In *A Common Destiny: Blacks and American Society*, edited by Gerald D. Jaynes and Robin M. Williams. Washington, D.C.: National Academy Press, 1989.

Schwartz, Bernard. *Swann's Way: The School Busing Case and the Supreme Court.* New York: Oxford University Press, 1986.

Scruggs, Otey M. "We the Children of Africa in This Land: Alexander Crummell." In *Africa and the Afro-American Experience: Eight Essays.* Edited by Lorraine A. Williams. Washington, D.C.: Howard University Press, 1977.

Simmons, Ron. *Affirmative Action: Conflict and Change in Higher Education After Bakke.* Cambridge, Mass.: Schenkman, 1982.

Sindler, Alan P. *Bakke, DeFunis, and Minority Admissions: The Quest for Equal Opportunity.* New York: Macmillan, 1978.

Stephan, Walter G., and Joe R. Feagin. *School Desegregation: Past, Present, and Future.* New York: Plenum Press, 1980.

Thorpe, Earl E. *Black Historians: A Critique.* New York: William Morrow, 1971.

Trillin, Calvin. *An Education in Georgia: Charlayne Hunter, Hamilton Holmes, and the Integration of the University of Georgia.* Athens: University of Georgia Press, 1991.

Tyack, David B., ed. *Turning Points in American Educational History.* Waltham, Mass: Blaisdell, 1967.

U.S. Commission on Civil Rights. *Twenty Years After Brown: The Shadows of the Past.* Washington, D.C.: U.S. Government Printing Office, 1974.

Urban, Wayne J. *Black Scholar: Horace Mann Bond, 1904-1972.* Athens: University of Georgia Press, 1992.

Whitman, David, and Dorian Friedman. "Busing's Unheralded Legacy: The Facts Are at Odds with the Unfavorable Image of Forced Desegregation." *U.S. News and World Report*, April 13, 1992, pp. 63-65.

Williams, Joyce E., and Ron Ladd. "On the Relevance of Education for Black Liberation." *Journal of Negro Education* 47, no. 3 (1978): 266-282.

FAMILY LIFE

Billingsley, Andrew. *Black Families in White America.* Englewood Cliffs, N.J.: Prentice Hall, 1968.

_____. *Climbing Jacob's Ladder: The Enduring Legacy of African-American Families.* New York: Simon & Schuster, 1993.

Caraway, Nancie. *Segregated Sisterhood: Racism and the Politics of American Feminism.* Knoxville: University of Tennessee Press, 1991.

Cheatham, Harold E., and James B. Stewart, eds. *Black Families: Interdisciplinary Perspectives.* New Brunswick, N.J.: Transaction, 1990.

Dash, Leon. *When Children Want Children: The Urban Crisis of Teenage Childbearing.* New York: William Morrow, 1989.

Davis, Angela Yvonne. *Women, Culture, and Politics.* New York: Random House, 1989.

Frazier, E. Franklin. *Black Bourgeoisie: The Rise of a New Middle Class.* Glencoe, Ill.: Free Press, 1957.

_____. *The Negro Family in the United States.* Chicago: University of Chicago Press, 1939.

Gutman, Herbert. *The Black Family in Slavery and Freedom, 1750-1925.* New York: Pantheon Books, 1976.

Harel, Zev, Edward A. McKinney, and Michael Williams, eds. *Black Aged: Understanding Diversity and Family Needs.* Newbury Park, Calif.: Sage Publications, 1990.

Hendricks, Leo E., and Teresa A. Montgomery. *Teenage Pregnancy from a Black Perspective: Some Reflections on Its Prevention.* Washington, D.C.: Institute for Urban Affairs and Research, Howard University, 1986.

Hine, Darlene Clark, ed. *Black Women in United States History.* 16 vols. Brooklyn, N.Y.: Carlson Publishing, 1990.

Jewell, K. Sue. *Survival of the Black Family: The Institutional Impact of U.S. Social Policy.* New York: Praeger, 1988.

Jones, Dionne J., and Stanley F. Battle, eds. *Teenage Pregnancy: Developing Strategies for Change in the Twenty-first Century.* New Brunswick, N.J.: Transaction Books, 1990.

Jones, Jacqueline. *Labor of Love, Labor of Sorrow: Black Women, Work, and Family from Slavery to the Present.* New York: Basic Books, 1985.

Lucas, Emma. *Elder Abuse and Its Recognition Among Health Service Professionals.* New York: Garland, 1991.

McAdoo, Harriette Pipes, ed. *Black Families.* Newbury Park, Calif.: Sage Publications, 1988.

Malson, Micheline R., et al., eds. *Black Women in America: Social Science Perspectives.* Chicago: University of Chicago Press, 1990.

Mangum, Garth L., and Stephen F. Seninger. *Coming of Age in the Ghetto: A Dilemma of Youth Unemployment.* Baltimore: The Johns Hopkins University Press, 1978.

Moore, Kristin A., Margaret C. Simms, and Charles L. Betsey. *Choice and Circumstances: Racial Differences in Adolescent Sexuality and Fertility.* New Brunswick, N.J.: Transaction Books, 1986.

Morton, Patricia. *Disfigured Images: The Historical Assault on Afro-American Women.* New York: Greenwood Press, 1991.

Nobles, W. W. "African-American Family Life: An Instrument of Culture." In *Black Families*, edited by Harriette Pipes McAdoo. Beverly Hills, Calif.: Sage Publications, 1981.

Sander, Joelle. *Before Their Time: Four Generations of Teenage Mothers.* New York: Harcourt Brace Jovanovich, 1992.

Tate, N. "The Black Aging Experience." In *Aging in Minority Groups*, edited by R. L. McNeely and John L. Colen. Beverly Hills, Calif.: Sage Publications, 1983.

Williams, Constance Willard. *Black Teenage Mothers: Pregnancy and Child Rearing from Their Perspective.* Lexington, Mass.: Lexington Books, 1991.

HEALTH

Agadzi, V. K. *AIDS: The African Perspective of the Killer Disease.* Accra: Ghana Universities Press, 1989.

Bell, Peter. *Chemical Dependency and the African American: Counseling Strategies and Community Issues.* Center City, Minn.: Hazelden, 1990.

Boston Women's Health Book Collective. *The New Our Bodies, Ourselves: A Book by and for Women.* New York: Simon & Schuster, 1984.

Brunswick, A. F. "Young Black Males and Substance Abuse." In *Young, Black and Male in America: An Endangered Species*, edited by Jewelle Taylor Gibbs. Dover, Mass.: Auburn House, 1988.

Cancer Facts and Figures for Minority Americans. New York: American Cancer Society, 1983.

Carpenter-Madoshi, Diana. "AIDS: The Black Community Fights Back." *The San Francisco Bay Guardian*, Oct. 4, 1989, p. 17.

Duh, Samuel V. *Blacks and AIDS: Causes and Origins.* Newbury Park, Calif.: Sage Publications, 1991.

Edelstein, Stuart J. *The Sickled Cell: From Myths to Molecules.* Cambridge, Mass.: Harvard University Press, 1985.

Edwards, Audrey, and Craig K. Polite. *Children of the Dream: The Psychology of Black Success.* New York: Doubleday, 1992.

Elliot, D. S., D. Huizinga, and S. S. Ageton. *Explaining Delinquency and Drug Use.*

Boulder, Colo.: Behavioral Research Institute, 1982.

Hobbs, Nicholas, and James M. Perrin, eds. *Issues in the Care of Children with Chronic Illness.* San Francisco, Calif.: Jossey-Bass, 1985.

Hobbs, Nicholas, James M. Perrin, and Henry T. Ireys. *Chronically Ill Children and Their Families.* San Francisco, Calif.: Jossey-Bass, 1985.

Hurtig, Anita Landau, and Carol Therese Viera, eds. *Sickle-Cell Disease: Psychological and Psychosocial Issues.* Urbana: University of Illinois Press, 1986.

Jaynes, Gerald D., and Robin M. Williams, eds. *A Common Destiny: Blacks and American Society.* Washington, D.C.: National Academy Press, 1989.

Leukefeld, C. G., R. J. Battjes, and Z. Amsel, eds. *AIDS and Intravenous Drug Use: Community Intervention and Prevention.* New York: Hemisphere Publishing, 1990.

McBride, David. *From TB to AIDS: Epidemics Among Urban Blacks Since 1900.* Albany: State University of New York Press, 1991.

Morais, Herbert M. *The History of the Negro in Medicine.* New York: Publishers Company, 1967.

Secundy, Marian Gray, ed. *Trials, Tribulations, and Celebrations: African-American Perspectives on Health, Illness, Aging, and Loss.* Yarmouth, Maine: Intercultural Press, 1992.

Serjeant, Graham R. *Sickle Cell Disease.* New York: Oxford University Press, 1985.

U.S. Congress. House. Committee on Energy and Commerce. Subcommittee on Health and the Environment. *Health Problems Confronting Blacks and Other Minorities: A Legislative Forum of the National Medical Association.* Washington, D.C.: U.S. Government Printing Office, 1985.

_____ . Select Committee on Narcotics Abuse and Control. *Intravenous Drug Use and AIDS: The Impact on the Black Community.* Washington, D.C.: U.S. Government Printing Office, 1988.

U.S. Department of Health and Human Services. *Healthy People 2000: National Health Promotion and Disease Prevention Objectives.* Washington, D.C.: U.S. Government Printing Office, 1991.

_____ . "Task Force on Black and Minority Health." *Report on the Secretary's Task Force on Black and Minority Health.* 8 vols. Washington, D.C.: U.S. Government Printing Office, 1990.

U.S. Public Health Service. *Healthy People 2000: National Health Promotion and Disease Prevention Objectives.* Washington, D.C.: U.S. Government Printing Office, 1990.

White, Jack. *Cancer in Non-White Americans.* Chicago: Year Book Medical Publications, 1980.

Willis, David P., ed. *Health Policies and Black Americans.* New Brunswick, N.J.: Transaction Books, 1989.

HISTORY

Adams, Russell L. *Great Negroes, Past and Present.* 3d ed. Chicago: Afro-American Publishing Co., 1969.

"Africans Taken in the Amistad" and "Argument of John Quincy Adams Before the Supreme Court of the United States." In *The Amistad Case: The Most Celebrated Slave Mutiny of the Nineteenth Century.* 2 vols. Reprint. New York: Johnson Reprint Corp., 1968.

Aptheker, Herbert, ed. *From the Colonial Times Through the Civil War.* Volume 1 in *A Documentary History of the Negro People of The United States.* New York: Citadel Press, 1951.

Asante, Molefi K. *The Afrocentric Idea.* Philadelphia: Temple University Press, 1987.

_____ . *Afrocentricity.* Rev. ed. Trenton, N.J.: Africa World Press, 1988.

Athearn, Robert G. *In Search of Canaan: Black Migration to Kansas, 1879-80.* Lawrence: Regents Press of Kansas, 1978.

Bemis, Samuel Flagg. *John Quincy Adams and the Union.* New York: Alfred A. Knopf, 1970.

Bennett, Lerone, Jr. *Before the Mayflower: A History of Black America.* 6th ed. Chicago: Johnson Publishing Company, 1987.

Bergman, Peter M. *The Chronological History of the Negro in America.* New York: Harper & Row, 1969.

Blassingame, John W. *The Slave Community: Plantation Life in the Antebellum South.* Rev. ed. New York: Oxford University Press, 1979.

Bontemps, Arna Wendell, and Jack Conroy. *Anyplace But Here.* New York: Hill & Wang, 1966.

Brownlee, Fred L. *New Day Ascending.* Boston: Pilgrim Press, 1946.

Caldwell, Erskine, and Margaret Bourke-White. *You Have Seen Their Faces.* New York: Arno Press, 1975.

Conrad, David Eugene. *The Forgotten Farmers: The Story of Sharecroppers in the New Deal.* Urbana: University of Illinois Press, 1965. Reprint. Westport, Conn.: Greenwood Press, 1982.

Cox, LaWanda, and John H. Cox, eds. *Reconstruction, the Negro, and the New South.* Columbia: University of South Carolina Press, 1973.

Davidson, Basil. *Africa in History: Themes and Outlines.* Rev. ed. New York: Collier Books, 1991.

_____ . *African Kingdoms.* Alexandria, Va.: Time-Life Books, 1978.

Diop, Cheikh Anta. *The African Origin of Civilization: Myth or Reality.* Translated by Mercer Cook. New York: Lawrence Hill, 1974.

Durham, Philip, and Everett L. Jones. *The Negro Cowboys.* New York: Dodd, Mead, 1965.

Foner, Eric. *Reconstruction: America's Unfinished Revolution, 1863-1877.* New York: Harper & Row, 1988.

Foner, Philip S. *Blacks in the American Revolution.* Westport, Conn.: Greenwood Press, 1975.

Franklin, John Hope. *Reconstruction After the Civil War.* Chicago: University of Chicago Press, 1961.

Franklin, John Hope, and Alfred A. Moss, Jr. *From Slavery to Freedom: A History of Negro Americans.* 6th ed. New York: Alfred A. Knopf, 1988.

Goodwin, E. Marvin. *Black Migration in America from 1915 to 1960: An Uneasy Exodus.* Lewiston, N.Y.: E. Mellen Press, 1990.

Grossman, James R. *Land of Hope: Chicago, Black Southerners, and the Great Migration.* Chicago: University of Chicago Press, 1989.

Grubbs, Donald H. *Cry from the Cotton.* Chapel Hill: University of North Carolina Press, 1971.

Harrison, Alferdteen, ed. *Black Exodus: The Great Migration from the American South.* Jackson: University Press of Mississippi, 1991.

Hartgrove, W. B. "The Negro Soldier in the American Revolution." *Journal of Negro History* 1, no. 2 (April, 1916): 110-131.

Hill, Daniel G. *The Freedom-Seekers: Blacks in Early Canada.* Agincourt, Canada: The Book Society of Canada, 1981.

Hine, Darlene Clark, ed. *Black Women in United States History.* 16 vols. Brooklyn, N.Y.: Carlson Publishing, 1990.

_____ , ed. *The State of Afro-American History: Past, Present, and Future.* Baton Rouge: Louisiana State University Press, 1986.

Hodges, Norman E. W. *Breaking the Chains of Bondage: Black History from Its Origins in Africa to the Present.* New York: Simon & Schuster, 1972.

Hutchinson, Louise Daniel. *Out of Africa: From West African Kingdoms to Civilizations.* Washington, D.C.: Smithsonian Institution Press, 1979.

Identity: The Black Experience in Canada. Toronto, Canada: Gage Educational Publishing, 1979.

Jackson, John G. *Introduction to African Civilizations*. New York: University Books, 1970.

James, G. M. *Stolen Legacy*. San Francisco: Julian Richardson Associates, 1976.

Jaynes, Gerald David. *Branches Without Roots: Genesis of the Black Working Class in the American South, 1862-1882*. New York: Oxford University Press, 1986.

Jones, Howard. *Mutiny on the Amistad: The Saga of a Slave Revolt and Its Impact on American Abolition, Law, and Diplomacy*. New York: Oxford University Press, 1987.

Kamau-Collier, M. A. Z. *Phoenix Arising: A Psycho-cultural Perspective on African American Issues up to the Twenty-first Century*. Baltimore: TransPress, 1990.

Kaplan, Sidney, and Emma N. Kaplan. *The Black Presence in the Era of the American Revolution*. Rev. ed. Amherst: University of Massachusetts Press, 1989.

Katz, William Loren. *The Black West*. 3d rev. ed. Seattle: Open Hand Publishers, 1987.

_____, ed. *Eyewitness: The Negro in American History*. New York: Pitman, 1967.

Karenga, Maulana. *Introduction to Black Studies*. Inglewood, Calif.: Kawaida Publications, 1982.

Kester, Howard. *Revolt Among the Sharecroppers*. New York: Arno Press, 1969.

Killiam, Crawford. *Go Do Some Great Thing: The Black Pioneers of British Columbia*. Vancouver, Canada: Douglas & McIntyre, 1978.

Kirkendall, Richard S. *The Global Power: The United States Since 1941*. Boston: Allyn and Bacon, 1973.

Leckie, William H. *The Buffalo Soldiers*. Norman: University of Oklahoma Press, 1967.

Lemann, Nicholas. *The Promised Land: The Great Black Migration and How It Changed America*. New York: Alfred A. Knopf, 1991.

Lewis, David L. *When Harlem Was in Vogue*. New York: Alfred A. Knopf, 1981.

Magubane, Bernard Makhosezwe. *The Ties That Bind: African-American Consciousness of Africa*. Trenton, N.J.: Africa World Press, 1987.

Marks, Carole. *Farewell—We're Good and Gone: The Great Black Migration*. Bloomington: Indiana University Press, 1989.

Martin, B. Edmon. *All We Want Is Make Us Free*. Lanham, Md.: University Press of America, 1986.

Maslowki, Pete. "National Policy Toward the Use of Black Troops in the Revolution." *South Carolina Historical Magazine* 73 (1972): 1-17.

Porter, Kenneth Wiggins. *The Negro on the American Frontier*. Reprint. New York: Arno Press, 1971.

Quarles, Benjamin. *The Negro in the American Revolution*. Chapel Hill: University of North Carolina Press, 1961.

Rabinowitz, Howard N., ed. *Southern Black Leaders of the Reconstruction Era*. Urbana: University of Illinois Press, 1982.

Savage, William Sherman. *Blacks in the West*. Westport, Conn.: Greenwood Press, 1976.

Stampp, Kenneth M. *The Era of Reconstruction, 1865-1877*. New York: Alfred A. Knopf, 1965.

_____. *The Peculiar Institution: Slavery in the Ante-Bellum South*. New York: Alfred A. Knopf, 1956.

Taylor, Roy G. *Sharecroppers: The Way We Really Were*. Wilson, N.C.: J-Mark, 1984.

Trotter, Joe William, Jr., ed. *The Great Migration in Historical Perspective: New Dimensions of Race, Class, and Gender*. Bloomington: Indiana University Press, 1991.

Van Sertima, Ivan. *They Came Before Columbus*. New York: Random House, 1976.

Walker, James W. St. G. *The Black Loyalists: The Search for a Promised Land in Nova Scotia and Sierra Leone, 1783-1870*. New York: Africana Publishing Company, 1973.

White, Deborah Gray. *Ar'n't I a Woman?: Female Slaves in the Plantation South*. New York: W. W. Norton, 1985.

Williams, John A., and Charles F. Harris, eds. *Amistad One*. New York: Random House, 1970.

_____, eds. *Amistad Two*. New York: Random House, 1971.

Williamson, Joel. *After Slavery: The Negro in South Carolina During Reconstruction, 1861-1877*. Chapel Hill: University of North Carolina Press, 1965.

Winks, Robin W. *The Blacks in Canada: A History*. New Haven, Conn.: Yale University Press, 1971.

Wyatt-Brown, Bertram. *Lewis Tappan and the Evangelical War Against Slavery*. New York: Atheneum, 1971.

LITERATURE

Bailey, Frankie Y. *Out of the Woodpile: Black Characters in Crime and Detective Fiction*. New York: Greenwood Press, 1991.

Baker, Houston A., Jr. "The Achievement of Gwendolyn Brooks." In *Singers of Daybreak: Studies in Black American Literature*. Washington, D.C.: Howard University Press, 1974.

_____. *Long Black Song: Essays in Black American Literature and Culture*. Charlottesville: University Press of Virginia, 1990.

Baraka, Imamu Amiri. *The Autobiography of LeRoi Jones-Amiri Baraka*. New York: Freundlich Books, 1984.

Bernotas, Bob. *Amiri Baraka (LeRoi Jones)*. New York: Chelsea House, 1991.

Blassingame, John W. *The Slave Community: Plantation Life in the Antebellum South*. Rev. ed. New York: Oxford University Press, 1979.

Brooks, Gwendolyn. *Report from Part One*. Detroit: Broadside Press, 1972.

Butterfield, Stephen. "James Baldwin: The Growth of a New Radicalism." In *Black Autobiography in America*. Amherst: University of Massachusetts Press, 1974.

Campbell, James. *Talking at the Gates: A Life of James Baldwin*. New York: Viking, 1991.

Cheney, Anne. *Lorraine Hansberry*. Boston: Twayne Publishers, 1984.

Christian, Barbara. "Novel for Everyday Use: The Novels of Alice Walker." In *Black Women Novelists: The Development of a Tradition, 1896-1976*. Westport, Conn.: Greenwood Press, 1980.

Clarke, John Henrik. "The Origin and Growth of Afro-American Literature." In *Black Voices: An Anthology of Afro-American Literature*. Edited by Abraham Chapman. New York: Mentor Books, 1968.

Cleaver, Eldridge. *Soul on Fire*. Waco, Tex.: Word Books, 1978.

Crowley, Daniel J. "Negro Folklore: An Africanist's View." *Texas Quarterly* 5 (Fall, 1962): 65-71.

De Veaux, Alice. "Alice Walker." *Essence* 20 (September, 1989): 56-62.

De Weever, Jacqueline. *Mythmaking and Metaphor in Black Women's Fiction*. New York: St. Martin's Press, 1992.

Dixon, Melvin. *Ride Out the Wilderness: Geography and Identity in Afro-American Literature*. Urbana: University of Illinois Press, 1987.

Du Bois, W. E. B. *The Souls of Black Folk: Essays and Sketches*. Chicago: A. C. McClurg, 1903.

Ellis, A. B. "Evolution in Folklore: Some West African Prototypes of the Uncle Remus Stories." *Popular Science Monthly* 48 (November, 1895): 93-104.

Fabre, Michel. *Richard Wright: Books and Writers*. Jackson: University Press of Mississippi, 1990.

_____. *The Unfinished Quest of Richard Wright*. Translated by Isabel Barzun. New York: William Morrow, 1973.

_____. *The World of Richard Wright*. Jackson: University Press of Mississippi, 1985.

Fiedler, Leslie A. *The Inadvertent Epic: From Uncle Tom's Cabin to Roots*. New York: Simon & Schuster, 1979.

Foster, Frances Smith. *Written by Herself: Literary Production by African American Women, 1746-1892*. Bloomington: Indiana University Press, 1993.

Fowler, Virginia C. *Conversations with Nikki*

Giovanni. Jackson: University Press of Mississippi, 1992.

Fuller, Miriam M. *Phillis Wheatley: America's First Black Poetess*. Champaign, Ill.: Garrard Publishing Company, 1971.

Gates, Henry Louis, Jr. *Figures in Black: Words, Signs, and the "Racial" Self*. New York: Oxford University Press, 1987.

Gerber, A. J. "Uncle Remus Traced to the Old World." *Journal of American Folklore* 6 (December, 1893): 245-257.

Haley, Alex. "What Roots Mean to Me." *Reader's Digest* 110 (May, 1977): 73-76.

Harris, William J. *The Poetry and Poetics of Amiri Baraka: The Jazz Aesthetic*. Columbia: University of Missouri Press, 1985.

Harrison, Eric. "Roots of Alex Haley Fame Headed for Auction Block." *Los Angeles Times*, September 27, 1992, p. A1, A26-A27.

Hull, Gloria T., and P. Gallagher. "Update on Part One—An Interview with Gwendolyn Brooks." *CLA Journal* 21 (September, 1977): 19-40.

Johnson, Charles. *Being and Race: Black Writing Since 1970*. Bloomington: Indiana University Press, 1988.

Kent, George E. *A Life of Gwendolyn Brooks*. Lexington: University of Kentucky, 1990.

Lacey, Henry C. *To Raise, Destroy, and Create*. Troy, N.Y.: Whitston, 1981.

Lewis, David L. *When Harlem Was in Vogue*. New York: Alfred A. Knopf, 1981.

Macebuh, Stanley. *James Baldwin: A Critical Study*. New York: Third Press, 1973.

McGuire, Willard, and M. S. Clayton. "Interview with Alex Haley." *Today's Educator* 66 (September, 1977): 45-47.

Massaquoi, Hans J. "Alex Haley: The Man Behind *Roots*." *Ebony* 32 (April, 1977): 33-36.

Miller, Eugene E. *Voice of a Native Son: The Poetics of Richard Wright*. Jackson: University Press of Mississippi, 1990.

Muller, Gilbert H. "The Greatest Show on Earth: The Detective Fiction." In *Chester Himes*. Boston: Twayne Publishers, 1989.

Nemiroff, Robert. *To Be Young, Gifted, and Black*. Englewood Cliffs, N.J.: Prentice-Hall, 1969.

O'Daniel, Therman B., ed. *James Baldwin: A Critical Evaluation*. Washington, D.C.: Howard University Press, 1977.

Owens, William. "Folklore of the Southern Negroes." *Lippincott's Magazine* 20 (December, 1877): 748-755.

Parker-Smith, Bettye J. "Alice Walker's Women: In Search of Some Peace of Mind." In *Black Women Writers (1950-1980): A Critical Evaluation*, edited by Mari Evans. Garden City, N.Y.: Anchor, 1984.

Porter, Horace A. *Stealing the Fire: The Art*

and Protest of James Baldwin. Middletown, Conn.: Wesleyan University Press, 1989.

Richmond, Merle A. *Bid the Vassal Soar: Interpretive Essays on the Life and Poetry of Phillis Wheatley and George Moses Horton*. Washington, D.C.: Howard University Press, 1974.

_____. *Phillis Wheatley*. New York: Chelsea House, 1988.

Robinson, William H. *Phillis Wheatley: A Bio-Bibliography*. Boston: G. K. Hall, 1981.

_____. *Phillis Wheatley and Her Writings*. New York: Garland, 1984.

_____. *Phillis Wheatley in the Black American Beginnings*. Detroit: Broadside Press, 1975.

Shaw, Harry B. *Gwendolyn Brooks*. Boston: Twayne, 1980.

Skinner, Robert E. *Two Guns from Harlem: The Detective Fiction of Chester Himes*. Bowling Green, Ohio: Bowling Green State University Popular Press, 1989.

Sundquist, Eric J. *To Wake the Nations: Race in the Making of American Literature*. Cambridge, Mass.: The Belknap Press of Harvard University Press, 1993.

Takaki, Ronald T. *Violence in the Black Imagination: Essays and Documents*. Rev. ed. New York: Oxford University Press, 1993.

Tate, Claudia. *Black Women Writers at Work*. New York: Continuum, 1983.

Van Deburg, William L. *Slavery and Race in American Popular Culture*. Madison: University of Wisconsin Press, 1984.

Walker, Margaret. *Richard Wright, Daemonic Genius: A Portrait of the Man, a Critical Look at His Work*. New York: Warner Books, 1988.

Warren, Kenneth W. *Black and White Strangers: Race and American Literary Realism*. Chicago: University of Chicago Press, 1993.

Williams, John A. *The Most Native of Sons: A Biography of Richard Wright*. New York: Doubleday, 1971.

Williams, John A., and Charles F. Harris, eds. *Amistad One*. New York: Random House, 1970.

Zimmerman, Paul D. "In Search of a Heritage." *Newsweek*, September 27, 1976, 94-96.

MILITARY

Allen, Robert L. *The Port Chicago Mutiny*. New York: Warner Books, 1989.

Barbeau, Arthur E., and Florette Henri. *The Unknown Soldiers: Black American Troops in World War I*. Philadelphia: Temple University Press, 1974.

Barbezat, Daniel, and Alexander George. "Who Died for Whose Way of Life? Re-

flections on the Burdens of Race." *Monthly Review* 43 (September, 1991): 34-36.

Bergman, Peter M. *The Chronological History of the Negro in America*. New York: Harper & Row, 1969.

Berry, Mary Frances. *Military Necessity and Civil Rights Policy: Black Citizenship and the Constitution, 1861-1868*. Port Washington, N.Y.: Kennikat Press, 1978.

Binkin, Martin. "The New Face of the American Military—The Volunteer Force and the Persian Gulf War." *The Brookings Review* 9 (Summer, 1991): 6.

Carroll, John Melvin, ed. *The Black Military Experience in the American West*. New York: Liveright, 1973.

Carter, Samuel. *Blaze of Glory: The Fight for New Orleans*. New York: St. Martin's Press, 1971.

Cornish, Dudley T. *The Sable Arm: Negro Troops in the Union Army, 1861-1865*. New York: Longmans, Green, 1956.

David, Jay, and Elaine Crane, eds. *The Black Soldier from the American Revolution to Vietnam*. New York: William Morrow, 1971.

Durden, Robert. *The Gray and the Black: The Confederate Debate on Emancipation*. Baton Rouge: Louisiana State University Press, 1972.

Foner, Jack D. *Blacks and the Military in American History*. New York: Praeger, 1974.

Foner, Philip S. *Blacks in the American Revolution*. Westport, Conn.: Greenwood Press, 1975.

Fowler, Arlen L. *The Black Infantry in the West, 1869-1891*. Westport, Conn.: Greenwood Press, 1971.

Garfinkel, Herbert. *When Negroes March: The March on Washington Movement in the Organizational Politics of FEPC*. Glencoe, Ill.: Free Press, 1959.

Gatewood, Willard B., Jr. *Black Americans and the White Man's Burden, 1898-1903*. Urbana: University of Illinois Press, 1975.

_____. *"Smoked Yankees" and the Struggle for Empire*. Urbana: University of Illinois Press, 1971.

Giffin, William W. "Mobilization of Black Militiamen in World War I: Ohio's Ninth Battalion." *Historian* 40 (August, 1978): 686-703.

Hartgrove, W. B. "The Negro Soldier in the American Revolution." *Journal of Negro History* 1, no. 2 (April, 1916): 110-131.

Hickey, Donald R. *The War of 1812: A Forgotten Conflict*. Urbana: University of Illinois Press, 1989.

Higginson, Thomas Wentworth. *Army Life in a Black Regiment*. Boston: Fields, Osgood, 1870. Reprint. Alexandria, Va.: Time-Life Books, 1982.

Horsman, Reginald. *The War of 1812*. New York: Alfred A. Knopf, 1969.

Kaplan, Sidney, and Emma N. Kaplan. *The Black Presence in the Era of the American Revolution*. Rev. ed. Amherst: University of Massachusetts Press, 1989.

Katz, William Loren. *The Black West*. 3d rev. ed. Seattle: Open Hand Publishers, 1987.

_____, ed. *Eyewitness: The Negro in American History*. New York: Pitman, 1967.

Koppes, Clayton R., and Gregory D. Black. "Blacks, Loyalty and Motion-Picture Propaganda in World War II." *The Journal of American History* 73 (September, 1986): 383-406.

Kornweibel, Theodore, Jr. "Apathy and Dissent: Black America's Negative Responses to World War I." *South Atlantic Quarterly* 80, no. 3 (1981): 322-338.

Leckie, William H. *The Buffalo Soldiers*. Norman: University of Oklahoma Press, 1967.

Lenoir, Gerald. "Blacks and the U.S. Military: From the Revolutionary War to the Persian Gulf Crisis." *The East Bay Guardian* 1 (February, 1991).

Maslowski, Pete. "National Policy Toward the Use of Black Troops in the Revolution." *South Carolina Historical Magazine* 73 (1972): 1-17.

Means, Howard. *Colin Powell: Soldier/ Statesman, Statesman/Soldier*. New York: Donald I. Fine, 1992.

Murray, Paul Thom, Jr. "Blacks and the Draft: A History of Institutional Racism." *Journal of Black Studies* 2, no. 1 (1971): 57-76.

Nalty, Bernard C. *Strength for the Fight: A History of Black Americans in the Military*. New York: Free Press, 1986.

Nell, William C. *Services of Colored Americans in the Wars of 1776 and 1812*. Boston: Prentiss & Sawyer, 1851. Reprint. New York: AMS Press, 1976.

Osur, Alan M. *Blacks in the Army Air Forces During World War II: The Problem of Race Relations*. Washington, D.C.: Office of Air Force History, 1977.

Patton, Gerald W. *War and Race: The Black Officer in the American Military, 1915-1941*. Westport, Conn.: Greenwood Press, 1981.

Potter, Lou, with William Miles and Nina Rosenblum. *Liberators: Fighting on Two Fronts in World War II*. New York: Harcourt Brace Jovanovich, 1992.

Quarles, Benjamin. *The Negro in the American Revolution*. Chapel Hill: University of North Carolina Press, 1961.

_____. *The Negro in the Civil War*. Boston: Little, Brown, 1953.

Ranelagh, John. "America's Black Eisenhower." *National Review* 43 (April 1, 1991): 26-28.

Rowan, Carl T. "Called to Service: The Colin Powell Story." *Reader's Digest* 135 (December, 1989): 121-126.

Thomas, Evan, and Tom Mathews. "The Reluctant Warrior." *Newsweek* 117 (May 13, 1991): 18-22.

Umberson, Debra, and Kristin Henderson. "The Social Construction of Death in the Gulf War." *Omega* 25, no. 1 (1992): 1-15.

Weaver, John D. *The Brownsville Raid*. College Station: Texas A&M University Press, 1992.

Williams, George Washington. *A History of the Negro Troops in the War of the Rebellion, 1861-1865*. Reprint. New York: Negro Universities Press, 1969.

Wilson, Joseph Thomas. *The Black Phalanx: A History of Negro Soldiers of the U.S. in the Wars of 1775-1812 and 1861-1865*. Hartford, Conn.: American, 1888. Reprint. New York: Arno Press, 1968.

Woodward, Bob. *The Commanders*. New York: Simon & Schuster, 1991.

Wynn, Neil A. *The Afro-American and the Second World War*. New York: Holmes & Meier, 1975.

MUSIC

Abdul, Raoul. *Blacks in Classical Music*. New York: Dodd, Mead, 1977.

Armstrong, Louis. *Satchmo: My Life in New Orleans*. New York: Prentice-Hall, 1954.

Barlow, William. *Looking Up at Down: The Emergence of Blues Culture*. Philadelphia: Temple University Press, 1989.

Bego, Mark. *Aretha Franklin: Queen of Soul*. New York: St. Martin's Press, 1989.

Berry, Chuck. *Chuck Berry: The Autobiography*. New York: Harmony Books, 1987.

Bigard, Barney. *With Louis and the Duke: The Autobiography of a Jazz Clarinetist*. New York: Oxford University Press, 1985.

Brooks, Tilford. *America's Black Musical Heritage*. Englewood Cliffs, N.J.: Prentice-Hall, 1984.

Brown, James, and Bruce Tucker. *James Brown: The Godfather of Soul*. New York: Thunder's Mouth Press, 1990.

Budds, Michael J. *Jazz in the Sixties*. Iowa City: University of Iowa Press, 1990.

Charters, Samuel Barclay. *The Country Blues*. New York: Da Capo Press, 1975.

Christgau, Robert. "Chuck Berry." In *The Rolling Stone Illustrated History of Rock & Roll*. Rev. ed. Edited by Jim Miller. New York: Random House/Rolling Stone Press, 1980.

Cole, Bill. *John Coltrane*. New York: Schirmer, 1976.

Collier, James Lincoln. *Duke Ellington*. New York: Oxford University Press, 1987.

Cone, James H. *The Spirituals and the Blues*. New York: Seabury Press, 1972.

Cuney-Hare, Maud. *Negro Musicians and Their Music*. Washington, D.C.: Associated Publishers, 1936.

De Lerma, Dominique-René. *Reflections on Afro-American Music*. Kent, Ohio: Kent State University Press, 1973.

DeVeaux, Scott, and William Howland Kenney, eds. *The Music of James Scott*. Washington, D.C.: Smithsonian Institution Press, 1992.

DeWitt, Howard A. *Chuck Berry: Rock 'n' Roll Music*. 2d ed. Ann Arbor, Mich.: Pierian Press, 1985.

Duberman, Martin Bauml. *Paul Robeson*. New York: Alfred A. Knopf, 1989.

Du Bois, W. E. B. *The Souls of Black Folk: Essays and Sketches*. Chicago: A. C. McClurg, 1903.

Early, Gerald. "One Nation Under a Groove: The Brief, Shining Moment of Motown—and America." *The New Republic* 205 (July 15 and 22, 1991): 30-41.

Ellington, Duke. *Music Is My Mistress*. Garden City, N.Y.: Doubleday, 1974.

Elsner, Constanze. *Steve Wonder*. New York: Popular Library, 1980.

Ewen, David. "Chuck Berry." In *American Songwriters*. New York: H. W. Wilson, 1987.

Floyd, Samuel A. *Black Music in the Harlem Renaissance: A Collection of Essays*. New York: Greenwood Press, 1990.

Garland, Phyl. *The Sound of Soul*. Chicago: Henry Regnery, 1969.

George, Don. *Sweet Man: The Real Duke Ellington*. New York: G. P. Putnam's Sons, 1982.

George, Nelson. *The Death of Rhythm and Blues*. New York: Pantheon Books, 1988.

_____. *Where Did Our Love Go?: The Rise and Fall of the Motown Sound*. New York: St. Martin's Press, 1985.

George, Nelson, Sally Banes, Susan Flinker, and Patty Romanowski. *Fresh, Hip Hop Don't Stop*. New York: Random House, 1985.

Giddins, Gary. *Celebrating Bird: The Triumph of Charlie Parker*. New York: Beech Tree Books, 1987.

Gitler, Ira. *Jazz Masters of the 40's*. New York: Macmillan, 1966.

Govenar, Alan. *The Early Days of Rhythm and Blues*. Houston, Tex.: Rice University Press, 1990.

Graham, Shirley. *Paul Robeson, Citizen of the World*. New York: J. Messner, 1946.

Guralnick, Peter. *Sweet Soul Music: Rhythm and Blues and the Southern Dream of Freedom*. New York: Harper & Row, 1986.

Hamilton, Virginia. *Paul Robeson: The Life and Times of a Free Black Man*. New York: Harper & Row, 1974.

Hampton, Lionel, with James Haskins.

Hamp: An Autobiography. New York: Warner Books, 1989.

Handy, W. C. *Blues: An Anthology.* Edited by William Ferris. New York: Da Capo Press, 1991.

Haralambos, Michael. *Right On: From Blues to Soul in Black America.* London: Eddison Press, 1974.

Harris, Sheldon. *Blues Who's Who.* New York: Da Capo Press, 1983.

Harrison, Daphne Duval. *Black Pearls: Blues Queens of the 1920s.* New Brunswick, N.J.: Rutgers University Press, 1988.

Harrison, Max. *Charlie Parker.* New York: A.S. Barnes, 1961.

Haskins, James. *Black Music in America.* New York: Thomas Y. Crowell, 1987.

Hirshey, Gerri. *Nowhere to Run: The Story of Soul Music.* London: Macmillan, 1985.

Hoskins, Robert. *Louis Armstrong: Biography of a Musician.* Los Angeles: Holloway House Publishing, 1979.

Hoyt, Edwin P. *Paul Robeson: The American Othello.* Cleveland: World Publishing Company, 1967.

Hurston, Zora Neale. *The Sanctified Church.* Berkeley, Calif.: Turtle Island, 1981.

Jacobs, Linda. *Stevie Wonder: Sunshine in the Shadow.* St. Paul, Minn.: EMC, 1976.

Jahn, Janheinz. *Muntu African Culture and the Western World.* New York: Grove Weidenfeld, 1990.

Jones, LeRoi. *Blues People: Negro Music in White America.* New York: William Morrow, 1963.

Jones, Max, and John Chilton. *Louis: The Louis Armstrong Story, 1900-1971.* Boston: Little, Brown, 1971.

Keil, Charles. *Urban Blues.* Chicago: University of Chicago Press, 1966.

Kenney, William Howland. *Chicago Jazz: A Cultural History, 1904-1930.* New York: Oxford University Press, 1993.

Levine, Lawrence W. *Black Culture and Black Consciousness: Afro-American Folk Thought from Slavery to Freedom.* New York: Oxford University Press, 1977.

Lincoln, C. Eric, and Laurence H. Mamiya. *The Black Church in the African American Experience.* Durham, N.C.: Duke University Press, 1990.

Litweiler, John. *The Freedom Principle: Jazz After 1958.* New York: William Morrow, 1984.

Maryman, Richard. *Louis Armstrong—A Self Portrait.* New York: Eakins Press, 1971.

Mathis, Sharon Bell. *Ray Charles.* New York: Thomas Y. Crowell, 1973.

Miller, Jim, ed. *The Rolling Stone Illustrated History of Rock and Roll.* Rev. ed. New York: Random House/Rolling Stone Press, 1980.

Parrish, Lydia. *Slave Songs of the Georgia Sea Islands.* Athens: University of Georgia Press, 1992.

Patterson, Lindsay. *International Library of Afro-American Life History: The Afro-American in Music and Art.* Cornwells Heights, Pa.: Publishers Agency, 1979.

Peisch, Jeffrey. *Stevie Wonder.* New York: Ballantine Books, 1985.

Pruter, Robert. *Chicago Soul.* Urbana: University of Illinois Press, 1991.

Reisner, Robert George. *Bird: The Legend of Charlie Parker.* New York: Citadel Press, 1962.

Roberts, John Storm. *Black Music of Two Worlds.* New York: Praeger, 1972.

Robeson, Paul. *Here I Stand.* London: D. Dobson, 1958.

Robeson, Susan. *The Whole World in His Hands: A Pictorial Biography of Paul Robeson.* Secaucus, N.J.: Citadel Press, 1981.

Robinson, Smokey, and David Ritz. *Smokey: Inside My Life.* New York: McGraw-Hill, 1989.

Rose, Cynthia. *Living in America: The Soul Saga of James Brown.* London: Serpent's Tail, 1990.

Rosenthal, David H. *Hard Bop: Jazz and Black Music, 1955-1965.* New York: Oxford University Press, 1992.

Russell, Ross. *Bird Lives!* New York: David McKay, 1971.

Salvo, Patrick William. "A Conversation with Chuck Berry." *Rolling Stone* n. 122 (November 23, 1972): 35-42.

Schuller, Gunther. *Early Jazz: Its Roots and Musical Development.* Vol. 1 in *The History of Jazz.* New York: Oxford University Press, 1968.

_____. *The Swing Era: The Development of Jazz, 1930-1945.* Vol. 2 in *The History of Jazz.* New York: Oxford University Press, 1989.

Shaw, Arnold. *Black Popular Music in America.* New York: Schirmer Books, 1986.

_____. *Honkers and Shouters: The Golden Years of Rhythm and Blues.* New York: Macmillan, 1978.

_____. "Soul Is..." In *The Popular Arts in America*, Edited by William M. Hammel. 2d ed. New York: Harcourt Brace Jovanovich, 1977.

Singer, Barry. *Black and Blue: The Life and Lyrics of Andy Razaf.* New York: Schirmer Books, 1993.

Singleton, Raynoma Gordy, with Bryan Brown and Mim Eichler. *Berry, Me, & Motown: The Untold Story.* Chicago: Contemporary Books, 1990.

Small, Michael. *Break It Down: The Inside Story from the New Leaders of Rap.* New York: Citadel Press, 1992.

Southern, Eileen. *The Music of Black Americans: A History.* 2d ed. New York: W. W. Norton, 1983.

Spencer, Jon Michael. *Black Hymnody: A Hymnological History of the African-American Church.* Knoxville: University of Tennessee Press, 1992.

Stambler, Irvin. *Encyclopedia of Pop, Rock and Soul.* New York: St. Martin's Press, 1974.

Story, Rosalyn M. *And So I Sing: African American Divas of Opera and Concert.* New York: Warner Books, 1990.

Swenson, John. *Stevie Wonder.* London: Plexus, 1986.

Thomas, J. C. *Chasin' the Trane: The Music and Mystique of John Coltrane.* Garden City, N.Y.: Doubleday, 1975.

Thurman, Howard. *Deep River and The Negro Spiritual Speaks of Life and Death.* Richmond, Ind.: Friends United Press, 1975.

Tirro, Frank. *Jazz: A History.* New York: W. W. Norton, 1977.

Trotter, James. *Music and Some Highly Musical People.* Boston: Lee and Shepard, 1878. Reprint. New York: Johnson Reprint Corp., 1968.

Whaley, Donald M. "'Memphis Soul Stew': Minstrelsy, Black Nationalism, and the Memphis Sound of Soul Music." In *Tennessee in American History,* edited by Larry H. Whiteaker and W. Calvin Dickinson. 2d ed. Needham Heights, Mass.: Ginn, 1991.

Williams, Martin. *The Jazz Tradition.* New York: Oxford University Press, 1970.

Wilson, John S. *Jazz: The Transition Years, 1940-1960.* New York: Appleton Century Crofts, 1966.

PERFORMING ARTS

Abramson, Doris. *Negro Playwrights in the American Theatre 1925-1959.* New York: Columbia University Press, 1969.

Acker, Ally. *Reel Women.* New York: Continuum, 1991.

Adler, Bill. *The Cosby Wit: His Life and Humor.* New York: Carroll & Graf, 1986.

Armstrong, Louis. *Satchmo: My Life in New Orleans.* New York: Prentice-Hall, 1954.

Aschenbrenner, Joyce. *Katherine Dunham: Reflections on the Social and Political Contexts of Afro-American Dance.* New York: CORD, 1981.

Baker, Jean-Claude, and Chris Chase. *Josephine: The Hungry Heart.* New York: Random House, 1993.

Barlow, William. *Looking Up at Down: The Emergence of Blues Culture.* Philadelphia: Temple University Press, 1989.

Beckford, Ruth. *Katherine Dunham: A Biography.* New York: Marcel Dekker, 1979.

Belker, Lisa. "Fame and Controversy for

Danny Glover." *The New York Times*, January 26, 1986, p. B21.

Bennett, Lerone. "Sammy Davis Jr., 1925-1990: The Legacy of the World's Greatest Entertainer." *Ebony* 45 (July, 1990): 118-120.

Berry, Chuck. *Chuck Berry: The Autobiography*. New York: Harmony Books, 1987.

Bigard, Barney. *With Louis and the Duke: The Autobiography of a Jazz Clarinetist*. New York: Oxford University Press, 1985.

Blum, David. "Today's Man: Bryant Gumbel's Different Strokes." *New York* 19 (August 4, 1986): 30-37.

Bogle, Donald. *Blacks in American Films and Television: An Illustrated Encyclopedia*. New York: Garland, 1988.

_____. *Brown Sugar: Eighty Years of America's Black Female Superstars*. New York: Harmony Books, 1980.

_____. *Toms, Coons, Mulattoes, Mammies, and Bucks: An Interpretive History of Blacks in American Films*. Rev. ed. New York: Continuum, 1989.

Branch, Taylor. *Parting the Waters: America in The King Years, 1954-63*. New York: Simon & Schuster, 1988.

Brown, James, and Bruce Tucker. *James Brown: The Godfather of Soul*. New York: Thunder's Mouth Press, 1990.

Campbell, Bebe Moore. "Spotlight: Billy Dee Williams." *Essence* 16 (July, 1985): 61.

Carter, Bill. "Forecast for Today: Cloudy." *The New York Times Magazine* 139 (June 10, 1990): 26.

Charters, Samuel Barclay. *The Country Blues*. New York: Da Capo Press, 1975.

Cherry, Gwendolyn. *Portraits in Color*. New York: Pageant Press, 1962.

Christgau, Robert. "Chuck Berry." In *The Rolling Stone Illustrated History of Rock & Roll*. Rev. ed. Edited by Jim Miller. New York: Random House/Rolling Stone Press, 1980.

Coe, Robert. "Katherine Dunham and Her People." In *Dance in America*. New York: E. P. Dutton, 1985.

Collier, Aldore. "Danny Glover: The Reluctant Movie Star." *Ebony* 41 (March, 1986): 82.

Collins, Glenn. "Lou Gossett, Jr. Battles the Hollywood Stereotype." *The New York Times*, February 19, 1989, p. B23.

Corliss, Richard. "Boyz of the New Black City." *Time* 137 (June 17, 1991): 64-68.

Cripps, Thomas. *Making Movies Black: The Hollywood Message Movie from World War II to the Civil Rights Era*. New York: Oxford University Press, 1993.

_____. *Slow Fade to Black*. New York: Oxford University Press, 1977.

Dandridge, Dorothy, and Earl Conrad. *Everything and Nothing: The Dorothy Dandridge Tragedy*. New York: Abelard-Schuman, 1970.

Dates, Jannette L., and William Barlow. *Split Image: African Americans in the Mass Media*. Washington, D.C.: Howard University Press, 1990.

Davis, Arthur P. *From the Dark Tower*. Washington, D.C.: Howard University Press, 1974.

Davis, Marianna W., ed. *Contributions of Black Women to America*. 2 vols. Columbia, S.C.: Kenday Press, 1982.

Davis, Sammy, Jane Boyar, and Burt Boyar. *Yes I Can: The Story of Sammy Davis, Jr.* New York: Farrar, Straus, & Giroux, 1965.

Davis, Thulani. "Denzel in the Swing." *American Film* 15 (August, 1990): 26-31.

DeWitt, Howard A. *Chuck Berry: Rock 'n' Roll Music*. 2d ed. Ann Arbor, Mich.: Pierian Press, 1985.

Duberman, Martin Bauml. *Paul Robeson*. New York: Alfred A. Knopf, 1989.

Edwards, Audrey. "Oprah Winfrey: Stealing the Show!" *Essence* 17 (October, 1986): 50-52.

_____. "Whoopi!" *Essence* 15 (March, 1985): 84-86.

Ely, Melvin Patrick. *The Adventures of Amos 'n' Andy: A Social History of an American Phenomenon*. New York: Free Press, 1992.

Emery, Lynne Fauley. *Black Dance: From 1617 to Today*. 2d rev. ed. Princeton, N.J.: Princeton Book Company, 1988.

Erickson, Steve. "Whoopi Goldberg." *Rolling Stone*, May 8, 1986, p. 38.

Estrada, Ric. "Three Leading Negro Artists, and How They Feel About Dance in the Community." *Dance* 42 (November, 1968): 45-60.

Ewen, David. "Chuck Berry." In *American Songwriters*. New York: H. W. Wilson, 1987.

Feather, Leonard. "Ray Charles." In *From Satchmo to Miles*. New York: Stein and Day, 1972.

Forman, James. *The Making of Black Revolutionaries*. New York: Macmillan, 1972.

Foxx, Redd and Norma Miller. *The Redd Foxx Encyclopedia of Black Humor*. Pasadena, Calif.: Ward Ritchie Press, 1977.

Funke, Lewis. *The Curtain Rises: They Story of Ossie Davis*. New York: Grosset & Dunlap, 1971.

George, Nelson. *The Death of Rhythm and Blues*. New York: Pantheon Books, 1988.

George, Nelson, and Sally Banes, Susan Flinker, and Patty Romanowski. *Fresh, Hip Hop Don't Stop*. New York: Random House, 1985.

Gourse, Leslie. *Sassy: The Life of Sarah Vaughan*. New York: Charles Scribner's Sons, 1992.

Graham, Shirley. *Paul Robeson, Citizen of the World*. New York: J. Messner, 1946.

Guralnick, Peter. *Sweet Soul Music: Rhythm and Blues and the Southern Dream of Freedom*. New York: Harper & Row, 1986.

Hager, Steven. *Hip Hop: The Illustrated History of Break Dancing, Rap Music, and Graffiti*. New York: St. Martin's Press, 1984.

Hallett, Lisa. "The World According to Danny." *Dial*, February, 1989, 10-12.

Hamilton, Virginia. *Paul Robeson: The Life and Times of a Free Black Man*. New York: Harper & Row, 1974.

Handy, W. C. *Blues: An Anthology*. Edited by William Ferris. New York: Da Capo Press, 1991.

Harnan, Terry. *African Rhythm, American Dance: A Biography of Katherine Dunham*. New York: Alfred A. Knopf, 1974.

Harris, Sheldon. *Blues Who's Who*. New York: Da Capo Press, 1983.

Harrison, Daphne Duval. *Black Pearls: Blues Queens of the 1920s*. New Brunswick, N.J.: Rutgers University Press, 1988.

Haskins, James. *Black Dance in America: A History Through Its People*. New York: Thomas Y. Crowell, 1990.

_____. *Black Theater in America*. New York: Thomas Y. Crowell, 1982.

_____. *The Cotton Club*. New York: Random House, 1977.

_____. *Richard Pryor: A Man and His Madness*. New York: Beaufort Books, 1984.

Hentoff, Nat. "An Inheritance Comes to P.S. 83." *American Education* 2 (February, 1966): 28-32.

Hewitt, Hugh. "Porcupine Strikes Back." *National Review* 44 (June 8, 1992): 6.

Hirshey, Gerri. *Nowhere to Run: The Story of Soul Music*. London: Macmillan, 1985.

Hoban, Phoebe. "Days of Glory: Denzel Washington—From Spike Lee's Blues to Richard III." *New York Magazine* 23 (August 13, 1990): 34-38.

Hoffman, William. *Sidney*. New York: L. Stuart, 1971.

Hoskins, Robert. *Louis Armstrong: Biography of a Musician*. Los Angeles: Holloway House Publishing, 1979.

Hoyt, Edwin P. *Paul Robeson: The American Othello*. Cleveland: World Publishing Company, 1967.

Hughes, Langston, and Milton Meltzer. *Black Magic: A Pictorial History of the African-American in the Performing Arts*. 1967. Reprint. New York: Da Capo Press, 1990.

Isaacs, Edith J. R. *The Negro in the American Theatre*. New York: Theatre Arts, 1947.

Johnson, James Weldon. *Black Manhattan*. 1930. Reprint. New York: Arno Press, 1968.

Jones, G. William. *Black Cinema Treasures:*

Lost and Found. Denton: University of North Texas Press, 1991.

Jones, LeRoi. *Blues People: Negro Music in White America.* New York: William Morrow, 1963.

Jones, Max, and John Chilton. *Louis: The Louis Armstrong Story, 1900-1971.* Boston: Little, Brown, 1971.

Kearney, Jill. "Whoopi: Color Her Anything." *American Film* 11 (December, 1985): 24-26.

Keil, Charles. *Urban Blues.* Chicago: University of Chicago Press, 1966.

Kettelkamp, Larry. *Bill Cosby: Family Funny Man.* New York: Wanderer Books, 1987.

Keyser, Lester J., and Andre H. Ruszkowski. *The Cinema of Sidney Poitier.* San Diego, Calif.: A. S. Barnes, 1980.

King, Norman. *Arsenio Hall.* New York: William Morrow, 1993.

_____. *Everybody Loves Oprah! Her Remarkable Life Story.* New York: William Morrow, 1987.

Klemesrud, Judy. "Earning Sergeant's Stripes for a Movie Role." *The New York Times,* July 25, 1982, p. B1.

Klotman, Phyllis, ed. *Screenplays of the African-American Experience.* Bloomington: Indiana University Press, 1991.

Kraus, Richard, Sarah Chapman Hilsendager, and Brenda Dixon. "Black Dance in America." In *History of the Dance in Art and Education.* Englewood Cliffs, N.J.: Prentice-Hall, 1991.

Kriegsman, Alan M. "The Master of Movement: Choreographer Alvin Ailey, the Spring in America's Steps." *The Washington Post,* December 2, 1989, p. C1.

Krista, Charlene. "Danny Glover: An Interview." *Films in Review,* April, 1985, 233-235.

Landay, Eileen. *Black Film Stars.* New York: Drake Publishers, 1973.

Latham, Caroline. *Bill Cosby, for Real.* New York: Tom Doherty Associates, 1985.

Leab, Daniel J. *From Sambo to Superspade: The Black Experience in Motion Pictures.* Boston: Houghton Mifflin, 1975.

Long, Richard A. *The Black Tradition in American Dance.* New York: Rizzoli, 1989.

Lydon, Michael. "Raw Truth and Joy: Ray Charles Cuts Through His Smoothness With Jolts of Musical Pleasure." *The Atlantic* 267 (March, 1991): 120-122.

_____. "Ray Charles." In *Boogie Lightning.* New York: Dial Press, 1974, pp. 187-229.

McBride, Joseph. "Stepin Fetchit Talks Back." *Film Quarterly* 25 (Summer, 1971): 20-26.

Major, Clarence. *The Cotton Club.* Detroit: Broadside Press, 1972.

Mapp, Edward. *Blacks in American Films:* *Today and Yesterday.* Metuchen, N.J.: Scarecrow Press, 1971.

Marill, Alvin H. *The Films of Sidney Poitier.* Secaucus, N.J.: Citadel Press, 1978.

Marshall, Herbert, and Mildred Stock. *Ira Aldridge: The Negro Tragedian.* 2d ed. Carbondale: Southern Illinois University Press, 1968.

Martin, Guy. "Blue Genius: Brother Ray Charles Sings the Gospel Truth." *Esquire* 105 (May, 1986): 92-100.

Maryman, Richard. *Louis Armstrong—A Self Portrait.* New York: Eakins Press, 1971.

Mills, Earl. *Dorothy Dandridge.* Los Angeles: Holloway House Publishing, 1970.

Mitchell, Loften. *Black Drama.* New York: Hawthorn Books, 1967.

Nazel, Joseph. *Richard Pryor: The Man Behind the Laughter.* Los Angeles: Holloway House, 1981.

Nemiroff, Robert. *Portrait of a Play.* New York: New American Library, 1966.

Nemy, Enid. "Whoopi's Ready, but Is Broadway?" *The New York Times,* October 21, 1984, p. B1.

Noble, Peter. *The Negro in Films.* New York: Arno Press, 1970.

Noel, Pamela. "Lights! Camera! Oprah!" *Ebony* 40 (April, 1985): 100-105.

Norment, Lynn. "Ebony Interview: Billy Dee Williams." *Ebony* 36 (January, 1981): 31-34.

_____. "Lou Gossett, Jr.: The Agony and Ecstasy of Success." *Ebony* 37 (December, 1982): 142.

_____. "Three Great Love Stories." *Ebony* 43 (February 1988): 150-152.

Patterson, Lindsay, ed. *Anthology of the American Negro in the Theatre.* New York: Publishers Company, 1970.

Pawley, Thomas D. *"The First Black Playwrights."* *Black World* 21 (November, 1972): 16-24.

Pieterse, Jan Nederveen. *White on Black: Images of Africa and Blacks in Western Popular Culture.* New Haven, Conn.: Yale University Press, 1992.

Poitier, Sidney. *This Life.* New York: Alfred A. Knopf, 1980.

Probosz, Kathilyn Solomon. *Alvin Ailey, Jr.* New York: Bantam Books, 1991.

Randolph, Laura B. "The Glory Days of Denzel Washington." *Ebony* 45 (September, 1990): 80-82.

_____. "The Whoopi Goldberg Nobody Knows." *Ebony* 46 (March, 1991): 110-112.

Reid, Mark A. *Redefining Black Film.* Berkeley: University of California Press, 1993.

Reilly, Rick. "The Mourning Anchor." *Sports Illustrated* 69 (September 26, 1988): 74-76, 79-82.

Riis, Thomas L. *Just Before Jazz: Black Musical Theater in New York: 1890-1915.* Washington, D.C.: Smithsonian Institution Press, 1989.

Robbins, Fred, and David Ragan. *Richard Pryor: This Cat's Got 9 Lives!* New York: Delilah Books, 1982.

Roberts, John Storm. *Black Music of Two Worlds.* New York: Praeger, 1972.

Robeson, Paul. *Here I Stand.* London: D. Dobson, 1958.

Robeson, Susan. *The Whole World in His Hands: A Pictorial Biography of Paul Robeson.* Secaucus, N.J.: Citadel Press, 1981.

Rose, Cynthia. *Living in America: The Soul Saga of James Brown.* London: Serpent's Tail, 1990.

Rosen, Marjorie, and Lois Armstrong. "Danny Glover." *People Weekly* 37 (February 10, 1992): 91-92.

Rosenberg, Robert. *Bill Cosby: The Changing Black Image.* Brookfield, Conn.: Millbrook Press, 1991.

Rovin, Jeff. *Richard Pryor, Black and Blue.* New York: Bantam Books, 1983.

Salvo, Patrick William. "A Conversation with Chuck Berry." *Rolling Stone* n. 122 (November 23, 1972): 35-42.

Sanders, Charles L. "Billy Dee Williams: The Serious Side of a Sex Symbol." *Ebony* 38 (June, 1983): 126-128.

Schiffman, Jack. *Uptown: The Story of Harlem's Apollo Theater.* New York: Cowles Book Co., 1971.

Schuller, Gunther. *Early Jazz: Its Roots and Musical Development.* Vol. 1 in *The History of Jazz.* New York: Oxford University Press, 1968.

_____. *The Swing Era: The Development of Jazz, 1930-1945.* Vol. 2 in *The History of Jazz.* New York: Oxford University Press, 1989.

Shah, Diane K. "Soldier, Healer, Seller of Rye." *GQ* 58 (October, 1988): 312-317.

Shook, Karel. *Elements of Classical Ballet Technique as Practiced in the School of the Dance Theatre of Harlem.* New York: Dance Horizons, 1977.

Small, Linda. "Black Dancers, Black Travelers." *Dance Magazine* 53 (October, 1979): 78.

Small, Michael. *Break It Down: The Inside Story from the New Leaders of Rap.* New York: Citadel Press, 1992.

Smith, Jessie Carney, ed. *Notable Black American Women.* Detroit: Gale Research, 1992.

Smith, Ronald L. *Cosby.* New York: St. Martin's Press, 1986.

Smith, Valerie, Camille Billops, and Ada Griffin, eds. *Black American Literature Forum.* Vol. 25, no. 2 (Summer 1991). "Black Film Issue."

Southern, Eileen. *The Music of Black Americans: A History.* 2d ed. New York: W. W. Norton, 1983.

Spencer, Jon Michael, ed. *The Emergency of Black and the Emergence of Rap.* Durham, N.C.: Duke University Press, 1991.

Stein, Charles W., ed. *American Vaudeville as Seen by Its Contemporaries.* New York: Alfred A. Knopf, 1984.

Steinem, Gloria, "Women in the Dark: Of Sex Goddesses, Abuse, and Dreams." in *Ms. Magazine,* January-February, 1991, pp. 35-37.

Stone, Judy. "Lou Gossett: Did We Always Eat Watermelon?" *The New York Times,* August 30, 1970, p. B13.

Tate, Greg. *Flyboy in the Buttermilk.* New York: Simon & Schuster, 1992.

Terry, Walter. "The Black Dance." *The Dance in America.* Rev. ed. New York: Harper & Row, 1971.

Thorpe, Edward. *Black Dance.* Woodstock, N.Y.: Overlook Press, 1990.

Tirro, Frank. *Jazz: A History.* New York: W. W. Norton, 1977.

Toop, David. *Rap Attack 2: African Rap To Global Hip Hop.* New York: Serpent's Tail, 1992.

Toppin, Edgar A. *A Biographical History of Blacks in America Since 1528.* New York: McKay, 1971.

Waldron, Robert. *Oprah!* New York: St. Martin's Press, 1987.

Waters, Harry F., and Patricia King. "Chicago's Grand New Oprah." *Newsweek,* December 31, 1984, 51.

Weller, Sheila. "Today's Man: The Double-Edged Charm of Bryant Gumbel." *McCall's* 114 (June, 1987): 69-71, 74.

"Whatever Happened to Lincoln (Stepin Fetchit) Perry," *Ebony* 27 (November, 1971): 202.

Wilkerson, Isabel. "A Grand Dame Fasts for Haitians and Suffering City Responds." *The New York Times,* March 8, 1992, p. A12.

Williams, John A., and Dennis A. Williams. *If I Stop I'll Die: The Comedy and Tragedy of Richard Pryor.* New York: Thunder's Mouth Press, 1991.

Wishengrad, Susan. "The Two Worlds of Ossie Davis and Ruby Dee." *Good Housekeeping* 192 (April, 1981): 2.

Woll, Allen. *Black Musical Theatre: From Coontown to Dreamgirls.* Baton Rouge: Louisiana State University Press, 1989.

Zoglin, Richard. "Lady with a Calling." *Time,* August 8, 1988, 62-64.

POLITICS AND GOVERNMENT

Ashmore, Harry S. *Hearts and Minds: The Anatomy of Racism from Roosevelt to Reagan.* New York: McGraw-Hill, 1982.

Baer, Donald. "Dealing with Souls on Fire." *U.S. News & World Report* 108 (May 28, 1990): 33-34.

Baker, James N. "Minority Against Minority: Rioting in D.C. Tests the New Mayor's Resolve." *Newsweek* 117 (May 20, 1991): 28.

Barker, Lucius J., ed. *Black Electoral Politics.* New Brunswick, N.J.: Transaction Publishers, 1990.

_____, ed. *Ethnic Politics and Civil Liberties.* New Brunswick, N.J.: Transaction Publishers, 1992.

Barnes, Frank. "The Wilder Side." *The New Republic* 201 (November 13, 1989): 9-10.

Barnett, Marguerite Ross. "The Congressional Black Caucus." In *Congress Against the President: Proceedings of the Academy of Political Science.* Edited by Harvey C. Mansfield, Sr. New York: Academy of Political Science, 1975.

Barone, Michael, and Gloria Borger. "The End of the Civil War." *U.S. News & World Report,* November 20, 1989, 45-48.

Barry, Marion. "Cock of the Walk." Interview. *National Review* 42 (February 5, 1990): 17-18.

Bennett, Lerone. "Inaugurating the Future." *Ebony* 45 (April, 1990): 8-12.

Booker, Simeon. "Washington Notebook." *Ebony* 35 (October, 1980): 25.

Borger, Gloria. "Sharon Dixon: Like Other City Leaders, D.C.'s New Boss Needs a Miracle." *U.S. News & World Report* 108 (December 31, 1990): 72.

Brenner, Marie. "Being There." *Vanity Fair* 54 (January, 1991): 86-96.

Brown, Frank Dexter. "The CBC: Past, Present and Future." *Black Enterprise* 20 (September, 1990): 25-28.

_____. "End of the New Deal?" *Black Enterprise* 16 (January, 1985): 23.

Browning, Rufus P., Dale Rogers Marshall, and David H. Tabb, eds. *Racial Politics in American Cities.* New York: Longman, 1990.

Brownmiller, Susan. *Shirley Chisholm: A Biography.* Garden City, N.Y.: Doubleday, 1971.

Chapman, Gil, and Ann Chapman. *Adam Clayton Powell, Saint or Sinner?* San Diego, Calif.: Publishers Export, 1967.

Chisholm, Shirley. *The Good Fight.* New York: Harper & Row, 1973.

_____. *Unbought and Unbossed.* Boston: Houghton Mifflin, 1970.

Clay, William L. *Just Permanent Interests: Black Americans in Congress, 1870-1991.* New York: Amistad Press, 1992.

Condit, Celeste Michelle, and John Louis Lucaites. *Crafting Equality: America's Anglo-African Word.* Chicago: University of Chicago Press, 1993.

Cornell, Jean Gay. *Ralph Bunche, Champion of Peace.* Champaign, Ill.: Garrard Publishing, 1976.

Davis, Flora. *Moving the Mountain: The Women's Movement in America Since 1960.* New York: Simon & Schuster, 1991.

Davis, Marianna W., ed. *Contributions of Black Women to America.* 2 vols. Columbia, S.C.: Kenday Press, 1982.

"Diggs Begins Comeback in Maryland State Race." *Jet* 78 (April 30, 1990): 18.

Dingle, D. T. "Governor Wilder: Champion of the 'New Mainstream.'" *Black Enterprise* 20 (March, 1990): 17.

Dreyfuss, Joel, and Charles Lawrence III. *The Bakke Case: The Politics of Inequality.* New York: Harcourt Brace Jovanovich, 1979.

Eastland, Terry, and William J. Bennett. *Counting by Race: Equality from the Founding Fathers to Bakke and Weber.* New York: Basic Books, 1979.

Edelman, Marian Wright. *The Measure of Our Success.* Boston: Beacon Press, 1992.

Ehrlich, Walter. *They Have No Rights: Dred Scott's Struggle for Freedom.* Westport, Conn.: Greenwood Press, 1979.

Elliot, Jeffrey M., ed. *Black Voices.* San Diego, Calif.: Harcourt Brace Jovanovich, 1986.

Fehrenbacher, Don E. *The Dred Scott Case: Its Significance in American Law and Politics.* New York: Oxford University Press, 1978.

_____. *Slavery, Law, and Politics: The Dred Scott Case in Historical Perspective.* New York: Oxford University Press, 1981.

Finch, Peter. "David Dinkins: How's He Doin'?" *Business Week* (June 18, 1990): 182-186.

Flowers, Ronald Barrie. *Minorities and Criminality.* Westport, Conn.: Greenwood Press, 1988.

Forman, James. *The Making of Black Revolutionaries.* New York: Macmillan, 1972.

Fox, J. A. "Do or Die for Diggs." *Black Enterprise* 10 (June, 1980): 55.

Franklin, John Hope, and Alfred A. Moss, Jr. *From Slavery to Freedom: A History of Negro Americans.* 6th ed. New York: Alfred A. Knopf, 1988.

French, Mary Ann. "Who Is Sharon Pratt Dixon?" *Essence* (April, 1991): 54.

Gardner, Carl. *Andrew Young.* New York: Sterling, 1980.

Garrow, David J., ed. *We Shall Overcome: The Civil Rights Movement in the United States in the 1950's and 1960's.* 3 vols. New York: Carlson Publishing, 1989.

Goode, W. Wilson, with Joann Stevens. *In Goode Faith.* Valley Forge, Pa.: Judson Press, 1993.

Grimshaw, William J. *Bitter Fruit: Black*

Politics and the Chicago Machine, 1931-1991. Chicago: University of Chicago Press, 1992.

Guy-Sheftall, Beverly. "Marian Wright Edelman." In *Notable Black American Women*, edited by Jessie Smith. Detroit: Gale Publishers, 1992.

Hacker, Andrew. *Two Nations: Black and White, Separate, Hostile, Unequal*. New York: Charles Scribner's Sons, 1992.

Hall, Kermit L., ed. *Civil Rights in American History: Major Historical Interpretations*. New York: Garland, 1987.

Hamilton, Charles V. *Adam Clayton Powell, Jr.: The Political Biography of an American Dilemma*. New York: Atheneum, 1991.

Haskins, James. *Adam Clayton Powell: Portrait of a Marching Black*. New York: Dial Press, 1974.

_____. *Fighting Shirley Chisholm*. New York: Dial Press, 1975.

_____. *Ralph Bunche: A Most Reluctant Hero*. New York: Hawthorn Books, 1974.

Haygood, Wil. *King of the Cats: The Life and Times of Adam Clayton Powell, Jr.* New York: Houghton Mifflin, 1993.

Haywood, R. L. "Inside Look as First Black Governor of Virginia Takes Charge." *Jet* 77 (February 5, 1990): 8-11.

Henry, Charles P. *Culture and African American Politics*. Bloomington: Indiana University Press, 1990.

Herzbrun, Phillip I., B. Kirk Rankin III, and Richard B. Thomas. *Ralph Bunche, World Servant*. Washington, D.C.: U.S. Information Agency, 1963.

Holli, Melvin G., and Paul M. Green, eds. *The Making of the Mayor, Chicago, 1983*. Grand Rapids, Mich.: Eerdmans, 1984.

Holli, Melvin G., and Peter d'A. Jones, eds. *Biographical Dictionary of American Mayors, 1820-1980*. Westport, Conn.: Greenwood Press, 1981.

"How Black Politicians Changed America." *Ebony* 46 (August, 1991): 34.

Hyman, Harold M., and William M. Wiecek. *Equal Justice Under the Law: Constitutional Development, 1835-1875*. New York: Harper & Row, 1982.

Jacobs, Andy. *The Powell Affair: Freedom Minus One*. Indianapolis: Bobbs-Merrill, 1973.

Jaffe, Harry. "Running on Empty." *Washingtonian* 27 (January, 1992): 50.

Jaffe, Harry, and Tom Sherwood. "Trust Me." *Washingtonian* 26 (May, 1991): 69.

Jaynes, Gerald D., and Robin M. Williams, eds. *A Common Destiny: Blacks and American Society*. Washington, D.C.: National Academy Press, 1989.

Joint Center of Political Studies. *Profiles of Black Mayors in the U.S.* Washington, D.C.: Joint Center for Political Studies, 1977.

Jordan, June. *Fannie Lou Hamer*. New York: Thomas Y. Crowell, 1972.

Kamen, Jeff. "Marion Barry Tries the Press." *Washington Journalism Review* 12, no. 9 (November, 1990).

Kirkendall, Richard S. *The Global Power: The United States Since 1941*. Boston: Allyn and Bacon, 1973.

Kugelmass, J. Alvin. *Ralph J. Bunche: Fighter for Peace*. New York: J. Messner, 1962.

Lanker, Brian. *I Dream a World: Portraits of Black Women Who Changed America*. New York: Stewart, Tabori & Chang, 1989.

Leerhsen, Charles. "When the House Is No Longer a Home." *Newsweek* 99 (January 18, 1982): 21.

Majors, Richard, and Janet Mancini Billson. *Cool Pose: The Dilemmas of Black Manhood in America*. New York: Lexington Books, 1992.

Masotti, Louis, et al. *Shoot-Out in Cleveland*. New York: Bantam Books, 1969.

Mendelson, Wallace. *The American Constitution and the Judicial Process*. Homewood, Ill.: Dorsey Press, 1980.

Miller, Alton. *Harold Washington: The Mayor, the Man*. Chicago: Bonus Books, 1989.

Mooney, Christopher F. *Inequality and the American Conscience: Justice Through the Judicial System*. New York: Paulist Press, 1982.

Mwadilifu, Mwalimu I. *Adam Clayton Powell, Jr.: A Black Power Political Educator*. New York: ECA Associates, 1983.

Nelson, William E., and Philip J. Meranto. *Electing Black Mayors*. Columbus: Ohio State University Press, 1977.

Noble, Jeanne L. *Beautiful, Also, Are the Souls of My Black Sisters*. Englewood Cliffs, N.J.: Prentice-Hall, 1978.

Norment, Lynn. "Charles Rangel: The Front-Line General in the War on Drugs." *Ebony* 44 (March, 1989): 128-131.

Norton, Eleanor Holmes. "Woman Who Changed the South." *Ms.* 6 (July, 1977): 51.

O'Neil, Timothy J. *Bakke and the Politics of Equality: Friends and Foes in the Classroom of Litigation*. Middletown, Conn.: Wesleyan University Press, 1985.

Osborne, Karen. "Harlem Gets Trade Center." *Black Enterprise* 20 (September, 1989): 22.

Parker, Frank R. *Black Votes Count: Political Empowerment in Mississippi After 1965*. Chapel Hill: University of North Carolina Press, 1990.

Payne, J. Gregory, and Scott C. Ratzan. *Tom Bradley, the Impossible Dream: A Biography*. Santa Monica, Calif.: Roundtable Publishing, 1986.

Pettigrew, Thomas F., and Denise A. Alston. *Tom Bradley's Campaigns for Governor: The Dilemma of Race and Political Strategies*. Washington, D.C.: Joint Center for Political Studies, 1988.

Poinsett, Alex. "The Changing Color of U.S. Politics." *Ebony* 46 (August, 1991): 30-35.

Powell, Adam Clayton, Jr. *Adam by Adam: The Autobiography of Adam Clayton Powell, Jr.* New York: Dial Press, 1971.

Powledge, Fred. *Free At Last? The Civil Rights Movement and the People Who Made It*. Boston: Little, Brown, 1991.

Ragsdale, Bruce A., and Joel D. Treese. *Black Americans in Congress, 1870-1989*. Washington, D.C.: U.S. Government Printing Office, 1990.

Randolph, Laura B. "Inside Gracie Mansion with New York's First Black Mayor." *Ebony* 45 (September, 1990): 54-58.

_____. "Top of Capitol Hill: Majority Whip and Five Black Committee Chairmen Are at Summit of Congressional Power." *Ebony* 45 (December, 1989): 144-147.

"Rangel Leads Illegal-Drug Probe Group in Caribbean." *Jet* 79 (January 16, 1989): 25.

Rivlin, Benjamin, ed. *Ralph Bunche, the Man and His Times*. New York: Holmes & Meier, 1990.

Rose, Thomas. *Black Leaders, Then and Now: A Personal History of Students Who Led the Civil Rights Movement in the 1960's—and What Happened to Them*. Garrett Park, Md.: Garrett Park Press, 1984.

Rowan, Carl T. *Dream Makers, Dream Breakers: The World of Justice Thurgood Marshall*. Boston: Little, Brown, 1993.

Royko, Mike. *Boss: Richard J. Daley of Chicago*. New York: E. P. Dutton, 1971.

Rubel, David. *Fannie Lou Hamer: From Sharecropping to Politics*. Englewood Cliffs, N.J.: Silver Burdett Press, 1990.

Ruffin, David C., and Frank Dexter Brown. "Clout on Capitol Hill." *Black Enterprise* 14 (October, 1984): 97-104.

Schwartz, Bernard. *Behind Bakke: Affirmative Action and the Supreme Court*. New York: New York University Press, 1988.

Silberman, Charles. *Criminal Violence, Criminal Justice*. New York: Vintage Books, 1978.

Simmons, Ron. *Affirmative Action: Conflict and Change in Higher Education After Bakke*. Cambridge, Mass.: Schenkman, 1982.

Sindler, Alan P. *Bakke, DeFunis, and Minority Admissions: The Quest for Equal Opportunity*. New York: Macmillan, 1978.

Sonenshein, Raphael J. *Politics in Black and White: Race and Power in Los Angeles*. Princeton, N.J.: Princeton University Press, 1993.

Stokes, Carl B. *Promises of Power, Then and Now*. Cleveland: Friends of Carl B. Stokes, 1989.

Swain, Carol M. *Black Faces, Black Interests: The Representation of African Americans in Congress*. Cambridge, Mass.: Harvard University Press, 1993.

Tate, Katherine. *From Protest to Politics: The New Black Voters in American Elections*. Cambridge, Mass.: Harvard University Press, 1993.

Taylor, Kristin Clark. *The First to Speak: A Woman of Color Inside the Bush White House*. New York: Doubleday, 1993.

Tompkins, Calvin. "Profiles: A Sense of Urgency." *The New Yorker*, March 27, 1989, pp. 48-74.

Travis, Dempsey. *An Autobiography of Black Politics*. Chicago: Urban Research Institute, 1987.

Weinberg, Kenneth G. *Black Victory: Carl Stokes and the Winning of Cleveland*. Chicago: Quadrangle Books, 1968.

Williams, Juan. "A Dream Deferred: A Black Mayor Betrays the Faith." *The Washington Monthly* 18, nos. 6-7 (July-August, 1986).

Williams, Michael. "Putting a New Face on Virginia's Future." *Black Enterprise* 21 (June, 1991): 284-294.

Wills, Garry. "Georgia Is Much on His Mind." *Time*, July 16, 1990, pp. 66-68.

Wilson, William Julius. *The Truly Disadvantaged: The Inner City, the Underclass, and Public Policy*. Chicago: University of Chicago Press, 1987.

Wood, Forrest G. *Black Scare: The Racist Response to Emancipation and Reconstruction*. Berkeley: University of California Press, 1968.

Young, Henry J., ed. *The Black Church and the Harold Washington Story: The Man, the Message, the Movement*. Bristol, Ind.: Wyndham Hall Press, 1988.

RACE, RACE RELATIONS, AND RACISM

Ashmore, Harry S. *Hearts and Minds: The Anatomy of Racism from Roosevelt to Reagan*. New York: McGraw-Hill, 1982.

Baer, Hans A., and Yvonne Jones, eds. *African Americans in the South: Issues of Race, Class, and Gender*. Athens: University of Georgia Press, 1992.

Bartley, Numan V. *The Rise of Massive Resistance: Race and Politics in the South During the 1950's*. Baton Rouge: Louisiana State University Press, 1969.

Bell, Derrick A., Jr. *Faces at the Bottom of the Well: The Permanence of Racism*. New York: Basic Books, 1992.

_____. *Race, Racism, and American Law*. 2d ed. Boston: Little, Brown and Co., 1980.

Bell, Malcolm. *The Turkey Shoot: Tracking the Attica Cover-up*. New York: Grove Press, 1985.

Benjamin, Lois. *The Black Elite*. Chicago: Nelson-Hall, 1991.

Berry, Mary Frances. *Black Resistance/White Law: A History of Constitutional Racism in America*. New York: Appleton-Century-Crofts, 1971.

Blauner, Bob. *Racial Oppression in America*. New York: Harper & Row, 1972.

Blaustein, Albert P. *Desegregation and the Law: The Meaning and Effect of the School Segregation Cases*. New Brunswick, N.J.: Rutgers University Press, 1957.

Branch, Taylor. *Parting the Waters: America in the King Years, 1954-63*. New York: Simon & Schuster, 1988.

Brooks, Roy L. *Rethinking the American Race Problem*. Berkeley: University of California Press, 1990.

Caraway, Nancie. *Segregated Sisterhood: Racism and the Politics of American Feminism*. Knoxville: University of Tennessee Press, 1991.

Carson, Clayborne, David J. Garrow, Gerald Gill, Vincent Harding, and Darlene Clark Hine, eds. "A Nation of Law?" In *The Eyes on the Prize: Civil Rights Reader*. New York: Penguin, 1991.

Carter, Dan T. *Scottsboro: A Tragedy of the American South*. Baton Rouge: Louisiana State University Press, 1969.

Chalmers, Allan K. *They Shall Be Free*. Garden City, N.Y.: Doubleday, 1951.

Clarke, John Henrik, ed. *Marcus Garvey and the Vision of Africa*. New York: Vintage Books, 1974.

Coons, William R. *Attica Diary*. New York: Stein & Day, 1972.

Covin, Kelly. *Hear That Train Blow! A Novel About the Scottsboro Case*. New York: Delacorte Press, 1970.

Cronon, Edmund David. *Black Moses: The Story of Marcus Garvey and the Universal Negro Improvement Association*. Madison: University of Wisconsin Press, 1955.

Davis, Angela Yvonne. *Women, Culture, and Politics*. New York: Random House, 1989.

_____. *Women, Race, and Class*. New York: Random House, 1981.

Dawson, Lallie P. *Bigotry and Violence on American College Campuses*. Washington, D.C.: Commission on Civil Rights, 1990.

Dinnerstein, Leonard, Roger L. Nichols, and David M. Reimers. *Natives and Strangers: Blacks, Indians, and Immigrants in America*. 2d ed. New York: Oxford University Press, 1990.

Dykstra, Robert R. *Bright Radical Star: Black Freedom and White Supremacy on the Hawkeye Frontier*. Cambridge, Mass.: Harvard University Press, 1993.

Early, Gerald, ed. *Lure and Loathing: Essays on Race, Identity, and the Ambivalence of Assimilation*. New York: Viking, 1993.

Eastland, Terry, and William J. Bennett. *Counting by Race: Equality from the Founding Fathers to Bakke and Weber*. New York: Basic Books, 1979.

Finkelman, Paul, ed. *Lynching, Racial Violence, and Law*. New York: Garland, 1992.

Flowers, Ronald Barrie. *Minorities and Criminality*. Westport, Conn.: Greenwood Press, 1988.

Franklin, John Hope. *The Color Line: Legacy for the Twenty-First Century*. Columbia: University of Missouri Press, 1993.

Frazier, E. Franklin. *On Race Relations: Selected Writings*. Chicago: University of Chicago Press, 1968.

Garvey, Marcus. *Philosophy and Opinions of Marcus Garvey*. 2 vols. Edited by Amy Jacques Garvey. New York: The Universal Publishing House, 1923-1925. Reprint. New York: Arno Press, 1968-1969.

Gates, Henry Louis, Jr., ed. *Bearing Witness*. New York: Pantheon Books, 1991.

Ginzburg, Ralph, ed. *100 Years of Lynchings*. Baltimore, Md.: Black Classic Press, 1988.

Greenberg, Jack. *Desegregation*. Eugene: University of Oregon Press, 1979.

_____. *Race Relations and American Law*. New York: Columbia University Press, 1959.

Grier, William H., and Price M. Cobbs. *Black Rage*. New York: Basic Books, 1968.

Hacker, Andrew. *Two Nations: Black and White, Separate, Hostile, Unequal*. New York: Charles Scribner's Sons, 1992.

Hall, Kermit L., ed. *Race Relations and the Law in American History: Major Historical Interpretations*. New York: Garland, 1987.

Hampton, Henry, and Steve Fayer, with Sarah Flynn, comps. *Voices of Freedom: An Oral History of the Civil Rights Movement from the 1950's Through the 1980's*. New York: Bantam Books, 1990.

Harris, Trudier. *Exorcising Blackness: Historical and Literary Lynching and Burning Rituals*. Bloomington: Indiana University Press, 1984.

Hate Groups in America: A Record of Bigotry and Violence. Rev. ed. New York: Anti-Defamation League of B'nai B'rith, 1989.

Helms, Janet E., ed. *Black and White Racial Identity*. New York: Greenwood Press, 1990.

Hill, Robert A., ed. *The Marcus Garvey and Universal Negro Improvement Association Papers*. 7 vols. Berkeley: University of California Press, 1983-1990.

Hooks, Bell. *Black Looks: Race and Representation*. Boston: South End Press, 1992.

Houston, Lawrence N. *Psychological Princi-*

ples and the Black Experience. Lanham, Md.: University Press of America, 1990.

Jaynes, Gerald D., and Robin M. Williams, eds. *A Common Destiny: Blacks and American Society*. Washington, D.C.: National Academy Press, 1989.

Jencks, Christopher. *Rethinking Social Policy: Race, Poverty, and the Underclass*. Cambridge, Mass.: Harvard University Press, 1992.

Jones, Leon. *From Brown to Boston: Desegregation in Education, 1954-1974*. Metuchen, N.J.: Scarecrow Press, 1979.

Jordan, Winthrop D. *White over Black: American Attitudes Toward the Negro, 1550-1812*. Chapel Hill: University of North Carolina Press, 1968.

Kelly, Alfred H., Winfred A. Harbison, and Herman Belz. *The American Constitution: Its Origins and Development*. New York: W. W. Norton, 1983.

Kluger, Richard. *Simple Justice: The History of Brown v. Board of Education and Black America's Struggle for Equality*. New York: Alfred A. Knopf, 1976.

Lewis, Rupert. *Marcus Garvey, Anti-Colonial Champion*. Trenton, N.J.: Africa World Press, 1988.

McNeil, Genna Rae. "Charles Hamilton Houston: Social Engineer for Civil Rights." In *Black Leaders of the Twentieth Century*, edited by John Hope Franklin and August Meier. Urbana: University of Illinois Press, 1982.

Majors, Richard, and Janet Mancini Billson. *Cool Pose: The Dilemmas of Black Manhood in America*. New York: Lexington Books, 1992.

Marr, Warren, II, and Maybelle Ward, eds. *Minorities and the American Dream: A Bicentennial Perspective*. New York: Arno Press, 1976.

Martin, Tony. *Race First: The Ideological and Organizational Struggles of Marcus Garvey and the Universal Negro Improvement Association*. Westport, Conn.: Greenwood Press, 1976.

Miller, Loren. *The Petitioners: The Story of the Supreme Court of the United States and the Negro*. New York: Pantheon Books, 1966.

New York (State) Special Commission on Attica. *Attica: The Official Report of the New York State Special Commission on Attica*. New York: Praeger, 1972.

Norris, Clarence, and Sybil D. Washington. *The Last of the Scottsboro Boys: An Autobiography*. New York: G. P. Putnam's Sons, 1979.

Oates, Stephen B. *Let the Trumpet Sound: The Life of Martin Luther King, Jr.* New York: Harper & Row, 1982.

Parrillo, Vincent N. *Strangers to These Shores: Race and Ethnic Relations in the U.S.* Boston: Houghton-Mifflin, 1980.

Patterson, Haywood, and Earl Conrad. *Scottsboro Boy*. New York: Bantam Books, 1950.

Persico, Joseph E. *The Imperial Rockefeller*. New York: Simon & Schuster, 1982.

Powell, Thomas. *The Persistence of Racism in America*. Lanham, Md.: University Press of America, 1992.

Raper, Arthur F. *The Tragedy of Lynching*. Chapel Hill: University of North Carolina Press, 1933.

Ringer, Benjamin Bernard. *"We the People" and Others: Duality and America's Treatment of Its Racial Minorities*. New York: Tavistock, 1983.

Rosenberg, Morris, and Roberta G. Simmons. *Black and White Self Esteem: The Urban School Child*. Washington, D.C.: American Sociological Association, 1971.

Russell, Kathy, Midge Wilson, and Ron Hall. *The Color Complex: The Last Taboo Among African-Americans*. New York: Harcourt Brace Jovanovich, 1992.

Schermerhorn, Richard A. *Comparative Ethnic Relations: A Framework for Theory and Research*. New York: Random House, 1970.

Scott, Elsie L. *Violence Against Blacks in the United States, 1979-1981*. Washington, D.C.: Mental Health Research and Development Center, Institute for Urban Affairs and Research, Howard University, 1982.

Shapiro, Herbert. *White Violence and Black Response: From Reconstruction to Montgomery*. Amherst: University of Massachusetts, 1988.

Silberman, Charles. *Criminal Violence, Criminal Justice*. New York: Vintage Books, 1978.

Simpson, George Eaton, and J. Milton Yinger. *Racial and Cultural Minorities: An Analysis of Prejudice and Discrimination*. 5th ed. New York: Plenum Press, 1985.

Steele, Shelby. *The Content of Our Character: A New Vision of Race in America*. New York: St. Martin's Press, 1990.

Stein, Judith. *The World of Marcus Garvey: Race and Class in Modern Society*. Baton Rouge: Louisiana State University Press, 1986.

Stengel, Richard. "Resentment Tinged with Envy." *Time* 126 (July 8, 1985): 56-57.

Taylor, Jared. *Paved with Good Intentions: The Failure of Race Relations in Contemporary America*. New York: Carroll & Graf, 1992.

Terkel, Studs. *Race: How Blacks and Whites Think and Feel About the American Obsession*. New York: New Press, 1992.

U.S. Commission on Civil Rights. *Intimidation and Violence: Racial and Religious Bigotry in America*. Washington, D.C.: U.S. Government Printing Office, 1990.

Warren, Robert P. *Segregation: The Inner Conflict in the South*. New York: Columbia University Press, 1956.

West, Cornel. *Race Matters*. New York: Beacon Press, 1993.

White, Joseph L. *The Psychology of Blacks: An Afro-American Perspective*. Englewood Cliffs, N.J.: Prentice-Hall, 1984.

White, Walter. *Rope and Faggot: A Biography of Judge Lynch*. New York: Alfred A. Knopf, 1929.

Wood, Forrest G. *Black Scare: The Racist Response to Emancipation and Reconstruction*. Berkeley: University of California Press, 1968.

Zangrando, Robert L. *The NAACP Crusade Against Lynching, 1909-1950*. Philadelphia: Temple University Press, 1980.

RADICALISM

Alkalimat, Abdul. *Perspectives on Black Liberation and Social Revolution: Malcolm X, Radical Tradition, and a Legacy of Struggle*. Chicago: Twenty-first Century Books and Publications, 1990.

Allen, Robert L. *A Guide to Black Power in America: An Historical Analysis*. London: Gollancz, 1970.

Aptheker, Bettina. *The Morning Breaks: The Trial of Angela Davis*. New York: International Publishers, 1975.

Bennett, Lerone, Jr. *Before the Mayflower: A History of Black America*. 6th ed. Chicago: Johnson Publishing Company, 1987.

Berry, Mary Frances, and John W. Blassingame. *Long Memory: The Black Experience in America*. New York: Oxford University Press, 1982.

Bracey, John H., Jr., August Meier, and Elliott Rudwick. *Black Nationalism in America*. The American Heritage series. Indianapolis: Bobbs-Merrill, 1970.

Breitman, George, Herman Porter, and Baxter Smith. *The Assassination of Malcolm X*. New York: Pathfinder Press, 1976.

Brown, Elaine. *A Taste of Power: A Black Woman's Story*. New York: Pantheon Books, 1993.

Brown, H. Rap. *Die, Nigger, Die!*. New York: Dial Press, 1969.

Butterfield, Stephen. "James Baldwin: The Growth of a New Radicalism." In *Black Autobiography in America*. Amherst: University of Massachusetts Press, 1974.

Carlisle, Rodney. *The Roots of Black Nationalism*. Port Washington, N.Y.: Kennikat Press, 1975.

Carmichael, Stokely. *Stokely Speaks*. New York: Random House, 1971.

Carmichael, Stokely, and Charles V. Hamilton. *Black Power: The Politics of Libera-*

tion in America. New York: Vintage Books, 1967.

Carson, Clayborne. *In Struggle: SNCC and the Black Awakening of the 1960's.* Cambridge, Mass.: Harvard University Press, 1981.

Churchill, Ward, and Jim Vander Wall. *Agents of Repression: The FBI's Secret Wars Against the Black Panther Party and the American Indian Movement.* Boston: South End Press, 1988.

Cleaver, Eldridge. *Soul on Fire.* Waco, Tex.: Word Books, 1978.

_____. *Soul on Ice.* New York: Dell, 1968.

Davis, Angela. *Angela Davis: An Autobiography.* New York: Random House, 1974.

_____. *If They Come in the Morning: Voices of Resistance.* New York: Third Press, 1971.

Erikson, Erik H. *In Search of Common Ground: Conversations with Erik H. Erikson and Huey P. Newton.* New York: W. W. Norton, 1973.

Foner, Philip Sheldon, ed. *The Black Panthers Speak.* Philadelphia: Lippincott, 1970.

Forman, James. *The Making of Black Revolutionaries.* New York: Macmillan, 1972.

Giddings, Paula. *When and Where I Enter: The Impact of Black Women on Race and Sex in America.* New York: William Morrow, 1984.

Haines, Herbert H. *Black Radicals and the Civil Rights Mainstream, 1954-1970.* Knoxville: University of Tennessee Press, 1986.

Hall, Raymond L., ed. *Black Separatism and Social Reality: Rhetoric and Reason.* New York: Pergamon Press, 1977.

Hilliard, David, and Lewis Cole. *This Side of Glory: The Autobiography of David Hilliard and the Story of the Black Panthers.* Boston: Little, Brown, 1993.

Lester, Julius. *Revolutionary Notes.* New York: R. W. Baron, 1969.

Lockwood, Lee. *Conversation with Eldridge Cleaver.* New York: McGraw-Hill, 1970.

Marable, Manning. *How Capitalism Underdeveloped Black America.* Boston: South End Press, 1983.

_____. *Race, Reform, and Rebellion: The Second Reconstruction in Black America, 1945-1990.* 2d ed. Jackson: University Press of Mississippi, 1984.

Marine, Gene. *The Black Panthers.* New York: New American Library, 1969.

Meier, August, and Elliot Rudwick, eds. *Conflict and Competition: Studies in the Recent Black Protest Movement.* Belmont, Calif.: Wadsworth, 1971.

Moore, Gilbert. *A Special Rage.* New York: Harper & Row, 1971.

Moses, Wilson J. *The Golden Age of Black Nationalism: 1850-1925.* Hamden, Conn.: Archon Books, 1978.

Newton, Huey P. *To Die for the People: The Writings of Huey P. Newton.* New York: Random House, 1972.

Newton, Michael. *Bitter Grain: Huey Newton and the Black Panther Party.* Los Angeles: Holloway House, 1991.

Obadele, Imari Abubakari. *America the Nation-State: The Politics of the United States from a State-Building Perspective.* Washington, D.C.: House of Songhay, Commission for Positive Education, 1988.

Parks, Gordon. "What Became of the Prophets of Rage?" *Life,* special issue, Spring, 1988, p. 32.

Rosebury, Celia. *Black Liberation on Trial: The Case of Huey Newton.* Berkeley, Calif.: Bay Area Committee to Defend Political Freedom, 1968.

Rout, Kathleen. *Eldridge Cleaver.* Boston: Twayne, 1991.

Seale, Bobby. *Seize the Time: The Story of the Black Panther Party and Huey P. Newton.* New York: Random House, 1970. Reprint. Baltimore, Md.: Black Classic Press, 1991.

Sellers, Cleveland, and Robert Terrel. *The River of No Return: The Autobiography of a Black Militant and the Life and Death of SNCC.* New York: William Morrow, 1973.

Shakur, Assata. *Assata: An Autobiography.* Westport, Conn.: Lawrence Hill, 1987.

Stuckey, Sterling, ed. *The Ideological Origins of Black Nationalism.* Boston: Beacon Press, 1972.

Tate, Gayle T. "Black Nationalism: An Angle of Vision." *Western Journal of Black Studies* 12 (Spring, 1988): 40-48.

Van Deburg, William L. *New Day in Babylon: The Black Power Movement and American Culture, 1965-1975.* Chicago: University of Chicago Press, 1992.

"Whatever Happened to . . . Eldridge Cleaver?" *Ebony,* March, 1988, pp. 66-68.

Wilmore, Gayraud S. *Black Religion and Black Radicalism: An Interpretation of the Religious History of Afro-American People.* 2d rev. ed. Maryknoll, N.Y.: Orbis Books, 1983.

Wiltse, Charles M., ed. *David Walker's Appeal to the Colored Citizens of the World.* New York: Hill & Wang, 1965.

RELIGION

Angell, Stephen. *Bishop Henry McNeal Turner and African-American Religion in the South.* Knoxville: University of Tennessee Press, 1992.

Baer, Hans A., and Merrill Singer. *African American Religion in the Twentieth Century: Varieties of Protest and Accommodation.* Knoxville: University of Tennessee Press, 1992.

Barrett, Leonard E. *Soul Force: African Heritage in Afro-American Religion.* Garden City, N.J.: Anchor Press, 1974.

Bowman, Thea, ed. *Families: Black and Catholic, Catholic and Black.* Washington, D.C.: U.S. Catholic Conference, Commission on Marriage and Family Life, 1985.

Bragg, George Freeman. *History of the Afro-American Group of the Episcopal Church.* Baltimore, Md.: Church Advocate Press, 1922. Reprint. New York: Johnson Reprint, 1968.

Burkett, Randall K. *Garveyism as a Religious Movement.* Metuchen, N.J.: Scarecrow Press, 1978.

Cone, James H. *For My People: Black Theology and the Black Church.* Maryknoll, N.Y.: Orbis Books, 1984.

Davis, Cyprian. *The History of Black Catholics in the United States.* New York: Crossroad, 1990.

Drake, St. Clair. *Redemption of Africa and Black Religion.* Chicago: Third World Press, 1970.

Du Bois, W. E. B. *The Negro Church.* Atlanta: Atlanta University Press, 1903.

Fitts, Leroy. *A History of Black Baptists.* Nashville, Tenn.: Broadman, 1985.

Frazier, E. Franklin. *The Negro Church in America.* New York: Schocken Books, 1974.

Freedman, Samuel G. *Upon This Rock: The Miracles of a Black Church.* New York: HarperCollins, 1993.

Green, Nathaniel E. *The Silent Believers: Background Information on the Religious Experience of the American Black Catholic with Emphasis on the Archdiocese of Louisville, Kentucky.* Louisville, Ky.: West End Catholic Council, 1972.

Harding, Vincent. *There Is a River: The Black Struggle for Freedom in America.* 2d ed. New York: Harcourt Brace Jovanovich, 1993.

Higginbothan, Evelyn Brooks. *Righteous Discontent: The Women's Movement in the Black Baptist Church, 1880-1920.* Cambridge, Mass.: Harvard University Press, 1993.

Hoskins, Charles Lwanga. *Black Episcopalians in Georgia: Strife, Struggle, and Salvation.* Savannah, Ga.: Hoskins, 1980.

Irvin, Dona L. *The Unsung Heart of Black America: A Middle-Class Church at Midcentury.* Columbia: University of Missouri Press, 1993.

Jackson, Joseph H. *A Story of Christian Activism: The History of the National Baptist Convention, U.S.A., Inc.* Nashville, Tenn.: Townsend Press, 1980.

Levine, Lawrence W. *Black Culture and Black Consciousness: Afro-American Folk Thought from Slavery to Freedom.* New

York: Oxford University Press, 1977.

Lincoln, C. Eric. *The Black Muslims in America.* Boston: Beacon Press, 1961.

Lincoln, C. Eric, and Laurence H. Mamiya. *The Black Church in the African American Experience.* Durham, N.C.: Duke University Press, 1990.

Mbiti, John S. *African Religions and Philosophy.* London: Heinemann, 1969.

Montgomery, William E. *Under Their Own Vine and Fig Tree: The African-American Church in the South, 1865-1900.* Baton Rouge: Louisiana State University Press, 1993.

Mukenge, Ida Rousseau. *The Black Church in Urban America: A Case Study in Political Economy.* Lanham, Md.: University Press of America, 1983.

Nelsen, Hart M., and Anne Kusener Nelsen. *Black Church in the Sixties.* Lexington: University Press of Kentucky, 1975.

Ochs, Stephen J. *Desegregating the Altar: The Josephites and the Struggle for Blacks Priests, 1871-1960.* Baton Rouge: Louisiana State University Press, 1990.

Payne, Wardell J., ed. *Directory of African American Religious Bodies: A Compendium by the Howard University School of Divinity.* Washington, D.C.: Howard University Press, 1991.

Raboteau, Albert J. *Slave Religion: The "Invisible Institution" in the Antebellum South.* New York: Oxford University Press, 1978.

Rigsby, Gregory U. *Alexander Crummell: Pioneer in Nineteenth Century Pan-African Thought.* New York: Greenwood Press, 1987.

Shuster, George, and Robert M. Kearns. *Statistical Profile of Black Catholics.* Washington, D.C.: Josephite Pastoral Center, 1976.

Sobel, Mechal. *Trabelin' On: The Slave Journey to an Afro-Baptist Faith.* Westport, Conn.: Greenwood Press, 1979.

Thurman, Howard. *Deep River and The Negro Spiritual Speaks of Life and Death.* Richmond, Ind.: Friends United Press, 1975.

Washington, James Melvin. *Frustrated Fellowship: The Black Baptist Quest for Social Power.* Macon, Ga.: Mercer University Press, 1986.

Washington, Joseph R., Jr. *Black Sects and Cults.* Garden City, N.Y.: Anchor Books, 1973.

West, Cornel. *Prophecy Deliverance! An Afro-American Revolutionary Christianity.* Philadelphia: Westminster Press, 1982.

Wilmore, Gayraud S., ed. *African American Religious Studies: An Interdisciplinary Anthology.* Durham, N.C.: Duke University Press, 1989.

_____ . *Black Religion and Black Radicalism: An Interpretation of the Religious History of Afro-American People.* 2d rev. ed. Maryknoll, N.Y.: Orbis Books, 1983.

SCIENCE, TECHNOLOGY, AND DISCOVERY

Allen, Will W. *Banneker: The Afro-American Astronomer.* Freeport, N.Y.: Books for Libraries Press, 1971.

Barksdale, Richard, and Kenneth Kinnamon, eds. *Black Writers of America: A Comprehensive Anthology.* New York: Macmillan, 1972.

Bedini, Silvio A. *The Life of Benjamin Banneker.* New York: Scribners, 1971.

Bergman, Peter M. *The Chronological History of the Negro in America.* New York: Harper & Row, 1969.

Brody, James Michael. *Created Equal: The Lives and Ideas of Black American Innovators.* New York: William Morrow, 1993.

Buckler, Helen. *Daniel Hale Williams, Negro Surgeon.* New York: Pitman, 1968.

_____ . *Doctor Dan, Pioneer in American Surgery.* Boston: Little, Brown, 1954.

Carwell, Hattie. *Blacks in Science: Astrophysicists to Zoologists.* Hicksville, N.Y.: Exposition Press, 1977.

Clark, Kenneth B., and Kate Clark Harris. "What Do Blacks Really Want?" *Ebony* 40 (January, 1985): 108.

"Contribution by a Psychologist in the Public Interest Gold Medal Award." *American Psychologist* 43 (April, 1988): 263-264.

Cruse, Harold. *The Crisis of the Negro Intellectual.* New York: Quill, 1984.

Davis, Marianna W., ed. *Contributions of Black Women to America.* 2 vols. Columbia, S.C.: Kenday Press, 1982.

Elliott, Lawrence. *George Washington Carver: The Man Who Overcame.* Englewood Cliffs, N.J.: Prentice-Hall, 1966.

Fenderson, Lewis R. *Daniel Hale Williams: Open-Heart Doctor.* New York: McGraw-Hill, 1971.

Ford, Nick A. *Black Studies: Threat or Challenge?* Port Washington, N.Y.: Kennikat Press, 1973.

Franklin, John Hope, and Alfred A. Moss, Jr. *From Slavery to Freedom: A History of Negro Americans.* 6th ed. New York: Alfred A. Knopf, 1988.

Goldsmith, Donald. *The Astronomers.* New York: St. Martin's Press, 1991.

Graham, Shirley. *Your Most Humble Servant.* New York: Messner, 1949.

Haber, Louis. *Black Pioneers of Science and Invention.* New York: Harcourt, Brace & World, 1970.

Hardwick, Richard. *Charles Richard Drew: Pioneer in Blood Research.* New York: Charles Scribner's Sons, 1967.

Hare, Nathan. "Is the Black Middle Class Blowing It? . . . Yes!" *Ebony* 42 (August, 1987): 85-86.

Hayden, Robert C. *Eight Black American Inventors.* Reading, Mass.: Addison-Wesley, 1972.

_____ . *Seven Black American Scientists.* Reading, Mass.: Addison-Wesley, 1970.

Ho, James K. K., ed. *Black Engineers in the United States: A Directory.* Washington, D.C.: Howard University Press, 1974.

Holt, Rackham. *George Washington Carver: An American Biography.* Garden City, N.Y.: Doubleday, Doran, 1943.

James, Portia P. *The Real McCoy: African American Invention and Innovation, 1619-1930.* Washington, D.C.: Smithsonian Institution Press, 1989.

King, William M. "Guardian of Public Safety: Garrett A. Morgan and the Lake Erie Crib Disaster." *The Journal of Negro History* 70 (Winter/Spring, 1985): 1-13.

Klein, Aaron E. *The Hidden Contributors: Black Scientists and Inventors in America.* Garden City, N.Y.: Doubleday, 1971.

Kremer, Gary R. *George Washington Carver in His Own Words.* Columbia: University of Missouri Press, 1987.

Lichello, Robert. *Pioneer in Blood Plasma: Dr. Charles Richard Drew.* New York: J. Messner, 1968.

McMurry, Linda O. *George Washington Carver: Scientist and Symbol.* New York: Oxford University Press, 1981.

Mahone-Lonesome, Robyn. *Charles Drew.* New York: Chelsea House, 1990.

Morais, Herbert M. *The History of the Negro in Medicine.* New York: Publishers Company, 1967.

Patterson, Lillie. *Sure Hands, Strong Heart: The Life of Daniel Hale Williams.* Nashville: Abingdon Press, 1981.

Pearson, Willie, Jr. *Black Scientists, White Society, and Colorless Science: A Study of Universalism in American Science.* Millwood, N.Y.: Associated Faculty Press, 1985.

Pizer, Vernon. *Shortchanged by History: America's Neglected Innovators.* New York: G. P. Putnam's Sons, 1979.

Sammons, Vivian Ovelton. *Blacks in Science and Medicine.* New York: Hemisphere Publishing Company, 1990.

Van Sertima, Ivan, ed. *Blacks in Science: Ancient and Modern.* New Brunswick, N.J.: Transaction Books, 1991.

Wynes, Charles E. *Charles Richard Drew: The Man and the Myth.* Urbana: University of Illinois Press, 1988.

Yount, Lisa. *Black Scientists.* New York: Facts on File, 1991.

SEGREGATION, DESEGREGATION, AND INTEGRATION

Altschiller, Donald, ed. *Affirmative Action.* New York: H. W. Wilson Co., 1991.

Bartley, Numan V. *The Rise of Massive Resistance: Race and Politics in the South During the 1950's.* Baton Rouge: Louisiana State University Press, 1969.

Becker, Gary Stanley. *The Economics of Discrimination.* Chicago: University of Chicago Press, 1957.

Bell, Derrick A., Jr. *Race, Racism, and American Law.* 2d ed. Boston: Little, Brown and Co., 1980.

Bentley, George R. *A History of the Freedmen's Bureau.* New York: Octagon Books, 1970.

Berlin, Ira. *Slaves Without Masters: The Free Negro in the Antebellum South.* New York: Pantheon, 1974.

Berry, Mary Frances. *Black Resistance/White Law: A History of Constitutional Racism in America.* New York: Appleton-Century-Crofts, 1971.

Blaustein, Albert P. *Desegregation and the Law: The Meaning and Effect of the School Segregation Cases.* New Brunswick, N.J.: Rutgers University Press, 1957.

Branch, Taylor. *Parting the Waters: America in the King Years, 1954-63.* New York: Simon & Schuster, 1988.

Breen, T. H., and Stephen Innes. *"Myne Own Ground": Race and Freedom on Virginia's Eastern Shore, 1640-1676.* New York: Oxford University Press, 1980.

Burstein, Paul. *Discrimination, Jobs, Politics.* Chicago: University of Chicago Press, 1985.

Carpenter, John A. *Sword and Olive Branch: Oliver Otis Howard.* Pittsburgh: University of Pittsburgh Press, 1964.

Clark, E. Culpepper. *The Schoolhouse Door: Segregation's Last Stand at the University of Alabama.* New York: Oxford University Press, 1993.

Clarke, John Henrik, ed. *Marcus Garvey and the Vision of Africa.* New York: Vintage Books, 1974.

Claypool, Jane. *The Worker in America.* New York: Franklin Watts, 1985.

Cronon, Edmund David. *Black Moses: The Story of Marcus Garvey and the Universal Negro Improvement Association.* Madison: University of Wisconsin Press, 1955.

Curry, Leonard P. *The Free Black in Urban America, 1800-1850: The Shadow of the Dream.* Chicago: University of Chicago Press, 1981.

Dreyfuss, Joel, and Charles Lawrence III. *The Bakke Case: The Politics of Inequality.* New York: Harcourt Brace Jovanovich, 1979.

Eastland, Terry, and William J. Bennett. *Counting by Race: Equality from the Founding Fathers to Bakke and Weber.* New York: Basic Books, 1979.

Garvey, Marcus. *Philosophy and Opinions of Marcus Garvey.* 2 vols. Edited by Amy Jacques Garvey. New York: The Universal Publishing House, 1923-1925. Reprint. New York: Arno Press, 1968-1969.

Gest, Ted. "Affirmative Verdict on Racial Hiring." *U.S. News & World Report* 101 (July 14, 1986): 17-18.

_____. "Why Drive on Job Bias Is Still Going Strong." *U.S. News & World Report* 98 (June 17, 1985): 67-68.

Graglia, Lino A. *Disaster by Decree: The Supreme Court Decisions on Race and the Schools.* Ithaca, N.Y.: Cornell University Press, 1976.

Greenberg, Jack. *Desegregation.* Eugene: University of Oregon Press, 1979.

_____. *Race Relations and American Law.* New York: Columbia University Press, 1959.

Gross, Barry, ed. *Reverse Discrimination.* Buffalo, N.Y.: Prometheus Books, 1977.

Hampton, Henry, and Steve Fayer, with Sarah Flynn, comps. *Voices of Freedom: An Oral History of the Civil Rights Movement from the 1950's Through the 1980's.* New York: Bantam Books, 1990.

Hill, Robert A., ed. *The Marcus Garvey and Universal Negro Improvement Association Papers.* 7 vols. Berkeley: University of California Press, 1983-1990.

Horton, James Oliver, and Lois E. Horton. *Black Bostonians: Family Life and Community Struggle in the Antebellum North.* New York: Holmes & Meier, 1979.

Jones, Leon. *From Brown to Boston: Desegregation in Education, 1954-1974.* Metuchen, N.J.: Scarecrow Press, 1979.

Kelly, Alfred H., Winfred A. Harbison, and Herman Belz. *The American Constitution: Its Origins and Development.* New York: W. W. Norton, 1983.

Kluger, Richard. *Simple Justice: The History of Brown v. Board of Education and Black America's Struggle for Equality.* New York: Alfred A. Knopf, 1976.

Lewis, Rupert. *Marcus Garvey, Anti-Colonial Champion.* Trenton, N.J.: Africa World Press, 1988.

Litwack, Leon F. *North of Slavery: The Negro in the Free States, 1790-1860.* Chicago: University of Chicago Press, 1961.

Lukas, J. Anthony. *Common Ground: A Turbulent Decade in the Lives of Three American Families.* New York: Alfred A. Knopf, 1985.

Lupo, Alan. *Liberty's Chosen Home: The Politics of Violence in Boston.* 2d ed. Boston: Beacon Press, 1988.

McFeely, William S. *Yankee Stepfather: General O. O. Howard and the Freedmen.* New Haven, Conn.: Yale University Press, 1968.

McNeil, Genna Rae. "Charles Hamilton Houston: Social Engineer for Civil Rights." In *Black Leaders of the Twentieth Century,* edited by John Hope Franklin and August Meier. Urbana: University of Illinois Press, 1982.

Martin, Tony. *Race First: The Ideological and Organizational Struggles of Marcus Garvey and the Universal Negro Improvement Association.* Westport, Conn.: Greenwood Press, 1976.

Massey, Douglas S., and Nancy A. Denton. *American Apartheid: Segregation and the Making of the Underclass.* Cambridge, Mass.: Harvard University Press, 1993.

Miller, Loren. *The Petitioners: The Story of the Supreme Court of the United States and the Negro.* New York: Pantheon Books, 1966.

Mooney, Christopher F. *Inequality and the American Conscience: Justice Through the Judicial System.* New York: Paulist Press, 1982.

Nash, Gary B. *Forging Freedom: The Formation of Philadelphia's Black Community, 1720-1840.* Cambridge, Mass.: Harvard University Press, 1988.

Nieman, Donald G. *To Set the Law in Motion: The Freedmen's Bureau and the Legal Rights of Blacks, 1865-1868.* Millwood, N.Y.: KTO Press, 1979.

Oates, Stephen B. *Let the Trumpet Sound: The Life of Martin Luther King, Jr.* New York: Harper & Row, 1982.

O'Neil, Timothy J. *Bakke and the Politics of Equality: Friends and Foes in the Classroom of Litigation.* Middletown, Conn.: Wesleyan University Press, 1985.

Oubre, Claude F. *Forty Acres and a Mule: The Freedmen's Bureau and Black Land Ownership.* Baton Rouge: Louisiana State University Press, 1978.

Schwartz, Bernard. *Behind Bakke: Affirmative Action and the Supreme Court.* New York: New York University Press, 1988.

_____. *Swann's Way: The School Busing Case and the Supreme Court.* New York: Oxford University Press, 1986.

Simmons, Ron. *Affirmative Action: Conflict and Change in Higher Education After Bakke.* Cambridge, Mass.: Schenkman, 1982.

Sindler, Alan P. *Bakke, DeFunis, and Minority Admissions: The Quest for Equal Opportunity.* New York: Macmillan, 1978.

Stein, Judith. *The World of Marcus Garvey: Race and Class in Modern Society.* Baton Rouge: Louisiana State University Press, 1986.

Trillin, Calvin. *An Education in Georgia: Charlayne Hunter, Hamilton Holmes, and the Integration of the University of Georgia.* Athens: University of Georgia Press, 1991.

Tushnet, Mark V. *The NAACP's Legal Strategy Against Segregated Education, 1925-1950.* Chapel Hill: University of North Carolina Press, 1987.

Warren, Robert P. *Segregation: The Inner Conflict in the South.* New York: Columbia University Press, 1956.

Whitman, David, and Dorian Friedman. "Busing's Unheralded Legacy: The Facts Are at Odds with the Unfavorable Image of Forced Desegregation." *U.S. News and World Report,* April 13, 1992, pp. 63-65.

Woods, Geraldine. *Affirmative Action.* New York: Franklin Watts, 1989.

SLAVERY

"Africans Taken in the Amistad" and "Argument of John Quincy Adams Before the Supreme Court of the United States." In *The Amistad Case: The Most Celebrated Slave Mutiny of the Nineteenth Century.* 2 vols. Reprint. New York: Johnson Reprint Corp., 1968.

Alkalimat, Abdul. *Introduction to Afro-American Studies: A Peoples' College Primer.* 6th ed. Chicago: Twenty-First Century Books and Publications, 1986.

Aptheker, Herbert. *American Negro Slave Revolts.* New York: International Publishers, 1963.

_____, ed. *From the Colonial Times Through the Civil War.* Volume 1 in *A Documentary History of the Negro People of The United States.* New York: Citadel Press, 1951.

Bemis, Samuel Flagg. *John Quincy Adams and the Union,* New York: Alfred A. Knopf, 1970.

Bennett, Lerone, Jr. *Before the Mayflower: A History of Black America.* 6th ed. Chicago: Johnson Publishing Company, 1987.

Berlin, Ira. *Slaves Without Masters: The Free Negro in the Antebellum South.* New York: Pantheon, 1974.

Berlin, Ira, and Philip D. Morgan, eds. *Cultivation and Culture: Labor and the Shaping of Slave Life in the Americas.* Charlottesville: University Press of Virginia, 1993.

Blassingame, John W. *The Slave Community: Plantation Life in the Antebellum South.* Rev. ed. New York: Oxford University Press, 1979.

Bontemps, Arna. *Black Thunder.* New York: Macmillan, 1936.

_____. *Free at Last: The Life of Frederick Douglass.* New York: Dodd, Mead, 1971.

Breen, T. H., and Stephen Innes. *"Myne Own Ground": Race and Freedom on Virginia's Eastern Shore, 1640-1676.* New York: Oxford University Press, 1980.

Breyfogle, William A. *Make Free: The Story of the Underground Railroad.* Philadelphia: J. B. Lippincott, 1958.

Brownlee, Fred L. *New Day Ascending.* Boston: Pilgrim Press, 1946.

Buckmaster, Henrietta. *Let My People Go: The Story of the Underground Railroad and the Growth of the Abolition Movement.* New York: Harper & Brothers, 1941.

Cable, Mary. *Black Odyssey: The Case of the Slave Ship Amistad.* New York: Viking Press, 1971.

Campbell, Edward D. C., and Kym S. Rice, eds. *Before Freedom Came: African-American Life in the Antebellum South.* Charlottesville: University Press of Virginia, 1991.

Crouch, Barry. *The Freedmen's Bureau and Black Texans.* Austin: University of Texas Press, 1993.

Curry, Leonard P. *The Free Black in Urban America, 1800-1850: The Shadow of the Dream.* Chicago: University of Chicago Press, 1981.

Curtin, Philip. *The Atlantic Slave Trade: A Census.* Madison: University of Wisconsin Press, 1969.

Daniel, Pete. *The Shadow of Slavery: Peonage in the South, 1901-1969.* Urbana: University of Illinois Press, 1972.

Dann, Martin E., ed. *The Black Press: 1827-1890.* New York: Putnam, 1971.

"Davidson, Basil. *The African Slave Trade.* Boston: Little, Brown, 1961.

Douglass, Frederick. *Frederick Douglass: The Narrative and Selected Writings.* Edited by Michael Meyer. New York: Vintage, 1984.

Ehrlich, Walter. *They Have No Rights: Dred Scott's Struggle for Freedom.* Westport, Conn.: Greenwood Press, 1979.

Fehrenbacher, Don E. *The Dred Scott Case: Its Significance in American Law and Politics.* New York: Oxford University Press, 1978.

_____. *Slavery, Law, and Politics: The Dred Scott Case in Historical Perspective.* New York: Oxford University Press, 1981.

Fogel, Robert William. *Without Consent or Contract: The Rise and Fall of American Slavery.* New York: W. W. Norton, 1989.

Foner, Philip S. *Frederick Douglass: A Biography.* 2d ed. New York: Citadel Press, 1969.

Franklin, John Hope, and Alfred A. Moss, Jr. *From Slavery to Freedom: A History of Negro Americans.* 6th ed. New York: Alfred A. Knopf, 1988.

Freehling, William W. "Denmark Vesey's Peculiar Reality." In *New Perspectives on Race and Slavery in America: Essays in Honor of Kenneth M. Stampp,* edited by Robert H. Abzug and Stephen E. Maizlish.

Lexington: University Press of Kentucky, 1986.

_____. *Prelude to Civil War: The Nullification Controversy in South Carolina, 1818-1836.* New York: Harper & Row, 1966.

Furnas, J. C. *The Road to Harpers Ferry.* New York: W. Sloane, 1959.

Gara, Larry. *The Liberty Line: The Legend of the Underground Railroad.* Lexington: University of Kentucky Press, 1961.

Genovese, Eugene D. *From Rebellion to Revolution: Afro-American Slave Revolts in the Making of the Modern World.* Baton Rouge: Louisiana State University Press, 1979.

_____. *Roll, Jordan, Roll: The World the Slaves Made.* New York: Pantheon Books, 1974.

Gutman, Herbert. *The Black Family in Slavery and Freedom, 1750-1925.* New York: Pantheon Books, 1976.

Hall, Kermit L., ed. *Civil Rights in American History: Major Historical Interpretations.* New York: Garland, 1987.

Harding, Vincent. *There Is a River: The Black Struggle for Freedom in America.* 2d ed. New York: Harcourt Brace Jovanovich, 1993.

Higginson, Thomas Wentworth. *Black Rebellion: A Selection from Travellers and Outlaws.* New York: Arno Press, 1969.

Hill, Daniel G. *The Freedom-Seekers: Blacks in Early Canada.* Agincourt, Canada: The Book Society of Canada, 1981.

Horton, James Oliver, and Lois E. Horton. *Black Bostonians: Family Life and Community Struggle in the Antebellum North.* New York: Holmes & Meier, 1979.

Huggins, Nathan Irvin. *Slave and Citizen: The Life of Frederick Douglass.* Boston: Little, Brown, 1980.

Hyman, Harold M., and William M. Wiecek. *Equal Justice Under the Law: Constitutional Development, 1835-1875.* New York: Harper & Row, 1982.

Jacobs, Donald M., ed. *Courage and Conscience: Black and White Abolitionists in Boston.* Bloomington: Indiana University Press, 1993.

Jones, Howard. *Mutiny on the Amistad: The Saga of a Slave Revolt and Its Impact on American Abolition, Law, and Diplomacy.* New York: Oxford University Press, 1987.

Lane, Ann J., ed. *The Debate over Slavery: Stanley Elkins and His Critics.* Urbana: University of Illinois Press, 1971.

Levine, Lawrence W. *Black Culture and Black Consciousness: Afro-American Folk Thought from Slavery to Freedom.* New York: Oxford University Press, 1977.

Littlefield, Daniel C. *Rice and Slaves: Ethnicity and the Slave Trade in Colonial South*

Carolina. Baton Rouge: Louisiana State University Press, 1981.

Litwack, Leon F. *North of Slavery: The Negro in the Free States, 1790-1860.* Chicago: University of Chicago Press, 1961.

Lofton, John. *Insurrection in South Carolina: The Turbulent World of Denmark Vesey.* Yellow Springs, Ohio: Antioch Press, 1964.

McPherson, James M. *The Struggle for Equality: Abolitionists and the Negro in the Civil War and Reconstruction.* Princeton, N.J.: Princeton University Press, 1964.

Martin, B. Edmon. *All We Want Is Make Us Free.* Lanham, Md.: University Press of America, 1986.

Mbiti, John S. *African Religions and Philosophy.* London: Heinemann, 1969.

Mullin, Gerald W. *Flight and Rebellion: Slave Resistance in Eighteenth-Century Virginia.* New York: Oxford University Press, 1972.

Nash, Gary B. *Forging Freedom: The Formation of Philadelphia's Black Community, 1720-1840.* Cambridge, Mass.: Harvard University Press, 1988.

Parish, Peter J. *Slavery: History and Historians.* New York: Harper & Row, 1989.

Quarles, Benjamin. *Black Abolitionists.* London: Oxford University Press, 1969.

_____. *Frederick Douglass.* Washington, D.C.: Associated Publishers, 1948. Reprint. New York: Atheneum, 1976.

_____. *Lincoln and the Negro.* New York: Oxford University Press, 1962.

_____. *The Negro in the Making of America.* 2d rev. ed. New York: Collier Books, 1987.

Raboteau, Albert J. *Slave Religion: The "Invisible Institution" in the Antebellum South.* New York: Oxford University Press, 1978.

Redding, Sanders. *They Came in Chains: Americans from Africa.* Philadelphia: J. B. Lippincott, 1950.

Ripley, C. Peter, et al., eds. *The Black Abolitionist Papers.* 5 vols. Chapel Hill: University of North Carolina Press, 1985-1992.

Rose, Willie Lee. *Slavery and Freedom.* New York: Oxford University Press, 1982.

Sirmans, M. Eugene. "The Legal Status of the Slave in South Carolina, 1670-1740." *Journal of Southern History* 28 (November, 1962): 462-473.

Sobel, Mechal. *Trabelin' On: The Slave Journey to an Afro-Baptist Faith.* Westport, Conn.: Greenwood Press, 1979.

Stampp, Kenneth M. *The Peculiar Institution: Slavery in the Ante-Bellum South.* New York: Alfred A Knopf, 1956.

Starobin, Robert S., ed. *Denmark Vesey: The Slave Conspiracy of 1822.* Englewood Cliffs, N.J.: Prentice-Hall, 1970.

Still, William. *The Underground Rail Road: A Record of Facts, Authentic Narratives, Letters, &c, Narrating the Hardships, Hair-breadth Escapes and Death Struggles of the Slaves in Their Efforts for Freedom.* Phildelphia: Porter & Coates, 1872.

Stuckey, Sterling. *Slave Culture: Nationalist Theory and the Foundations of Black America.* New York: Oxford University Press, 1987.

TePaske, John T. "The Fugitive Slave: Intercolonial Rivalry and Spanish Slave Policy, 1689-1764." In *Eighteenth-Century Florida and Its Borderlands.* Edited by Samuel Proctor. Gainesville: University Presses of Florida, 1975.

Tise, Larry E. *Proslavery: A History of the Defense of Slavery in America, 1701-1840.* Athens: University of Georgia Press, 1987.

Trefousse, Hans L. *Lincoln's Decision for Emancipation.* Philadelphia: J. B. Lippincott, 1975.

Wade, Richard C. "The Vesey Plot: A Reconsideration." *Journal of Southern History* 30 (May, 1964): 148-161.

Weir, Robert M. *Colonial South Carolina: A History.* Millwood, N.Y.: KTO, 1983.

Wesley, Charles H., and Patricia W. Romero. *Negro Americans in the Civil War: From Slavery to Citizenship.* 2d rev. ed. New York: Publishers Company, 1969.

White, Deborah Gray. *Ar'n't I a Woman?: Female Slaves in the Plantation South.* New York: W. W. Norton, 1985.

Wikramanayake, Marina. *A World in Shadow: The Free Black in Antebellum South Carolina.* Columbia: University of South Carolina Press, 1973.

Wilmore, Gayraud S., ed. *African American Religious Studies: An Interdisciplinary Anthology.* Durham, N.C.: Duke University Press, 1989.

_____. *Black Religion and Black Radicalism: An Interpretation of the Religious History of Afro-American People.* 2d rev. ed. Maryknoll, N.Y.: Orbis Books, 1983.

Wood, Forrest G. *Black Scare: The Racist Response to Emancipation and Reconstruction.* Berkeley: University of California Press, 1968.

Wood, Peter H. *Black Majority: Negroes in Colonial South Carolina from 1670 through the Stono Rebellion.* New York: W. W. Norton, 1975.

Wyatt-Brown, Bertram. *Lewis Tappan and the Evangelical War Against Slavery.* New York: Atheneum, 1971.

_____. "The Mask of Obedience: Male Slave Psychology in the Old South." *American Historical Review* 93 (1988): 1228-1252.

Yee, Shirley J. *Black Women Abolitionists: A Study in Activism, 1828-1860.* Knoxville: University of Tennessee Press, 1992.

SPORTS

Aaron, Hank, with Lonnie Wheeler. *I Had a Hammer: The Hank Aaron Story.* New York: HarperCollins, 1991.

Ashe, Arthur. *A Hard Road To Glory: A History of the African-American Athlete.* 3 vols. New York: Warner Books, 1988.

Atyeo, Don, and Felix Dennis. *The Holy Warrior, Muhammad Ali.* New York: Simon & Schuster, 1975.

Baldwin, Stanley C., and Jerry B. Jenkins. *Bad Henry.* Radnor, Pa.: Chilton Book Co., 1974.

Bruce, Janet. *The Kansas City Monarchs: Champions of Black Baseball.* Lawrence, Kans.: University Press of Kansas, 1985.

Bunch, Lonnie G., and Louie Robinson. *The Black Olympians, 1904-1984.* Los Angeles: California Afro-American Museum, 1984.

Chadwick, Bruce. *When the Game Was Black and White: The Illustrated History of Baseball's Negro Leagues.* New York: Abbeville, 1992.

Chalk, Ocania. *Black College Sport.* New York: Dodd, Mead, 1976.

_____. *Pioneers of Black Sport: The Early Days of the Black Professional Athlete in Baseball, Basketball, Boxing, and Football.* New York: Dodd, Mead, 1975.

Cottrell, John. *Man of Destiny.* London: Muller, 1967.

Davis, Marianna W., ed. *Contributions of Black Women to America.* 2 vols. Columbia, S.C.: Kenday Press, 1982.

Fleischer, Nat. *Black Dynamite: The Story of the Negro in the Prize Ring from 1782 to 1938.* 5 vols. New York: C. J. O'Brien, 1938-1947.

Frommer, Harvey. *Jackie Robinson.* New York: Franklin Watts, 1984.

George, Nelson. *Elevating the Game: Black Men and Basketball.* New York: HarperCollins, 1992.

Green, Tina Sloan, Alpha Alexander, and Nikki Franke. *Black Women in Sport.* Reston, Va.: AAHPERD Publications, 1981.

Gutman, Bill. *Modern Basketball Superstars.* New York: Dodd, Mead, 1975.

Hahn, James, and Lynn Hahn. *Henry!: The Sports Career of Henry Aaron.* Mankato, Minn.: Crestwood House, 1981.

Harris, Merv. *The Lonely Heroes: Professional Basketball's Great Centers.* New York: Viking, 1975.

Haskins, James. *Babe Ruth and Hank Aaron: The Home Run Kings.* New York: Lothrop, Lee & Shepard, 1974.

Hauser, Thomas. *Muhammad Ali: His Life and Times.* New York: Simon & Schuster, 1991.

Henderson, Edwin Bancroft. *The Negro in Sports.* Washington, D.C.: Associated Publishers, 1939.

Hoberman, John M. *The Olympic Crisis: Sport, Politics, and the Moral Order.* New Rochelle, N.Y.: A. D. Caratzas, 1986.

Holway, John. *Voices from the Great Black Baseball Leagues.* New York: Dood, Mead, 1975.

Isenberg, Michael T. *John L. Sullivan and His America.* Chicago: University of Illinois Press, 1988.

Jones, Wally, and Jim Washington. *Black Champions Challenge American Sports.* New York: David McKay, 1972.

Kahn, Roger. *The Boys of Summer.* New York: Harper & Row, 1972.

Lipsyte, Robert. *Free to Be Muhammad Ali.* New York: Harper & Row, 1977.

Mailer, Norman. *The Fight.* Boston: Little, Brown, 1975.

Matthews, Peter. *Track and Field Athletes: The Records.* Enfield, England: Guinness Superlative, 1985.

Mead, Chris. *Champion: Joe Louis, Black Hero in White America.* New York: Scribner's, 1985.

Money, Don, with Herb Anastor. *The Man Who Made Milwaukee Famous: A Salute to Henry Aaron.* Milwaukee: Agape Publishers, 1976.

Olsen, Jack. *The Black Athlete: A Shameful Story.* New York: Time-Life Books, 1968.

Page, James A. *Black Olympian Medalists.* Englewood, Colo.: Libraries Unlimited, 1991.

Peterson, Robert. *Only the Ball Was White.* Englewood Cliffs, N.J.: Prentice-Hall, 1970.

Plimpton, George. *One for the Record: The Inside Story of Hank Aaron's Chase for the Home-Run Record.* New York: Harper & Row, 1974.

Roberts, Randy. *Papa Jack: Jack Johnson and the Era of White Hopes.* New York: Macmillan, 1983.

Robinson, Jackie. *I Never Had It Made.* New York: G. P. Putnam's Sons, 1972.

Rogosin, Donn. *Invisible Men: Life in Baseball's Negro Leagues.* New York: Antheneum, 1983.

Rust, Art, Jr., and Edna Rust. *Art Rust's Illustrated History of the Black Athlete.* Garden City, N.Y.: Doubleday, 1985.

Seymour, Harold. "Part-Five—The House of Baseball: The Outbuilding." In *The People's Game.* Vol. 3 in *Baseball.* New York: Oxford University Press, 1990.

Sheed, Wilfred. *Muhammad Ali.* New York: Thomas Y. Crowell, 1975.

Somers, Dale A. *The Rise of Sports in New Orleans, 1850-1900.* Baton Rouge: Louisiana State University Press, 1972.

Tygiel, Jules. *Baseball's Great Experiment: Jackie Robinson and His Legacy.* New York: Oxford University Press, 1983.

Young, Andrew Sturgeon Nash. *Negro Firsts in Sports.* Chicago: Johnson, 1963.

VISUAL ARTS

Alexander, Lois K. *Blacks in the History of Fashion.* New York: Harlem Institute of Fashion, 1982.

Charles, Roland, and Toyomi Igus, eds. *Life in a Day of Black L.A.: The Way We See It: L.A. Black Photographers Present a New Perspective on Their City.* Berkeley: University of California Press, 1992.

Dallas Museum of Art. *Black Art Ancestral Legacy: The African Impulse in African-American Art.* New York: Harry N. Abrams, 1989.

Doty, Robert. *Contemporary Black Artists in America.* New York: Dodd, Mead for the Whitney Museum of American Art, 1971.

Dover, Cedric. *American Negro Art.* Reprint. Greenwich, Conn.: New York Graphic Society, 1969.

Driskell, David C. *Two Centuries of Black American Art.* New York: Alfred A. Knopf for the Los Angeles County Museum of Art, 1976.

Fine, Elsa Honig. *The Afro-American Artist: A Search for Identity.* New York: Hacker Art Books, 1982.

Hageney, Wolfgang, ed. *Black Africa Impressions: Graphic and Color and Fashion and Design.* 2d ed. Rome, Italy: Belvedere, 1983.

Hall, Robert L. *Gathered Visions: Selected Works by African American Women Artists.* Washington, D.C.: Smithsonian Institution Press, 1992.

Haskins, James. *James Van DerZee: The Picture-Takin' Man.* New York: Dodd, Mead, 1979.

Ketner, Joseph D. *The Emergence of the African-American Artist: Robert S. Duncanson, 1821-1872.* Columbia: University of Missouri Press, 1993.

Lippard, Lucy R. *Mixed Blessings: New Art in a Multicultural America.* New York: Pantheon, 1990.

Moutoussamy-Ashe, Jeanne. *Viewfinders: Black Women Photographers.* New York: Dodd, Mead, 1986.

Myers, Walter Dean. *Crystal.* New York: Viking Kestrel, 1987.

Natanson, Nicholas. *The Black Image in the New Deal: The Politics of FSA Photography.* Knoxville: University of Tennessee Press, 1992.

Parks, Gordon, Sr. *Voices in the Mirror: An Autobiography.* New York: Doubleday, 1991.

Patterson, Lindsay. *International Library of Afro-American Life History: The Afro-American in Music and Art.* Cornwells Heights, Pa.: Publishers Agency, 1979.

Reynolds, Gary A., and Beryl J. Wright. *Against All Odds: African-American Artists and the Harmon Foundation.* Newark, N.J.: The Newark Museum, 1989.

Roberts, Richard Samuel. *A True Likeness: The Black South of Richard Samuel Roberts, 1920-1936.* Chapel Hill, N.C.: Algonquin Books of Chapel Hill, 1986.

Robinson, Aminah Brenda Lynn, comp. *The Teachings: Drawn from African-American Spirituals.* New York: Harcourt Brace Jovanovich, 1993.

Rollock, Barbara. *Black Authors and Illustrators of Children's Books.* New York: Garland, 1988.

Salley, Columbus, ed. *Accent African Fashions.* New York: Col-Bob Associates, 1975.

Starke, Barbara M., Lillian O. Holloman, and Barbara K. Nordquist. *African American Dress and Adornment: A Cultural Perspective.* Dubuque, Iowa: Kendall/Hunt, 1990.

Studio Museum in Harlem, The. *Harlem Renaissance: Art of Black America.* New York: Harry N. Abrams, 1987.

Vlach, John Michael. *The Afro-American Tradition in Decorative Arts.* Athens: University of Georgia Press, 1992.

Williams, Helen E. *Books by African-American Authors and Illustrators for Children and Young Adults.* Chicago: American Library Association, 1991.

Willis-Thomas, Deborah. *Black Photographers, 1840-1940: A Bio-Bibliography.* New York: Garland, 1985.

_____. *An Illustrated Bio-Bibliography of Black Photographers, 1940-1988.* New York: Garland, 1988.

People by Profession

ABOLITIONISTS

Allen, Richard
Brown, Henry "Box"
Brown, William Wells
Carey, Lott
Cornish, Samuel Eli
Crummell, Alexander
Cuffe, Paul
Delany, Martin Robison
Douglass, Frederick
Equiano, Olaudah
Garnet, Henry Highland
Harding, Vincent
Harper, Frances E. W.
Jacobs, Harriet
Nell, William C.
Quarles, Benjamin
Remond, Charles Lenox
Ruggles, David
Shadd, Mary Ann
Stewart, Maria Miller
Still, William
Truth, Sojourner
Tubman, Harriet
Walker, David
Ward, Samuel Ringgold

ACTIVISTS. *See* CIVIL RIGHTS ACTIVISTS

ACTORS

Aldridge, Ira Frederick
Amos, John
Anderson, Eddie "Rochester"
Anderson, Jim
Angelou, Maya
Avery, Margaret
Bailey, Pearl
Beals, Jennifer
Beavers, Louise
Belafonte, Harry George, Jr.
Belafonte-Harper, Shari
Berry, Halle
Blacque, Taurean
Brooks, Avery
Brown, Georg Stanford
Brown, Ruth Weston
Browne, Roscoe Lee
Burge, Gregg
Burrows, Vinie
Burton, LeVar
Bush, Anita
Caesar, Adolph
Cambridge, Godfrey
Cara, Irene
Carroll, Diahann
Carroll, Vinnette Justine

Carter, Nell
Casey, Bernie
Cosby, Bill
Crosse, Rupert
Crothers, Benjamin Sherman "Scatman"
Dandridge, Dorothy
Davis, Clifton
Davis, Ossie
Davis, Sammy, Jr.
Day, Morris
Dee, Ruby
Dixon, Ivan, III
Dorn, Michael
Duke, William "Bill"
Duncan, Todd
Evans, Michael Jonas
Fetchit, Stepin
Fisher, Gail
Foster, Gloria
Foxx, Redd
Freeman, Albert Cornelius, Jr.
Freeman, Morgan
Gilpin, Charles Sidney
Glover, Danny
Goldberg, Whoopi
Gordon, Dexter
Gossett, Louis, Jr.
Graves, Teresa
Grier, Pam
Guillaume, Robert
Gunn, Moses
Guy, Jasmine
Hardison, Kadeem
Harewood, Dorian
Harney, Ben
Harrison, Richard B.
Haynes, (Samuel) Lloyd
Hemsley, Sherman
Hernandez, Juano
Holder, Geoffrey Lamont
Hooks, Kevin
Hooks, Robert
Horne, Lena Mary Calhoun
Horsford, Anna Maria
Hunter, Eddie
Hyman, Earle
Ice-T
Ingram, Rex
Jackée
Jackson, Janet
Jacobs, Lawrence-Hilton
Johnson, Anne-Marie
Jones, Grace
Jones, James Earl
Julien, Max
Kelly, Jim
Kelly, Paula

Kennedy, Leon Isaac
Kirby, George
Kitt, Eartha
Kotero, Patricia "Apollonia"
Kotto, Yaphet
LaBelle, Patti
Lange, Ted W., III
Lee, Canada
Lee, Shelton Jackson "Spike"
Little, Cleavon Jake
Lockhart, Calvin
Long, Avon
Lumbly, Carl
McDaniel, Hattie
McGee, Vonetta
McKee, Lonette
McKinney, Nina Mae
McNair, Barbara
McNeil, Claudia Mae
McQueen, Thelma "Butterfly"
Marshall, William
Mayo, Whitman
Mills, Stephanie
Mr. T.
Moore, Melba
Morris, Garrett
Morris, Greg
Morrison, E. Frederick "Sunshine Sammy"
Morton, Edna
Morton, Joe
Murphy, Edward Regan "Eddie"
Muse, Clarence
Nicholas, Denise
Nichols, Nichelle
O'Neal, Frederick
O'Neal, Ron
Pace, Judy
Perry, Shauneille
Peters, Brock
Poitier, Sidney
Pryor, Rain
Pryor, Richard Franklin Lennox Thomas
Rashad, Phylicia
Rasulala, Thalmus
Ray, Gene Anthony
Reid, Daphne Maxwell
Reid, Tim
Rich, Matty
Richards, Beah
Robeson, Paul
Robinson, Bill "Bojangles"
Rolle, Esther
Rollins, Howard Ellsworth, Jr.
Roundtree, Richard
Russell, Nipsey
St. Jacques, Raymond

Sands, Diana
Sanford, Isabel
Simms, Hilda
Sinclair, Madge
Smith, Anna Deavere
Snipes, Wesley
Sykes, Brenda
Thigpen, Lynne
Townsend, Robert
Tyson, Cicely
Uggams, Leslie
Underwood, Blair
Van Peebles, Mario
Van Peebles, Melvin
Vanity
Vereen, Ben
Walker, George
Walker, James Carter "Jimmie"
Ward, Douglas Turner
Warren, Michael
Washington, Denzel, Jr.
Washington, Fredricka Carolyn "Fredi"
Waters, Ethel
Wayans, Damon
Wayans, Keenen Ivory
Weathers, Carl
Whitaker, Forest
White, Melvin "Slappy"
Whitfield, Lynn
Williams, Billy Dee
Williams, Clarence, III
Williams, Egbert Austin "Bert"
Williamson, Fred
Wilson, Demond
Winfield, Paul
Winfrey, Oprah Gail

ANTHROPOLIGISTS. *See* SOCIAL SCIENTISTS

ARCHITECTS and ENGINEERS

Alexander, Archie Alphonso
Callender, Leroy Nathaniel
Crosthwait, David Nelson, Jr.
Hall, Titus C.
Lankford, John Anderson
McCoy, Elijah
Mackey, Howard Hamilton, Sr.
Matzeliger, Jan Earnst
Morgan, Garrett Augustus
Robinson, Hilyard R.
Slaughter, John Brooks
Williams, Paul Revere

ARTISTS

Alston, Charles
Andrews, Benny
Artis, William E.
Ball, James Presley
Bannister, Edward Mitchell
Barthé, Richmond
Bearden, Romare
Biggers, John

Billops, Camille J.
Blackburn, Robert
Braxton, William E.
Browne, Vivian
Bullock, Star(manda)
Burke, Selma
Burroughs, Margaret Taylor Goss
Carter, William
Catlett, Elizabeth
Chandler, Dana
Chase-Riboud, Barbara
Clark, Edward
Cortor, Eldzier
Crichlow, Ernest
Crite, Allan Rohan
Cruz, Emilio
Delaney, Beauford
Delaney, Joseph
DePillars, Murry Norman
Dickerson-Thompson, Julee
Douglas, Aaron
Duncanson, Robert
Edmunson, William
Edwards, Melvin E.
Evans, Minnie Jones
Fax, Elton
Flemister, Fred
Fuller, Meta Vaux Warrick
Gafford, Alice
Gilliam, Sam
Hammons, David
Hardison, Inge
Harper, William
Hathaway, Isaac
Hayden, Palmer C.
Hunt, Richard Howard
Hunter, Clementine
Jackson, May Howard
Johnson, Charles Richard
Johnson, Daniel LaRue
Johnson, Malvin Gray
Johnson, Sargent
Johnson, William Henry
Johnston, Joshua
Jones, Lois Mailou
Joseph, Ronald
Lawrence, Jacob
Lee-Smith, Hughie
Lewis, (Mary) Edmonia
Lewis, Samella Sanders
McCullough, Geraldine
Mayhew, Richard
Miller, Earl B.
Moorhead, Scipio
Morgan, Norma Gloria
Motley, Archibald John, Jr.
Oubre, Haywood Louis
Overstreet, Joseph "Joe"
Perkins, Marion
Pippin, Horace
Porter, James Amos
Ringgold, Faith
Saunders, Raymond

Savage, Augusta
Scott, William Edouard
Sebree, Charles
Silverstein, Shel(by)
Simpson, William
Smith, Vincent DaCosta
Tanner, Henry Ossawa
Thompson, Robert "Bob"
Thrash, Dox
Warbourg, Eugene
Waring, Laura Wheeler
Webb, Clifton
White, Charles
Whitten, Jack
Wilson, Ellis
Wilson, John
Woodruff, Hale

ASTRONAUTS and AVIATORS

Bluford, Guion Stewart, Jr.
Brown, Willa B.
Bullard, Eugene Jacques
Coleman, Bessie
Gregory, Frederick Drew
Jemison, Mae C.
Julian, Hubert Fauntleroy
Lawrence, Robert H., Jr.
McNair, Ronald E.
Payne, Betty J.

ASTRONOMERS. *See* SCIENTISTS

ATHLETES. *See also* BASEBALL PLAYERS, BASKETBALL PLAYERS, BOXERS, FOOTBALL PLAYERS, *and* TRACK and FIELD ATHLETES

Ashe, Arthur Robert, Jr. (tennis)
Brown, Pete (golf)
Campbell, Chris (wrestling)
Coage, Allen James (judo)
Davenport, Willie D. (bobsleding)
Davis, John Henry, Jr. (weightlifting)
DeFrantz, Anita Luceete (rower)
Elder, (Robert) Lee (golf)
Elder, Rose Harper (golf)
Flack, Rory (skating)
Francis, Herbert (cycling)
Fuhr, Grant Scott (hockey)
Galimore, Ron (gymnastics)
Garrison, Zina (tennis)
Gibson, Althea (tennis)
Glass, Cheryl (auto racing)
Hyman, Flora "Flo" (volleyball)
Jones, Uriah (fencing)
Keaser, Lloyd Weldon (wrestling)
Lewis, Oliver (jockey)
Long, James (jockey)
McCurdy, Robert C. (jockey)
MacNeil, Lori (tennis)
Mosley, Donna Lynn (gymnastics)
Murphy, Isaac (jockey)
Okino, Elizabeth "Betty" (gymnastics)

O'Ree, William Eldon "Willie" (hockey)
Peete, Calvin (golf)
Powell, Renee (golf)
Scott, Wendell (auto racing)
Sifford, Charlie (golf)
Taylor, Marshall W. "Major"
Thomas, Debi (skating)
Thorpe, Jim (golf)
Washington, Ora (tennis)
White, Cheryl (jockey)
White, Ruth (fencing)
Winkfield, Jimmy (jockey)

AUTHORS. *See* WRITERS

AVIATORS. *See* ASTRONAUTS

BASEBALL PLAYERS
Aaron, Henry Louis "Hank"
Allen, Richard Anthony, "Richie"
Ashford, Emmett
Banks, Ernest "Ernie"
Baylor, Don
Bell, James "Cool Papa"
Blue, Vida
Bonds, Bobby Lee
Brock, Lou
Campanella, Roy
Carew, Rodney Cline
Cepeda, Orlando
Charleston, Oscar McKinley
Clemente, Roberto
Cooper, Cecil
Dawson, Andre Fernando "The Hawk"
Doby, Lawrence Eugene "Larry"
Flood, Curtis Charles
Foster, Andrew "Rube"
Foster, George
Gaston, Clarence "Cito"
Gibson, Joshua "Josh"
Gibson, Robert "Bob"
Gooden, Dwight Eugene "Doc"
Gwynn, Tony
Henderson, Rickey
Howard, Elston
Irvin, Merrill Monford "Monte"
Jackson, Bo
Jackson, Reggie
Jenkins, Ferguson Arthur
Johnson, William Julius "Judy"
Leonard, Walter Fenner "Buck"
McCovey, Willie
McGee, Willie
Marichal, Juan
Mays, Willie Howard, Jr.
Minoso, Minnie
Morgan, Joe
Murray, Eddie
Newcombe, Donald "Don"
Oliva, Pedro "Tony"
Paige, Leroy Robert "Satchel"
Parker, David Gene "Dave"
Perez, Tony

Puckett, Kirby
Rice, James Edward
Robinson, Frank, Jr.
Robinson, Jackie
Smith, Carl Reginald "Reggie"
Smith, Osborne Earl "Ozzie"
Stargell, Wilver Dornel "Willie"
Stewart, David Keith
Stone, Toni
Strawberry, Darryl
Tiant, Luis
Walker, Moses Fleetwood
Whitaker, Louis Rodman
White, William DeKova "Bill"
Wills, Maurice Morning "Maury"
Winfield, David Mark "Dave"

BASKETBALL PLAYERS
Abdul-Jabbar, Kareem
Archibald, Nathaniel "Tiny"
Attles, Alvin A., Jr.
Barkley, Charles Wade
Barksdale, Don
Baylor, Elgin
Bellamy, Walter "Walt"
Bias, Len
Bing, David "Dave"
Chamberlain, Wilt
Cooper, Charles H. "Chuck"
Cooper, Charles Theodore "Tarzan"
Dandridge, Robert L., Jr.
Dantley, Adrian Delano
Davis, Walter Paul
Drexler, Clyde
Dumars, Joe, III
Erving, Julius
Ewing, Patrick Aloysius
Frazier, Walt
Gaines, Clarence "Big House"
Gervin, George "Iceman"
Gilmore, Artis
Greer, Harold Everett "Hal"
Harlem Rens
Harlem Globetrotters
Harris, Luisa "Lucy"
Hawkins, Cornelius "Connie"
Hayes, Elvin Ernest
Haywood, Spencer
Hudson, Lou
Johnson, Earvin "Magic," Jr.
Johnson, Gus, Jr.
Jones. K. C.
Jones, Samuel "Sam"
Jordan, Michael
Lanier, Robert Jerry "Bob," Jr.
Lemon, Meadowlark
Lewis, Charlotte
Love, Bob
McAdoo, Bob
Malone, Jeff
Malone, Karl
Malone, Moses Eugene
Marquis, Gail

May, Scott Glenn
Miller, Cheryl DeAnne
Miller, Reginald Wayne "Reggie"
Moncrief, Sidney A.
Monroe, Earl "The Pearl"
Murphy, Calvin Jerome
Nixon, Norman Ellard "Norm"
Olajuwon, Hakeem
Parish, Robert L., Jr
Reed, Willis, Jr.
Roberts, Patricia
Robertson, Oscar Palmer
Robinson, David Maurice
Rodman, Dennis "Worm"
Russell, Bill
Scott, Byron
Scott, Charles Thomas "Charlie"
Tatum, Reese "Goose"
Thomas, Isiah Lord, III
Thompson, David
Thompson, John Robert, Jr.
Thurmond, Nathaniel "Nate"
Unseld, Westley Sissel "Wes"
Walker, Chester "Chet"
Washington, Ora
Webb, Spud
Wilkens, Leonard Randolph "Lenny"
Wilkins, (Jacques) Dominique
Woodard, Lynette
Worthy, James Ager

BIOLOGISTS. *See* SCIENTISTS

BOXERS
Ali, Muhammad
Armstrong, Henry
Bowe, Riddick
Carter, Rubin "Hurricane"
Charles, Ezzard Mack
Ellis, Jimmy
Foreman, George
Foster, Robert Wayne "Bob"
Frazier, Joseph "Joe"
Gans, Joe B.
Hagler, "Marvelous" Marvin
Hearns, Thomas "Hit Man"
Holmes, Larry
Holyfield, Evander
Johnson, John Arthur "Jack"
Leonard, Ray Charles "Sugar Ray"
Liston, Charles "Sonny"
Louis, Joe
Molyneux, Tom
Moore, Archie
Patterson, Floyd
Robinson, Sugar Ray
Spinks, Leon
Spinks, Michael
Trimiar, Marian "Tyger"
Tyson, Michael Gerard "Mike"
Walcott, "Jersey Joe"
Wills, Harry
Wilson, Jack "Jackie"

BROADCAST JOURNALISTS. *See*
TELEVISION PERSONALITIES

BUSINESSPEOPLE and LABOR
LEADERS
Amos, Wallace, Jr.
Bolden, Dorothy Lee
Bolden, J. Taber, Jr.
Brown, George L.
Cuffe, Paul
Davis, Preston Augustus
Dunham, Robert
Du Sable, Jean Baptiste Pointe
Edwards, Nelson Jack
Finley, Clarence C.
Ford, Barney
Forten, James
Fortune, Amos
Fuller, S. B.
Gaston, Arthur George
Gourdine, Simon Peter
Graves, Earl G., Sr.
Green, Ernest G.
Hall, David McKenzie
Hernandez, Aileen Clark
Herndon, Alonzo F.
Hulbert, Maurice "Hot Rod"
Jackson, Eugene
Johnson, George Ellis
Johnson, John Harold
Julian, Percy Lavon
Lee, Bertram M.
Lewis, Reginald F.
Morrow, E(verett) Frederic
O'Neal, Frederick
Parks, Henry Green, Jr.
Price, Lloyd
Randolph, Asa Philip
Rattley, Jessie Meinfield
Reynolds, Barbara Ann
Robertson, Stanley
Russell, Herman
Shocklee, Hank
Sherwood, Kenneth N.
Simmons, Russell
Spaulding, Asa
Spaulding, Charles C.
Sutton, Pierre Montea "PePe"
Taylor, Hobart, Jr.
Toote, Gloria E. A.
Townsend, Willard Saxby
Travis, Dempsey Jerome
Walker, Madam C. J.
Walker, Maggie Lena Draper
Weaver, George Leon-Paul
Wilkinson, Frederick D., Jr.
Williams, Franklin H.
Wood, Thomas Alexander
Wormley, James

CHEMISTS. *See* **SCIENTISTS**

CHOREOGRAPHERS. *See* **DANCERS**

CIVIL RIGHTS ACTIVISTS
Abernathy, Ralph
Anderson, Jim
Baker, Ella
Barry, Marion
Bass, Charlotta Spears
Bates, Daisy
Berry, Mary Frances
Bevel, James
Bolden, Dorothy Lee
Bond, Julian
Briggs, Cyril V.
Brown, Charlotte Hawkins
Brown, Elaine
Brown, H. Rap
Brown, Hallie Q.
Bunche, Ralph J.
Burroughs, Nannie Helen
Burrows, Vinie
Carmichael, Stokely
Cary, William Sterling
Chavis, Benjamin Franklin, Jr.
Clark, Mark
Clark, Septima Poinsette
Cleage, Albert Buford, Jr.
Cleaver, Eldridge
Cobb, William Montague
Cooper, Anna Julia Haywood
Crummell, Alexander
Davis, Angela Yvonne
Davis, Henrietta Vinton
Davis, Ossie
Delany, Martin Robison
Douglass, Frederick
Du Bois, W. E. B.
Edelman, Marian Wright
Evers, (James) Charles
Evers, Medgar Wylie
Farmer, James
Forman, James
Forten, James
Fortune, T. Thomas
Franklin, C. L.
Gardner, Edward
Garvey, Amy Jacques
Garvey, Marcus
Green, Ernest G.
Gregory, Dick
Hall, Prince
Hamer, Fannie Lou
Hamilton, Charles Vernon
Hampton, Fred
Harding, Vincent
Haynes, George Edmund
Height, Dorothy Irene
Hernandez, Aileen Clark
Hill, Herbert
Hilliard, David
Holman, M. Carl
Hood, James Walker
Hooks, Benjamin Lawson
Hutton, Bobby James
Innis, Roy Emile Alfredo

Jackson, George
Jackson, Jesse
Jacob, John Edward
Johnson, James Weldon
Jones, Claudia
Jones, Eugene Kinckle
Jordan, June
Jordan, Vernon Eulion, Jr.
Karenga, Ron Ndabetta
Kimbro, Warren
King, Coretta Scott
King, Martin Luther, Jr.
King, Martin Luther, Sr.
King, Melvin H.
Lewis, John Robert
Lincoln, C(harles) Eric
McKissick, Floyd
Malcolm X
Marshall, Thurgood
Meredith, James Howard
Mitchell, Clarence
Moses, Robert Parris
Motley, Constance Baker
Murray, Pauli
Newton, Huey P.
Obadele, Imari Abubakari
Parks, Rosa
Randolph, A. Philip
Ricks, Willie
Robeson, Eslanda Cardoza Goode
Robeson, Paul
Robinson, Aubrey E., Jr.
Robinson, Jo Ann Gibson
Robinson, Randall
Robinson, Ruby Doris Smith
Rustin, Bayard
Seale, Bobby
Sellers, Cleveland, Jr.
Shakur, Assata Olugbala
Sharpton, Al
Shuttlesworth, Fred L.
Sullivan, Leon Howard
Terrell, Mary Church
Trotter, William Monroe
Truth, Sojourner
Tubman, Harriet
Turner, Henry McNeal
Waddles, Mrs. Payton "Mother"
Wallace, Michele
Walters, Alexander
Walters, Ronald
Washington, Booker T(aliaferro)
Watkins, Bruce R., Sr.
Wattleton, (Alyce) Faye
Wells, Ida B(ell)
White, Walter Francis
Wiley, George
Wilkins, Roy
Williams, Hosea
Williams, Robert Franklin
Wilson, Margaret Bush
Young, Whitney Moore, Jr.

COMEDIANS

Allen, Byron
Anderson, Eddie "Rochester"
Brown, Ernest
Cambridge, Godfrey
Cosby, Bill
Fetchit, Stepin
Fletcher, Clinton "Dusty"
Foxx, Redd
Goldberg, Whoopi
Gregory, Richard Claxton "Dick"
Hall, Arsenio
Kirby, George
Mabley, Jackie "Moms"
Markham, Dewey "Pigmeat"
Mills, Florence
Morris, Garrett
Murphy, Edward Regan "Eddie"
Pryor, Richard Franklin Lennox Thomas
Russell, Nipsey
Thomas, Rufus
Townsend, Robert
Walker, George
Walker, James Carter "Jimmie"
Wallace, George
Wayans, Damon
White, Melvin "Slappy"
Williams, Egbert Austin "Bert"
Wilson, Clerow "Flip"
Wiltshire, George

COMPOSERS and SONGWRITERS.
See also **CONDUCTORS** *and*
MUSICIANS and SINGERS

Anderson, Thomas Jefferson
Ashford and Simpson
Baker, David
Basie, William "Count"
Bechet, Sidney Joseph
Benton, Brook
Berry, Charles Edward Anderson
 "Chuck"
Blake, Eubie
Bland, James
Blythe, Arthur
Bonds, Margaret Allison
Bradford, (John Henry) Perry "Mule"
Brown, James
Brown, Oscar, Jr.
Burleigh, Harry T.
Carter, Bennett Lester "Benny"
Chapman, Tracy
Charles, Ray
Cleveland, James
Coleridge-Taylor, Samuel
Cordero, Roque
Crouch, Andrae
Davis, Clifton
Davis, Miles Dewey
Dixon, "Big" Willie
Dixon, Charles Edward "Charlie"
Dixon, Jessy
Dorsey, Thomas Andrew

Ellington, Edward Kennedy "Duke"
Ellington, Mercer Kennedy
Europe, James Reese
Gamble and Huff
Gillespie, John Birks "Dizzy"
Gordon, Dexter
Gordy, Berry, Jr.
Gottschalk, Louis Moreau
Grant, Micki
Green, Al
Guy, George "Buddy"
Handy, W(illiam) C(hristopher)
Harris, James "Jimmy Jam," III, and
 Lewis, Terry
Harris, Margaret R.
Harris, Robert Allen
Hathaway, Donny
Hayes, Isaac
Heath, James Edward "Jimmy"
Hines, Earl Kenneth "Fatha"
Holland-Dozier-Holland
Hopkins, Claude Driskett
Ingram, James
Jackson, Michael Joseph
Jackson, Millie
Jaxon, Frankie "Half-Pint"
Johnson, Albert J. "Budd"
Johnson, Georgia
Johnson, J(ohn) Rosamond
Johnson, James Louis "J. J."
Johnson, James P(rice)
Johnson, James Weldon
Jones, Quincy Delight, Jr.
Jones, Richard Myknee
Joplin, Scott
Kay, Ulysses
Kendrick(s), Eddie
Khan, Chaka
King, Ben E.
LaBelle, Patti
Lateef, Yusef
Lewis, Terry. *See* Harris, James
Lincoln, Abbey
McPhatter, Clyde
Marsalis, Wynton
Mayfield, Curtis
Millinder, Lucius Venable "Lucky"
Mingus, Charlie
Monk, Thelonious Sphere
Morton, Ferdinand Joseph La Menthe
 "Jelly Roll"
Oliver, Melvin James "Sy"
Ory, Edward "Kid"
Parker, Ray, Jr.
Parks, Gordon, Sr.
Perkinson, Coleridge-Taylor
Perry, Julia
Price, Lloyd
Prince
Redman, Donald Matthew "Don"
Robinson, William "Smokey," Jr.
Sampson, Edgar Melvin "The Lamb"
Schuyler, Philippa Duke

Shorter, Wayne
Silver, Horace
Silverstein, Shel(by)
Sissle, Noble
Smith, Hale
Snow, Phoebe
Still, William Grant
Strayhorn, Billy
Summer, Donna
Swanson, Howard
Tindley, Charles Albert
Toussaint, Allen
Waller, Thomas Wright "Fats"
Ward, Clara
Webb, William Henry "Chick"
White, Barry
White, Maurice
Whitfield, Norman
Williams, Mary Lou
Wilson, Olly
Winbush, Angela
Womack, Bobby

CONDUCTORS, MUSICAL

Baker, David
Brown, Joyce
Carter, Bennett Lester "Benny"
Coleridge-Taylor, Samuel
Cordero, Roque
DePriest, James
Dixon, Dean
Harris, Margaret R.
Harris, Robert Allen
Millinder, Lucius Venable "Lucky"
Moten, Benjamin "Bennie"
Perkinson, Coleridge-Taylor
Redman, Donald Matthew "Don"
Sissle, Noble
Still, William Grant

COWBOYS. *See* PIONEERS

DANCERS and CHOREOGRAPHERS

Ailey, Alvin, Jr
Allen, Debbie
Atkins, Charles "Cholly"
Baker, Josephine
Bates, Clayton "Peg Leg"
Berry Brothers, The
Briggs, Bunny
Brown, Bobby
Brown, Ernest
Bubbles, John
Burge, Gregg
Cara, Irene
Coles, Charles "Honi"
Collins, Janet
Cook, Charles "Cookie"
Davis, Sammy, Jr.
De Lavallade, Carmen
Duncan, Arthur
Dunham, Katherine
Glover, Savion

Green, Charles "Chuck"
Guy, Jasmine
Hammer
Hines Brothers, The
Hines, Gregory Oliver
Hinkson, Mary
Holder, Geoffrey Lamont
Jackson, "Baby" Laurence
Jackson, Janet
Jackson, Michael
Jamison, Judith
Johnson, Louis
Johnson, Virginia Alma Fairfax
Jones, Bill T.
Kelly, Paula
Lane, William Henry "Master Juba"
Lemon, Ralph
LeTang, Henry
Long, Avon
Millinder, Lucius Venable "Lucky"
Mills, Florence
Mitchell, Arthur
Nicholas Brothers, The
Nugent, Pete
Primus, Pearl
Ray, Gene Anthony
Rector, Eddie
Robinson, Bill "Bojangles"
Sims, Howard "Sandman"
Slyde, Jimmy
Step Brothers, The
Vereen, Ben
Washington, Lula
Watley, Jody
Whitman Sisters, The
Winfield, Hemsley

DIRECTORS, FILM, TELEVISION, and STAGE

Allen, Debbie
Brown, Georg Stanford
Carroll, Vinnette Justine
Dash, Julie
Davis, Collis H., Jr.
Davis, Ossie
Dawson, Daniel D.
Dickerson, Ernest
Duke, William "Bill"
Fletcher, Robert E.
Gordone, Charles
Gordy, Berry, Jr.
Harris, Doug
Henderson, Leroy W.
Holder, Geoffrey Lamont
Hooks, Kevin
Hudlin, Reginald
Hudlin, Warrington
Lange, Ted W., III
Lee, Shelton Jackson "Spike"
Mannas, Jimmie
Micheaux, Oscar
O'Neal, Frederick
Parks, Gordon, Sr.

Perry, Shauneille
Poitier, Sidney
Rich, Matty
Richards, Lloyd
Robertson, Stanley
Singleton, John
Smith, Anna Deavere
Townsend, Robert
Van Peebles, Mario
Van Peebles, Melvin
Ward, Douglas Turner
Watkins, Perry
Wayans, Keenen Ivory
Williamson, Fred

ECONOMISTS. *See* SOCIAL SCIENTISTS

EDUCATORS

Alston, Charles
Andrews, Benny
Arrington, Richard
Artis, William E.
Asante, Molefi Kete
Avery, Margaret
Baker, Augusta Braxton
Baker, David
Baker, Houston Alfred, Jr.
Barksdale, Richard K.
Ben-Jochannan, Yosef
Berry, Mary Frances
Bethune, Mary McLeod
Biggers, John
Billingsley, Andrew
Billops, Camille J.
Bond, Horace Mann
Bouchet, Edward Alexander
Bradley, David
Brawley, Benjamin Griffith
Brimmer, Andrew Felton
Brooks, Avery
Brown, Charlotte Hawkins
Brown, Dorothy Lavinia
Brown, Hallie Q.
Brown, Sterling Allen
Browne, Vivian
Bullock, Star(manda)
Burke, Selma
Burroughs, Nannie Helen
Butcher, Philip
Canady, Hortense
Carter, Lisle Carleton, Jr.
Carver, George Washington
Chandler, Dana
Cheek, James
Cheek, King
Chennault, Madelyn
Clark, Kenneth Bancroft
Clarke, John Henrik
Cobb, William Montague
Coker, Daniel
Cole, Johnnetta Betsch
Cole, Thomas W., Jr.

Collins, Marva
Comer, James Pierpont
Cook, Mercer
Cook, Samuel DuBois
Cooper, Anna Julia Haywood
Cortor, Eldzier
Crim, Alonzo
Cross, Theodore L.
Curtis, Austin Maurice, Sr.
Davis, Arthur Paul
Davis, Charles Twitchell
Davis, Frances Reed Elliott
Davis, Lenwood G.
DePillars, Murry Norman
Drew, Charles Richard
Edwards, Alfred Leroy
Edwards, Cecile Hoover
Edwards, Melvin E.
Evans, Mari
Fletcher, Robert E.
Forten, Charlotte
Frazier, E(dward) Franklin
Futrell, Mary Hatwood
Gates, Henry Louis, Jr.
Georgiou, Tyrone
Gloster, Hugh
Greener, Richard
Grimké, Angelina (Emily) Weld
Hamilton, Charles Vernon
Hare, Nathan
Harper, Frances E. W.
Harris, James A.
Harris, Robert Allen
Haskins, James S.
Hathaway, Isaac
Heath, James Edward "Jimmy"
Hill, Anita Faye
Hill, Herbert
Hilliard, Asa Grant, III
Hine, Darlene Clark
Hinton, William Augustus
Holland, Jerome H.
Hooks, Bell
Inman, Dorothy J. "Lee"
Irvis, K. Leroy
Jackson, May Howard
Jackson, Reginald L.
Jeffries, Leonard
Jenifer, Franklyn Green
Jenkins, Martin David
Johnson, Charles Spurgeon
Johnson, James Weldon
Johnson, Mordecai Wyatt
Jones, Lois Mailou
Jordan, June
Kent, George E.
Killens, John Oliver
Lane, Isaac
Laney, Lucy Craft
Langston, John Mercer
Lawrence, Jacob
Lewis, Samella Sanders
Lincoln, C(harles) Eric

Locke, Alain Leroy
Loury, Glenn C.
McCullough, Geraldine
McGee, Henry Wadsworth, Jr.
McHenry, Donald F.
Madhubuti, Haki R.
Marable, Manning
Martin, Tony
Mayfield, Julian
Mays, Benjamin Elijah
Merritt, Emma Frances Grayson
Miller, Earl B.
Miller, Kelly
Morrison, Toni
Morrow, John Howard, Sr.
Moses, Robert Parris
Moton, Robert
Nabrit, Samuel
Neal, Larry
Noble, Jeanne L.
Norton, Eleanor Holmes
Parsons, James Benton
Payne, Daniel Alexander
Peery, Benjamin Franklin, Jr.
Peoples, John Arthur, Jr.
Player, Willa Beatrice
Pontiflet, Ted
Porter, James Amos
Poussaint, Alvin Francis
Primus, Pearl
Quarles, Benjamin
Raboteau, Albert Jordy
Redding, Jay Saunders
Redmond, Eugene
Riles, Wilson
Ringgold, Faith
Robeson, Paul
Robinson, Jo Ann Gibson
Rodney, Walter
Savage, Augusta
Scarborough, William Sanders
Schomburg, Arthur
Shadd, Mary Ann
Smythe, Hugh H.
Sowell, Thomas
Spearman, Leonard Hall O'Connell
Sudarkasa, Niara
Sullivan, Louis Wade
Thomas, Bettye Collier
Thurman, Howard
Turner, Darwin Theodore Troy
Turner, James Milton
Walker, Margaret Abigail
Walters, Ronald
Washington, Booker T(aliaferro)
Washington, Mary Helen
West, Cornel
Wharton, Clifton Reginald, Jr.
Wideman, John Edgar
Williams, John Alfred
Willie, Charles Vert
Wilson, John
Wright, Nathan, Jr.

Wright-Jones, Jane Cooke
Young, Nathan Benjamin

ENGINEERS. *See* ARCHITECTS

FASHION DESIGNERS and MODELS
Brock, Gertha
Chanticleer, Raven
Iman
Johnson, Beverly
Jones, Grace
Lowe, Ann
Sebree, Charles
Sims, Naomi
Smith, Willi
Tadlock, Robert
Watkins, Perry

FOOTBALL PLAYERS
Allen, Marcus
Brown, Jim
Brown, Robert
Campbell, Earl Christian
Casey, Bernie
Cunningham, Randall
Davis, Ernie
Dickerson, Eric Demetric
Dorsett, Anthony Drew "Tony"
Eller, Carl Lee
Gaither, Alonzo "Jake"
Green, Darrell
Greene, Charles Edward "Mean Joe"
Grier, Roosevelt "Rosey"
Griffin, Archie Mason
Harris, Franco
Harris, James "Shack"
Hayes, Bob
Jackson, Bo
Joiner, Charles "Charlie," Jr.
Kelly, Leroy
Lane, Richard "Night Train"
Little, Floyd Douglas
Marshall, James Laurence "Jim"
Mitchell, Robert Cornelius "Bobby"
Moore, Lenny
Page, Alan
Parker, James Thomas
Payton, Walter
Perry, Fletcher Joseph "Joe"
Pollard, Frederick "Fritz," Sr.
Powell, Arthur L. "Art"
Rashad, Ahmad
Rice, Jerry
Robinson, Edward Gay "Eddie"
Rodgers, John "Johnny"
Sayers, Gale Eugene
Shell, Arthur "Art"
Simpson, Orenthal James "O.J."
Taylor, Charles Robert "Charley"
Taylor, Lawrence "L. T."
Tunnell, Emlen "Em"
Walker, Herschel
Warfield, Paul D.

Washington, Kenneth S. "Kenny"
Williams, Douglas Lee
Young, Claude Henry "Buddy"
Younger, Paul "Tank"

FUGITIVE SLAVES
Brown, Henry "Box"
Burns, Anthony
Cato
Cinque, Joseph
Gabriel
Henson, Josiah
Tubman, Harriet
Turner, Nat
Vesey, Denmark

HISTORIANS. *See* SOCIAL SCIENTISTS

INVENTORS. *See also* SCIENTISTS
Baker, David
Banneker, Benjamin
Beard, Andrew Jackson
Blair, Henry C.
Boone, Sarah
Carruthers, George R.
Crosthwait, David Nelson, Jr.
Ferrell, Frank J.
Goode, Sarah E.
Hillery, John Richard
Jackson, Benjamin F.
Jones, Frederick McKinley
Latimer, Lewis Howard
Leslie, F. W.
McCoy, Elijah
Matzeliger, Jan Earnst
Morgan, Garrett Augustus
Rhodes, J. B.
Richardson, W. H.
Rillieux, Norbert
Robinson, Elbert R.
Spikes, Richard B.
Temple, Lewis
Thrash, Dox
Woods, Granville T.

JOURNALISTS. *See also* TELEVISION PERSONALITIES and BROADCAST JOURNALISTS
Abbott, Robert Sengstacke
Anthony, Michael
Baker, Denise
Barksdale, Richard K.
Barnett, Ferdinand Lee
Beasley, Delilah Leontium
Bluford, Lucile H.
Bolden, J. Taber, Jr.
Bond, Anna Monique
Bradley, Ed
Brown, William Anthony "Tony"
Clarke, John Henrik
Fortune, T(imothy) Thomas
Gilbert, Jarobin, Jr.

Gilliam, Dorothy Butler
Goode, Malvin R.
Gordon, Edwin Jason
Graham, Gordon
Gumbel, Bryant Charles
Hatcher, Andrew T.
Higgins, Chester A., Sr.
Hunter-Gault, Charlayne
Jackson, Fay M.
Johnson, James Weldon
Jordan, June
Kennedy, Royal
King, Emery
Matney, William C., Jr.
Matthews, (Ann) Victoria Earle
Mossell, Gertrude Bustill
Murphy, Carl
Nell, William C.
Payne, Ethel
Perez, Anna
Perkins, Joseph
Petry, Ann
Pierce, Ponchitta Anne
Quarles, Norma
Reynolds, Barbara Ann
Rogers, Joel A.
Rowan, Carl Thomas
Ruggles, David
Russwurm, John Brown
Schuyler, George Samuel
Schuyler, Philippa Duke
Shadd, Mary Ann
Simpson, Carole
Taylor, Susan L.
Teague, Robert "Bob"
Thompson, Era Bell
Tolliver, Melba
Tucker, Lemuel "Lem"
Wallace, Michele
Watkins, Joseph Philip
Williams, John Alfred
Woods, Howard B.

JUDGES and LAWYERS
Allen, Milton Burk
Anderson, Sarah A.
Bolin, Jane Matilda
Bryant, William Benson
Carey, Archibald J., Jr.
Carter, Robert Lee
Christian, Almeric
Collins, Robert Frederick
Cook, Julian Abele, Jr.
Cooper, Julia
Dudley, Edward Richard
Erwin, Richard C.
Green, Clifford Scott
Hargrove, John R.
Hastie, William Henry
Hatchett, Joseph Woodrow
Horton, Odell
Hoyt, Kenneth
Jones, Nathaniel Raphael

Kearse, Amalya Lyle
Keith, Damon Jerome
McCree, Wade Hampton, Jr.
McDonald, Gabrielle Kirk
McKissick, Floyd Bixler, Sr.
McMillian, Theodore
Marshall, Thurgood
Motley, Constance Baker
Nix, Robert Nelson Cornelius, Jr.
Parker, Barrington Daniels
Parsons, James Benton
Pierce, Lawrence Warren
Pierce, Samuel Riley, Jr.
Richardson, Scovel
Robinson, Aubrey E., Jr.
Robinson, Spottswood W., III
Sampson, Edith
Simmons, Paul A.
Tanner, Jack Edward
Thomas, Clarence
Waddy, Joseph C.
Watson, James L.
Williams, Albert P.
Williams, Ann Claire
Williams, David Welford
Wingate, Henry T.

LABOR LEADERS. *See* BUSINESS-PEOPLE

LAWYERS. *See* JUDGES

LIBRARIANS. *See* EDUCATORS

MATHEMATICIANS. *See* SCIENTISTS

MAYORS. *See also* POLITICIANS
Arrington, Richard
Barnes, Thomas
Barry, Marion Shepilov, Jr.
Barthelemy, Sidney John
Berry, Theodore M.
Blackwood, Ronald A.
Box, Charles E.
Bradley, Thomas J.
Burney, William D., Jr.
Busby, Jim
Chase, James E.
Cooper, Algernon J.
Dinkins, David
Dixon, Richard Clay
Dixon, Sharon Pratt
Floyd, James A.
Foley, Lelia Kasenia Smith
Gaines, Paul L., Sr.
Gantt, Harvey Bernard
Garner, James N.
Gibson, Kenneth A.
Goode, W(illie) Wilson
Hatcher, John C., Jr.
Inman, Dorothy J. "Lee"
James, Sharpe
Larkins, E. Pat

Lee, Howard N., Jr.
Livingston, George
McGee, James Howell
Milner, Thirman L.
Moore, Walter Louis
Morial, Ernest Nathan "Dutch"
Officer, Carl E.
Perry, Carrie Saxon
Primas, Melvin Randolph "Randy," Jr.
Rice, Norman Blann
Sawyer, Eugene
Schmoke, Kurt Liddell
Shackelford, Lottie Holt
Stokes, Carl Burton
Summers, Edna White
Taylor, Noel C.
Vincent, Edward
Washington, Harold
Washington, Walter E.
West, Roy A.
Wilson, Lionel J.
Young, Coleman Alexander

MEDICAL PRACTITIONERS
Adams, Numa Pompilius Garfield
Adams-Ender, Clara Leach
Augusta, Alexander Thomas
Barnett, Constantine Clinton
Bowen, Clotilde Marian Dent
Boyd, Robert Fulton
Brown, Dorothy Lavinia
Cardozo, W(illiam) Warrick
Carson, Benjamin Solomon
Chennault, Madelyn
Clark, Kenneth Bancroft
Cobb, William Montague
Cole, Rebecca J.
Comer, James Pierpont
Crumpler, Rebecca Lee
Curtis, Austin Maurice, Sr.
Dailey, Ulysses Grant
Davis, Frances Reed Elliott
Drew, Charles Richard
Fisher, Rudolph
Green, Henry Morgan
Hale, Clara McBride
Hall, George Cleveland
Hinton, William Augustus
Jemison, Mae C.
Kountz, Samuel Lee, Jr.
Lathen, John William
Lattimer, Agnes Delores
Lawless, Theodore K.
Lewis, Julian Herman
Lynk, Miles Vandahurst
McGee, James Howell
Mossell, Nathan Francis
Nichols, Barbara Lauraine
Payne, Clarence H.
Payne, Howard Marshall
Poussaint, Alvin Francis
Smith, James McCune
Wattleton, (Alyce) Faye

Welsing, Frances Cress
West, Lightfoot Allen
Williams, Daniel Hale
Wright, Louis Tompkins
Wright-Jones, Jane Cooke

MILITARY PERSONNEL
Adams, Robert Bradshaw
Adams-Ender, Clara Leach
Anderson, James, Jr.
Anderson, Webster
Arnold, Wallace Cornelius
Attucks, Crispus
Becton, Julius Wesley, Jr.
Boddie, James Timothy, Jr.
Bowen, Clotilde Marian Dent
Brailsford, Marvin Delano
Brooks, Elmer T.
Brooks, Harry William, Jr.
Brooks, Leo Austin
Brown, Coverdale, Jr.
Brown, John Mitchell, Sr.
Brown, William E., Jr.
Bryant, Cunningham Campbell
Bussey, Charles David
Byrd, Melvin Leon
Cadoria, Sherian Grace
Carney, William H.
Cartwright, Roscoe Conklin
Chambers, Andrew Phillip
Charlton, Cornelius H.
Charlton, Samuel
Clifford, Thomas E.
Cromartie, Eugene Rufus
Cromwell, Oliver
Curry, Jerry Ralph
Davis, Benjamin O., Jr.
Davis, Benjamin O., Sr.
Davis, Rodney M.
Davison, Frederic Ellis
Delandro, Donald Joseph
Doctor, Henry, Jr.
Durham, Archer L.
Ferguson, Alonzo L.
Flipper, Henry Ossian
Flora, William
Forte, Johnnie, Jr.
Fraunces, Samuel
Freeman, Jordan
Gaskill, Robert Clarence
Gorden, Fred Augustus
Gravely, Samuel L., Jr.
Greer, Edward
Gregg, Arthur James
Hall, David McKenzie
Hall, James Reginald, Jr.
Hall, Titus C.
Hamlet, James Frank
Haynes, Lemuel
Hector, Edward
Hines, Charles Alfonso
Holmes, Arthur
Honor, Edward

Honore, Charles Edward
Hull, Agrippa
Hunton, Benjamin Lacy
James, Avon C., Jr.
James, Daniel "Chappie"
Jiggetts, Charles B.
Johnson, Hazel Winifred
Johnson, Henry
Klugh, James Richard
Lafayette, James Armistead
Lawson, John
Lew, Barzillai
McCall, James Franklin
Matthews, Saul
Miller, Doris "Dorie"
Nash, Charles Edmund
Olive, Milton L., III
Paige, Emmett, Jr.
Parker, Julius, Jr.
Petersen, Frank E.
Pitts, Riley Leroy
Poor, Salem
Powell, Colin Luther
Powers, Winston D.
Randolph, Bernard P.
Ranger, Joseph
Robinson, Hugh Granville
Robinson, James
Robinson, Roscoe, Jr.
Rogers, Charles Calvin
Rozier, Jackson Evander, Jr.
Salem, Peter
Sheffey, Fred Clifton, Jr.
Short, Alonzo Earl, Jr.
Sisson, Tack
Smalls, Robert
Smith, Isaac Dixon
Stanford, John Henry
Tarrant, Caesar
Theus, Lucius
Thomas, Gerald Eustis
Thompson, William H.
Waller, Calvin Augustine Hoffman
Whipple, Prince
Williams, Charles Edward
Williams, George Washington
Williams, Harvey Dean
Young, Charles

MODELS. *See* **FASHION DESIGNERS**

MUSICIANS and SINGERS. *See also*
    COMPOSERS and
    SONGWRITERS *and*
    CONDUCTORS

Blues and Rhythm and Blues
Ammons, Albert
Baker, LaVern
Blackwell, Francis Hillman "Scrapper"
Bland, Bobby "Blue"
Broonzy, Big Bill
Campbell, James "Little Milton"

Carr, Leroy
Cox, Ida
Cray, Robert
Crudup, Arthur "Big Boy"
Davis, "Reverend" Gary
Dixon, "Big" Willie
Dorsey, Thomas A.
Guy, Buddy
Handy, W. C.
Harpo, Slim
Hooker, John Lee
Hopkins, Sam "Lightnin' "
House, Eddie "Son"
Howlin' Wolf
Hunter, Alberta
Hurt, "Mississippi" John
Hutto, Joseph Benjamin "J. B."
James, Elmore
Jaxon, Frankie "Half-Pint"
Jefferson, "Blind" Lemon
Johnson, Lonnie
Johnson, Robert
King, B. B.
Leadbelly
Little Walter
McTell, Blind Willie
Memphis Minnie
Memphis Slim
Milburn, Amos
Muddy Waters
Odetta
Patton, Charley
Professor Longhair
Rainey, Ma
Reed, Jimmy
Rush, Otis
Rushing, Jimmy
Scott, Hazel
Seals, Frank "Son"
Shaw, Marlena
Shines, Johnny
Smith, Bessie
Smith, Mamie
Spand, Charlie
Tampa Red
Taylor, Koko
Thornton, Willie Mae "Big Mama"
Walker, Aaron Thibeaux "T-Bone"
Wallace, Beulah "Sippie"
Wells, Junior
Williamson, John Lee "Sonny Boy"
Williamson, Sonny Boy, II
Wright, Betty

Gospel
Burleigh, Harry T.
Caesar, Shirley
Caravans, The
Clark Sisters, The
Cleveland, James
Coates, Dorothy Love
Cooke, Sam
Crouch, Andrae

Dixie Hummingbirds, The
Dixon, Jessy
Dorsey, Thomas A.
Fisk Jubilee Singers
Gates, J. M.
Green, Al
Hawkins, Edwin R.
Hawkins, Tramaine Davis
Houston, Cissy
Jackson Harmoneers
Jackson, Mahalia
Kings of Harmony, The
Knight, Marie
Martin, Sallie
Mighty Clouds of Joy, The
Nightingales, the
Original Gospel Harmonettes, The
Roberta Martin Singers
Smith, Willie Mae Ford
Soul Stirrers, The
Sweet Honey in the Rock
Taylor, Johnnie
Tharpe, Sister Rosetta
Ward, Clara
Winans, Benjamin "BeBe" and Cecelia
  "CeCe"
Winans, The

Jazz
Adderley, Julian Edwin "Cannonball"
Adderley, Nathaniel "Nat," Sr.
Albright, Gerald
Anderson, Ivie
Anderson, William "Cat"
Armstrong, Louis
Austin, Patti
Baker, David
Barefield, Edward Emmanuel "Eddie"
Basie, William "Count"
Bechet, Sidney Joseph
Benson, George
Blakey, Art
Blythe, Arthur
Bolden, Charles Joseph "Buddy"
Bradford, (John Henry) Perry "Mule"
Brown, Clifford "Brownie"
Brown, Marion
Brown, Ray
Byas, Don
Byrd, Donald
Callender, George Sylvester "Red"
Calloway, Cabell "Cab," III
Carn, Jean
Carney, Howell "Harry"
Carter, Bennett Lester "Benny"
Carter, Betty
Charles, Ray
Christian, Charles "Charlie"
Clarke, Stanley Marvin
Coleman, Ornette
Coltrane, Alice
Coltrane, John William
Daniels, Billy

Daniels, Jimmy
Davis, Miles Dewey
Dixon, Charles Edward "Charlie"
Dodds, Johnny
Durham, Eddie
Eckstine, Billy
Eldridge, Roy
Ellington, Edward Kennedy "Duke"
Ellington, Mercer Kennedy
Europe, James Reese
Farmer, Art
Fitzgerald, Ella
Foster, George Murphy "Pops"
Gaillard, Slim
Garner, Erroll
Gillespie, John Birks "Dizzy"
Gordon, Dexter
Gottschalk, Louis Moreau
Hampton, Lionel
Hancock, Herbie
Handy, John Richard, III
Harney, Ben
Hartman, Johnny
Hawkins, Coleman
Hawkins, Erskine
Heath, James Edward "Jimmy"
Henderson, Fletcher
Hill, Bertha "Chippie"
Hines, Earl "Fatha"
Hinton, Milton J.
Hodges, John Cornelius "Johnny"
Holiday, Billie
Hopkins, Claude Driskett
Horn, Shirley
Horne, Lena
Jackson, Milt
Jamal, Ahmad
Jarreau, Al
Jazz Crusaders, The
Johnson, Albert J. "Budd"
Johnson, James Louis "J. J."
Johnson, James P.
Johnson, William Geary "Bunk"
Jones, Elvin Ray
Jones, Henry "Hank"
Jones, Quincy Delight, Jr.
Jones, Richard Myknee
Joplin, Scott
Jordan, Stanley
King Curtis
Kirk, Rahsaan Roland
Klugh, Earl
Lateef, Yusef
Lewis, Ramsey
Lincoln, Abbey
Lunceford, James Melvin "Jimmie"
McCann, Leslie Coleman "Les"
McFerrin, Bobby, Jr.
McGriff, Jimmy
McRae, Carmen
Marsalis, Branford
Marsalis, Wynton
Mills Brothers

Mingus, Charlie
Mingus Dynasty
Modern Jazz Quartet
Monk, Thelonious
Montgomery, John Leslie "Wes"
Moody, James
Morgan, Lee
Morton, Benny
Morton, Ferdinand Joseph La Menthe
  "Jelly Roll"
Moten, Benjamin "Benny"
Navarro, Theodore "Fats"
Noone, Jimmie
Oliver, King
Oliver, Melvin James "Sy"
Ory, Edward "Kid"
Page, Oran "Hot Lips"
Parker, Charlie "Bird"
Peterson, Oscar
Powell, Earl "Bud"
Redman, Don
Reeves, Dianne
Richmond, June
Roach, Max
Rollins, Sonny
Rushing, Jimmy
St. Cyr, John Alexander "Johnny"
Sampson, Edgar Melvin "The Lamb"
Scott, Hazel
Shaw, Marlena
Shepp, Archie
Short, Bobby
Shorter, Wayne
Silver, Horace
Smith, James Oscar "Jimmy"
Smith, Willie "the Lion"
Stitt, Edward "Sonny"
Strayhorn, Billy
Sullivan, Maxine
Take 6
Tatum, Art, Jr.
Taylor, William "Billy"
Tyner, (Alfred) McCoy "Sulaimon Saud"
Vaughan, Sarah
Waller, Thomas Wright "Fats"
Washington, Dinah
Washington, Grover, Jr.
Webb, William Henry "Chick"
Webster, Ben
Williams, Joe
Williams, Mary Lou
Williams, Stanley R. "Fess"
Wilson, Nancy
Wilson, Theodore Shaw "Teddy"
World Saxophone Quartet
Young, Lester "Pres" or "Prez"

Opera and Classical
Addison, Adele
Allen, Betty Lou
Anderson, Marian
Arroyo, Martina
Battle, Kathleen

Bethune, Thomas Green "Blind Tom"
Bonds, Margaret Allison
Bryant, Joyce
Bumbry, Grace Ann
Conrad, Barbara
Cordero, Roque
Dobbs, Mattiwilda
Duncan, Todd
Estes, Simon
Evanti, Lillian
Greenfield, Elizabeth Taylor
Grist, Reri
Harris, Margaret R.
Hayes, Roland
Hyers Sisters
Jones, Sissieretta
Kay, Ulysses
McFerrin, Robert, Sr.
Maynor, Dorothy
Mitchell, Nellie E. Brown
Norman, Jessye
Price, Leontyne
Schuyler, Philippa Duke
Selika, Marie
Shirley, George
Verrett, Shirley
Warfield, William
Watts, Andre

Popular

Adams, Faye
Adams, Oleta
Ashford and Simpson
Atlantic Starr
Bailey, Pearl
Baker, Anita
Baker, Josephine
Baker, LaVern
Bar-Kays, The
Bassey, Shirley
Belafonte, Harry
Bell Biv DeVoe
Benton, Brook
Berry, Charles Edward Anderson
    "Chuck"
Blackbyrds, The
Blake, Eubie
Bland, Bobby "Blue"
Bland, James
Booker T. and the MGs
Boys, The
Brooks, Avery
Brown, Bobby
Brown, James
Brown, Roy
Brown, Ruth Weston
Bryant, Joyce
Bryson, Robert Peabo
Butler, Jerry
Cameo
Campbell, James "Little" Milton
Campbell, Tevin
Cara, Irene

Carroll, Diahann
Carter, Nell
Chantels, The
Chapman, Tracy
Charles, Ray
Checker, Chubby
Chenier, Clifton
Chiffons, The
Chi-Lites, The
Clark, Delectus "Dee"
Coasters, The
Cole, Nat "King"
Cole, Natalie
Commodores, The
Cooke, Sam
Crawford, Randy
Crudup, Arthur "Big Boy"
Crystals, The
Davis, Sammy, Jr.
Day, Morris
DeBarge
Delfonics, The
Dells, The
Diddley, Bo
Domino, Antoine "Fats"
Dramatics, The
Drifters, The
Dynasty
Earth, Wind, and Fire
Emotions, The
En Vogue
Fifth Dimension
First Choice
Flack, Roberta
Four Tops, The
Frankie Lymon and the Teenagers
Franklin, Aretha
Gaye, Marvin
Gaynor, Gloria
Gladys Knight and the Pips
Green, Al
Harney, Ben
Hathaway, Donny
Havens, Richie
Hayes, Isaac
Hendrix, Jimi
Hewett, Howard
Holliday, Jennifer
Holloway, Brenda
Holman, Eddie
Horne, Lena
Houston, Whitney
Howard, Miki
Hyers Sisters
Hyman, Phyllis
Impressions, The
Ingram, James
Ink Spots, The
Isley Brothers, The
Jackson 5, The
Jackson, Freddie
Jackson, Janet
Jackson, Jermaine La Jaune

Jackson, Michael
Jackson, Millie
James, Etta
James, Rick
Jaye, Miles
Johnson, J. Rosamond
Johnson, Jesse
Jones, Bobby
Jones, Grace
Junior Walker and the All-Stars
Kelly, Paula
Kendrick(s), Eddie
Khan, Chaka
King, Ben E.
King, Evelyn "Champagne"
Kitt, Eartha
Kool and the Gang
Kotero, Patricia "Apollonia"
Kravitz, Lenny
LaBelle, Patti
Lakeside
Lattisaw, Stacy
Levert
Little Anthony and the Imperials
Little Eva
Little Richard
Living Colour
Long, Avon
McKee, Lonette
McNair, Barbara
McPhatter, Clyde
Martha and the Vandellas
Marvelettes, The
Mathis, Johnny
Mayfield, Curtis
Midnight Star
Mills Brothers
Mills, Florence
Mills, Stephanie
Miracles, The
Mitchell, Abbie
Moore, Melba
Morgan, Meli'sa
Nash, Johnny
Neville, Aaron
Neville Brothers, The
New Edition
Odetta
O'Jays, The
O'Neal, Alexander
Orioles, The
Parker, Ray, Jr.
Parliament/Funkadelic
Paul, Billy
Pendergrass, "Teddy"
Persuaders, The
Persuasions, The
Peterson, Oscar
Phillips, Esther
Pickett, Wilson
Platters, The
Pointer Sisters, The
Preston, Billy

Price, Lloyd
Pride, Charley
Prince
Raeletts, The
Rawls, Lou
Redding, Otis
Reese, Della
Richie, Lionel
Riley, Cheryl "Pepsii"
Riperton, Minnie
Robeson, Paul
Robinson, William "Smokey," Jr.
Rockwell
Ronettes, The
Ross, Diana
Ruffin, David
Rufus
Sam and Dave
Scott-Heron, Gil
Shalamar
Sheila E(scovedo)
Shirelles, The
Simone, Nina
Sister Sledge
Sledge, Percy
Sly and the Family Stone
Snow, Phoebe
Spinners, The
Staples, The
Starr, Edwin
Stylistics, The
Summer, Donna
Supremes, The
Sylvers, The
Sylvester
Syreeta
Taylor, Johnnie
Temptations, The
Terrell, Tammi
Thomas, Carla
Thomas, Rufus
Thornton, Willie Mae "Big Mama"
Tresvant, Ralph
Troop
Turner, Ike
Turner, Tina
Uggams, Leslie
Vandross, Luther
Vanity
Vereen, Ben
War
Warwick, Dionne
Washington, Dinah
Waters, Ethel
Watley, Jody
Wells, Mary
Whispers, The
White, Barry
White, Maurice
Williams, Deniece
Williams, Vanessa
Williams, Vesta
Wilson, Jackie

Wilson, Mary
Wilson, Shanice
Winbush, Angela
Womack, Bobby
Wonder, Stevie
Yancey, James Edward "Jimmy"

Rap
Bambaataa, Afrika
Blow, Kurtis
Chubb Rock
Digital Underground
Doug E. Fresh
E.P.M.D.
Fat Boys, The
Father MC
Grandmaster Flash and the Furious Five
Hammer
Heavy D.
Ice-T
Kane, Big Daddy
Kool Moe Dee
KRS-One
Last Poets
L.L. Cool J.
M.C. Lyte
Naughty by Nature
NWA
Public Enemy
Queen Latifah
Run-D.M.C.
Salt-N-Pepa
Shocklee, Hank
Simmons, Russell
2 Live Crew
Walters, Ricky "Slick Rick"
Whodini
Young M.C.

PHOTOGRAPHERS
Agins, Michell
Allen, Jules
Allen, Winifred Hall
Austin, Hansen
Bailey, John B.
Ball, James Presley
Cryor, Cary Beth
Davis, Billie Louise Barbour
Davis, Collis, H., Jr.
Davis, Griffith J.
Davis, Pat
Dawson, Daniel D.
DeCarava, Roy
Draper, Louis H.
DuMetz, Barbara
Ferrill, Mikki
Fletcher, Robert E.
Freeman, Roland
Georgiou, Tyrone
Grice, Francis
Hardison, Inge
Harris, Doug
Harris, Frank

Henderson, Leroy W.
Higgins, Chester, Jr.
Hinton, Milton J.
Jackson, Reginald L.
Jefferson, Louise
Lewis, Roy
Lion, Jules
Mannas, Jimmie
Martin, Louise
Moutoussamy-Ashe, Jeanne
Muhammad, Ozier
Parks, Gordon, Sr.
Pontiflet, Ted
Roberts, Richard Samuel
Roberts, Wilhelmina Pearl Selena
Robinson, Rudolph
Saunders, Richard
Scales, Jeffrey Charles
Shepherd, Harry
Sherman, Edward Forrester
Simpson, Coreen
Simpson, Lorna
Sleet, Moneta, Jr.
Smith, Beuford
Stewart, Chuck
Stewart, Frank
Sunday, Elisabeth
Van Der Zee, James Augustus Joseph
Weems, Carrie Mae

PHYSICISTS. *See* **SCIENTISTS**

PIONEERS and COWBOYS
Beckwourth, James Pierson
Brown, Clara
Bush, George W.
Campbell, "Aunt" Sally
Dart, Isom
Fields, Mary
Henson, Matthew Alexander
Love, Nat
Pickett, Bill
Washington, George
York

POLITICIANS. *See also* **MAYORS**
Alexander, Clifford L., Jr.
Alexander, Lenora Cole
Allen, Milton Burk
Amerson, Lucius D.
Anderson, Sarah A.
Arrington, Richard
Atkins, Hannah Diggs
Austin, Richard H.
Baker, James E.
Barrett, Brenetta Howell
Barry, Marion Shepilov, Jr.
Barthelemy, Sidney John
Bass, Charlotta Spears
Berry, Mary Frances
Bethune, Mary McLeod
Bond, (Horace) Julian
Borges, Francisco L.

Bradley, Melvin L. P.
Bradley, Thomas J.
Braun, Carol E. Moseley
Brokenburr, Robert Lee
Brooke, Edward William
Brown, George L.
Brown, Ronald H.
Bruce, Blanche Kelso
Bunche, Ralph J.
Burke, Yvonne Brathwaite
Burris, Roland W.
Cain, Richard Harvey
Cardozo, Francis Louis
Carey, Archibald J., Jr.
Carter, Lisle Carleton, Jr.
Chapin, Arthur A.
Cheatham, Henry Plummer
Chisholm, Shirley
Clay, William Lacy
Coleman, William Thaddeus, Jr.
Collins, Cardiss Robertson
Collins, George Washington
Conyers, John, Jr.
Cook, Mercer
Crockett, George William, Jr.
Curry, Jerry Ralph
Davis, Henrietta Vinton
Davis, Preston Augustus
Dawson, William Levi
Days, Drew Saunders, III
De Large, Robert Carlos
Dellums, Ronald V.
Depriest, Oscar
Diggs, Charles Coles, Jr.
Dinkins, David
Dixon, Julian C.
Dixon, Sharon Pratt
Dudley, Edward Richard
Dymally, Mervyn
Edwards, Alfred Leroy
Elliott, Robert Brown
Espy, Mike
Evans, Melvin Herbert
Evers, (James) Charles
Farrelly, Alexander A.
Fauntroy, Walter
Fauset, Crystal Bird
Ferguson, Clarence Clyde, Jr.
Flake, Floyd Harold
Ford, Harold
Franks, Gary A.
George, Zelma Watson
Gibson, Truman K., Jr.
Glaudé, Stephen A.
Gourdine, Simon Peter
Granger, Lester Blackwell
Gray, William H., III
Green, Ernest G.
Greener, Richard
Gunn, Wendell Wilkie
Hall, Katie Beatrice Green
Haralson, Jeremiah
Harris, Patricia Roberts

Hastie, William Henry
Hatcher, Andrew T.
Hatcher, Richard Gordon
Hawkins, Augustus Freeman
Hayes, Charles Arthur
Herman, Alexis M.
Higginbotham, A. Leon, Jr.
Higgins, Chester A., Sr.
Hill, Anita Faye
Hodge, Derek M.
Holland, Jerome H.
Holman, M. Carl
Humphrey, Melvin
Hunton, Benjamin Lacy
Hyman, John Adams
Irvis, K. Leroy
Jackson, Jesse Louis
Jackson, Maynard Holbrook, Jr.
Jackson, Samuel Charles
Jenkins, Howard, Jr.
Jordan, Barbara
King, Melvin H.
Kitchen, Robert Wilson, Jr.
Knox, Clinton Everett
Lafontant, Jewel
Langston, John Mercer
Leland, George "Mickey"
Lewis, James B.
Lewis, John Robert
Long, Jefferson Franklin
Lowery, Robert O.
Lucas, William
Lynch, John Roy
McClure, Frederick Donald
McCree, Wade Hampton, Jr.
McGee, Henry Wadsworth, Jr.
McHenry, Donald F.
Mahoney, Charles H.
Marr, Carmel Carrington
Metcalfe, Ralph Horace
Mfume, Kweisi
Miller, Thomas Ezekiel
Millin, Henry Allan
Mitchell, Arthur Wergs
Mitchell, Parren James
Monroe, Loren Eugene
Montero, Frank
Morrow, E(verett) Frederic
Morrow, John Howard, Sr.
Murray, George Washington
Nabrit, James Madison, Jr.
Nash, Charles Edmund
Newhouse, Richard H.
Newman, Constance Berry "Connie"
Nichols, Barbara Lauraine
Nix, Robert Nelson Cornelius, Sr.
Norton, Eleanor Holmes
O'Hara, James Edward
Owens, Major Robert Odell
Parker, Henry Ellsworth
Partee, Cecil A.
Paterson, Basil
Payne, Donald

Pendleton, Clarence McLane, Jr.
Perkins, Edward Joseph
Perkins, Joseph
Perry, Carrie Saxon
Phillips, Vel Rogers
Pierce, Samuel Riley, Jr.
Pinchback, P(inckney) B(enton) S(tewart)
Poston, Ersa Hines
Powell, Adam Clayton, Jr.
Rainey, Joseph Hayne
Rangel, Charles
Ransier, Alonzo Jacob
Rapier, James Thomas
Rattley, Jessie Meinfield
Revels, Hiram Rhoades
Savage, Augustus F. "Gus"
Shakur, Assata Olugbala
Smythe, Hugh H.
Spearman, Leonard Hall O'Connell
Spencer, James Wilson
Stewart, Bennett McVey
Stokes, Carl Burton
Stokes, Louis
Sullivan, Louis Wade
Summers, Edna White
Sutton, Percy Ellis
Taylor, Hobart, Jr.
Taylor, Kristen Clark
Toote, Gloria E. A.
Towns, Edolphus "Ed"
Tucker, Cynthia DeLores Nottage
Tucker, Walter, III
Turner, Benjamin S.
Turner, James Milton
Usry, James L.
Vincent, Edward
Waldon, Alton Ronald, Jr.
Wallace, C. Everett
Walls, Josiah Thomas
Washington, Craig Anthony
Washington, Harold
Waters, Maxine
Watkins, Bruce R., Sr.
Watkins, Joseph Philip
Watson, Barbara M.
Weaver, George Leon-Paul
Weaver, Robert Clipton
Westerfield, Samuel Z.
Wharton, Clifton Reginald, Sr.
Wheat, Alan Dupree
White, George Henry
Wilder, L(awrence) Douglas
Williams, Eddie Nathan
Williams, Franklin H.
Wilson, Lance Henry
Woodson, Robert L.
Wright, Robert Courtlant
Young, Andrew Jackson, Jr.

PSYCHOLOGISTS. *See* **MEDICAL PRACTITIONERS**

PUBLISHERS

Abbott, Robert Sengstacke
Barnett, Ferdinand Lee
Bass, Charlotta Spears
Bennett, Lerone, Jr.
Cornish, Samuel Eli
Gordon, Edwin Jason
Graves, Earl G., Sr.
Johnson, John Harold
Murphy, John Henry, Sr.
Myers, Walter Dean
Perry, Christopher James
Sengstacke, John
Wells, Ida B.
Williams, Hosea
Woods, Howard B.
Woodson, Carter G(odwin)

RELIGIOUS LEADERS

Abernathy, Ralph David
Ali, Noble Drew
Allen, Richard
Allensworth, Allen
Bryan, Andrew
Burgess, John M.
Burns, Anthony
Caesar, Shirley
Carey, Lott
Cary, William Sterling
Cleage, Albert Buford, Jr.
Cleveland, James
Clinton, George Wylie
Coker, Daniel
Cornish, Samuel Eli
Crowdy, William S.
Drexel, Katherine
Fard, Wallace D.
Farrakhan, Louis Abdul
Father Divine
Fisher, Elijah John
Forbes, James A., Jr.
Franklin, C. L.
Gardner, Edward
Garnet, Henry Highland
Gates, J. M.
Grace, Charles Emmanuel "Sweet
   Daddy"
Harding, Vincent
Harris, Barbara
Haynes, Lemuel
Healy, James Augustine
Hoggard, James Clinton
Hood, James Walker
Howze, Joseph Lawson
Hurley, George W.
Israel, Prince Ashiel Ben
Jackson, Jesse
Jackson, Joseph Harrison
Johnson, Mordecai
Jones, Absalom
Kelly, Leontine
King, Martin Luther, Sr.
King, Martin Luther, Jr.

Lane, Isaac
Lincoln, C(harles) Eric
McGuire, George A.
Malcolm X
Marino, Eugene Antonio
Moore, Emerson
Muhammad, Elijah
Muhammad, Wallace D.
Paul, Thomas, Sr.
Perry, Harold Robert
Powell, Adam Clayton, Sr.
Raboteau, Albert Jordy
Revels, Hiram R.
Reverend Ike
Rush, Christopher
Shaw, Herbert Bell
Smith, Willie Mae Ford
Spottswood, Stephen Gil
Stallings, George Augustus, Jr.
Sullivan, Leon Howard
Taylor, Gardner Calvin
Thurman, Howard
Tindley, Charles Albert
Truth, Sojourner
Turner, Henry McNeal
Turner, Thomas Wyatt
Waddles, Mrs. Payton "Mother"
Walters, Alexander
Ward, Samuel Ringgold
Watkins, Joseph Philip
Williams, Hosea
Wilson, Demond

SCIENTISTS. *See also* INVENTORS

Banneker, Benjamin
Bouchet, Edward Alexander
Carruthers, George R.
Carver, George Washington
Drew, Charles Richard
Granville, Evelyn Boyd
Hall, Lloyd Augustus
Johnson, Katherine G.
Julian, Percy Lavon
Just, Ernest Everett
Latimer, Lewis Howard
Miller, Kelly
Peery, Benjamin Franklin, Jr.
Slaughter, John Brooks
Turner, Thomas Wyatt

SINGERS. *See* MUSICIANS

SOCIAL SCIENTISTS

Ben-Jochannan, Yosef
Bennett, Lerone, Jr.
Blassingame, John W.
Brimmer, Andrew Felton
Brown, Sterling Allen
Carson, Clayborne
Clark, Kenneth Bancroft
Clarke, John Henrik
Dean, William Henry
Du Bois, W. E. B.

Dunham, Katherine
Fields, Barbara Jeanne
Franklin, John Hope
Frazier, E. Franklin
Freeman, Jewel Virginia Mulligan
Hale, Clara McBride
Harding, Vincent
Harris, Middleton A. "Spike"
Hensen, Matthew Alexander
Hine, Darlene Clark
Hurston, Zora Neale
Jackson, Reginald L.
Johnson, Charles Spurgeon
Johnson, Guy Benton
Lewis, Samella Sanders
Lewis, Sir W(illiam) Arthur
Logan, Rayford Whittingham
Loury, Glenn C.
Miller, Kelly
Nell, William C.
Painter, Nell Irvin
Quarles, Benjamin
Rogers, Joel A.
Skinner, Elliott Percival
Sowell, Thomas
Thomas, Bettye Collier
Wesley, Charles Harris
Westerfield, Samuel Z.
Williams, Chancellor
Williams, Eddie Nathan
Williams, George Washington
Willie, Charles Vert
Wilson, William Julius
Woodson, Carter G(odwin)

SONGWRITERS. *See* COMPOSERS

TEACHERS. *See* EDUCATORS

TELEVISION PERSONALITIES and
BROADCAST JOURNALISTS

Baker, Denise
Bolden, J. Taber, Jr.
Bond, Anna Monique
Bradley, Ed
Brown, William Anthony "Tony"
Clayton, Xernona
Daniels, Randy
Gilbert, Jarobin, Jr.
Gist, Carole
Goode, Malvin R.
Graham, Gordon
Gumbel, Bryant Charles
Hall, Arsenio
Hulbert, Maurice "Hot Rod"
Hunter-Gault, Charlayne
Jackson, Eugene
Jenkins, Carol Ann
Johnson, John
Kennedy, Royal
King, Emery
Matney, William C., Jr.
Noble, Gilbert E. "Gil"

Payne, Ethel
Quarles, Norma
Reynolds, Barbara Ann
Robertson, Stanley
Robinson, Max C.
Shaw, Bernard
Simpson, Carole
Simpson, Orenthal James "O.J."
Sutton, Pierre Montea "PePe"
Teague, Robert "Bob"
Tolliver, Melba
Tucker, Lemuel "Lem"
Turner, Debbye
Vincent, Marjorie
Williams, Vanessa
Winfrey, Oprah Gail

TRACK and FIELD ATHLETES
Ashford, Evelyn
Beamon, Robert "Bob"
Boston, Ralph
Brisco-Hooks, Valerie
Brown, Earlene
Burrell, Leroy Russell
Carlos, John Wesley
Coachman, Alice
Davenport, Willie D.
Foster, Greg
Francis, Herbert
Gourdin, Edward Orval
Griffith-Joyner, Florence Delorez
Hayes, Bob
Hubbard, William DeHart
Jackson, Nell
Johnson, Michael
Johnson, Rafer Lewis
Joyner-Kersee, Jackie
Lewis, Frederick Carlton "Carl"
McDaniel, Mildred Louise
Metcalfe, Ralph Horace
Mims, Madeline Manning
Moses, Edwin Corley
Owens, James Cleveland "Jesse"
Poage, George Coleman
Rudolph, Wilma
Smith, Tommie C.
Stadler, Joseph F.
Stoakes, Louise
Taylor, John Baxter, Jr.
Tyus, Wyomia
White, Willye B.

WRITERS
Andrews, Raymond
Angelou, Maya
Anthony, Michael
Baldwin, James Arthur
Bambara, Toni Cade
Banneker, Benjamin
Baraka, Amiri
Bennett, Lerone, Jr.
Bontemps, Arna Wendell
Bradley, David

Braithwaite, William Stanley Beaumont
Brawley, Benjamin Griffith
Brooks, Gwendolyn
Brown, Claude
Brown, Hallie Q.
Brown, William Wells
Bullins, Ed
Butcher, Philip
Butler, Octavia E(stelle)
Carson, Clayborne
Chase-Riboud, Barbara
Chesnutt, Charles Waddell
Childress, Alice
Christian, Barbara T.
Clarke, John Henrik
Cleage, Albert Buford, Jr.
Cleaver, Eldridge
Cooper, J(oan) California
Cotter, Joseph Seamon, Jr.
Cotter, Joseph Seamon, Sr.
Cross, Theodore L.
Cullen, Countée
Davis, Arthur Paul
Davis, Ossie
Delany, Samuel R(ay), Jr.
Dodson, Owen
Du Bois, Shirley Graham
Dumas, Henry Lee
Dunbar, Paul Laurence
Elder, Lonne, III
Ellison, Ralph
Equiano, Olaudah
Evans, Mari
Fair, Ronald L.
Fauset, Jessie Redmon
Fax, Elton
Ferguson, Clarence Clyde, Jr.
Fisher, Rudolph
Fuller, Charles
Fuller, Meta Vaux Warrick
Gaines, Ernest J.
Gates, Henry Louis, Jr.
Gayle, Addison, Jr.
Giovanni, Nikki
Gloster, Hugh
Gordone, Charles
Greenlee, Sam
Grimké, Angelina (Emily) Weld
Guy, Rosa Cuthbert
Haley, Alex Palmer
Hamilton, Charles Vernon
Hammon, Jupiter
Hansberry, Lorraine
Hare, Nathan
Harper, Frances E. W.
Harper, Michael S.
Haskins, James S.
Hayden, Robert Earl
Himes, Chester Bomar
Holman, M. Carl
Hooks, Bell
Horton, George Moses
Hughes, (James Mercer) Langston

Hunter, Eddie
Hunter, Kristin Elaine Eggleston
Hurston, Zora Neale
Irvis, K. Leroy
James, Rick
Johnson, Charles Richard
Johnson, Fenton
Johnson, Georgia
Johnson, James Weldon
Jones, Gayl
Jordan, June
Julien, Max
Kelley, William Melvin
Killens, John Oliver
Knight, Etheridge
Lange, Ted W., III
Lester, Julius
Locke, Alain Leroy
Logan, Rayford Whittingham
Lorde, Audre
Lovelace, Earl
Lynch, John Roy
McKay, Claude
McMillan, Terry
McPherson, James Alan
Madhubuti, Haki R.
Major, Clarence
Marable, Manning
Marshall, Paule
Mayfield, Julian
Mays, Benjamin Elijah
Meriwether, Louise
Micheaux, Oscar
Mitchell, Loften
Morrison, Toni
Motley, Willard Francis
Murray, Albert
Myers, Walter Dean
Naylor, Gloria
Neal, Larry
Nicholas, Denise
Parks, Gordon, Sr.
Perry, Shauneille
Petry, Ann
Pontiflet, Ted
Porter, James Amos
Randall, Dudley
Redding, Jay Saunders
Redmond, Eugene
Reed, Ishmael
Rich, Matty
Richardson, Willis
Ringgold, Faith
Rivers, Conrad Kent
Rodgers, Carolyn M.
Rodney, Walter
Rowan, Carl Thomas
Sanchez, Sonia
Schuyler, George Samuel
Scott, Nathan Alexander, Jr.
Scott-Heron, Gil
Sebree, Charles
Shange, Ntozake

Shepp, Archie
Silverstein, Shel(by)
Smith, Anna Deavere
Sowell, Thomas
Tarry, Ellen
Taylor, Mildred D.
Taylor, Theodore
Terry, Lucy
Thurman, Wallace Henry
Tolson, M(elvin) B(eaunorus)
Toomer, Nathan Eugene "Jean"

Townsend, Robert
Van Peebles, Melvin
Walker, Alice Malsenior
Walker, David
Walker, Margaret Abigail
Walrond, Eric
Walters, Ronald
Ward, Douglas Turner
Ward, Theodore
Wayans, Keenen Ivory

Wheatley, Phillis
Wideman, John Edgar
Williams, John Alfred
Willie, Charles Vert
Wilson, August
Wright, Jay
Wright, Nathan, Jr.
Wright, Richard
Yerby, Frank
Young, Al

Index